sport,

culture and society

sport,
culture and society:

a reader on the sociology of sport

JOHN W. LOY, JR.
University of Illinois
Champaign, Illinois

GERALD S. KENYON
BARRY D. McPHERSON
University of Waterloo
Waterloo, Canada

SECOND AND REVISED EDITION

Lea & Febiger   ●   1981 Philadelphia

Lea & Febiger
600 Washington Square
Philadelphia, PA 19106
U.S.A.

Library of Congress Cataloging in Publication Data
Main entry under title:

Sport, culture, and society.

Includes bibliographies.
1. Sports—Social aspects—Addresses, essays,
lectures. I. Loy, John W. II. Kenyon, Gerald S.
III. McPherson, Barry D.
GV706.5.S7   1981   305'.4   81-3692
ISBN 0-8121-0781-0   AACR2

PRINTED IN THE UNITED STATES OF AMERICA

Print No. 2 1

preface

A decade ago, in the preface to the first edition of *Sport, Culture and Society,* we drew attention to the fact that sport had made substantial inroads into our various social institutions, whether they were economic, educational, political, familial, or religious. Since then, sport has become even more pervasive, from the witnessing of a single high performance event by hundreds of millions, to the rapid growth of the "sport-for-all" movement.

On the scholarly side, the level of scholarship has been raised, and the range of subject matter broadened. The results remain uneven, however, both nationally and internationally. Moreover, just as sport itself tends to mirror society, the sociology of sport has a tendency to reflect sociology. That is, areas of inquiry and questions of method, which became part of mainstream sociology during the period, were paralleled in the sociology of sport. For example, sport issues such as discrimination and social control were particular manifestations of larger social problems addressed by the parent discipline. The result however, is a much more diverse body of literature, with many contributions reflecting new levels of theoretical and methodological sophistication.

Such developments notwithstanding, progress has not been as great as envisioned by many in the late 1960s. In a recent analysis* of why this

*Loy, J. W., McPherson, B. D., and Kenyon, G. S., The Sociology of Sport as an Academic Specialty: An Episodic Essay on the Development and Emergence of an Hybrid Subfield in North America. Ottawa, Canada: Canadian Association for Health, Physical Education and Recreation, 1978.

has been the case, some factors were identified, the most important of which was the lack of a sufficiently large "critical mass" of sport sociologists and all that implies for any academic specialty. That is, with only a small number of active scholars, the scope of the subject matter and the extent to which theoretical and methodological alternatives are employed are limited; this in turn, has an impact upon the literature, both quantitatively and qualitatively.

Although advancement may have fallen short of the ideal, and despite retaining less than a third of the material from the first edition, selecting the content for this revision was not without difficulty. While we believe worthy representatives of our conceptual framework have been chosen, some excellent writings could not be included. Although different approaches can be seen in the readings reprinted, our preference was for the work of the more productive scholars whose thrust has been theoretically based empirical work. To draw the reader's attention to other approaches, as well as to provide a list of closely related studies, some of which were too long to be included, we have provided a *Further Readings* section following each part of the text.* Compared with ten years ago, however, we feel less of a need to be comprehensive with respect to either developmental or bibliographic material since several readers and textbooks have become available to the student.

With respect to uses of this reader, we believe it can stand alone as a resource volume for

*In addition, the student should scan the references cited in each of the papers included in this reader.

those desiring an introduction to the sociology of sport, either independently, or as part of a first course in the subject. Alternatively, it could supplement a textbook on sport sociology. For this reason, we have structured the Reader to parallel closely the form of our own book, *Sport and Social Systems,*† written especially to provide a comprehensive analysis of the major problems receiving attention and the results of theoretical and empirical inquiry into sport phenomena.

As in the aforementioned text, we have used the *social system* and its basic components as an organizing framework for the readings. Human social behavior, including that within sport milieus, whether it involves two individuals or an entire society, is organized and structured into systems varying in structure, composition, complexity, and function. Consequently, the interests of sport sociologists range from the traits of individuals (e.g., athletes) and how they interact in face-to-face groups (e.g., teams), to the relationship between sport and the characteristics of major social institutions (e.g., the family, the school, the economy, and the mass media). The former we refer to as *micro-social systems;* the latter as *macro-social systems.*

Thus, we have separated the reader into three parts: Part One—"The Sociological Analysis of Sport"—contains two sections; the first includes statements on the sociology of sport as an academic specialty; the second addresses conceptual problems in the sociological study of sport. Part Two—"Sport and Micro-Social Systems"—comprises three sections dealing with sport groups, sport organizations, and sport subcultures, respectively. Part Three—"Sport and Macro-Social Systems"—consists of four sections; the first three address the relationship be-

tween sport and socializing, regulative, and cultural institutions; the fourth contains contributions to the literature on the relationship between sport and institutionalized forms and processes of social stratification.

Finally, a major objective of the first edition was to whet the academic appetite for the study of sport from the perspective of the social sciences. While we hope the second edition will serve this purpose as well, we believe it also represents a reasonable expression of the state of the art, though restricted to North America for the most part. Nevertheless, we sincerely hope that the advances made in the future will necessitate a third edition long before another decade elapses. Or, put another way, we would like to think we will have come a little closer to that "some day" described by Wector over 40 years ago:

Some day.... He will show us how cricket, with its white clothes and leisured boredom, and sudden crises met with cool mastery to the ripple of applause among the teacups and cucumber sandwiches, is an epitome of the British Empire. Or the bull-fight with its scarlet cape and gold braid, its fierce pride and cruelty, and the quixotic futility of its perils, is the essence of Spain. Or that football with its rugged individualism, and baseball with its equality of opportunity, are valid American symbols.... Most of these things have been felt or hinted before, but their synthesis has never been made.*

> John W. Loy, Jr.
> Gerald S. Kenyon
> Barry D. McPherson

Champaign, Illinois
Waterloo, Canada

---

† Loy, J. W., McPherson, B. D., and Kenyon, G.S., *Sport and Social Systems.* Reading, MA, Addison-Wesley Publishing Co., 1978. (Each chapter includes an extensive bibliography on each of the topics covered in this reader.)

---

* Wector, Dixon, *The Saga of American Society: A Record of Social Aspirations, 1607–1937.* New York, Charles Scribner and Sons, 1937, p. 428.

contents

Contents

PART THREE: Sport and Macro-Social Systems

Contents

PART ONE
the sociological analysis of sport

Although the first edition provided a brief historical basis for an emerging sociology of sport, since then more thorough analyses have been published,* obviating the need to detail such material here. Nevertheless, an introduction to the literature of any field is enhanced by a "setting of the scene." Thus, *Section One: Sociology of Sport*, contains articles addressed to characterizing the sociology of sport as an academic specialty. The readings in *Section Two: Sport as a Social Phenomenon*, treat some of the conceptual issues underlying the serious study of sport from a social science perspective.

In the first article of *Section One*, Kenyon and Loy call for the joining together of a number of disparate initiatives into a systematic sociology of sport. The extent to which this has occurred fifteen years later, and the prospects for the future are reflected upon by McPherson in the paper that follows. The reader should note that there have appeared a number of critiques and alternative orientations to the theoretical and methodological positions taken in these contributions. For example, the limitations of a so-called "value-free" sport sociology have been argued by several writers (Melnick, 1975; Whitson, 1978), and likewise, alternatives to "bour-

geois sociology" have been presented by Eastern European observers (Erbach, 1966; Wohl, 1966, 1975).

As is the case with any emerging field, a number of writers have wrestled with the necessary but difficult task of clarifying concepts and stating orientations—the precursors of systematic inquiry. Devoting considerable space to the subject may seem trivial at first, but upon reflection, one realizes that the term "sport" has a variety of meanings and uses; from "good sport," "blood sport," and being "sporty," to "sports car," "sporting chance," and "sporting house." To illustrate, *Section Two* contains two analyses: in the first, Loy describes how the term "sport" takes on different meanings, depending upon the level of discourse. Thus, the meaning of "sport" depends upon whether it is a "game occurrence," an "institutionalized game," a "social institution," or a "social system." In the second article, Kenyon approaches sport from the perspective of individual involvement and endeavours to classify the several roles played in sport situations. Limitations of space prevent the inclusion of more writings on these topics, but the reader can obtain a taste of the problems as they are summarized in the two papers included, and by consulting the publications listed in *Further Readings* (in particular, see Caillois, 1961; Huizinga, 1955; and McIntosh, 1963). However, despite several attempts to conceptualize sport phenomena, most writers probably would agree that a universally accepted framework has yet to appear.

---

* For example, see Loy, J. W., McPherson, B. D., and Kenyon, G. S., The Sociology of Sport as an Academic Specialty: An Episodic Essay on the Development and Emergence of an Hybrid Subfield in North America. Ottawa, Canada: Canadian Association For Health, Physical Education and Recreation, 1978.

1

SECTION ONE
sociology of sport

toward a
sociology of sport

GERALD S. KENYON and JOHN W. LOY

To declare that sport, during the present century, has become a cultural phenomenon of great magnitude and complexity is an affirmation of the obvious. Sport is fast becoming a social institution, permeating education, economics, art, politics, law, mass communications, and international diplomacy. Its scope is awesome; nearly everyone has become involved in some way, even if only vicariously. As a business enterprise alone it represents an annual expenditure by the American public of over $20 billion. For the services of a single performer, $400 thousand apparently is not too much to pay. Sport has become a potent social force with a capacity to create needs ranging from seats on the fifty-yard line to stretch pants in pastel colors.

Despite the magnitude of the public's commitment to sport, as a social phenomenon it has received little serious study. The ubiquitous presence of sports has largely been taken for granted by social scientists and physical educators alike. A clear description, let alone explanation of this social force, is largely nonexistent. Many of its manifest and most of its latent functions have been ignored. For the physical educator, sport provides a medium for pursuing educational goals. For almost anyone else it probably serves quite different purposes. In neither case is its social significance understood. Therefore, we urge the development of a

Reprinted from the *Journal of Health-Physical Education-Recreation* 36:24–25, 68–69, 1965. Copyright, 1965, by American Alliance for Health, Physical Education, Recreation and Dance, Reston, VA. 22091

"sociology of sport" as a division of an academic discipline such as that recently described by Franklin Henry.[1]

THE NATURE OF SPORT SOCIOLOGY

If sociology is the study of social order—the underlying regularity of human social behavior—including efforts to attain it and departures from it,[2] then the sociology of sport becomes the study of the regularity, and departures from it, of human social behavior in a sports context. Since we see the social psychology of sport as having much in common with its sociology, we include the content and method of the former within the realm of our subdiscipline.[3] Thus, if social psychology is "an attempt to understand and explain how the thought, feeling, and behavior of individuals are influenced by the actual, imagined, or implied presence of other human beings,"[4] then the social psychology of sport is the study of individuals in social and cultural settings associated with sport. Just as exercise physiology deals with something less than the whole of physiology, the concern of a psychosociological study of sport is with something less than the whole of social psychology or sociology.

A psychosociological inquiry into sport and physical activity requires a concern for such concepts as *basic social units* (including individuals, groups, institutions, societies, and cultures), *primary social psychological attributes* (such as interpersonal response traits, motives, attitudes, and values), and *fundamental social processes* (socialization, social control,

5

social conflict, social stratification, and social change).

For an illustration of the significance of this framework, we refer to the work of Roberts and Sutton-Smith,[5] an anthropologist and a psychologist collaborating to study the role of games in various societies. They have shown that the types of games played reflect values inherent in a particular culture and at the same time serve to teach certain cultural values and attitudes. For example, with respect to child rearing practices, obedience training is associated with a culture stressing games of strategy, responsibility training with games of chance, and achievement training with games of physical skill. Thus Roberts and Sutton-Smith argue that individuals in different cultures (basic social units) perceive games differently, depending upon the values and attitudes prevalent within a particular culture (primary social-psychological attributes) and that such games serve to relieve social conflict and consequently enhance socialization (fundamental social processes). It follows that such a framework could be useful for the study of the many social facets of sport.

We suggest, therefore, that the observational techniques and the theoretical rationale available to the sport sociologist could provide unique possibilities for viewing the social significance of sport. To illustrate, the classification of activities into such schemes as individual, dual, or team sports so familiar to the physical educator, or into factors such as intensity, frequency, and duration, so familiar to the exercise physiologist, will give way to classifications appropriate for a social context, such as Caillois' conception of games as competition, chance, drama (mimicry), and the pursuit of vertigo.

WHAT THE SOCIOLOGY OF SPORT IS NOT. Having briefly described what the sociology of sport *is,* we turn now to what it is *not,* in an effort to distinguish between the goals of science and those of education or physical education. The sport sociologist does not base his inquiries upon the assumption that "physical activity is good." Sport sociology, as we view it, is a value-free social science. It is not an effort to influence public opinion or behavior, nor is it an attempt to find support for the "social development" objective of physical education, as described in the writings of Hetherington, Williams, Nash, Oberteuffer, and others. The sport sociologist is neither a spreader of gospel

nor an evangelist for exercise. His function is not to shape attitudes and values but rather to describe and explain them. By taking such a position, in no way do we suggest that physical education ought to be value free; it must have its objectives, certainly. We *do* suggest, however, that the choice of both ends and means may be enhanced considerably by drawing from the findings of a well-developed sport sociology.

PREPARING THE SPORT SOCIOLOGIST. To perform the functions of a sport sociologist obviously requires some preparation. Students of sport sociology, in addition to an interest in and understanding of sport, should have a strong background in the behavioral and social sciences, especially psychology, sociology, social psychology, and cultural anthropology. The exciting developments occurring in both the theoretical and empirical aspects of these fields make it essential that the student pay considerable attention to each. With the degree of mathematical thinking in the social sciences increasing rapidly, adequate preparation in mathematics and statistics is essential to understand certain theoretical models and data analysis procedures.

A BRIEF HISTORICAL PERSPECTIVE

Although a work entitled *Soziologie des Sports* was published in Germany in 1921, few publications referring directly to sport sociology can be found. Up to the present, much of the writing, varying widely in scope and depth, has been largely descriptive in nature.[6] Nevertheless, these writers have often provided cogent observations, suggesting hypotheses worthy of test. With the exception of some of Cowell's work,[7] serious empirical study of sport sociology per se has not been popular. Few investigators from physical education have devoted a substantial period of their career to the subject. The work of others, such as sociologists, usually has been conducted in the broader context of use of leisure.[8] While it would be false to assert that the sociology of sport has acquired a substantial subject matter, some work—both theoretical and empirical—does exist.

THEORETICAL EFFORTS. Theories of sports and games have long been of interest to social scientists. At the beginning of the century G. T. W. Patrick wrote on the "psychology of football." Numerous theories of play as means to certain social ends have been advanced. These theories came to be discarded when found contradictory to evidence provided by empirical psychology. In the 1930's, however, Huizinga argued that play ought to be considered for its own sake, as an end in itself rather than a means to some other end. He showed how play pervades all cultural institutions. Although his work is frequently alluded to, little effort has been made to extend his theory and test the hypotheses it suggests. Another work linking sport and culture is that of Caillois who attempts to demonstrate that the health of a society is reflected in the types of games it encourages.

EMPIRICAL STUDIES. Much of the work cited by Roberts, Sutton-Smith, and co-workers was based upon empirical cross-cultural data. Their hypothesis that games model the major maintenance problems of a given society is illustrated using the highly competitive society of the United States, where sports and games permit youth to rehearse competitive roles without experiencing the adverse anxiety experienced by adults striving for success. Other studies include Weinberg and Arond's discussion of the occupational culture of the boxer; Grusky's treatment of managerial succession and organizational effectiveness in baseball; Riesman's description of the cultural diffusion of football and its bearing on ethnic differentiation and social mobility; and Stone's work, which offers a number of interesting hypotheses about the relationships between sport and socioeconomic status.

EUROPEAN INTEREST. Although workers in this country have been leaders in several aspects of the science of physical activity, it is interesting to note that at present the greatest interest in sport sociology seems to be centered in Europe. In addition to work cited elsewhere in this paper, a number of other essays and research studies have been published during the past few years.[9]

AVENUES FOR FUTURE INQUIRY

Sport sociology as an empirical science is in its infancy, but it need not remain this way. The interested researcher soon becomes aware of the numerous possibilities, first, by taking cognizance of the many theoretical models explaining group and individual behavior, and second, by taking advantage of such technical advances as electronic computers and multivarious methods of data reduction and analysis. For fruitful inquiry the relevant developments in other disciplines cannot be ignored any more than the curriculum worker can afford to ignore concept learning, teaching machines, programed learning, and team teaching.

Our consideration of the numerous possibilities for research has been a natural outgrowth of the thought associated with some modest studies under way at the University of Wisconsin. At present, work is in progress in four areas: the diffusion of innovations in American sport; the significance of physical activity for adults as a function of age, sex, education, socioeconomic status, and national origin; the development of models for the characterization of values held for physical activity; and cross-national studies of attitudes toward physical activity as a function of certain cultural and educational factors. It has been our further observation that many promising avenues of inquiry are opened by becoming familiar with general sociological theory.

THE USE OF SOCIAL THEORY IN EXPLAINING THE ROLE OF SPORT IN SOCIETY. The role of theory is the same for the sport sociologist as for the scientist in general. Theory provides a logical foundation for research, that is, it circumscribes and characterizes the phenomenon in question; it suggests significant hypotheses; it relates seemingly discrete findings by summarizing facts into generalizations and systems of generalizations; and it identifies gaps in knowledge. Perhaps most important, theory "by providing a rationale . . . introduces a *ground for prediction* which is more secure than mere empirical extrapolation from previously observed trends."[10]

Fortunately for the sport sociologist, several contemporary sociological theories are relevant for studying the many ramifications of sport in modern society. Although these may require slight modification by virtue of use in a sports situation, they should be applicable if there is regularity to human social behavior. For example, Parson's theoretical scheme differentiating four levels of structural organization—primary, managerial, institutional, and societal—permits analysis of any social system in terms of the functional problems such systems must solve in order to survive.[11] He labels these problems as adaptive, goal-attainment, pattern-maintenance and tension management, and integrative.

Less general theories applicable to the sport setting include those concerned with collective behavior, such as the recent and rather complete framework of Smelser.[12] Admittedly, a riot such as that which occurred at a Peruvian soccer match in the spring of 1964 bringing death to several hundred persons is relatively rare. However, other forms of collective behavior associated with sports are quite common.

POSSIBLE RESEARCH AREAS. Other approaches which we believe warrant some investigation include the following:

1. *Computer Simulation.* The technological advances in computer design and application are more rapid than had been anticipated. Recent developments in computer simulation techniques [13] could be applied to team dynamics, sport development and decline and spectator behavior.

2. *Game Situation Laboratory.* The development of a facility capable of simulating the environment surrounding the game would afford a compromise between the uncontrollable actual condition and the artificial conditions of the laboratory.

3. *Interdisciplinary Studies.* Instead of independent work by exercise physiologists, psychologists, sociologists, and sport sociologists, work in concert would yield knowledge heretofore unknown. As Roger Bannister recently pointed out, "maximum athletic performance cannot be explained by physiology alone." [14]

4. *Social Model Development.* The construction of models, both static and dynamic, could produce one basis for describing and explaining the significance of sport for individuals and groups. McPhee's "addiction model" represents one approach for predicting the course of "enthusiasms" or "passions" for a given pastime, intellectual or physical. [15]

5. *Cross-National and Cross-Cultural Studies.* Whatever laws that may be discovered and theories developed, the crucial test lies in their potential for generalizing to other countries and other cultures.

6. *Game Theory.* The application of the now well-established theory of games apparently has failed, to a large extent, to interest investigators studying sport.

7. *The Significance of Sport and Physical Activity as a Leisure Pursuit.* During the past few years considerable interest has been shown in the sociology of leisure, both in this country and abroad. [16] Although a leisure use theory depends upon acquiring more data, a number of studies have been completed, and several national and international conferences held.

8. *Social Change and Sport.* Among the most profound characteristics of contemporary Western civilization is the rapidity of social change, change in the nature of social institutions and social values. What is it about the "Great Society" that explains the Mets outdrawing the Yankees?

This list of potential research areas is not meant to be exhaustive, or to contain mutually exclusive subjects for investigation. Moreover, it will be noted that we are suggesting not only points of departure for future research but also some techniques of inquiry, many of which have only recently become available for practical use.

In summary, we have suggested that the explanation of the contemporary pervasiveness of sport requires a sociology of sport in the tradition of the social sciences. We have attempted to show what the characteristics of such a subdiscipline might be, drawing examples from studies both completed and proposed. With the vastness of sport today, together with its anticipated growth in the future, the potentiality of a sociology of sport becomes apparent. To become firmly established, however, will require well-prepared and dedicated workers using a value free approach to an often value charged subject matter.

NOTES

1. Henry, F. M.: Physical education: An academic discipline. J. Health Educ. Rec., September:32, 1964.

2. Inkeles, A.: What is Sociology? Englewood Cliffs, N.J., Prentice-Hall, 1964, p. 27.

3. It is assumed that for most subsequent references to the *sociology* of sport, the *social psychology* of sport is implied also.

4. Allport, Gordon W.: The historical background of modern social psychology. *In* Handbook of Social Psychology, Vol. 2. Edited by G. Lindzey. Reading, Mass., Addison-Wesley, 1954, p. 5.

5. See Roberts and Sutton-Smith, p. 47.

6. For example, see Cozens, F. W., and Stumpf, F. S.: Sports in American Life. Chicago, University of Chicago Press, 1953, for a well-documented account of the diversity of sport in the United States with frequent reference to historical developments. For more recent reflections on sport as a social institution, particularly from an international viewpoint, see McIntosh, P. C.: Sport in Society. London, Bowes & Bowes, 1958.

7. For example, see Cowell, Charles C.: The contributions of physical activity to social development. Res. Q., May:286, 1960, a review of literature which includes five of his own research reports.

8. For an early example (1934) see Lundberg, G., et al.: the amount of uses of leisure. *In* Mass Leisure. Edited by E. Larrabee and R. Meyersohn. Glencoe, Ill., The Free Press, 1958; more recently, de Grazia, S.: Of Time, Work, and Leisure. Garden City, N.Y., Doubleday, 1962.

9. For example, see Helanko, R.: Sports and socialization. Acta Sociol., *2*:1, 1956; and Maheu, Rene: Sport and culture; Leemars, E.J.: A sociological approach to sports; Vlot, N.J.: A sociological analysis of sport in the Netherlands; and Dumazedier, Joffre: The point of view of a social scientist, *in* International Research in Sport and Physical Education. Edited by E. Jokl and E. Simon. Springfield, Ill., Charles C Thomas, 1964.

10. Merton, Robert K.: Social Theory and Social Structure. Glencoe, Ill., Free Press, 1957, p. 98.

11. Talcott, Parsons: General theory in sociology. *In* Sociology Today. Edited by R. K. Merton et al. New York, Basic Books, 1959.

12. Smelser, Neil J.: Theory of Collective Behavior. New York, Free Press of Glencoe, 1963.

13. For example, see Newell, A., and Simon, H. A.: Computers in psychology. *In* Handbook of Mathematical Psychology, Vol. 1. Edited by R. Luce et al. New York, Wiley, 1963.

14. The Meaning of Athletic Performance. Paper presented at the International Conference of the International Council for Sport and Physical Education, Paris, October, 1963.

15. McPhee, W. N.: Formal Theories of Mass Behavior. New York, Free Press of Glencoe, 1963.

16. For a summary of studies together with an extensive bibliography, see Larabee, E. and Meyersohn, R. (eds.): Mass Leisure. Glencoe, Ill., Free Press, 1958.

REFERENCES

Caillois, Roger: Man, Play and Games. Glencoe, Ill., Free Press, 1961.

Grusky, Oscar: Managerial succession and organizational effectiveness. American Journal of Sociology, *69* (1):21, 1963.

Huizinga, Johan: Homo Ludens. Boston, Beacon Press, 1960.

Patrick, G. T. W.: The psychology of football. American Journal of Psychology, *14* (3-4):104, 1903.

Rapaport, Anatole: Fights, Games and Debates. Ann Arbor: University of Michigan Press, 1960.

Riesman, David and Reul, Denny: Football in America. American Quarterly, 3:309, 1951.

Roberts, John M., et al.: Games in culture. American Anthropologist, *61*:597, 1959.

Roberts, John M. and Sutton-Smith, Brian: Child Training and Game Involvement. Ethnology, *1*:166, 1962.

Roberts, John M., et al.: Strategy in games and folk tales. Journal of Social Psychology, *61*:185, 1963.

Stone, Gregory P.: Some meanings of American sport. College Physical Education Association 60th Annual Proceedings. Washington, D. C.: CPEA, 1957.

Sutton-Smith, Brian, et al.: Game Involvement in Adults. Journal of Social Psychology, *60*:15, 1963.

Weinberg, S. K., and Arond, H.: The occupational culture of the boxer. American Journal of Sociology, *57*:460, 1962.

past, present and future perspectives for research in sport sociology

BARRY D. McPHERSON

INTRODUCTION

Unlike many of the other sub-disciplines in the field of human movement studies, the sociology of sport is a relatively new area of academic interest. Although sport has been an integral facet of life in most societies throughout history, only in the last ten to twenty years have sociologists, and physical educators trained in the social sciences, given serious consideration to sport as a social phenomenon. In fact, it is quite likely that an undergraduate course in sociology or sport sociology was neither a required nor an elective subject for the majority of those working in the field today who were physical education majors at one time. Therefore, the purpose of this paper is first, to define the boundaries of sport sociology; second, to present a brief historical overview of the institutionalization of the sub-discipline; and, third, to attempt to define the sub-discipline by discussing the occupational socialization, the research methodologies, and the substantive concerns of past, present and future sport sociologists.

SPORT SOCIOLOGY DEFINED

Common to many other sub-disciplines within the sport sciences (e.g., exercise physiology), sport sociology has been defined to a great extent by the topics that have been investigated, both by those formally trained in the area, and by those who identify with the area in order to legitimate their own work. As a result, in the early years any study involving a group (e.g., sport team) was classified under the rubric of sport sociology, regardless of whether the level of analysis was an individual's motives, attitudes, or personality (i.e., psychology), or the interactions within the group (i.e., social psychology), or the processes and patterns of group or collective factors influencing human behaviour in a sport context (i.e., sociology).

In order to define sport sociology, one must consider the level of analysis that is examined, and the topics of concern to sociologists. Theodorson and Theodorson (1969:401) state that:

Sociology studies the processes and patterns of individual and group interaction, the forms of organization of social groups, the relationships among them, and group influences on individual behavior . . . it has focused on the understanding of group or other collective factors in human behavior . . . it may deal with any social system, including the small group, or any aspect of social organization or social behavior. Sociology seeks to develop a body of interrelated scientific propositions, or generalizations, that explain social behavior and that may under specified conditions predict or aid in understanding behavior.

Thus, if sport sociology is a sub-set of sociology, then sport sociologists should study "the processes and patterns . . . that explain social behavior and that may under specified conditions predict or aid in understanding behavior" (Theodorson and Theodorson, 1969:401) in a sport context. More specifically, sport sociologists deal with basic social units (individuals, groups, institutions, societies, cultures) and fundamental social processes (socialization, social control, stratification, social conflict, social change) present in a variety of sport milieu. In short, sport sociology is not interested in a specific individual or group, but rather in the social structure, social patterns and social organization of groups engaged in sport, whether it be a micro-system (e.g., a hockey team), a large complex organization (e.g., professional sport league, an international sporting association), a sub-culture (e.g., ethnic groups), or a society (e.g., a nation).

THE INSTITUTIONALIZATION OF SPORT SOCIOLOGY

Although a definitive history of sport sociology has not been completed a preliminary attempt was made by Kenyon and Loy (1965) and Loy and Kenyon (1969) in their early efforts to define and provide an overview for the subdiscipline. For example, they reported that a publication entitled *Soziologie des Sports* was published in Germany as early as 1921. Despite the appearance of this isolated work, and a few others that followed, it wasn't until the 1950's that individuals began to publish articles dealing with sport as a social phenomenon. For example, in 1953, A. Wohl, in Poland, wrote a paper entitled "The Problems of Development of Physical Culture in The Socialist System," and subsequently wrote many other papers concerned with the role and function of sport and sportsmen in Poland. At about the same time, G. Stone wrote "American Sports: Play and Dis-play" (1955), and "Some Meanings of American Sport" (1957). It was not until the mid-1960's that others such as Heinilä (Finland), Kenyon, Lüschen and Schafer (United States) began to add to the body of knowledge.

As a result of this increasing interest in a common phenomenon, and the increasing interest in meeting to present papers, initiate research and exchange ideas, the International Committee on Sport Sociology was created as a formal organization. The membership on this Committee was, and is, international in character and includes both sociologists and physical educators. As a result of this institutionalization, seminars and symposia have been held, the most recent of which include, the 3rd International Symposium held in Canada in 1971, the 4th Symposium held in Rumania in August, 1973, and the 5th Symposium to be held in Finland in 1975. Each symposium has been organized around a common theme or problem of interest to a group of international scholars. Furthermore, *International Review of Sport Sociology* was initiated as an annual journal in 1966, and in 1973 became a quarterly journal to meet the need for the expanding body of knowledge being produced. In addition to the above, as will be seen in the following section, sport sociology is now an integral facet of higher education as evidenced by the many undergraduate and graduate courses offered in Departments of Physical Education and Sociology; by the concomitant increase in textbooks, bibliographies, and readers; by the development of a computerized information retrieval system (SIRLS) containing approximately 3,000 references in the sociology and social psychology of sport; and, by the initiation of cooperative research projects, two of which are designed to gather cross-national data.

THE OCCUPATIONAL SOCIALIZATION OF SPORT SOCIOLOGISTS

The evolution of the career pattern of sport sociologists is not unlike that experienced by exercise physiologists. To date, the occupational role has been filled by three generations, each of which underwent a unique process of occupational socialization. In this section, then, the formal training patterns for three generations are outlined.

The first generation (e.g., Lüschen, Kenyon, Page, Schafer, and Stone in North America; Erbach, Novikov, Wohl, and Heinilä in Eastern and Western Europe; Takenoshita in Japan) were trained at both the undergraduate and graduate level in either a Department of Physical Education, which emphasized the biological and physical sciences, or in a Department of Sociology, where sport as a social phenomenon was seldom, if ever, discussed. It was not until at some point after their highest earned degree that these scholars became interested in studying sport from a sociological perspective. That is, this generation was characterized by individuals who either had formal training in sociology and a strong interest in sport, or who had formal training in physical education and sport, and a strong interest in social phenomena. It is not surprising then, that their early careers were characterized by role conflict (especially the sociologist) as they sought to legitimate both the introduction of new courses and the type of research they were undertaking. In fact, they were marginal men, neither sociologists nor physical educators. More specifically, those trained in sociology gained little status as sociologists because they dealt with a frivolous, non-work topic; while those trained in physical education were labelled as pseudo-intellectuals because they were more concerned with the social interactions, processes, problems and structure of sport, than with muscles, skills and how to become a more successful coach. In short, neither group was fully accepted by the parent profession, and thus the marriage of the two groups into the International Committee on Sport Sociology was not surprising.

The present, or second generation, of sport sociologists (i.e., those who earned their doctorate since approximately 1967) were trained jointly in Departments of Sociology, Social Psychology, and Physical Education. Many of these scholars were introduced to the social sciences while an undergraduate physical education major, yet in all likelihood never completed an undergraduate course in their area of specialization. Thus, at the graduate level they further developed their modest undergraduate experiences in the social sciences by attending an institution which encouraged an in-depth penetration in the basic discipline (sociology or social psychology), along with graduate courses in the sociology and social psychology of sport. In all instances, they studied under a first generation sport sociologist, usually within a Department of Physical Education. Unfortunately, in some cases they were bound by departmental regulations which required that a certain number of core courses (e.g., philosophy or history of physical education, measurement and evaluation) be completed before graduation. This requirement reduced the number of cognate courses in the basic discipline, and often meant that courses in social theory and sociological methods were either not taken, or at best only an introductory course was completed. Thus, whereas this generation was well prepared in the substantive areas of sociology and sport sociology, their training in theory and methodology was less than ideal. Nevertheless, most of the

second generation earned either a minor or joint major in sociology, and therefore have been able to obtain cross-appointments in Departments of Sociology at a much earlier stage in their career than did the first generation. This, of course, is an indirect indicator of both the quality of their formal occupational socialization, and an indicator that sport sociology is being currently accepted as a sub-discipline within sociology. This career step has been facilitated by administrators in physical education who are more discriminating in their hiring process. That is, they now seek individuals formally trained in sociology and sport sociology (i.e., those from a discipline-oriented programme), rather than those, however great their interest in sport sociology, who have graduated from a "generalist" programme in physical education (i.e., a professionally-oriented programme) with little or no training in the social sciences in general, and perhaps, sport sociology in particular.

To summarize, two generations of sport sociologists have been trained in the last ten years, and are now employed in universities throughout the world. A recent content analysis of the entire SIRLS file at Waterloo indicated that among those listed who had presented or published at least two papers in sport sociology or social psychology, twenty were employed in European institutions, 23 in the United States and 20 in Canada. Thus, there are approximately 63 active researchers in the sub-discipline. Of course there are many others who are just getting started or who only teach a course in the area, but never engage in the research process. In addition to the production of sport sociologists, a related trend has been the appearance of historians who are interested in looking at social phenomena in a sport context from an historical perspective via retrospective longitudinal studies (e.g., Berryman, Betts, Lewis, Metcalfe).

Turning to the future, and a consideration of the third generation which has already begun its training, we can foresee additional improvements in the socialization process. First, these individuals will in all likelihood have had an undergraduate major or minor in one of the social sciences, and will in most cases, have had from one to three undergraduate courses in the social science of sport (e.g., sociology of sport, social psychology of sport, psychology of sport, sociology of leisure). Thus, they will enter graduate school, at both the Master's and Doctoral level, with a strong knowledge base which can then be expanded by an in-depth penetration through both formal courses and independent research. Furthermore, these students will pursue their degree in either Departments of Sociology or Physical Education, usually under the supervision of a first or second generation sport sociologist.

Concurrent with the increasing emphasis on quantitative techniques and theory construction in sociology, this generation will pursue these areas in depth, and will be as well trained as any sociologist. In fact, the more rigorous their programme in these areas, the greater their marketability after graduation. Thus, being no longer restricted by the professional requirements of physical education departments, they will be free to maximize their potential as sociologists with a substantive interest in sport, regardless of the department in which they are registered. In addition to the increased competency in the quantitative and methods area, they will also have a better understanding of the science game. For example, whereas the first and second generation were exposed to philosophy of physical education courses, future generations will be exposed to the philosophy of science, the philosophy of the social sciences, and the sociology of science.

Other possible developments in the future that will facilitate the training and work of sport sociologists include:

1. the increased availability of funding for sociological research, including that which is sport-oriented, thereby negating a common excuse of past generations for failing to be as productive as other subdisciplines;
2. the job requirements will become more specific in that responsibilities will more closely approximate that in other departments (e.g., they will not play the role of coach), thereby leaving time and energy for the research enterprise;
3. post-doctoral fellowships may become available, thereby enabling a student to pursue substantive and methodological concerns to an even greater depth, and at the same time these will enable a fellow to initiate a number of research studies prior to entering the "real" university world where teaching and administrative responsibilities (i.e., committees) tend to

reduce the energy of the young scholar; and,
4. data banks, housing data sets from completed studies, will be established, thereby enabling the student to engage in independent, yet inexpensive, empirical and theoretical studies early in his graduate career.

RESEARCH METHODS

The research methods utilized by sport sociologists have been, are, and will continue to be those used in sociology, namely surveys (interviews or questionnaires), secondary analyses (content analysis, data analysis), controlled field studies, participant observation, and laboratory studies for social psychologists interested in micro-sport systems. In view of the comprehensive review and analysis of research methodology in the sociology of sport by Loy and Segrave (1974), this section is limited to a discussion of problems associated with past and current methods, and a discussion of some approaches which may be increasingly used in the future.

The major method employed by the first generation was the social survey, with the questionnaire format predominating over the structured interview format. Many of these studies employed intact, convenient groups (e.g., athletes at one school, in one region, of one sex, in one sport, at one class level). Thus, the samples were seldom representative or random (even within one community), nor, more importantly, was there the development of a theoretical rationale as to why the particular group or sub-group comprised the sample. As a result, the findings often could not be generalized beyond the local scene. In defense of this weakness, however, it must be noted that funding was difficult to obtain. Furthermore, since many of these studies were exploratory, they were often descriptive rather than explanatory in nature. For example, frequency counts of the number and frequency of activities, the attitudes of individuals in groups, and the demographic characteristics of the sample were the major pieces of information collected and reported. Other than crosstabulations by class background, little explanation was attempted. Again, however, this stocktaking in the early years was necessary and is a common pattern in many disciplines. In summary, the research completed by the first generation was, for the most part, descriptive, atheoretical, and on the macro-level. In addition, the major tool was the questionnaire administered to convenient groups.

With the arrival of the second generation, committed to a career in sport sociology early in life, and committed to a more analytic and explanatory approach, a variety of methods were, and are, being used to examine sport phenomena. Although the survey continued to be a popular method, an increasing number of studies began to use either the interview (Loy, 1968) or mailed questionnaire (Loy and Sage, 1972; Petrie and Reid, 1972) format, partially because of increased funding. More importantly, representative sampling procedures were utilized, often with large samples (N=500+), and groups were selected on some theoretical basis. Other methods used by this generation were content analysis (Hart, 1967; Haerle, 1973), secondary data analysis (Grusky, 1963; Loy and McElvogue, 1970; Ball, 1971), and for those more interested in social psychology, controlled laboratory (Martens, 1969), or field studies (McIntyre, 1970; Vander Velden, 1971). At the same time, a group of journalists (Schecter, 1970; Amdur, 1971), and ex-athletes (Meggesey, 1970; Shaw, 1972) utilized participant observation to describe the social milieu within professional sport. With the exception of the interesting study by McFarlane (1955) on the sociology of sport promotion, this technique has not been used to study sport phenomena from a sociological perspective. In addition to their interest in macro-social systems, there has been increased activity to understand the structure and processes inherent in micro-social systems. Again, this is partly a reflection of their concern with explanation and prediction.

Finally, in recent years this generation has become increasingly concerned with such issues as causation, operationalism, and theory construction, again paralleling the concerns of sociologists in other substantive areas. That is, there has been an increasing interest in organizing concepts into propositions, inter-relating these propositions into a verbal explanatory system (i.e., theory), building causal models, and testing and evaluating these theories, often using the multivariate approach known as path analysis (Kenyon, 1970; McPherson, 1972). This has enabled the empiricist and theorist roles to be merged into one—the theoretical empiricist or the empirical theorist.

In summary, at the present time a variety of

methods are being employed, especially secondary data analysis and social surveys; the analyses are more analytic and explanatory, multivariate rather than bivariate models are being employed; and, there is an increasing concern with developing sound theoretical bases, often in the form of a metatheory constructed for a specific study by the investigator.

Turning to the future, what might we expect from the second and third generation in terms of design and methods? First, the recent commitment to theoretical orientations and the subsequent emphasis on theory construction and causal modeling will continue with increasing mathematical sophistication. In fact, sport sociologists trained in the quantitative area may well make contributions to the field of methodology (i.e., methodology via sport). At the same time as they are committing themselves to a model of the social world which applies to their study, they should be prepared to present or discuss alternative models. In the past, very few studies, especially those which explained only a small percentage of variance, ever suggested alternative models. Both sport sociologists and social psychologists should be aware of the potentialities of computer simulation (Abelson, 1968), and network analyses (Harary, 1965; Granovetter, 1973) for studying social systems, interaction processes, and inter-personal relationships in sport situations. For example, simulation games can model different types of social systems and can be used to generate and test theories. While some of these simulated games have used athletes as subjects, none have studied social processes in a sport context.

Now that a body of knowledge has accumulated over a fifteen year period, some attempt should be made to pursue an in-depth penetration of the more scientifically-interesting topics, and to replicate studies completed at an earlier time in order to understand and explain social change. Similarly, studies should be replicated to verify the findings and to extend the results, within and between other sub-cultures (e.g., sex, ethnic, and regional differences). This process of replication could be greatly facilitated if more effort was directed toward utilizing not only better indicators, but also to arriving at some consensus as to what indicators might be used in a variety of studies. For example, various measures of social class are used, and even when similar measures are used, the breaking points are often different from one study to the next.

Similarly, there must be greater attention paid to the operationalization of commonly used variables, such as, degree of sport involvement. For example, does this refer to organized recreational sport, organized competitive sport, spontaneous sport involvement, all of these, some of these, or none of these!

With the increasing availability of funding for sport research, there should be an attempt to initiate longitudinal studies, especially since there is a young cohort of investigators readily available (even if they choose to wait until after tenure is earned). That is, there is little reason for continuing to rely on retrospective or cross-sectional data, especially when examining such processes as socialization, social mobility and social change. Similarly, there is no excuse for continuing to undertake myopic team, institutional or community studies in one region or at one institution. Since almost all regions of the country are represented by at least one sport sociologist, national and regional [research] should be proposed and undertaken. Furthermore, this [research] should be extended to the international scene with a greater emphasis on cross-national studies. This can be facilitated greatly by working with colleagues who are corresponding members of the International Committee on Sport Sociology. The current cross-national study of Leisure Role Socialization is an example of what can be accomplished given enough time and effort. For example, at the moment, six countries are at various stages of data collection, while another six are about to enter the project. To pursue this theme of co-operative research efforts one step further, sport sociologists should give some thought to entering multi-disciplinary studies, at least within the narrower rubric of the social sciences. That is, in any attempt to explain the success of elite athletes, there should be greater verbal interaction and research efforts between the psychologist who is concerned with personality, attitudes and motives; the social psychologist who is concerned with the dynamics of interaction within the sport group; and, the sociologist who is interested in the structural influences of the earlier and present social systems on the athlete. Thus, rather than each explaining a small percentage of the variance; together, employing a multivariate approach, they may explain a considerably higher percentage.

To conclude this section, four other developments that may occur in the near future are iden-tified. First, there should be a greater emphasis on the macro-level of analysis (social organizations, social institutions) and less on the micro-elements (groups) within one specific social system. Second, there should be an increased or new use of existing sociological methods such as, controlled field studies by social psychologists (cf. Lenk and Lüschen, 1973); secondary data analyses for national and cross-national studies and to study historical trends; content analyses to examine both current (McKay et al., 1973) phenomena and elements of social change (Haerle, 1973; Palmer, 1973); and participant observation to obtain real insights (qualitative rather than quantitative) into sport phenomena and thereby facilitate theory generation. A third development may be an increasing interest in the study of applied social problems (e.g., change agent research) and the initiation of policy research, both stimulated by the changing philosophy and policies of funding agencies who want some immediate feedback and action. Finally, on the international scene, there may be an increasing tendency for sport sociologists in some Eastern European countries to increasingly adopt Western empirical, non-normative approaches to the study of sport. This change will be facilitated by the increasing number of social scientists who attend international meetings held in Western countries, thereby becoming more familiar with our methods and concerns. In addition, the rapidly improving technology in their own countries will increase their willingness to get involved in macro studies with large data sets since machine-processing of data is becoming more available.

SUBSTANTIVE INTERESTS

Human behaviour, whether at work or play, is greatly influenced by the social milieu in which the individual finds himself at a specific point in time, and by the social environments he has been exposed to in the past. For example, whereas psychological, biomechanical and physiological processes may account for success or failure in sport at a given point in time, the sociological processes and the past experiences in a variety of social systems often dictate who gets involved, at what stage in life, and whether the individual ever attains the opportunity to compete at a high level of competition. Furthermore, although the biological sciences may be able to explain physical and structural differences between men and women, between the young and the old, and, even between different races; they cannot explain all of the variation accounting for differences in sport performance in these same parameters. Nor can they totally explain why individuals from one country (e.g., G.D.R.) are more successful in international competition than those from another country (e.g., Canada) with a similar population and geographical characteristics; or, why one region of a country is more involved in physical activity than another region. That is, much of the variation between groups is accounted for by social and cultural factors. In summary, sport sociology is distinguished from most of the other sub-disciplines in the sport sciences in that it must be concerned with the influence of temporal variables at various stages in the life cycle. That is, whereas other subdisciplines (physiologists, psychologists) are interested in describing and explaining the present elite performance of those who have achieved success, sport sociologists are interested in the process by which they attained this status, and why others did not. In summary, the above suggests that the property space of substantive concern to sport sociologists is broad, and therefore the topics investigated have been, and continue to be, quite varied in nature.

In the early years, the work of the first generation was devoted to attempts to conceptualize the sub-discipline; justify its existence; present appropriate concepts and methodologies; describe the social organization of sport sociology in various countries (see *International Review of Sport Sociology*, 1(1966)); and to offer polemic concerns about the role or function of sport in society, especially in the East European countries. Furthermore, much of the empirical work was devoted to: the interaction processes within small groups; the present and changing attitudes toward sport of various sub-groups; the class basis of sport involvement; the amount of time spent in play and sport; and, the relationship between sport involvement and educational attainment. Again, many of these studies are descriptive and atheoretical.

From the late 1960s until the present time, many of the second generation were, and still are, interested in such domains as:

1. the relationship between social class and sport involvement, especially as it influences social mobility;
2. the relationship between sport involvement

and educational attainment and aspirations;
3. the dynamics of small groups; and,
4. attitudes toward, and emanating from, sport involvement.

However, more recent studies have examined such domains as:

1. the relationship between institutionalized sport and such social processes as socialization, integration, assimilation, conflict, and social change; and,
2. social problems, such as, racial and ethnic discrimination, institutionalized aggressive behaviour, and delinquency; and, the structure and interactions within complex social organizations.

As a result of these efforts, numerous readers and textbooks (Loy and Kenyon, 1969; Kenyon, 1969; Lüschen, 1970; Sage, 1970; Dunning, 1972; Hart, 1972; Stone, 1972; Edwards, 1973; and, Page and Talamini, 1973), have appeared, with little overlap in substantive material.

Turning to the future, the following are some potential avenues of inquiry with respect to the field in general. Many of these questions will interest those who are discipline-oriented, as well as those who wish to pursue a more applied route. In the future, more studies, regardless of substantive concern, should be longitudinal in nature and comparative in perspective, both within and between societies and organizations.

Within the general rubric of sport and social processes there are a number of questions worthy of investigation, especially in the areas of social change, socialization and social stratification. First, scholars interested in social change should be attuned to the changing leisure patterns of consumption and participation of a variety of sub-groups, especially as they interact with changing value systems at the societal and sub-cultural level concerning the role of sport in society, and in particular, the role of minor sport and school sport (cf. Sack, 1973). For example, to what extent are values concerning sport undergoing change—is the humanistic trend suggested by many authors (e.g., Scott, 1973) a myth or reality, and, if real, to what extent and in what social environments has it gained acceptance? Additional questions related to changing values include the role of women in minor, school and professional sport programmes; the relationship between the values held by minor sport executives and the goals and effectiveness of the organization; the impact of recent immigrants on the values held for specific sports in the host society; and, the impact, both immediate and in the long run, of system disruption on sport participation and sport organization (e.g., the work-to-rule policy of school teachers, including coaches). Other problems related to social change include: the relationship between the growth of urbanism and sport phenomena; the impact of recent and future technological changes on sport; the relationship between work involvement and sport involvement (e.g., if mechanization fosters alienation at work, what role does sport play in reducing alienation, if any); the rise and role of sport in the Third World; the increasing politicization of sport and the shifts in power in the sport hierarchy at the local, national and international level; the growth and diffusion of new sports introduced by immigrants (e.g., European handball, soccer, orienteering) and the impact of this diffusion on existing sports; the diffusion and assimilation of sport interests over generations within specific ethnic groups; and, the changing influence of the professional athlete as role model and trend-setter (cf. G. Smith, 1973, who discusses this phenomenon but presents no data as to where and to what extent it is occurring).

While the process of socialization via sport and into sport has received considerable attention in recent years, the question of de-socialization and re-socialization has been ignored. For example, how and why do people become de-socialized from specific sport roles, or re-socialized from one role to another? Similarly, the career shift of professional athletes from the role of athlete to whatever work role they play in the middle and later years of the life cycle (cf. Milhovilovic, 1968; Kahn, 1972) should be examined from more than a social mobility perspective. These studies should be longitudinal in nature, or cross-sectional at best, in order to examine the influence of the sport career on their subsequent participation in the labour force (cf. Kenyon, 1972). Finally, since certain variables are more important at different stages in the life and work cycle than at other stages, studies should consider the influence of such temporal and situational factors as school-leaving, first job, career formation, retirement, marriage, and child-rearing on sport and leisure involvement over the life cycle for both males and females.

A consideration of the current social stratification literature as it relates to sport raises the following questions with respect to this social process: (1) is there a stratification system within sport (i.e., one sport carries more prestige than others) or within a given sport (e.g., a quarterback has more prestige than a tackle); (2) is the fact that someone is French Canadian or Polish more important for his involvement in a specific sport than the fact that his parents earn a specific income or live in a specific section of a community—that is, we must partial out the influence of ethnicity, father's income and occupation, and place of residence; (3) to what extent are there cross-national or regional differences in class-based involvement in sport (e.g., soccer may be an upper-class sport in one society, yet a lower-class sport in another); (4) are there inter-generational changes in class-oriented involvement in sport and, if so, to what extent are they related to upward mobility; (5) is social inequality in sport a reality, and, if so, does this vary by region, country or sex; (6) to what extent will government or private sector intervention lead to egalitarian grassroots participation (i.e., a "class" to "mass" trend in sport participation); (7) to what extent is sport involvement by women class-based; (8) are there differential associations between social origins and the frequency and pattern of sport consumption; (9) what support is there for the proposition that the newer the sport, the higher the social class of the participants; and, (10) is the democratization of sport occurring and if so, does this vary by region and by sex. In short, there are many interesting questions within the stratification literature that need to be answered.

Another major area of inquiry should be the study of sport phenomena as experienced by specific sub-groups. For example, except for the study by Hatt (1972) of the Metis' agrarian society in Northern Alberta, there has been virtually no interest in Canada in Indian or Eskimo societies from a sociological perspective. Similarly, there have been few studies concerned with Francophones or other ethnic groups within a particular society.

Similarly, an increased interest in women and sport might lead to an examination of: (1) the influence of mothers on children's sport involvement (i.e., both type and degree); (2) the extent to which the limiting factors for women's involvement and competitive achievements in sport are socially-induced (e.g., sanctions, norms, expectations, opportunity set), rather than biologically-based; (3) a comparison of the expectations concerning role equivalence and the achievements of males and females in Socialist and Western countries, both in general and in sport milieu; and, (4) a study of the implications of sex tests for females on their perceived sex-role. Other sub-groups which might merit study in the future include rural inhabitants and the aged. For example, the rural sociology literature might provide fruitful ideas, paradigms (cf. Loy, 1966) and theories to examine the role and influence of sport on life-styles (cf. Fox, 1961; Hatt, 1972) in various rural communities, while the sociology of aging literature might suggest similar stimuli and guidelines (e.g., disengagement vs. activity theory) for a consideration of sport involvement at various stages in the life-cycle, especially the later years (e.g., de-socialization).

Another domain which should receive greater attention in the near future is that of social problems inherent in sport. While many problems might be enumerated, this section will be delimited to a discussion of three which are interrelated: minor sport organizations, athletic drop-outs, and mass consumption. First, the structure and social organization of voluntary minor and adult sport associations should be studied. Many of these organizations are mini-bureaucracies comprised of individuals who volunteer their services and retain their tenured position of power for many years. From the perspective of formal organizations then, an examination of the relationship between limited turnover and organizational effectiveness would be interesting, as would the study of the dynamics of participation, replacement, and control (power) within an association. Thus, whereas recent attempts have been made to examine professional and college sport as formal organizations, little attention has been paid to the organizational structure or problems inherent in the plethora of voluntary minor sport associations which exist throughout the world. This area, then, would appear to offer many avenues of inquiry for both those interested in the structure and processes of organizations, and those interested in identifying and alleviating practical problems found in the minor sport associations in their community (e.g., change agent research). A somewhat related problem is the increasing number of athletic "drop-outs" or, non-participants in the child-hood and adolescent years. For example, what factors inherent in the social organization of minor sport predispose young athletes (e.g., those in age-group, all-star and house league programmes) to stop participating or competing at a very young age so that either future elite athletes are lost from the pool of talent available for international competition, or, more seriously, physical activity ceases to be an integral facet of their life-style and thus, the society becomes increasingly less active. Some possible factors, among many, might include a shift from a "work ethic" to a "fun ethic"; the increasing, but unbearable, normative pressures to achieve; changing values and norms within the peer groups reflected in competing or alternative leisure-time life-styles; and, lack of reinforcement from significant others.

A third problem worthy of study is the increasing trend toward high mass-consumption (Rostow, 1971), sport being just one facet of this trend. Avenues of inquiry in this domain might include an understanding of: (1) sport consumption as a form of expressive behaviour; (2) the dynamics of the sport consumer—a comparison by sport and country would be worthwhile; (3) collective violence in the consumption milieu (cf. M. Smith, 1973); and, (4) the impact of the four-day work week on sport consumption patterns (e.g., will there be further expansion by professional sport organizations in order to present Tuesday or Thursday afternoon entertainment for the masses).

SUMMARY AND CONCLUSIONS

In summary, this paper has discussed the past, present and future of sport sociology with respect to the training of scholars, the methodologies employed, and the substantive concerns. It was noted that the process of occupational socialization for sport sociologists is increasingly paralleling that of others in sociology, that the techniques of scientific inquiry are becoming increasingly theoretical and quantitative, and that the substantial concerns are expanding in new directions, but at the same time, being pursued to a greater depth with respect to the understanding of specific problems in specific social systems.

In conclusion, it must be remembered that sport, at whatever level, occurs in a social context. That is, a variety of social parameters and social processes influence human performance in sport, whether they be vendor, volunteer minor coach or team owner. Thus, sport sociology, despite its recent appearance, is a viable domain of inquiry in the area of human movement studies, especially as they seek to identify and explain the parameters influencing variation in success, whether it be at the local, regional, national, international, amateur or professional level.

REFERENCES

1. Abelson, R. P.: Simulation of social behavior. *In* Handbook of Social Psychology, Volume 2. Edited by G. Lindzey and E. Aronson. Reading, Mass., Addison-Wesley, 1968, pp. 274–356.
2. Amdur, N.: The Fifth Down: Democracy and The Football Revolution. New York, Dell, 1971.
3. Ball, D. W.: Olympic Games Competition: Structural Correlates of National Success. Paper presented at the 66th Annual Meeting, American Sociological Association, Denver, August 1971.
4. Dunning, E.: Sport: Readings from a Sociological Perspective. Toronto, The University of Toronto Press, 1972.
5. Edwards, H.: Sociology of Sport. Georgetown, Ontario, Irwin-Dorsey Limited, 1973.
6. Fox, J. R.: Pueblo baseball: a new use for old witchcraft. J. Am. Folklore, *74*:9, 1968.
7. Granovetter, M. S.: The strength of weak ties. Am. J. Sociol., *78* (May):1360–1380, 1973.
8. Grusky, O.: Managerial succession and organizational effectiveness. Am. J. Sociol., *69* (July):21, 1963.
9. Haerle, R.: Heroes, Success Themes, and Basic Cultural Values in Baseball Autobiographies: 1900–1970. Presented at the Third National Meeting of the Popular Culture Association, Indianapolis, Indiana, April 14, 1973.
10. Harary, F.: Graph theory and group structure. *In* Readings in Mathematical Psychology. Edited by R. Luce et al. New York, Wiley, 1965, Vol. 2.
11. Hart, M.: An Analysis of the Content of Sport Magazines: 1889–1965, Unpublished Ph.D. Dissertation, University of Southern California, 1967.
12. Hart, M., (ed.): Sport in the Socio-Cultural Process. Dubuque, Iowa, W. C. Brown Co., 1972.
13. Hatt, F. K.: The Game as a Critical Element in the Sociology of Sport. Presented at the 67th Annual Meeting of the American Sociological Association. August 28–31, 1972.
14. Kahn, R.: The Boys of Summer. New York, Fitzhenry and Whiteside, 1972.
15. Kenyon, G. S.: Values Held for Physical Activity by Selected Urban Secondary School Students in Canada, England, Australia, and the United States. Final Report, United States Office of Education, Contract OE–6–10–179, University of Wisconsin, 1968.
16. Kenyon, G. S.: Aspects of Contemporary Sport Sociology. Chicago, The Athletic Institute, 1969.
17. Kenyon, G. S.: The use of path analysis in sport sociology with special reference to involvement socialization. Int. Rev. Sport Sociol., *5*:191, 1970.
18. Kenyon, G. S.: Sport and Career: Patterns of Role Progression. Paper presented at Scientific Congress of 20th Olympiad, Munich, August 21–25, 1972.
19. Kenyon, G. S. and Loy, J. W.: Toward a sociology of sport. J. Health, Phys. Educ. Rec., *36*:24, 1965.
20. Lenk, H. and Lüschen, G.: The Problem of Explanation in Social Psychology and the Personality and Social System Levels. Paper presented at the Conference on Social Psychology of Sport, Allerton House, University of Illinois, Urbana, May 15, 1973.
21. Loy, J. W.: A paradigm of technological change in the sport situation. Int. Rev. Sport Sociol., *1*:177, 1966.
22. Loy, J. W.: Sociopsychological attributes associated with the early adoption of a sport innovation. J. Psychol., *70*:141, 1968.
23. Loy, J. W. and Kenyon, G. S. (eds.): Sport, Culture and Society. New York, Macmillan, 1969.
24. Loy, J. W. and McElvogue, J. F.: Racial segregation in American sport. Int. Rev. Sport Sociol., *5*: 5, 1970.
25. Loy, J. W. and Sage, G.: Social Origins, Academic Achievement, Athletic Achievement and Career Mobility Patterns of College Coaches. Paper presented at the 67th Annual Meeting of the American Sociological Association, New Orleans, August 28–31, 1972.
26. Loy, J. W. and Segrave, J. O.: Research methodology in the sociology of sport, *In* Exercise and Sport Sciences Review. Edited by J. Wilmore. New York, Academic Press, 1974. Vol. II.
27. Lüschen, G. S.: Cross-Cultural Analysis of Sport and Games. Champaign, Ill., Stipes, 1970.
28. Martens R.: Effect on performance of learning a complex motor task in the presence of spectators. Research Quarterly, *49* (May):272, 1969.
29. McFarlane, B. A.: The Sociology of Sports Promotion. Unpublished Master of Arts Thesis, McGill University, 1955.
30. McKay, J. et al.: Da da Canada—Nyet nyet Soviet: A Study of Ethnocentrism in the first U.S.S.R.—Canada Hockey Series. Presented at the First Canadian Congress for the Multi-Disciplinary Study of Sport and Physical Activity, Montreal, October 12–14, 1973.
31. McIntyre, T. D.: A Field Experimental Study of Cohesiveness, Status, and Attitude Change in Four Biracial Small Sport Groups, Unpublished Ph.D. Dissertation, Pennsylvania State University, 1970.
32. McPherson, B. D.: Socialization Into the Role of Sport Consumer: A Theory and Causal Model. Unpublished Ph.D. Dissertation, University of Wisconsin, 1972.
33. Meggesey, D.: Out of Their League. Berkeley, California, Ramparts Press, 1970.
34. Milhovilovic, M. A.: The status of former sportsmen. Int. Rev. of Sport Sociol., *3*: pp. 73–96, 1968.
35. Page, C. and Talamini, J.: Sport and Society. Boston, Little, Brown, 1973.

36. Palmer, M. D.: The sports novel: mythic heroes and natural men. Quest, *19*:49–58, 1973.
37. Petrie, B. and Reid, E. L.: The political attitudes of Canadian athletes. *In* Proceedings of Fourth Canadian Symposium on Psycho-Motor Learning and Sports Psychology. Edited by I. Williams and L. Wankel. Ottawa, Department of Health and Welfare, Fitness and Amateur Sport Directorate, 1972.
38. Rostow, W. W.: The Stages of Economic Growth. London, Cambridge University Press, 1971.
39. Sack, A. L.: Yale 29—Harvard 4: The professionalization of college football. Quest, *19* (January): 24–34, 1973.
40. Sage, G.: Sport and American Society. Reading, Massachusetts, Addision-Wesley, 1970.
41. Schecter, L.: The Jocks. New York, Paperback Library, 1970.
42. Scott, J.: Sport and the radical ethic. Quest, *19* (January):71–76, 1973.
43. Shaw, G.: Meat on the Hoof: The Hidden World of Texas Football. New York, St. Martins Press, 1972.
44. Smith, G.: The sport hero: an endangered species. Quest, *19* (January):59–70, 1973.
45. Smith, M. D.: Hostile outbursts in sport. Sport Sociol. Bull., *2* (Spring):6–10, 1973.
46. Stone, G.: American sports—play and display. Chicago Rev., *9* (Fall):83–100, 1955.
47. Stone, G.: Sport, Games and Power. New Brunswick, New Jersey, Transaction Books, 1972.
48. Stone, G.: Some Meaning of American Sport. College Phys. Assoc. 60th Annu. Proc., 1957, (October), 6–29.
49. Theodorson, G. A. and Theodorson, A. G.: Modern Dictionary of Sociology. New York, T. Y. Crowell, 1969.
50. Vander Velden, L.: Relationships Among Member, Team and Situational Variables and Basketball Team Success, Unpublished Ph.D. Dissertation, University of Wisconsin, 1971.
51. Wohl, A.: The problems of development of physical culture in the socialist system. Kultura Fizyczna, *6*:182–187, 1953.

SECTION TWO
sport as a social phenomenon

the nature of sport: a definitional effort

JOHN W. LOY, JR.

Sport is a highly ambiguous term having different meanings for various people. Its ambiguity is attested to by the range of topics treated in the sport sections of daily newspapers. Here, one can find accounts of various sport competitions; advertisements for the latest sport fashions, advice on how to improve one's skills in certain games, and essays on the state of given organized sports, including discussions of such matters as recruitment, financial success, and scandal. The broad, yet loose encompass of sport reflected in the mass media suggests that sport can and perhaps should be dealt with on different planes of discourse if a better understanding of its nature is to be acquired. As a step in this direction we discuss sport as a *game occurrence,* as an *institutionalized game,* as a *social institution* and as a *social situation* or social system.

I. SPORT AS A GAME OCCURRENCE

Perhaps most often when we think of the meaning of sport we think of sports. In our perspective sports are considered as a specialized type of game. That is, *a sport* as one of the many "sports" is viewed as an actual game occurrence or event. Thus in succeeding paragraphs we briefly outline what we consider to be the basic characteristics of games in general. In describing these characteristics we continually make reference to sports in particular as a special type of game. A *game* we define as any form of playful

competition whose outcome is determined by physical skill, strategy or chance employed singly or in combination.[1]

A. PLAYFUL

By "playful competition" we mean that any given contest has one or more elements of play. We purposely have not considered game as a subclass of play,[2] for if we had done so sport would logically become a subset of play and thus preclude the subsumption of professional forms of sport under our definition of the term. However, we wish to recognize that one or more aspects of play constitute basic components of games and that even the most highly organized forms of sport are not completely devoid of play characteristics.

The Dutch historian, Johan Huizinga, has probably made the most thorough effort to delineate the fundamental qualities of play. He defines play as follows:

Summing up the formal characteristics of play we might call it a free activity standing quite consciously outside "ordinary" life as being "not serious," but at the same time absorbing the player intensely and utterly. It is an activity connected with no material interest, and no profit can be gained by it. It proceeds within its own proper boundaries of time and space according to fixed rules and in an orderly manner. It promotes the formation of social groupings which tend to surround themselves with secrecy and to stress their difference from the common world by disguise or other means (Huizinga, 1955, p. 13).

Reprinted from *Quest, 10*:1–15, 1968.© 1968 Human Kinetics Publishers, Box 5076, Champaign, IL 61820.

Caillois has subjected Huizinga's definition to critical analysis (Caillois, 1961, pp. 3–10) and has redefined play as an activity which is free, separate, uncertain, unproductive, governed by rules and make-believe (Caillois, 1961, pp. 9–10). We shall briefly discuss these qualities ascribed to play by Huizinga and Caillois and suggest how they relate to games in general and sports in particular.

1. **FREE.** By free is meant that play is a voluntary activity. That is, no one is ever strictly forced to play, playing is done in one's free time, and playing can be initiated and terminated at will. This characteristic of play is no doubt common to many games, including some forms of amateur sport. It is not, however, a distinguishing feature of all games, especially those classified as professional sport.

2. **SEPARATE.** By separate Huizinga and Caillois mean that play is spatially and temporally limited. This feature of play is certainly relevant to sports. For many, if not most, forms of sport are conducted in spatially circumscribed environments; examples being the bullring, football stadium, golf course, race track and swimming pool. And with few exceptions every form of sport has rules which precisely determine the duration of a given contest.

3. **UNCERTAIN.** The course or end result of play cannot be determined beforehand. Similarly a chief characteristic of all games is that they are marked by an uncertain outcome. Perhaps it is this factor more than any other which lends excitement and tension to any contest. Strikingly uneven competition is routine for the contestants and boring for the spectators; hence, efforts to insure a semblance of equality between opposing sides are a notable feature of sport. These efforts typically focus on the matters of size, skill and experience. Examples of attempts to establish equality based on size are the formation of athletic leagues and conferences composed of social organizations of similar size, and the designation of weight classes for boxers and wrestlers. Illustrations of efforts to insure equality among contestants on the basis of skill and experience are the establishment of handicaps for bowlers and golfers; the designation of various levels of competition within a given organization as evidenced by freshmen, junior varsity and varsity teams in scholastic athletics; and the drafting of players from established teams when adding a new team to a league as done in professional football and basketball.

4. **UNPRODUCTIVE.** Playing does not in itself result in the creation of new material goods. It is true that in certain games such as poker there may occur an exchange of money or property among players. And it is a truism that in professional sports victory may result in substantial increases of wealth for given individuals. But the case can be made, nevertheless, that a game *per se* is nonutilitarian in nature.[3] For what is produced during any sport competition is a *game;* and the production of the game is generally carried out in a prescribed setting and conducted according to specific rules.

5. **GOVERNED BY RULES.** All types of games have agreed-upon rules, be they formal or informal. It is suggested that sports can be distinguished from games in general by the fact that they usually have a greater variety of norms and a larger absolute number of formal norms (i.e., written prescribed and proscribed norms).[4] Similarly, there is a larger number and more stringent sanctions in sports than games in general. For example, the basketball player must leave the game after he has committed a fixed number of fouls, the hockey player must spend a certain amount of time in the penalty box after committing a foul, and a football player may be asked to leave the game if he shows unsportsmanlike conduct.

With respect to the normative order of games and sports one explicit feature is that they usually have definite criteria for determining the winner. Although it is true that some end in a tie, most contests do not permit such an ambivalent termination by providing a means of breaking a deadlock and ascertaining the "final" victor. The means of determining the winner in sportive endeavors are too numerous to enumerate. But it is relevant to observe that in many sport competitions where "stakes are high" a series of contests are held between opponents in an effort to rule out the element of chance and decide the winner on the basis of merit. A team may be called "lucky" if it beats an opponent once by a narrow margin, but if it does so repeatedly then the appellations of "better" or "superior" are generally applied.

6. **MAKE-BELIEVE.** By the term make-believe Huizinga and Caillois wish to signify that play stands outside "ordinary" or "real" life and is distinguished by an "only pretending quality." While some would deny this characteristic of play as being applicable to sport, it is interesting to note that Veblen at the turn of the century stated:

Sports share this characteristic of make-believe with the games and exploits to which children, especially boys, are habitually inclined. Make-believe does not enter in the same proportion into all sports, but it is present in a very appreciable degree in all. (Veblen, 1934, p. 256)

Huizinga observes that the "... 'only pretending' quality of play betrays a consciousness of the inferiority of play compared with 'seriousness' ..." (1955, p. 8). We note here that occasionally one reads of a retiring professional athlete who remarks that "he is giving up the game to take a real job,"[5] and that several writers have commented on the essential shallowness of sport.[6] Roger Kahn, for example, has written that:

The most fascinating and least reported aspect of American sports is the silent and enduring search for a rationale. Stacked against the atomic bomb or even against a patrol in Algeria, the most exciting rally in history may not seem very important, and for the serious and semi-serious people who make their living through sports, triviality is a nagging, damnable thing. Their drive for self-justification has contributed much to the development of sports. (Kahn, 1957, p. 10)

On the other hand, Huizinga is careful to point out that "... the consciousness of play being 'only pretend' does not by any means prevent it from proceeding with the utmost seriousness..." (Huizinga, 1955, p. 8). As examples, need we mention the seriousness with which duffers treat their game of golf, the seriousness which fans accord discussions of their home team, or the seriousness that national governments give to Olympic Games and university alumni to collegiate football?[7,8]

Accepting the fact that the make-believe quality of play has some relevance for sport, it nevertheless remains difficult to empirically ground the "not ordinary or real life" characteristic of play. However, the "outside of real life" dimension of a game is perhaps best seen in its "as-if" quality, its artificial obstacles and in its potential resources for actualization or production.

(a) In a game the contestants act as if all are equal and numerous aspects of "external reality" such as race, education, occupation and financial status are excluded as relevant attributes for the duration of a given contest.[9]

(b) The obstacles individuals encounter in their daily work-a-day lives are not usually predetermined by them and are "real" in the sense that they must be adequately coped with if certain inherent and socially conditioned needs are to be met; whereas, in games obstacles are artificially created to be overcome. Although these predetermined obstacles set up to be conquered can sometimes attain "life and death" significance as in a difficult Alpine climb they are not usually essentially related to an individual's daily toil for existence.[10]

(c) Similarly, it is observed that in many "real" life situations the structures and processes needed to cope with a given obstacle are often not at hand; whereas, in a play or game situation all of the structures and processes necessary to deal with any deliberately created obstacle and to realize any possible alternative in course of action are potentially available.[11]

In sum, then, games are playful in nature in that they typically have one or more elements of play: freedom, separateness, uncertainty, unproductiveness, order, and make-believe. In addition to having elements of play, games have components of competition.

B. COMPETITION

Competition is defined as a struggle for supremacy between two or more opposing sides. We interpret the phrase "between two or more opposing sides" rather broadly to encompass the competitive relationships between man and other objects of nature both animate and inanimate. Thus competitive relationships include:

1. competition between one individual and another, e.g., a boxing match or 100-yard dash;
2. competition between one team and another, e.g., a hockey game or yacht race;
3. competition between an individual or team and an animate object of nature, e.g., a bullfight or deer hunting party;
4. competition between an individual or team and an inanimate object of nature, e.g., a canoeist running a set of rapids or a mountain climbing expedition; and finally,
5. competition between an individual or team and an ideal standard, e.g., an individual attempting to establish a world land speed record on the Bonneville salt flats or a basketball team trying to set an all-time scoring record. Competition against an "ideal"

standard might also be conceptualized as man against time or space, or as man against himself.[12]

The preceding classification has been set forth to illustrate what we understand by the phrase "two or more opposing sides" and is not intended to be a classification of competition *per se*. Although the scheme may have some relevance for such a purpose, its value is limited by the fact that its categories are neither mutually exclusive nor inclusive. For instance, an athlete competing in a cross-country race may be competitively involved in all of the following ways: as an individual against another individual; as a team member against members of an opposing team; and as an individual or team member against an "ideal" standard (e.g., an attempt to set an individual and/or team record for the course).[13]

C. PHYSICAL SKILL, STRATEGY AND CHANCE

Roberts and Sutton-Smith suggest that the various games of the world can be classified

... on the basis of outcome attributes: (1) games of *physical skill*, in which the outcome is determined by the players' motor activities; (2) games of *strategy*, in which the outcome is determined by rational choices among possible courses of action; and (3) games of *chance*, in which the outcome is determined by guesses or by some uncontrolled artifact such as a die or wheel. (Roberts and Sutton-Smith, 1962, p. 166)

Examples of relatively pure forms of competitive activities in each of these categories are weight lifting contests, chess matches and crap games, respectively. Many, if not most, games are, however, of a mixed nature. Card and board games, for instance, generally illustrate a combination of strategy and chance. Although chance is also associated with sport, its role in determining the outcome of a contest is generally held to a minimum in order that the winning side can attribute its victory to merit rather than to a fluke of nature. Rather interestingly, it appears that a major role of chance in sport is to insure equality. For example, the official's flip of a coin prior to the start of a football game randomly determines what team will receive the kickoff and from what respective side of the field, and simi-

larly, the drawing of numbers by competitors in track and swimming is an attempt to assure them equal opportunity of being assigned a given lane.

D. PHYSICAL PROWESS

Having discussed the characteristics which sports share in common with games in general, let us turn to an account of the major attribute which distinguishes sports in particular from games in general. We observe that sports can be distinguished from games by the fact that they demand the demonstration of physical prowess. By the phrase "the demonstration of physical prowess" we mean the employment of *developed* physical skills and abilities within the context of gross physical activity to conquer an opposing object of nature. Although many games require a minimum of physical skill they do not usually demand the degree of physical skill required by sports. The idea of "developed physical skills" implies much practice and learning and suggests the attainment of a high level of proficiency in one or more general physical abilities relevant to sport competition such as strength, speed, endurance, or accuracy.

Although the concept of physical prowess permits sports to be generally differentiated from games, numerous borderline areas exist. For example, can a dart game among friends, a horseshoe contest between husband and wife, or a fishing contest between father and son be considered sport? One way to arrive at an answer to these questions is to define *a sport* as any highly organized game requiring physical prowess. Thus a dart game with friends, a horseshoe contest between spouses or a fishing contest between a father and son would not be considered sport; but formally sponsored dart, horseshoe or fishing tournaments would be legitimately labeled sport. An alternative approach to answering the aforementioned questions, however, is to define *a sport* as an institutionalized game demanding the demonstration of physical prowess. If one accepts the latter approach, then he will arrive at a different set of answers to the above questions. For this approach views a game as an unique event and sport as an institutional pattern. As Weiss has rather nicely put it:

A game is an occurrence; a sport is a pattern. The one is in the present, the other primarily past, but instantiated in the present. A sport defines the conditions to which the participants must submit if there is to be a game; a game gives rootage to a set of rules and thereby enables a sport to be exhibited (1967, p. 82).

II. SPORT AS AN INSTITUTIONALIZED GAME

To treat sport as an institutionalized game is to consider sport as an abstract entity. For example, the organization of a football team as described in a rule book can be discussed without reference to the members of any particular team; the relationships among team members can be characterized without reference to unique personalities or to particular times and places. In treating sport as an institutionalized game we conceive of it as distinctive, enduring patterns of culture and social structure combined into a single complex; the elements of which include values, norms, sanctions, knowledge and social positions (i.e., roles and statuses).[14] A firm grasp of the meaning of "institutionalization" is necessary for understanding the idea of sport as an institutional pattern, or blueprint if you will, guiding the organization and conduct of given games and sportive endeavors.

The formulation of a set of rules for a game or even their enactment on a particular occasion does not constitute *a sport* as we have conceptualized it here. The institutionalization of a game implies that it has a tradition of past exemplifications and definite guide lines for future realizations. Moreover, in a concrete game situation the form of a particular sport need not reflect all of the characteristics represented in its institutional pattern. The more organized a sport contest in a concrete setting, however, the more likely it will illustrate the institutionalized nature of a given sport. A professional baseball game, for example, is a better illustration of the institutionalized nature of baseball than a sandlot baseball game, but both games are based on the same institutional pattern and thus may both be considered forms of sport. In brief, a sport may be treated analytically in terms of its degree of institutionalization and dealt with empirically in terms of its degree of organization. The latter is an empirical instance of the former.

In order to more adequately illustrate the institutionalized nature of sport we contrast the organizational, technological, symbolic and educational spheres of sports with those of games. In doing so we consider both games and sports in their most formalized and organized state. We

are aware that there are institutionalized games other than sports which possess characteristics similar to the ones we ascribe to sports, as for example chess and bridge, but we contend that such games are in the minority and in any case are excluded as sports because they do not demand the demonstration of physical prowess.

A. ORGANIZATIONAL SPHERE

For present purposes we rather arbitrarily discuss the organizational aspects of sport in terms of teams, sponsorship and government.

1. TEAMS. Competing sides for most games are usually selected rather spontaneously and typically disband following a given contest, whereas, in the case of sports, competing groups are generally selected with care and, once membership is established, maintain a stable social organization. Although individual persons may withdraw from such organizations after they are developed, their social positions are taken up by others and the group endures.[15]

Another differentiating feature is that as a rule sports show a greater degree of role differentiation than games. Although games often involve several contestants (e.g., poker), the contestants often perform identical activities and thus may be considered to have the same roles and statuses. However, in sports involving a similar number of participants (e.g., basketball) each individual or combinations of just a few individuals perform specialized activities within the group and may be said to possess different roles. Moreover, to the extent that such specialized and differentiated activities can be ranked in terms of some criteria, they also possess different statuses.

2. SPONSORSHIP. In addition to there being permanent social groups established for purposes of sport competition there is usually found in the sport realm social groups which act as sponsoring bodies for sport teams. These sponsoring bodies may be characterized as being direct or indirect. Direct sponsoring groups include municipalities who sponsor Little League Baseball Teams, universities who support collegiate teams, and business corporations who sponsor AAU teams, whereas indirect sponsoring groups include sporting goods manufacturers, booster clubs and sport magazines.

3. GOVERNMENT. Although all types of games have at least a modicum of norms and sanctions associated with them, the various forms of sport are set apart from many games by the fact that they have a larger number, more formal and more institutionalized sets of these cultural elements. In games, rules are often passed down by oral tradition or spontaneously established for a given contest and forgotten afterward, or, even where codified, are simple and few in number. In the case of sports, however, rules are usually many in number and formally codified and typically enforced by a regulatory body. There are international organizations governing most sports, and in America there are relatively large social organizations governing both amateur and professional sports. For example, amateur sports in America are controlled by such groups as the NCAA, AAU, and NAIA, and the major professional sports have national commissioners with enforcing officials to police competition.

B. TECHNOLOGICAL SPHERE

In *a sport* technology denotes the material equipment, physical skills and body of knowledge which are necessary for the conduct of competition and potentially available for technical improvements in competition. Although all types of games require a minimum of knowledge and often a minimum of physical skill and material equipment, the various sports are set apart from many games by the fact that they typically require greater knowledge and involve higher levels of physical skill and necessitate more material equipment. The technological aspects of *a sport* may be dichotomized into those which are intrinsic and those which are extrinsic. Intrinsic technological aspects of *a sport* consist of those physical skills, knowledge and equipment which are required for the conduct of a given contest *per se*. For example, the intrinsic technology of football includes: (a) the equipment necessary for the game—field, ball, uniforms, etc.; (b) the repertoire of physical skills necessary for the game—running, passing, kicking, blocking and tackling abilities, etc.; and (c) the knowledge necessary for the game—rules, strategy, etc. Examples of extrinsic technological elements associated with football include: (a) physical equipment such as stadium, press facilities, dressing rooms, etc.; (b) physical skills such as those possessed by coaches, cheerleaders and ground crews; and (c) knowledge such as that possessed by coaches, team physicians and spectators.

C. SYMBOLIC SPHERE

The symbolic dimension of *a sport* includes elements of secrecy, display and ritual. Huizinga contends that play "promotes the formation of social groupings which tend to surround themselves with secrecy and to stress their difference from the common world by disguise of other means" (1955, p. 13). Caillois criticizes his contention and states to the contrary that "... play tends to remove the very nature of the mysterious." He further observes that "... when the secret, the mask or the costume fulfills a sacramental function one can be sure that not play, but an institution is involved" (1961, p. 4).

Somewhat ambivalently we agree with both writers. On the one hand, to the extent that Huizinga means by 'secrecy' the act of making distinctions between "play life" and "ordinary life" we accept his proposition that groups engaged in playful competition surround themselves with secrecy. On the other hand, to the extent that he means by "secrecy" something hidden from others we accept Caillois' edict that an institution and not play is involved.

1. The latter type of secrecy might well be called "sanctioned secrecy" in sports. For there is associated with many forms of sport competition rather clear norms regarding approved clandestine behavior. For example, football teams are permitted to set up enclosed practice fields, send out scouts to spy on opposing teams and exchange a limited number of game films revealing the strategies of future opponents. Other kinds of clandestine action such as slush funds established for coaches and gambling on games by players are not always looked upon with such favor.[16]

2. A thorough reading of Huizinga leads one to conclude that what he means by secrecy is best discussed in terms of display and ritual. He points out, for example, that "the 'differentness' and secrecy of play are most vividly expressed in 'dressing up';" and states that the higher forms of play are "... a contest *for* something or a representation *of* something"—adding that "representation means display" (1955, p. 13). The "dressing-up" element of play noted by Huizinga is certainly characteristic of most sports. Perhaps it is carried to its greatest height in bullfighting but it is not absent in some of the less overt forms of sport. Veblen writes:

It is noticeable, for instance, that even very

mild-mannered and matter-of-fact men who go out shooting are apt to carry an excess of arms and accoutrements in order to impress upon their own imagination the seriousness of their undertaking. These huntsmen are also prone to a histrionic, prancing gait and to an elaborate exaggeration of the motions, whether of stealth or of onslaught, involved in their deeds of exploits (1934, p. 256).

A more recent account of "dressing-up" and display in sports has been given by Stone (1955) who treats display as spectacle and as a counterforce to play. Stone asserts that the tension between the forces of play and display constitute an essential component of sport. The following quotation gives the essence of his account:

> Play and dis-play are precariously balanced in sport, and, once that balance is upset, the whole character of sport in society may be affected. Furthermore, the spectacular element of sport, may, as in the case of American professional wrestling, destroy the game. The rules cease to apply, and the "cheat" and the "spoilsport" replace the players.... The point may be made in another way. The spectacle is predictable and certain; the game, unpredictable and uncertain. Thus spectacular dis-play may be reckoned from the outset of the performance. It is announced by the appearance of the performers—their physiques, costumes, and gestures. On the other hand, the spectacular play is solely a function of the uncertainty of the game (p. 98).

In a somewhat different manner another sociologist, Erving Goffman, has analyzed the factors of the uncertainty of a game and display. Concerning the basis of "fun in games" he states that "... mere uncertainty of outcome is not enough to engross the players" (1961, p. 68); and suggests that a successful game must combine "sanctioned display" with problematic outcome. By display Goffman means that "... games give the players an opportunity to exhibit attributes valued in the wider social world, such as dexterity, strength, knowledge, intelligence, courage, and self-control" (1961, p. 68). Thus, for Goffman, display represents spectacular play involving externally relevant attributes, while, for Stone, display signifies spectacular exhibition involving externally nonrelevant attributes with respect to the game situation.

3. Another concept related to display and spectacle and relevant to sports is that of ritual. According to Leach, "ritual denotes those aspects of prescribed formal behavior which have no direct technological consequences" (1964, p. 607). Ritual may be distinguished from spectacle by the fact that it generally has a greater element of drama and is less ostentatious and more serious in nature. "Ritual actions are 'symbolic' in that they assert something about the state of affairs, but they are not necessarily purposive, i.e., the performer of ritual does not necessarily seek to alter the state of affairs" (Leach, 1964). Empirically ritual can be distinguished from spectacle by the fact that those engaged in ritual express an attitude of solemnity toward it; an attitude which they do not direct toward spectacle.

Examples of rituals in sport are the shaking of hands between team captains prior to the start of a game, the shaking of hands between coaches after a game, the singing of the national anthem before the beginning of a game, and the singing of the school song at the conclusion of a game.[17]

D. EDUCATIONAL SPHERE

The educational sphere focuses on those activities related to the transmission of skills and knowledge to those who lack them. Many, if not most people learn to play the majority of socially preferred games in an informal manner, that is, they acquire the required skills and knowledge associated with a given game through casual instruction of friends or immediate associates. In the case of sport, however, skills and knowledge are often obtained by means of formal instruction. In short the educational sphere of sport is institutionalized, whereas in most games it is not. One reason for this situation is the fact that sports require highly developed physical skills which games often do not, and to achieve proficiency requires long hours of practice and qualified instruction, i.e., systematized training. Finally, it should be pointed out that associated with the instructional personnel of sport programs are a number of auxiliary personnel such as managers, physicians and trainers, a situation not commonly found in the case of games.

III. SPORT AS A SOCIAL INSTITUTION

Extending our notion of sport as an institutional pattern still further we note that in its broadest sense, the term sport supposes a social institution. Schneider writes that the term *institution:*

> ... denotes an aspect of social life in which distinctive value-orientations and interests, centering upon large and important social concerns ... generate or are accompanied by distinctive modes of social interaction. Its use emphasizes 'important' social phenomena; relationships of 'strategic structural significance' (1964, p. 338).

We argue that the magnitude of sport in the Western world justifies its consideration as a social institution. As Boyle succinctly states:

> Sport permeates any number of levels of contemporary society, and it touches upon and deeply influences such disparate elements as status, race relations, business life, automotive design, clothing styles, the concept of the hero, language, and ethical values. For better or worse it gives form and substance to much in American life (1963, pp. 3, 4).

When speaking of sport as a social institution we refer to the *sport order*. The sport order is composed of all social organizations in society which organize, facilitate, and regulate human action in sport situations. Hence, such organizations as sporting goods manufacturers, sport clubs, athletic teams, national governing bodies for amateur and professional sports, publishers of sport magazines, etc., are part of the sport order. For analytical purposes, four levels of social organization within the sport order may be distinguished: namely, the primary, technical, managerial and corporate levels.[18] Organizations at the primary level permit face-to-face relationships among all members and are characterized by the fact that administrative leadership is not formally delegated to one or more persons or positions. An example of social organization associated with sport at the primary level is an informally organized sport team as evidenced in a sandlot baseball game.

Organizations at the technical level are too large to permit simultaneous face-to-face relationships among its members but small enough so that each member knows of every other member. Moreover, unlike organizations at the primary level, organizations at the technical level officially designate administrative leadership positions and allocate individuals to them. Most scholastic and collegiate athletic teams, for example, would be classified as technical organizations with coaches and athletic directors functioning as administrative leaders.

At the managerial level organizations are too large for each member to know every other member but small enough so that all members know one or more of the administrative leaders of the organization. Some of the larger professional ball clubs represent social organizations related to sport at the managerial level.

Organizations at the corporate level are characterized by being bureaucratic in nature with centralized authority, a hierarchy of personnel, protocol, and procedural emphases, and stress on rationalization of operations and impersonal relationships. A number of the major governing bodies of amateur and professional sport at the national and international level illustrate sport organizations of the corporate type.

In summary, the sport order is composed of the congeries of primary, technical, managerial, and corporate social organizations that arrange, facilitate, and regulate human action in sport situations. The value of the concept lies in its use in macro-analyses of the social significance of sport. We can make reference to the sport order in an historical and/or comparative perspective. For example, we can speak of the sport order of nineteenth-century America or contrast the sport order of Russia with that of England.

IV. SPORT AS A SOCIAL SITUATION

As was just noted, the sport order is composed of all social organizations in society which organize, facilitate and regulate human action in sport situations. Human "action consists of the structures and processes by which human beings form meaningful intentions and, more or less successfully, implement them in concrete situations" (Parsons, 1966, p. 5). A sport situation consists of any social context wherein individuals are involved with sport. And the term *situation* denotes "... the total set of objects, whether persons, collectivities, culture objects, or himself to which an actor responds" (Friedsam, 1964, p. 667). The set of objects related to a specific sport situation may be quite diverse, ranging from the elements of the social and physical environments of a football game to those associated with two sportniks[19] in a neighborhood bar arguing the pros and cons of the manager of their local baseball team.

Although there are many kinds of sport situations most if not all may be conceptualized as social systems. A social system may be simply defined as "... a set of persons with an identifying characteristic plus a set of relationships established among these persons by interaction" (Caplow, 1964, p. 1). Thus the situations represented by two teams contesting within the confines of a football field, a father and son fishing from a boat, and a golf pro giving a lesson to a novice each constitute a social system.

Social systems of prime concern to the sport sociologist are those which directly or indirectly relate to a game occurrence. That is, a sport sociologist is often concerned with why man gets involved in sport and what effect his involvement has on other aspects of his social environment. Involvement in a social system related to a game occurrence can be analyzed in terms of degree and kind of involvement.

Degree of involvement can be assessed in terms of frequency, duration and intensity of involvement. The combination of frequency and duration of involvement may be taken as an index of an individual's "investment" in a sport situation, and intensity of involvement may be considered an index of an individual's "personal commitment" to a given sport situation.[20]

Kind of involvement can be assessed in terms of an individual's relationship to the "means of production" of a game. Those having direct or indirect access to the means of production are considered "actually involved" and are categorized as "producers," and those individuals lacking access to the means of production are considered "vicariously involved" and are categorized as "consumers." We have tentatively identified three categories of producers and three classes of consumers.

Producers may be characterized as being primary, secondary or tertiary with respect to the production of a game. (1) "Primary Producers" are the contestants who play the primary role in the production of a game, not unlike the role of actors in the production of a film or play. (2) "Secondary Producers" consist of those individuals, who while not actually competing in a sport contest, perform tasks which have direct technological consequences for the outcome of a game. Secondary producers include club owners, coaches, officials, trainers and the like. It may be possible to categorize secondary producers as entrepreneurs, managers and technicians. (3) "Tertiary Producers" consist of those

persons who are actively involved in a sport situation but whose activities have no direct technological consequences for the outcome of a game. Examples of tertiary producers are cheerleaders, band members, and concession workers. Tertiary producers may be classified as service personnel.

Consumers like producers are designated as being primary, secondary, or tertiary. (1) "Primary Consumers" are those individuals who become vicariously involved in a sport through "live" attendance at a sport competition. Primary consumers may be thought of as "active spectators." (2) "Secondary Consumers" consist of those persons who vicariously involve themselves in a sport as spectators via some form of the mass media, such as radio or television. Secondary consumers may be thought of as "passive spectators." (3) "Tertiary Consumers" are those individuals who become vicariously involved with sport other than as spectators. Thus an individual who engages in conversation related to sport or a person who reads the sports section of the newspaper would be classified as a tertiary consumer.

In concluding our discussion of the nature of sport we note that a special type of consumer is the *fan*. A fan is defined as an individual who has both a high personal investment in and a high personal commitment to a given sport.

REFERENCES

Berne, Eric: Games People Play. New York, Grove Press, 1964.

Beisser, Arnold R.: The Madness in Sport. New York, Appleton-Century-Crofts, 1967.

Boyle, Robert H.: Sport—Mirror of American Life. Boston, Little, Brown, 1963.

Caillois, Roger: Men, Play and Games (translated by Meyer Barash). New York, Free Press, 1961.

Caplow, Theodore: Principles of Organization. New York, Harcourt, Brace & World, 1964.

Friedsam, H.J.: Social situation. *In* A Dictionary of the Social Sciences. Edited by Julius Gould and William L. Kolb. New York, Free Press, 1964.

Fromm, Eric: The Sane Society. New York, Fawcett, 1965.

Goffman, Erving: Encounter. Indianapolis, Bobbs-Merrill, 1961.

Huizinga, Johan: Homo Ludens—A Study of the Play-Element in Culture. Boston, Beacon Press, 1955.

Johnson, Harry M.: Sociology: A Systematic Introduction. New York, Harcourt, Brace & Co., 1960.

Kahn, Roger: Money, muscles—and myths. Nation, *185*:9. 1957.

Leach, E.R.: Ritual. *In* A Dictionary of the Social

Sciences. Edited by Julius Gould and William L. Kolb. New York, Free Press, 1964.

Lüschen, Günther: The Interdependence of Sport and Culture. A paper presented at the National Convention of the American Association for Health, Physical Education and Recreation, Las Vegas, 1967.

McCall, George J. and Simmons, J.L.: Identities and Interactions. New York, Free Press, 1966.

McIntosh, Peter C.: Sport in Society. London, C.A. Watts, 1963.

Parsons, Talcott: Societies—Evolutionary and Comparative Perspectives. Englewood Cliffs, N.J., Prentice-Hall, 1966.

Piaget, Jean: Play, Dreams and Imitation in Childhood (translated by C. Gattegno and F.M. Hodgson). New York, W.W. Norton, 1951.

Riezler, Kurt: Play and seriousness. J. Philosophy, 38:505, 1941.

Roberts, John, et al.: Games in culture. Am. Anthropol., 61:597, 1959.

Roberts, John M. and Sutton-Smith, Brian: Child training and game involvement. Ethnology, 1:166, 1962.

Sapora, Allen V. and Mitchell, Elmer D.: The Theory of Play and Recreation, 3rd ed. New York, Ronald Press, 1961.

Schiffer, Donald: Sports. Colliers Encyclopedia, 21:449, 1965.

Schneider, Louis: Institution. In A Dictionary of the Social Sciences. Edited by Julius Gould and William L. Kolb. New York, Free Press, 1964.

Smelser, Neil J.: The Sociology of Economic Life. Englewood Cliffs, N.J., Prentice-Hall, 1963.

Stone, Gregory P.: American sports: play and display. Chicago Rev., 9:83, 1955.

Sumner, William Graham: Folkways. New York, Mentor, 1960.

Torkildsen, George E.: Sport and Culture. M.S. Thesis, University of Wisconsin, 1967.

Veblen, Thorstein: The Theory of the Leisure Class. New York, The Modern Library, 1934.

Weiss, Paul: Sport: A Philosophic Study. Unpublished manuscript, 1967.

NOTES

1. This definition is largely based on the work of Caillois (1961) and Roberts and others (1959). Other definitions and classifications of games having social import are given in Berne (1964) and Piaget (1951).

2. As have done Huizinga (1955), Stone (1955) and Caillois (1961).

3. Cf. Goffman's discussion of "rules of irrelevance" as applied to games and social encounters in general (1961, pp. 19–26).

4. E.g., compare the rules given for games in any edition of Hoyle's *Book of Games* with the NCAA rule books for various collegiate sports.

5. There is, of course, the amateur who gives up the "game" to become a professional.

6. For an early discussion of the problem of legitimation in sport, see Veblen, 1934, pp. 268–270.

7. An excellent philosophical account of play and seriousness is given by Kurt Riezler (1941, pp. 505–517).

8. A sociological treatment of how an individual engaged in an activity can become "caught up" in it is given by Goffman in his analysis of the concept of "spontaneous involvement" (1961, pp. 37–45).

9. For a discussion of how certain aspects of "reality" are excluded from a game situation see Goffman's treatment of "rules of irrelevance." Contrariwise see his treatment of "rules of transformation" for a discussion of how certain aspects of "reality" are permitted to enter a game situation (1961, pp. 29–34).

10. Professional sports provide an exception, of course, especially such a sport as professional bull-fighting.

11. Our use of the term "structures and processes" at this point is similar to Goffman's concept of "realized resources" (1961, pp. 16–19).

12. Other possible categories of competition are, of course, animals against animals as seen in a horse race or animals against an artificial animal as seen in dog racing. As noted by Weiss: "When animals or machines race, the speed offers indirect testimony to men's excellence as trainers, coaches, riders, drivers and the like—and thus primarily to an excellence in human leadership, judgment, strategy, and tactics" (1967, p. 22).

13. The interested reader can find examples of sport classifications in: Schiffer (1965), McIntosh (1963) and Sapora & Mitchell (1961).

14. This definition is patterned after one given by Smelser, 1963, p. 28.

15. Huizinga states that the existence of permanent teams is, in fact, the starting-point of modern sport (1955, p. 196).

16. Our discussion of "sanctioned secrecy" closely parallels Johnson's discussion of "official secrecy" in bureaucracies (1960, pp. 295, 296).

17. For an early sociological treatment of sport, spectacle, exhibition and drama see Sumner (1960, pp. 467–501). We note in passing that some writers consider the totality of sport as a ritual; see especially Fromm (1955, p. 132); and Beisser (1967, pp. 148–151 and pp. 214–225).

18. Our discussion of these four levels is similar to Caplow's treatment of small, medium, large and giant organizations (Caplow, 1964, pp. 26, 27).

19. The term sportnik refers to an avid fan or sport addict.

20. Cf. McCall and Simmons, (1966, pp. 171, 172).

sport involvement:
A Conceptual Go and Some Consequences Thereof

GERALD S. KENYON

On the assumption that those interested in the social nature of sport seek to achieve more meaningful descriptions and more powerful explanations, a necessary and obvious prerequisite is a viable conceptual system. If well formulated, it will, in all likelihood, consist of both unique and borrowed terms, and serve as the basis for formulating propositions which in turn, should facilitate inquiry and enhance communication.

As we seek to improve our understanding of sport we have a wide array of concepts and frames of reference from which to choose. The choice will depend upon, among other considerations, whether we are concerned with sport as a social system, as a vehicle for the occurrence of social processes, or as a cultural product. If we are primarily interested in the actions of persons in sport situations, a concept which may be of some use is that of *involvement*. Certainly the currency of the concept in the serious literature on games and sport seems to be increasing; probably the most familiar example is its appearance in the work of Roberts and Sutton-Smith (Roberts and Sutton-Smith, 1962; Sutton-Smith et al., 1963) in conjunction with their conflict-enculturation hypothesis.

Recently, a sub-committee of the International Committee for the Sociology of Sport has been in the process of planning a cross-national study of involvement socialization. After hearing the term being used in differing contexts by those participating in the planning workshops, I came

Reprinted from Aspects of Contemporary Sport Sociology. Edited by Gerald S. Kenyon. Copyright 1969 by the Athletic Institute, Chicago, Illinois.

to the conclusion that all may not have been using it in quite the same way. Moreover, having already employed the concept in some of my own work I have developed certain reservations about the manner in which I have been using it. I believe, therefore, that before we go any further, we need to do some conceptual spade work, which should result in either developing a more definitive and useful construct, or rejecting the term altogether. Thus, with this objective in mind, I would like to report the results of what at times was a most perplexing journey through a semantic labyrinth, in which vagueness and ambiguity were the major source of illumination. More specifically, I would like to present a conceptual schematic, if you will, of the concept *involvement*, and then explore how such a system might be used; first, to describe and explain human action in sport, and second, to discover the consequences of human action in sport. In each case I will illustrate with what I hope are plausible propositions. However, I would like to stress the point that what I am proposing is not an explanation of sport, but rather a tool that might be useful in the pursuit of explanations.

THE CONCEPT OF INVOLVEMENT

The problem, as I view it, is to find a better way to talk about what people do and what people feel when confronted with sport. Insofar as the term *involvement* might be useful for such purposes, it behooves us to say what we mean when we employ such a concept, particularly in a research context. Casual observations reveal that the word enjoys widespread use in the English language. Its shades of meaning are several, ranging from getting involved *in something* to getting involved *with someone,* both of which are of no small significance. However, if we consult an unabridged dictionary, we may find something useful, although dictionaries probably make greater contributions to supplying us with information on word origin, pronunciation, and syllabification, than on word meaning. In any case, the lexicographer for the new *Random House Dictionary,* as might be expected, provides fifteen definitions (in the verb form), including "to bring into difficulties," and "to swallow up, engulf or overwhelm." Although such definitions are obviously inadequate for our purposes, others show more promise, including "to combine inextricably," "to engage the interest or emotions or commitment of," and "to preoccupy or absorb fully." Reading on, the following synonyms were suggested: "complicated," "knotty," "tangled," and "perplexing." Interestingly, the sole antonym was "simply," a definition which I came to accept most readily.

Dictionary definitions at least partially aside, it seems to me that in general, when we speak of being involved, we are talking about an actor's relationship with one or more manifestations of sport. Thus, involvement becomes *social action related to some manifestation of sport.* However, it consists of more than active participation in sport situations. In addition to its *behavioral* dimensions, there are *cognitive* and *dispositional* dimensions. I would like to elaborate a little, by treating each separately.

INVOLVEMENT AS OVERT BEHAVIOR

There are two basic *modes* of behavioral involvement. *Primary* involvement refers to actual participation in the game or sport as a player or contestant, while *secondary* involvement refers to all other forms of participation, of which there are several; including participation via the *consumption* of sport and participation via the *production* of sport. One consumes at any point in time in one of two ways—*directly,* through attendance at the performance of others (those who are primarily involved), or *indirectly,* by exposure to one of the several forms of mass media which permits people to be involved secondarily.[1] The *producer,* on the other hand,

is responsible for bringing the spectacle up to expectations.

Obviously, people can behave in sport situations in several different ways. While doing so they are playing one or more *sport roles.* Those associated with primary involvement are, of course, the *athlete* or *player.* These, in turn, may be *winners, losers, first-stringers, substitutes, superstars,* etc. Roles reflecting secondary involvement are both consuming and producing. The *spectator* represents the *direct* consuming role, while the *viewer, listener,* and *reader* represent *indirect* consuming roles. Producing roles are of three kinds: leadership roles—*instructor, coach, captain, cheerleader,* or *manager;* arbitration roles—*referee, umpire,* or *scorekeeper;* and entrepreneurial roles—*promoter, manufacturer, wholesaler, retailer,* and *concessionaire.* Figure 1 shows the various modes of involvement together with representative roles.

COGNITIVE INVOLVEMENT

The cognitive world of most people includes sport. The amount of sport information made available to persons in most countries makes it almost impossible to avoid learning something about it. It seems to be knowledge of two kinds: on the one hand, people acquire information on the major features and requirements of a sport contest, and the situation in which it occurs; while on the other hand, persons acquire a knowledge of the outcomes of sport contests. At this time, little is known about the level, variability, and source of such knowledge. Suffice it to say that this is a most fertile field for research, particularly in view of the attention paid today to the field of linguistics and the nature and function of mass communication. Despite this state of affairs it seems obvious that the playing of sport roles, whether they be primary or secondary, producer or consumer oriented, depends upon the nature of the role player's cognitive system pertaining to sport in general, and to the sport situation in which he finds himself in particular.

INVOLVEMENT DISPOSITIONS

Whether a person is overtly involved in sport at a given point in time is not a necessary condition for harboring certain feeling states or dispositions toward one or more manifestations of sport. Even without actually engaging in sport

MODE	PRIMARY	SECONDARY				
		CONSUMER		PRODUCER		
ROLE		Direct	Indirect	Leader	Arbitrator	Entrepreneur
	contestant	spectator	viewer	instructor	members of —sports governing body	manufacturer
	athlete		listener	coach	—rules committee	promoter
			reader	manager	referee	wholesaler
	player			team leader	umpire	retailer
					scorekeeper	
					other officials	

FIG. 1—SOME SOCIAL ROLES ASSOCIATED WITH PRIMARY AND SECONDARY MODES OF SPORT INVOLVEMENT

actors may become deeply involved in an emotional sense. Just as sport becomes a part of most people's cognitive systems, these same people have likely acquired various values and attitudes, general and specific, relevant to sport as the social object.

Drawing upon Campbell's "residues of experience," or what he calls "acquired behavioral dispositions" (Campbell, 1963), it is possible to characterize dispositions toward sport, like all others, into two dimensions: *acquired means* of behaving and *acquired goals*. Acquired means include acquired behavioral routines, programs or sequences of response, and schedules for behavior. For the most part these are akin to the previously discussed cognitive elements of involvement. Acquired goals, or end concepts, include acquired drives, motives, purposes, needs, need-dispositions, and cathectic orientations (Campbell, 1963, pp. 136–137).

One of the more frequently studied dispositions associated with sport is *attitude*. Again, as is the case with any other social object, the possessing of attitudes toward sport does not imply observable behavior in sport situations. In other words, one could develop favorable dispositions toward involvement in sport but never be *overtly* involved. However, although a disposition toward involvement does not imply behavioral in-

volvement, behavioral involvement in most sport situations is a function of one's disposition to be involved. This is not particularly profound since most conceptions of social action have a motivational or normative element (e.g., Parsons and Shills, 1951; Smelser, 1962). Although I have divided the two for analytic purposes it behooves us to recognize their linkage.

A CONCEPTUAL MODEL: WHAT IS THE PAYOFF?

Having had a go at conceptualizing sport involvement, it remains to be shown what the consequences might be of using such a conceptualization to pursue our goal as stated at the outset—namely, a better understanding of sport and related phenomena. Basically, there are two possibilities from which to choose. It seems to me that we can either seek to improve our understanding of the phenomenon *per se*, or, in a more general sense, seek to improve our understanding of other social phenomena through the study of sport involvement. Stated in another way, the first approach employs involvement as the dependent variable, while the latter approach employs it as the independent variable—the means-ends dichotomy.

Whichever approach is chosen we are, for

the most part, still at sea—having considered involvement in much of a vacuum. What is needed is a broader frame of reference, within which we can begin to formulate and test propositions. One way (but obviously only one of several) of achieving this, I suggest, is to view involvement from a *temporal perspective*. This will allow us to consider involvement in three stages: *becoming involved, being involved,* and *becoming uninvolved.*[2]

First, let us consider becoming involved, or in more familiar language *involvement socialization*. If we set as our goal the understanding of sport involvement *per se,* at this stage we are asking how people become involved or more specifically, how do people learn to play sport roles? How does one become an athlete? How does one become a member of the International Olympic Committee?

Although role theory is not well developed, we should be able to identify the major situational and personal factors that prepare someone to play a particular role. For example, if we adopt Kemper's reference group approach (1968), wherein he argues that roles are learned and levels of achievement reached through the acting together of three types of reference groups; namely *normative, comparison,* and *audience groups,* then the most effective socialization should occur as a result of considerable exposure to all three. For an athlete, we would expect normative groups, such as his family, and certainly his coaches, to set high standards of performance. There would need to be present a comparison group made up of attractive role models, such as national sport stars and superstars, or even the players of the next higher level of ability. Finally, there would be an audience, known and unknown, who themselves play various secondary involvement roles. Although not particularly profound, in propositional form, we might have the following:

> In part, effective involvement socialization is a function of exposure to, interaction with, and reinforcement from members of normative, comparison, and audience groups who play other sport roles within both primary and secondary modes of involvement.

Some limited support for such a proposition comes from data acquired from 110 track and field athletes who participated in the final trials for the 1968 U. S. Olympic Team. Based upon a preliminary look at the data, most of the group reported that all during their career, they have subscribed to high ideals, reinforced by a variety of reference groups from the family to girl friends, were provided with plenty of role models whom they could identify by name, and finally depended heavily upon audiences both immediate and remote, including family, peers, and consumers of mass media.

So much for involvement socialization. As more work is carried out in this area, we should be able to formulate many more propositions capable of explaining the process in a more complete way.

I turn now to the second stage of involvement, that is, having become involved, some persons continue to relate to sport through *persistent patterns of action* (Moore, 1963, p. 3). But not all people persist in the same way. Thus we have the proposition that:

> Sport involvement is pattern like, but differential.

Although at the moment there is little empirical support for such a proposition, McPhee (1963) has put forward an "addiction model" wherein he postulates various "paths of consumption" of sport or leisure pursuits. He has labeled such patterns as "explosive," "chronic," "divergent," "normal," "abortive," and "aversive." The McPhee model is based on the assumption that if we examine the involvement behavior of a large group of persons primarily involved in a particular sport or physical activity, we could expect to find different patterns of involvement over time, that is, not everyone would participate with the same frequency or at the same intervals. For some persons involvement would be on a rather regular basis and well-integrated into the life style. Other persons may play a few games separated by a period of inactivity or, in other words, be involved on more of a cyclical basis; while still others become involved in an activity only to find the time required for it increasing exponentially or in McPhee's words, "... carried away toward consumption ever rising beyond any bounds and without return, for example, drinking to unconsciousness and then hospitalization" (McPhee, 1963, p. 194). Here at Wisconsin, we have recently tried to fit some time series involvement data to stochastic models, which permitted us to test the "patterns of involvement'' hypothesis (Kenyon and Schutz, 1968). The results, based upon relatively short term play in two sports, suggest that some order is present in data generated by observing persistent involvement.

Although patterns of persistent *secondary* involvement may exist, I know of no empirical work that has investigated same. However, the findings may be less rich than those from primary involvement, as sport situations facilitating secondary involvement may impose more limitation on the actor by virtue of their more rigid structure. While he can choose when he will play golf or tennis, at least to some extent, he can only attend football games (or sell programs there) when his team plays at home, and can only read *Sports Illustrated* once per week.

It is conceivable that some success may be had in efforts to *describe* persistent primary and secondary involvement, but *explaining* the discovered patterns presents us with a much more formidable task. However, since we are dealing with an aspect of social behavior, and insofar as there are common elements among many manifestations of social behavior, the efforts of social psychologists and sociologists in their quest for understanding more general social phenomena might be helpful. For example, within the context of Festinger's Cognitive Dissonance Theory we might generate propositions such as:

Actors secondarily involved as partisan spectators are more likely to attribute a loss by their team to factors unrelated to overall team ability than are non-partisans.

Moving to the third stage of involvement, namely *becoming uninvolved*, we find few if any attempts, either theoretical or empirical, to deal with processes of withdrawal and termination. It is conceivable that the description of withdrawal could be accomplished using concepts found suitable for describing involvement persistence. When it comes to explanation, however, I would suspect we might consider theories of social change.

THE OTHER SIDE OF THE COIN

I would like to pause a moment to remind you that in examining involvement from a temporal perspective, thus far my examples were oriented toward involvement phenomena as dependent variables. It also is possible to look at the other side of the coin, raising questions about sport involvement as the independent variable. This leads to a consideration of a variety of consequences of involvement, for individuals, social systems, large and small, and for sport itself.

Taking involvement stage by stage and considering *involvement socialization* first, it seems reasonable to expect an array of consequences as sport roles are learned, particularly for such institutions as the family and the school— witness the role of games in enculturation during childhood as shown by Roberts and Sutton-Smith. *Persistent involvement*, that is the enactment of sport roles over time, likely has implications, though not clear at the moment, for achieving and maintaining status within various social systems, for explaining certain instances of social mobility and perhaps for achieving some measure of identification with family, school, community or nation. The third stage, namely *withdrawal*, can't help but have some impact upon one's life style, and in turn affect other groups and institutions for example, the economy.

To illustrate involvement as an independent variable consider the following proposition:

Identification is a function of group related persistent secondary sport involvement.

Although for purposes of analysis I have suggested that involvement could be either the dependent variable or the independent variable, it would be well to point out the naiveté of assuming a clear cut distinction here. Clearly, the results of any well formulated research project should have implications for both sport and the situation within which it exists. However, whether it would be fruitful to consider developing a theory of involvement remains a moot point. A decision to inter-relate confirmed propositions concerning involvement in sport should no doubt await the time when more than a few have been established. Of first consideration, however, will be whether or not to simply incorporate these verified propositions into existing social theory explaining social action in general, or whether or not to make some effort to develop a more modest theory explaining sport itself. One might expect the person whose primary interest is in sport would choose the latter route; while he whose first interest is in what is common to social systems in general, might prefer the former approach. In any case the two are mutually compatible.

SUMMARY

On the argument that before one can study anything seriously, he needs to have a way of talking about that which concerns him, it has been my purpose this afternoon to look at a concept frequently used in the study of sport phenomena—namely the concept of *involvement*. Although my intentions were honorable, it should be clear that the task is far from complete. In any case, the degree to which my characterization of involvement will prove useful will depend not only upon further logical analysis of sport phenomena, but upon the utility of such a scheme when used in empirical inquiry.

REFERENCES

Campbell, Donald T.: Social attitudes and other acquired behavioral dispositions. *In* Psychology: A Study of a Science. Edited by S. Koch. New York, McGraw-Hill, 1963, Vol. 6, pp. 94–172.

Kemper, T. D.: Reference groups, socialization and achievement. Am. Sociol. Rev., *33*:31, 1968.

Kenyon, Gerald S. and Robert W. Schutz: Patterns of involvement in sport: a stochastic view. Paper presented at the Second International Congress of Sport Psychology, Washington, D.C., 1968.

McPhee, W. N.: Formal Theories of Mass Behavior. New York, Free Press, 1963.

Moore, W. E.: Social Change. Englewood Cliffs, New Jersey, Prentice-Hall, 1963.

Parsons, T. and E. A. Shils (eds.).: Toward a General Theory of Action. Cambridge, Mass., Harvard University Press, 1951.

Roberts, John M. and Sutton-Smith, Brian.: Child training and game involvement. Ethnology, *I*:185, 1962.

Smelser, N. J.: Theory of Collective Behavior. New York, Free Press, 1962.

Sutton-Smith, Brian et al.: Game involvement in adults. J. Soc. Psychol., *60*:15, 1963.

NOTES

1. The distinction between direct and indirect consumption may be appreciated better when we consider that the spectator is a part of the sport situation and may have some immediate and spontaneous effect upon the event, while this is not the case for other consumers. Indeed, they may consume at an entirely different point in time (relevance of time and place).

2. Although the time at which an actor may enter each stage may correspond roughly to stages of his life cycle, it is also possible for the passage through all stages to occur early or late in life or somewhere in between.

further readings for part one

Section One: Sociology of Sport

Erbach, G.: The science of sport and sport sociology: questions related to development—Problems of structure. Int. Rev. Sport Sociol., *1*:59, 1966.

Dunning, E.: Notes on some conceptual and theoretical problems in the sociology of sport. Int. Rev. Sport Sociol., *2*:143, 1967.

Gruneau, R.S.: Conflicting standards and problems of personal action in the sociology of sport. Quest, *30*:80, 1978.

Hendry, L.B.: Sports sociology in Britain—career or commitment? Int. Rev. Sport Sociol., *8*:117, 1973.

Lowe, B.: Sports sociology: the first ten years. New Zealand HPER, *7*:32, 1974.

Loy, J.W., and Kenyon, G.S. (eds.): Sport, Culture and Society: A Reader on the Sociology of Sport. New York, Macmillan, 1969. (See the Appendix of this reader for contents.)

Loy, J.W.: A case for the sociology of sport. Part IV of Leisure Today, a special supplement of the J. Health, Phys. Educ. Rec., May/June, 1972.

Loy, J.W., and Seagrave, J.: Research Methodology in the sociology of sport. *In* Exercise and Sport Sciences Reviews. Edited by J. Wilmore. New York, Academic Press, 1974, Vol. 2.

Loy, J.W., McPherson, B.D. and Kenyon, G.S.: The Sociology of Sport as an Academic Specialty: An Episodic Essay on the Development and Emergence of an Hybrid Subfield in North America. Ottawa: Canadian Association for Health, Physical Education and Recreation, 1978.

Loy, J.W.: An exploratory analysis of the scholarly productivity of North American based sport sociologists. Int. Rev. Sport Sociol., *14*(3-4): 97, 1979.

Loy, J.W.: The emergence and development of the sociology of sport as an academic specialty. Res. Q. Exer. Sport, *51*:91, 1980.

Lüschen, G.: On sociology of sport. *In* The Scientific View of Sport: Perspectives, Aspects, Issues. Edited by O. Grupe, et al. Berlin, Springer, 1973.

Lüschen, G.: The development and scope of a sociology of sport. Am. Correc. Ther. J., *29*:39, 1975.

Lüschen, G.: Sociology of sport: development, present state and prospects. *In* Annu. Rev. Sociol. Edited by A. Inkeles. Palo Alto, Calif., Annual Reviews, 1980. Vol. 6.

Lüschen, G., and Sage, G.: Sport in sociological perspective. *In* Handbook of Social Science of Sport. Edited by G. Lüschen and G. Sage. Champaign, Ill., Stipes, 1981.

McIntosh, P.: The sociology of sport in the ancient world. *In* Handbook of Social Science of Sport. Edited by G. Lüschen and G. Sage. Champaign, Ill., Stipes, 1981.

McPherson, B.D.: Avoiding chaos in the sociology of sport brickyard. Quest, *30*:72, 1978.

Melnick, M.J.: A critical look at the sociology of sport. Quest, *24*:34, 1975.

Sage, G.: Sport and the social sciences. The Annals, *445*:1, 1979.

Snyder, E.E., and Spreitzer, E.: Sociology of sport: an overview. Sociol. Q., *15*:467, 1974.

Snyder, E.E., and Spreitzer, E.: Sport sociology and the discipline of sociology: present status and speculations about the future. Rev. Sport Leisure, *4*:10, 1979.

Spreitzer, E., Snyder, E., and Jordan, C.: Reflections on the integration of sport sociology into the larger discipline. Sociol. Symp., *39*:1, 1980.

Whitson, D.J.: Sociology, psychology and Canadian sport. Can. J. Appl. Sport Sci., *3*:71, 1978.

Wohl, A.: Conception and range of sport sociology. Int. Rev. Sport Soc., *1*:5, 1966.

Wohl, A.: Some remarks on the methodology of research on the sociology of sport. Int. Rev. Sport Soc., *10*:5, 1975.

Section Two: Sport as a Social Phenomenon

Caillois, R.: The structure and classification of games. Diogenes, *12*:62, 1955.

Caillois, R.: Man, Play and Games. New York, Free Press, 1961.

Guttman, A.: Play, games, contests, sports. *In* Ritual to Record. Edited by A. Guttman. New York, Columbia University Press, 1978.

Huizinga, J.: Homo Ludens—A Study of the Play Element in Culture. Boston, Beacon Press, 1955.

Keating, J.: Winning in sport and athletics. Thought, *38*:201, 1963.

Loy, J.W.: The cultural system of sport. Quest, *29*:73, 1978.

McIntosh, P.: Sport in Society. London, C.A. Watts, 1963.

Pearson, K.: The institutionalization of sport forms. Int. Rev. Sport Soc., *14*:51, 1977.

Roberts, J.M., et al.: Games in culture. Am. Anthropol., *61*:597, 1959. (See also, Roberts and Sutton-Smith, 1962, reprinted in Loy and Kenyon, 1st Edition.)

PART TWO

sport and micro-social systems

Behavior in situations involving two or more persons tends to become structured, routinized, and predictable—that is, it becomes *systematic*, with respect to form and process. Thus, one of the most useful constructs for the study of social behavior has been the *social system* and its three basic components: *persons, social structure,* and *culture*. This is as obvious in sport as it is in any other social context.* It is not surprising, therefore, that sociologists of sport have drawn heavily upon the notion of social system and its several characteristics as delineated by sociologists over the years. Although there is no clear demarcation line, social systems have come to be divided into *micro-* and *macro-*systems, with differences largely based upon magnitude (complexity is encountered in even the smallest of groups). Thus, the remainder of the reader is divided into two parts, one addressed to sport and micro-systems, the other to sport and macro-systems.

With regard to sport and *micro-*social systems, we have separated the readings into three sections: sport groups, sport organizations, and sport subcultures. *Section One: Sport Groups* contains five articles, all of which were published in the 1970s or late 1960s. As a reading of these will reveal, much of the recent work is based upon earlier studies carried out in the active field of small group research, a traditional domain of social psychologists. As well as those

reprinted here, the student should consult earlier sources (listed under *Further Readings*) such as the work of Fiedler, Meyers, McGrath, Klein and Christiansen, and Lenk; together with two papers reprinted in Section Two (Blalock and Grusky). In one way or another, each writer was attempting to account for team success, by studying the structure of the group, the social processes occurring within the group, or both.

Of the structural elements, the characteristics of individuals (the most basic component of the social system) have been the subject of many inquiries during the 1960s. In fact, administering readily available personality inventories to athletes became rather commonplace, often without much attention given to the theoretical bases for doing so. While in some cases the personalities of athletes were shown to differ from those of nonathletes, to expect personality alone to account for individual, and, in turn, team success, became recognized as an oversimplification of the complexities of small groups. Nevertheless, we present two studies of personality factors in sport situations reflecting some of the better work in this area (Kroll *et al.* and Loy).

From the perspective of group characteristics and processes, researchers have studied such factors as cohesion, status consensus, interaction patterns, self versus task orientations, achievement motivation, and the compromising of values under stress. Two examples are included: one is in the context of basketball using lower-level performers but in a "natural" context (Martens and Petersen), while the other is based upon volleyball teams of varying ability

---

*For a fuller amplification of the concept of social system, its nature and significance for the study of sport, see Loy, McPherson, and Kenyon, *Sport and Social Systems*, Chapter 2.

(Bird). The results confirm the importance of *structural* variables, and in these examples, cohesion in particular. However, after many studies of individual and group characteristics, most investigators have concluded that predicting team performance is a complex matter. Thus, the remaining paper in Section One (Nixon) illustrates an attempt to bring some order to the situation through the development of a propositional theory to explain team success, based upon many of the empirical findings reported in the literature. The value of such an approach, in addition to providing a more systematic and comprehensive explanation, lies in the identification of empirically testable hypotheses that can lead to confirmation, modification, or rejection of all or part of the theory—the business of social science.

Turning to *Section Two: Sport Organizations,* if the sport team is viewed as the independent variable in a causal relationship, (that is, participation in sport *causes* ...), then, as a social organization, it facilitates a variety of social actions that precipitate consequences beyond those of a single game occurrence. For example, an element of any organization is *social differentiation,* a unifying theme of the four papers in this section. In the first article, Blalock develops a series of propositions accounting for minority discrimination, using professional baseball as a setting. Next, Grusky reports on the impact of formal structure upon career advancement. His findings, which suggest that occupants of positions calling for high interaction (those more "central") were more likely to experience upward mobility, have stimulated a number of investigators to replicate and expand upon his work. In the next reading, Loy and McElvogue build upon the work of both Blalock and Grusky to show a strong relationship between racial segregation and centrality, employing data from both baseball and football. Ball, in some further analyses of professional football, confirms the Loy and McElvogue findings using Canadian data, and goes on to report that national origin, as another ascribed characteristic, is also related to centrality of playing position, i.e., the phenomenon of "stacking." For additional material, some of which challenges the work of those described above (e.g., Gamson and Scotch, 1964), the reader is again referred to the items listed under *Further Readings* and to the references in the articles themselves.

The concept of "subculture" is not clearly defined in the social sciences. Nevertheless, the term has come to imply the prevalence of values and norms arising within a unique social situation. Thus, both structural and cultural components of the social system are relevant here. Writers have debated such definitional issues as the boundary between a subculture and the dominant culture; the degree to which face-to-face interaction is a necessary condition; and the extent of member commitment, given membership in, or identification with, other subcultures. The answers vary, of course, depending upon whether the subculture in question arises from occupational, avocational, or deviant concerns. Difficulties notwithstanding, for the sport sociologist, the concept has been found to be useful, regardless of whether sport is central to the subculture (e.g., surfing), or merely an element of a more general subculture (e.g., youth).

Most investigators have been interested in sport subcultures *per se.* In fact, some of the earliest serious sport sociology was carried out in this context. For example, in 1952, Weinberg and Arond published an account of the boxer's subculture from an occupational perspective. In *Street Corner Society*—one of the classic community studies in American sociology—Whyte (1955) describes in detail the varieties of social relationships in a Chicago bowling subculture. Later, Polsky (1964) gave a vivid account of the pool hustler and his world, while Stone (1972) described the unique culture of professional wrestling.

The readings reprinted in *Section Three: Sport Subcultures,* provide more recent examples of sport subcultures, representing a variety of sport situations, including horse racing (Scott), rugby football (Sheard and Dunning), soccer (Pooley), and surfing (Pearson). By way of introduction the Pearson paper is presented first, in that he includes an attempt to rationalize sport and the concept of subculture.

As a concluding note, the reader should observe the marked difference in research methods and style among the readings included in Part Two. For example, notice the extensive use of qualitative methods by writers in Section Three in contrast to the almost exclusive use of quantitative approaches in Sections One and Two. Taken together, they reveal the eclectic quality of present-day sociology of sport.

SECTION ONE
sport groups

multivariate analysis of the personality profiles of championship czechoslovakian athletes *

W. KROLL and J. LOY
V. HOSEK and M. VANEK

A basic belief held by many individuals associated with athletics is that participants in different sports can be distinguished in terms of particular personality characteristics. If this basic belief were a proven premise then it would afford an important aid in the understanding of the psychodynamics of athletes, and establish a basis for examining the interrelationships between personality and social structure in sport situation. Moreover, it would provide empirical grounds for making practical applications in athletics. For example, knowledge of modal personality types in athletics would give an initial understanding of the kinds of persons possessing a propensity for participating in particular athletic activities. This understanding should in turn suggest means for identifying potential athletic talent and methods of athletic counseling, i.e., channeling individuals into appropriate athletic activities. Another possibility is that knowledge of athletic personality types would further the understanding of the probable psychological demands of selected sports upon their participants. Such understanding would provide a basis for athletic guidance, as for example prescribing individualized training routines. Unfortunately, however, the notion that sport groups can be differentiated according to modal personality types associated with them is not well founded.

* A revised version of a paper presented at the Third Annual Canadian Psycho-Motor Learning and Sports Psychology Symposium, Vancouver, British Columbia, Canada.

Reprinted from International Journal of Sport Psychology, 4:131-147, 1973. Copyright 1973 by International Journal of Sport Psychology.

Results of research regarding athletic personality types are, to say the least, inconclusive.

The rather ambiguous nature of current findings concerning athletic personality types may stem from several sources. First, there is the very strong possibility that different types do not in fact exist. A second alternative is that they exist, but have not been discovered to date because present methods of personality measurement are inadequate for the task. Finally, even assuming that athletic types do exist and that current personality tests are adequate for their assessment, there remains the possibility that definitive findings about athletic types have not been obtained as a result of inadequate theorizing, data collection, and/or data analysis. Thus, seldom has a given study: (1) considered a variety of models of athletic personality; (2) examined many kinds of athletes both male and female; and, (3) applied a number of different methods of multivariate analysis to data obtained from relatively large samples of top-caliber sportsmen.

The present investigation reflects an attempt to deal with some of the stated limitations of athletic personality research. Specifically, the purpose of the study was to make between, within and across sport comparisons of the personality profiles of 358 nationally ranked, male and female, Czechoslovakian athletes participating in a variety of sports.

ANALYSIS AND RESULTS

The Cattell Sixteen Personality Factor Questionnaire was administered to 278 male athletes representing 20 different sports and 80 female athletes representing 8 different sports. These

358 Czechoslovakian sport participants were selected from athletes participating in the final trials for the 1968 Olympic Games and /or who were members of nationally ranked sport teams.

Raw test scores on each scale of Cattell's Sixteen Personality Factor Questionnaire for a sample of 278 male athletes in 20 sports, and a sample of 80 female athletes in 8 sports, were subjected to stepwise multiple discriminant function analysis using the Biomedical Computer Program BMD07M. In this program one variable at a time in stepwise fashion is entered into the set of discriminating variables. The variable entered at any step is selected by the first of the following equivalent criteria: (1) the variable with the largest F-value, (2) the variable which partialed on the previously entered variables has the highest multiple correlation with the groups, (3) the variable which gives the greatest decrease in the ratio of within to total generalized variance (Dixon, 1967, 214a).

Tables 1 and 2 summarize the findings for the male athletes, while Tables 3 and 4 summarize the findings for the female athletes. The discriminative power of the total battery of psychological variables, as well as the discriminative power of any given variable, is reported in terms of the U-statistic. The F-value for a given U-statistic related to a specific variable associated with a given cumulative proportion of total dispersion permits the determination of whether or not there are statistically significant differences among sport groups.

DISCRIMINATORY POWER. Tables 1 and 3 show that all sixteen personality factors constitute statistically significant variables in the set of discriminatory variables for both male and female samples. However, it is clear from a comparison of the two tables that a much smaller subset of variables accounts for maximum possible dispersion among women than men. Interestingly, Factor B (intelligence) accounts for the greatest amount of total dispersion of any given variable for both samples. Other variables possessing a relatively high degree of discriminatory power for both male and female athletes include: Factor A (sociability), Factor G (superego strength), Factor Q_1 (radicalism), and Factor Q_2 (self-sufficiency). Traits having discriminatory power for males but not females include Factor E (dominance) and Factor Q_3 (personal integration); whereas Factor M (imaginativeness) and Factor F (surgency) possess discriminatory power for women but not men. Rather strikingly,

TABLE 1

Stepwise Multiple Discriminant Function Analysis of 16 Personality Factor Profiles for Male Athletes

Step Number	Variable (personality factor)	Value of U-statistic *	Cumulative Proportion of Total Dispersion
1	B —Intelligence	0.6785	0.27518
2	G —Superego Strength	0.5066	0.44269
3	E —Dominance	0.4255	0.58067
4	Q_3—Integration	0.3720	0.67963
5	Q_2—Self-Sufficiency	0.3303	0.76930
6	Q_1—Radicalism	0.2945	0.83254
7	A —Sociability	0.2648	0.88370
8	N —Sophistication	0.2392	0.91737
9	L —Suspiciousness	0.2158	0.94257
10	F —Surgency	0.1952	0.96369
11	I —Sensitivity	0.1765	0.97761
12	C —Ego Strength	0.1635	0.98901
13	O —Guilt Proneness	0.1522	0.99555
14	Q_4—Ergic Tension	0.1400	0.99942
15	H —Venturesomeness	0.1308	0.99991
16	M —Imaginativeness	0.1246	1.00000

* All U-Statistics significant at the .01 level.

TABLE 2
Classification of Male Athletes

Sport Group	1	2	3	4	5	6	7	8	9	10	11	12	13	14	15	16	17	18	19	20	Percent Correctly Classified
1. Basketball	2	0	0	1	0	0	0	0	1	0	1	1	0	0	5	1	1	0	0	0	15%
2. Boxing	0	4	0	0	0	0	0	0	0	1	0	0	0	0	1	0	0	1	0	0	57
3. Canoeing (C)	0	1	10	0	0	0	0	1	2	0	0	0	0	3	1	1	0	0	0	1	50
4. Canoeing (R)	0	0	1	5	0	0	1	1	0	0	0	3	2	0	2	1	0	1	1	1	26
5. Cycling	0	1	1	1	3	0	1	1	2	2	0	0	1	1	0	1	2	1	1	0	16
6. Gymnastics	0	1	0	0	0	6	0	0	0	0	0	0	0	0	0	0	0	1	0	0	75
7. Ice-hockey	0	2	3	1	2	2	6	1	1	3	0	1	6	1	1	0	1	1	3	2	16
8. Motorcycling (C)	0	0	2	0	0	0	1	2	1	0	0	0	2	0	1	0	0	1	3	0	15·
9. Motorcycling (T)	0	1	3	1	0	0	1	2	3	1	1	0	0	2	0	0	1	0	0	0	19
10. Mountaineering	1	0	0	0	0	0	0	0	1	6	0	0	0	0	0	1	1	0	1	0	46
11. Orienteering	0	0	0	0	1	0	0	1	1	0	5	0	0	0	0	0	0	0	0	0	83
12. Rowing	1	0	2	1	0	0	1	0	0	1	1	7	0	1	0	3	1	1	1	0	33
13. Shooting	0	0	1	0	1	4	1	2	0	0	0	0	3	0	1	0	0	0	0	1	21
14. Skiing (D)	1	0	0	1	1	0	0	2	0	2	0	0	1	4	1	0	0	1	3	0	24
15. Ski Jumping	1	0	0	0	0	0	0	0	1	0	0	0	1	0	4	0	0	0	1	0	50
16. Skiing (N)	0	0	0	0	0	0	0	0	1	0	0	0	0	0	0	4	0	0	0	0	80
17. Track & Field	0	0	1	0	0	1	0	0	0	0	0	0	0	1	0	0	6	0	2	1	50
18. Volleyball	0	2	0	0	0	1	1	0	0	0	1	0	0	0	0	0	1	7	2	1	44
19. Weight Lifting	0	1	0	0	0	0	0	0	0	0	1	0	0	0	0	0	1	0	2	0	40
20. Wrestling	2	0	0	0	0	0	0	0	1	0	0	0	1	0	0	0	0	0	0	5	55

Number of Correct Classifications by Sport Group (columns 1–20)

TABLE 3
Stepwise Multiple Discriminant Function Analysis of 16 Personality Factor Profiles for Female Athletes

Step Number	Variable (personality factor)	Value of U-statistic*	Cumulative Proportion of Total Dispersion
1	B —Intelligence	0.6190	0.38575
2	M —Imaginativeness	0.5116	0.59898
3	F —Surgency	0.4246	0.74857
4	G —Superego Strength	0.3587	0.85897
5	A —Sociability	0.3133	0.97908
6	Q_1—Radicalism	0.2713	1.00001
7	Q_2—Self-Sufficiency	0.2351	1.00001
8	O —Guilt Proneness	0.2087	1.00001
9	L —Suspiciousness	0.1758	1.00001
10	I —Sensitivity	0.1602	1.00001
11	E —Dominance	0.1451	1.00001
12	Q_4—Ergic Tension	0.1348	1.00001
13	H —Venturesomeness	0.1255	1.00001
14	C —Ego Strength	0.1182	1.00001
15	N —Sophistication	0.1125	1.00001
16	Q —Integration	0.1078	1.00001

TABLE 4
Classification of Female Athletes

Sport Group	1	2	3	4	5	6	7	8	Number of Ss	Percent Correctly Classified
		Number of Correct Classifications								
1. Basketball	7	1	0	1	2	1	1	1	14	50%
2. Canoeing (C)	0	5	0	0	1	0	0	0	6	83
3. Canoeing (R)	1	0	7	2	0	0	0	1	11	64
4. Gymnastics	3	1	2	3	1	1	1	1	13	23
5. Orienteering	0	1	0	0	4	0	1	1	7	57
6. Skiing (D)	1	0	0	0	0	6	0	0	7	86
7. Track & Field	0	0	0	0	0	0	5	0	5	100
8. Volleyball	2	2	0	4	0	1	0	8	17	46

Factor H (venturesomeness) has virtually no discriminatory power for either athletic sample.

CLASSIFICATION Examination of the cumulative proportion of total dispersion for each sample shown in Tables 1 and 3 indicates that there are statistically significant differences among sport groups. However, the data presented in Tables 2 and 4 which compare the assignment of subjects on the basis of sport participation with their assignment on the basis of personality do not offer substantial support for the supposition that there are distinctive personality types associated with selected sport groups.

Table 2 reveals the fit between personality types and participation types among male athletes. On the one hand, 5 out of 6 orienteers, 4 out of 5 Nordic skiers, 6 out of 8 gymnasts, and 4 out of 7 boxers are correctly classified. On the other hand, only 6 out of 37 ice hockey players, 2 out of 13 basketball players, 3 out of 19 cyclists, and 7 out of 21 rowers are correctly classified.

Table 4 reflects the match between sport particpation and personality assignment for female athletes. On the one hand, 7 out of 7 downhill skiers, 5 out of 5 trackwomen, and 5 out of 6 channel canoeists are correctly classified. On the other hand, only 3 out of 13 gymnasts, 8 out of 17 volleyball players, and 7 out of 14 basketball players are correctly classified.

STAGE 2: NUMERICAL TAXONOMY ANALYSIS

The results of the discriminant function analysis for sport groups do not provide substantial support for the premise that participants in given sports have similar personality profiles. Part of the cause for such weakness in discriminating between participants in various sport groups may be due to a deficiency in the classification scheme utilized. As Vanek and Cratty (1970) have suggested, some sports may actually belong in similar classification categories. They suggest that athletes in different sports may demonstrate similar personality profiles because the sport groups are characterized by similar psychological demand characteristics. For example, archery and shooting may be considered homogeneous sports since they both are sporting activities which involve hand-eye coordination.

The problem of identifying suitable classification criteria is not unique to athletic inquiries seeking to establish sport types. Several scientific and scholarly disciplines such as anthropology, botany, entomology and zoology have been faced with the task of sorting similar objects into groups and dissimilar objects into other groups when the important discriminant characteristics of the groups and/or the number of groups is unknown. The physical anthropologist, for example, may be in possession of a number of skulls and seeks to establish some meaningful classification scheme. Relevant characteristics of the skulls could be assessed—diameter of the skull, distance between eye sockets, angle of jaw, etc.—and the means sought to sort these various skulls on the basis of the profile of characteristics measured. Similarly, a botanist may come into possession of a new plant and he must "match" the new plant to its most homogeneous generic species.

In any arbitrary classification of groups, issue may be taken with the criteria for classification. With the present data the problem may be seen as one in which satisfactory discrimination between various sport groups was not possible because some of the supposedly distinct sport groups were actually members of the same category if one used different classification criteria; that is, discrimination between gymnasts and ski jumpers may not have been possible since they both fall within Vanek and Cratty's (1970) "category 2" of sports that require "total body coordination and consideration" (see Table 5). The fact that we call one group "gymnasts" and the other "skiers" may be irrelevant as far as a taxonomy based upon personality profiles is concerned.

Numerical taxonomy, classification, or cluster analysis techniques offer the alternative *of first* forming mutually exclusive and optimally homogeneous groups *and then* considering the criteria capable of explaining the resultant classifications. A number of such classification techniques exist (for example, Cole, 1969; Ward and Hook, 1963) although infrequently used by athletic personality researchers (Kroll and Carlson, 1967). One such numerical taxonomy technique developed by Parks (1970), the Q-mode cluster analysis on distance functions, was employed to classify the Czech sport groups in the present study. Parks' technique offers several advantages over other procedures, since it transforms the raw score characteristic measures into an uncorrelated set of orthogonal variables via a principal components analysis. Such a transformation not only reduces the number of relevant dimensions necessary in the classification procedure, but also ameliorates the deficiency existing in most data where the profile measures are intercorrelated. Factor scores are then secured for each sample and simple distance functions computed comparing each sample with other samples across the reduced orthogonal set of factor scores. The analysis technique sorts the distance functions between all possible pairs of samples and the array is processed for plotting of a dendogram. The dendogram, a technique first used in systematic zoology, resembles a listing for an elimination tournament in which the relationships among entries based upon similarly assessed via distance functions are illustrated.

Separate numerical taxonomy analyses were made on (a) female sport groups, (b) male sport groups, and (c) combined male and female sport groups. Figures 1 through 3 illustrate the results. Note that the simple distance function can range from 0.0, shortest distance or closest similarity, to +1.0, longest distance or greatest dissimilarity.

The obtained distance functions show the degree of similarity in 16 PF profiles among sport groups. It can be seen from the female dendogram (see Fig. 1) that orienteering and channel canoeists had the smallest distance function

TABLE 5
Vanek-Cratty Sport Typology

Type 1	Sport Activities Involving Hand-Eye Coordinations Examples = archery, shooting
Type 2	Sport Activities Requiring Total Body Coordination Examples = diving, figure skating, ski-jumping
Type 3	Sport Activities Requiring Total Mobilization of Body Energy Example = distance running, rowing, swimming
Type 4	Sport Activities in which Injury is Imminent Examples = boxing, motorcycling, parachute jumping
Type 5	Sport Activities Involving the Anticipation of Movements of Other Individuals A. Games employing a net: e.g., tennis, volleyball and table tennis B. Games involving direct aggression against an opponent: e.g., football, ice hockey, wrestling C. Games involving parallel competition: e.g., bowling, cricket and golf

*Adapted from Vanek and Cratty, pp. 39–45.

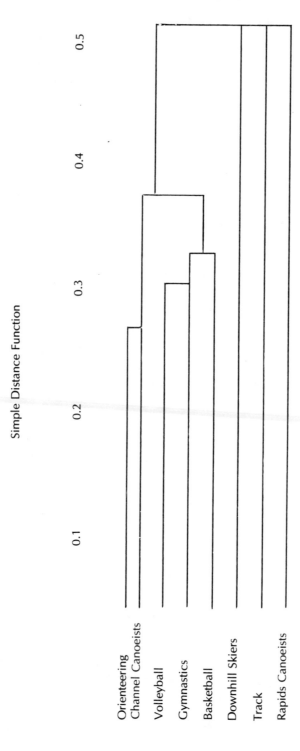

FIG. 1.   DENDOGRAM OF FEMALE SPORT GROUPS.

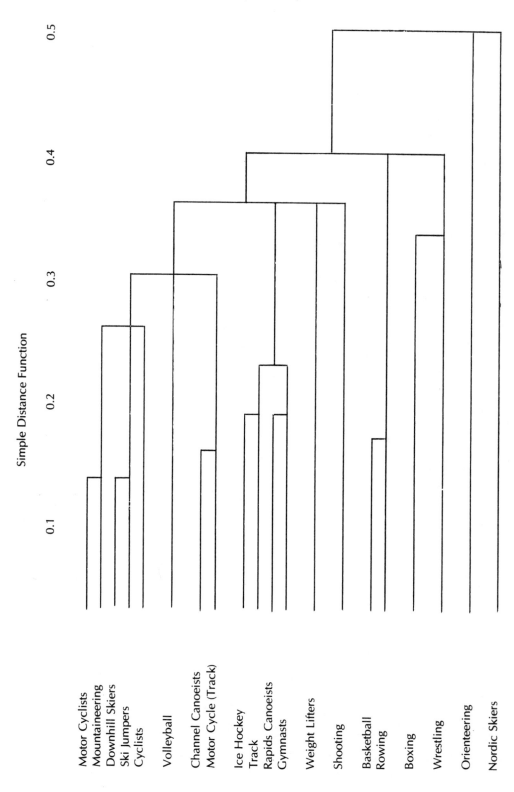

Simple Distance Function

0.1   0.2   0.3   0.4   0.5

Motor Cyclists
Mountaineering
Downhill Skiers
Ski Jumpers
Cyclists

Volleyball

Channel Canoeists
Motor Cycle (Track)

Ice Hockey
Track
Rapids Canoeists
Gymnasts

Weight Lifters

Shooting

Basketball
Rowing

Boxing

Wrestling

Orienteering

Nordic Skiers

FIG. 2.   DENDOGRAM OF MALE SPORT GROUPS.

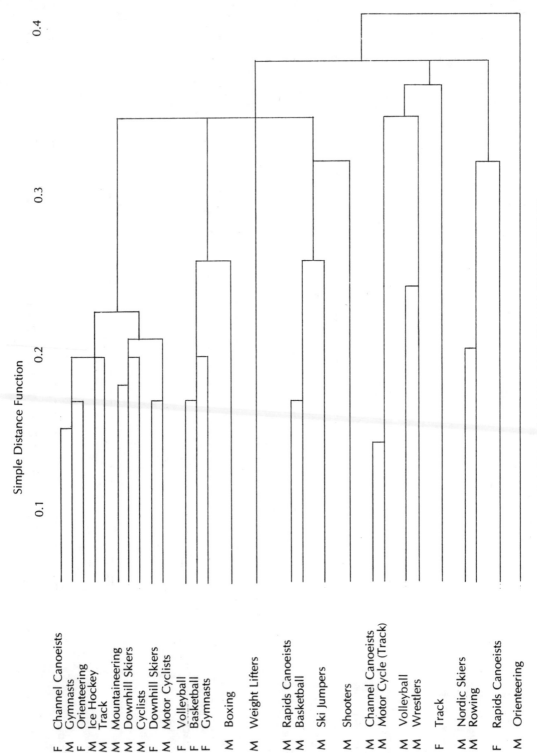

FIG. 3.   DENDOGRAM OF MALE AND FEMALE SPORT GROUPS.

(DF=.270) and were thus the most similar in factor profile. Volleyball players and gymnasts were next most similar (DF=.284), quickly joined by the basketball players (DF=.295). The orienteering and channel canoeist cluster was then joined with the volleyball-gymnast-basketball cluster (DF=.363). Downhill skiers, rapids canoeists, and track athletes represented the most divergent groups and were joined to the first major cluster with a simple distance value of approximately .48.

Similar interpretations can be made for the male data (see Fig. 2) and the combined male-female data (see Fig. 3). In the combined analysis, for example, the first pairs matched were: female channel canoeists and male gymnasts (DF=.1032); male channel canoeists and male track motor cyclists (DF=.1097); male rapids canoeists and male basketball players (DF=.1247); and, female volleyball players and female basketball players (DF=.1260).

Attempts to deduce meaningful classification criteria for the results of these analyses await mature counsel. Utilizing the typologies suggested by Vanek and Cratty (see Table 5) produces some typological incongruencies. The first match of female channel canoeists and male gymnasts apparently represents a match between Type 3 sports requiring total mobilization of body energy and Type 2 sports requiring total body coordination. Male channel canoeists represent Type 3 (total mobilization of body energy) or Type 4 (sports where injury or death are imminent) while male track motor cyclists probably represent Type 4. Male rapids canoeists are Type 4 (injury or death imminent) while male basketball players are classified in Type 5a (anticipation of movements of other people with no direct aggression). The fourth pair of female volleyball players and female basketball players are both Type 5a. Even though some of the initial pairing of sport groups appear to fit Vanek and Cratty's (1970) typology scheme, subsequent clustering of sport groups is seemingly incongruent with such a typology scheme.

Perhaps the most interesting cluster of sport groups is the matching of male motor cyclists, mountaineers, downhill skiers, ski-jumpers and cyclists (see Fig. 2). Although these sport groups appear to be quite diverse at first glance, they may be analytically viewed as agonetic activities involving physical experiences which provide « . . . at some risk to the participant, an element of thrill through the medium of speed, accelera-tion, sudden change of direction, or exposure to dangerous situations, with the participant usually remaining in control » (Kenyon, 1968, p. 100). Thus the clustering of these specific sport groups offers empirical evidence for the "category of vertigo" in Caillois' (1955) classification of games, and for the subdomain entitled "pursuit of vertigo" in Kenyon's (1968) conceptual model for characterizing physical activity. Interestingly, Kenyon notes that: "The participant may not recognize vertigo as the common element, but rather views sports such as skiing, diving from a high platform, heavy weather sailing, mountain climbing, sky diving, etc., as apparently unrelated." (1968, p. 100)

STAGE 3: FACTOR ANALYSIS AND FACTOR MATCHING

Results of the discriminant function and numerical taxonomy analysis cannot be said to be encouraging to attempts at identifying sport types based upon 16 PF profile data. It was decided, then, to factor analyze the 16 PF profile for the male and female Czech athletes separately, regardless of sport group affiliation, and compare the factor structure for males and females.

Principal component and varimax rotation analysis produced 16 factors in both male and female data.[a] Each factor accounted for approximately six percent of the total variance and the rotated factors were identified by their near-unity loadings on one of the 16 PF profile components. The varimax rotation loadings suggest, in accordance with Cattell's theory and test construction procedures, that the 16 PF factors each assess independent components of personality.

Utilizing a technique developed by Ahmavaara (1957), the separate factor analyses of male and of female 16 PF profiles were compared for similarity of factor structures. Results of the factor matching analysis are presented in Table 6. High similarity of the corresponding factors for male and female Czech athletes is evidenced by the near-unity diagonal correlation values. Near-zero values for off-diagonal correlation values indicate dissimilarity of the other factors. The factor matching analysis thus indicates a marked similarity in the factorial composition of personality, as assessed by the 16 PF, in male and female Czech athletes.

---

[a] For logical rather than statistical reasons, 100 percent of the total variance was extracted.

TABLE 6

Factor matching for Normalized Varimax Rotation of 16 PF Profiles for Male and Female Czech Athletes

Factor	A	B	C	E	F	G	H	I	L	M	N	O	Q₁	Q₂	Q₃	Q₄
A	9805	0789	0630	-0213	-0419	-0170	0242	-0939	0219	-0473	-0129	-1139	0277	0108	0039	0069
B	-0713	9889	-0492	-0053	0097	0333	-0486	0447	-0135	-0263	0105	-0311	0375	-0662	-0181	-0246
C	0201	-0396	9714	-0257	-1151	0650	-0051	0201	-0212	0975	0151	-0514	-0452	-0991	0998	-0345
E	0099	-0231	0206	-0918	1205	0230	-0069	1439	1181	-0312	0311	-0828	-0278	0236	0180	-1269
F	0612	-0117	0338	9606	-9714	-0530	0643	0953	0179	0087	-0237	0735	-0100	0831	0392	1092
G	-0188	0271	-0314	0200	0420	9750	0013	-0134	1824	-0282	0472	-0037	-0633	0608	-0030	0325
H	-0598	0446	-0276	-1209	-0055	-0115	-9686	-0102	-0557	-0224	0774	1189	1313	0037	-0287	0782
I	0763	-0552	-0129	-0856	0698	-0020	-0394	-9810	0346	0337	-0070	-0042	0315	-0460	-0130	
L	-0384	0103	0307	1116	-0290	1862	-0065	-0187	9381	1037	0644	-0822	-0673	-1007	1328	-1258
M	0308	0351	-0752	0120	0313	0375	-0884	0000	-0900	-9824	-0640	-0016	0601	-0085	0170	0184
N	0031	0021	0593	0715	0155	0397	-0631	0390	0084	0554	9868	-0052	-0553	-0419	-0178	0408
O	1205	-0018	0619	-0105	0783	-0323	0583	0075	0288	0003	-0354	-9767	0426	0000	-0701	-0031
Q₁	-0448	-0546	0548	0192	-0364	0537	0964	0278	0630	0367	0651	0538	-9800	0823	0345	-0039
Q₂	0214	-0813	-1045	-0008	-0396	0473	0252	0077	-0745	-0051	-0590	0347	-0835	9726	0596	1022
Q₃	-0309	-0370	0552	-1042	-0288	-0089	0019	0621	0763	-0342	-0313	0611	-0398	0569	9865	0087
Q₄	0213	-0835	-0218	-1042	-1523	0978	-0546	0249	-1194	0398	0603	0233	0481	0716	0500	9565

REFERENCES

1. Ahmavaara, Y.: On the unified factor theory of mind. Ann. Akad. Sci. Fennicae (Helsinki), Sevlal B, 106, 1957.
2. Caillois, R.: The structure and classification of games. Diogenes, 12:62, 1955.
3. Cole, A. J. (ed.): Numerical Taxonomy. Academic Press, New York, 1969.
4. Dixon, W. J. (ed.): Biomedical Computer Program. Los Angeles, University of California Press, 1967.
5. Kenyon, G. S.: A conceptual model for characterizing physical activity. Res. Q., 39:96, 1968.
6. Kroll, Walter, and Petersen, Kay H.: Personality factor profiles of collegiate football teams. Res. Q., 36:433, 1965.
7. Kroll, Walter, and Carlson, B. Robert: Discriminant function and hierarchial grouping analysis of karate participants' personality profiles. Res. Q., 38:405, 1967.
8. Parks, James M.: Fortran IV Program for Q-Mode Cluster Analysis on Distance Function with Printed Dendogram. (Computer contribution 46, State Geological Survey). University of Kansas, Lawrence, 1970.
9. Tiedeman, David V.: The utility of the discriminant function in psychological and guidance investigations. Harvard Educ. Rev., 21:71, 1951.
10. Vanek, Miroslav, and Cratty, Bryant J.: Psychology of the Superior Athlete. Macmillan, New York, 1970.
11. Ward, Joseph H. Jr., and Hook, Marion E.: Application of an hierarchical grouping procedure to a problem of grouping profiles. Educ. Psychol. Meas., 23:69, 1963.

social psychological characteristics of innovators *

JOHN W. LOY, JR.

In his work, *Diffusion of Innovations* (1962), Rogers reviews several hundred publications related to innovativeness, i.e., "the degree to which an individual is relatively earlier in adopting new ideas than other members of his social system" (p. 2). Rogers argues that "when research on this topic reaches the point where we may predict 'when' and 'who' will adopt new ideas in a social system, valuable theoretical and practical consequences should result" (pp. 285–286). He cautiously observes though: (1) that in view of the quantity of literature on diffusion research, there have been relatively few attempts to predict innovativeness; (2) predictive efforts[1] to date have been only moderately successful at best; (3) "there are few studies that have related adequate measures of personality variables to innovativeness" (p. 178); and (4) nearly all predictive studies have been limited to farmer respondents, and thus "there is little evidence to date that (discovered) relationships

will hold in other types of social systems" (p. 289).

This investigation represents an effort to both replicate and extend research related to the prediction of innovativeness. First, it puts to test—in an English social system related to sport—generalizations derived from work in rural sociology with American farmers. Although it has been observed that "the spread of sport through the world and changes in its nature are major phenomena of the twentieth century" (Smithells and Cameron, 1962:438), and although sportsmen and others have acknowledged the changes which innovations such as new training methods have wrought in sport, little theoretical or empirical work has been done regarding these changes.

Second, the investigation places emphasis on the adequate assessment of theoretically relevant personality variables. A number of theorists of social change have stressed the importance of personality traits as antecedents to change (e.g., Barnett, 1953; Hagen, 1962; McClelland, 1961). Also, the need for studies assessing the relationship of personality characteristics to the differential adoption of innovations has been stated by several writers (e.g., Miles, 1964; Rogers, 1962; Straus, 1956). Yet, the investigator knows of only one study regarding the adoption of an innovation wherein an objective multiple-factor personality inventory was administered in the process of gathering data concerning personal attributes of adopters (cf. Straus, 1956). This investigation attempted to meet the aforementioned criterion by using Cattell's *Sixteen Per-*

Reprinted from American Sociological Review, 34:73–82, 1969. Copyright 1969 by the American Sociological Review, Washington, D.C. 20036.

* This research study was a part of a doctoral dissertation completed at the University of Wisconsin, June 1967. Partial support for the investigation was provided by funds from the NDEA Title IV Supplementary Fund for the General Improvement of Graduate Education. Appreciation is accorded to Joseph W. Elder and A. Eugene Havens, Department of Sociology, and Gerald S. Kenyon, Department of Physical Education, University of Wisconsin, for guidance in the investigation. Thanks is also expressed to the staff of the University of Wisconsin Computing Center for assistance rendered.

sonality Factor Questionnaire to obtain data on personality measures hypothesized to be related to technological change.

Third, the study examines innovativeness by determining whether multiple adopter categories can be empirically differentiated in terms of selected socio-psychological characteristics. Past efforts of predicting innovativeness have been largely conducted by rural sociologists making multiple correlation analyses of data collected from farmer respondents (cf. Rogers, 1962: 287–292). Although multiple correlation procedures provide an indication of what variables are associated with the early adoption of an innovation, they ignore the matter of group membership. That is, multiple correlational analysis indicates the group in which an individual will perform best, but provides little knowledge as to the group which he most nearly resembles (Rulon, 1951).

It is true that some studies have been conducted in an attempt to answer the preceding question, but they typically have had certain common conceptual and methodological weaknesses. A major conceptual weakness has been that past investigations of differences between adopter categories have often considered only dichotomized categories, such as early and late adopters, or acceptors and rejectors. Rogers demonstrates that innovativeness may be empirically treated as a continuous variable, and contends that the concept may be better understood if its underlying continuum is partitioned so that individuals are grouped into several adopter categories (1962:148–168). Specifically, Rogers posits and discusses the salient values of five ideal-type adopter categories. He operationally defines his categories as follows: Innovators, first 2½% to adopt a given innovation; Early Adopters, next 13½% to adopt; Early Majority, following 34% to adopt; Late Majority, next 34% to adopt; and finally, Laggards, last 16% to adopt (1962:159–172).

Previous empirical efforts to differentiate between various categories of early and late adopters have been limited to comparing differences between means on given traits, or comparing profiles on several traits for different adopter categories. The first approach to data analysis precludes the assessment of all attributes simultaneously for different categories; whereas the major weakness of the second manner of data treatment is that "profile factors may be highly

related, and the possibility exists that less than the entire set of different variables is meaningful or that other variables, non-significant by themselves, may be discriminating when viewed as an entire profile rather than individually" (Kroll and Petersen, 1965:433–434). An alternative to the aforementioned methods of data analysis is the configurational approach to prediction proposed by Rogers (1962:292–295). Rogers' approach, however, does not seem to be a practical one when large numbers of independent variables are considered and it tends to possess the drawbacks of profile analysis. To avoid the methodological weaknesses outlined, this investigation used multiple discriminant function analysis to test whether multiple adopter categories can be empirically differentiated.

PROCEDURES

SUBJECTS

Data were collected from 89 male and 17 female English swimming coaches by means of personal interviews (35 cases) and mailed questionnaires (71 cases) in the spring and summer of 1966. Analyses of data, however, were confined to a sample of 42 men and six women drawn from a population of chief (including three co-chief) swimming coaches,[2] with a minimum of eight years coaching experience,[3] associated with competitive clubs affiliated to the Amateur Swimming Association of England (ASA).[4] This sample represents approximately 50 percent of the coaches associated with competitive clubs affiliated to the ASA.[5]

VARIABLES

Seventeen socio-psychological attributes were considered in the investigation: innovativeness, socio-economic status, educational status, professional status, peer status, cosmopoliteness, sociability, intelligence, dominance, surgency, perseverance, venturesomeness, sensitivity, imaginativeness, shrewdness, experimentiveness, and self-sufficiency.[6]

The variables, largely sociological in nature, were selected on the basis of findings of past research as revealed by Rogers' review (1962) of the literature. The variables of a psychological nature, reflecting personality traits, were chosen because they have been shown important in the prediction of creativity (IPAT, 1963), which

Hagen has theorized as being a crucial factor in social change (1962).

INSTRUMENTS

Measures of the above variables were obtained using a questionnaire developed by the investigator and Form A of Cattell's *Sixteen Personality Factor Questionnaire* (16 PF). The latter instrument was selected for use in the investigation because: (1) the factors it purports to measure are relevant to the assessment of venturesomeness and creativity; (2) the instrument has been shown to be a reliable and valid inventory for purposes of "group" investigation; (3) the instrument may be self-administered and is thus suitable for a study using mailed questionnaires; and (4) the instrument appeared appropriate for the population concerned, as it had been previously used for research purposes in England and is designed for adult populations (Cattell and Eber, 1957, 1962a, 1962b).

MEASURES

An operational indicator was developed for each of the seventeen variables listed above.

1. Following Rogers, *Innovativeness* was defined as "the degree to which an individual is relatively earlier in adopting a new idea than other members of his social system." Innovativeness was taken as the dependent variable and operationalized as time of adoption of the controlled interval method (CIM) recorded to the nearest year.[7] The CIM is a sophisticated form of interval training wherein pulse rate is used as a means of determining the intensity of a training bout, the length of recovery period between bouts, and as a motivation device and an indicator of a swimmer's level of cardiovascular fitness (ASA, 1962). The CIM was selected for consideration in the investigation because: (1) having potential for bringing about change in competitive swimming via better performance records, it appeared to be a notable sport innovation; (2) it was distinctive—there being no other methods of training quite like it; (3) it did not have major economic constraints attached to it, thus eliminating certain factors which would have had to be controlled; (4) it had attained a moderate diffusion; (5) it had a pattern of diffusion which could be accurately traced; and (6) it was officially recommended but not required for adoption by the national body governing swimming in England.

2. *Socio-economic status* denotes an individual's position in a social system with respect to level of wealth and occupation. Two operational measures of socio-economic status were obtained by means of criteria given by *Classification of Occupations 1966*, General Register's Office. First, each subject was classified on the basis of his occupation, according to what that volume terms "social class," as follows: (1) professional occupations and alike, (2) intermediate occupations, (3) skilled occupations, (4) partly skilled occupations, and (5) unskilled occupations. The resulting index was called *social status*. Second, each subject was classified according to what the above publication terms "socio-economic group." The following categories were employed: (1) employers and managers of large establishments, (2) employers and managers of small establishments, (3) professional workers self-employed, (4) professional workers—employees, (5) intermediate non-manual workers, (6) junior non-manual workers, (7) personal service workers, (8) foremen and supervisors, (9) skilled manual workers, (10) semi-skilled manual workers, and (11) unskilled manual workers. The resulting index was labeled *occupational status*.

3. *Educational status* denotes an individual's position in a social system with respect to level of educational achievement. A subject's educational status was ascertained by his response to questions regarding years of schooling, types of schools attended, and diplomas and degrees earned. On the basis of replies received, an operational index of educational status was developed by assigning numerical values one through nine to the following categories: primary school, secondary modern school, secondary technical school, grammar school, public school, technical college, training college, advanced college of technology, and university (cf. Burgess, 1964).

4. *Professional status* denotes an individual's position in a social system with respect to level of professional achievement. Professional status was operationalized by determining the degree to which a subject's ability to teach and coach swimming was recognized by the ASA. The governing body of amateur swimming in England has established committees which annually appoint a national panel of examiners which administer tests, both theoretical and practical, at

three levels of proficiency. Subjects were ranked in terms of professional proficiency and assigned a numerical value of "0," "1," "2," or "3."[8]

5. *Peer status* denotes an individual's position in a social system with respect to the degree of deference accorded him. A subject's peer status was measured by how many times he was mentioned by other coaches when they were asked: "Excluding yourself, who do you think are the three best coaches in your district?"[9]

6. *Cosmopoliteness* denotes the degree to which an individual's orientation is external to the local situation in which he generally operates. Three operational measures of "cosmopoliteness" were used in the present study. The first was a measure of how far away a subject had traveled from his locality during the past year to participate in a professional function. Each subject was asked: "What is the most distance (one way) you have traveled at any time during the past year to participate in or attend a swimming gala or coaching course?" Replies were recorded to the nearest mile reported.

The second and third measures were designed to ascertain to what extent a subject employed cosmopolite information sources related to swimming. Each respondent was asked the following two questions: (1) "Have you written during the past year to any nationally or internationally known coach or other swimming expert for information or advice about some aspect of swimming?" and (2) "Are you a member of the British Swimming Coaches Association (B.S.C.A.)?" Replies to these questions were recorded yes or no and scored one or zero respectively.

7. *Personality Traits.* Empirical indicators for each of the psychological attributes were based on raw scores for given factor scales of the 16 P.F. The following personality variables and their respective 16 P.F. factor scales were taken into account: Sociability (A), Intelligence (B), Dominance (E), Surgency (F), Perseverance (G), Venturesomeness (H), Sensitivity (I), Imaginativeness (M), Shrewdness (N), Experimentiveness (Q1), and Self-sufficiency (Q2).

TREATMENT

Subjects were placed into adopter categories on the basis of what appeared to be "natural" groupings in terms of when they adopted the CIM.[10] Table 1 shows how the subjects were classified on the basis of when they adopted the CIM. As is evident from this table, the first three (6½%) to adopt CIM were classified as Innovators; the next twenty-four (50%) to adopt were labeled Early Majority; the following fifteen (31%) to adopt were termed Late Majority; and the last subject to adopt as well as five nonadopters (12½%) were defined as Laggards. It is noted that if the strong assumption is granted that the category labeled Early Majority in this study is composed of both Early Adopters and Early Majority in terms of Rogers' classification,

TABLE 1

Distribution of Adopter Categories

Year of Adoption	Number Adopting per Year	Adopter Category
1957	1	
1958	2	Innovators (n=3)
1959	11	
1960	13	Early Majority (n=24)
1961	3	
1962	3	
1963	3	Late Majority (n=15)
1964	6	
1965	0	
1966	1	Laggards (n=6)
Not Adopting	5	
	Total=48	

then the two methods of adopter categorization are approximate.

Multiple discriminant function analysis was employed to determine whether the four categories were empirically different. This technique was considered appropriate since ". . . discriminant analysis takes into account variability of group means on the n variables, variation of individuals about group means on the n variables, and interrelationships of the n variables . . ." (Tiedeman, 1951:76). In short, discriminant function analysis provides three kinds of information. First, it determines whether in fact certain groups are really distinct with respect to selected characteristics. Second, it tells us on what factors the groups may be best discriminated. And third, it indicates whether an individual is like other individuals in the group to which he has been assigned. That is, it indicates the extent to which individuals have been theoretically misclassified.

The multivariate generalized null hypothesis tested was that no socio-psychological differences existed among the four adopter categories. The .05 level of significance was selected as being sufficient to warrant the rejection of the statistical hypothesis. All socio-psychological attributes considered as independent variables in the investigation were treated in the discriminant function analysis. Differences among adopter categories are reported in terms of D-squares for each pair of groups. The discriminative power of the total battery of socio-psychological variables, as well as the discriminative power of any given variable, are reported in terms of Wilk's lambdas. The statistical significance of a given lambda is given in terms of its F-ratio.

RESULTS

ADOPTER CATEGORIES·

The multivariate generalized null hypothesis of no socio-psychological differences among the four adopter categories was rejected, as the obtained lambda for the overall test was found to be statistically significant beyond the .01 level. In addition, differences between all but one pair of adopter categories were found to be statistically significant at or beyond the .05 level. The F-value of differences between Late Majority Adopters and Laggards is statistically significant at the .05 level when rounded to only two decimal places but just fails to reach the significant level when carried to three decimal places, as shown in Table 2.

TABLE 2

Discrimination Between Paired Adopter Categories, Nineteen Independent Variables

	\multicolumn{4}{c}{D-Squares for Each Pair of Adopter Categories †}
	1	2	3	4
1	. . . .	31.674	62.309	91.937
2		. . . .	15.735	24.731
3			. . . .	15.014
4				. . . .

	\multicolumn{4}{c}{F-Tests for Each Pair of Adopter Categories (19+26 d.f.)}
	1	2	3	4
1	. . . .	2.627 *	4.845 **	5.719 **
2		. . . .	4.517**	3.692 **
3			. . . .	2.001 ††
4				. . . .

\multicolumn{2}{c}{F-Test for Over-all Analysis (57+78 d.f.)}
Lambda=.032	F=2.977 **

† 1=Innovators (n=3); 2=Early Majority (n=24); 3=Late Majority (n=15); and 4=Laggards (n=6).
* .05 level of significance.
** .01 level of significance.
†† With 19+26 d.f. an F-value of 2.0027 is required for p≤.05.

TABLE 3

Discriminant Function Analysis, Nineteen Independent Variables

Variable	Lambda	F
1. Venturesomeness (H)	.539	7.405 **
2. Professional Status	.543	7.300 **
3. Imaginativeness (M)	.566	6.639 **
4. Educational Status	.580	6.285 **
5. Dominance (E)	.621	5.288 **
6. Sociability (A)	.623	5.252 **
7. Cosmopoliteness #3	.648	4.700 **
8. Self-Sufficiency (Q2)	.688	3.926 *
9. Perseverance (G)	.773	2.538
10. Cosmopoliteness #1	.794	2.247
11. Peer Status	.794	2.240
12. Intelligence (B)	.802	2.133
13. Occupational Status	.828	1.800
14. Social Status	.829	1.791
15. Cosmopoliteness #2	.845	1.590
16. Shrewdness (N)	.847	1.569
17. Experimentiveness (Q1)	.914	.815
18. Surgency (F)	.958	.383
19. Sensitivity (I)	.990	.085

* .05 level of significance
** .01 level of significance   (3+26 d.f.)

DISCRIMINATORY POWER

Regarding the discriminative power of individual variables, it can be seen from Table 3 that the lambdas for the variables of venturesomeness, professional status, imaginativeness, educational status, dominance, sociability, cosmopoliteness #3 (membership in B.S.C.A.), and self-sufficiency were statistically significant beyond the .05 level.

CLASSIFICATION

Table 4 compares the assignment of subjects on the basis of their time of adoption of CIM with their empirical classification determined by discriminant function analysis. As is evident from that table, only one subject out of the forty-eight was misclassified; namely, one individual classified as a Late Majority Adopter was shown to possess the socio-psychological attributes of an Early Majority Adopter.

TABLE 4

Classification of Subjects, Nineteen Independent Variables

Adopter Category	A Priori Assigned	Empirically Differentiated	Wrongly Classified
Innovators	3	3	0
Early Majority	24	25 *	0
Late Majority	15	14	1 *
Laggards	6	6	0
Total	48	48	1

*An individual theoretically classified as a Late Majority Adopter was empirically found to possess attributes in common with Early Majority Adopters.

DISCUSSION

The discovery of empirically distinguishable adopter categories lends support to Rogers' argument that innovativeness is a continuous variable and that it may be both theoretically and empirically fruitful in diffusion research to study multiple rather than dichotomous adopter categories.

It is also of interest to observe that the findings give some support to Hagen's argument that "technological progress results from the actions of men characterized by varying degrees of creativity" (1962:88). For the most discriminative variables in the investigation are not unlike several of those reported by Taylor and Holland in their analysis of the creative individual:

> There is some evidence that creative persons are more autonomous than others, more self-sufficient, more independent in judgment . . . more open to the irrational in themselves, more stable, more feminine in interests and characteristics . . . more dominant and self-assertive, more complex, more resourceful and adventurous . . . (1964:27–28).

Moreover, it is of special interest to note that venturesomeness had the most discriminative power of all the independent variables considered, which supports Rogers' contention that "the major value of the innovator is venturesomeness" (1962:169).

In addition to providing a means of establishing the empirical validity of *a priori* established adopter categories, discriminant function analysis provides a useful method for the better understanding of the data. For example, it isolates deviant individuals within given groups who can be further analyzed in an effort to account for exceptional findings. The single individual misclassified in this investigation well illustrates this point. The coach was classified on the basis of his date of adoption of CIM as a Late Majority Adopter, but analysis showed him to be more like Early Majority Adopters in terms of the socio-psychological attributes he possessed. A case analysis based on data obtained from the subject in a personal interview is suggestive as to why the subject was wrongly classified.

The subject is near retirement age and, although he has coached for several years, he did not become active in highly competitive swimming until he began tutoring a young female swimmer in 1962. He recognized this swimmer to have great talent and perceived the CIM to be applicable to her training program; whereas before this time he had no swimmers under his charge whom he felt capable of benefiting from the CIM training program. An outcome ascribed in part to his act of adoption of CIM was that the female swimmer concerned represented Great Britain at the 1964 Olympic Games.

In view of the moderately striking findings of the investigation, a cursory discussion of the arbitrariness associated with adopter categorization is called for as a cautionary note. Discriminant analysis allows one to determine whether discrimination among social categories is possible in terms of selected characteristics. But ". . . the multiple discriminant function can not be used as a substitute for theory in selecting the groups or the attributes for study . . ." (Rettig, 1964:398). Although there is some theoretical basis for considering innovativeness as a continuous dimension, which may be partitioned into several categories for more fruitful examination, there exists no truly adequate rationale for partitioning an adopter continuum one way or another. Even Rogers, who has probably given the most thought to adopter categorization, concedes that "five" was an arbitrary number for his suggested categories (1962:162–163). Likewise, the categorization made in the present study was a discretionary decision, more empirical than theoretical in nature. It seemed reasonable, however, to conceive of a small group of individuals at one extreme of the distribution who actively sponsor technological change, a second small group at the opposite extreme who actively resist change, and two large groups between the extremes—one favoring early adoption and the other late adoption. Also, it seemed sensible, in view of the small sample, to select adopter categories in terms of more or less "natural groupings," rather than imposing precise operational cut off points, such as those given by Rogers.

Even assuming that one has solid theoretical grounds for choosing certain categories and attributes for study, there is still the decision regarding how many characteristics to take into account. For, in discriminant function analysis, an investigator often has the problem of striking a happy medium between variable parsimony and maximum likelihood classification. As an example, only one adopter was misclassified in

TABLE 5

Discrimination Between Paired Adopter Categories, Twelve Independent Variables

F-Tests for Each Pair of Adopter Categories† (12+33 d.f.)				
	1	2	3	4
1	.....	3.341**	6.135**	6.071**
2	.....	.....	5.530**	3.484**
3	.....	.....	.....	2.007
4	.....	.....	.....	.....

F-Test for Over-all Analysis (36+98 d.f.)	
Lambda=.082	F=3.626**

Classification of Subjects			
Adopter Category*	A Priori Assigned	Empirically Differentiated	Wrongly Classified
1	3	3	0
2	24	23	3 (three 3's)
3	15	17	2 (two 2's)
4	6	5	1 (one 3)
Total	48	48	6

† 1=Innovators (n=3); 2=Early Majority (n=24); 3=Late Majority (n=15); and 4=Laggards (n=6).
* .05 level of significance.
** .01 level of significance.

the aforementioned analysis, but a total of nineteen social psychological characteristics were used for purposes of discrimination. When a second analysis was made using fewer factors, the number of significant discriminatory variables was increased, but the number of misclassified adopters was also increased (see Tables 5 and 6).

Since past efforts accounting for innovativeness have largely relied on multiple correlation procedures, a comparison between discriminant function analysis and multiple correlation analy-

TABLE 6

Discriminant Function Analysis, Twelve Independent Variables

Variable	Lambda	F
1. Professional Status	.553	8.898**
2. Educational Status	.601	7.300**
3. Venturesomeness (H)	.640	6.196**
4. Imaginativeness (M)	.669	5.441**
5. Cosmopoliteness #1	.711	4.472**
6. Self-Sufficiency (Q2)	.734	3.991*
7. Cosmopoliteness #3	.749	3.677*
8. Sociability (A)	.757	3.538*
9. Perseverance (G)	.761	3.448*
10. Dominance (E)	.763	3.411*
11. Intelligence (B)	.838	2.122
12. Peer Status	.908	1.117

* .05 level of significance
** .01 level of significance
(3+33 d.f.)

sis is perhaps in order at this point. The former technique is appropriate for answering the question: "Can various adopter categories be empirically differentiated on the basis of a battery of social psychological characteristics collectively considered," whereas the latter method is appropriate for answering the question: "Can a substantial proportion of the variance associated with innovativeness be explained by a cluster of social psychological characteristics?"

When eighteen of the nineteen previously treated social psychological factors were used in multiple correlation analysis,[11] a corrected multiple correlation of .77 was obtained between date of adoption of CIM and the several independent variables considered in combination (see Table 7). Thus sixty percent of the adoption variance associated with the sport innovation was accounted for.

A comparison of Tables 3, 6 and 7 reveals that the attributes of professional status and venture-someness have the greatest explanatory power among the several attributes considered in each analysis. However, there is some discrepancy between the rank order of the other predictor variables when discriminant function analysis is contrasted with multiple correlation analysis. This discrepancy is perhaps to be expected in light of the basic differences between the two methods of analysis. As Rulon (1951) observes:

> The fact of group membership is not entered into the data matrix for multiple correlation analysis, but the criterion score for goodness and badness is. In the multiple discriminant analysis it is the other way around. The criterion score is not entered in the data matrix but the fact of group membership is (p. 89).[12]

In any event, it is notable that the findings resulting from both methods of analysis are similar in several instances to those reported in past diffusion studies. (For major summaries of the find-

TABLE 7

Multiple Correlation Analysis, Eighteen Independent Variables†

Independent Variable	Partial Correlation with Innovativeness	t-value with 29 d.f.
1. Professional Status	.556	3.700**
2. Venturesomeness (H)	.396	2.319*
3. Sociability (A)	−.390	−2.281*
4. Experimentiveness (Q1)	.356	2.049*
5. Shrewdness (N)	−.355	−2.043*
6. Imaginativeness (M)	.347	1.995
7. Cosmopoliteness #2	.336	1.923
8. Dominance (E)	−.327	−1.865
9. Occupational Status	.303	1.715
10. Sensitivity (I)	−.293	−1.649
11. Peer Status	.202	1.109
12. Self-Sufficiency (Q2)	.164	.897
13. Intelligence (B)	−.158	−.861
14. Educational Status	.135	.734
15. Cosmopoliteness #3	−.114	−.619
16. Perseverance (G)	.009	.537
17. Cosmopoliteness #1	.006	.358
18. Surgency (F)	−.002	−.117

Multiple Correlation Coefficient=.868	Corrected R =.774 ††
Coefficient of Determination=.753	Corrected R²=.599 ††

† Dependent variable is date of adoption of CIM (i.e., innovativeness).

†† Correction of coefficients for inflated R due to small sample size was made using formulas given by Guilford, 1956, p. 399.

* .05 level of significance.

** .01 level of significance.

ings from diffusion research, see Havens, 1962; Rogers, 1962; Rogers and Ramos, 1965; Rogers and Bettinghaus, 1966.)

In summary, the present investigation permits four conclusions: First, the effort to account for innovativeness in this study appears to be somewhat more successful than those of earlier studies. Second, a number of generalizations regarding the diffusion and adoption of innovations, largely based on work in rural sociology in America, have been supported by this study in sport sociology conducted in England. Third, the investigation suggests that consideration of theoretically relevant personality variables, when adequately assessed, may be fruitful in predicting innovativeness. Fourth, the study implies that it is worthwhile to consider multiple adopter categories rather than just bi-polar groups, such as early and late adopters. Finally, the investigation suggests that future studies of a similar nature might find it profitable to use multivariate statistical techniques, and more particularly, to employ, as did this investigation, the multiple discriminant function technique.

REFERENCES

Amateur Swimming Association of England: Competitive Swimming. London, Educational Productions, 1962.

Barnett, H. G.: Innovation—The Basis of Cultural Change. New York, McGraw-Hill, 1953.

Burgess, Tyrell: A Guide to English Schools. London, Penguin Books, 1964.

Cattell, Raymond, and Eber, Herbert W.: Handbook for the Sixteen Personality Factor Questionnaire. Champaign, Ill., Institute for Personality and Ability Testing, 1957.

Cattell, Raymond, and Eber, Herbert W.: Manual for Forms A and B of the Sixteen Personality Factor Questionnaire. Champaign, Ill., Institute for Personality and Ability Testing, 1962.

Cattell, Raymond, and Eber, Herbert W.: Supplement of Norms for Forms A and B of the Sixteen Personality Factor Questionnaire. Champaign, Ill., Institute for Personality and Ability Testing, 1962.

General Register Office: Classification of Occupations, 1966. London, Her Majesty's Sationery Office, 1966.

Guilford, J. P.: Fundamental Statistics in Psychology and Education. 3rd Edition. New York, McGraw-Hill, 1956.

Hagen, Everett E.: On the Theory of Social Change. Homewood, Ill., Dorsey Press, 1962.

Havens, A. Eugene: A review of factors related to innovativeness. Mimeo Bulletin A. E. 329. Columbus, Ohio, Department of Agricultural Economics and Rural Sociology, Ohio Agricultural Experimental Station, 1962.

IPAT: Data for psychologists selecting students for creativity and research potential. Bulletin #10. Champaign, Ill., Institute for Personality and Ability Testing, 1963.

Kroll, Walter, and Peterson, Kay H.: Personality factor profiles of collegiate football teams. Res. Q., 36:433, 1965.

McClelland, David C.: The Achieving Society. New York, D. Van Nostrand, 1961.

Miles, Matthew B.: Innovation in education: some generalizations. In Innovation in Education. Edited by Matthew B. Miles. New York, Bureau of Publications, Teachers College, Columbia University, 1964.

Rettig, Salomon: Multiple discriminant analysis: an illustration. Am. Sociol. Rev., 29:398, 1964.

Rogers, Everett M.: Diffusion of Innovations. New York, Free Press, 1966.

Rogers, Everett M., and Bettinghaus, Erwin P.: Comparison of generalizations from diffusion research on agricultural and family planning innovations. Paper presented at the American Sociological Association Annual Meeting, Miami Beach, 1966.

Rogers, Everett M., and Bonilla de Ramos, Elasy: Prediction of the adoption of innovations: a progress report. Paper presented at the Rural Sociological Society meetings, Chicago, 1965.

Rulon, Phillip J.: Distinctions between discriminant and regression analyses and a geometric interpretation of the discriminant function. Harvard Educ. Rev., 21:80, 1951.

Smithells, Phillip A., and Cameron, Peter E.: Principles of Evaluation in Physical Education. New York, Harper, 1962.

Straus, Murray A.: Personality testing the farm population. Rural Sociol., 21:293, 1956.

Taylor, Calvin W., and Holland, John: Predictors of creative performance. In Creativity: Progress and Potential. Edited by Calvin W. Taylor and John Holland. New York, McGraw-Hill, 1964.

Tiedman, David V.: The utility of the discriminant function in psychological and guidance investigations. Harvard Educ. Rev., 21:71, 1951.

NOTES

1. More accurately, most, if not all predictive efforts to date, including the present investigation, have been postdictive in nature.

2. The sample was limited to chief coaches because assistant coaches often lacked the authority to make the decision to adopt the innovation considered.

3. Since the innovation considered was first introduced in 1957–1958, only those subjects who had coached at least eight years, and thus had nearly equal opportunity of being an early adopter, were considered for data analysis.

4. Analysis was limited to coaches associated with competitive clubs in that the innovation considered was not relevant for non-competitive clubs. For purposes of this investigation, a competitive club was defined as one who had one or more swimmers, placing at least third in one or more events at its district championships in 1964.

5. The proportion of competitive clubs represented in the sample according to districts within the ASA is

as follows: North-Eastern District—11/12, Northern District—7/17, Midland District—13/32, Western District—6/12, and Southern District—8/15.

6. Empirically speaking, one dependent and nineteen independent variables were considered as two measures of socio-economic status and three measures of cosmopoliteness were used in data analysis.

7. Several items (innovations) are usually used to construct a composite index of innovativeness in diffusion research (cf. Rogers, 1962). Thus, the index employed here probably has a relatively low degree of reliability in comparison to composite indices of innovativeness. However, this fact should lead to a conservative rather than a liberal correlation between the dependent variable and any given independent variable.

8. The relationship between innovativeness and professional status is perhaps inflated to the extent that obtaining an advanced award of the ASA implies knowledge and use of the CIM. It is noted, however, that most subjects earned their awards before the CIM became prominent or adopted the CIM before passing examinations for the advanced award of the ASA.

9. The measurement of peer status is limited by the fact that some districts had more coaches than others and by the fact that there were differential rates of returns by districts.

10. This categorization is, moreover, the most reliable one. Follow-up post cards were mailed to each coach asking again when he first used CIM. While some coaches gave a date of adoption which varied by a year from their earlier statement of their time of adoption, in no case did their second statement of adoption date change the adopter category to which they were assigned.

11. The variable of social status was excluded for purposes of analysis since it was found to be nearly identical with occupational status. Also for purposes of analysis, a set of "dummy variables" was defined over the group of eighteen independent variables. Scores exceeding the mean on a given personality variable were assigned a "1" and those at or below the mean, a "0." Other variables were similarly dichotomized at or near the median.

12. Rulon further states that ". . . in view of these basic differences between the two approaches, and the fairly clear distinction between the kinds of information yielded by the two techniques, it is remarkable or refreshing—or something—that people sometimes say the two approaches are the same, or that we don't need the discriminant function because you can do the same thing with multiple correlation" (1951:89).

group cohesiveness as a determinant of success and member satisfaction in team performance

RAINER MARTENS and JAMES A. PETERSON

The effectiveness of sport teams in competition is dependent upon many factors, one of which is the ability of individual members to work together. The coach often refers to this ability as teamwork, togetherness, or morale, while the researcher refers to it as group integration or group cohesiveness. Physical educators and coaches alike have long postulated that the most effective team is not necessarily composed from a combination of the best skilled individuals. The ability of individuals to effectively interact with teammates to obtain a group-desired goal has been recognized as contributing to team effectiveness. A common held assumption is that the higher the cohesiveness of a team the more effective it will be. The purpose of the present study was to investigate this assumption among intramural basketball teams. The problem was to determine if different levels of group cohesiveness affected the effectiveness and individual member satisfaction of these teams.

Lott and Lott (1965), in their review of the group cohesion literature, cite considerable research directed at the relationship between cohesiveness and performance. The conclusion reached by these reviewers is that the findings have been contradictory—i.e., in some situations a high level of cohesiveness was beneficial, while in other cases this same level of cohesiveness impaired performance. Lott and Lott state that:

Reprinted from International Review of Sport Sociology, 6:49–59, 1971. Copyright, 1971, by International Review of Sport Sociology, Warsaw, Poland.

It seems likely that in a task situation other variables such as the demands of the situation itself (instructions or job specifications), the standards of performance preferred by liked co-workers, and the degree to which sociability may interfere with the required behavior for a particular job, may be highly significant (p. 298).

The experimental literature concerning the relationship between cohesiveness and team performance for sport groups is also contradictory. Klein and Christiansen (1966), Myers (1962), and Chapman and Campbell (1957) using basketball teams, rifle teams, and a novel motor task, respectively, have reported a positive relationship between the cohesiveness of these teams and their effectiveness. An equal number of studies, however, have found that increasing levels of cohesiveness among sport teams produced no increase in effectiveness or actually impaired effectiveness. Lenk (1966) cites several examples of highly effective Olympic rowing teams having extremely low levels of cohesiveness. Fiedler (1953, 1954) and McGrath (1962) have found that a high degree of cohesiveness often interfered with effective performance of basketball teams and rifle teams. To explain this apparent paradox, both McGrath and Fiedler have suggested that players on high cohesive teams may be more concerned with maintaining good interpersonal relations than with effectively playing basketball.

Certainly the need for further study as to the consequences of various levels of cohesiveness on the effectiveness of sport teams is obvious. However, another measure of the consequences that various levels of cohesiveness may have on participation is member satisfaction. It would appear that the degree of satisfaction individuals derive from participating in a sport with a particular group is of equal importance to the number of games won or lost. Therefore, the present study determined if different levels of group cohesiveness are partial determinants of member satisfaction as well as team effectiveness.

METHOD

SUBJECTS AND DESIGN

In cooperation with the Division of Intramurals at the University of Illinois, Urbana, over 1200 male university undergraduate students divided into 144 basketball teams were used as subjects. These teams participated in league play on the basis of their residential affiliation: fraternity (FRAT), men's residence halls (MRH), and men's independent associations (MIA). The members of each team, therefore, resided together and most had previously participated in intramural basketball together. Consequently, the members of a team were not unfamiliar with each other since a certain degree of social interaction had occurred previously.

A questionnaire instrument, used to assess each team's level of cohesiveness, was administered one day before the first league game of the spring intramural basketball program. Cohesiveness was assessed by a number of different questions. On the basis of these responses teams were categorized into low, moderate, or high cohesive teams. The number of games won was the measure of effectiveness. The degree of satisfaction was obtained from a questionnaire administered at the end of the season. Team effectiveness for the three levels of cohesiveness (using each measure of cohesiveness) was analyzed by a one-way analysis of variance disregarding the teams' residential affiliation. Member satisfaction was analyzed in a 3×3 factorial design. The first factor was composed of the three measures of cohesiveness, while the second factor was comprised of the three residential organizations.

MEASUREMENT OF GROUP COHESIVENESS

The most common nominal definition of group cohesiveness is Festinger's (1950). He defines cohesiveness as "the resultant of all the forces acting on members to remain in the group" (p. 164). Operationally defining this array of forces acting on members to remain in the group has not been very successful. As a result, the most prevalent approach for measuring group cohesiveness has been to assess the degree of interpersonal attraction between members of a group. Obviously interpersonal attraction does not constitute the only force acting upon members to remain in the group. Therefore, most previous research has operationally defined cohesiveness by measuring only one component of the nominal definition.

This arbitrary operational definition has been criticized by Gross and Martin (1952). They argue against the attempt by researchers to measure only one component of cohesiveness and, then, on the basis of the results obtained, make inference to the total concept. They suggest it is better to assess cohesiveness by a direct question to each member regarding the cohesiveness of the group. Rather than the researcher making an inference about the cohesiveness of a group on the basis of partial information, Gross and Martin advocate each member of the group making such an inference based upon his intimate acquaintance with the group.

In the present project a number of measures of cohesiveness which were suggested by previous research were used. The questionnaire was constructed in the form of a 9-choice alternative between two polarities. For example, to assess interpersonal attraction the following question was asked:

On what type of a friendship basis are you with each member of your team? If you know him very well and are good friends, rate him high on the scale. If you do not know him or are not good friends, rate him low on the scale.

1	2	3	4	5	6	7	8	9
Good Friend					Not Good Friend			

The questions asked were of three different types. Four questions assessed each team member's evaluation of every other member regarding: (a) the degree of interpersonal attraction, (b) contribution of each member based on his ability, (c) the contribution of each member based on enjoyable to play with, and (d) the influence or power of each member. The second type of question asked each member to indicate his relationship to the team. The two questions of this type asked each member's opinion of: (a) how strong a sense of belonging he had toward the group, and (b) the value of membership on the team. The third type of question asked each member's evaluation of the group as a whole regarding (a) the level of teamwork, and (b) how closely knit the group was.

PROCEDURE

Questionnaires were administered by four assistants supervised by the experimenter. Each team was contacted through the Division of Intramurals and asked to participate in the study. A time was arranged for each group to answer the questionnaire together. Once together the assistant had the names of every team member written and numbered on a poster visible to the entire group. Each member evaluated every other member according to the number assigned. Those individuals who could not attend the group meeting (a very small number) completed the questionnaire alone immediately before the first game.

All records of games won and lost were tabulated by the Division of Intramurals. The post-questionnaire was administered approximately two days after the last game of the season. All teams completed the season, even though a small number of individuals quit teams during the season.

The questionnaire data were transferred from IBM digital answer sheets to IBM computer cards. A mean for each question for each team was computed. The teams were then ranked for each measure of cohesiveness for each residential group and divided into the three categories: low, moderate, and high cohesiveness. This categorization of the eight cohesiveness questions then served as the three levels of the independent variable.

RESULTS

TEAM EFFECTIVENESS

The one-way analyses of variance for the eight measures of cohesiveness are summarized in Table 1.

The first four questions assessed each

TABLE 1

Summary of the Analyses of Team Effectiveness Variance for the Eight Measures of Cohesiveness

Item	Df	Ms	F
Interpersonal attraction	2	0.65	0.28
Residual	141	2.29	
Contribution based on ability	2	0.44	0.19
Residual	141	2.30	
Contribution based on enjoyment	2	0.58	0.25
Residual	141	2.30	
Power of influence	2	3.01	1.33
Residual	141	2.27	
Sense of belonging	2	2.31	1.02
Residual	141	2.28	
Value of membership	2	16.86	8.15 **
Residual	141	2.07	
Teamwork	2	7.26	3.29 *
Residual	141	2.21	
Closely knit	2	6.33	2.86 *
Residual	141	2.22	

* Significant at the .05 level.
** Significant at the .01 level.

member's rating of every other member in the group. None of the questions regarding interpersonal attraction, contribution based on ability or satisfaction or power significantly differentiated between successful and unsuccessful teams. The sense-of-belonging question also failed to show any differences between winning and losing teams.

The two questions designed to directly assess cohesiveness as a general construct—degree of teamwork and closeness—significantly differentiated between successful and unsuccessful teams. Figure 1 graphically illustrates the differences between the three levels of teamwork and closeness on the number of games won. For both cohesion criterion, a Newman-Keuls test (Winer, 1962, p. 80–85) was used to determine the simple effects of the overall F. For the teamwork criterion, accepting the .05 level of significance, the high (2.89) and moderate (2.66) cohesive teams won significantly more games than the low cohesive teams (2.13). The difference between the high and moderate teams, however, was not significant. For the closeness criterion, the Newman-Keuls test revealed that high cohesive teams won significantly more games (2.96) than the moderate (2.46) and low cohesive teams (2.26). The difference between the moderate and low cohesive teams was not significant.

The most significant F value was obtained from the question regarding the "value of membership" each individual attributed to his basketball team. Those teams whose individual members attributed greater value in belonging to the group won significantly more games (3.26) than those with moderate (2.18) or low scores (2.27). The difference between the moderate and low teams was not significant for this criterion.

INDIVIDUAL MEMBER SATISFACTION

The post-questionnaire asked each individual to indicate how satisfied he was personally with playing on his team. A team mean was calculated which was the score used for the analysis of member satisfaction variance.

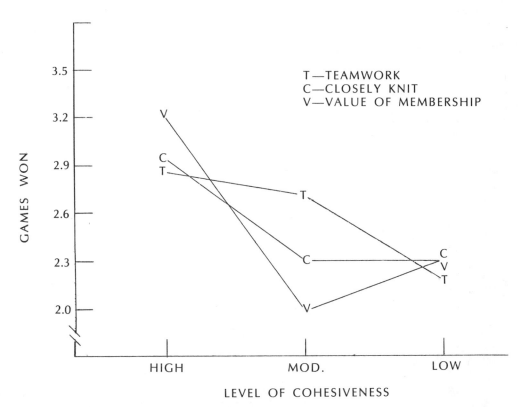

FIG. 1. NUMBER OF GAMES WON FOR THREE DIFFERENT LEVELS OF COHESIVENESS BASED ON THREE CRITERIA.

The eight analyses of variance on individual member satisfaction for each of the cohesiveness criteria are summarized in Table 2. Accepting the .05 level of significance, seven of the eight measures found significant differences on individual member satisfaction. The only item failing to show a significant difference was interpersonal attraction.

The Newman-Keuls procedure for a factorial design (Winer, 1962, p. 309) was used to deter-

mine the simple effects of the over-all significant F. For the contribution-based-on-ability criterion the Newman-Keuls test indicated that the teams rating themselves high on ability were significantly more satisfied (4.11)[1] than moderately-rated teams (4.58) and low-rated teams (4.78). The difference between the moderate and low-rated teams was not significantly different at the .05 level. The exact same pattern of significant differences was found for

TABLE 2
Summary of Analyses of Member Satisfaction for the Eight Measures of Cohesiveness

Item	Df	Ms	F
Interpersonal Attraction (A)	2	0.40	0.46
Residential Affiliation (B)	2	0.35	0.40
A × B	4	1.36	1.56
Residual	135	0.87	
Contribution based on ability (A)	2	5.09	6.54 **
Residential Affiliation (B)	2	0.40	0.52
A × B	4	1.81	2.33
Residual	135	0.78	
Contribution based on satisfaction (A)	2	3.02	3.57 *
Residential Affiliation (B)	2	0.40	0.47
A × B	4	0.80	0.94
Residual	135	0.85	
Influence or power (A)	2	3.30	3.99 *
Residential Affiliation (B)	2	0.41	0.50
A × B	4	1.00	1.21
Residual	135	0.83	
Sense of belonging (A)	2	6.36	8.12 **
Residential Affiliation (B)	2	0.34	0.43
A × B	4	1.48	1.89
Residual	135	0.78	
Value of membership (A)	2	3.54	4.21 *
Residential Affiliation (B)	2	0.38	0.44
A × B	4	0.82	0.98
Residual	135	0.84	
Teamwork (A)	2	2.92	3.46 *
Residential Affiliation (B)	2	0.45	0.53
A × B	4	0.65	0.77
Residual	135	0.84	
Closely Knit (A)	2	11.07	4.33 *
Residential Affiliation	2	6.57	2.57
A × B	4	1.93	0.76
Residual	135	2.56	

*Significant at the .05 level.
**Significant at the .01 level.

the contribution-based-on-satisfaction criterion. The mean for the high-rated group was 4.21, while the moderate group had a mean of 4.52, and the low-rated group had a mean of 4.74.

The Newman-Keuls test on the significant influence of power criterion revealed that the teams high on this measure were significantly more satisfied (4.24) than the low teams (4.79) while the moderate teams were also significantly more satisfied (4.43) than the low teams. The difference between the high and moderate teams was not significant.

For the sense-of-belonging criterion the high, moderate, and low teams each differed significantly from the other two groups. Unlike the other criteria, the high teams were most satisfied (4.10), but the low teams were next (4.51), while the moderate teams were least satisfied (4.88).

The teamwork criterion was the only measure in which the high cohesive teams were not the most satisfied. The Newman-Keuls test on this criterion indicated that the moderate teams were significantly more satisfied (4.26) than the low teams (4.77) and the high teams were significantly more satisfied (4.44) than the low teams. The difference between the moderate and high teams was not significant.

The closeness criterion found the very close teams to be significantly more satisfied (3.81) than the teams low in this criterion (4.83). The Newman-Keuls test on this criterion found no significant difference between the very close teams and the moderately close teams (4.30) and between the moderately close teams and the teams low in this criterion.

The value-of-membership criterion revealed that the teams who valued their membership the most were significantly more satisfied (4.16) than the moderate- (4.65) and low-rated teams (4.67) on this criterion. The difference between the low and moderate teams was not significant.

DISCUSSION

The results from the team effectiveness data are equivocal and focus upon the methodological problem of operationally defining cohesiveness. The general operational definitions were used: (a) each member rated every other member of the team on some component of cohesiveness—e.g., interpersonal attraction; (b) each member indicated his relationship to the team—e.g., value of membership; and (c) each member directly rated the cohesiveness of the group as a whole—e.g., level of teamwork, Our hypothesis that high cohesive teams win significantly more games than low cohesive teams was supported when assessing cohesiveness by the third approach and one question from the second approach. Results of the other measures of cohesiveness found no significant differences in games won between high and low cohesive teams.

The four components of cohesiveness assessed by the first approach were interpersonal attraction, contribution based on ability, contribution based on satisfaction, and influence or power. The questions concerning the contribution based on ability and satisfaction were used as additional indicators of interpersonal attraction. The degree to which members of the team attributed power or influence to the group was the fourth component of cohesiveness. The nexus being that the more cohesive the team the greater its influence on the members. The failure of these measures to find any systematic variance between high, moderate and low cohesive teams as far as team effectiveness is concerned does not concur with previous research.

For example, Fiedler (1953, 1954), Lenk (1966), McGrath (1962), and Viet (1968) have all suggested from their research that high levels of cohesiveness may be detrimental to effective performance. On the other hand, Chapman and Campbell (1957), Klein and Christiansen (1966), and Myers (1962) have found a positive relationship between cohesiveness and effectiveness. The sole operational definition of cohesiveness in each of these studies has been some form of interpersonal attraction. Our interpersonal attraction results (and the measurement of any component of cohesiveness) present a third finding, mainly that differences in interpersonal attraction among teams do not significantly affect team effectiveness.

Another portion of our results appeared ambiguous. The sense-of-belonging and value-of-membership questions were designed to measure each individual member's relationship to the team, and consequently, were expected to reveal similar results. This was not the case, however. The sense-of-belonging question did not differentiate between successful and unsuccessful teams, whereas the value-of-membership question found a very significant difference. Why the apparent discrepancy between two questions thought to assess the same phenomenon? One possible explanation is that sense of belonging seems to focus upon the individual's relationship with other members in the group and the status he has in the group. If this be the case, his status, which is really an indication of this relationship with the other members, may be a general evaluation of his interpersonal attraction toward the group. Possibly then the nonsignificant finding from the sense-of-belonging question is consistent with the interpersonal attraction results. The value-of-membership question, on the other hand, implies not only the importance of affiliating with the other members of the team, but with the goals and outcomes of the team. If the activities of the team are of intrinsic enjoyment to an individual even though he does not particularly feel a strong sense of commitment to that group, he may indeed value his membership while not having a strong sense of belonging.

The somewhat consistent pattern obtained from the different operational definitions lead us to the following conclusion. At the present time our knowledge of the operational measurement of cohesiveness is not sufficient to measure only certain components of cohesiveness and have it significantly discriminate between effective and ineffective teams. These data suggest that individual members are better able to integrate the components of cohesiveness to determine the level of cohesiveness present within a team.

In reviewing the previous relevant research we find no apparent explanation for the contradictory results; nor do we know why the previous research has consistently found differences between high and low cohesive teams when using interpersonal attraction as the criterion and the present study failed to find any difference. However, the significant results obtained in this study suggest that Gross and Martin's argument for a direct assessment of cohesiveness has merit.

Results of the analyses of individual member satisfaction showed that seven of the eight cohesion criteria significantly discriminated between satisfied and unsatisfied teams. These results suggest a circular relationship between satisfaction, cohesiveness, and success (see Fig. 2).

Those teams who are more cohesive are more successful, and teams which are successful have greater satisfaction from participation than unsuccessful teams. Greater satisfaction, in turn, leads to higher levels of cohesiveness, thus maintaining a circular relationship. In actuality, though, this cause-effect triangulation is bombarded with a number of other important factors that may influence this sequence of events.

In conclusion, we have found that when cohesiveness is directly assessed, it is an important determinant of team effectiveness. However, it is not contended that cohesiveness is the primary factor in successful basketball performance. The ability of the players and their opponents, the quality of coaching, the officials, and many other factors contribute to the effective-

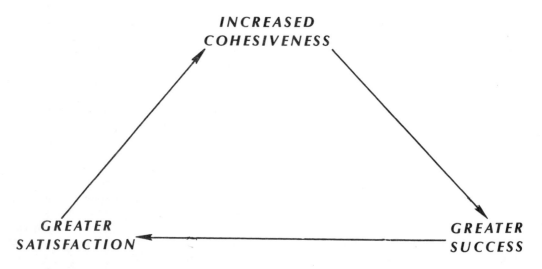

FIG. 2.   RELATIONSHIP BETWEEN COHESIVENESS, SUCCESS, AND SATISFACTION.

ness of a team. Our finding, however, does suggest that higher levels of cohesiveness are associated with greater success and satisfaction.

REFERENCES

Chapman L. J., and Campbell D. T.: An attempt to predict the performance of three-man teams from attitude measurements. J. Soc. Psychol., 46:277, 1957.

Festinger L., Schachter S., and Back K.: Social Pressures in Informal Groups: Study of a Housing Project. New York, Harper, 1950.

Fiedler F. E.: The psychological distance dimension in interpersonal relations. J. Pers., 22:142, 1953.

Fiedler F. E: Assumed similarity measures as predictors of team effectiveness. J. Abnorm. Soc. Psychol., 49:381, 1954.

Gross N. and Martin W. E.: On group cohesiveness. Am. J. Soc., 57:546, 1952.

Klein M. and Christiansen G.: Group composition, group structure and group effectiveness of basketball teams. In Sport, Culture, and Society. Edited by J. W. Loy and G. S. Kenyon. London, Macmillan, 1969, pp. 397-408.

Lenk H.: Top performance despite internal conflict: An antithesis to a functionalistic proposition. In Sport, Culture, and Society. Edited by J. W. Loy and G. S. Kenyon. London, Macmillan, 1969, pp. 393-397.

Lott A. J. and Lott B. E.: Group cohesiveness as interpersonal attraction: A review of relationships with antecedent and consequent variables. Psychol. Bul., 64:259, 1965.

McGrath J. E.: The influence of positive interpersonal relations on adjustment effectiveness in rifle teams. J. Abnorm. Soc. Psychol., 65:365, 1962.

Myers A.: Team competition, success, and the adjustment of group members. J. Abnorm. Soc. Psychol., 65:325, 1962.

Veit, Hans.: Some remarks upon the elementary interpersonal relations within ball games teams. Paper presented at 2nd International Congress of Sport Psychology, Washington, D. C., October 1968.

Winer B. J.: Statistical Principles In Experimental Design. New York, McGraw-Hill, 1962.

NOTE

1. The lower the score the greater the satisfaction.

development of a model for predicting team performance

ANNE MARIE BIRD

Most sport behavioralists accept the notion that social psychological variables do operate within athletic teams and do affect team performance outcomes in terms of winning and losing. Yet, little research has been undertaken in an effort to identify and measure such variables.

Factors which have inhibited the initiation of research endeavors in this area have been primarily methodological in nature. The assessment instruments which are presently available ordinarily were designed to be used with nonsport samples. Thus, their selection for use as predictors for sport group success is somewhat questionable. In addition, these instruments are most often nonprojective (paper and pencil) in construction and are, therefore, subject to the weaknesses inherent in all such measures. As discussed elsewhere[3] they are subject to errors associated with the respondent's conception of reality and the instrument's capability of measuring that conception. Given this potential for error within single instruments, perhaps initially, multiple measures designed to assess the same variable should be used. If these multiple measures yield similar results, then our confidence in the concurrent and predictive validity of each should be increased. We would then have greater confidence that we are indeed measuring that which we say we are measuring. Further, we would have established some basis by which we can defend the selection and use of an instrument.

Based upon this rationale, it would appear reasonable that a sensible avenue for sport behavioral research would be that which attempts to identify multiple social psychological variables thought to influence team performance outcome and to then employ multiple measures of each. Such an approach would provide not only a more sound methodological basis, but also a defensible conceptual model in terms of complex social interactions which take place within small groups such as sport teams.

The social psychological variable most often thought to influence competitive athletic team success is that of cohesion. An early definition of cohesion was that proposed by Festinger, Schachter, and Back[7]. They viewed cohesion as "the total field of forces which act on members to remain in a group" (7:164). Subsequent to this definition, researchers[6,9] have rendered criticism of such an approach due to a failure in the research methodology employed to adequately articulate between the nominal definition and the operational measurement of cohesion. Put more simply, researchers[1,22] had attempted to measure the "total field of forces" by means of a single predictive index.

Hagstrom and Selvin[10] factor analyzed 19 possible indicators of cohesiveness. Their

This research was financed by a research grant from Western Society for Physical Education of College Women. The author also wishes to express appreciation to the athletic directors and coaches of the Southern California Women's Intercollegiate Athletic Conference for their cooperation.

results indicated two distinct dimensions of cohesiveness as it operates in interdependent small groups: "social satisfaction," and "sociometric cohesion." Social satisfaction involves satisfaction with the group and influence of the group on significant behavior. Sociometric cohesion was so labeled because it correlated with what the authors felt were important sociometric measures, proportion of best friends in the group and proportion who seek personal advice from other group members. More importantly perhaps in a sport group, the latter factor took into account the amount of time spent in group activities. This is of particular importance because of the general acceptance in psychological theory that rewards are capable of modifying behavior. Therefore, if a group or interacting sport team is indeed functional or successful, members would tend to remain with that group. Thus, cohesion in the Festinger and others[7] sense would occur.

Research endeavors which have attempted to ascertain the relationship between sport team success and degree of cohesion at first appeared to yield contradictory results. However, Landers and Lueschen[14] clarified the supposed conflicts in the literature when they related team structural dimensions to degree of cohesion. With few exceptions, such as track and field or gymnastics, sport teams can be dichotomized into either interacting or coacting groups.

Coacting teams are structured so that team members act independently and usually perform a similar skill. Team performance is determined by the sum or average of all member's contributions. Riflery and bowling teams are examples of coacting teams. Summary of the current research evidence [13, 14, 17, 18] indicates that coacting teams are more successful when low team cohesion is present.

Thomas[21] described interacting groups as those which are characterized by what he labeled "means-controlling facilitation." By this he meant that when a group is formed for the purpose of obtaining a goal, and when members must coordinate their efforts during performance in order to secure that goal, then members are interdependent upon one another. As such, when one member progresses toward the goal, all members are facilitated. Conversely, if a member fails at his task or is hindered in his goal-seeking efforts, then the team itself is affected negatively. In sport, teams such as volleyball, basketball, and hockey are classified as interacting. Studies which have focused upon the relationship between interacting teams and degree of cohesion have found that more successful teams evidenced greater cohesion.[12, 16, 23]

It would appear a sound assumption that within competitive sport, the leadership style employed by the coach may influence team outcome. Although researchers have emphasized the necessity of investigating this variable,[4, 20] little research has been completed. Penman, Hastad, and Cords[19] found that coaches of more successful basketball and football teams were more authoritarian. Danielson, Zelhart, and Drake[5] proposed that more effective coaching style may vary according to situation and team. This finding was substantiated further by Bird.[2] Such an idea supports the rationale underlying the work of Fiedler.[8] He constructed a contingency model for leadership effectiveness based upon certain group-situational factors. In essence, if the coach perceives himself to be accepted by the group and also has relatively high position power, then the more successful leader of an interacting team will employ a task-oriented mode of leadership style.

Based upon the necessity of identifying those measures most capable of discriminating between successful and unsuccessful interactive sport teams and the evidence presented, the following hypotheses were tested:

1. Successful volleyball teams will possess team cohesion and will be coached by a task-oriented leader.
2. Measures of cohesion and leadership most capable of discriminating between successful and unsuccessful teams can be identified.

PROCEDURE

Players within the two most highly skilled or competitive divisions of the Southern California Women's Intercollegiate Athletic Conference volleyball league comprised the sample. Performance success was determined by the percentage of games won during the regular volleyball season. Initial data were secured from all 16 teams within Division I and II. Division I was the most highly skilled. This division consisted of seven teams, the two most successful and two least successful were respectively designated as winners and losers. Division II consisted of nine teams; two winners and two losers were determined in the exact manner described for Division I. Of the total of 16 teams, therefore, four were winners, four were losers and eight were eliminated from the analyses.

Level of significance was established at .05 for all analyses. Results were analyzed by means of a 2 × 2 (team success × level of skill) multivariate analysis of variance (MANOVA) and a discriminant function analysis with stepwise F tests. The multivariate analysis of variance was used to test five dependent variables (team atmosphere, leadership style, leader behavior-consideration, leader behavior-initiating structure, and cohesion). Results of the multivariate analysis were used to establish criteria for inclusion and order of factors for the final discriminant function analysis and the stepwise F tests.

The criteria used for inclusion of variables in the discriminant function analysis were: the attainment of statistical significance for the main effect of team success (winners/losers), and the presence of no disordinal interactive effect for team success × level of skill. A disordinal interaction is one in which the "rank order of the treatments changes." [15] The purpose for conducting the discriminant function analysis was to identify that linear combination of dependent variables most capable of maximally discriminating between winning and losing teams regardless of the skill level of the players. The presence of a significant disordinal interaction would indicate that a variable was not constant across skill levels. As such, it would mean that the variable operates differently according to the skill level of the players. Therefore, when a disordinal interaction exists, it indicates that the variable should not be included in the discriminate function analysis.

ASSESSMENT INSTRUMENTS

COHESION

GROUP ATMOSPHERE SCALE.[a, 8] The purpose of this scale was to measure the player's perception of her acceptance and comfort within the group, similar to that dimension labeled social satisfaction by Hagstrom and Selvin.[10]

COHESION.[16] This scale was a modified version of that devised by Martens and Peterson.[16]

---

[a] From A Theory of Leadership Effectiveness by F. E. Fiedler. Copyright 1967 by McGraw-Hill, Inc. Used with permission of McGraw-Hill Book Company.

This scale was thought to be capable of ascertaining the second dimension identified by Hagstrom and Selvin as sociometric cohesion, particularly in regard to proportion of friends on the team and value of team membership.

LEADERSHIP

LEAST PREFERRED COWORKER SCALE.[8] The (LPC) scale results in a single inventory score. A high score indicates a therapeutic, socio-emotional leader, whereas a low score indicates a task-oriented leader. Players used the scale to rate their head coach's leadership style.

LEADER BEHAVIOR DESCRIPTION QUESTIONNAIRE.[11] The *Leader Behavior Description Questionnaire* (LBDQ) measures two separate components of leadership behavior: Initiating Structure (task leader) and Consideration (socio-emotional leader). The two components were treated as individual scores. Players were instructed to assess their head coach's leadership behavior.

RESULTS

Results of the multivariate analysis of variance indicated a significant main effect for the factor of team success (winners/losers), $F(5,63) = 10.48$, $p<.001$. The results of the subsequent univariate analysis indicated significant main effects for the team success factor for all five dependent variables. Table 1 indicates the F ratios and means for winners and losers for each of the five dependent variables included in the multivariate analysis. In all instances, a higher mean value reflects a more positive perception of the variable.

No significant multivariate main effect was found for the factor of level of skill (Division I/Division II), $F(5,63) = 1.09$, $p>.05$. However, a significant multivariate interaction effect for team success × level of skill was shown, $F(5,63) = 6.42$, $p<.001$. Observation of the univariate analysis indicated significant interactive effects for the variables of Team Atmosphere, $F(1,67) = 14.02$, $p<.001$; Least Preferred Coworker (LPC), $F(1,67) = 25.28$, $p<.001$; and Leader Behavior—Consideration, $F(1,67) = 18.61$, $p<.001$. No interactive effects were demonstrated for either Leader Behavior—Initiating Structure, $F(1,67) = 1.81$, $p>.05$, or Cohesion, $F(1,67) = 3.22$, $p>.05$.

TABLE 1

F Ratios and Means for Winners and Losers for Five Dependent Variables

| Variable | $F_{(1, 67)}$ | Mean | | p |
		Winners	Losers	
Team Atmosphere	47.33	6.77	4.96	.001
Least Preferred Coworker	8.55	6.51	5.80	.005
Leader Behavior—Consideration	5.35	41.04	36.93	.024
Leader Behavior—Initiating Structure	11.23	43.87	34.80	.001
Cohesion	33.55	6.86	4.64	.001

Figure 1 indicates the interaction for team success × level of competition for the variable of team atmosphere. Observation of this figure shows that this relationship is ordinal for the skill levels tested. That is, the rank order of the variable of team atmosphere was constant for Division I and Division II. Winners in Division 1 ($\bar{X} = 7.28$) and Division II ($\bar{X} = 6.23$) both perceived greater team cohesion than did losers for either Division I ($\bar{X} = 4.49$) or Division II ($\bar{X} = 5.43$).

Figure 2 shows the significant interactive effect for team success × level of competition for the variable of leadership style as measured by the Least Preferred Coworker Scale (LPC). The interaction is disordinal in that winning players within Division I ($\bar{X} = 7.23$) and losing players within Division II ($\bar{X} = 6.30$) both perceived their coaches to be more socio-emotional in style. Winning players within Division II ($\bar{X} = 5.81$) and losing players within Division I ($\bar{X} = 5.31$) perceived their coaches to be more task-oriented.

Figure 3 presents graphically the interactive effect for team success × level of competition for the variable of Leader Behavior—Consideration. These results appear geometrically similar to the disordinal interaction presented in Figure 2. Winners in Division I ($\bar{X} = 45.14$) and losers in Division II ($\bar{X} = 40.35$) perceived their coaches to be more considerate, whereas winners in Division II ($\bar{X} = 36.94$) and losers in Division I ($\bar{X} = 33.50$) saw coaches to be less considerate.

Based upon the presence of significant and disordinal interactions for the variables of Leadership Style (LPC) and Leader Behavior—Consideration, these variables were eliminated from further analyses. This was done to eliminate any effect attributable to the factor of skill level which might affect the attempt to isolate that combination of variables most capable of discriminating between all successful and unsuccessful teams.

The factors of Leader Behavior—Initiating Structure, Team Atmosphere, and Cohesion were so ordered and entered into the discrimi-

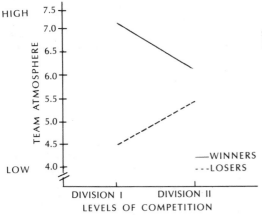

FIG. 1. TEAM SUCCESS × LEVEL OF COMPETITION FOR TEAM ATMOSPHERE

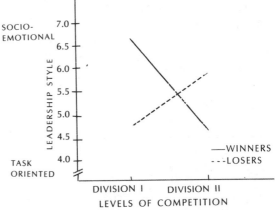

FIG. 2. TEAM SUCCESS × LEVEL OF COMPETITION FOR LEADERSHIP STYLE (LPC).

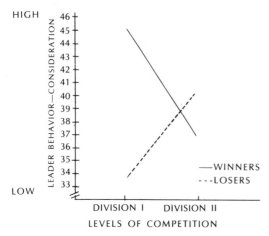

FIG. 3. TEAM SUCCESS × LEVEL OF COM-
PETITION FOR LEADER BEHAVIOR—CON-
SIDERATION.

criminant function than did Leader Behavior—
Initiating Structure (.013).

Observation of Table 3 reveals that of the total sample of players grouped as winners or losers, 77.46% would have been correctly classified in terms of team success by their scores on the three predictor variables (Leader Behavior—Initiating Structure, Team Atmosphere, Cohesion) included in the discriminant analysis. Of the actual winners, 82.5% could be accurately predicted, whereas 17.5% would have been inaccurately classified as losers. For actual losers, 71% could be correctly predicted, while 29% would have been incorrectly classified as winners.

DISCUSSION

The first hypothesis predicted that successful volleyball teams would perceive greater team cohesion and also would be coached by more task-oriented leaders. Results of the data analysis warrant unqualified support for the presence of greater cohesion within successful interacting volleyball teams. Based upon the presence of an overall significant multivariate F, the univariate results for the two measures of cohesion both revealed significantly greater cohesion within successful teams (Team Atmosphere: winners $\bar{X} = 6.77$, losers $\bar{X} = 4.96$; Cohesion: winners $\bar{X} = 6.86$, losers $\bar{X} = 4.64$). Results of the multivariate analysis indicated somewhat confounding data relative to the prediction that successful teams would be coached by task-oriented leaders. The design included three separate measures for leadership: Least Preferred Coworker Scale (LPC), Leader Behavior—Consideration, and Leader Behavior—Initiating Structure. Results for both the Least Preferred Coworker and Leader Behavior—Consideration indicated significant disordinal interactive effects for team success × level of skill. The interactions were

nant function analysis with stepwise F tests. The factor of Leader Behavior—Initiating Structure was ordered first for purposes of theoretical consistency. This was done so that factors associated with cohesion (Team Atmosphere and Cohesion) would be assessed in relation to the amount of discriminatory power their presence contributed beyond that generated by this aspect of leadership. The discriminant stepwise method used was Wilk's Lambda. This method employs the criterion of the overall multivariate F ratio for testing the differences between group centroids.

Table 2 summarizes the results of the stepwise discriminant analysis. Results indicate all variables to be significant. However, Team Atmosphere (.62) and Cohesion (.60) more effectively reduced Wilk's Lambda than did Leadership Behavior (.92). In addition, observation of the discriminant function coefficients indicates that both Team Atmosphere (−.65) and Cohesion (−.41) contributed substantially more to the dis-

TABLE 2

Summary Table for Discriminant Analysis

Variable	d/f	F	Wilk's Lambda	p	Discriminant Function Coefficient
Leader Behavior—Initiating Structure	1/69	5.85	.92	.017	.013
Team Atmosphere	2/68	20.36	.62	.000	−.65
Cohesion	3/67	14.95	.60	.000	−.41

TABLE 3

Prediction Results from Discriminant Function Analysis

Actual Group Membership	No. of Cases	Predicted Group Membership*	
		Winners	Losers
Winners	40	33	7
		82.5%	17.5%
Losers	31	9	22
		29.0%	71.0%

*Total percentage of "grouped" cases correctly classified: 77.46%.

consistent, however, in that in both cases winners within Division I and losers within Division II perceived coaches to be more socio-emotional or considerate, whereas losers within Division I and winners within Division II perceived coaches to be less considerate or more task-oriented.

Some explanation for these results might lie within structural changes which may occur owing to skill level of players. Perhaps on less highly skilled teams, effective coaching strategy demands greater use of designated positions such as hitters or setters, whereas on more highly skilled teams, such as Division I, positions are more flexible because of the type of playing strategy employed. If this is so, then the prediction which was generated from Fiedler's[8] contingency model for highly structured groups would indeed be applicable to less highly skilled teams such as those in Division II. An alternative explanation may be that players on more highly skilled teams may be sufficiently motivated and, therefore, respond more to a supportive, socio-emotional coach. In either case, the results strongly suggest that effective leadership or coaching style is somewhat related to situational factors such as player skill.

The second hypothesis proposed that measures of both leadership and cohesion could be identified which were most capable of discriminating between successful and unsuccessful teams. This hypothesis received some support, specifically in regard to measures of cohesion. Owing to the presence of disordinal interactions attributable to division membership, the variables of Least Preferred Coworker and Leader Behavior—Consideration were excluded from further analysis. The rationale underlying this procedure was based upon the desire to identify

discriminating variables which would not be affected by level of player skill, but which would instead be able to predict team performance for all interacting competitive teams.

Results of the discriminant analysis indicated that the two measures of cohesion were most capable of discriminating between successful and unsuccessful teams. Although the Leader Behavior—Initiating Structure was perceived significantly different by winning and losing players, its presence added very little to the total predictive power of the discriminant function. However, using the three predictor variables included in the total function, 77.46% of the players tested could have been correctly classified as members of winning or losing teams.

The overall results of the present study strongly support the premise that cohesion is related to the success of interacting sport teams. Further research is needed, however, in order to ascertain the importance of leadership style and variations in its effectiveness relative to player skill level. Similarly, other still-untested social psychological variables should be investigated to determine if their inclusion in the present model would generate increased predictive power.

NOTES

1. Back, K. W.: The exertion of influence through social communication. J. Abnorm. Soc. Psychol., 46:9, 1951.
2. Bird, A. M.: Leadership and cohesion within successful and unsuccessful teams: Perceptions of coaches and players. Proc. North Am. Soc. Psychol. Sport Phys. Activity, Austin, Texas, 1976.
3. Bird, A. M.: Nonreactive research: Applications for sociological analysis of sport. Int. Rev. Sport Sociol., 1(11):83, 1976.
4. Cratty, B. J.: Psychology in contemporary sport:

Guidelines for coaches and athletes. Englewood Cliffs, New Jersey, Prentice-Hall, 1973.

5. Danielson, R. R.; Zelhart, Jr., P. F.; and Drake, C. J.: Multidimensional scaling and factor analysis of coaching behavior as perceived by high school hockey players. Res. Q., *46*:323, 1975.

6. Eisman, B.: Some operational measures of cohesiveness and their correlations. Hum. Relations, *12*:183, 1959.

7. Festinger, L.; Schachter, S.; and Back, K.: Social Pressures in Informal Groups: Study of a Housing Project. New York, Harper, 1950.

8. Fiedler, F. E.: A Theory of Leadership Effectiveness. New York, McGraw-Hill, 1967.

9. Gross, N., and Martin, W.: On group cohesiveness. Am. J. Sociol., *57*:533, 1952.

10. Hagstrom, W. O., and Selvin, H.C.: The dimensions of cohesiveness in small groups. Sociometry, *28*:30, 1965.

11. Halpin, A. W.: Manual for the Leader Behavior Description Questionnaire. Columbus, The Ohio State University, 1957.

12. Klein, M., and Christiansen, G.: Group composition, group structure and group effectiveness of basketball teams. *In* Sport, Culture and Society. Edited by J. Loy Jr. and G. S. Kenyon. London, Macmillan, 1969.

13. Landers, D. M., and Crum, T. F.: The effect of team success and formal structure on interpersonal relations and cohesiveness of baseball teams. Int. J. Sport Psychol., *2*:88, 1971.

14. Landers, D. M., and Lueschen, G.: Team performance outcome and the cohesiveness of competitive coacting groups. Int. Rev. Sport Sociol., *9*:57, 1974.

15. Lubin, A.: The interpretation of significant interaction. Educ. Psychol. Meas., *21*:807, 1961.

16. Martens, R., and Peterson, J. A.: Group cohesiveness as a determinant of success and member satisfaction in team performance. Int. Rev. Sport Sociol., *6*:49, 1971.

17. McGrath, J. E.: The influence of positive interpersonal relations on adjustment and effectiveness in rifle teams. J. Abnorm. Soc. Psychol., *65*:365, 1962.

18. Myers, A.: Team competition, success and the adjustment of group members. J. Abnorm. Soc. Psychol., *65*:325, 1962.

19. Penman, K. A.; Hastad, D. N.; and Cords, W. L.: Success of the authoritarian coach. J. Soc. Psychol., *92*:155, 1974.

20. Percival, L.: The coach from the athlete's viewpoint. *In* Proc., Symp. Art Sci. Coaching. Edited by J. W. Taylor. Toronto, Fitness Institute, 1971.

21. Thomas, E. J.: Effects of facilitative role interdependence on group functioning. Hum. Relations, *10*:347, 1957.

22. Schachter, S.: Deviation, rejection and communication. J. of Abnorm. Soc. Psychol., *46*:190, 1951.

23. Stogdill, R. M.: Team achievement under high motivation. Business Res. Mono., Ohio State University, 1963.

an axiomatic theory of team success

HOWARD L. NIXON, III

While Loy and Kenyon (1969: 349–351) have observed the limited sociological attention to sports groups as social systems, the main theme of the "Sport and Small Groups" section of their reader suggests that a primary concern of those social scientists who have studied sports groups has been team effectiveness. It may be difficult to understand the general inattention in social science to small groups in sport; however, it is easy to understand the focus on team effectiveness in the work that has been done in this area. Sports teams are explicitly goal- or task-oriented; and the outcome of the goal attainment process, victory of defeat (or a tie), can be measured readily and precisely.

In view of the fact that a number of investigators have examined psychological and social factors associated with team success and that there appear to be some inconsistencies in the findings of ostensibly similar investigations, it would seem appropriate to begin formulating an integrated and coherent conception of the relationships between team success and the factors affecting, and affected by, it. In this vein, I am proposing here an axiomatic theory of team success which is aimed at providing the basis for a more systematic understanding of some prominent intrapersonal, interpersonal, and structural causes and consequences of team success. This theory is meant to be an extension of existing

knowledge concerning team success; and it is hoped that it will stimulate the kind of research that will enlarge and refine our understanding of this central aspect of sports contests, the process of pursuit of the goal of team victory.

Much of the team effectiveness research that has been done deals with the relationship between team effectiveness and cohesiveness. However, a first glance at the findings concerning this relationship seems to indicate that they are somewhat contradictory.[1] The research of Fiedler (1954) concerning basketball teams, McGrath (1962) concerning rifle teams, Lenk (1969) concerning Olympic rowing crews, and Veit (1970) concerning sport teams suggests that there is an inverse relationship between cohesiveness and team success. The studies of Myers (1962), who used rifle teams, Klein and Christiansen (1969), who used basketball teams, seem to imply that cohesiveness and team success are positively related. Finally, Martens and Peterson (1971) investigated basketball teams and uncovered mixed results concerning the relationship between cohesiveness and success. They believed that a careful examination of the findings produced in these various studies should indicate that they are not as contradictory as a first glance seems to suggest.

In order to understand the precise meaning of the results of the research that has just been cited, one must know the following things about each study: (a) how cohesiveness has been interpreted; (b) whether it has been viewed as an independent or dependent variable; and (c) whether the results enable us to make judg-

Reprinted from Sport Sociology, Bulletin, 3(1):1–12, 1974. Copyright 1974 by Sport Sociology Bulletin, Recreative Studies, College of Human Learning and Development, Governors State University, Park Forest South, Illinois 60466.

ments about the *dynamic* interrelations of cohesiveness, the task orientation, and team effectiveness.

The work of Fiedler, McGrath, and Veit suggests that members of winning athletic teams tend to prefer more instrumentally-oriented teammates, while members of less successful teams tend to be more concerned than those of successful teams with warm, friendly relationships with each other. Lenk's research has shown that conflict within athletic teams will not necessarily have an inhibiting effect upon performance. In particular, it showed that the intensification of internal conflict within athletic teams can be accompanied by an improvement in group performance (with very high levels of success) *if* teams are able to stay together despite the conflict. The results of these four studies imply that social distance among players, fueled by intense interpersonal rivalries in certain cases, may be positively associated with team success and that successful teams may be characterized more by business-like, than friendly, relationships among team members.

Taken together, the findings of Fiedler, McGrath, Veit, and Lenk seem to suggest that Bales' (e.g., 1950, 1966) interpretation of the negative relationship between the affective and instrumental (or task) emphases in group behavior may be at least partially correct. For their research appears to point to the conclusions that members of highly cohesive teams may be hurting their chances for success by concentrating too much on getting along with each other, and that interpersonal rivalries may reflect a dominant concern for achievement that could enhance a team's chances for success. However, none of this research provides support for Bales' assumption of a seesaw-like movement of group behavior between affective and instrumental orientations. This is because none of it focuses on the *process* of goal attainment. Furthermore, none of these studies indicates that group solidarity is an essential aspect of group success.

In this context, Klein and Christiansen's work is particularly relevant. It not only shows that cohesiveness can be positively related to success; it also provides an empirical basis for considering the dynamic interrelationship between affective and instrumental activities during the goal attainment process, a perspective made salient by Bales' general theoretical and empirical work with task-oriented groups. Signifi-

cantly, Klein and Christiansen have examined the relationship of interpersonal sentiments to instrumental activities, *but* they have interpreted cohesiveness, per se, as attraction to the team *as a whole*.

Klein and Christiansen's findings indicate that a high average desire to win among team members is not a sufficient basis for achieving success, even assuming the existence of considerable individual talent on the team. For teams where coordinated interactions of the members are the means for attaining victory, as in basketball and unlike riflery, the structure of the group determines whether or not individual performances lead to victory. In particular, success seems to depend significantly upon the interrelated factors of status consensus, interpersonal sentiments, integration of group activities, and team cohesion, with the effects of interpersonal sentiments being diminished by confrontation with strong opponents.

The data concerning ease of interaction and interpersonal sentiments provide tentative support for Bales' conception of the swaying movement of task-oriented groups between affective and instrumental orientations. They have shown that when teams were not especially pressed by their opponents, players tended to pass most frequently to teammates whom they liked best (regardless of ability); and this implies that team success in such circumstances tended to be at least indirectly determined by the existence of favorable sentiments of players toward each other. However, these data also showed that this tendency to make passes on the basis of personal liking disappeared when stronger opponents were being played. This last finding can be interpreted as implying that when the "chips are down" and considerable concentration on the team's task of winning is needed, team members (on successful teams) will shift from their affective orientation to a more purely instrumental one. When the stakes are high and the opponent is very challenging, teammates will temporarily forget their personal likes and dislikes or, perhaps, persevere despite them to achieve the glory of victory. Presumably, when the competitive challenge eases, their orientation will become more affective once again.

The evidence concerning team success and interpersonal sentiments uncovered by Myers indicates that winning can do more than suppress unfavorable feelings about teammates and the team as a whole. He found that the reward of team success makes it easier for team members to be friendly to one another and to feel happy about being a member of the group. He also found that competition seems to draw teams together whenever it means that performance will be evaluated on a group rather than on an individual basis.

The purpose of Martens and Peterson's investigation was to determine if different levels and kinds of group cohesiveness affected the success and individual member satisfaction of basketball teams. Their measures of cohesiveness were of three different kinds: (a) evaluation of other team members (in terms of interpersonal attraction, contribution of teammates based on ability, contribution of teammates based on how enjoyable they were to play with, and influence or power of teammates); (b) perceived relationship to the team (in terms of sense of belonging and value of team membership); and (c) evaluation of the team as a whole (in terms of level of teamwork and how closely knit the team was). Martens and Peterson's hypothesis that high cohesiveness would be associated with a higher rate of success than low cohesiveness was supported by evidence derived from three of the eight items measuring the three kinds of cohesiveness. Results from the two items concerning the evaluation of the team as a whole and from one of the items concerning a member's perception of his relationship to the team, i.e., value of membership, were consistent with this hypothesis. Results of the other measures of cohesiveness showed no significant differences in games won between high and low cohesive teams.

Martens and Peterson also found that there is a circular relationship among individual member satisfaction, cohesiveness (viewed as attraction to the team as a whole), and team success. Those teams that were more cohesive (in this sense) tended to be more successful; and teams which were more successful tended to produce greater satisfaction from participation. Greater satisfaction, in turn, tended to generate higher levels of cohesiveness; and thus, the circular relationship was maintained. However, as Martens and Peterson have pointed out, this triangular relationship is affected by numerous other factors which can alter its basic pattern. In addition, as they noted at the end of their article, while cohesiveness can be viewed as an important aspect of

successful teams, it may not be the primary ingredient of team success. They suggested that other factors such as the ability of opposing players, the quality of coaching and officiating, and the inspiration or discouragement of spectators, could also figure prominently into the formula of team success. Indeed, a myriad of psychological, physical, environmental, and social factors could affect, or be affected by, team success. However, the axiomatic theory that will be presented here deals almost exclusively with the intrapersonal, interpersonal, and structural factors examined in the research previously cited in this paper. Thus, this set of interrelated assumptions can be seen as a partially substantiated starting point for the development of a systematically formulated and tested dynamic theory of sports team (and, more generally, task group) success. Although Bales has not studied sports teams, his work with task groups, in general, clearly indicates the importance of assuming a dynamic perspective and it provides a theoretical model to use in thinking about the dynamic interrelationship of affective and task orientations and group success *in sports team contexts*.

While the present theory of team success is not meant to be exhaustively inclusive of the psychological and social factors associated with team success, its scope is still relatively broad. This breadth of scope reflects the diverse perspectives of the previously-mentioned investigators of team effectiveness. A clear indication of the range of variables treated by this theory of team success should be provided by the variable list which appears below:

A. Intrapersonal Factors (Aggregated Over Group)

1. Degree of Importance of Team v. Individual Success, or Group Achievement Orientation (GAO)—Suggested primarily by Klein and Christiansen (1969).

2. Amount of Perceived Discrepancy between the Task Ability Levels of One's Own Group and a Competitive Group, or Perceived Ability Discrepancy (AD)—Suggested primarily by Klein and Christiansen (1969).

3. Degree of Closeness in Expected Relative Group Competitive Outcome, or Expected Competitive Outcome (EO)

—Suggested primarily by Klein and Christiansen (1969); Myers (1962).

4. Degree of Fulfillment of Expectation of Group Competitive Success, or Success Expectation Fulfillment (or Overfulfillment) (F)—Suggested primarily by Klein and Christiansen (1969).

5. Amount of Individual Member Satisfaction with Group Involvement, or Satisfaction (S)—Suggested primarily by Martens and Peterson (1971).

B. Interpersonal Factors

1. Degree of Interpersonal Rivalry, or Interpersonal Rivalry (IR)—Suggested primarily by Klein and Christiansen (1969); Lenk (1969).

2. Amount of Discrepancy Between Positive Affective and Task Orientations, or Affective-Task Discrepancy (A-TD)—Suggested by Bales (1950, 1966); Fiedler (1954, 1960); Klein and Christiansen (1969); Lenk (1969); Martens and Peterson (1971); McGrath (1962); Myers (1962); Veit (1970).

3. Amount of Perceived Integration of Group Activities, or Perceived Teamwork (TW)—Suggested primarily by Martens and Peterson (1971).

C. Social Structural Factors

1. Amount of Status Consensus, or Status Consensus (SC)—Suggested primarily by Fiedler (1954, 1960); Klein and Christiansen (1969).

2. Amount of Attraction to the Group as a Whole, or Group Cohesion (C)—Suggested primarily by Klein and Christiansen (1969); Martens and Peterson (1971).

3a. Amount of Success in Group Goal Attainment Efforts, or Group Success (GS)—Suggested by Bales (1950, 1966); Fiedler (1954, 1960); Klein and Christiansen (1969); Lenk (1969); Martens and Peterson (1971) McGrath (1962); Myers (1962); Veit (1970).

3b. Amount of Immediate Past Group Success, or Past Group Success (PGS)—Suggested primarily by Martens and Peterson (1971). Note that right after task efforts with respect to a given group goal have been completed, group success becomes immediate past group success.

The following assumptions collectively represent an axiomatic version of a dynamic theory of team (or, more generally, competitive task group) success. (Though most of the possible logical derivations have been specified, not every one has been specified because some derivations are presently considered theoretically uninteresting.)

1. The greater the group achievement orientation, the less the interpersonal rivalry in a group.

2. The less the interpersonal rivalry, the greater the status consensus.

3. Therefore, the greater the group achievement orientation, the greater the status consensus. (From 1 & 2)

4. The greater the status consensus, the greater the perceived teamwork and group cohesion.

5. Therefore, the greater the group achievement orientation, the greater the perceived teamwork and group cohesion. (From 3 & 4)

6. Therefore, the less the interpersonal rivalry, the greater the perceived teamwork and group cohesion. (From 2 & 4)

7. The greater the perceived teamwork and group cohesion, the greater the group success.

8. Therefore, the greater the group achievement orientation, the greater the group success. (From 5 & 7)

9. Therefore, the less the interpersonal rivalry, the greater the group success. (From 6 & 7)

10. Therefore, the greater the status consensus, the greater the group success. (From 4 & 7)

11. The smaller the perceived ability discrepancy, the closer the expected competitive outcome.

12. The closer the expected competitive outcome, the smaller (or more negative) the affective-task discrepancy.

13. Therefore, the smaller the perceived ability discrepancy, the smaller (or more negative) the affective-task discrepancy. (From 11 & 12)

14. The smaller (or more negative) the affective-task discrepancy, the greater the group success.

15. Therefore, the smaller the perceived ability discrepancy, the greater the group success. (From 13 & 14)
16. Therefore, the closer the expected competitive outcome, the greater the group success. (From 12 & 14)
17. The greater the past group success, the greater the success expectation fulfillment (or overfulfillment).
18. The greater the success expectation fulfillment, the greater the satisfaction of group members.
19. Therefore, the greater the past group success, the greater the satisfaction of group members. (From 17 & 18)
20. The greater the satisfaction of group members, the greater the group achievement orientation.

21. Therefore, the greater the past group success, the greater the group achievement orientation. (From 19 & 20)
22. Therefore, the greater the past group success, (a) the less the interpersonal rivalry (From 21 & 1); (b) the greater the status consensus (From 21 & 3); (c) the greater the perceived teamwork and group cohesion (From 21 & 5); and (d) the greater the future group success. (From 21 & 8)

This paper concludes with a symbolic representation of the theory just presented. Hopefully, the presentation of this theory will stimulate the development of more systematic sociological knowledge of team success.

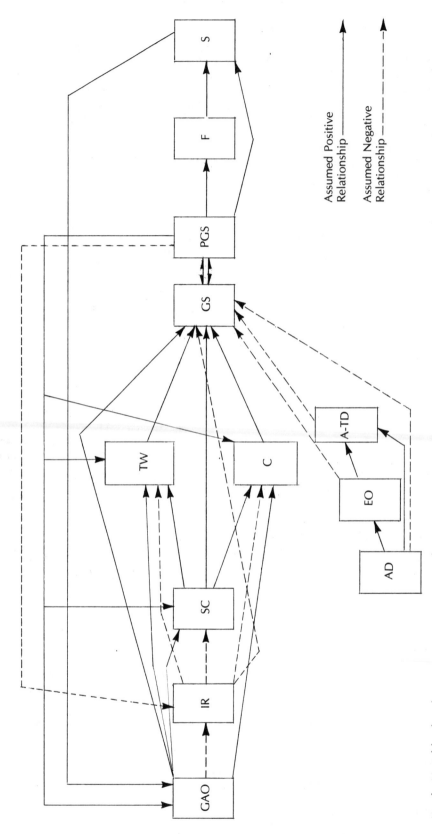

Key for Variable Identification: (1) GAO=Group Achievement Orientation; (2) AD=Perceived Ability Discrepancy; (3) EO=Expected Competitive Outcome; (4) F=Success Expectation Fulfillment; (5) S=Satisfaction; (6) IR=Interpersonal Rivalry; (7) A-TD=Affective-Task Discrepancy; (8) TW=Perceived Team-work; (9) SC=Status Consensus; (10) C=Group Cohesion; (11) GS=Group Success; (12) PGS=Past Group Success.

FIG. 1. SYMBOLIC REPRESENTATION OF THEORY

REFERENCES

Bales, Robert F.: Interaction Process Analysis. Reading, Mass., Addison-Wesley, 1950.

Bales, Robert F.: Adaptive and integrative changes as sources of strain in social systems. *In* Small Groups. Edited by A. Paul Hare, et al. New York, Alfred A. Knopf, 1966.

Fiedler, Fred E.: Assumed similarity measures as predictors of team effectiveness. J. Abnorm. Soc. Psychol., *49*:381, 1954.

Fiedler, Fred E.: The leader's psychological distance and group effectiveness. *In* Group Dynamics. Edited by O. Cartwright and A. Zander. Evanston, Ill., Row, Peterson, 1960.

Klein, Michael, and Christiansen, Gerd: Group composition, group structure, and group effectiveness on basketball teams. *In* Sport, Culture, and Society. Edited by John W. Loy and Gerald S. Kenyon. New York, Macmillan, 1969.

Lenk, Hans: Top performance despite internal conflict. *In* Sport, Culture, and Society. Edited by John W. Loy and Gerald S. Kenyon. New York, Macmillan, 1969.

Martens, Rainer, and Peterson, James: Group cohesiveness as a determinant of success and member satisfaction in team performance. Int. Rev. Sport Sociol., *6*: 49, 1971.

McGrath, Joseph E.: The influence of positive interpersonal relations on adjustment effectiveness in rifle teams. J. Abnorm. Soc. Psychol., *65*:365, 1962.

Myers, Albert: Team competition, success, and the adjustment of group members. J. Abnorm. Soc. Psychol., *65*:325, 1962.

Nixon, Howard L. III: Sport and Social Organization. Indianapolis, In., Bobbs Merrill, 1976.

Veit, Hans: Some remarks upon the elementary interpersonal relations within ball game teams. *In* Contemporary Psychology of Sport. Edited by Gerald S. Kenyon. Chicago, Athletic Institute, 1970.

NOTE

1. The review of the literature which follows is largely adapted from an initial formal draft of Howard L. Nixon III, *Sport and Social Organization* (Indianapolis, Indiana: Bobbs-Merrill, 1976), Chap. IV.

SECTION TWO
sport organizations

occupational discrimination: some theoretical propositions

H. M. BLALOCK, JR.

Historically, most American minorities have entered the labor force at or very near the bottom of the occupational ladder. Prior to the restriction of immigration during the first quarter of the 20th Century, each immigrant group was followed by more recent arrivals to take its place at the base of the pyramid. Therefore as the immigrant group became assimilated and developed industrial skills, while simultaneously losing its visibility as a minority, its relative position generally improved in the expanding economy. The Negro has been exposed to a different situation in several important respects. Not only is the economy expanding at a much slower rate, with the major sources of immigration cut off, but the Negro's major handicap—his skin-color—cannot be overcome so readily as language and other cultural characteristics which have given immigrant minorities their visibility. Furthermore, the Northern-born Negro with several generations of urban experience is often more or less automatically classed with more recent Southern migrants of his race. The saliency of skin-color as a characteristic, together with existing prejudices, is sufficiently pronounced to osbcure the very real differences between native and migrant Negroes. Thus crimes committed by recent migrants are attributed to the entire group, there being no distinctive labels for members of successive generations.

Under these circumstances Negroes face the possibility of becoming a more or less permanent lower-class group. With the exception of occupations which service the minority community, it is certainly conceivable that only the least desirable positions will generally be reserved for such a racial minority. On the other hand there are certain types of occupations which, particularly during periods of labor scarcity, have begun to open up to Negroes. The purpose of the present paper is to examine one of these occupations, professional baseball, in some detail and to list a number of theoretical propositions which are immediately suggested by this analysis.

Let us begin with the assumption that a highly visible minority with an initially low occupational status is at a competitive disadvantage as compared with other persons in the labor force. In a competitive situation, therefore, the minority member will be hired only in the least desirable positions unless he possesses some compensatory advantage over his competitors. We can distinguish between two general types of such advantages, positive and negative. From the standpoint of the employer, *positive advantages* can be measured in terms of performance per unit of cost; the minority may possess certain special skills or be willing to work for lower wages. Under *negative advantages* we include those factors which would adversely affect the employer should he fail to hire a certain number of minority members, regardless of performance or cost considerations. For example he may lose minority customers, or he may undergo public censure for failing to comply with fair employ-

Reprinted from Social Problems, 9:240–247, 1962. Copyright 1962 by The Society for the Study of Social Problems; State University College at Buffalo, Buffalo, New York, 14222.

ment practice laws. Or he may be refused government contracts if his policies are obviously discriminatory.

It is of the nature of most negative advantages possessed by Negroes under present circumstances that these advantages diminish in value once a small token minority labor force has been hired. For example, if an employer can point to one or two Negroes in semi-responsible positions, he can usually clear himself of the charge of discrimination. If such Negroes are highly visible to members of the minority (e.g., the Negro personnel man or the salesman in the Negro community), the employer may actually gain favor with the minority group, given the existing level of discrimination by his competitors. Under these circumstances the strength of the negative advantages diminishes with decreasing discrimination, and occupational opportunities for the minority become stabilized at a point where there are a sufficient number of token representatives to relieve pressure on the employer. Further gains for the minority must come at the expense of increased outside pressure on the employer and increased vigilance in locating and demonstrating discriminatory behavior.

If the minority possesses positive advantages, however, an unstable equilibrium situation is likely to prevail once the initial resistance to employment has been broken unless, of course, more powerful counterforces are brought into operation. Thus if Negroes are willing to work for lower wages than whites, and if the efficiency of operation is not impaired by vehement protests and work stoppages on the part of whites, Negroes will be hired in larger and larger numbers until they have saturated the position concerned, until they demand equal wages, or until the opposition of white workers is aroused to the point where the advantage of hiring Negroes at lower wages is effectively counterbalanced.

Perhaps a more interesting illustration of an unstable equilibrium situation produced by a positive advantage has occurred in professional sports, especially in the case of major league baseball. Professional baseball has provided Negroes with one of the relatively few avenues for escape from traditional blue-collar occupations. Why should this be the case? In part, the answer can be given in terms of negative advantages: pressure by the growing number of Negro spec-

tators in franchise cities. But such pressure, alone, would not account for the very rapid gains since World War II.

Negro players were completely excluded from both major leagues prior to 1947. As a result, there built up a pool of first-rate Negro athletes whose abilities were superior to those of many whites of major league caliber. Negroes within such a pool actually possessed a positive advantage over a number of white players. Once the racial barrier was broken when Jackie Robinson joined the Brooklyn Dodgers, there was an almost immediate rush to tap this reservoir of skilled manpower. The result has not been a mere effort to hire a token number of Negroes to warm the benches and to ward off the charge of discrimination, but a genuine integration of Negroes into the major leagues. Many are among the highest salaried athletes in the country, having won at least their share of Most Valuable Player awards and other major honors. This is not to say that Negro players do not face some discrimination on the part of their teammates or that they are completely integrated off the job as well as on the field. But we seem to have in professional baseball an occupation which is remarkably free of racial discrimination. And the change occurred almost overnight.

In order to gain insight into the nature of occupations for which a comparable situation might hold, it will be helpful to analyze the case of professional baseball in some detail. We shall then be in a position to state some theoretical propositions which, hopefully, might apply more generally.

THE CASE OF PROFESSIONAL BASEBALL

Perhaps the most obvious fact about the baseball profession is its highly competitive nature. Not only is there a high degree of competition among employers for the top athletes, but individual skill is of utmost importance to the productivity of the "work group." [1] Furthermore, skill and performance are easily evaluated. There is a whole series of precise quantitative measures of performance which can be standardized across teams and players—batting averages, slugging averages, home runs, runs batted in, fielding averages, earned run averages, strikeouts, won and lost records, etc. Each player can thus easily be compared with his competitors. There is no question whatsoever as to which batters or pitchers have the best records.

In few occupations known to the writer is individual performance so easily evaluated by all concerned, so variable among persons, and so important to the success of the work group.

It is also the case that a high level of performance clearly works to the advantage of one's teammates, both in terms of prestige and income. Although intra-team rivalries inevitably develop, the fact that teammates share in the rewards of outstanding performance tends to channel such competition into more or less good-natured rivalry. No matter how envious they may be, players must outwardly show respect for the batting or pitching star. His performance yields him high status; the higher the productivity, the higher his prestige. This is in marked contrast to situations in which norms develop which regulate output, thereby equalizing the performances of all members and reducing the importance of individual differences in skill. [2]

Because of the highly competitive nature of the occupation and the fact that when performance slips there are numerous other candidates available to take one's place, it would be highly difficult for the work group to develop effective sanctions restricting performance. Nor does high productivity on the part of some individuals mean fewer jobs for others, as in instances where production is limited by consumer demand. Also, there seems to be little or no systematic hostility directed toward the employer as the superordinate agent forcing performance against the will of the players. The norm of high performance is simply part of the game, and it is seldom perceived as a case of employees versus employers.

Players on any one team are not in direct competition with most of their teammates. Although there may be perhaps a dozen or so pitchers in competition for starting positions, the more usual case involves competition among only two or three players who are candidates for a given position. Competition is primarily with a host of more or less anonymous players on other teams or in other leagues. A player knows that if his performance slips he will inevitably be replaced, possibly by someone on his own team but equally as likely by someone else. There is no major hierarchy of positions such that if the top man is replaced, every other person moves up one notch. In effect, this means that one gets ahead on the basis of his own performance alone. He cannot generally rely on moving permanently into a position merely if the performance of his nearest rival is lowered. Nor will it help to place barriers or restrictions in the path of his competitors, unless he can simultaneously handicap a large percentage of these persons. The power position of the individual player is obviously not such that this is possible. His job tenure thus remains inherently insecure. This would seem to be one of the major reasons why the introduction of Negro players did not create an uproar among these professional athletes. Their jobs were threatened, but they had always been threatened, if not by Negroes then by countless others of their own race. [3]

As is true for most other sports, in professional baseball top performance leads to high prestige, income, and acclaim, but it does not imply a corresponding degree of power or control over other players. A team is essentially equalitarian in nature, with persons in authority (coaches, managers) usually being drawn from the ranks of retired rather than active players. [4] There is thus little or no threat of the Negro teammate becoming the white player's boss, and an additional source of resistance to his employment is thereby removed.

In some occupations workers may successfully prevent the hiring of minority group members by threatening to quit work or even to work for a rival employer. The prestige of major league baseball would seem to be too high, however, for such threats to appear realistic. Nor do league rules permit a player to change jobs by joining a competing team if he happens to object to some of his teammates. His freedom of choice is thus very much limited. [5]

In baseball it is also difficult to control the minority's access to the training necessary for high-level performance. Such skill depends to a large extent on innate abilities which vary considerably from individual to individual. Nor does training in baseball require a college education, as in the case of football, or expensive equipment (as with golf), or access to restricted facilities (golf, swimming). Baseball is almost as much a lower-class as a middle-class sport. Although a long period of training or apprenticeship is required, it is difficult for whites to obtain a monopoly on training facilities, as they have in the case of a number of trades and professions. There are few, if any, trade secrets which are not well known to the public.

Another important factor has worked to the

advantage of the Negro in organized baseball. In this profession performance depends only to a slight degree on interpersonal relations and manipulative skills. In contrast, a salesman's performance—also easily evaluated—depends to a large extent on his ability to persuade a prospective client. If the client is prejudiced, the Negro salesman is especially handicapped. Although a particular pitcher may be prejudiced against Negroes, there is little he can do to hamper the performance of the Negro slugger, short of an attempt at foul play. Many of baseball's top performers would never win a popularity contest, but for essentially the same reason the Negro athlete's performance is not as directly dependent upon the good-will of whites as would be the case in most managerial-type positions. We might predict, however, that Negroes will find it much more difficult working into coaching and managerial positions in baseball and will have an exceedingly difficult time obtaining positions in the "front office."[6]

Finally, it may be of some significance that although there is a considerable amount of interaction among players both on and off the field, much of this interaction does not involve the wives and other members of the opposite sex. Players must spend a good deal of the season traveling, eating together, living in hotels, and in general recreating away from their home communities. The specter of intermarriage does not so easily arise as would be the case if, for example, a Negro male were hired as a member of an office staff.

SOME THEORETICAL PROPOSITIONS

The foregoing analysis of professional baseball suggests some general propositions which might apply to other occupations. In listing these propositions, it is necessary to keep in mind that we are assuming other factors to remain constant. In particular, we shall suppose that the prestige-level of the job and general labor market conditions do not vary. It is especially important that the general prestige-level be considered constant since, because of the positive correlation between the competitive nature of an occupation and its prestige, many of these propositions would otherwise seem obviously false.[7] Detailed analyses of other occupations which have suddenly been opened to minority group members should suggest qualifications as well as addi-tional propositions which, hopefully, can then be subjected to empirical testing.

1. The greater the importance of high individual performance to the productivity of the work group, the lower the degree of minority discrimination by employers.

2. The greater the competition among employers for persons with high performance levels, the lower the degree of minority discrimination by employers.

3. The easier it is accurately to evaluate an individual's performance level, the lower the degree of minority discrimination by employers.

4. To the degree that high individual performance works to the advantage of other members of the work group who share rewards of high performance, the higher the positive correlation between performance and status within the group, and the lower the degree of minority discrimination by group members. NOTE: It is important, here, that there not be disadvantages of high performance which outweigh the advantages (e.g., where total productivity is limited by consumer demand or where there is extensive hostility toward the employer).

5. The fewer the restrictions placed on performance by members of the work group, the lower the degree of minority discrimination. (Restrictions reduce the minority member's advantage with respect to performance.) NOTE: Where high individual performance works to the advantage of the group, restrictions on performance are unlikely. Hence propositions 4 and 5 are closely related.

6. To the degree that a work group consists of a number of specialists interacting as a team and that there is little or no serious competition among these members, the lower the degree of minority discrimination by group members.

7. To the degree that a group member's position is threatened by anonymous outsiders rather than other members of his own group, the lower the degree of minority discrimination by group members.

8. To the extent that an individual's success depends primarily on his own performance, rather than on limiting or restricting the performance of specific other indi-

viduals, the lower the degree of minority discrimination by group members. NOTE: Condition 8 is likely whenever there is intense competition and a large number of potential competitors available outside the work group (e.g., a tenure position at an outstanding university).

9. To the degree that high performance does not lead to power over other members of the work group, the lower the degree of minority discrimination by group members. NOTE: Condition 9 is especially likely when there is no hierarchy of power among group members, but where control is exercised by another category of persons altogether.

10. To the degree that group members find it difficult or disadvantageous to change jobs in order to avoid minority members, the lower the degree of minority discrimination by employers.

11. To the extent that it is difficult to prevent the minority from acquiring the necessary skills for high performance, the lower the degree of discrimination. This is especially likely when:

    (a) skill depends primarily on innate abilities,
    (b) skill can be developed without prolonged or expensive training, or
    (c) it is difficult to maintain a monopoly of skills through secrecy or the control of facilities.

12. To the extent that performance level is relatively independent of skill in interpersonal relations, the lower the degree of discrimination. (Lower discrimination is predicted where one works with things rather than where one works with or manipulates persons.) NOTE: Proposition 12 is based on the assumption that performance level can be more easily affected by prejudice when such performance depends on interpersonal skills.

13. The lower the degree of purely social interaction on the job (especially interaction involving both sexes), the lower the degree of discrimination. NOTE: A high degree of social interaction may not only result in the minority member feeling left out and desiring to leave the job, but it may also affect his performance.

CONCLUDING REMARKS

A major question raised by the analysis of professional baseball is that of the typicality of such an occupation. What other occupations have characteristics similar to those of baseball and how many minority group members can be absorbed into these positions? Other entertainment fields immediately come to mind. Competition is intense, box-office appeal is relatively easy to evaluate, and—at least in many types of entertainment—expensive training is less important than talent or native abilities.

Academic and scientific professions also would seem to offer the Negro similar opportunities. Performance is readily evaluated in terms of research contributions or publications and does not depend primarily on interpersonal skills. There is also extensive competition for outstanding personnel, and total productivity is not sharply limited by consumer demand. It is noteworthy that although Negroes have not as yet entered these fields in any numbers, Jews are if anything "overrepresented" in academic and scientific circles. Although there is no question that anti-semitism has proved a handicap, the emphasis within the Jewish subculture given to learning and independent thinking has provided this particular minority with a compensatory positive advantage. Unlike baseball, however, training for academic and scientific careers is both prolonged and expensive. This fact, plus the lack of an intellectual tradition among Negroes, may account for the relatively small number of Negro intellectuals. But with the growing influence of state and national governmental agencies on the hiring of intellectuals (e.g., in large state universities, through military contracts), Negroes should obtain additional leverage which, if added to a greater emphasis on intellectual pursuits, should give rise to increasing numbers of Negro academics.

A large number of white-collar occupations are not of this highly competitive nature, however. Especially on the lower rungs of the white-collar ladder, where a low-status minority might be expected to make its greatest initial gains, many positions are either relatively noncompetitive (e.g., stenographer, sales clerk) or highly dependent upon interpersonal skills (e.g., supervisor, realtor, insurance agent). Furthermore, the Negro finds himself in direct competition with another "minority group," women, entering the lower-level white-collar occupations in ever increasing numbers. Not only are women willing to work for lower salaries, but they constitute a relatively docile labor force. Although labor turnover among females may be high, in many instances such a turnover does not constitute a major problem in positions in which personnel are more or less interchangeable and where performance levels are not highly variable. The fact that heterosexual contacts are frequent in these white-collar occupations further militates against the Negro male.

The number of occupations in which Negroes can make use of important positive advantages may thus be quite limited. If this should be the case, perhaps the best strategy would be to encourage Negroes to seek out those white-collar occupations for which the demand is far greater than the supply because of the hesitancy of majority group members to fill these positions. Well-trained and capable Negroes may find it not too difficult to enter such professions as teaching or social work because of the fact that whites with whom they are competing are far less qualified than themselves. Although such a strategy might appear to involve accepting second-best opportunities, it may also help to reduce the Negro's handicaps in entering a wider range of occupations.

NOTES

1. Becker theorizes that there should in general be less discrimination in competitive industries than in monopolistic ones. See G. Becker, *The Economics of Discrimination*. Chicago, University of Chicago Press, 1957, Chapter 3.

2. Hughes notes a tendency for Negro workers to fail to adhere to norms requiring a restriction of output in part because of the fear that they were being put on trial by management and that greater productivity was required of them as compensation for their minority status. See E. C. Hughes, The knitting of racial groups in industry. Am Sociol Rev, *11:*512, 1946.

3. Of course the pool of qualified Negro players was not unusually large. In addition, the norm of good sportsmanship—in part also a resultant of the necessity for regulating competition—undoubtedly worked in favor of nondiscrimination.

4. The position of team captain seems to be primarily honorific and is often given to a player (usually an infielder) who can best inspire team morale. Authority, however, rests with the coaches and manager.

5. Such a situation might be contrasted with one involving residential segregation, where whites may readily move away from a neighborhood being invaded by Negroes.

6. A possible exception, here, would be the star performer who is used by management primarily as a figurehead.

7. It is a moot point whether or not it makes sense to conceive of prestige being controlled if competition among employers and importance of individual performance are allowed to vary. However, we shall conceive of comparisons among occupations having roughly the same general prestige.

the effects of formal structure on managerial recruitment:
a study of baseball organization *

OSCAR GRUSKY

The formal structure of an organization consists of a set of norms which define the system's official objectives, its major offices or positions, and the primary responsibilities of the position occupants. [1] Official norms or rules are often of such generality that informal practices inevitably develop as solutions for particular cases. The officially acceptable standards of the present frequently were the unofficial, informal practices of the past. Hence, a fundamental characteristic of formal structures is that they constantly undergo change. At any single point in time the behavior of a position occupant is governed by a combination of official and unofficial standards. [2]

The formal structure, conceived of as the environment within which the informal develops, patterns the behavior of its constituent positions along three interdependent dimensions: (1) spatial location, (2) nature of task, and (3) frequency of interaction. We distinguish between central and peripheral spatial locations, independent and dependent tasks, and frequent and less frequent interpersonal interaction. In accordance with the formulations of Bavelas and Leavitt, central positions are defined as those located close to other positions. [3] Independent

Reprinted from Sociometry, 5:5–24, 1971. Copyright 1971 by the American Sociological Association, 1722 N. Street, N.W., Washington, D.C. 20036.
* I am grateful to Judith Kairath for doing the coding, to Don Zimmerman for computational work, and the University of California, Los Angeles for research funds. The members, too numerous to name, of the Department of Anthropology and Sociology's informal seminar, directed by Joan Moore, were kind enough to criticize an earlier draft of this paper.

tasks are of the kind performed without the necessity of coordination with the activities of other positions. All else being equal, the more central one's spatial location: (1) the greater the likelihood dependent or coordinative tasks will be performed and (2) the greater the rate of interaction with the occupants of other positions. [4] Also, performance of dependent tasks is positively related to frequency of interaction. Combining these three criteria, we define two types of positions in a formal structure, those with high and low interaction potential. We shall refer to *high interactors* and *low interactors*.

In most cases, formal structures are able to maintain themselves despite the fact that succession among position occupants is a continuous process. We assume that both the formal structure and the position occupant mutually influence one another in varying degrees. [5] The particular pattern of characteristics associated with the position a person occupies should affect not only his degree of job satisfaction but also the nature of his career pattern. Hence, Leavitt found that persons occupying central positions were more satisfied and more likely to be selected as leaders than were those in peripheral positions. [6] Our general hypothesis maintains that position in the formal structure of an organization contributes to the development of role skills which are essential to career movement. [7] Since interaction is positively related to liking, high interactors should be selected more often than low interactors as the most respected and popular members of the organization. [8] Also, high interactors should be more likely to learn cooperative social skills and develop a strong commitment to the welfare of the organization. Low interactors should be more likely to focus on individualistic rather than team values and tend to be psychologically distant or aloof. In formal organizations which utilize these or related characteristics as official or unofficial criteria for managerial selection, high interactors should be selected for executive positions more often than low interactors.

We decided to test the managerial recruitment proposition of this theory, in an admittedly preliminary and exploratory manner, on baseball teams. Professional sports organizations have a number of unique features which make them useful sources for testing hypotheses of concern to organization theory. For example, they tend to have fairly stable formal structures, are of similar size, keep accurate public records, and utilize relatively objective performance standards. [9] This study examines the relationship between the internal structure of baseball organization and the recruitment of field managers. Specifically, we hypothesized that the occupants of certain key formal positions (infielders and catchers) were more likely than others to become managers.

BASEBALL ORGANIZATION. The playing organization of professional baseball teams consists of three major interaction units, outfielders, infielders, and the pitcher and catcher. [10] The constituent positions of each unit differ with respect to the attributes of spatial location, type of task, and frequency of interaction.

The outfielders constitute the most isolated unit. They are not only located at a distance from each other but also are far away from the infield. [11] As a result, outfielders probably have the lowest rate of team interaction during the defensive part of the game, although perhaps the highest rate of interaction with the fans. [12]

Field positions in baseball differ considerably with respect to the nature of the primary tasks expected of the occupant. A major dimension is the extent to which the tasks are dependent or independent. Although outfielders do have some dependent functions, for example, when they must throw the ball into the infield to complete a play, independent tasks are more characteristic of their position. In sharp contrast, infielders' functions are predominantly of the dependent type. [13] The third baseman must be able to throw the ball accurately and rapidly to the first base-

man and the shortstop must not only field ground balls cleanly but also be able to toss the ball at the proper angle so the second baseman can handle it, pivot, avoid the onrushing runner, and throw quickly to the first baseman.

Because they are densely concentrated close to the center of the game's activity, infielders tend to interact more frequently with each other, rival players, and even the umpires. Their offensive as well as their defensive tasks can be distinguished from that of the outfielders. Where the outfielder is supposed to hit homeruns, an independent function, the infielder is more often expected to hit singles, or bunt, and thereby sacrifice his turn at bat for the team's benefit. It is true that the first baseman, often a converted outfielder, deviates from this overall pattern.

Independent tasks in baseball are more likely to be of the glamorous, heroic type and most frequently are offensive rather than defensive in nature. It is the sluggers who are likely to provide the daily headlines. Where the outfielder is typically expected to excel offensively and not as a fielder, the reverse is the case for the infielder. He is commonly described as a "gloveman."

The third interaction unit, officially called the battery, possesses a number of special characteristics. In general, the catcher's position takes on more of the attributes of the infielder while the pitcher's position resembles that of the outfielder. Two factors are relevant to the classification of the pitcher. First, like the outfielders, his functions are primarily independent. It is not his abilities in team-play that are critical to his success. His offensive tasks are considered of minor importance and are generally of a dependent nature. Second, despite a central location, his interaction rate is severely limited by the fact that he participates in only about one game in four, unless he is a relief pitcher. In the latter case, he typically performs only for a few innings.

Both the spatial location and the dependent nature of the defensive tasks of the catcher place him in a situation of close interdependence and frequent interaction with the infielders. On the other hand, his offensive tasks are frequently of the independent variety. This unique combination, as we shall see, may especially prepare occupants of this position for managerial selection.

As noted earlier, spatial location and nature of task are mutually correlated with frequency of interaction. Applying these criteria, we classify infielders and catchers as *high interactors,* and outfielders and pitchers, *low interactors.* Assuming that the formal characteristics of the position directly affect the nature of the role skills developed by the occupants, then high interactors should be well-liked, more likely to learn cooperative social skills, and should develop a strong commitment to team welfare, while low interactors should be less popular, focus more on individualistic rather than team values, and tend to be psychologically distant or aloof.

Elsewhere we have described the major sources of managerial role strain. [14] The considerable discrepancy that exists between the manager's responsibility, and his authority, on the one hand, and the availability of an objective assessment of managerial and team performance to the organization's clientele and higher levels of authority, on the other, combine to lessen the possibility of domination of the players by the occupant of this position. Instead, managerial control in baseball is likely to be based on mutual respect and liking. Since interaction is positively related to liking, it is the high interactors whom we would expect to be selected as the most respected and popular. In general, it is this group whose formal position should enable them to develop appropriate managerial skills. Hence, we hypothesized that field managers would be more likely to be recruited from among high than low interactors.

METHODS AND FINDINGS

A simple random sample was drawn from all players listed in *The Official Encyclopedia of Baseball,* which purports to cover". . . every man who ever appeared in a regularly scheduled major league game since the birth of professional league play in 1871." [15] From a random start every twentieth player listed was included in the sample. Of the 465 persons selected, a total of thirteen had been managers. The major sample of field managers was provided from data collected for a previous study. This sample consisted of the total population of field managers of the sixteen professional baseball teams during the periods 1921–1941 and 1951–1958. [16]

Table 1 presents the basic data of the study. The table shows that field managers are almost entirely recruited from among professional players. Comparing the larger sample of managers and the players, we find that, as predicted, both pitchers and outfielders were underrepresented among the managerial group, while catchers, first basemen, second basemen, third basemen, and shortstops, were overrepresented. Not a single major position deviated from the expected pattern.

TABLE 1
Distribution of Major Field Positions of Managers and Players

Position	All Managers * 1921– 41, 1951– 58	Random Sample ** Managers	Players
Pitcher	6.5%	(2)	38.5%
Catcher	26.2	(5)	11.3
First base	11.2	(1)	4.4
Second base	10.3	(1)	8.2
Third base	13.1	—	4.4
Shortstop	14.0	(1)	8.0
Outfielder	15.9	(1)	22.1
Pinch hitter	—	—	2.9
Non-player	2.8	(2)	—
Non ascertained	—	—	.2
Totals	100.0%		100.0%
N=	107	(13)	452

*Includes all field managers of the sixteen professional baseball teams during the periods indicated.
**From *The Official Encyclopedia of Baseball* which covers the 1871–1958 period.

Table 2 combines the positions into two groups, high and low interactors. This table demonstrates: (1) the similarity of the large and small samples of managers with respect to distribution among the two types of positions, (2) strong support for the hypothesis that managers were more likely to have had experience in high than low interaction positions. The hypothesis was supported both when the large sample of managers and the small sample were compared with the random sample of players.

To return briefly to Table 1, we see that this table also suggests that managers were more likely to be recruited from catchers than from any other field position. [17] Where only about eleven per cent (11.3%) of the random sample of players were catchers, over one-fourth (26.2%) of the large sample of managers had held this position. We noted earlier that the catcher, although identified as a high interactor because of spatial location and defensive tasks, tended also to possess a major attribute of the low interactors in his offensive function. Like the outfielders, he is typically expected to be a slugger. Perhaps this combination of characteristics develops the types of social skills defined as especially appropriate for field managers. As a high interactor, the catcher tends to be in the very center of team action, participates directly in the coordination of the efforts of the team, and therefore becomes closely identified with the welfare of the organization as a whole. Also important, however, may be the attitude of psycho-

logical remoteness—a trait assumed to be developed primarily among low interactors. It may be that the catcher's characteristically independent offensive performance encourages him to adopt an aloof social style. Homans' formulation suggests the following interpretation. [18] The catcher, because of his key position, earns authority through the acquisition of esteem. He acquires esteem by giving advice which is helpful to others. Hence, he is viewed as someone to be listened to. At the same time, since he is involved in advising and coordinating the efforts of others, the others incur costs in accepting his influence. As a consequence, the others develop mixed feelings toward him. He is esteemed and respected because his advice is personally rewarding as well as contributing to the team's objectives, but, at the same time, he is resented. As Homans further indicates, an aloof social style on the part of the leader tends to be exceedingly helpful to him. This approach and F. Fiedler's supporting research would suggest that all else being equal, managers who had been catchers should be highly effective leaders. [19]

CONCLUSIONS

This study has attempted to show the possible effects of formal structure on managerial recruitment patterns. A theory of formal structure was described focusing on three interdependent attributes of positions: spatial location, nature of task, and rate of interaction. Two conditions of interdependency, high and low interaction, were

TABLE 2
Relationship Between Type of Field Position and Managerial Experience[a]

Type of Position	A. All Managers[b] 1921– 41, 1951– 58 (N=104)	Random Sample[c]	
		B. Managers (N=11)	C. Players (N=438)
High Interactors (Infielders and Catchers)	76.9%	73%	37.4%
Low Interactors (Outfielders and Pitchers)	23.1	27	62.6
	100.0%	100%	100.0%

[a] A x C, Chi Square=52.92, df=1, p<.0001; B x C, Chi Square=4.26, df=1, p<.025, Yates' correction applied. Values of p are based on one-sided critical region.

[b] Excludes three managers who were not players.

[c] B. excludes two managers who were not players; C. excludes thirteen pinch hitters and one player for whom data were not obtainable.

distinguished and seen as affecting the acquisition of role skills which, in turn, influence the recruitment of managers. The theory was applied to baseball organizations and the proposition that occupants of high interaction positions are more likely than those in low interaction positions to become field managers was strongly supported.

It should be pointed out that our discussion omitted the obviously important and perhaps mitigating effects of the informal group structure, assuming that, at least in part, the development of this structure will be influenced by the shape of the formal structure. Likewise we have been unable to consider the potential influence of personality predispositions on managerial recruitment. It may be, for example, that players with strong needs for affiliation seek infield positions and that these needs are merely reinforced by later experiences. Despite these reservations and others associated with the problem of correlated bias, the data presented may be viewed as tentative support for the theory outlined. It appears that in professional baseball organizations the interactional constraints associated with the type of position occupied as a player are related significantly to chances for obtaining managerial office.

REFERENCES

1. Broom, Leonard, and Sleznick, Philip: Sociology. A Text with Adapted Readings. 2nd Edition. Evanston, Ill., Row, Peterson, 1958, pp. 208–213.
2. Blau, Peter, and Scott, W. Richard: Formal Organizations. San Francisco, Chandler, 1962, pp. 5–8.
3. Bavelas, Alex: Communication patterns in task-oriented groups. J. Acoustical Soc. Am., 22:725, 1950; Leavitt, Harold J.: Some effects of certain communication patterns on group performance. J. Abnorm. Soc. Psychol., 46:38, 1951. See also Mulder, Mark: Communication structure, decision structure and group performance. Sociometry, 23:1, 1960; and Guetzkow, Harold, and Simon, Herbert A.: The impact of certain communication nets upon organization and performance in task-oriented groups. Management Sci., 1:233, 1955.
4. See Blau and Scott, pp. 126–128. Also, on the relationship between spatial location and liking, see Festinger, Leon, Schachter, Stanley, and Back, Kurt W.: Social Pressures in Informal Groups. New York, Harper & Bros., 1950, pp. 33–59. On some effects of type of task, termed degree of "facilitation in rule interdependence," see Thomas, Edwin J.: Effects of facilitative role interdependence on group functioning. In Group Dynamics. 2nd Edition. Edited by Dorwin Cartwright and Alvin Zander. Evanston, Ill., Row, Peterson, 1960, pp. 449–471.
5. See Argyris, Chris: Personality and Organization. New York, Harper, 1957; Merton, Robert K.: Social Theory and Social Structure. Revised Edition. Glencoe, Illinois, The Free Press, 1957, pp. 195–206; Sussman, Leila E.: The personnel and ideology of public relations. Public Opinion Q, 12:697, 1948–1949; and Swanson, Guy E.: Agitation through the press: a study of the personalities of publicists. Public Opinion Q, 20:441, 1956.
6. See Leavitt, op. cit. Also, Norman H. Berkowitz and Warren G. Bennis report a positive relationship between the status of the other party and satisfaction with interaction. People receive more satisfaction from interaction with persons of higher status. See, Interaction patterns in formal service-oriented organizations. Administrative Sci. Q., 6:25, 1961.
7. A good summary and critique of role skills deemed desirable for business success can be found in Stark, Stanley: Research criteria of executive success. J. Bus. of the University of Chicago, 32:1, 1959.
8. A number of studies supporting this relationship are discussed in Homans, George C.: Social Behavior: Its Elementary Forms. New York, Harcourt, Brace and World, 1961, pp. 181–190.
9. Some implications of these attributes for sports organizations are discussed in a companion paper, Managerial succession and organizational effectiveness. Am. J. Sociol., 69:21, 1963.
10. The official rules specify that there be nine players but define only the functions of these four. See Turkin, Hy, and Thompson, S.C.: The Official Encyclopedia of Baseball. 2nd Revised Edition. New York, A.S. Barnes, 1959, pp. 554–586.
11. This fact is recognized in a rather amusing fashion by the official rule which defines the outfielder as ". . . a fielder who occupies a position in the outfield, which is the area of playing field most distant from home base." Ibid., p. 559.
12. Although not tested in this study, this assumption can be examined empirically. An observer could conceivably take a battery-operated interaction process recorder to a sample of ballgames. Or, of course, a simple interaction matrix could be used.
13. This statement like many others is based largely on personal observation. As a start, one might utilize box-score data to determine more precisely which positions have the highest proportion of independent and dependent acts.
14. Managerial succession and organizational effectiveness, op. cit.
15. Turkin and Thompson, p. 57.
16. Managerial succession and organizational effectiveness, op. cit.
17. It is apparent that our theory is a tentative one and that other explanations are equally possible. An anonymous reviewer, for example, suggests as a possible alternative explanation that perhaps there is a norm in professional baseball that catching is the best position for training managers or that persons of managerial potential should be encouraged to become catchers. The theory presented is somewhat more satisfactory than these on several grounds. (1) It explains more. The alternatives

above do not explain why infielders are dispropor-tionately more likely than others to become managers. Of course, one might suggest that a norm is the explanation for this also. But then one must explain the genesis of the norm, which would bring you full circle back to the theory presented. (2) It fits in systematically to a comprehensive body of generalizations in the field of organiza-tions.Theory and research by Bavelas, Leavitt, Selznick, Blau and Scott, Homans, and numerous others may be mentioned. (3) It suggests a number of additional empirical propositions. For example,

is there a relationship between position played and managerial effectiveness? Is amount of experience as an infielder or number of different positions played a contributory factor affecting managerial recruitment? To what extent does the formal struc-ture influence the development of the informal?

18. Homans, pp. 307–315.
19. Fiedler, F.: The leader's psychological distance and group effectiveness. In Group Dynamics. 2nd Edition. Edited by Dorwin Cartwright and Alvin Zander. Evanston, Ill., Row, Peterson, 1960, pp. 586–606.

racial segregation in american sport*

JOHN W. LOY and JOSEPH F. McELVOGUE

Numerous journalists have commented on the social functions which sport fulfills for minority groups in American society. Boyle, for example, forcefully writes:

Sport has often served minority groups as the first rung on the social ladder. As such, it has helped further their assimilation into American life. It would not be too far-fetched to say that it has done more in this regard than any other agency, including church and school (1963, p. 100).

Recently, journalists have placed special emphasis on the many contributions sport has made for the Negro. As Olsen observes:

Every morning the world of sport wakes up and congratulates itself on its contributions to race relations. The litany has been so often repeated that it is believed almost universally. It goes: "Look what sports has done for the Negro" (1968, p. 7).

In view of the many journalistic accounts of the contributions of sport to the social success of minority groups, it is somewhat surprising that sociologists and physical educators have largely ignored the issue of minority group integration in American sport. The purpose of this paper is to

Reprinted from International Review of Sport Sociology, 5:5–24, 1971. Copyright 1971 by International Review of Sport Sociology, Warsaw, Poland.

* Appreciation is accorded to Mr. Schroeder, director, and Mr. Dyer, assistant director of Helms Hall for assistance in the collection of data for this paper.

direct the attention of sport sociologists to the issue by presenting a theoretical and empirical examination of racial segregation in America's major professional baseball and football teams.

THEORETICAL OVERVIEW

Theoretically considered, our examination largely draws upon Grusky's (1963) theory of formal structure of organizations and Blalock's (1962) set of theoretical propositions regarding occupational discrimination.

According to Grusky, "the formal structure of an organization consists of a set of norms which define the system's official objectives, its major offices or positions, and the primary responsibilities of the position occupants" (p. 345). The formal structure ". . . patterns the behavior of its constituent positions along three interdependent dimensions: (1) spatial location, (2) nature of task, and (3) frequency of interaction" (p. 345). The theoretical import of Grusky's model is contained in his statement that:

All else being equal, the more central one's spatial location: (1) the greater the likelihood dependent or coordinative tasks will be performed and (2) the greater the rate of interaction with the occupants of other positions. Also, the performance of dependent tasks is positively related to frequency of interaction (p. 346).

Combining these three criteria, Grusky distinguishes positions of high interaction potential and positions of low interaction potential within the social structure of organizations. He defines

103

the occupants of these two types of positions as high and low interactors, respectively.

For our purposes, we prefer to use the concept of "centrality" in dealing with Grusky's three interdependent dimensions of organizational positions. With an extension to permit us to embrace all three of Grusky's criteria, we accepted Hopkins' (1964) definition of this concept:

Centrality designates how close a member is to the "center" of the group's interaction network and thus refers simultaneously to the frequency with which a member participates in interaction with other members and the number or range of other members with whom he interacts (p. 28) [and the degree to which he must coordinate his tasks and activities with other members].

BLALOCK'S THEORETICAL PROPOSITIONS

Several years ago, Blalock (1962) made a very astute analysis of why "professional baseball has provided Negroes with one of the relatively few avenues for escape from blue-collar occupations." From his analysis, Blalock developed thirteen theoretical propositions concerning occupational discrimination which can be empirically tested in other occupational settings. His analysis is an excellent example of how the critical examination of a sport situation can enhance the development of sociological theory in an area of central concern. Blalock was, however, perhaps naive in assuming that professional baseball is ". . . an occupation which is remarkably free of racial discrimination" (p. 242).

We sought to test Blalock's assumption that professional baseball is relatively free of racial discrimination by drawing upon three of his propositions to predict where racial segregation is most likely to occur on the baseball diamond. The three particular propositions which we considered were:

1. The lower the degree of purely social interaction on the job . . . , the lower the degree of discrimination (p. 246).
2. To the extent that performance level is relatively independent of skill in interpersonal relations, the lower the degree of discrimination (p. 246).
3. To the extent that an individual's success depends primarily on his own performance,

rather than on limiting or restricting the performance of specific other individuals, the lower the degree of discrimination by group members (p. 245).

On the one hand, the consideration of proposition 1 in conjunction with proposition 2 suggested that discrimination is directly related to level and type of interaction. On the other hand, the combined consideration of propositions 2 and 3 suggested that there will be less discrimination where performance of independent tasks are largely involved; because such tasks do not have to be coordinated with the activities of other persons, and therefore do not hinder the performance of others, nor require a great deal of skill in interpersonal relations.

Since the dimensions of interaction and task dependency treated by Blalock are included in our concept of centrality, we subsumed his three propositions under a more general one, stating that: "discrimination is positively related to centrality."

STATEMENT OF THEORETICAL HYPOTHESIS

Broadly conceived, discrimination ". . . denotes the unfavourable treatment of categories of persons on arbitrary grounds" (Moore, 1964, p. 203). Discrimination takes many forms, but a major mode is that of segregation. Segregation denotes the exclusion of certain categories of persons from specific social organizations or particular positions within organizations on arbitrary grounds, i.e., grounds which have no objective relation to individual skill and talent.

Since we were chiefly concerned with the matter of racial segregation in professional sports, we took as our specific theoretical hypothesis the proposition that: *racial segregation in professional team sports is positively related to centrality*. In order to test this hypothesis, we empirically examined the extent of racial segregation within major league baseball and major league football.

THE CASE OF PROFESSIONAL BASEBALL

Baseball teams have a well defined social structure consisting of the repetitive and regulated interaction among a set of nine positions combined into three major substructures or interaction units: (1) the battery, consisting of pitcher and catcher; (2) the infield, consisting of

1st base, 2nd base, shortstop and 3rd base; and (3) the outfield, consisting of leftfield, centerfield and rightfield positions.

EMPIRICAL HYPOTHESIS

As is evident from Figure 1, one can readily see that the outfield contains the most peripheral and socially isolated positions in the organizational structure of a baseball team. Therefore, on the basis of our theoretical hypothesis, we predicted that Negro players in comparison to white players on major league teams are more likely to occupy outfield positions and less likely to occupy infield positions.

METHODS

Data. On the basis of the *1968 Baseball Register* all professional players in the American and National Leagues who played at least fifty games during the 1967 season were categorized according to race and playing position. [1]

Treatment. The X^2 test for two independent

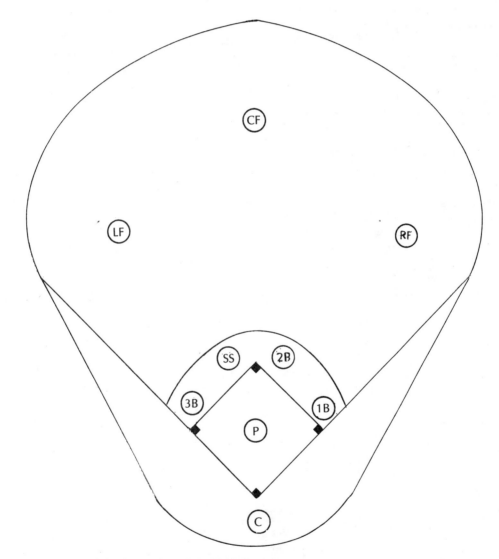

FIG.1 SCHEMATIC OUTLINE OF FIELD POSITIONS IN BASEBALL
P—pitcher; C—catcher; 1B—first base; 2B—second base; SS—shortstop; 3B—third base; Lf—leftfield; Cf—centerfield; Rf—rightfield.

samples was used to test the null hypothesis that there is no difference between white and black ballplayers in terms of the proportion who occupy infield and outfield positions. The .01 level of significance, using a one-tailed test, was selected as being sufficient to warrant the rejection of the null hypothesis.

FINDINGS

Table 1 presents the number of white and black athletes occupying specific positions in the major leagues in 1967. It is clearly evident from the table that Negro players are predominantly found in the outfield. The highly significant X^2, resulting from the test of our null hypothesis, gives strong support to our empirical hypothesis and provides some confirmation of our theoretical hypothesis that racial segregation in professional sports is related to centrality. As a further test of our hypothesis we examined the extent of racial segregation in professional football.

THE CASE OF PROFESSIONAL FOOTBALL

Like baseball teams, football teams have well defined organizational structures. However, whereas the positions in baseball organization are determined by defensive alignment, there ex-

ists both a distinctive offensive and a distinctive defensive team within modern professional football organization. Figure 2 shows the constituent positions of the offensive and defensive teams of any given professional football organization.

EMPIRICAL HYPOTHESIS

It is clear from Figure 2 that the most central positions on the offensive team consist of center, right guard, left guard and quarterback; while the most central position on the defensive team are the three linebacker positions. Therefore, on the basis of our theoretical hypothesis, we predicted that Negro football players in comparison to white players are more likely to occupy noncentral positions than central positions on both offensive and defensive teams.

Data. Using the *Official 1968 Autographed Yearbooks* of the American and National Football Leagues in conjunction with Zanger's *Pro Football 1968* we classified all starting offensive and defensive players according to race (black or white) and playing position (central or noncentral). [2]

Treatment. The X^2 test for two independent samples was used to test the null hypothesis that there is no difference between white and black occupancy of centrally located positions on

TABLE 1

A Comparison of Race and Position Occupancy in Major League Baseball in 1967

Playing Position	American League		National League		Both Leagues	
	White	Black	White	Black	White	Black
Catcher	13	0	14	1	27	1
Shortstop	7	0	10	1	17	1
1st Base	11	2	7	5	18	7
2nd Base	10	3	6	1	16	4
3rd Base	9	2	7	4	16	6
Outfield	26	14	12	22	38	36
$N=$	76	21	56	34	132	55

RACE

Position	White	Black	Total
Infield	94	19	113
Outfield	38	36	74
	132	55	187

$$\chi^2 = 20,32; p < .0005 \ (df = 1)$$

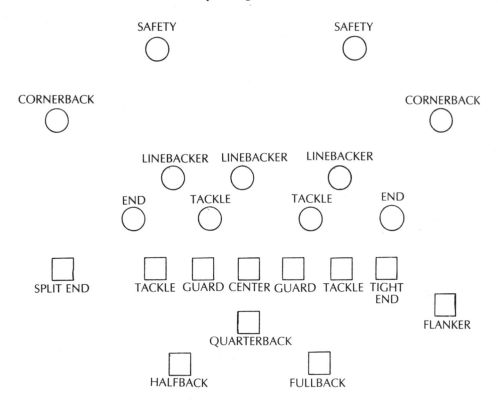

FIG. 2 SCHEMATIC OUTLINE OF FIELD POSITIONS IN PROFESSIONAL FOOTBALL

either offensive or defensive teams. The .01 level of significance, using a one-tailed test, was selected as being sufficient to warrant the rejection of the null hypothesis.

FINDINGS

Tables 2 and 3 present the number of white and black athletes occupying central and non-central offensive and defensive positions, respectively, in the major professional football leagues in 1968. It is evident from the tables that very few Negro players occupy central positions, either defensively or offensively. The significant X^2 tests of our null hypothesis give strong support to our empirical hypothesis and provide further confirmation of our theoretical hypothesis.

DISCUSSION

The preceding findings leave little doubt that only a very small proportion of black athletes occupy central positions in America's professional baseball and football organizations. However, notwithstanding our theoretical but-

tress, a number of telling questions can be raised regarding the revealed relationships between race and position occupancy. Three such questions are: (1) Does the discovered relationship between race and position occupancy indicate the actual presence of racial segregation? (2) If racial segregation is actually present, what are the "social mechanisms" linking it to centrality? (3) If racial segregation does exist in professional sports, what are its social consequences? Let us briefly consider each of these questions in turn.

DOES RACIAL SEGREGATION ACTUALLY EXIST IN SPORT?

One can argue that showing that Negro athletes infrequently occupy central positions does not confirm that they are racially segregated. They may be excluded from central positions for objective rather than arbitrary reasons. On the one hand, Negroes may not have as great a talent or skill for certain tasks as white players, and are thus excluded from selected positions for that reason. On the other hand, Negroes may possess greater athletic ability than whites for certain

TABLE 2

A Comparison of Race and Position Occupancy within Offensive Teams in Major League Football in 1968

Playing Position	American League		National League		Both Leagues	
	White	Black	White	Black	White	Black
Center	10	0	16	0	26	0
Quarterback	9	1	16	0	25	1
Right Guard	9	1	15	1	24	2
Left Guard	10	0	15	1	25	1
Right Tackle	10	0	11	5	21	5
Left Tackle	8	2	11	5	19	7
Tight end	7	3	13	3	20	6
Split end	8	2	10	6	18	8
Fullback	4	6	11	5	15	11
Halfback	3	7	7	9	10	16
Flankerback	7	3	10	6	17	9
$N =$	85	25	135	41	220	66

RACE

Position	White	Black	Total
Central	100	4	104
Non-central	120	62	182
	220	66	286

$$\chi^2 = 32,37; p < .0005 \text{ (df} = 1)$$

activities, and are accordingly found proportionately more often in some positions than others. A third alternative, of course, is that Negro athletes exclude themselves from selected positions by personal preference.

Although we are not presently prepared to fully assess the validity of each of these three perspectives, we must frankly state we find them tenuous. For example, we have found no evidence which would lead us to believe that Negro athletes have inferior ability in comparison to white athletes for any role assignment in professional baseball or football. We observe that time and again in the world of sport athletic stereotypes of Negroes have been refuted. It will be recalled that, not too long ago, there existed the myth among track authorities that Negroes were racially suited for the sprints and perhaps the shorter distance races, but did not possess the capabilities for the endurance events. The success of black athletes in long distance running events, including the Olympic marathon, in re-

cent years has dispelled the notion that Negro trackmen are speed merchants without stamina.

Similarly, we have discovered little support for the view that Negro athletes possess certain abilities in greater abundance than white athletes. We have, however, encountered some findings which indicate that a black athlete must be superior to his white counterpart before he is permitted to occupy a given position. For example, a recent study shows that the cumulative major league batting averages in 1968 were higher for Negroes at every position as follows: catcher—whites .238, blacks .279; first and third bases—whites .265, blacks .277; second and shortstop—whites .246, blacks .258; outfield—whites .253, blacks .266 (Los Angeles Times, May 15, 1969, part 3, p. 3). [3]

Finally, we find it difficult to believe that Negro athletes are largely selecting the positions which they occupy in baseball and football on the basis of personal preference. What seems to be operating is a self-fulfilling belief. A black

TABLE 3

A Comparison of Race and Position Occupancy within Defensive Teams in Major League Football in 1968

Playing Position	American League		National League		Both Leagues	
	White	Black	White	Black	White	Black
Middle Linebacker	8	2	16	0	24	2
Right Linebacker	10	0	15	1	25	1
Left Linebacker	8	2	15	1	23	3
Right End	6	4	12	4	18	8
Right Tackle	7	3	13	3	20	6
Left Tackle	7	3	10	6	17	9
Left End	8	2	11	5	19	7
Right Safety	7	3	10	6	17	9
Left Safety	7	3	10	6	17	9
Right Cornerback	2	8	6	10	8	18
Left Cornerback	1	9	3	13	4	22
$N =$	71	39	121	55	192	94

RACE

Position	White	Black	Total
Central	72	6	78
Non-central	120	88	208
	192	94	286

$$\chi^2 = 29,26; \ p < .0005 \ (df = 1)$$

athlete assumes that he doesn't have much chance at being accepted at certain positions and thus tries out for other positions where his estimate of success is much higher. As Olsen succinctly states: "He *anticipates* the white man's categorization of him, and acts accordingly" (1968, p. 170). An interesting study, we suggest, would be to compare the playing positions of white and black athletes in professional football with those they filled in college football. Our prediction is that a greater proportion of black than white athletes will be discovered to have acquired new role assignments.

Some would perhaps contend that we are overstating our case regarding racial segregation in professional sports; because:

The degree to which Negroes have moved into pro sports is astonishing. More than half the players in the National Basketball Association are Negroes—as were eight of the 10 starters in the last NBA All-Star Game. A quarter of the players in the National Football League are Negroes, and the 1967 NFL team was 40 per cent black. Nearly 25 per cent of all players in major league baseball are American Negroes, and here too a disproportionate number of the stars are not white. For example, of the top ten hitters in the National League for the 1967 season, only one was a Caucasian (Olsen, 1968, p. 170).

Nevertheless, we point out that sport seems to mirror American life at large, in that, integration has been very slow, and where it has been rather fully achieved there remain many forms of discrimination other than that of segregation.

Professional baseball is a good example of how slowly the process of integration takes place. Many herald 1947 as the year "the color line was broken" with the entrance of Jackie Robinson into major league baseball. But, as illustrated in Table 4, ten years later there were only a dozen Negro players in the National League and as late as 1960 there were only a half dozen black athletes in the American League.

TABLE 4

Distribution of White, Black and Latin American Players by Position in Major League Baseball 1956–1967

National League

Year	Catcher	Shortstop	2nd Base	3rd Base	1st Base	Outfield	Total No.
	14	10	6	7	7	12	56
1967	1	1	1	4	5	22	34
	0	1	4	1	3	7	16
	13	9	8	8	5	15	58
1966	2	2	2	3	4	21	34
	0	2	4	2	3	8	19
	15	10	10	8	7	13	63
1965	1	1	1	3	5	19	30
	1	3	3	0	5	8	19
	13	8	11	8	8	18	66
1964	2	2	1	3	5	20	33
	0	3	2	2	2	8	16
	14	8	8	14	10	22	76
1963	1	2	2	2	4	18	29
	0	3	2	0	1	3	9
1962	Data not available						
	11	5	8	8	6	18	56
1961	1	2	2	2	2	11	20
	0	3	2	0	2	5	12
	12	6	7	9	9	21	64
1960	1	2	2	1	2	11	19
	0	1	2	0	2	4	9
1959	Data not available						
	12	7	8	9	10	18	64
1958	2	1	1	0	2	8	14
	2	1	1	0	1	2	5
	11	6	8	8	11	25	69
1957	1	2	1	2	1	5	12
	1	1	0	1	0	2	5
	11	9	8	9	9	20	66
1956	1	1	3	1	1	5	12
	0	0	2	0	0	2	2

Ethnic Group	Catcher	Shortstop	2nd Base	3rd Base	1st Base	Outfield	Total No.
White	13	7	10	9	11	26	76
Black	0	0	3	2	2	14	21
Latin	2	4	1	1	1	6	15
White							
Black			Data not available				
Latin							
White	12	12	10	10	14	29	87
Black	2	0	1	1	1	12	17
Latin	1	3	2	2	1	6	13
White	12	9	13	10	12	29	85
Black	2	0	1	1	2	10	16
Latin	1	2	0	1	1	7	12
White	14	10	11	6	13	31	87
Black	2	0	2	1	1	7	13
Latin	2	2	0	1	1	5	1
White	13	11	11	9	11	34	85
Black	2	0	1	2	0	3	8
Latin	2	3	0	1	1	2	9
White	13	9	13	12	12	29	89
Black	2	1	1	1	0	9	14
Latin	1	3	0	0	1	3	8
White	10	6	9	11	11	27	74
Black	2	0	1	0	0	3	6
Latin	0	3	0	0	2	2	7
White	13	12	12	9	10	28	84
Black	0	0	0	0	2	3	5
Latin	0	2	0	1	2	2	7
White							
Black			Data not available				
Latin							
White							
Black			Data not available				
Latin							
White							
Black			Data not available				
Latin							

Table 4 does reveal, however, that there has been a substantial increase in the number of Latin American players in recent years and indicates that there exists an intermediate "brown zone" between the "white and black belts" of major league baseball. [4]

WHAT ARE THE SOCIAL MECHANISMS OF SEGREGATION?

Assuming that there is racial segregation in professional baseball and football, one is led to inquire as to what are the underlying causes of this form of discrimination. We have argued that segregation is a function of centrality and its associated interdependent dimensions of spatial location, rate of interaction and task dependency. Sociologically viewed, our theoretical rationale is probably a fairly satisfactory one; but those of a more social psychological orientation would likely want to know what sort of personal qualities and behavioral dispositions are associated with centrality which influence segregation.

There are no doubt many kinds of normative beliefs and attitudes which act as antecedent and/or intervening variables in the relationship between segregation and centrality. We specifically speculate that there is a relationship between interaction and attitudes regarding personal intimacy; and a relationship between task dependency and beliefs concerning the qualities of judgment and decision-making ability.

A major generalization of discrimination research states that: "there is a range within discriminatory practice such that there is most discrimination and most prejudice as the practice comes closer to intimate personal contact" (Berelson and Steiner, 1964, p. 511). Thus, we reason that Negroes may be excluded from central positions because these positions involve high rates of interaction which lead to greater personal contact among players than do peripheral positions in an organization.

We conject, in passing, that there may even be normative beliefs regarding the interaction of Negro athletes among themselves. In the case of professional football, for instance, black athletes are most often found at the two cornerback positions. Similarly, in the case of professional baseball, we point out that in the infield Negroes are most often found at first and third bases. While the relationship may be a spurious one, it is interesting that Negroes are placed in the extreme corners of the field in both baseball and football. A related observation is that seldom does one find two Negroes playing side-by-side in either major league baseball or football.

In treating interaction, one should, of course, distinguish between task interaction and social interaction since there is probably only a moderate correlation between the two. Although we expect that there may be a substantial degree of prejudice regarding the intermixing of white and black players off the field, we are not sure that there is marked prejudice among players concerning racial interpersonal contact on the field. [5]

We speculate that segregation in professional sports is more a function of management than playing personnel. For example, there appears to be a myth among coaches that Negro players lack judgment and decision-making ability. This myth results in black athletes being excluded from positions requiring dependent or coordinative tasks as such activities generally require greater judgment than independent tasks. In short, the central positions in major league baseball and football are typically the most responsible or so-called "brains positions." The following quotations from Olsen with respect to central and peripheral defensive positions within football organization well illustrate the matter:

"Most defensive football players have a single job to do, with little variation, but the linebacker has to exercise judgment" says a thoughtful NFL player. "He may wind up tackling the quarterback fifteen yards behind the line of scrimmage, and he may wind up knocking down a pass twenty-yards up the field. He has to be able to read plays well, everybody knows all the things the linebacker has to do. It's one of the most responsible defensive positions. Therefore, he can't be a Negro" (p. 172).

"Cornerback is not a brains position" says Bill Koman, retired St. Louis Cardinal linebacker. "You pick up the split end or the flanker and you stay with him all the way. That's it" (p. 173).

"Yassuh, white man, boss," says one NFL cornerback derisively when asked about the situation, "We ain't got the brains to play center, 'cause we can't count, but we can follow that flanker's ass all the way down the field, *yuck, yuck*" (p. 173).

In our discussion herein we have emphasized the interaction and task dependency dimensions of centrality; whereas in our empirical examination of racial segregation we stressed the dimension of spatial location. Additional limitations of our empirical analysis include the fact that our measure of spatial location was dichotomous rather than continuous in nature; and the fact that we only looked at major league baseball and football for specific one-year periods. In an effort to overcome these limitations, we extended our analysis of the racial composition of professional baseball to cover a twelve year period; and we developed an operational index of centrality which is continuous in nature and which reflects the interaction and task dependency dimensions of centrality.

Table 5 shows the approximate number of individual white and black athletes at each field position in the major leagues over a twelve year period. [6] The table also shows the rank order of playing positions in terms of the proportion of Negro players at each position. This rank order is nearly identical to that given in Table 1.

Having reaffirmed the relationship between segregation and spatial location, we turned our attention to the interaction and task dependency dimensions of centrality. We decided that the total number of "assists" made by occupants of given field positions during a season would serve as an adequate operational indicator of centrality. [7] On the one hand, assists are an indicator of the rate of interaction and the number and range of other group members with whom a position occupant interacts. On the other hand, assists are an index of the degree to which dependent tasks are associated with given positions.

We discovered that the rank order of field positions with respect to number of annual assists remained the same for both leagues for every year covered. [8] More strikingly, however, we found a perfect rank order correlation between our measures of segregation and centrality (see Table 6). Thus, we concluded that we had obtained substantial support for our theoretical hypothesis that racial segregation in professional team sports is positively related to centrality.

WHAT ARE THE SOCIAL CONSEQUENCES OF SEGREGATION?

It is exceedingly difficult to assess the social consequences of racial segregation in professional baseball and football because data is limited; and because the consequences are both manifest and latent, acute and chronic. It would appear, however, that one of the major disadvantageous consequences of segregation is the retardation of upward career mobility in professional sports. Grusky (1963) has shown that approximately three-fourths of all major league baseball managers are recruited from infield positions. [9] Therefore, to the degree that Negro athletes are denied access to central positions, they are also limited in obtaining positions of leadership in professional baseball. [10]

Grusky assumes that the position which an individual occupies influences his development of varying kinds of role skills; and further assumes that the occupancy of central positions enhances the obtainment of key role skills related to upward career mobility. These rather broad assumptions are likely related to Hopkins' (1964) set of fifteen theoretical propositions

TABLE 5

Distribution of Individual White and Black Players by Position in Major League Baseball 1956–1967

Playing Position	White Players	Black Players	Total No. of Players	% of Black Players	Rank Order % White Players
Catcher	85	5	90	.0555	1
Shortstop	39	4	43	.0930	2
2nd Base	61	7	68	.1029	3
3rd Base	41	9	50	.1800	4
1st Base	54	13	67	.1940	5
Outfield	129	61	190	.3210	6
N =	409	99	508	.1948	

TABLE 6

Ranks for Position Occupancy and Annual Assists in Professional Baseball

Field Position	Rank Order		d_1	$d_i{}^2$
	% of Whites*	Annual Assists**		
Catcher	1	1	0	0
Shortstop	2	2	0	0
2nd Base	3	3	0	0
3rd Base	4	4	0	0
1st Base	5	5	0	0
Outfield	6	6	0	0

$$rs = 1 - \frac{6\sum_{i=1}^{n} d_i{}^2}{N^3 - N} = 1 - \frac{6(0)}{6(3) - 6}; \text{ rho} = 1.00$$

(Siegel, 1956, pp. 202–213)

   * See Table 5.

  ** See Footnote 8.

regarding small groups. For example, Hopkins states that: "For any member of a small group, the greater his centrality:

1. the greater his observability;
2. the greater his conformity;
3. the greater his influence; and,
4. the higher his rank" (1964, p. 51).

Another related proposition is that centrality is positively related to liking (Grusky, 1963, p. 347; Homans, 1950, p. 133).[11]

This latter proposition suggests that there may be a "vicious cycle" operating in professional sports. Negroes, because they are not liked by the white establishment, are placed in peripheral positions; and, as a result of this placement, do not have the opportunity of high rates of interaction with teammates, and do not receive the potential positive sentiment which might accrue from such interaction. In view of the nature of our problem, our discussion is likely too brief and superficial. However, we hope that we have been successful in directing the attention of sport sociologists to the matter of integration in American sport, and in providing stimulation for further theoretical and empirical analyses of the subject.

REFERENCES

American Football League Official Autographed Yearbook 1968. Dallas, Sports Underwriters, Inc., 1968.

American League Red Book. Boston, American League Publicity Department.

Baseball Register. St. Louis, Sporting News.

Berelson, B. and Steiner, G. A.: Human Behavior—an Inventory of Scientific Findings. New York, Harcourt, Brace & World, 1964.

Blalock, H. M. Jr.: Occupational discrimination: some theoretical propositions. Soc. Prob., 9:240, 1962.

Boyle, R. H.: Sport—Mirror of American Life. Boston, Little, Brown Co., 1963.

Charnofsky, H.: The major league professional baseball player: self-conception versus the popular image. Int. Rev. Sport Sociol. 3, 1968.

Grusky, O.: The effects of formal structure on managerial recruitment: a study of baseball organization. Sociometry, 26:345, 1963.

Homans, G. C.: The Human Group. New York, Harcourt, Brace & World, Inc., 1950.

Hopkins, T. K.: The Exercise of Influence in Small Groups. Totowa, N.J., Bedminster Press, 1964.

Loy, J. W. and Sage, J. N.: The Effects of Formal Structure on Organizational Leadership: An Investigation of Interscholastic Baseball Teams. Paper presented at the 2nd International Congress of Sport Psychology, November 1, 1968, Washington, D.C.

Moore, H. E.: Discrimination, In A Dictionary of the Social Sciences. Edited by Julius Gould and William L. Kolb. Glencoe, New York, The Free Press 1964.

Olsen, J.: The Black Athlete—A Shameful Story. New York: Time, Inc., 1968.

National Football League Official Autographed Yearbook 1968. Dallas, Sports Underwriters, Inc., 1968.

National League Green Book. Cincinnati, National League Public Relations Department.

Rosenblatt, A.: Negroes in baseball: the failure of success. Trans-Action, 4:51, 1967 with a reply by Whitehead, 4:63, 1967.

Siegel, S.: Nonparametric Statistics. New York, McGraw-Hill Book Co., Inc., 1956.

Study Indicates Cracking Majors Harder for Blacks. Los Angeles Times, May 15, 1969, Part III, p. 3.

Zanger, J.: Pro Football 1968. New York, Pocket Books, 1968.

NOTES

1. The criterion of fifty games was established in order to eliminate the partial participant, such as the pinch hitter or runner, the player brought up from the minor leagues on a part-time basis, the occasional utility man, and the unestablished rookie trying to make the team at any position.

Players were ethnically classified as Caucasians, Negroes or Latin Americans. The latter group was excluded from most analyses, however, as it was impossible in terms of the sources available to determine which Latin American athletes were Negroes.

Players at all positions were considered except for pitchers. They were excluded for purposes of analysis because: (1) data comparable to that collected for other players was not available, (2) the high rate of interchangeability among pitchers precluded accurate recording of data, and (3) pitchers are in a sense only part-time players, in that they typically play in only one game out of four, or if relief pitchers play only a few innings in any given game. In order that the reader may make certain comparisons later in the paper, we note at this point that "only 13 of the 207 pitchers in 1968 major league rosters were Negroes" (Olsen, 1968, p. 170).

2. The major difficulties we experienced in data collection were associated with the problems of determining the race of the players and in determining who were the first string or starting players. In the case of major league football, we used the "official yearbooks" to ascertain the race of given players as these sources contained photographs of the members of every team in a given league. Zanger's text was used as a means of determining the first string or starting lineup for each team. However, Zanger's lineups were preseason forecasts based upon the players' performance the previous season. A more accurate means of recording would have been to determine the players having the most playing time at each position for every team during the 1968 season.

An indication, however, that the data which we present in Tables 2 and 3 is reasonably accurate are the following facts cited from a study made independently of our own.:

"On one typical weekend in the 1967 NFL season, no Negro center started a game. Of the 32 offensive guards in the starting lineups of NFL teams, 29 were white" (Olsen, 1968, p. 171)

". . . (on that same typical weekend in the 1967 season, 48 linebackers lumbered out on the field to start NFL games, and 45 of them, or 94 per cent, were white). . ." (Olsen, 1968, p. 172)

3. For a more complete account of how Negro athletes must be superior to white athletes in professional baseball in order to maintain their positions, see Rosenblatt, 1967. Finally, we note that the three outfield positions were considered as a single category since data were not available for each of the three outfield positions taken separately.

4. It would be interesting to find out whether or not "darker" Latin American athletes are more often found in the outfield than the "lighter" Latin players.

There are some small indications that "quota systems" are operating for American Negro players and Latin American players, in that, if members of one group are prominent occupants of a given field position within a league, then the members of the other group tend to be predominant at another playing position. For a discussion of the social relations between American Negro and Latin American players, see Boyle, 1963, pp. 108–113.

5. Charnofsky (1967), for example, presents evidence which suggests that while there exists a degree of racial prejudice among a number of players, the majority of athletes in professional baseball hold favorable attitudes toward minority group members on their teams. We note, however, that off the field the problem of discrimination may be a horse of a different color. For example, the 1969 season is the first where several teams have set forth explicit policies assuring the racial integration of teammates on the road via mixed room assignments.

6. As is evident from Table 4, we were unable to obtain relevant data for a number of seasons for the two major leagues between 1956 and 1967. However, there does not appear to be much change in playing personnel from one year to the next. Moreover, our figures provide a conservative estimate of the racial composition of professional baseball, in that the missing data includes more white players.

It was not difficult to keep track of a small number of players switching leagues over the period sampled, but a small number of players switching playing positions over the period covered did pose a bit of a problem. We arbitrarily assigned them the position where they had played the most games in their major league career.

7. An assist is the official credit awarded in the scoring of a game to a player who throws a ball in such a way that it results in a putout. Data regarding assists were obtained from the *American League Red Book* and the *National League Green Books*. These are annual publications of the two major leagues which report vital statistics about all players, teams and games each season.

8. In the scoring of a game, the strikeouts made by the pitcher which are caught by the catcher are recorded as putouts for the catcher. For purposes of analysis we considered such putouts as assists. We reasoned that the catcher calls the pitch and assists in making the strikeouts by receiving the thrown ball from the pitcher. We note that a strikeout is recorded regardless of whether the ball is caught or not.

An example of the consistency of the number of annual assists by position for both leagues is the following data for the 1963, 1964 and 1965 seasons:

Year	American League	Position	National League
1963	10,508	C	9,946
	4,724	SS	4,749
	4,427	2nd	4,253
	3,176	3rd	3,029
	1,119	1st	1,002
	325	Out	323
1964	10,713	C	10,112
	4,775	SS	4,939
	4,425	2nd	4,404
	3,225	3rd	3,096

Year	American League	Position	National League
1964	1,059	1st	1,018
	308	Out	322
1965	10,461	C	10,454
	4,696	SS	4,886
	4,274	2nd	4,831
	3,341	3rd	3,093
	1,050	1st	1,045
	274	Out	292

9. In Grusky's study about twenty-five per cent of the managers were found to be ex-catchers. Recent investigations by Loy and Sage concerning collegiate baseball show that college coaches and college team captains are most often recruited from infield positions; especially that of catcher. Moreover, their findings indicate that, although there are relatively few Negroes playing college baseball, there are proportionately more Negroes in outfield than infield positions.

10. It is only recently that a token number of former Negro athletes have been hired as coaches in professional sports; and to date there are no Negro head coaches in major league football or Negro managers in major league baseball.

11. See Hopkins, 1964, pp. 112–117 for a critique of this proposition.

ascription and position: a comparative analysis of "stacking" in professional football *

DONALD W. BALL

One of the emergent characteristics of the sociology of the sixties was the development of a substantive focus on sport. Among the major reasons for this development were the increasingly large number of persons and volume of resources involved in sport and the recognition of the pre-eminently social nature of sport as a form of conduct.

Sport as a social activity is particularly amenable to general sociological scrutiny because sports *qua* games may be heuristically treated as closed systems, with explicit and codified normative regulations, for example, rulebooks, and precise and public measures of outcomes, performances, efficiency, and the like. Such an approach is basically one of a "sociology *through* sport," using sport data to address more general sociological questions.

Although sport may be treated "as if" it is a

bounded system, empirically it is embedded in the larger society—acting and reacting and mirroring that broader societal context. Sport is neither trivial nor merely a laboratory for the sociologist, but an important dimension of human experience and concern. This perspective is one that focuses on "sport and society" or the "sociology *of* sport," viewing sport as a social reality *sui generis*.

The following discussion will be concerned with patterns of differential treatment of professional football players in Canada and the United States. Such differences will be considered both with regard to (1) the variables of race and national origins, that is, a sociology *of* sport; and (2) in terms of which of two theoretical models can best account for any differences found; that is, a sociology *through* sport.

I

In considering the differential treatment of professional athletes on the basis of race, there are two broad approaches. One, "the Jackie Robinson story" basically says (regarding blacks), "you never had it so good" (Boyle, 1963; Olsen, 1968). This view emphasizes the opportunities for mobility made available to minority group members by professional sport. Thus, professional sport is seen as an accessible "legitimate opportunity structure" (Cloward and Ohlin, 1960).

The other view might be called "the Harry Edwards corrective" (Edwards, 1969). This perspective acknowledges the availability of entrance into sport for minority members, but

Reprinted from Canadian Review of Sociology and Anthropology, *10*:97–113, 1973. Copyright 1973 by Canadian Review of Sociology and Anthropology, Montreal, Quebec H3G1M8.

*I am indebted to Cameron Ball, Neil Ball, and Philip Pollard for their help in procuring some of the data on players in the Canadian Football League used in this article. This project was partially supported by a University of Victoria Faculty Research Grant (08 518). Helpful comments were received from colleagues when earlier versions of this material were presented in seminars at the University of Alberta and the University of Calgary; from Brian Currie of the University of Victoria, and John Loy of the University of Massachusetts. A more extensive formulation was presented to the symposium on Man, Sport, and Contemporary Society, Queens College of the City University of New York, March 1972.

points to continued discriminatory practices within the context of the structure of sport. Of special attention by this school have been their allegations of "stacking."

Stacking, the practice of positioning athletes in team sports on the basis of particularistic rather than universalistic characteristics has been alleged and described by Edwards (1969), Meggysey (1970), and Olsen (1968); and empirically demonstrated by Loy and McElvogue (1970), along with confirmatory research by Brower (1972). Essentially, *stacking in sports involves assignment to a playing position, an achieved status, on the basis of an ascribed status* (Davis, 1949:96–117). A focal concern by sociologists of sport has been the stacking of team members on the ascriptive basis of race, (for example, Loy and McElvogue, 1970; Brower, 1972; and Edwards, 1969). As is the case with much material of a sociological perspective, the works cited above are primarily or exclusively referring to situations in the United States.

In the following discussion, the theoretical formulation and empirical investigation begun on United States professional football by Loy and McElvogue (1970) will be applied to Canadian sport, replicated on race (also see Smith and Grindstaff, 1970; Barnes, 1971), and *extended to national origins* with comparative data drawn from professional football in the United States and in Canada from the Canadian Football League (CFL). Additionally, an alternative theory will be proposed as of equal or greater power in explaining Canadian patterns.

II

The Centrality Theory

Drawing upon Grusky's theory of organization structure (1963) and Blalock's propositions regarding occupational discrimination (1962), Loy and McElvogue (1970:5–7) have formulated a theory to explain the disproportionate presence—stacking—of blacks in some positions, and their practical absence from others in professional football and baseball. In doing so, they conceive of teams as work organizations, and the positions within them as analogous to occupations.

Employing baseball teams *qua* formal organizations for his empirical examples, Grusky has asserted that the formal structure of an organiza-

tion systematically patterns the behaviours associated with its constituent positions along three interdependent dimensions: spatial location, nature of organizational tasks, and frequency of interaction. The major theoretical thrust of Grusky's organizational model is contained in the statement that "all else being equal, the more central one's spatial location: (1) the greater the likelihood dependent or coordinative tasks will be performed and (2) the greater the rate of interaction with occupants of other positions. Also, the performance of dependent tasks is positively related to frequency of interaction" (1963:346).

Centrality, then refers to (1) spatial location and (2) the attendant kinds of tasks and interaction rates. From a structural standpoint it is best operationalized, at least in the case of fixed-position team sports taken-as-formal-organizations (for example, football or baseball), by spatial location.

Like Grusky, Blalock's consideration of interaction, task dependency, and occupational discrimination turned to baseball for empirical examples to bolster the theoretical propositions. Blalock's propositions can be readily synthesized with Grusky's model. As Loy and McElvogue put it, "since the dimensions of interaction and task dependency treated by Blalock are included in the concept of centrality, we integrated his propositions under a more general one, stating that *discrimination is positively related to centrality*" (1970:7; emphasis added).

Centrality and Professional Team Sports

In professional team sports a specific variant of occupational discrimination is *stacking:* the arbitrary inclusion or exclusion of persons vis-a-vis a playing position on the basis of ascriptive status, for example, race. Thus, Loy and McElvogue predicted as their specific theoretical proposition that stacking, a form of "racial segregation in professional team sports is positively related to centrality" (1970:7).

The Original Test of the Proposition

For their first test of the prediction, Loy and McElvogue turned to major league baseball in the United States. Using 1967 data and treating catchers and infield positions as central, the outfield as non-central (and excluding pitchers as unique and neither), they found that 7 out of 10 white players ($N = 132$) occupied central positions, while only 1 out of 3 blacks ($N = 55$) were so located (1970:8–10; also see 15–24). Statistically significant beyond the .0005 level, the baseball data were strongly supportive of their model and the stacking prediction it generated. They next turned their attention to United States professional football.

III

The Case of Professional Football

Although there are differences between the rules and positions regarding professional football in Canada and the United States, these are increasingly more historical than actually differentiating (on the convergence between the two games, see Cosentino, 1969). Table 1 indicates the central and non-central positions which characterize both offensive and defensive formations, and subsumes the minor differences between the two sets of procedures in force on each side of the border.

Data

Loy and McElvogue's American football data (1970:11–13) were drawn from yearbooks for the 1968 seasons of the American Football League and the National Football League and classified all starting players (except specialty teams) by offensive or defensive position, along with race, black or white. All data on American professional football employed in the following is taken from their study.

The data on the Canadian Football League personnel presented here is for the 1971 season. It is drawn from the *Canadian Football League Player Photos, Official 1971 Collection*, a widely distributed promotional device, and checked where possible against other and similar sources

(on the rationale for using such mass-circulation-based data see Ball, 1967:452–453). These materials provide a 75 per cent sample of the 32-man roster allowed each of the nine teams in the league, and like the Loy and McElvogue data, are based upon pre-season, but accurate, forecasts. For each player information is available on position, on race (from a photograph), and usually on national origin and on prior education and playing experience. Although a 75 per cent sample should yield an $N = 216$, due to missing information it is reduced slightly here to $N = 209$. On the whole, visual inspection suggests the sample is representative. However, it is slightly biased toward imports in terms of national origins.

Although this attribute, national origin, is an important independent variable, its bias is neutralized by percentaging against the unbalanced marginal totals. However, because of the limitations of the sample, the following is claimed to be no more than a "demonstration" (Garfinkel, 1964), rather than a more rigorous "investigation." (On the methodological problems of using rosters, for example the lack of stability within seasons, see Smith and Grindstaff, 1970:60–62). Finally, though the data cover only one season in each case, other research has shown aggregate sport data to be quite stable over time (on international figure skating, see Ball, 1971; on baseball, see Loy and McElvogue, 1970:15–22).

Centrality, Stacking, and Race: A Comparison

According to the Loy-McElvogue hypothesis, blacks in professional football will be stacked at non-central positions and excluded from central ones. Comparing their data on the American NFL

TABLE 1
Central and Non-Central Positions on Offence and Defence *

	Offence	Defence
Central	centre quarterback guards	linebackers
Non-central	tackles ends flankers, wide receivers running backs	tackles ends backs, safeties

*Adapted from Loy and McElvogue (1970:10–12).

(columns B and D of Table 2) with data on the CFL (columns A and C) indicates a similar pattern in each case: blacks are virtually excluded from central positions in professional football on either side of the border. The similarity of the patterns is as striking as the moral implications are obvious; neither virtues nor vices are respecters of national borders (also see Smith and Grindstaff, 1970:47–66; and more generally, Cosentino, 1969, on the "Americanization" of Canadian football).

IV

Centrality, National Origins, and Stacking

Unlike professional football in the United States, Canadian football has been historically cross-cut by another ascriptive status of its players; national origin, Canadians and imports (for the latter, read Americans). Americans have been playing football in Canada at least since 1912, in the forerunners of the CFL, the rugby unions (Cosentino, 1969:48–49).

It should be understood that the categorization of national origins to be used here, Canadians and imports, is not the same as that used by the CFL itself. The League's definition emphasizes prior experience as well as citizenship and nativ-

ity, the criterion herein employed. Thus, an American player without United States high school or college experience becomes a non-import under League definitions. Put another way, national origins are ascriptive, while League definitions may be achieved. Consistency suggests the utility of opting for the former as an analytical variable.

Canadians and Imports: The Data

When nativity is considered, the null form of the stacking hypothesis predicts no differences between the proportion of centrally located Canadians and imports. In other words, the relationship should be one of parity.

Following Loy and McElvogue (1970), Table 3 presents the distribution of imports (Americans) and Canadians in the CFL in terms of the centrality model. It is clear that whether one looks at over-all patterns, or at offensive or defensive alignments separately, imports predominate over Canadian players in terms of the proportion of central positions they occupy. The difference on offence is particularly interesting, since almost half of the central Canadians are at one position only ($N = 8$), that of centre. Smith and Grindstaff (1970:36) have described the centre as a position usually manned by Canadians and "generally acknowledged to require less skill."

TABLE 2
Race of Players by Centrality of Position for Canadian and US Professional Leagues (adjusted percentages) *

	Percentage of whites		Percentage of blacks	
Position	(A) Cdn.	(B) US †	(C) Cdn.	(D) US †
Offence				
Central	47	45	06	02
Non-Central	53	55	94	98
Total percentage	100	100	100	100
N	97*	220	19*	66
Defence				
Central	28	37	—	06
Non-Central	72	63	100	94
Total percentage	100	100	100	100
N	83*	192	12	94

*Percentage adjusted to compensate for the additional position in Canadian football. This position is non-central; thus the non-central raw number is multiplied by .875 (7/8) to equalize with US formations. Adjusted base numbers, upon which percentages are calculated are: $97 \approx 90$; $83 \approx 75$; and $19 \approx 17$. This procedure is not necessary in subsequent tables where comparisons are limited to CFL players only.
†US data for 1968 from Loy and McElvogue (1970:10–12).

TABLE 3

National Origins of CFL Players and Centrality of Position

Position	Percentage of Canadians	Percentage of Imports
Central, all	27	35
Non-Central, all	73	65
Total	100	100
N	94	110
Offence		
Central	34	41
Non-Central	66	59
Total	100	100
N	50	64
Defence		
Central	18	26
Non-Central	82	74
Total	100	100
N	44	46

Thus, if central positions are assumed to be in some ways more "difficult" as well as more "desirable," Canadians predominate at only the least of these. Additionally, because of the restrictive quota on imports (maximum of 14 out of 32 players *per* team in 1971), quantitative differences are actually more extreme than their apparent magnitude. [1]

To demonstrate that Canadians and imports are differentially distributed is not to demonstrate "stacking" *per se*, however. It is frequently alleged that imports are the more skilled players by virtue of their superior training rather than their ability; especially in terms of their college and university football experience (see former import Hardimon Curetan, quoted in Barnes, 1971:43–54). At the same time, although perhaps not widely recognized, the fact is that approximately half of the Canadians in the Canadian Football League played football while attending college or university in the United States. Such "crash courses" have often been the instigation of CFL teams themselves (Barnes, 1971).

Thus, examining Canadian players in terms of prior playing experience would allow for an assessment of a *training* versus *stacking* hypothesis. Table 4 presents data on Canadian players in terms of centrality and whether or not they played collegiate football in the United States or had some other form of prior experi-

ence, for example, Canadian university, junior football, or high school participation.

If training accounts for the differential positioning of imports and Canadians, it should virtually disappear in the cases of Canadians with United States collegiate experience. From these data can be seen: (1) over-all, American collegiate experience is associated with centrality; (2) that this association is especially marked on offence; but (3) slightly reversed for the defensive unit. However, recalling Table 3, neither the over-all nor the offensive proportions of American-trained Canadians at central positions reaches the percentage of such positions occupied by imports. Although these data do not compel the acceptance of a stacking hypothesis, they do argue the rejection of one based upon training alone.

The reversal of the association between American training and centrality when the defence is considered is somewhat anomalous. However, upon closer examination it appears to be at least partly artificial. Few American-trained Canadians play defence: less than half as many as the "others" without such experience (13 to 20). Further, most Canadians *cum* American collegians in central positions are on offensive units, while the reverse is true for those without such experience.

This last is part of a more general pattern. "Most teams play more of their imports on of-

TABLE 4

Prior Background Experience of CFL Players and Centrality of Position

Position	Percentage US college	Percentage Other
Central, all	31	20
Non-Central, all	69	80
Total	100	100
N	45	44
Offense		
Central	37	21
Non-Central	62	79
Total	100	100
N	32	14
Defence		
Central	15	20
Non-Central	85	80
Total	100	100
N	13	30
Central Positions		
Offence	86	33
Defence	14	67
Total	100	100
N	14	9

fense rather than defense because coaches feel that normally it takes more talent and experience to play offense, and that it is possible to train Canadian players with less experience to do an adequate job of defense" (Smith and Grindstaff, 1970:60). The data in Table 5 substantiate this statement. Imports predominate over Canadians on offence, but American-trained Canadians do so especially compared to those without such experience.

Centrality: An Overview

In general, the ascriptive statuses of Canadians and imports do appear to be differentially positioned in terms of the centrality model. Assuming, for whatever reasons, that central positions are more desirable or more rewarding, the ascribed status of imports is associated with such location, and that of Canadians with the alternative of non-centrality. When Canadians are categorized as those with United States collegiate football experience, or those without it, the deficit position is explained and reduced, but not removed.

Still, the differences are not of sufficient magnitude to warrant an exclusive employment of the centrality model as an explanatory tool in the case of differential positioning by national

TABLE 5

Offensive and Defensive Players in the CFL by National Origin and Prior Background Experience

Position	Percentage by national origin		Percentage by background, Canadians only	
	Imports	Canadians	US College	Others
Offence	58	53	71	26
Defence	42	47	29	74
Total	100	100	100	100
N	110	94	45	44

origins in the CFL. In sum, centrality shows more power as regards stacking and the ascriptive criterion of race than it does regarding nativity.

V

Primary and Supporting Players: An Alternative Model

As does the Loy and McElvogue model, this model looks at football teams as a set of positions constituting a formal work organization. However, where the centrality model looks to spatial location, the primary-supporting model looks to organizational goals and the nature of organizationally defined tasks.

The overreaching goal of a football team is to win games. To accomplish this, teams are divided into subunits or separate organizations within organizations: the offensive and defensive units.

Within each of these organizations, offence and defence, positions can be differentiated on the basis of task-orientation into primary and supporting positions. The former, the *primary positions*, are those within the organization charged with the basic achievement and realization of the organization's goals. *Supporting positions*, on the other hand, are defined as those responsible for assisting the primary positions in their efforts toward goal-achievement, but not ordinarily directly involved in such accomplishment. Put grossly, primary positions (and thus their occupants, the players) are doers; supporting positions are helpers (for a more generalized and abstract, but similar approach, see Etzioni, 1961:93–96).

When the offensive unit of a football team is considered in terms of the primary-supporting model, with its goal of moving the ball and scoring points, the primary positions are the quarterback, the running backs, and the pass catchers, that is, the ends, flankers, and wide receivers. These are the positions sometimes called by the coaches the "skill positions" (see, for instance, Oates, 1972). The supporting positions, whose task is to assist the goal-directed activities of the primary positions, are the offensive guards, the offensive tackles, and the centre. These are the basic positions charged with blocking so that others may advance the ball. Although the centre handles the ball on every play, it is only to deliver it to the quarterback (except in kicking situations), at the quarterback's initiative, and from a symbolically subordinate posture. It may

be noted that although the offensive guards and centre are central in terms of spatial location their tasks are supporting rather than primary.

A further refinement within the primary offensive positions is the distinction between those that are *proactive* and initiate goal-directed activity and/or carry it out independently, and those that are *reactive* or dependent upon the activities of other primary positions for participation. Quarterbacks initiate activity and act independently, and running backs act independently once in possession of the ball: these positions are proactive. Ends, flankers, and wide receivers must wait for a pass to realize their primary, goal-related tasks: they are reactive.

The language of football points to the primary-supporting distinction within the defensive alignment. The common collective term for the defensive backs and safeties is the "secondary." By implication other defensive positions are primary—and so they are. In combination or alone it is the task of the defensive tackles and ends, the "front four," along with the linebackers, to stop running plays before the ball carrier can get past them, and/or get to the quarterback before he can throw a pass. Only if these positions fail to do so does the secondary formally come into play to stop a runner who has progressed downfield or to break up or intercept a pass or to stop a successful receiver from making further progress. Thus, on defence the primary positions are the defensive tackles and ends and the linebackers. The supporting positions are the defensive backs and safeties of the secondary. (Table 6 summarizes the above six paragraphs.)

VI

The data in Table 7 array the same information in terms of the primary-supporting model which were shown in Tables 3 and 4 with the centrality model.

As the data show, in all cases imports are more likely to occupy primary rather than supporting positions, while in only one case, offence, do Canadians reach the parity of a 50–50 split. This despite the fact that over half (56 per cent in 1971) of each roster must be Canadian. The difference between imports and Canadians is most dramatic in the case of the initiating, independent proactive offence positions and the dependent reactors: where imports are proactors in almost three out of every four cases, Canadians are reactors two out of three times. The effect of United States collegiate experience is mixed and

TABLE 6

Primary and Supporting Positions on Offence and Defence

	Offence	Defence
Primary	quarterback * running backs * flankers, wide receivers † ends †	tackles ends linebackers
Supporting	centre guards tackles	backs safeties

* Proactive
† Reactive

relatively slight except in the case of the proactive-reactive distinction, where United States collegiate experience is almost twice as likely to be associated with the occupancy of proactive positions compared to a lack of such experience. But never does this former group equal the proportion of imports at primary positions in general.

Comparison with the Loy-McElvogue centrality model (Tables 3 and 4) indicates that the primary-supporting model shows much greater differentiation with regard to national origins of

TABLE 7

Primary and Supporting Players in the CFL by National Origin and Prior Background Experience

	Percentage by national origin		Percentage by background, Canadians only	
Position	Imports	Canadians	US College	Others
Primary, all	68	49	47	50
Supporting, all	32	51	53	50
Total	100	100	100	100
N	110	94	45	44
Offence:				
Primary	73	50	47	57
Supporting	27	50	53	43
Total	100	100	100	100
N	64	50	32	14
Defence:				
Primary	61	48	46	47
Supporting	39	52	54	53
Total	100	100	100	100
N	46	44	13	30
Offence, Primary Only:				
Proactive	72	36	47	25
Reactive	28	64	53	75
Total	100	100	100	100
N	47	25	15	8

CFL players. However, the centrality scheme was originally developed to explain racial differentiation in professional team sports. Thus, Table 8 compares Canadians and imports while controlling for race.

As Table 8 shows, we might speak, none too figuratively it seems, about the "white niggers of the CFL" (after Vallières, 1971). If the assumption is again made that, like central positions, primary positions are the more desirable and rewarding—then only in the case of defence where Canadians are stacked (see Table 5 and accompanying discussion) does the proportion of Canadians exceed that of blacks in primary positions. Further, blacks themselves are traditionally stacked in the supporting defensive secondary (Loy and McElvogue, 1970:13).

VII

The assumption that central and/or primary positions are somehow more rewarding and more desirable has been invoked several times in the preceding pages (also see Homans,

1950:140–144). If the assumption is valid, the question becomes one of measurement: what data might be brought to bear to compare (1) the differential rewards of central and non-central along with primary and secondary positions in terms of national origins of the players; and (2) the magnitude of these differences when it is the two models that are compared.

Salary provides just such a measure. Barnes (1971:144–145) lists average salaries by position for each team and for the CFL as a whole for the 1967 season. Table 9 presents this salary information. In interpreting these figures, a *caveat* should be kept in mind. Barnes's definitions of Canadians and imports are those of the League, not the criterion of national origin used here. Thus, some Canadians as *per* League classification may be imports or Americans in terms of actual nativity. Therefore, salary differentials are, if anything, conservative, since some high-salaried Americans could be classified as Canadians by the League's standards.

The findings emerging from Table 9 are of

TABLE 8

Primary and Supporting Players in the CFL by National Origin and Race of Imports

Position	Percentage of imports		Percentage of Canadians
	whites	blacks	
Primary, all	71	60	49
Supporting, all	29	40	51
Total	100	100	100
N	80	30	94
Offence			
Primary	71	79	50
Supporting	29	21	50
Total	100	100	100
N	45	19	50
Defence			
Primary	71	27	48*
Supporting	29	73	52
Total	100	100	100
N	35	11	44
Offence, primary only			
Proactive	75	67	36
Reactive	25	33	64
Total	100	100	100
N	32	15	25

*Includes one black.

TABLE 9

Differences in Average Salaries: Centrality and Primary-Supporting Models by National Origins *

	Centrality Model				Primary-Supporting Model		
	Imports	Canadians	Difference		Imports	Canadians	Difference
Offence				*Offence*			
Central	$13,300	$13,200	$ 100	Primary	$13,612	$12,295	$1,317
Non-Central	13,087	8,958	4,129	Supporting	12,783	8,516	5,267
			$\bar{X}=2,114$				$\bar{X}=3,483$
Defence				*Defence*			
Central	11,375	8,625	2,750	Primary	12,191	8,708	3,483
Non-Central	12,783	8,516	4,267	Supporting	13,750	8,050	5,700
			$\bar{X}=3,508$				$\bar{X}=4,591$
Combined average			2,811				3,941

*Calculated from Barnes, 1971:144–145.

several kinds. First, in all comparisons imports are rewarded more highly than Canadians. Vallières has described "white niggers" as "the cheap labor that the predators of industry, commerce, and high finance are so fond of" (1971:19). Originally applied to Francophones vis-a-vis Anglophones, "white nigger" also fits the salary situation of Canadians in the Canadian Football League.

Secondly, in the case of imports on defence, the expected salary differential is reversed for both models. Since blacks are traditionally stacked here the finding is all the more surprising. In all other cases (six out of eight), however, differences are as expected, with central and primary players, whether Canadians or imports reported as more highly rewarded.

Thirdly, when the two models are compared, the magnitude of differential rewards is greater for the primary-supporting model compared to that based upon centrality—in effect, validating the greater utility of the former over the latter, at least in the case of Canadian football.

VIII

OVERVIEW

The purpose of this paper has been twofold: (1) from the standpoint of the sociology *of* sport, to investigate patterns of stacking of imports and Canadians in the Canadian Football League, using the basic ascriptive difference of nativity rather than race; and (2) from the perspective of sociology through sport to compare two models

of ascription-based organizational-occupational differentiation.

DISCUSSION

Are Canadians discriminated against in the CFL? The data are relatively clear-cut. They are less likely to occupy central positions than imports, and still less likely to perform at primary positions compared to secondary ones. Further, their average salaries are lower than those of imports, especially within the context of the primary-supporting model. At the same time, Canadian players with American collegiate football experience are more likely than other Canadians to be located at central or primary positions, though never to the same extent as imports. Thus, while United States collegiate experience reduces the differences between imports and Canadians, these differences do not disappear. Is this discrimination? Unless discrimination is operationally defined it remains a moral meaning, subject to the relativization of all such terms. However, a majority of roster positions coupled with a minority of primary or central positions does demonstrate a *prima facie* case worthy of further consideration.

Both Loy and McElvogue (1970:18) and Smith and Grindstaff (1970), although referring to race, argue that stacking is a function of team management rather than of the players themselves. In 1969 in the CFL all 9 head coaches were Americans, as were 31 of the 32 assistant coaches, and 6 of the 9 general managers (the most recent year for which data were readily available (Smith and Grindstaff, 1970:4).

In effect what seems to happen is this: when Americans coaching in the CFL have a first-year prospect from the United States, they also have a set of expectations about his abilities based upon their knowledge of the calibre of football characteristic of the rookie's school, the level of competition, the coaching he likely received, etc. Alternatively, a new American prospect may have had professional experience in the United States to generate such expectations among the coaches. For the Canadian collegiate football player (or one up from junior football) no such expectations exist. In a word, the American coaches know a lot about American football. They know little about football in Canada outside of the CFL. Thus, they are more likely to (1) go with the American import, who if not a proven quantity is likely to generate great expectations; and (2) assume that Canadians, especially those without American collegiate experience, are simply less skilled or talented since they haven't been measured on the recognized testing grounds of the United States playing fields.

If discrimination is too strong a word, *benign neglect* is not. These same coaches are, after all, responsible for the similar distribution of blacks at central and non-central positions in both American and Canadian professional football.

The question can also be raised as to why the centrality model is most powerful with regard to stacking and race and works best in the United States, and the primary-supporting model is more useful in accounting for stacking by national origin in the CFL.

First of all, though both models are concerned with ascription, there is a vast difference between race and nativity. And although there are many stereotypical assumptions about black athletes, especially in the United States (see for instance, Edwards and Russell, 1971; Brower, 1972), it is not clear that there are similarly extensive attributions about Canadians, and by Americans concerning the former's athletic ability (however, see Barnes, 1971).

Secondly, the centrality model was first (and most thoroughly) tested with regard to baseball, while the primary-supporting model was formulated specifically with regard to Canadian football, thus helping to account for its greater power regarding the CFL.

Thirdly, the centrality scheme emphasizes ascriptive differentiation on the basis of extra-organizational social characteristics, for example, race and interaction patterns. The primary-supporting model starts with organizational characteristics and then looks for ascriptive differentiation among members—and in the case of American-controlled but quota-bound Canadian football it finds them.

In the United States situation there are no formal rules which require blacks to be on team rosters. In Canada, a fixed proportion of each roster must be Canadian. The primary-supporting model points to where those least talented or skilled will, in effect, be likely to do the least damage. Thus, blacks in the United States (and American imports in Canada) play strictly on the basis of ability—in fact they may have to be better than their white counterparts (Rosenblatt, 1967)—but Canadians in the CFL are guaranteed their quota. Therefore, a task-based model should be more useful in predicting where they may be stacked, as the primary-supporting scheme in fact is.

In sum, Canadians in the CFL are stacked: on defence, in supporting and reactive positions; and even with American collegiate experience they are excluded from the more rewarding and desirable positions. This differential treatment is also reflected in the lower salaries they receive compared to those of imports. Whether caused by discrimination or benign neglect is a matter of definition—even if functionally equivalent in terms of consequences.

Needless to say, the usual *caveats* concerning further research apply here. The explanation of stacking which postulates a lack of expectations about Canadian players is speculative, but worthy of further interest. If valid, it is just one more tile in the mosaic of the branch plant economy. Finally, as will be obvious to many, this is not a "fan's-eye" view, but a sociological one. The fan may look for, and to, exceptions such as high-salaried, Canadian-trained quarterback Russ Jackson; the sociologist points instead to patterns. And, as has often been the case, the exposition of deviant-case analysis by laymen often functions to bolster the state of things as they are.

REFERENCES

Ball, Donald W.: Toward a sociology of toys: inanimate objects, socialization and the demography of the doll world. Sociol. Q., *8*:447, 1976.

Ball, Donald W.: "The cold war on ice: the politics of international figure skating." Paper presented to the third Canadian Symposium on Sport Psychology, Vancouver, 1971.

Barnes, LaVerne: The Plastic Orgasm. Toronto, McClelland and Stewart, 1971.

Blalock, Hubert M., Jr.: Occupational discrimination: some theoretical propositions. Soc. Prob., 9:240, 1962.

Boyle, Robert H.: Sport—Mirror of American Life. Boston, Little, Brown, 1963.

Brower, Jonathon J.: The racial basis of the division of labor among players in the National Football League as a function of racial stereotypes. Presented to the Pacific Sociological Association, Portland, April 13–15, 1972.

Cloward, Richard A., and Ohlin, Lloyd E.: Delinquency and Opportunity. Glencoe, New York, The Free Press, 1960.

Cosentino, Frank: Canadian Football: The Grey Cup Years. Toronto, Musson, 1969.

Davis, Kingsley: Human Society. New York, Macmillan, 1949.

Edwards, Harry: The Revolt of the Black Athlete. New York, The Free Press, 1969.

Edwards, Harry, and Russell, Bill: Racism: a prime factor in the determination of black athletic superiority. Presented to the American Sociological Association, Denver, September, 1971.

Etzioni, Amitai: A Comparative Analysis of Complex Organizations. Glencoe, N.Y., The Free Press, 1961.

Garfinkel, Harold: Studies of the routine grounds of everyday activities. Soc. Prob., 11:225, 1964.

Grusky, Oscar: The effects of formal structure on managerial recruitment: a study of baseball organization. Sociometry, 26:345, 1963.

Homans, George C.: The Human Group. New York, Harcourt, Brace and World, 1950.

Loy, John W., and McElvogue, Joseph F.: Racial segregation in American sport. Int. Rev. Sport Sociol., 5:5, 1970.

Meggysey, Dave: Out of Their League. Berkeley, Ramparts Press, 1970.

Oates, Bob: Column on the 1971 National Football League all-star team. Sporting News, 173 (January 15):17, 1972.

Olsen, Jack: The Black Athlete—A Shameful Story. New York, Time, 1968.

Rosenblatt, Aaron: The failure of success. Transaction, 4:51, 1967.

Smith, Gary, and Grindstaff, Carl F.: Race and sport in Canada. London, University of Western Ontario (mimeo), 1970.

Vallières, Pierre: White Niggers of America. (Trans. by Joan Pinkham). New York and London, Monthly Review Press, 1971.

NOTE

1. Unfortunately, sample data do not allow for this factor to be weighted or otherwise controlled. Its effect is to minimize actual differences, and to make apparent differences more conservative.

SECTION THREE
sport subcultures

subcultures and sport

KENT PEARSON

This article has four objectives. The first is to review the concept subculture and some of the major issues involved in using the term. These issues are related to physical activity subcultures. The second is to demonstrate that cultural dimensions are basic in defining and understanding sport phenomena. A third objective is to illustrate aspects of the concept by drawing on details from empirical research. The illustrations are drawn from a recent study of two surfing subcultures in Australia. The fourth objective is to show that the cases chosen for detailed treatment each reflect a more general type of sport subculture. The article itself is divided into two parts. Part 1 is concerned with the first objective and Part 2 with the remaining objectives.

PART 1

PARADOXES OF THE TERM "SUBCULTURE"

An overview of the way the term "subculture" has been used by theorists reveals a number of paradoxes. On the one hand, the concept draws attention to cultural patterns which in some way contrast with, or are different from, the broader culture (of which the subculture is a part). Culture therefore appears not as an evenly woven cloth but as including a variety of patterns in which identifiable parts are somehow different. At the level of the individual such a focus on differences and contrasts may be seen to encourage a perspective which takes some account of individual subjectivity, of the way individuals define situations and contribute to shared "worlds of meaning."

On the other hand the concept also directs

Adapted from Sub-Cultures, Drug Use, and Physical Activity, keynote address from Sub-Theme Two, International Congress of Physical Activity Sciences, Quebec, Canada, July 1976.

attention to the level of "system." Subculture involves structure. Systematized patterns are pictured as external to individuals and as imposing on them. Individuals are "socialized" into the system; that is, they adopt the cultural definitions and perspectives of those with whom they interact. The language used here is typically that which Dawe has called a "sociology of social system."[1] It is a language which leads to a Durkheimian emphasis on culture as a thing-like facticity, as something concrete which exists and can be analysed. It is a view which tends to lead to an "over-socialized" conception of man. It is a view which also tends to overlook the fact that "subculture" is ultimately an analytic device of a researcher.

From another viewpoint, the term subculture suggests a unit of analysis somewhat smaller and more manageable than the whole of culture; yet the very process of attempting to limit and define subcultural boundaries can lead to an escalation of measurement requirements to include both cultural and subcultural attributes: for in one sense, it is not possible to say how a subcultural attribute differs from a parent "culture" without first having appropriate measures of the parent culture. These paradoxes suggest that subculture is not a theoretical area involving a particular approach or perspective. There are numerous different sociological orientations and approaches which may be used in understanding and explaining subcultures.

One recent writer observing the difficulties of using the term suggested that had the concept not been a feature of everyday language, thereby permitting it to be introduced as a new concept in sociology, it would probably be rejected as useless.[2] Perhaps a major reason for its continued use, despite the difficulties involved, is a widespread recognition of the pluralistic nature of complex modern society. Subculture "squares" with a conception of a differentiated

131

society in which there exists a variety of cultural systems.

Support for some of the key notions implied in the concept is also provided by numerous studies which demonstrate the significance of specific cultural contexts, (e.g., the culture of a particular drug using group) in understanding behaviour. Even the apparently objective pharmacological properties of drugs cannot be adequately understood in isolation, for responses to them are inseparable from individual subjectivity which in turn is understandable only as a part of a cultural or a subcultural context.[3]

Subculture as a concept is an abstract construction and many of the stumbling blocks to clarity and unambiguous definition derive from the level of abstraction of the term. Perhaps the most obvious area of confusion is the failure of users of the concept to maintain a consistent and logical distinction between social systems and cultural systems. A theme of this article is that the careful maintenance of the distinction is crucial to clear thinking on matters of subculture.

THE SOCIAL-CULTURAL DISTINCTION

A social system may simply be pictured as a static arrangement of positions or, as Robertson has stated, "sociologically depicted relationships between and among roles, collectivities and social sectors."[4]

Cultural systems represent the system of ideas, beliefs, values, expressive symbols and grounds of meaning according to which individuals define situations, act and evaluate both their own and others' actions. Cultural patterns may be seen to emerge as action settles into regulated and persisting patterns.

Logically, the use of the term subculture indicates that a "cultural" rather than a "social" perspective is being used. This in turn implies that the definition and delineation of subculture must be based on "cultural" and not "social" criteria.[5]

In many cases however, (probably the vast majority) interactive social behavior will correspond closely with cultural systems.[6]

The tendency for there to be a close relationship between a subcultural system and overt group behaviour is a consideration which is of some importance in theories accounting for the emergence and development of subcultures. Such theories often emphasize the development of culture as a result of structural factors. However, subculture can be independent of a particular system of interactive social behavior, for value sharing does not necessarily require social interaction. This means that not only are subcultural boundaries and interaction boundaries distinct because they are different orders of phenomena, but also that those who share in a particular subculture do not necessarily take part in a system of interactive social behaviour.

Activity-based subcultures in general involve a system of "meanings and ways" concerned with the activity.[7] There are "intricacies" which are known and considered by persons who share in the subculture. In many respects subcultures are specialized knowledge areas which include a distinctive history, lore, ritual, techniques and other specific forms of information, associated with or around which, behaviour occurs. They also include the symbols which permit such intricacies to be stored, transmitted, and communicated. Patterns of symbolic communication permit the nature of the intricacies to be continually modified as individuals ongoingly pursue their objectives. That is, the web of meanings which individuals have spun is continually being respun through interaction and/or communication.

A number of statements may be made about the meaning of subculture on the basis of the discussion to this point.

The concept subculture involves abstract construction. A subculture is typological in the sense that it involves selection and abstraction of cultural aspects of socio-cultural systems.[8] Only some of a great range of cultural features are selected, such selection normally being made according to what the researcher sees as the main distinguishing features of the subculture. Insofar as the selected and frequently accentuated (abstract) features are woven into a patterned construct, "subculture" may be regarded as an "ideal type."[9]

In effect, the construction permits the delineation of a boundary on the basis of cultural criteria. The criteria enabling such a boundary to be drawn around what is and what is not subculture, are of a more abstract conceptual order than those usually used in the selection of sample populations. Cultural phenomena are not directly observable or measurable and therefore, tend to be associated with a subjective methodology.

While there are difficulties in categorizing at

such an abstract level, grappling with such difficulties may be judged to be worthwhile if the object is to focus on phenomena which are the "stuff" of subcultures; ideas, interests, beliefs, symbols, norms, values, and other categories constituting cultural phenomena.

At the level of individuals, the point of subcultural analysis becomes apparent when an objective involves a focus on systems of meanings shared by individuals who use such meanings (under particular circumstances) in "defining the situation." Such systems of meanings may be used as frameworks for interpreting (understanding) action.

The very notion of subculture depends on the legitimacy of building abstract concepts which depend on selection, emphasis, and categorization into systems which may not exist (as such) in the minds of those who share in the subculture, and which cannot be directly seen or measured. The concept is an heuristic device useful in some types of explanation.

EXPLANATIONS OF SUBCULTURES— EMERGENCE AND DYNAMICS

Most theories concerning the genesis of subcultures depend in some way on the interrelationship between culture and structure.[10] What is probably the most systematic and sustained treatment given to the process of subcultural emergence has been provided by Cohen. Cohen begins by focusing on the problems to which people are continually trying to find solutions and which always involve an interaction between the actor's frame of reference, and the situation he confronts.

This situation includes:

the world we live in and where we are located in that world. It includes the physical setting within which we must operate, a finite supply of time and energy with which to accomplish our ends, and above all, the habits, the expectations, the demands and the social organization of the people around us. Always our problems are what they are because the situation limits the things we can do and have and the conditions under which they are possible.[11]

Cohen also considers the process whereby the situation of a number of interacting actors with similar problems of adjustment leads to mutually supportive innovation. He asks "How does one

know (emphasis in original) whether a gesture toward innovation will strike a responsive and sympathetic chord in others or whether it will elicit hostility, ridicule and punishment?" This question he answers in terms of exploratory gestures. Innovatory "feelers" to test the reactions of others could be put out "by increments so small, tentative and ambiguous as to permit the actor to retreat if the signs become unfavourable, without having become associated with an unpopular position."[12]

The really hard problems Cohen considers to be those with no ready-at-hand solution. For such problems the solution "must entail some change in (the actor's) frame of reference itself." The crucial condition for the emergence of new cultural forms is "the existence in effective interaction with one another, of a number of actors with similar problems of adjustment."[13]

In this manner, and through social interaction, group standards or shared frames of reference emerge.

Shibutani,[14] writing within a symbolic interactionist perspective, differs from most other theorists writing on subcultures in his emphasis on the role of communication in the development of a social world. Whereas face to face interactive social behavior is implied by Cohen, Shibutani sees a communication network as a crucial ingredient in the formation of a social world. While acknowledging that probably the greatest sense of identification and solidarity is to be found in the various communal structures—the underworld, ethnic minorities, the social elite, in which there is frequently spatial segregation— social worlds also form around associational structures. The world of medicine, of organized labour, in which such things as specialized journals and feature sections in newspapers are important, provide examples. "Each social world, then, is a culture area, the boundaries of which are set neither by territory nor by formal group membership, but by the limits of effective communication."[15]

SUMMARY OF MAIN POINTS

Drawing on the discussion based on the analytical distinction between social and cultural systems and from the brief look at explanations of subcultures presented above, a number of issues of importance to subcultural phenomena may be listed:

1. Many so-called theories of subcultures confuse systems of interactive social behaviour and subcultural systems when each of these levels is analytically distinct.
2. Many theories explaining the origin and development of subcultures, (and especially that of Cohen considered above) stress differential interaction as being important, such differential interaction being brought about or stimulated by such things as structural position or social situation, including individuals with like psychological problems of adjustment (Cohen).
3. Interaction of persons with like (similar) interests can lead to the emergence of shared perspectives. Cohen in his discussion of the role of exploratory gestures, mutual explanation and joint elaboration, and Shibutani in his use of a symbolic interactionist framework, provide some insight into the processes involved in the emergence of shared perspectives, norms, etc.
4. The theorists reviewed imply that once a circle of interaction among individuals is in existence, leading to the development of shared norms, values, etc., there is a reciprocal effect generating a continuance of the process, i.e., the development of some degree of common knowledge of group standards, values, ingroup symbols etc., tends to lead to greater interaction and a more codified subculture. Some reasons for this are given by Cohen (sympathetic moral climate in which subcultural forms may flourish) and by Shibutani (the internalization of particular perspectives leading to the maintenance of social distance through segregation, conflict, or differential communication).
5. While theories explaining subcultural genesis stress face to face social interaction among individuals with like interests or problems as being prior to the emergence of subcultures, Shibutani's emphasis on communication patterns provides an avenue for conceptualizing the development and diffusion of subcultural forms independent of systems of interactive social behaviour.

Many of the above points are illustrated in the model depicted in Figure 1.

Three levels are depicted: individual, social and cultural. A prerequisite of subcultural development is a collection of individuals who possess like (or similar) interests.[16]

According to the theorists considered above, what is further needed is for these individuals to be brought into social interaction with one another so that "like" interests and problems may become "common." A great variety of events, situations and structures facilitate or impede such social interaction. A natural disaster or a shipwreck on an isolated island could be precipitating events which provide the background conditions for such interaction. More obvious, in terms of traditional explanations of subcultures, would be interaction among similarly located juveniles in a large city. Interaction could also be stimulated by the intentional establishment of a specific purpose organization—for example, a sporting club (see (a) in Fig. 1).

Any situation, event, or set of structures which leads to the interaction of individuals with like interests in such a way that interaction with others not similarly involved is reduced (see (b) in Fig. 1) carries with it the likelihood of the development of shared perspectives, group standards etc.; that is, aspects of subculture (see (d) in Fig. 1). The development of shared perspectives is the beginning of subcultural forms.

Individuals involved in the social interaction generating the subculture manifest various behaviours reflecting the subculture. Further social interaction serves to consolidate or modify the cultural forms and to further effect individual attitudes, beliefs, behaviour, etc., generating a cycle between the factors at the three levels depicted (b, c, d).

With the development of channels of communication the possibility exists for persons to share in the subculture without being part of the group which initially generated its existence.

PART 2

The subculture of a physical activity in terms of the ideas reviewed above is the system of "meanings and ways" concerned with the activity and shared by interactants in the activity. This may involve little or no formal organization or may involve a complex sport bureaucracy. Understanding the subculture of a physical activity is crucial to understanding the nature of the activity itself, for the meanings which people find in and give to the activity are sociologically a part of the activity. Indeed it may further be claimed that sport itself can only be defined

Antecedent Conditions   The Process of Subcultural Development

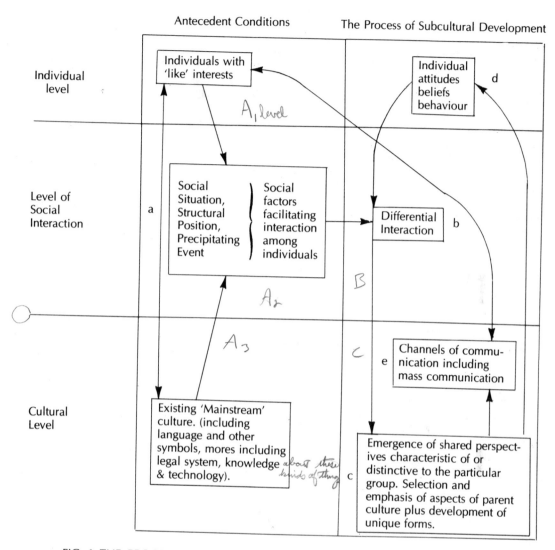

FIG. 1 THE PROCESS OF SUBCULTURAL EMERGENCE AND DEVELOPMENT

sociologically in terms of cultural criteria. This statement will briefly be justified.

Throughout history, definitions of sport have stressed in some way or another, physical activity or movement. The general characteristic which may be seen as the common thread basic to most or all definitions and descriptions, is some emphasis on physical prowess dimensions. At some point however these definitions break down.

What is it about the physical that makes it sport or not sport? The normal approach for answers to such questions is to look at type and/or amount of movement. Many writers have seen "gross" movement as being a requirement.

Physical skill prowesses may however be conceptualized as lying on a continuum from less developed to more developed. To what extent do particular skills need to be developed before they are classifiable as "developed?" What are the characteristics of gross physical activity, and when precisely does a particular movement become gross? Different sports are based on different prowesses.

Simply, such approaches break down because they are not sociological enough. More specifically sport is ultimately best defined by reference to values, i.e., cultural criteria. It is not the nature, type or degree of physical prowess that is important in defining sport but the value that is attached to the prowesses; a value that is to be seen in terms of game rules (interpreted broadly to include game lore) in relation to specifiable game objectives. When the pattern of activity involves overt or covert "rules of the game" and there is an institutionalized value on particular physical prowesses which are basic to the achievement of the games objectives, the necessary and sufficient conditions for it to be classifiable as a sport are present.

Sport may be defined as that part of physical activity which is performed with a view to achieving particular game outcomes and which involves as part of the process of achieving these outcomes a value on physical prowesses relevant to such achievement. The prowesses that are valued are related to the objectives or the outcomes to which the activity is directed, and these in turn are related to particular game contexts (in the broadest sense) in which the activity occurs.

THE SUBCULTURES OF SURF LIFESAVING AND SURFBOARD RIDING

Some approaches which have been taken in an analysis of two contrasting surfing subcultures in Australia and New Zealand will serve to illustrate various aspects of subcultures mentioned to this point. Sharing in each of these subcultures are two different types of surfer. Each type represents a rather extreme contrasting tendency. Each is involved in a very different type of sport organization. The surfboard rider is typically youthful, hedonistic, mobile and, simply put, somewhat anti-establishment. The surf lifesaver is more conservative and conventional with regard to mainstream social values. He is obviously more achievement-oriented and gets many of his rewards from involvement with a surfing club (in turn a part of a large bureaucratic lifesaving and sport organization) and is normally involved in the highly institutionalized, formally organized competitive sport of surf lifesaving. These two milieux form a striking contrast. Both surf lifesaving and surfboard riding are sports according to the definition given above. In both forms of surf activity there are rules of the game and a value on specifiable physical prowesses. As sports however they are very different. The contrasts are highlighted both by the fact that each has the surf as the focus of his activity and also because each type of surfer presents an outgroup focus for the other. Many of the more striking contrasts between surf lifesaving and surfboard riding are summarized in Table 1.

The subcultures in many respects represent extreme tendencies within the world of sport and some of the tendencies seen in terms of "play sport" and "athletic sport" appear generalizable to other sport situations. This is considered later in the article.

The chief sociological problem which was addressed in the research was accounting for the origins and development of surf lifesaving and surfboard riding as distinctive sport forms. For most of the history of surfing in Australia and New Zealand, surfing has been virtually synonymous with surf lifesaving. Persons more interested in surfing than the casual beachgoer joined a surf lifesaving club and surfed with other surf lifesavers. The sort of surfing developed by the Surf Life Saving Association (S.L.S.A.) was very different from the surfing which was pursued in other parts of the world, notably Hawaii and California. American and Hawaiian surfers early in this century were focusing on the rediscovery of the ancient Polynesian sport of surfboard riding.

Surf lifesaving in Australia had its genesis at the end of the 19th century in organizations which were centrally concerned with fighting the puritanical dawn to dusk bathing curfew which existed in New South Wales (N.S.W.) and other places in Australia at that time. After fighting the prosecution of several offenders against these laws and having won some concessions from governments, some of these groups were organized into clubs for the pursuit of surf bathing. The names of many of these clubs (surf bathing clubs) reflected the primary interest of their members. In 1907, when the existing clubs in N.S.W. were formed into a single association, the title was The New South Wales Surf Bathing Association. As restrictions against use of the beaches were relaxed and surf bathing became more popular, there were numerous drowning fatalities, manifesting a clear social problem for the authorities who had jurisdiction over these areas. Surf Bathing Clubs were able to legitimate their activities first by providing lifesaving services, and secondly by developing a competitive surfing sport (the time of the formation of the

TABLE 1

Structural-Functional Characteristics of the Sports of Surfboard Riding and Surf Lifesaving [17]

Surfboard Riding	Surf Lifesaving
Little formal organization. Majority of board riders do not belong to any formal organization	Highly formalized organization. Institutionally differentiated at the local (club), branch, state, national and international levels.
Interaction among board riders and the social structure a result of enforced "closeness" of participants at surfing locations. Evolution of norms as a result of like (individualized) interests of participants in wave riding rather than common group action to achieve specified competition goals.	Formal and elaborate written rules worked out pragmatically and legitimated via rational-bureaucratic channels.
Fluctuating patterns of interactive social behaviour due to many factors of geography, physics of wave shape, size, etc., number and standard of ability etc., of participants.	Patterns of change institutionalized through rational-bureaucratic channels.
Identifiable regional variation in the nature and type of 'norms' according to localized lore (e.g., one area approves leg ropes, another doesn't, etc.) especially obvious in matters of fashion (e.g., board design, clothes etc.).	Standardization of gear and equipment specification—especially in relation to craft. Standardization of rules and procedures at all levels of association functioning up to national and international levels.
No precise definition of territory. The area of interaction dependent on physical and geographical factors which fluctuate greatly over time and place. Duration of interaction flexible—left to individuals to decide if and when they will participate, the length of time they will participate and when they will leave the activity. Other natural factors (e.g., wind, tide) influence this.	Precise definition of territory on which competition takes place. Starts, finishes and courses clearly marked. Predetermination of numbers of contestants, themselves normally selected according to standardized 'impartial' methods. Any advantage due to conditions randomized through balloting etc., to ensure equality of opportunity.
Any surfing session strongly influenced by explicit manifestations of physical prowess of participants and overtly aggressive behaviour in wave-taking and riding (the establishment of a pecking order).	Minimization, principally through formal rules, of the influence of any social or individual differences on the game pattern, norms of equality and fairness.
Loose distinction between active and spectating roles. A fluctuating gradation from most actively involved surfboard riders to those merely spectating.	Strict distinction between playing, officiating and spectating roles.
Low role differentiation and low structural differentiation (many elements rolled into one).	High role differentiation (division of labour) e.g., active competitors on basis of competition class—boat, rescue and resuscitation, board, ski etc. Officials on basis of nature of specialist function. Marshall, judge, arena controller, computing steward, etc.

(Continued on p. 138)

TABLE 1 *(Continued)*

Surfboard Riding	*Surf Lifesaving*
Informal control by surfers within the context of on-going activity. Recourse to physical force frequent.	Formal social control by "impartial" officials appointed and certified by legislative bodies (at club, branch, regional, national and international levels) who have power to investigate and/or intervene when a breach of the rules has apparently occurred. Formal imposition of penalties according to the seriousness of the offence—ranging from admonishment to disqualification from event, suspension of membership, etc. Physical violence not a legitimate form of sanction.
Generation of spontaneous expression of emotion (ready expression of emotion).	Generation of a more controlled "sublimated" form of excitement tension. A high degree of restraint and controlled expression of emotion.

S.L.S.A. was a period of high legitimacy of organized sport).

The S.L.S.A. proved to be an extremely successful organization in respect both to its development as a competitive sport organization and as a rescue organization. It quickly built up a phenomenal rescue record, a record of which it continues to be (justifiably) proud. As a competitive sport it flourished. Surf lifesavers came to be seen as a group apart—"The Samurais of the surf."[18] The "hard muscled" surf lifesaver became a national symbol for Australia. From 1910 to the mid 1950s the S.L.S.A. dominated the surf in Australia and New Zealand. As a competitive sport it broadened and developed around different forms of gear and equipment (generally craft).

The surf lifesaving associations' monopolization of the surf in Australia and New Zealand set the stage for the events which took place in the late 1950s and early 1960s and which led to the development of two surfing sports. The S.L.S.A. had altered in numerous respects during the period from 1910 to 1956, but had functioned and developed primarily as an organization for high performance competitive sport and for beach patrol and rescue purposes. At the end of World War II numerous changes in the broader fabric of Australian society were beginning to affect the S.L.S.A. There was a greater degree of consumer affluence. Mass production and the availability of motor cars together with an improvement in road transport led to greater

mobility. There was also a shift in cultural values in the direction of increasingly legitimating "hedonistic" pursuits.[19] All of these aspects contributed to the surfboard riding revolution which occurred in the early sixties. While the design and use of surf craft in Australia had taken place within contexts circumscribed by the S.L.S.A., surf craft design and surfboard riding in the United States had evolved (especially since the end of World War II) in the direction of designing boards for wave riding. Progressively smaller, lighter, more maneuverable boards for wave riding had been developed. After the war, a technological "breakthrough" represented by a combination of revolutionary advances in materials, design improvement for wave riding, and methods of mass production led to a new type of craft. It was the introduction of this craft which precipitated the development of a new surfing sport in Australia.

The board riding movement grew initially as a result of conflict within the S.L.S.A., eventually leading to a basic split within the movement. The introduction of this type of craft, however, was not sufficient reason for the split which occurred.

A polarity between persons primarily interested in surfing and those who were basically concerned with the rescue and competitive sport objectives of the S.L.S.A. had been a characteristic of much of the previous fifty years of surf life saving history. In addition, the S.L.S.A. had in many respects been capable of adapting to, even stimulating in some cases, innovation and design in relation to surf craft. Why then did it not embrace or adjust to the introduction of the Malibu board?

Many things apparently favoured such adoption. The boards were introduced and demonstrated by a team of U.S. lifeguards who were sponsored by the S.L.S.A. The S.L.S.A. at once responded favourably and introduced wave riding competitions into its competition programme, indicating an initial preparedness to adopt the new craft.

To consider the reasons for the emergence of two surfing subcultures, details were sought on the way each type of surf participant viewed his involvement in the surf. The interests, values and goals which led to the involvement of each type of surfer were explored.

In doing this a variety of different types of data were collected and a variety of different techniques of data collection were used. The methods included: participant observation, detailed questionnaires aimed at eliciting responses to both closed and open questions, and structured and unstructured interviews. In addition to the data collected directly from surfers, documentary sources were also used. Participant observation assisted in considering the normative frameworks governing interaction among surfers during surfing sessions at board riding locations. The closed questionnaire data were computer analysed and provided a large amount of statistical information. The open ended data were analysed with a view to gaining information about two related areas.[20] These were: (1) the meanings people found in, and gave to, their surfing activity, and (2) the in-group/out-group focus of each type of surfer.

The split between the Surf Life Saving Association and the surfboard riding movement can be explained, in large measure, in terms of contrasting value orientations which such data reflect. Each of these areas of data will be discussed in turn.

MEANINGS IN SURFING. Simply, what resulted from an analysis of the "meanings" data was that surf lifesavers were much more instrumentally oriented in their surfing activity than surfboard riders. Surf lifesavers' responses emphasised the development of technical skills and prowesses in the context of a competitive relationship with nature, often with socially competitive ends in view. There was a tendency to regard physical prowesses instrumentally in terms of their usefulness for "handling" the surf. Competition was of crucial importance in most responses and in general was regarded as an inextricable part of surf lifesaving. Expressions of a desire to master, conquer or in some other way challenge the power or might of nature were much more frequent and received greater emphasis from surf lifesavers. On the other hand surfboard riders emphasised the joyful and immediately rewarding nature of surfboard riding activities. They stressed an essentially harmonious relationship between man and nature and appeared far more attuned to appreciate nature in terms of aesthetic criteria. The mastery of board riding skills was often considered in terms of facilitating self-expression. In general, surfboard riders' descriptions of the nature of their involvement were unashamedly hedonistic, in contrast to explicitly instrumental reasons given by surf lifesavers.

IN-GROUP/OUT-GROUP FOCUS. The following examples provide good illustrations of the responses of board riders:

Person 1: Clubbies are clean cut, better dressed, they usually keep to a tight circle of themselves, do not like surfies and get their kicks from races and carnivals. Surfies are more natural, they have a more casual approach to life and get their kicks from the waves themselves.

Person 2: Clubbies are lifesavers and do a good job of protecting beaches. They have short hair, are more regimented (than board riders) and stick close to their mates . . . have a slight resentment to surfers, are more career minded and drink a lot of beer. Surfies like a free life. They are usually nomadic easy going fellows who like quiet out-of-the-way places. They have a completely different mental attitude to the ocean than clubbies . . . they (surfies) usually have longer hair and are easier going concerning jobs, money, personal possessions. They are definitely dedicated to surfing as a way of life rather than a sport.

The views of surf lifesavers were obviously different as the following responses illustrate.

Person 1: Clubbies are community service oriented and display better teammanship, they can be disciplined. Better personal appearance. Surfies are most undisciplined, pleasure seeking and alone. They have a strong feeling of distrust in anything that is regimented and organized in a way that interferes with their pursuit of the perfect wave. They are foot-loose and irresponsible with a poor attitude on community affairs.

Person 2: Clubbies take part in competitions and do patrols. They swim as much as they use craft and they stay at one beach. They are more competent in the water than surfies, many of whom cannot even swim very well. Clubbies have a sense of responsibility. Surfies often have shoulder length hair and untidy appearances and a selfish attitude towards others. They travel in groups in panel vans from beach to beach to follow surf and often appear to resent the authority given to clubbies for policing craft areas.

There were some minor differences in the detail attended to by each type of surfer. For example, surfboard riders paid more attention to appearances (short hair versus long hair, speedos versus board shorts) and conspicuous behaviour (surfing for training rather than surfing for fun or to express oneself) than surf lifesavers. There were also more references to "establishment versus anti-establishment images" and behaviour than was the case for surf lifesavers. Surf lifesavers, on the other hand, were more likely to see differences in terms of discipline, organization, formal authority, and responsibility. In many cases however, there was a large amount of agreement between the views surf lifesavers had of themselves and the views board riders had of them and the views board riders had of themselves and the way clubbies viewed them.

Even the words used to categorize and label were often the same or similar. The major differences were not in the nature of detail which could be objectively considered but in the evaluations which were explicitly made or connoted by the terms used and which in turn, reflected the "evaluative" contexts from which the judgements were made. For example, the mobility of the surfies was described in a neutral or positive manner by surfboard riders in terms such as "free wheeling" or "nomadic" while for surf lifesavers this mobility led to the use of such terms as "gypsies," "bums," or "drifters." The "slim" build as a characteristic of surfies was interpreted as "weak-looking" by many surf lifesavers while a more typical evaluation by surfboard riders was that surfies characteristically possessed "slim lithsome bodies." It was frequently the use of particular evaluative terms which gave insight into subjective feeling states and orientations of participants.[21]

The evaluative comments made by surf lifesavers were typically those which could have been expected from persons sharing in an athlete subculture (as described by writers such as Schafer and Alderman), while the surfboard riders' evaluations were much closer to those of the youth counterculture as described by such persons as Reich, Roszak, Schafer and Berger, et al.,[22] Turner's typology which contrasts loci of self in terms of "impulse" or "institutions" points to other dimensions which are important in considering the self concepts of each type of surfer.[23]

The conclusions drawn from the responses of each type of surfer assisted an explanation of the emergence of surfboard riding as a distinctive surfing (sport) subculture; a subculture which contrasts in numerous respects with the historically much earlier established sport of surf lifesaving.

Surf lifesaving flourished as a competitive sport and developed rapidly at a time when there was widespread acceptance of competitive sport values. Twenty years after it came into existence it had become a highly institutionalized, bureaucratically organized, sport form.

Processes of institutionalization in regard to competitive sport are familiar themes in the sociology of sport literature.[24] I have given some attention to the directions of institutionalization elsewhere[25] and see these processes as usually leading towards more athleticized forms of sport. The athleticization process involves increasing increments on at least three associated clusters of variables; those concened with social competition, those to do with valued physical prowesses of the sport and those concerned with bureaucratization of sport organizations. These are illustrated in Figure 2.

The process of athleticization of sport inevi-

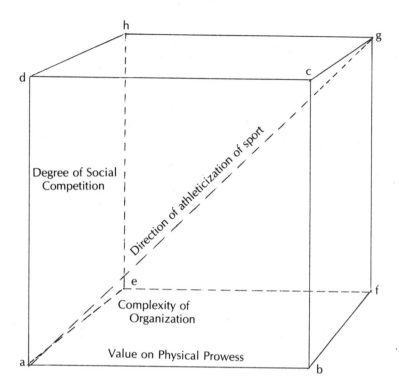

FIG. 2 THREE DIMENSIONAL FIELD FOR CHARACTERIZING AND LOCATING SPORTS AND FORMS OF ATHLETICS

tably leads to an increase in the instrumental factors involved in physical activity. The normal consequence of this process is that playful forms of sport become less playful as they become more institutionalized. Sport organizations typically grow in size and complexity and as institutionalization processes continue they tend to become increasingly rationalized, bureaucratized, formalized and standardized.

The development of surf lifesaving from 1910 onwards was increasingly in the direction of an athletic sport organization, and the reasons for participating in surfing activity were increasingly characterized by utilitarian considerations. Although there had always been a polarity between surf play and more instrumental objectives of the S.L.S.A. the discrepancy increased as (1) the S.L.S.A. gave greater emphasis to instrumental objectives, and (2) the value climate of the broader culture altered in the direction of increasingly legitimating "play" pursuits.

The introduction of the short-finned Malibu board and its adoption and development for wave riding highlighted the discrepancy between playful forms of surfing and more instrumental forms of involvement. The short board itself became the very symbol of a threat perceived by administrators of the Surf Life Saving Association. The perceived threat was added to by the unashamed desire of many surfers to do little else than ride boards (i.e., persons manifesting play values), something which had not only been impossible technologically a few years earlier but was also "unthinkable" when the S.L.S.A. dominated what happened in the Australian surf.

It was a combination of factors which set the stage for the conflict which occurred between the S.L.S.A. administration and those wishing to ride boards. In brief, these included: increasing material affluence, the technological revolution in surfing equipment, a changing value climate in regard to the legitimacy of "play" pursuits, and most importantly the growing discrepency between the instrumental ideology of the S.L.S.A. and the values of those wanting mainly to surf.

The resultant conflict functioned to crystalize

TABLE 2
Some Contrasts Between Play-Sport and Athletic-Sport

Play-Sport	Athletic Sport
Orientation toward time	
Stress on the present—less oriented to clock time, more to social or "natural" rhythms, e.g., ebb and flow of tide, light and dark, summer, winter, etc.	Orientation to the present mixed with a stress on the future. Instrumental attitude toward time. Timetable of training habits to suit a daily routine. Disciplined schedules in close adherence to objective (timed) performances and objective measures of conditioning (relaxed pulses, recovery rate of pulses, etc.)
Awareness of and focus on the body	
Body a vehicle for experiencing. Less aware of the body as an object of performance in terms of objective measures in either absolute or comparative terms. Awareness and focus on body through involvement in sport processes.	Body a vehicle (machine) to perform specific tasks. Objective measures and knowledge of condition and performance relative to one's own baseline and to others in competition. Importance of 'shaping' body machinery.
The nature of self	
Location of self in impulse tendency to reject relationships based largely on structural, impersonal and functional lines. Source of identity more closely linked to the way an individual experiences self. Self linked more to expressive activity.	Institutional location of self—self more tied to specific role relationships. Source of identity closely linked to formal organizational structures. Self linked to achievement of specific games objectives and role performances. Excellence in terms of comparative merit.
Significant others likely to be those able to appreciate expressive efforts, often who empathise and share 'like' or similar experiences	Acceptance of self more conditional on performance. Significant others likely to be role partners in an enterprise aimed at achieving victory. Respect for others based on an appreciation of professional skill.
Innovation	
a) *Technology*	
Favourable orientation to experimentation with equipment. Experimentation takes place within broad limits.	Experimentation and innovation viewed equivocally (depending on position within organization). What experimentation occurs takes place within clearly specified boundaries.
b) *Technique.*	
Anything goes—individual expression and experience what is valued.	Innovation in technique restricted to the 'laws of the sport'. What innovation does take place is often as a result of the application of rational scientific investigation.
Relationship with natural environment.	
Tendency to stress harmonious relationship with natural environment	Tendency to stress neutral or antagonistic relationship with the natural environment

the covert differences between each as well as to assist the development of a coherent surfboard riding philosophy. The foundations of two contrasting surfing subcultures were thereby laid. Further development was stimulated by the official reaction of the S.L.S.A. which influenced government at various levels to control surfboard riding. This was seen as retribution by many surfboard riders and led to an intensification of conflict. The mass production of boards and the commercialization of surfboard riding during the 60's resulted in surfboard riders quickly outnumbering surf lifesavers. The "ingroup"—"out-group" focus contributed to the coherence of each subculture in various ways and the resultant stereotypes themselves became a part of each subculture.

In this manner many of the contrasts between "athletic sport" and "play sport," which had been implicit tensions within the S.L.S.A. throughout much of its history, became explicit and institutionalized as separate aspects of contrasting sport subcultures.

CONCLUSION

The second part of this paper has given an explanation of the emergence and development of two contrasting surfing sports. The explanation was facilitated by conceptualizing each as an activity-based subculture and analysing the contrasting value orientations of each type of surfer.

At a more abstract level it has been argued that some of the key features of subcultures, especially subculturally institutionalized value orientations, are important in understanding aspects of behaviour. Moreover it has been suggested that the two specific sport subcultures which have been treated above are each representative of a "type" of sport subculture. Some of the main features of these types will be abstracted in concluding this article.

The term "type" is used in the sense which McKinney has given to "constructed types":

The constructed type is a pragmatically devised system of characteristics, made up of abstracted elements and formed into a unified conceptual pattern wherein there may be an intensification of one or more attributes for purposes of utility.[26]

Table 2 lists a set of abstractions based on the sports of surf lifesaving and surfboard riding which are sufficiently general to be usefully considered in combination as parts of a type of "play sport" and a type of "athletic sport."

Returning to the discussion presented earlier in which aspects basic in defining and understanding forms of sport were considered, six dimensions (see Table 3) appear important in the comparison of sports. These dimensions may be added to the contrasts in Table 2 to build more complete 'play-sport' and 'athletic-sport' types.

The various attributes and dimensions which

TABLE 3

Some Dimensions of Contrast Between Play-Sport and Athletic-Sport

	Play-sport	Athletic-sport
Measure of bureaucratization e.g., organizational complexity (social system measures)	Low	High
Coherence of central values and norms (cultural system measures)	May be low or high	High
Rationalization of techniques geared to the achievement of precisely specifiable performance outcomes	Low	High
Emphasis on qualitative aspects of performance including value placed on 'flow' experience. (process rather than product)	High	Low
Importance of social competition	Low	High
Complexity and specification of formal games rules	Low	High

appear in Tables 2 and 3 have been abstracted in part from the sport literature and in part from data on the sports of surf lifesaving and surfboard riding. These abstractions appear as important parts of two contrasting general types of sport. Many modern sport forms appear to resemble one or the other type.

NOTES

1. Dawe, A.: The Two Sociologies. Br J Sociol, *21*:207, 1970.

2. Clarke, M.: On the Concept of Subculture. Br J Sociol, *25*(4):428, 1974.

3. Young, J.: See, for example Chapter 2, The social basis of drug dependency. The Drugtakers. London, Paladin, 1971.

4. Robertson, R.: Toward the identification of the major axes of sociological analysis. *In* Approaches to Sociology. Edited by J. Rex. Routledge and Kegan Paul, London, 1974, pp. 107–123. See also Mouzelis, N.: Social and system integration: Some reflections on a fundamental distinction. Br J Sociol, *25*(4):398, 1974.
The treatment which Mouzelis has given to the social/cultural distinction implies an analytical distinction only, i.e., the distinction refers to aspects of social reality which are only conceptually distinguishable from other aspects. Robertson (op. cit.) has left open the question of whether there is an empirical basis to the distinction; but by his criticism of the way ethnomethodologists deny the significance of analytic distinctions thereby foreclosing the possibility that such distinctions may be in the nature of socio-cultural reality, he clearly suggests such a distinction may have an empirical basis.
More specifically in relation to subcultures Clarke has argued that the social/cultural contrast represents "only an analytical distinction, that is they cover the same actual social relations from a different standpoint, selecting different aspects for consideration." (Clarke, p. 428)
While holding that the contrasts between the two perspectives are quite sharp, each taking a very different route over similar ground, Clarke also considers their complementarity equally clear. "The abstraction of social structure, the getting to the essentials of social relations, can only preceed on the basis of an understanding of culture, and a cultural analysis can only be fully successful and explicit if it accepts at certain points other definitions of the people who enact the culture than the culture itself presumes. The style of the two is also clearly quite different. The structural perspective looks at social events, the cultural into the analysis of meaning." (Clarke, p. 429)

5. In this regard it may be interesting to note that Milton Gordon who was the first author to present a sustained treatment of the concept subculture in 1947 also confused cultural and social elements in his definition (See Milton M. Gordon, "The Concept of the Sub-culture and its Application" *Social Forces* Vol. 26, Oct. 1947, pp. 40–42). Seventeen years later, however, Gordon re-examined the concept and was particularly careful in distinguishing between social structure and culture. On the basis of the distinction, he presented a formal analysis of three levels of social units and three levels of "culture" associated with these units. "Subculture" was identified as the intermediate level of culture. (See Gordon, M.: Assimilation in American Life. Oxford University Press, London, 1964, pp. 30–54).

6. The phrase "interactive social behaviour" is used to mean a social system of persons who interact directly with each other. As such, the concept excludes symbolic communication in non face to face situations.

7. The phrase "meanings and ways" is used here to indicate what is involved in "subculture". It includes normative guides to social behaviour, the overarching values such guidelines reflect and the various symbols and modes of operation which represent and convey meaning.

8. The term "socio-cultural" is used to refer to a social system together with its associated culture.

9. For a discussion on the nature and meaning of Ideal Types, see Martindale, D.: Sociological theory and the ideal type. *In* Symposium on Sociological Theory. Edited by L. Gross. New York, Harper & Row, 1957.

10. See for example Arnold, D. V. (ed.): Subcultures. Berkley, Calif., Glendessary Press, 1970, pp. 92–93.

11. Cohen, A. K.: Delinquent Boys. The Culture of the Gang. London, Routledge & Kegan Paul, 1956, pp. 51–52.

12. Ibid., p. 60.

13. Ibid., p. 59.

14. Shibutani, T. Reference groups as perspectives. Am J Sociol, *60*:562, 1955.

15. Ibid., p. 565.

16. MacIver and Page make a distinction between "like" and "common" relative to interests. "The 'like' is what we have distributively privately, each to himself. The 'common' is what we have collectively, what we share without dividing up." See MacIver, R. and Page, C. Society—An Introductory Analysis. Macmillan., 1962, p. 32.

17. Some inspiration for this table comes from E. Dunning (The structural functional properties of folk games and modern sports., *Sportwissenschaft*, *3*:215, 1973) who compares folk games and modern sports.

18. Margan, F. and Finney, B. Surfing. Paul Hamlyn, Sydney, 1970, p. 155.

19. This point is more fully documented in Pearson, K.: Leisure in Australia. *In* Outdoor Recreation: Australian Perspectives. Edited by D. Mercer. Melbourne, Sorrett, 1976.

20. All open-ended data were transcribed longhand onto McBee key sort cards. Categories were generated on the basis of (1) relevant literature and (2) obvious clustering of responses. Cards were then punched for computational procedures. These cards then served as a response retrieval system.

21. Major differences in orientation revealed by subjective responses of participants were differences in orientation to time, to the body, to competition, to formal organizations, and toward the natural environment. See Pearson, K.: Sport: Play and Athletics— A Sociological Approach. Paper presented at A.C.P.H.E.R. Conference, Brisbane, 1977.

22. Schafer, W. Sport & Youth Counterculture: Contrasting Socialization Themes. Paper presented at Conference on Sport & Social Deviancy, State University of New York, Brockport, 1971. Alderman, R. The Modern Young Athlete in our Society. Paper presented at Conference on Sport Society and Personality. La Trobe University, Melbourne, 1975. Reich, C. *The Greening of America*. New York, Random House, 1970. Roszak, T. The Making of a Counter Culture. New York, Anchor Books, 1969. Berger, P. K., Berger, B., and Kellner, H.: The Homeless Mind. Hammondsworth, Middlesex, England, Penguin, 1974.

23. Turner, Ralph.: The real self: From institution to impulse. Am J Sociol, *81*(5), 1976.

24. See for example Ingham, A. & Loy, J.: The social system of sport: A humanistic perspective. Quest, *19*:3, 1973.

25. See Pearson, K.: Subcultures, drug use and physical activity. Keynote address to I.C.P.A.S. Conference, S.T. 2. Quebec, 1976. Also Sport: Play and Athletics—A Sociological Approach, op. cit.

26. McKinney, J.: Constructive Typology and Social Theory. New York, Appleton-Century-Crofts, 1966.

the man on the horse

MARVIN B. SCOTT

CHARACTER AND COOLNESS

Worship, as Durkheim has taught us,[1] involves the collective reaffirmation of moral values. Now if we ask where the virtues of moral character—courage, integrity, dignity, and so forth—are reaffirmed in action, we arrive at a curious irony that the racetrack and not the church is a place of worship.

Attributes of moral character are established only in risk-taking situations: before we are ready to impute to a person the quality of strong character, he must be seen as voluntarily putting something on the line.[2]

At the racetrack, we find a sphere of life where men are out to establish character, demonstrate virtue, and achieve honor. These men are the jockeys; and while on stage they are putting on the line their money, their reputations, and their lives.

The jockey is one of the few survivals of the traditional concept of "the man of honor"—which interestingly has always been synonymous with "the man on the horse": *cavalier*, *caballero*, knight.

Feats of gallantry—or the capacity to follow the rules of decorum when it is costly to do so—are not uncommon at the track. Thus a jockey in a neck-and-neck duel down the stretch has been known to casually hand his whip to a rider who dropped his in the course of the race—and

then resume a strenuous hand ride to a winning finish, demonstrating a prideful self-confidence of succeeding though under a handicap.[3]

Integrity, another attribute of moral character, is not mere honesty, but honesty when it is costly to oneself to be honest. An illustration of what I have in mind involves the case of a leading jockey whose license was revoked for betting on mounts other than his own. A wiretap revealed that the jockey had made twenty-seven bets *against* his own mounts; but in eleven of these races he rode the winner.[4] This case dramatically illustrates one of the stable features of horse racing: when a jockey is placed in a situation where he must choose between playing for himself or playing for some other party that employs him, he will opt for the other party. That is, he chooses integrity. Thus we can expect integrity even from a dishonest jockey.

Above all, the jockey with strong character possesses the perceived virtue of coolness. A jockey who possesses this attribute is said to always "keep his cool," "to ride like an ice man," or to have ice in his veins. The ideal horse-jockey combination is a fiery animal and an icy rider.

The cool jockey can wait patiently with a horse in a pocket and get through on the inside, risking the possibility that there will be no opening. Coolness is waiting far back in the pack, risking the possibility that his horse will not "get up" in time. Coolness is sparing the whip on a front-running horse when another animal has pressed into the lead, risking the possibility that once his horse is passed he will not get started again. All these activities are taken by observers as instances of a jockey's character. In short, moral character is coolness in risky situations.

Morning glories are horses that perform well offstage but fail to demonstrate heart in the heat of competition. The term is also used for jockeys who display all the necessary skills in the morning workouts but lack coolness in the heat of battle. Horsemen believe—no doubt expressing a stereotypical bias—that Negroes lack the moral character necessary for being jockeys, though they are thought to possess a "sweet seat" and "strong hands." (Thus there are many Negro exercise boys, but very few Negro jockeys.) By a kind of self-fulfilling hypothesis, the belief is maintained. When a Negro exercise boy is given opportunities to "don the silks" in the afternoon, he tries so hard to make a good showing that as a result he shows a lack of coolness. Interestingly, in the nineteenth century most jockeys were Negroes, and one of the reputed all-time greats was Isaac Murphy, a Negro. Horsemen acknowledge this, but contend that the style of racing has changed in such a way that qualities are called for today that were less important in an earlier day, qualities that are captured by the term "coolness."

After a jockey has suffered a serious fall, many players feel they should avoid betting on his later mounts. They feel that he has lost his moral character. Horsemen themselves share this belief and are reluctant to give mounts in important races to jockeys who are making a comeback. Naturally, jockeys fear the physical consequences of a serious spill. But what is not so obvious is that they fear that a spill will cause them to lose their character; similarly, they fear that others will perceive them as losing their character.

What the above discussion has implied and what will now be made explicit is that traits of moral character are generated by social organization.

To begin with, a jockey's success depends upon his getting mounts on winning horses. The greenest boy can outride the greatest reinsman— if the former has a superior horse. How, then, does a jockey get the best horses? Simply by having the widest selection of mounts from which to choose. What a jockey wants is a choice between several mounts in a race; he wants to be in demand. And to be in demand he must somehow mobilize his activities so as to

appear to possess those virtues of character that horsemen deem important for jockeys— integrity, gameness, coolness. In other words, a jockey must commit himself to a line of risk taking because not to do so would constitute an even greater loss to self.[5]

BECOMING A JOCKEY

To start his career as a jockey, a young man need only convince an employer to take him on. A boy need not ever have been on a horse so long as he meets the physical requirements of size and the psychological requirement of desire.[6]

Once employed he starts as a stable boy— carrying water, mucking stalls, polishing tack, walking hots (horses that are cooled out after working or racing). He also rides about with the horse when shipped and sleeps on straw. Trainers view these demeaning activities as a kind of initiation period. As one put it: "If a boy is willing to travel 300 miles in the back of a van sleeping on piss-soaked straw, or if he wades through a stall full of shit at 5:30 every morning for no pay, you know he wants to be a jock." These activities are known as "learning horse."

The stable boy himself does not think of these activities as particularly demeaning, so long as it is clear that they are part of the first step of his career. Some fail to get beyond the stage of stable boy and are permanently placed here; others get here as a result of downward mobility (for example, exercise boys who have gone bad). For the young man performing demeaning activities, one of the protective factors to self is age: culturally, we expect boys to engage in dirty work. To distinguish himself from the "failures," the upwardly mobile stable boy will walk about with riding boots (though he is not yet permitted to ride), and during breaks in the routine he will prominently be squeezing rubber balls (as an aid to strengthen his hands for his anticipated future role).

Eventually, the boy is tried on a horse in a workout. If the horse responds to his urging and if the boy follows instructions, he is ready for official apprenticeship. He is placed under contract and apprenticed to the employer for three to five years. The contract, formulated by the Jockey Club, is standard throughout the country. In the contract, the boy pledges to keep the employer's secrets and to obey orders given by his representative (the trainer). The employer in turn provides room and board, a small salary, and traveling expenses.

Before the boy gets a mount in a race, he will spend months exercising horses. His designation is shifted from stable boy to exercise boy, but he must continue to muck stalls, polish tack, etc. The role of exercise boy is the most prestigious role below the rank of jockey, and is thus a status alternative that cushions the loss of face suffered by a jockey who failed to make the grade.

Horsemen say that the most important reason for exercise boys failing to become jockeys, or for jockeys dropping back to become exercise boys, is their inability to make the weight. The interesting question is why do they fail to make the weight?

To begin with, size (within limits) is no barrier to becoming a jockey; for though it is atypical, jockeys—including some of the leading ones— are as tall as five feet, eleven inches. While the growing boy cannot control his height, he can control weight, given the desire that he has amply demonstrated in going through the initiation period. My observations and interviews have led me to hypothesize that a boy does not first pick up weight and then have his career blocked. Rather, career opportunities first close up and then he gains weight—though lay beliefs hold the reverse to be the case.[7] The stable boy who finds himself exercising horses for a year or so without getting a mount can see the writing on the wall; the next step in the career ladder is not being opened for him; he sees himself as lacking the skill or character necessary for the competitive scene. By picking up weight, he has a face-saving device for not going on.

Another common instance of sudden weight increase is that of the jockey recently graduated from the apprentice ranks. Until one year from the day he has his first mount or upon winning forty races, whichever is the longer, the apprentice jockey is given what is called a weight allowance or "bug." A five-pound allowance means that any horse ridden by an apprentice will carry five pounds less than that stipulated in the race conditions. As we shall see later, horsemen are hyperconscious of weight and believe that five pounds equal one length—the difference between victory and defeat in most races. Thus a "bug" is likely to get many offers to ride, and having several mounts to choose from in a race will increase his probability of getting hot

horses. Frequently the leading jockey at any given meet is a bug, not because of his skill but because of the advantages that come with his weight allowance. But when a jockey loses his bug, suddenly he finds few if any mounts forthcoming. Overnight—at the loss of a bug—the jockey who was yesterday's hottest rider is today's inexperienced kid. At this point, the young jockey begins to pick up weight—which generally is attributed to his being a growing boy.

The acceptable weight for an exercise boy makes face-saving easy for an erstwhile jockey. While the virtual upper limit for a jockey is 117 pounds, exercise boys can be as heavy as 130. Thus, if a boy weighs 120, he might be continually asked why he doesn't lose weight and get mounts. But if he is over 120, he is considered beyond the point of losing weight; yet he is secure in his position as exercise boy.

If a jockey weighs more than the horse is to carry according to the conditions of the race, the difference is known as "overweight." Bettors believe that "overweight" has a decided effect on the performance of a horse, and information about overweight is taken into account before a final selection is made. Before the first post at all tracks, the overweights of all horses are announced over the public address system. This information is repeated before every race and is also shown in colored-chalk notations on boards located at various places around the track. Some handicapping systems sold to the betting public have as one of the rules: eliminate all horses carrying overweight. Many horsemen share these beliefs about the adverse effects of overweight, and a trainer on some occasions may in fact seek an overweight jockey when he wants his horse to lose.

The overweight limit is five pounds. A pound or two makes a big difference in the mounts a boy can accept. If a horse is scheduled to carry 110 pounds and the jockey scheduled to ride the mount "weighs in" at 116 (his weight and saddle and other gear are included in the weighing), he will be disqualified from riding the horse. A jockey's weight is classified in the following way: a light-weight jockey weighs less than 110 pounds; a middleweight is 110 to 113; and a heavyweight weighs above 113. To lose that extra pound or so before a race, some jockeys go through the process of "wasting," which involves daily sessions in a steam cabinet or sweating between rubber sheets.

BENCHMARKS IN A RIDER'S CAREER

A jockey who wins his first race, like a horse, is said to have broken his maiden. The news of a first win is broadcast by the public address announcer, and the crowd cheers the young man; a broken maiden is also a significant item in newspaper sports pages. In the jockeys' room, the ritual is to give the boy a cold shower—with his winning silks on.

The second major event in a jockey's career is winning the first handicap or stakes race. A jockey receives 10 percent of the purse for a winning ride. In the heavy-purse stakes and handicap races, of say $100,000, the jockey can earn about $10,000 for a minute's work. But more than money is involved. A race for the big chips poses a real test of moral character. Here coolness is considered to be more crucial than in other races. The winning of the first handicap race is a *rite de passage* where the self-image of one who possesses moral character is dramatically confirmed.

The third important event in the jockey's career is his first bad fall. The significance of this event, as already suggested, is not whether the jockey will be injured badly enough to impede his riding. More important is whether he can—psychologically—ride at all. After a bad spill, some jockeys don't "come back"; they don't feel at home any more on a horse. But to come back after a bad fall and continue to ride with the same success as before fully authenticates one as a jockey in the eyes of horsemen; he has demonstrated the moral attribute of gameness.

In interviewing jockeys (who are difficult to interview in any case, since they are instructed to maintain a distance from strangers who might be prospective con men or fixers), the most difficult subject to get them to talk about is falls. "We never talk about those things," one rider told me. "It happens, it happens. There's nothing to talk about."

Another jockey who after a fall failed to make a comeback said: "For a while you only get pigs to ride. The trainers with hot horses ain't out to give you a break. Only the gyps like [he mentioned a certain hand-to-mouth trainer] will put you on their plugs. I'm out of the business now. Who wants to get killed riding plugs?"

INCOME AND EXPENSES

Whether they ride plugs or hot mounts, jockeys' riding fees are the same. The usual guide lines, as established by the racing associations, are $20 for an unplaced horse, $25 for third, $35 for second, and $50 for first. By tradition, the winning jockey also receives 10 percent of the purse.

Jockeys have many expenses. Except for the silks, they own everything that goes on the horse. A jockey has about $1,000 invested in his "stage clothes": boots, pants, saddles, and other tack.

A much more expensive overhead is the jockey's agent, who receives 20 percent of the earnings—on winning or losing mounts. Jockeys typically do not resent such fees; most believe that their success or failure on the turf depends as much on the agent as anything else. Only occasionally does a jockey refer to his agent as "my pimp." The agent's job is to solicit mounts for the rider. If the boy is hot, the agent has no problem and may insist that a trainer wanting the jockey's services pay a flat fee, usually 10 percent of the purse, win or lose. Usually handling only one jockey, the agent closely identifies with his boy. When discussing the successes or failures of his boy, an agent often refers to him as "I"[8]—I'm getting nothing to ride these days but cripples," "I was just nosed out of three mounts yesterday," etc.

One aspect of the agent's role is to cool out the losing jockey. When a jockey loses on a favorite, the agent will say that the horse shouldn't have been a favorite; for it wasn't the best horse in the race. If the jockey falls into a slump, the agent will point out the names of all the jockeys who are in a slump, recall the time that some leading jockey had fifty-two consecutive losers, and expound on a philosophy that deals with the swinging pendulum of luck.

Typically, jockeys don't enter into contracts with agents. The arrangement is based on common understandings. Some jockeys change agents frequently, especially when in a slump, or when they believe that the agent isn't getting enough good mounts. Some agents will go to great lengths to get mounts for their boys, at times going so far as to exercise horses free to establish a relation of indebtedness with trainers. The success of an agent can easily be determined by his demeanor. The agent with the hot boy is quiet, tight-lipped, and noncommittal. The struggling agent is a friendly hail-fellow-well-met, ready to slap a trainer on the back and offer him a favor. Unless one is aware of the structural elements that determine the agents' "personalities," one might conclude—in observing the same agents over a period of years—that they are a manic-depressive breed.

The jockey's other expense is the valet. The valet is employed by the track, but receives about $5 a mount and $10 a winner from the jockey. At getaway day (that is, the last day of a meet), the jockey customarily gives his valet a bonus of $100 or more, depending on his success. The valets are frequently former jockeys who have grown too big, too old, or too inept to continue as riders. The valets are treated with a good deal of charity; many jockeys feel that "there but for the grace of God. . . ."

About twenty minutes before post time, the jockeys are weighed for the race in the scale room, and the clerk checks the reading against the assigned weight. If the jockey is light, the clerk will tell the valet, "Give him a shade," and if the boy is heavy, the clerk may suggest, "Try a lighter saddle pad." [9]

After being fitted out at the proper weight, the jockey hands his equipment to a valet, who goes to the paddock where he assists the trainer in saddling the horse. Later, when the jockey has weighed in after the race, the valet takes his equipment and returns it to the jockeys' quarters. In his free time, the valet looks after the tack, arranges clothes, helps the jockey dress, etc.

TYPES OF JOCKEYS

Horsemen recognize three categories of jockeys: "honest boys," "money jocks," and "businessmen."

To get the reputation of an honest boy (most jockeys are so categorized) a jockey must satisfy two conditions: he must accept all mounts offered him, and he must ride in strict accord to instructions.

If a jockey's services are called upon, he must not refuse, lest his reputation as "honest" be damaged. The only legitimate reason for not accepting a mount is to have already accepted a bid to ride some other trainer's horse. Given this cultural expectation, we might expect that all trainers would freely attempt to gain the services of the hottest jockeys, ensuring the best possible chance of their horses finishing in the money. Moreover, we might expect that given a choice between mounts, the jockeys will always choose the hot horse. In actuality, trainers will often call upon second-rate jockeys to ride their horses; and jockeys will often choose to ride a second-rate horse. These anomalous choices deserve some explanation.

When a trainer has a horse whose expected performance for a particular event is highly uncertain, often he will prefer to call upon the services of a lesser-known jockey. Should he choose a superior jockey and should the horse perform very poorly, then the superior jockey will—when given a choice in the future—choose to ride for another trainer. The trainer's disinclination to ask a hot jockey to ride an uncertain animal has the consequence of resolving the jockey's dilemma: to be "honest" he must accept all mounts—usually on a first-come, first-served basis—but to maintain a good winning record he needs a choice from among *hot* mounts. In sum, trainers in the pursuit of their own self-interest help jockeys maintain their reputation as being both "honest" and "hot."

From time to time, however, a trainer will call upon the services of a hot boy even when he knows for certain that his animal will do little running on a particular day. In the erratic horse's next race, where the winning effort is planned, the trainer may shift to a no-name jockey. This shifting from a hot jockey to a no-name boy is a maneuver to get better odds. The playing public reasons this way: "If hot jock Jones can't bring the animal home, the horse is a nothing." When the horse wins next time at a big price with the no-name jock, the public attributes the victory to some factor of racing luck and not to the manipulations of the man behind the horse. Naturally, the trainer can't pull this maneuver too often, for fear of alienating the good jockey. Moreover, each time the trainer employs this maneuver, he is tacitly indebted to "pay off" the jockey by furnishing him with a hot mount in the future.

As I have already suggested, the hot jock will sometimes choose to ride what he takes to be an inferior mount. Such decisions typically involve horses from the leading money-winning stables. The jockey "trades" a bad mount today for a good mount tomorrow. That is, the winning stable, when it has a hot horse, will go back with the boy who is willing to ride those horses whose performance is uncertain.

In general, a type of equilibrium is established whereby the leading trainers get the leading jocks to ride for them, and the leading jocks get the best mounts. But, as I indicated, this state of affairs is the result of many sorts of exchanges and tacit negotiations.

The second criterion of a jock's reputation as "honest"—strictly following instructions of the trainer—can be explained more briefly. Trainers, for reasons that will be made clear later, often have something to gain when their horses lose on a particular occasion. One way of making a horse lose or appear to be off form is to instruct the jockey to run the animal in a manner contrary to the horse's best efforts. If a horse runs best in front, the trainer who wants to lose will instruct the jockey to come from behind; if the horse runs best close to the rail, the trainer will instruct the jockey to keep the horse wide; if the horse responds only to energetic whipping, the trainer will instruct the jockey not to use the whip. The jockey may well realize that the instructions are contrary to the horse's best efforts; he might realize that by *not* following instructions he can win an otherwise losing race. However, he will *not* race in accord with his own best judgment, because what he has at stake is his reputation as an "honest boy."

The second type of jockey—the "money jock"—is not concerned with the number of mounts he receives but with getting the best mounts in the best races. If he had his way, the money jock would accept only mounts in the feature Saturday race. In receiving mounts, his agent is often instructed to demand a flat fee for his services. For instance, the stable demanding the services of the money jock must meet a set fee of, say, $250 (10 percent of the winning share in most ordinary races) on a win-or-lose basis. This demand usually means that the jock will get hot mounts, for owners are slow to put up a win-or-lose fee unless they have a hot horse and expect to win. By getting hot horses, the money jock will be on a mount where he can display his skills and character to best advantage. These are some of the backstage manipulations that make his on-stage performance appear so stunning.

Money jocks are preferred by moneyed stables. The leading handicap and stakes horses are to be found in the barns of those owners who regard horse racing literally as a game. Being able to foot the bills, their concern is with the honor that goes with owning (and frequently breeding) the *winner*. Second- or third-place money is seldom a target for these owners.

The characteristic of the money jock is his in-and-out performance. When he is "in," it is frequently because he has—as a consequence of his coolness—staged a ride that saved the horse perhaps as much as five lengths. Many horsemen say that a money jock can give a horse a five-length advantage. They believe the money jock can remain cool in a pocket and plunge through on the inside rail when and if the opportunity comes, rather than taking a horse on the outside where the certainty of racing room may cost a horse five lengths. Since one length equals five pounds (by rule of thumb calculation accepted by racing secretaries), the right kind of ride can—in lay theory at least—make up for a deficit of twenty-five pounds spotted to the opposition. In short, the moneyed stables depend on the money jocks to bring home *first* money.

The third type of jockey—the "businessman"—is a boy who "gets what he can, any way he can," as one observer put it. This is the lay image most spectators have of all jockeys. Even Devereux, in his study of gambling, suggests that because the jockey's racing days are numbered, he will be inclined to conspire with gamblers in their betting coups. By entering into the plans of gamblers by, let us say, pulling a horse on orders (presumably to protect the bookies against a large loss), the jockey can solidify his relations with the gamblers who may be of help to him after retirement.[10]

Devereux's remarks represent an interesting theory of an activity that occurred in a real *past* or a *fictionalized* present. To begin with, jockeys—unlike most other athletes—are neither limited as to age nor do they believe they are. Unlike boxers, baseball players, and football pros., who are called old men at thirty-five and are retired by forty, jockeys have been active and in fact won some of the richest handicap races while in their late fifties; two of the most prominent boys (jockeys are boys at any age) were Pat Remmilard and Johnny Longden, both of whom were racing until their sixtieth years. Asked when jockeys should retire, they respond not by mentioning an age, but say, "When you can't get any more mounts." Second, retirement funds and pension plans (for jockeys disabled in a spill) cushion the pressure of "getting it" while you can. Finally, and most important, the surveillance system of the various racing associations and the severity of sanctions (being ruled off the turf for misconduct) virtually have done away with the "businessman" who has conspired with gamblers to fix a race.

As the term is used today, "businessman" refers to the type of jockey whose overwhelming motivation is the profit motive. This motive is expressed in the jock's assertion, heard in the business world but seldom among the other jocks, "I'm not in business for my health." Further, businessmen believe that, at least for them, the way to make money is by betting on their mounts. So far as possible, businessmen will seek mounts on horses they think are ready to win at a good price.

Among those jockeys who have no agents, by far the largest group are the businessmen. Preferring to hustle their own mounts, they seek out the small-time owner-trainer who stables "platers" (cheap claiming horses). This type of trainer can't pay the win-or-lose fee demanded by the money jocks, nor does he expect to get the hot jocks who are cultivating greener pastures. A more likely choice of rider is the businessman. Moreover, since the owner-trainer has to foot all the bills, he finds in the businessman an opportunity to cut corners. Frequently the businessman will exercise horses free or simply wait for payment until the stable is having some success. In exchange, the owner-trainer takes the jockey into his confidence and strategies are worked out together. Although not under contract to the owner-trainer, the jock often will travel the various circuits with him.

The owner-trainer with whom the businessman associates is invariably one who doesn't bet and often has the reputation of being poor but honest. This sets the stage for a mutually advantageous arrangement. A betting trainer would take great pains to conceal his intentions and limit the information flow; for a leak of intentions would affect the odds on the horse, and he wishes to get the most for his betting investment. Since the nonbetting trainer has little to lose by revealing his intentions to a jockey, he can get the services of a skillful jockey for little cost: namely, information concerning his intentions.

The businessman is quick to see the advantage in hooking up with the honest trainer. A brief explanation of the problems of putting over a coup will show why this is the case. When betting trainers manipulate horses for the purpose of winning bets, the investigative activities of the racing association quickly get wind of this and place pressure on the stable (just what pressures can be applied will be discussed later). To avoid such investigations, betting stables today engage in *partial* concealment of a horse's true form. A partial concealment, however, implies a partial disclosure of form, which legitimates a horse's winning (that is, nothing is incongruous about a horse winning if it has displayed a recent fair effort). On the other hand, the fact that form has been partly concealed helps assure a fair price (conceived typically at odds of about 4 to 1). Betting stables do not run "in-and-outers" or "sharp wake-ups" that pay "boxcar mutuels" (winners with very big pay-offs). Thus the gambling stables work to maintain the impression of simon-pure honesty. The known nonbetting, honest trainer, however, can run hot-and-cold horses and win at boxcar mutuels with impunity; officials will take for granted that the erratic performance of his horses is due to low-grade stock, thought to be naturally unpredictable. Also, as long as the boxcar mutuels are coming from the horses of honest stables, in-and-out performances are tolerated—indeed, welcome—for they give variety in the payoffs. To the businessman jockey, one or two bets on one or two 40-to-1 shots during a fifty-five-day racing meet are big dividends. Thus the betting jockey prefers to stick with the honest trainer. Indirectly, then, in the manner I have suggested, honesty is in the service of "vice."

When two or three businessmen are in the same race, the scene is set for possible chicanery. One may find here the closest thing to a fixed race, what is called a "jockeys' race." Here two or three boys, surveying the situation in the jocks' room before going to the paddock, will come to an understanding through a kind of tacit bargaining. The conversation among businessmen Tom, Dick, and Harry might run something like this:

Tom: How do you like your mounts today, fellers?

Dick: Well, I have a ready horse, but I'm not going to bet a dime. There's nothing that will keep up with the favorite.

Harry: My horse is pretty fair, too, but no use killing him for show dough. He'll be saved for next week. Think I'll bet him then.

Tom: You know, guys, my horse can turn it on in the stretch. If only something would go with the favorite for a mile and knock the wind out of him! You know, Dick, if your horse went with the favorite for half a mile and then you, Harry, picked him up at the far turn, the favorite would be a dead duck. And if I can get home with Slow Bones, I'll be glad to "save" with you boys.

That is all that need be said. The favorite is knocked out of competition by the top of the stretch, and Tom waltzes home on Slow Bones at 20 to 1. Next time, perhaps it will be Harry's turn to come home first.

A jockeys' race—when it occurs at all—takes place in the last race. One reason for this is that the cheapest race of the day is typically the last race, and here we would be more likely to find two or three businessmen in the same race. Second, the last race is almost always a distance race, at least $1^1/_{16}$ miles. The longer distance is necessary for working out a strategy (however vaguely suggested). In a sprint race most of the horses are rushing from start to finish, and strategies to control the pace of the race are not easy to put into operation (unless the planning is highly deliberate and carefully worked out). The most important feature of the last race is that it is the *last* race. At this time the stewards tend to relax their usual vigilance, and the crowd is dispersing and is less likely to shout disapproval at what appears to be a jockeys' race. In fact, many fans assume that the last race will be a jockeys' race and will be stabbing for a long shot to get even on the assumption that a long shot has a better chance in the last race than it would otherwise. And when a long shot does suddenly pop home a winner the crowd—even when they haven't bet on the particular horse—voices a kind of approval. On homeward-bound buses and trains, the conversation will center on how the player bet or almost bet the winning long shot in the last race. On the other hand, a favored horse winning the last race is unpopular; the mass of players are betting long shots to get even. A subtle pressure is exerted on the stewards not to inquire too closely into the last race, since one of their jobs is to keep the public content. A jockeys' race sometimes gives the appearance of a well-rehearsed performance, and yet there is nothing specific to put one's finger on. Nothing is, strictly speaking, illegal.

Another feature of the last race is that the riders, often having only one mount that day, have been sitting in the jockeys' room together for six hours, and as time has passed, eventually have turned their conversation to the race they will run. According to the rules of racing, the jockey—even if he has only one mount—must report to the jockeys' room one hour before the first race, and remain there until riding his last mount of the day. The sheer amount of time jockeys spend together is conducive to "discussing things."

Finally, the businessman is generally better informed than any other type of jockey about the condition of the animal he is to ride and the intentions of the stable. Moreover, since the businessman often has the trainer in his debt, he can get away with not running the race exactly to orders, which in any case will be something like: "You know what the horse can do. Just do your best."

The businessman jockey doesn't see anything wrong with the staging of a race and would probably be mildly shocked if accused of dishonest dealings. The cooperative arrangement is viewed as just another version of the traditional practice of "saving." During a race, a rider may try to make a bargain to share the purse. For instance, two horses may enter the stretch head and head, and one jock will call out: "How about saving?" The other might say: "You're on."

Although the practice of saving is frowned upon officially in most races, it is a mandatory practice among jockeys who ride as an entry in a stakes or handicap race. For example, a stable might enter two (or more) horses in a race, and the jockeys arrange a 60-40 split if one should win.

The bargaining arrangement that occurs among businessmen is to them but a form of the legitimate practice of saving. They legitimate the arrangements they make by referring to them as "saving," just as trusted bank employees justify their embezzlement by referring to it as "borrowing." [11]

In sum, an analysis of the deviant practice of the jockeys' race involves the conditions typically thought to be relevant in the analysis of most kinds of deviance. [12] First the *conduciveness* and *opportunity* associated with knowing something about the trainer's intentions and being thrown into interaction together, permitting the teaming up in a deviant act; the *strain* placed on the businessman who wins only a few races and has relatively few mounts and must make these count; the *legitimation* of the course of action through a "neutralization technique"[13] of saving; and finally, a *laxity of social control*—characteristic of the last race milieu—on the part of the racing officials.[14]

COMMUNICATION STRATEGIES

During a race, the jockeys must keep in mind three separate audiences—the fans, the horse-men and the officials—each of which is demanding a certain kind of performance. The crowd wants an energetic effort; the officials, an honest, free-from-fouling ride; the trainer, a ride to orders. These different audiences frequently make demands at cross-purposes. The trainer may instruct the jockey not to press the horse, and this may appear to the crowd as the absence of an energetic ride; and if the horse is heavily bet on, the jockey might be booed. On the other hand, the trainer may give the jockey instructions to get out in front at once, which often involves cutting across the field rapidly and may lead to officials' sanctioning for rough riding.

Whatever the orders, the jockey must at least *appear* to be riding energetically and cleanly. To bring off these appearances the jockey has developed certain communication strategies—*dramatic accentuation* and *concealment* or a combination of both. (Thus the jockey engages in impression management even in situations of total involvement.)

Dramatic accentuation refers to the exaggeration of an aspect of one's performance. Horse-men sometimes speak of this strategy as riding in the style of Don Meade. In 1930, Don Meade was ruled off the turf for betting on horses other than his own. After several years of applying to be reinstated, he was finally given a license to ride on the strength of a promise that "if they just give me one more chance, they'll see a jockey ride as none had ever ridden in history." To keep his promise he dramatically accentuated an always-trying riding style. "Stigmatized as a jockey who would throw a race, he always pushed his mounts to their utmost, and made a display of this that became part of his characteristic riding style—of shoving a horse. ..."[15] Today jockeys who think they are under suspicion suddenly adopt the Meade style. To some degree, all jockeys adopt this style to appear honest and energetic. This style, emphasizing the energetic use of hands and legs, does not

improve the horse's performance. It is all part of impression management.

Oddly enough, this strategy not only takes in the audience of fans, but also the other jockeys. Some jockeys become specialists in appearing to be working so hard on a horse that the other jockeys in a race may assume that the horse being worked on is tiring fast. The jockey on a front-running mount may begin to wave his elbows furiously (known as "pumping"), and the other jockeys, believing that the horse will soon slow up, will wait before making a move. Suddenly, just as the horse appears to be finished and the other horses make their move, the front horse jumps out to a bigger lead and now is really being pressed by its jockey for the first time. Even when the other jockeys suspect that pumping may be a deception, they can never be sure. Hence, at the very least, the strategy undercuts certainty. While pumping can be used as a strategy to win a race, it is equally serviceable for the jock who has instructions to lose a race. He can save a horse for another race and at the same time give the appearance to the fans and officials of pressing hard.

The example of pumping illustrates that techniques of dramatic accentuation might also serve as a strategy of concealment—one of the strategies that a jockey must learn. Concealment strategies are particularly important in handicap races and trainers will caution riders *not to win by too much*; for an easy win will lead the track handicapper to add extra poundage on the horse in his next outing. If the jockey fails to conceal the true form of a handicap horse, the trainer will mete out sanctions, as jockey Eddie Arcaro recalls:

> I won the Metropolitan with Third Degree by five lengths. That was a mile race. Handicapper John B. Campbell was so impressed by this performance that he tacked on more weight for Third Degree's Suburban Handicap engagement. That added weight proved to be the difference between victory and defeat. John Gaver [the trainer] gave me hell for that.[16]

A DAY IN THE LIFE OF A JOCKEY

Unless the jockey exercises horses in the morning or is called upon to have a dry run with a horse in preparation for some big engagement, his working day begins at noon. At that time, he checks into the jockeys' quarters located near the paddock (where the horses will be saddled before each race). By the time the jock arrives, the valets will already have been at work for a few hours, polishing boots and saddles and checking the colors to be worn by the riders. The silks (the shirts that bear the colors of the owner) are brought in from the "color room" and hung on racks in the order of each race and each starting position. When the jock arrives, he heads straight for the steam room or the whirlpool bath, and then sits down in the locker room to leaf through the *Racing Form* or josh with the valets.

By 12:30, the patrol judge or one of the stewards announces he is going to screen films of the previous day's races. This is known as the jockeys' matinee. Attendance is optional, except for those jockeys who are specifically ordered to attend. From time to time, the judge will stop the film to point out incidents of misconduct, or—in the case of apprentice jocks—he may point out mistakes and offer advice.

Before each race, the jockey's weight is checked in the weighing room. He weighs in wearing his colors, carrying his equipment—and nothing else. If he has a cigarette in his mouth, he won't be weighed.

Afterwards, he goes to the paddock where the trainer and sometimes the owner will be waiting in a stall with the same number as the post position of the horse. The horse has already been saddled and either is standing in the stall or is being paraded around the paddock, led by the groom or hot walker. Now the trainer instructs the jockey: "This horse has been primed for this race; keep him close to the pace and when the early runners fade go to the whip—and come home early."

Parading to the starting gate, the jock looks over at the tote board and sees his horse is 3 to 1. He feels a little more confident knowing that so many fans have thought highly of his chances. Also, with all that money riding on him, he knows he must look good. Now he's at the starting gate, and finally, in his stall. All the mounts are in. Some of the boys are chanting: "No chance yet, sir; no chance; no chance, sir." Suddenly all is quiet and the starter presses the button releasing the gate.

It is a close race, but the jock's mount lasts to win. Returning to the winner's circle, he salutes the placing judges with his whip; failing to do so results in a fine. In the winner's circle, he is photographed along with the trainer, the owner and his wife, and friends of the family. Returning to the jockeys' quarters, he can relax if he doesn't ride in the next race. In the jockeys' quarters, he sees some of the other jocks relaxing, watching television, playing cards, pool, or Ping-Pong. Others are in the heat box or in a bunk bed swathed in rubber sheets.

After his last mount of the day, the jock can leave the jockeys' quarters. He then goes to the clubhouse or turf club where his agent has been playing the horses and talking to the trainers. He consults with the agent as to his future mounts. He stays to watch a race or two, very often as a guest in the private box of one of the owners or trainers. Once the jockey leaves the park, his racing day is over.

NOTES

1. Durkheim, Emile: The Elementary Forms of Religious Life. New York, The Free Press of Glencoe, 1957. I am indebted to Erving Goffman for the general point suggested in this paragraph.

2. This is the central point of Goffman's essay, Where the Action Is. *In* Interaction Ritual. Chicago, Aldine Publishing Company, 1967.

3. For an illustration see Atkinson, Ted: All the Way. New York, Paxton Slade, 1961, p. 66.

4. Ainslie, Tom: Ainslie's Jockey Book. New York, Trident Press, 1967.

5. Commitment, then, involves some kind of side bet, such as one's reputation. See Becker, Howard S.: Notes on the concept of commitment. Am J Sociol, July 1960, pp. 32–40.

6. There is no lower age limit to begin one's career, though most boys are "brought up" (that is, taken on as an apprentice) in their teens. Some boys seek employment after they have passed the legal age when they can quit school. Since most of the boy's chores take place from 5 to 9 A.M. and again in the early evening, he may continue with his formal schooling without gross interference with his racing career.

7. It should be emphasized that I am here presenting a tentative hypothesis. Hard data to support the hypothesis is difficult to come by. It would be necessary to obtain weights of the boys and establish correlations (in the statistical sense) between shifts in weight and career events.

8. Ainslie, op. cit., p. 6.

9. Atkinson, op. cit., p. 171.

10. Devereux, Edward C. Jr.: Gambling and the Social Structure—A Sociological Study of Lotteries and Horse Racing in Contemporary America. Unpublished doctoral dissertation, Harvard University, 1949, p. 424.

11. Cressey, Donald: Other People's Money. New York, The Free Press of Glencoe, 1953.

12. Cohen, Albert K.: The sociology of the deviant act. Am Sociol Rev, February 1965, pp. 9–14.

13. Sykes, Gresham M.: and Matza, David: Techniques of neutralization. Am Sociol Rev, December 1957, pp. 667–669.

14. Taken together, these components of a deviant act constitute what Neil J. Smelser, in Theory of Collective Behavior, New York: Free Press of Glencoe, 1963, calls a value-added process, which he uses in his explanatory model of all kinds of collective behavior.

15. Parmer, Charles B.: For Gold and Glory. New York, Carrick and Evans, 1939, p. 212.

16. Arcaro, Eddie: I Ride to Win. New York, Greenberg, 1951, p. 39. The strategy of winning by the shortest possible margin is the key deceptive move of the poolroom hustler. See Polsky, Ned: The hustler. *In* Hustlers, Beats, and Others. Chicago, Aldine Publishing Company, 1967.

the rugby football club as a type of "male preserve":

some sociological notes

K. G. SHEARD AND E. G. DUNNING

Sport is an area of social life which is rich in opportunities for sociological research. So far, however, little work of a genuinely sociological character has been carried out into the problems which it raises.[1] This, it seems to us, is particularly the case as far as the subcultures which arise in connection with sport are concerned. The present paper is an attempt—a preliminary one—to remedy that deficiency. It is the study, not of a sport *per se*, but of the development, functions and subsequent modification of the subculture which has grown up around it.

The sport in question is Rugby Union football. In Britain, players of this sport have gained a reputation for regularly violating a number of taboos, especially those regarding violence, physical contact, nakedness, obscenity, drunkenness, and the treatment of property.[2] Taboo-breaking of this kind tends to take a highly ritualized form. It has come to form an integral part of the subculture that has grown up around the rugby game. One of its functions is that of providing an avenue of satisfaction for the players in addition to the game itself. However, much of the behaviour it involves offends against the "everyday" standards of the upper and middle classes, the social strata to which rugby players mainly belong. It also runs counter to the standards of *mens sana in corpore sano* which have become so firmly embedded in sports ideology though not, in Britain at least, to the same

Reprinted from International Review of Sport Sociology, 8(3–4):5–24, 1973. Copyright 1973 by International Review of Sport Sociology, Warsaw, Poland.

extent in sporting practice. It would be interesting to see whether the type of sports subculture we are about to describe is a uniquely British phenomenon or whether there are counterparts in other countries as well.

Rugby football began to become established in Britain as a game for upper and middle class adults in the years between 1850 and 1870. It seems likely that it grew in popularity in that period largely on account of its comparative roughness and the strenuous physical exertion it involved. It was a game which provided the young man with the opportunity to engage in vigorous physical activity, an opportunity which was increasingly denied him in other fields, particularly that of work. More often than not, his occupation was sedentary, involving mental rather than physical effort. The running entailed in playing rugby enabled him to experience that pleasure which tends to accompany "motility" in any activity which is voluntarily undertaken.[3] At the same time, the competitive rough and tumble of the game enabled him to derive pleasure from the excitement of an organized mock battle and permitted him to measure up better to traditional ideals of masculinity than his everyday occupation. This latter aspect was probably crucial. The fact that the English concept of the "gentleman" is derived, in part, from the ethos of an elite with military roots is probably of some significance with respect to the development of these ideals. Despite the expansion of the empire, the latter half of the nineteenth century witnessed a greater growth of non-military occupations for the middle and upper classes than had

157

occurred in any previous stage in the development of British society. Under the urban-industrial conditions that were coming increasingly to prevail, it became more and more difficult for traditional upper and middle class norms of masculinity to find expression in the normal run of everyday life, and rugby football began to emerge, not without considerable conflict, as one of the principal social enclaves where they could be legitimately expressed.

This analysis may provide the beginnings of an explanation of why, in the second half of the nineteenth century, young adult males from the middle and upper classes should have begun in considerable numbers to take up a rough and energetic contact sport. It does not, however, explain the emergence of those aspects of the rugby subculture which developed off the field of play. The game, came, as we have seen, to embrace a customary disrespect for taboos regarding nakedness. These taboos have to be relaxed to some extent in any activity where a communal dressing room forms the location where the "actors" change from their everyday clothes. What is noticeable about rugby football, however, is the fact that these taboos are contravened and not simply relaxed. The male "strip-tease" became a firmly institutionalized part of the rugby subculture and the singing of a song entitled "the Zulu Warrior" became the traditional signal for a ritualistic strip by a member of the group. This ritual is usually enacted after the match, either in the club-house bar or, if the team has been playing away, on the coach which is carrying the players home. Initiation ceremonies also became customary on such occasions. In the course of such ceremonies, the initiate is stripped—often forcibly—and his body, especially his genitals, defiled with shoe polish and vaseline. Drinking to excess also came to be firmly embedded in the rugby club tradition. While drunk, the players sing obscene songs which involve, as a central theme, the mocking, objectification and defilement of women and homosexuals. Articles of property are often either stolen or wantonly destroyed. Perhaps the most striking aspect of this pattern, however, is the fact that it became accepted as normal for members of this group by the rest of society. It did not come to be regarded as either criminal or deviant but, on the contrary, to be condoned as evidence of excusable "high spirits". As long as they confine it largely to the club-house, the players are allowed to behave with impunity in a manner which would bring immediate condemnation and punishment were it to occur among other social strata or even among members of the upper and middle classes in a different social setting. Little effort is made to bring their behaviour into line with the dominant social standards. As far as one can tell, it is even accorded a large measure of tolerance in such public places as the carriages of railway trains and the bars of hotels. It is certainly not condemned as "hooliganism" or regarded as a "social problem" as has recently occurred with respect to the behaviour of those working class youths who smash the light bulbs, tear the seats and defile the lavatories of "football specials."[4]

Rugby Union footballers probably owe this privileged treatment mainly to historical association of their game with the public schools. It originally developed, as its name suggests, at Rugby, which became a leading public school in the early part of the nineteenth century. It began to spread from Rugby during the 1840's and 50's, initially to other public schools which had taken that school as their model,[5] later to the universities of Oxford and Cambridge. During most of the second half of the nineteenth century, the game could only be learned in these elite schools and universities. It was seldom adopted by those not introduced to it in such a social setting.[6] Indeed, the earliest adult clubs were founded mainly by "old boys" from the public schools. Players were unambiguously identified as members of the national ruling elite and the game itself came to be regarded as an elite leisure activity. It is unlikely that members of the upper and middle classes would have branded their own sons as delinquents. Members of the lower classes moreover, were not sufficiently powerful either to label or to punish behaviour of this kind, whatever their feelings about it may have been.

The social status of Rugby Union players and the related class connotations which became attached to the game may help to explain why players were able to flaunt social conventions without fear of punishment but they cannot adequately explain the pressures—whether of a social or a psychological character—which drove young adult males from the middle and upper classes, most of them in their twenties and early thirties, towards such violation of taboos. Nor can they explain why such men should have wanted to break specifically the taboos referred to above. In order to approach such aspects of the problem, it is useful to conceptualize the rugby club as a kind of "male preserve" which came to function as a social setting for the expression, often in an extreme form, of the then current norms of masculinity.

Ned Polsky, in his study of "poolrooms" in the United States, has shown how the poolroom in that country—the "billiard hall"—came to act as an "escape hatch from the world of feminine values." [7] He points out that the open frontier once performed this function but that, with the closure of the frontier and increasing urbanization, the poolroom gradually became the principal refuge for American men who wanted to "curse, spit tobacco, fight freely, dress sloppily, gamble heavily, get drunk, whore around." His main concern was to explain why the poolroom has declined in popularity in recent years. He dismissed several popular explanations in favour of his own which centres on the hypothesis that poolrooms came to form the keystone of a heterosexual but all-male subculture. They became so bound up with this subculture, he suggests, that they could not adapt to changed conditions. When the subculture died, the poolrooms nearly died with it. The traditional poolroom had depended upon men who were heterosexual but, nonetheless, committed to remaining unmarried. They were men whose sexual needs were met partly by masturbation and, partly or mainly, by recourse to prostitutes. Today, Polsky, maintains, American men use prostitutes pre-maritally, extra-maritally and post-maritally but hardly ever any more as a means of maintaining life-long bachelorhood. The social conditions of urban life have led the majority of men to favour marriage. With the decline of the "life-long bachelor" as a social type, came the decline of the traditional poolrooms. Some attempt was made by entrepreneurs to "re-vamp" and glamourize them as a means of attracting a new clientele but it was, argues Polsky, almost bound to fail. This was because it simultaneously alienated such traditional clients as still remained and was too firmly associated, particularly in the minds of women, with the earlier, all-male subculture.

The British rugby club developed as a form of male-preserve in a different social setting. Its development, therefore, is not directly equivalent to that of poolrooms in the U.S.A. Britain, for example, had no open frontier during the nineteenth century although it did have an expanding empire which, to some extent, may have served a similar social function. However, the development of rugby football as a male preserve came at the height of imperial expansion and not, as in the case of American pool, with the closure of the frontier. Furthermore, the clientele of British rugby clubs in the late nineteenth century was drawn predominantly from the ranks of the upper and middle classes as compared with the mainly working class clientele of the poolrooms in America. The rugby clubs, however, did embrace a bachelor subculture that was similar in many respects. Most British rugby players, unlike the groups described by Polsky, were not committed to remaining unmarried but the social norms of the class from which they came did dictate the deferral of marriage until the late twenties or early thirties. By that time, it was believed, a man would be earning a salary sufficient for maintaining a wife and children in a manner considered appropriate for a member of his class. [8] Even within marriage, a high degree of conjugal role segregation remained the norm since the balance of power between the sexes [9] had not yet altered sufficiently to lead to the current, increasingly dominant pattern of role-sharing between husband and wife. Consequently, even for the married man, there was less pressure to share his leisure with his wife and children than tends nowadays to be the case. Conditions were ripe, in short, for the emergence of a subculture that was both all-male and composed of heterosexuals. Again, however, although this may provide an explanation of some of the conditions necessary for the emergence of the rugby football club as a type of male preserve, it does not represent an explanation of the sufficient conditions for this process. In particular, it cannot explain why this type of male-preserve came traditionally to involve the contravention of a specific set of social taboos. For a more complete explanation, it is necessary to probe a little deeper.

Lionel Tiger has recently attempted to develop a "socio-biological" theory of the all-male group. [10] He begins by noting that the "male-bond" is a "cultural universal". Its universality, he argues, strongly suggests that the mechanisms which produce it are in large part biological. There is reason to believe, he suggests, that the male-bond became genetically implanted at an early stage in human evolution. The development of co-operative hunting, he maintains, was probably decisive in this respect mainly because groups where men inherited the propensity to form close relations with other men would have been more successful in their hunting and would therefore have had greater potential for survival than groups where men were genetically programmed in some less advantageous way. The genetic inheritance of women, he suggests, followed a different course of evolution. They became programmed to bond with their mates and their children but not with other women. Moreover, as a means of further increasing potential for survival, the propensity to exclude women from their hunting groups became a hereditary part of the males' biological equipment. Women are not physiologically equipped for the efficient performance of the tasks involved in hunting. They cannot run as fast as men. They cannot throw as well. Their temperature control is less adaptable. The menstrual cycle affects their social, psychological, and physical efficiency. They are adapted for child-bearing and child-rearing, and these have always been a full-time occupation. Tiger points out that, despite the apparent success of the suffragettes, women do not seem to have managed yet to gain many top jobs in areas such as government, high finance, major industry, the law and the military. He concludes that this is because men are genetically programmed to rule and women to obey, that men are genetically programmed to co-operate and that women are not, and that the need of men to form "secret societies" and other forms of sex-exclusive association is part of our biological heritage.

In expounding this "socio-biological" hypothesis, Tiger has made a brave and highly imaginative attempt to combat sociological orthodoxy. However, most research to date suggests very strongly that the mechanisms whereby all-male groups are formed are social and not biological in character. We know a good deal, for example, about the ways in which socialization serves to maintain a culture and a social structure in which men are dominant. So far, however, no one has succeeded in identifying the "genetic programme" hypothesized by Tiger.[11] If one compares the short decades which have elapsed since the first strivings in the campaign for women's rights with the centuries during which males have been dominant, it is hardly surprising that relatively little has been achieved so far with

respect to ending sexual discrimination in patterns of role recruitment. The failure of women to form effective, solidary groups among themselves is reminiscent of the failure of subordinate groups throughout history to unite in opposition to their oppressors. It is not only women in industrial societies but also the working classes and Negroes in societies of this type who have begun, only relatively recently,[12] to organize in order to combat their subordinate status. Would Tiger want to argue that their subordination is "genetically programmed," too? It is a sociological truism that groups with power usually fight hard to retain it and that, as a rule, they only relinquish or share it if they are forced to do so. Moreover, the ideological legitimation of their rule and the techniques of control they utilize to maintain it are often so effective that the legitimacy of their dominance is accepted by members of the subordinate group. In the case of the Negro slave, he comes to develop the "Sambo" personality,[13] while the working class "deference voter" who supports the Conservative Party acknowledges the "eternal right" of the upper classes to rule and his own "eternal duty" to obey. In similar fashion, large numbers of women, because of their socialization, a social structure which limits their opportunities, and the sanctions which are brought to bear if they challenge male "superiority", accept the right of men to be dominant in the major spheres of social life. Indeed, in many cases, they learn to need to be dominated and controlled by men.

There can be little doubt that the processes involved in the initial emergence and subsequent transformation of rugby football as a male preserve were social process *sui generis*. It is probably not without significance in this respect that rugby football developed as a game for adults in the second half of the nineteenth century. For it was during that period that the first significant demands began to be made by women for a greater share in political and economic power. Most of the suffragettes came from the ranks of the middle and upper classes, the social strata from which rugby players were predominantly drawn. Their movement reflected a deep ground swell of dissatisfaction with the social opportunities traditionally open to women from the middle and upper classes. We should like to hypothesize that the historical conjuncture represented by the simultaneous rise of rugby football as a game for upper and middle class adult males, and the rise of the suffragette movement within those social strata, may have been of some significance with respect to the emergence of the specific pattern of socially tolerated taboo-breaking—or at least of some central aspects of it—which came to characterize the subculture of Rugby Union football. For women, particularly at these levels in the social hierarchy, were increasingly becoming a threat to men, and men, we should like to suggest, responded, among other ways, by developing rugby football as a male preserve in which they could bolster up their threatened masculinity and, at the same time, mock, objectify and vilify women, the principal source of the threat.

Obscene songs were not widely condemned in England until about the 1850s. From the sixteenth to the middle of the nineteenth century, such songs were common in the theatre and the music hall. As Ivan Bloch has written:

In the first half of the nineteenth century it was customary among men of the "upper classes" to visit a music hall after an opera performance for "supper and song". A music hall of evil repute was "Little Tom's Tavern" in White-chapel. But all music halls during the first half of the nineteenth century had a bad reputation owing to the obscene songs performed in them. [14]

Bloch goes on to show how the performance of these songs was only stopped when the doors of the music hall were opened to women. As is frequently the case when women are admitted to a previously all-male institution, manners changed and behaviour began to become more refined—i.e. less "masculine" in terms of previously existing standards.

But women were accorded less opportunity to enter the rugby clubs which were beginning to spring up at that time. Such clubs came to serve as one of the principal social enclaves where the obscene song tradition could be perpetuated and where, at the same time, the threat posed to men by increasingly powerful women could be rendered symbolically harmless. Such songs, moreover, helped to keep the women out and simultaneously to increase the *esprit de corps* of the men. Because obscene songs violated conventional norms and standards, they increased the cohesion of the all-male group by making them, as it were, "partners in crime".

The rugby club in this situation also functioned in part as a perpetuation of the all-male community of the boarding school. Such an all-male community, we can assume from recent research, was accorded positive value by the boys and regarded as something worth defending. Thus, according to a public schoolboy quoted in a recent study:

Society is warm and close-knit—not ridden by jealousies. Boys aren't catty like girls. Girls couldn't create this sense of community and comradeship—real affection and loyalty to each other. A marvellous sense of togetherness and teamwork. [15]

It was not, however, only the comradeship that was appealing but the fact that the absence of women and girls enhanced the "masculinity" of the group. This was of great importance in the value scheme of rugby players. Another pupil in the same study had this to say of the all-male boarding school:

It makes us more masculine. If we are to be males, for God's sake let's go the whole hog. Let's learn to understand, command, live with males. We *must* understand our own sex fully and cannot if females are tripping and flirting around. [16]

Remarks such as this are probably indicative of the fact that the balance of power between the sexes is now beginning to veer towards a more egalitarian form of relationship than used formerly to prevail. No one would think it necessary to defend all-male institutions if they were not under attack. We should like to hypothesize that one of the principal initial responses of many men as the attack from women first began to be mounted was to withdraw into the all-male culture and celebrate its values. The rugby clubs became central foci of this culture. In them, the singing of obscene songs which symbolically expressed masculinity in a virulent form, men's fear of women, and their simultaneous dependency on them, became one of the central elements in the club subculture.

The obscene songs and ballads which became traditional in rugby clubs display at least two central characteristics. At first sight, these characteristics may appear to be unrelated. We should like to suggest, however, that they both reflect the increasing power of women and their growing threat to the traditional social position and self-image of men. The first is their embodiment of a hostile, brutal but, at the same time, fearful attitude towards women and the sexual act. The second is the fact that they came to mock homosexuals and homosexuality. The psychiatrist David Stafford-Clark, in a discussion of the "narrative poem," "Eskimo Nell," concluded that:

> What characterises her story on reflection is the absolute joylessness of the whole thing. The deliberate and complete absence of any note of compassion, of humour except for that implicit in the grotesque nature of the sexual descriptions, and the lack of any suggestion of love or delight in life. The poem is the negation of everything except the destructive aspects of sado-masochistic sexuality.[17]

In many of these songs and poems, women tend to be objectified and depicted as a threat to men. In "Eskimo Nell," for example, even the champion womanizer, "Dead Eye Dick," is unable to provide Nell with sexual satisfaction. This is left to his henchman, "Mexican Pete," who performs the task with his "six-shooter." In the "Engineer's Hymn," the central character, an engineer whose wife "was never satisfied," had to build a machine in order to fulfil the erotic component of his marital role. Seldom, if ever, is the "normal" man or woman featured in these songs. Super-human or extra-human powers are required before the "hero" can satisfy the "heroine's" voracious sexual appetite. Nothing could be more revealing of the function of these songs in symbolically expressing but also, to some extent, in symbolically reducing the fear of women who were experienced as powerful and demanding. Such fears are likely to have grown as the power of women began, factually, to increase. They were probably particularly strong in the case of public schoolboys, for they had been brought up largely in an all-male environment. In such an environment, the opportunities available for learning to relate to women of equal social status from outside their own families were relatively restricted. Such relationships, moreover, were surrounded by a complex etiquette which placed women "on a pedestal" but, at the same time, expressed their subordination to men.[18]

The rugby club can reveal itself to the outsider as a very close, affectionate gathering of males who bathe together, strip in all-male company, and generally indulge in what may appear to be homo-erotic behaviour, perhaps of an unconsciously motivated kind. Even the game-situation of the scrummage where the players grasp each other in a hot, sticky mass, their heads between each others thighs, has become the butt for frequent jokes. Thus, as the other side of the coin, the feminine or homosexual male has come to be mocked in rugby songs. For, especially given the growing power of women, homosexuality, or the fear of it, represents another source of threat to the male's sense of masculine identity. One of the songs, traditional in rugby circles, has as its chorus:

> For we're all queers together,
> Excuse us while we go upstairs,
> For we're all queers together,
> That's why we go round in pairs.[19]

The function of this song appears to be to counter the charge before it is made, to stress and reinforce masculinity by mocking, not only women but also homosexuals. In an age when women were beginning to become more powerful and able to challenge their factual subordination, if not their symbolic objectification, with a growing measure of success, men who clung to the old style and continued to enjoy participation in all-male groups would have had doubts cast on their masculinity. Many of them probably began to doubt it themselves. Doubts of this kind must have been doubly threatening in a situation such as that of the rugby club where the principal function was the expression of masculinity and the perpetuation of traditional norms in this regard. In the case of public schoolboys, the threat is likely to have been even greater for, in the public schools, as an author has recently written:

> ... the incidence of homosexuality is likely to be high: in some schools, either overt homosexuality or partially repressed homosexuality is the general practice. Nearly everywhere homosexual friendships are frequent and it is not infrequent ... for such friendships to reach the point of physical action.[20]

In all probability, much of the homosexuality that occurs in public schools is merely a temporary substitute for heterosexual behaviour. It has not been proved that boys' boarding schools produce more adult homosexuals than non-boarding schools. But the fact remains that, at these schools, boys do frequently experience desire for other boys. This must have the effect on many of making them apprehensive concerning their masculinity. When, as is the case with rugby footballers, they participate in a subculture which epitomizes rugged manliness and still "unnatural" desires of this kind, the resultant conflicts are likely to accentuate the need to prove their masculinity.

From the very beginning, the ethos of rugby football has consistently stressed masculinity. In 1863, at one of the series of meetings held in London in order to set up a uniform code of rules for football on a national level, F. W. Campbell of the Blackheath Rugby club spoke as follows in defence of "hacking," the practice which the majority of members of the embryo Football Association wished to abolish:

> As to not liking hacking as at present carried on, I say that ... it savours far more of the feeling of those who like their pipes and grog or schnappes more than the manly game of football. [21]

H. H. Almond, headmaster of Loretto Academy, the Scottish public school, wrote in 1892 that, "... the great end of the game (is) to produce a race of robust men, with active habits, brisk circulations, manly sympathies and exuberant spirits." [22]

It is probably significant in the light of this concern with masculinity that rugby-playing and beer-drinking have long been regarded as synonymous. As early as 1893, *The Cambrian* reported a speech by a Mr. Michael Craven in which he stated that rugby football was "the fascination of the devil and twin sister of the drinking system and that without the latter it would have a job to succeed." [23] More recently, Morgan and Nicholson have pointed out that:

> The schoolboys who are boldest at going into pubs for a beer are so often to be the best footballers that the amateur sociologist could be forgiven for hazarding a bit of cause and effect. In college the beer drinking competitions were always staged under the aegis of the Rugby Club. [24]

Many commentators seem to regard drunkenness as the greatest single factor behind the "vandalism" which occurs in rugby-playing fraternities. However, it would be dangerous to assume that the mere fact of men in groups, drinking heavily together, will produce the type of behaviour which is characteristic of rugby players after the match. Here is an example from one of our case records:

> An after-rugger match striptease ended in uproar as an undergraduate footballer was carried naked past girl students in a university bar. Yesterday, the rumpus was condemned as "disgusting behaviour" by a female student leader at Keele University ..., She wrote: "Soon after the bar opened at 6 o'clock, the players were singing characteristic songs. So far all was normal. But the high spirits zoomed into orbit. A player in the bar removed all his clothing except for his underpants. Then two players undressed to vocal accompaniment. They made obscene movements. They began throwing beer at each other, smashing glasses and throwing sugar. Then the students (both sexes) sitting at the tables were treated to the sight of a naked man being carried around the snack bar. He was drunk but consenting." [25]

It seems fairly clear that, in cases such as this, the drinking serves, partly as a means of testing, expressing and accentuating masculinity, and partly as a means of loosening internalized restraints. The loosening of restraints with alcohol appears to be a necessary precondition for the ritual enactments which follow. The rituals in the case described above centrally involved the mocking of the female stripper and, symbolically through her, of the "fallen" women who is easy prey to men. It is significant that they took place in the actual presence of women and that many of the women present appeared to regard them simply as a matter of course. As far as one can tell, such women did not have, or gain, a reputation as "easy" sexual objects among the players they were accompanying. It is perhaps even more significant that some of the women present reacted vocally and with disgust. This would seem to reveal that, increasingly, women are willing and able to fight against their symbolic reification and ritual vilification by men.

Asked to justify his participation in such activities, a student rugby player interviewed by one of the authors replied:

> I don't try to personally. If one analyzes it outside the context of being there, then you're dissatisfied with what you've done, but when you've had ten or eleven pints and you're in this situation then the way to justify it is to say

you were pissed out of your mind at the time. One isn't necessarily proud of what one has done but you do tend to look back on it and say "we had a good night there."

This appears to indicate that the activities of the rugby club offend against the "everyday" values of its own members as well as against those of the dominant groups in society at large. The very fact, however, that this type of activity runs counter to dominant values and that this is recognized by the participants themselves, probably serves even further to reinforce the close-knit character of the group. Such fellowship and closeness are enhanced by the consumption of alcohol so that "respectability" and "propriety" can make way for a value that is more highly regarded than both—masculinity and, since traditional standards of masculinity are increasingly threatened in modern society, as its corollary, the mocking, objectification and ritual vilification of women.

However, great changes have begun to take place in British rugby clubs in recent years. They are no longer clear-cut male preserves. Much of the behaviour which, formerly, was typical of them is now either dead or in the process of dying out. Rugby players tend to remain a special "type" but the type has begun to alter. Their off-the-field behaviour has begun to change, largely in the direction of greater restraint and greater control.

The breakdown and loosening of the structures and ideologies that once held rugby players together into close-knit, all-male groups is a complex social process. We should like to suggest that one of the more important aspects of it has been the continuing emancipation of women in British society.[26] A stage has now been reached where women are frequent and, what is more important, *welcome* visitors to rugby clubs. In part, it was financial necessity that began to bring about this change. But this economic fact reflects wide changes in social structure, particularly in the position of women within that structure.

Ten or so years ago, if a young person wanted to go dancing, he or she typically went to a youth club, a church hall or a commercial dance. Today, young people can usually find ample opportunities for dancing at any of the rugby clubs in their district. The senior clubs especially, faced with the prospect of falling gates and rising costs, opted for dances as a means of raising money. Fear of the dangers supposedly inherent in professionalism[27] and the corresponding emphasis placed on Rugby Union as a "players game," ruled out, at least until recently, attracting more spectators to the game through the introduction of a more competitive framework designed to enhance excitement.[28] The junior and the "old boy" clubs, with little or no chance of spectator appeal but with valuable contributions to make as social centres, had only one acceptable course open to them and that was to hold dances. Other ways of raising funds such as bingo and football pools had lower class connotations and did not, therefore, represent a feasible alternative.

Dances, of course, brought women into the male preserve with official approval. This does not mean that their presence had been entirely disallowed before. On the contrary, they have always been welcome to make tea, prepare and serve meals, and to cheer on their men-folk. But traditionally, their presence was only tolerated if they were content to remain in a subordinate position. They had to leave the club-house when ordered to do so by the men. In fact, a particular exclusion ritual grew up in order to let them know that they had overstayed their welcome and that beer-drinking and the singing of obscene songs were about to commence. The signal was a song entitled "Good Night, Ladies." Any women who insisted on remaining after the enactment of this ritual suffered loss of status. In any event, their presence was only tolerated as long as they passively accepted the objectification of themselves by men.

The more emancipated women who have now begun to enter the club-houses, whether in order to attend the dances or simply in order to drink with their men, are increasingly not prepared to accept this subordinate position. They tend to be more independent, better off financially, more desirous of equality, more aware of the power which their desirability as mates gives them in relation to men. They are unwilling to accept behaviour which they regard as aggressively intentioned or, alternatively, they use obscenities themselves as a sign of their emancipation. However, the principal consequence of the admission of increasing numbers of women into rugby clubs has been to prevent the rugby club Saturday night from assuming its traditional shape. Writing for a Sunday paper in 1969, Lionel Tiger observed that:

One of the most obvious distinguishing characteristics of men is their great ability, even urge, to get together with their own sex. The cheerful, noisy Rugby players at the wash-up and sing-in ... have featured on the covers of best-selling Rugby song-books. The half-million copies that have been bought are a tribute to the appeal of the all-male get together.[29]

However, he appears to have missed the point. The majority of such books are sold outside rugby circles. In this respect, they form part of that overall cultural change which began in the early 1960's and led to the advent of the so called "permissive society." Previous generations of rugby players found books of this kind unnecessary. "True" rugby men even today—the guardians of a dying tradition—hold them in amused contempt. Traditionally, the obscene songs were passed from generation to generation by word of mouth. Each club had its own version of the favourite songs and these were picked up *in situ* by the younger members who perpetuated the tradition. But, in large part because women are now beginning to become an integral part of rugby club life, newcomers are not exposed to the songs with the same intensity as previously. The tradition is difficult to maintain in its earlier oral form. Insofar as such books are sold to rugby players, this is indicative, not of the strength but of the growing weakness of the rugby club as a male preserve.

Excessive drinking and the antics which accompanied it have also begun to decline in rugby clubs in recent years. This is clearly due, in part, to the advent of a more competitive framework in the game and to the greater emphasis on coaching and training which this has begun to entail. Physical fitness is increasingly at a premium and this limits the degree to which players can engage in heavy drinking. But, we would venture to suggest, the decline of heavy drinking is also connected with the changing pattern of relations between the sexes. Women today, especially in the middle classes, demand increasingly to be regarded as central in the lives of their men. The young man, whose status among other young men is now increased by having a regular girl friend, is forced to go in search of a mate on Saturday nights instead of drinking at the rugby club. Even the young married man is much more willing than previously to share his leisure with his family and more inclined to accord with the wishes of his wife. This appears to be indicative not only of the increasing power of women in our society, but also of the increasing willingness of men to succumb to that power. Gradually men are ceasing to regard women as objects and are coming, more and more, to regard them as persons. Increasingly, they *want* to be with their wives and girl friends rather than with other men. According to a student rugby player interviewed in the course of our researches:

I tend to go out with my girl friend on Saturday nights. I always put my girl friend before rugby crowd, because I don't think that the boozing and socialising in rugby after the game is so important that you've got to give something up in order to be there. I think it's alright if you've nothing better to do.

Today, middle class men have to be more attentive towards their wives and girl friends and more responsive to their needs and wishes. During the 1960's, this developed to a stage where growing numbers even of the more "traditional" men began to become afraid to admit that they would rather spend their time in an all-male group than with a member of the opposite sex. Women, for their part are beginning to become aware that, by gaining entry to the rugby clubs, they have begun to breach a bastion of male dominance. At times, they are openly exultant. In a letter to the student newspaper attacking the University rugby club, a female student at Leicester University recently wrote:

Let's face it, the cult of the hairy-legged hard man is dying a natural death and the minority who are still desperately prodding the corpse can do little to save the species from extinction.

It appears likely that, with the increasing emancipation of women and the altering focus of marriage and family life, the old-style rugby player will become just an historical curiosity. All the signs seem to indicate that he is gradually being replaced by a much more restrained model, one who is more "conformist" with respect to the dominant social standards and much more serious and dedicated in his approach to the game. It is true that obscene songs and rowdy behaviour still occur in rugby circles but, increasingly, they are being limited to special occasions. The "hot pot suppers" and the Easter tours are, in most cases, the only situations where the rugby club still tends frequently to get out of hand but even these last sanctuaries are beginning to be invaded. At Leicester University, it was recently proposed, admittedly tentatively, that women be allowed to attend the annual dinner of the rugby club and, at Easter 1969, the "old boy" side with which one of the authors is associated allowed women to accompany the team to an Easter rugby tournament on the Isle of Man. Wives and girl friends went along and enjoyed the "family occasion." This remained a type of male dominance, of course, in that the women accompanied the men rather than vice versa. Nonetheless, it provides a clear enough indication of the degree to which male dominance in British society has begun to be eroded. Of course, it shows at the same time how far women still have to go in order to achieve something approaching a measure of full equality with men. For one of the reasons why, in this case, they had to follow the men, is the fact that few comparable leisure activities are available to women. This, in its turn, we should like to suggest, is largely the result of centuries of male dominance and an overall social structure which, by and large, continues to reflect and reinforce that dominance. It also reflects the development of patterns of socialization which fit women for the performance of subordinate roles and which limit their aspirations, not only in the occupational field but in the sphere of leisure activities as well.

NOTES

1. Günther Lüschen, in his The Sociology of Sport: A Trend Report and Bibliography. (Current Sociology Series, the Hague and Paris, 1968), lists 892 books and articles on the sociology of sport. However, as Lüschen himself points out, most of the contributions listed were written, not by sociologists, but by specialists in physical education. At a fairly generous estimate, only something like twenty to thirty of the articles referred to were written by sociologists and published in sociology journals. Some of the books listed are by recognized sociologists but none of them deals with the sociology of sport as such. They were included by the author because he considered them relevant to the field.

2. Behaviour of this kind is not found in such a highly developed form in Rugby League, the semi-professional offshoot of Rugby Union football played mainly in the North of England. There is insufficient space here for a detailed examination of the reasons why such behaviour did not become so firmly estab-

lished in Rugby League. It must be enough simply to say that the semi-professional nature of the latter game with its correspondingly greater emphasis on fitness and training, and the fact that most of its players traditionally come from the working classes, are among the major factors.

3. For a discussion of this concept, see Elias, N. and Dunning, E.: Leisure in the sparetime spectrum. In Sociology of Sport: Theoretical and Methodological Foundations. Edited by R. Albonico and K. Pfister-Binz. Magglingen, 1972.

4. For a highly imaginative discussion of "soccer hooliganism" as a social problem, see Taylor, I.: Football mad: A speculative sociology of football hooliganism. In The Sociology of Sport: A Selection of Readings. Edited by E. Dunning. London, 1971. Taylor has developed his ideas further in another article, Soccer consciousness and soccer hooliganism, which appears in Images of Deviance. Edited by S. Cohen. Harmondsworth, 1971.

5. Principal among them were schools such as Marlborough, Cheltenham, Haileybury and Sherborne which were not founded or did not become public schools until the middle of the nineteenth century.

6. From about 1880 onwards, members of the working classes, particularly in Lancashire and Yorkshire, did begin to play rugby in increasing numbers. As their participation increased, however, so did the tendency towards the professionalization of the game. It was this which led to the break between Rugby Union and Rugby League.

7. Polsky, N.: Poolrooms: End of the male sanctuary. Trans-action, March 1967, p. 38. "Pool" is an American version of the game which, in Britain, we call "billiards."

8. Banks, J. A.: Prosperity and Parenthood. London, 1958.

9. This term is taken from an as yet unpublished paper by Norbert Elias entitled The Balance of Power Between the Sexes. As far as we know, he is the first sociologist to attempt to conceptualize the relations between the sexes in terms of an explicit "power model."

10. See Tiger, Lionel: Men in Groups. London, 1969.

11. We do not wish to give the impression that Tiger is unaware of the speculative nature of much of his work. As he writes himself: "My method ... owes more to the enthusiastic shotgun than the sabre." (op. cit., p. 141). Or again, "... we do not know the actual cortical-amygdaloid processes involved in bonding among men, or even the neurological differences among males and females in this respect." (Ibid., p. 51).

12. The term "recently" as used here with respect to the working classes refers, of course, to the last one hundred and fifty years.

13. See Elkins, S. M.: Slavery: A Problem in American Institutional and Intellectual Life. Chicago, 1969.

14. Bloch, I.: Sexual Life in England, Past and Present. London, 1953, p. 607.

15. Lambert, R.: The Hothouse Society. London, 1968, p. 105.

16. Ibid., p. 309.

17. Stafford-Clark, D.: The Twentieth Century,

Summer edn., 1965, pp. 17–22, no title. While we agree with Stafford-Clark's analysis of "Eskimo Nell," we would not wish to argue that all rugby songs similarly lack humour and compassion. Nor would we accept that all the songs negate "everything except the destructive elements of sado-masochistic sexuality." This is a recurrent element, it is true, but rugby songs are part of a complex oral tradition which frequently displays considerable humour and both verbal and rhyming skill. We do not wish to claim that our own analysis offers more than a possible explanation of one or two strands in this complex tradition. Thus, many of the songs and rhymes mock, not only women and homosexuals, but also men and male sexuality, even human sexuality as such. Others reveal a mixture of fear and disgust at the possibilities of contracting venereal disease. Yet another possible strand is revealed in one of the favourite songs, "The Sexual Life of the Camel." This song not only displays considerable humour and literary skill but is sung to the tune of the "Eton Boating Song." It does not seem too far-fetched to suggest that the use of this tune may have been introduced by pupils at Rugby or by Old Rugbyians as a means of mocking their traditional rivals, the Etonians.

18. Of course, access to female servants and to prostitutes was probably never restricted to the same extent nor surrounded by such a complex etiquette. This was probably the case only as far as women who were status equals were concerned.

19. It may be of some significance that the tune to which this song, too, is traditionally sung is that of the "Eton Boating Song."

20. Wilson, J.: Public Schools and Private Practice. London, 1962, p. 70.

21. Green, G.: A History of the Football Association. London. 1953, p. 29.

22. Mackenzie, R. J.: Almond of Loretto, London, 1906, p. 73.

23. Quoted in Morgan, W. J. and Nicholson, G.: Report on Rugby. London, 1958, p. 18.

24. Ibid., p. 26.

25. As we shall try to show, the presence of women on this occasion did not result simply from the fact that the venue was a university bar rather than the bar of a rugby club. None of the rituals which have grown up as a means of excluding women from such events was brought into play. Their presence was actually tolerated, even welcomed, if not without ambivalence. This is indicative, we should like to suggest, of the fundamental changes which have begun to take place in the relations between the sexes.

26. It may seem as if we are committing the logical error here of principally explaining both the rise and decline of the male preserve in rugby football in terms of the same "factor", the increasing power of women. What we are, in fact, suggesting is that the relationship between them is "curvi-linear", that the same social process had different consequences at different stages. This is perfectly logical, especially if one thinks in terms of social processes rather than in terms of discrete, ahistorical "factors" or "variables".

27. i.e., principally of the fact that, as Gregory Stone would put it, professionalism might lead to a change in the balance between "play" and "display" in favour of the latter, with the consequent destruction of rugby as a "sport" and its transformation into a mass, commercial spectacle. For a discussion of these concepts, see Stone, G. P.: American sports: Play and dis-play, in Dunning, E.: op. cit., pp. 47–65.

28. The introduction of formal competitions such as "leagues" and "cups" was resisted by the Rugby Union authorities until the 1971–72 season. Now they have begun, reluctantly, to give way in the face of mounting pressure from players and the press.

29. Observer Colour Magazine, 29th June, 1969.

ethnic soccer clubs in milwaukee: a study in assimilation *

JOHN C. POOLEY

INTRODUCTION

Sport has shown itself to be a factor in forming a point of contact between ethnic groups who find themselves living in close proximity. Expatriate groups in African countries, missionaries and traders in isolated communities and military forces representing different nations[1] are good examples of this. Immigrants who become lodged in already established "advanced" societies are equally affected. For example, West Indians who emigrate to Britain, Southern Europeans who emigrate to Australia and diverse ethnic groups immigrating to the United States would fall into this category. Whenever members of an ethnic group move to another society, some degree of assimilation occurs and their survival depends upon it.

The primary purpose of this study was to determine the role of sport in assimilation. More specifically, the study endeavored to determine the significance of the structure and function of ethnic soccer clubs in the assimilation of their members.

Reprinted from Sport in the Socio-Cultural Process, Edited by M. Hart. Second Edition. Dubuque, Iowa, W. C. Brown, 1976, pp 475–492. Copyright 1976 by John C. Pooley.

* Part of this paper was read at the AAHPER Annual Convention, Boston, April 11, 1969. The author wishes to acknowledge the valuable assistance of Gerald S. Kenyon, University of Waterloo, who acted as advisor for the study which formed part of a Masters Degree at the University of Wisconsin, Madison, completed in 1968

The terms used in this study are defined below:

Assimilation

Assimilation is a process of interpenetration and fusion in which persons and groups acquire the memories, sentiments, and attitudes of other persons or groups, and, by sharing their experiences and history, are incorporated with them in a common cultural life.[2]

From the definition, it is clear that "acculturation" is included. As Gordon[3] has commented, the phrases "sharing their experiences" and "incorporating with them in a common cultural life" suggest the added criterion of social structure relationships.

ETHNIC GROUP. An ethnic group[4] is a group with a shared feeling of peoplehood.[5] According to Tumin,

The term is most frequently applied to any group which differs in one or several aspects of its patterned, socially-transmitted way of life from other groups, or in the totality of that way of life or culture. Frequently, the group in question formerly enjoyed or still enjoys a separate political-national identity as well. Thus, various national-ethnic stocks in the United States would be considered as ethnic groups, e.g., Greeks, Poles, Haitians, Swedes, etc.[6]

CORE SOCIETY. This term refers to "the dominant subsociety which provides the standard to which other groups adjust or measure their relative degree of adjustment."[7] According to Fishman,[8] the culture of this society is that "into which immigrants are assimilated, and it forms the one accepted set of standards, expectations, and aspirations, whether they pertain to clothing, household furnishings, personal beauty, entertainment or child rearing."

In this study an attempt was made to assess the factors which accelerate or retard the rate of assimilation. Saxon[9] and Warner and Srole[10] have recognized that the recreational habits of a group have considerable import in the degree to which such a group may identify itself with, or be isolated from, the core society. This point has greater relevance in an age when increased leisure time is available to the majority of the population.[11]

The existence of a sport club provides varying degrees of social intercourse between active and non-active members of the same club and between different clubs. The amount and type of social interaction practiced depends upon the size of the club, makeup of its members, arrangement of social events, and type of club accommodation.

More specifically, this study was concerned with determining the factors which influence assimilation. Questions asked were as follows:

1. To what degree does participation in ethnic soccer influence assimilation?
   a. Positively
   b. Negatively
2. What forces within ethnic soccer explain this influence?
   a. Structural factors
   b. Functional factors

While other studies have focused attention on the significance of religion,[12] color,[13] occupation,[14] and concentration,[15] on the acculturation or assimilation of ethnic groups, little has been written on the use of sport as a vehicle in this process. Participation in a single sport, albeit from a professional standpoint, as a means to assimilate, has been discussed by Andreano,[16] Handlin,[17] Saxon,[18] Boyle,[19] Shibutani[20] and Weinberg.[21] These studies have been directed toward the individual's motives and attitude, whereas the present study was a departure from this approach in that it examined the role of the sport club as exemplified by the constitution of the club through the voice of the committee. Also, researchers have invariably confined themselves to a single ethnic group[22] or they have analyzed the many factors which have contributed to the acculturation or assimilation process of an ethnic group or groups in a city or rural community.[23]

This study was concerned with the role of the sport club (soccer), in a culturally heterogeneous setting; it sought to uncover club policy rather than individual attitude; it incorporated six ethnic groups in a confined area.

Milwaukee was chosen as the location for the study. Soccer was introduced in the city in 1913; the Wisconsin State Football Association was organized in 1914, and the Wisconsin State Soccer Football League was initiated in 1924.[24] With a population of 1,149,977 in Milwaukee, 326,666, or 28.4 percent comprised the element of foreign stock.[25] It was they who originally were responsible for the introduction of soccer into the area.

The choice of soccer allowed the study to pay some attention to the "foreign game" element. Soccer is a world game, being played on all five continents.[26] Of the larger countries, it is probably played least in America. By contrast, the countries of origin of the ethnic groups, represented by the sport clubs in Milwaukee, all have soccer as their major national outdoor game.

Since the sport of soccer is alien to the core society; and since soccer is the major national game of the countries of origin of the ethnic groups; and since members of the ethnic groups in question were involved in the activities of soccer clubs, either in the role of player, club official, manager, coach, spectator or social member; it is, therefore, hypothesized that ethnic soccer clubs in Milwaukee inhibit structural assimilation.

POPULATION

The population used for this investigation was the ten soccer clubs located within the City of Milwaukee. Some statistical information relating to the ten clubs is included in Tables 1, 2, and 3. It will be seen from Table 1 that only three clubs were founded in the 1920's. Five clubs came into being within a span of seven years from 1947 to 1953 inclusive. The remaining two clubs, founded in 1961 and 1964, respectively, were formed from members of two existing clubs. Club I was originally the second team Club C. When friction developed between the first and the second teams, three men contacted members of the second team and invited them to form a new club.[27]

TABLE 1
Dates of Foundation and Ethnic Orientation[a] of the Soccer Clubs in Milwaukee

Club	Date When Founded	Ethnic Orientation
A	1922	Croatian
B	1926	Hungarian
C	1929	German
D	1947	German
E	1950	Polish
F	1950	Serbian
G	1952	Italian
H	1953	German
I	1961	German
J	1964	Serbian

[a] Demonstrated by ethnicity of committee members, players, ordinary members, original members, or a combination of these.

Club J was founded as the result of a split in the Eastern Orthodox Church which served the Serbian community. Club F represented the original community; the splinter group formed Club J because a sufficient number of players wished to play soccer.[28] Therefore, the last occasion when an entirely new club was formed was in 1953.

The ethnic orientation of the soccer clubs is seen in Table 1. Four ethnic groups are represented by one club as follows: Croatian, Hungarian, Polish and Italian. One ethnic group is represented by two clubs: Serbian. Another ethnic group is represented by four clubs: German.

This does not mean that a club represented exclusively a single ethnic group. It does mean that each club in question was predominantly represented by a single ethnic group, according to the criteria indicated in Table 1.

Details of club membership are indicated in Table 2. These figures are approximate only because it was difficult to obtain precise figures. Normally the payment of dues provides an exact indication of membership. However, in the case of some of the clubs, committee members indicated that dues were not demanded because clubs did not wish to restrict the use of the term "member" to those who had become paid

TABLE 2
Details of Club Membership[a]

Club	Total Membership	Membership According to Age				
		Under 18	18–25 Years	25–35 Years	35–45 Years	Over 45
A	84	14	10	10	10	40
B	71	16	0	40	15	0
C	540	150	100	100	100	90
D	300	50	60	50	40	100
E	160	50	20	45	35	10
F	410	100	30	120	60	100
G	135	25	30	35	30	15
H	240	40	45	75	60	20
I	25	0	12	12	·1	0
J	200	20	50	50	40	40

[a] Membership figures are an approximation. Several clubs did not have membership lists.

TABLE 3

Details of the Number of Teams Sponsored by Each Club and the Leagues[a] in Which They Play

Club	Number of Teams Sponsored	Major Division	Major Reserve	First Division	Junior	Intermediate	Midget
A	3	1	1				1
B	3	1	1				1
C	5	1	1		1	1	1
D	5	1	1		1	1	1
E	4	1	1			1	1
F	4			1	1		2
G	3	1	1				1
H	5	1	1		1	1	1
I	1			1			
J	2			2			

[a] The most senior division is the Major Division. At the end of each season, the last placed club is relegated to the First Division. The team which wins the First Division is promoted to the Major Division. Each Major Division team is required to sponsor a reserve team.

members. In most instances, therefore, the figures were agreed upon following a consultation between the clubs' committee members. To be classed as a member, a person was required to demonstrate continuous interest in the club through support of club games or social functions, or through payment of dues.

A total of thirty-five teams were sponsored by the ten soccer clubs in 1967. These included eighteen adult teams and seventeen boys' teams. Details are indicated in Table 3.

NATURE OF THE BASIC VARIABLES

The nature of the dependent variable and the independent variable, and the procedures used for operationalizing them, are given below.

DEPENDENT VARIABLE: STRUCTURAL ASSIMILATION

The concept of "structural assimilation" was defined for this study as follows: entrance of an ethnic group into primary group relations with the core society.

In his model of the seven assimilation variables, Gordon demonstrates the key role of structural assimilation in the total process of assimilation.[29] He reiterates: "Once structural assimilation has occurred, . . . all of the other types of assimilation will follow." [30] The implication of this is that the price of such assimilation is the disappearance of the ethnic group as a separate entity and the evaporation of its distinctive values.[31]

The level of assimilation of club members was sought by directly questioning the club committees. The committees were asked to state whether the other six stages of assimilation had occurred. These variables, together with a brief definition of each, are listed here and in Table 4. They are taken from Gordon's model.[32]

Cultural assimilation (acculturation): Change of cultural patterns to those of the core society.

Marital assimilation (amalgamation): Large scale intermarriage between club members and members of the core society.

Identificational assimilation: Development of a sense of peoplehood based exclusively on the core society.

Attitude receptional assimilation: An absence of prejudice by the core society.

Behavior receptional assimilation: An absence of discrimination by the core society.

Civic assimilation: An absence of value and power conflict between club members and the core society.

INDEPENDENT VARIABLE: CLUB POLICY

The concept of "club policy" was defined for this study as follows: Courses or actions of a

TABLE 4
The Assimilation Variables

Subprocess or Condition	Type or Stage of Assimilation	Special Term
Change of cultural patterns to those of host society	Cultural or behavioral	Acculturation
Large scale entrance into cliques, clubs, and institutions of host society, on primary group level.	Structural assimilation	None
Large scale intermarriage	Marital assimilation	Amalgamation
Development of sense of peoplehood based exclusively on host society	Identificational assimilation	None
Absence of prejudice	Attitude receptional assimilation	None
Absence of discrimination	Behavioral receptional assimilation	None
Absence of value and power conflict	Civic assimilation	None

club, either explicit or implicit, in matters pertaining to its organization and activities, demonstrated by the actions it has taken in the past and the opinions held by its present committee.

It was found desirable to divide the concept into two aspects. These were operationalized by utilizing a number of elements in each case, as follows:

A. Characteristics of and Policies Concerning Membership
  1. Membership characteristics
    a. Naturalization and generation
    b. Occupation
    c. Ability to speak English
  2. Choice of language, either English or ethnic, demonstrated on the following occasions:
    a. At club meetings
    b. When playing soccer
    c. On social occasions
  3. Policy when accepting new members
  4. Policies for the actions taken to attract new members from:
    a. Other ethnic groups
    b. Core society
B. Policies Pertaining to Structure and Maintenance of Club
  1. Need for existence
  2. Election of officers

  3. Changes in organization
  4. Degree to which club perceives itself either as:
    a. Soccer club
    b. Social club
  5. Degree of organized social contact between the club and:
    a. Other clubs
    b. Core society

THE INSTRUMENT

Data collected in this investigation consisted of responses to a structured interview which was employed between April 7–23, 1967. The structured interview schedule consisted of two parts. The questions for Part One were sent to the President of each club at least seven days before the date of the interview. These questions related to the club's history, the number of teams being sponsored, the size of the club, the age, and other details concerning members.

The questions for Part Two were answered spontaneously because it was considered that prior knowledge of them might have adversely affected the answers. The questions were related to club policy concerning membership: questions directed toward the assimilation of members; constitutional procedures; and the language used at club meetings, on social occasions and in the dressing room before a game.

The questions used in both parts of the interview were designed by the investigator. The assimilation variables in Part Two were culled from Gordon's paradigm.[33] An average of four committee members were interviewed from each club.

TREATMENT AND ANALYSIS OF DATA

This study utilized the responses of the club committees to the structured interview. Primarily, questions devoted to club policy formed the basis of the analysis. The study examined the relationship between the dependent and the independent variables and a logical analysis of that relationship.

The information accrued was analyzed in two stages: first, a measure of the level of assimilation already achieved by club members was determined by utilizing questions directly related to the six assimilation variables (excluding structural assimilation). Second, the effect of the policies of the clubs on structural assimilation was determined by utilizing the elements defined under the sub-heading "Independent Variable."

The hypothesis stated earlier, namely that ethnic soccer clubs in Milwaukee inhibit structural assimilation, was more specifically defined for this study as: club policy inhibits the structural assimilation of members.

The information was treated descriptively. In the first stage, the level of assimilation which had already occurred was analyzed deductively. In the second stage, each question was analyzed in terms of the independent variable. In conclusion, the relationship between certain elements of the independent variable and the dependent variable were deduced, and the hypothesis tested.

RESULTS

The hypothesis was tested by determining the degree of relationship between the dependent variable and the independent variable.

The results of this investigation showed that:

1. The perceived level of assimilation of soccer club members varied among clubs. (See Table 5.) The two clubs whose members had assimilated most represented the German ethnic group, although they were less ethnic oriented than any of the clubs. The two clubs whose members had assimilated least represented the Serbian ethnic group.

TABLE 5

Degree of Assimilation of Ethnic Soccer Clubs in Milwaukee Based Upon the Model by Gordon

Club and Main Ethnic Group Represented[a]	Type of Assimilation[b]						
	Cultural			Identifi-cational	Attitude Receptional	Behavior Receptional	Civic
	Intrinsic	Extrinsic	Marital				
"A" — Croatian	No	Partly	No	Partly	Yes	Mostly	Yes
"B" — Hungarian	No	Partly	No	No	Yes	Yes	Yes
"C" — German	No	Partly	Partly	Yes	Yes	Yes	Yes
"D" — German	Partly	Partly	No	No	Yes	Yes	Yes
"E" — Polish	Partly	Mostly	No	No	Yes	Yes	Yes
"F" — Serbian	No	Partly	No	No	Mostly	Yes	Mostly
"G" — Italian	No	Partly	Partly	No	Yes	Yes	Yes
"H" — German	Partly	Yes	Partly	Partly	Yes	Yes	Yes
"I" — German	Yes	Yes	Partly	Yes	Yes	Yes	Yes
"J" — Serbian	No	Partly	No	No	Mostly	Yes	Yes

[a] Clubs H and I were least representative of a single ethnic group. Club I was the smallest of the ten clubs by a substantial margin.

[b] Although Gordon identified seven types of assimilation, "structural assimilation" was omitted because it will be examined in the role of dependent variable.

TABLE 6
Characteristics of Club Members: Percentage Naturalized and by Generation

Club	Percent Naturalized	Percent by Generation [a]		
		First	Second	Third
A	90	50	15	5
B	75	90	10	0
C	90	60	20	20
D	75	80	19	1
E	75	75	20	5
F	50	80	15	5
G	70	65	25	10
H	75	90	7	3
I	98	99	1	0
J	65	90	10	0

[a] First generation, i.e., original adult immigrant.
Second generation, i.e., children of the original adult immigrant.
Third generation, i.e., children of the second generation.

TABLE 7
Characteristics of Club Members: Most Frequent Occupations [a]

Club	Most 1	2	3	Least 4
A	Unskilled Labor	Skilled Labor	Private Business	Professional
B	Skilled Labor	Unskilled Labor		
C	Skilled Labor	Private Business	Unskilled Labor	Professional
D	Skilled Labor	Private Business	Professional	Unskilled Labor
E	Skilled Labor	Unskilled Labor	Private Business	
F	Skilled Labor	Private Business	Unskilled Labor	Professional
G	Skilled Labor	Private Business	Unskilled Labor	Professional
H	Skilled Labor	Unskilled Labor	Private Business	Professional
I	Skilled Labor	Professional	Unskilled Labor	
J	Skilled Labor	Unskilled Labor	Private Business	Professional

[a] Homemakers and (high school) students not included.

174

2. In terms of three assimilation variables, namely civic, behavioral receptional and attitude receptional, the majority of club members were alleged to have assimilated in large measure (see Table 5). In terms of three other assimilation variables, namely cultural, marital and identificational, the record of assimilation was poor. Of these, marital assimilation (amalgamation) had occurred least of all.

3. A review of the characteristics of soccer club members indicated that: (a) a large percentage were naturalized and first generation immigrants (see Table 6); (b) their most frequent occupation was in the area of "skilled labor" (see Table 7); (c) they spoke English only moderately well (see Table 8); and (d) approximately one-third were playing members and two-thirds were social members (see Table 9).

4. When accepting new members, approximately half of the clubs had developed a clear-cut, if not rigid, policy, whereas the other clubs had a very open policy.

5. Half of the clubs took no action to attract new members, either from other nationality groups, or the core society (see Table 10). Three clubs took action to attract players to their clubs, but otherwise ignored other potential members. One club encouraged players but discouraged non-players. One club took positive action to attract new members, whether players or non-players.

6. Seven clubs were identified with a specific ethnic group by their choice of name. Three had neutral names.

7. The language used at club meetings, when playing soccer, and on social occasions

TABLE 9

Characteristics of Club Members: Percentage of Playing Members and Social Members

Club	Percentage Playing	Percentage Social
A	45	55
B	65	35
C	12	88
D	25	75
E	45	55
F	25	75
G	40	60
H	35	65
I	65	35
J	20	80
TOTALS	37.7	62.3

TABLE 8

Characteristics of Club Members: Ability to Speak English

Club	Very Good	Good	Fair	Poor	Very Poor
A	20%	20%	40%	10%	10%
B	10	60	20	10	—
C	40	50	10	—	—
D	15	40	40	5	—
E	50	10	35	4	1
F	25	25	25	20	5
G	30	30	20	10	10
H	30	40	20	10	—
I	100	—	—	—	—
J	15	40	30	10	5

Mean Percentage:

	Very Good	Good	Fair	Poor	Very Poor
	33.5	31.5	24.0	7.9	3.1

Mean Percentage without Club I:

	Very Good	Good	Fair	Poor	Very Poor
	26.1	35.0	26.6	8.8	3.5

TABLE 10
Action Taken to Attract New Members to the Clubs from Other Ethnic Groups
and the Core Society

Club	Other Ethnic Groups	Core Society
A	None	None
B	None	None
C	None (unless player)	None (unless player)
D	None	None
E	None (unless player)	None (unless player)
F	Players encouraged Non-players discouraged	Players encouraged Non-players discouraged [a]
G	None (unless player)	None (unless player)
H	None	None
I	Action taken to attract players and non-players, young and old.	Action taken to attract players and non-players, young and old.
J	None	None

[a] Unless parents of players.

TABLE 11
Language Used at Club Meetings, When Playing Soccer and on Social
Occasions

Club	Club Meetings	Playing Soccer	Social Occasions
A	Croatian	Croatian and Others [a]	Croatian and Others
B	English and Hungarian	Hungarian	Hungarian
C	English	English	English
D	English	German and English	German and English
E	Polish	Polish	Polish
F	English and Serbian	English and Serbian	English and Serbian
G	English and Italian	English	English
H	English	English	English and German
I	English	English	English
J	Serbian	Serbian	Serbian and English

[a] This expression was used by the committee of Club A, presumably because English and other languages were spoken according to the ethnicity of those present.

varied according to the club (see Table 11). Only two clubs spoke English exclusively. Four clubs spoke their own ethnic language for the most part. The remaining four clubs spoke their own ethnic language and English.

8. There was little social contact between the clubs; with one exception, there was no contact between the clubs and the core society.

CONCLUSIONS

Within the limitations of this study, the following conclusions seem warranted:

With some exceptions, involvement in ethnic soccer is not conducive of furthering assimilation, and that more specifically, club policies of ethnic soccer clubs inhibit the structural assimilation of members.

NOTES

1. The point of contact made possible through sport can lead to discord as Reid found. In his book which tells the story of an Allied prisoner of war camp in Germany, he relates how arguments developed as a result of a "wall game" competition *between* different nationalities, whereas in games played by prisoners from within a single group (in this case Britain), arguments never occurred. Reid, P. R.: Escape from Colditz. New York, Berkeley Publishing Corporation, 1952, p. 64.

2. Park, Robert E., and Burgess, Ernest W.: Introduction to the Science of Sociology. Chicago, University of Chicago Press, 1921, p. 735.

3. Gordon, Milton M.: Assimilation in American Life. New York, Oxford University Press, 1964, p. 62.

4. From the Greek work "ethnos" meaning "people" or "nation."

5. Gordon, op. cit., p. 24.

6. Tumin, Melvin M.: Ethnic group. *In* A Dictionary of the Social Sciences. Edited by Julius Gould and William L. Kolb. Free Press of Glencoe, 1965, p. 243.

7. Gordon, op. cit., p. 72. Gordon prefers the term "core group," which was used by A. B. Hollingshead to describe the old Yankee families of colonial, largely Anglo-Saxon ancestry who have traditionally dominated the power and status system of the community. See Hollingshead, August B.: Trends in social stratification: A case study. Am. Soc. Rev., *17* (December, 1952): 686.

8. Fishman, Joshua A.: Childhood indoctrination for minority-group membership. *In* Ethnic groups in American life. Daedalus: J. Am. Acad. Arts Sci., Spring, 1961, 329.

9. Saxon, George: Immigrant culture in a stratified society. Mod. Rev., *11:*122, 1948.

10. Warner, W. Lloyd, and Srole, Leo: The Social Systems of American Ethnic Groups. New Haven, Yale University Press, 1945, pp. 254–282.

11. This point is taken up by Martin when he says, "At present, we are participating in an extremely drastic and rapid cultural change, affecting our entire Western society. The rapid advance of technological science, spear-headed by automation, is causing a steady shrinkage of the workaday world. Plans now underfoot for a six-week vacation and a three-day weekend indicate that before long our work force will have 200 free days in the year." He goes on to qualify this as follows: "These changes do not apply, to the same extent, to professional executive and management groups. However, the fact remains that, coincidental with a rising standard of living, higher employment, and a steadily increasing national product, the American people are finding themselves with more and more time off the job. In other words, we have already acquired, in large measure, the latest and the greatest freedom of all—free time, unstructured time, discretionary time, time for leisure." (Alexander Reid Martin: Man's leisure and his health. Quest 5: 26, 1965.) Three publications by Brightbill, Miller and Robinson, and Dumazedier, which discuss societal problems and current theories related to leisure, either directly or indirectly, point to the increase in leisure time during the current era. "It seems curious that at a time when many people have more leisure than ever before ..." (Brightbill, Charles K.: Man and Leisure. Englewood Cliffs, N. J., Prentice-Hall, 1961, p. v.) "The twentieth century finds man turning more and more to his increasing free time, to fulfill himself." (Miller, Norman P. and Robinson, Duane M.: The Leisure Age. Belmont, Calif., Wadsworth Publishing Co., 1963, p. v.) "Leisure today is a familiar reality in our advanced societies." (Dumazedier, Joffre: Toward a Society of Leisure. New York, The Free Press, 1967, p. 1.)

12. For example, Rosenthal, Erich: Acculturation without assimilation: The Jewish community of Chicago, Illinois. Am. J. Sociol. *66:*275–288, 1960. Chyz, Yaroslav, and Lewis, Read: Agencies organized by nationality groups in the United States. Ann. Am. Acad. Political Soc. Sci. March, 1949, *262*. Wilensky, Harold L.: and Ladinsky, Jack: From religious community to occupational group: Structural assimilation among professors, lawyers and engineers. Am. Sociol. Rev. *32:*541–542, 1967.

13. For example, Walker, Harry J.: Changes in the structure of race relations in the South. Am. Sociol. Rev. *14:*377–383, 1949, Senior, Clarence: Race relations and labor supply in Great Britain. Social Problems *4:*302–312, 1957. Banton, Michael P.: White and Colored. New Brunswick, N. J., Rutgers University Press, 1960, Neprash, J. A.: Minority group contacts and social distance. Phylon *14*(19):207–212, 1953. Davison, R. B.: Black British: Immigrants in Britain. London, Oxford University Press, 1966, p. 170. Martin Luther King, Jr., Where Do We Go From Here: Chaos or Community? New York, Harper and Row p. 269.

14. For example, Breton, Raymond, and Pinard, Maurice: Group formation among immigrants: Criteria and process. Can. J. Economics Political Sci. *26:*465–477, 1960. Weinstock, Alexander, S.: Role elements: A Link between acculturation and occupational status. Br. J. Soc. *14:*144–149, 1963: Wilensky, loc. cit.

15. For example, Duncan, Otis Dudley, and Lieberson, Stanley: Ethnic segregation and assimilation. Am J Sociol. *64:*364–374, 1959: Lieberson, Stanley: Ethnic

Patterns in American Cities. New York, Free Press of Glencoe, 1963.

16. Andreano, Ralph: No Joy in Mudville. Cambridge, Massachusetts, Schenkman Publishing Co., 1965, p. 133.

17. Handlin, Oscar: The family in old world and new. *In* Social Perspectives on Behavior. Edited by Herman D. Stein and Richard A. Cloward. New York, The Free Press, 1958, p. 103.

18. Saxon, loc. cit.

19. Boyle, Robert H.: Sport-Mirror of American Life. Boston, Little, Brown and Company, 1963, p. 97.

20. Shibutani, Tamotsu, and Kwan, Kian-M.: Ethnic Stratification. New York, Macmillan, 1965, pp. 543–544.

21. Weinberg, S. Kirson, and Arond, Henry: The occupational culture of the boxer. Am J Sociol *57:*462, 1951.

22. For example, Young, Pauline V.: The Pilgrims of Russian Town. Chicago, University of Chicago Press, 1932. Roucek, Joseph S.: The Yugoslav immigrants in America. Am J Sociol, *40:*602–11, 1935: Hawgood, John S.: The Tragedy of German-America. New York, G. P. Putnam's Sons, 1940; Eisenstadt, S. N.: The place of elites and primary groups in the absorption of new immigrants in Israel. Am J Sociol *57:*222–231, 1951: Richardson, Alan: The assimilation of British immigrants in Australia. Hum. Relations, *10:*157–165, 1957: Weinstock, S. Alexander: The Acculturation of Hungarian Immigrants: A Social-Psychological Analysis. Columbia University, Ph.D. (1962), University Microfilms, Inc., Ann Arbor, Michigan; Talf, R.: The assimilation of Dutch male immigrants in a western Australian community. Hum Relations, *14:*265–281, 1961: Broom, Leonard and Shevky, E.: Mexicans in the United States: A problem in social differentiation. Sociology and Social Research *36:*150–158, 1952. In some instances, two ethnic groups have been studied allowing some comparative analysis. For example, Borrie, Wilfred D.: Italians and Germans in Australia: A Study of Assimilation. Melbourne, Published for the Australian National University by F. W. Cheshire, 1954, pp. 217–231.

23. For example, Stanley Lieberson, loc. cit.

24. Wisconsin State Football Association, Soccer Souvenir Book, issued on the occasion of the United States Football Association Convention, June 30-July 1 (Milwaukee: Wisconsin State Football Association, 1928). Pages not numbered.

25. U. S. Bureau of the Census, U. S. Census of Population: 1960. Vol. 1. Characteristics of the Population, Part 51: Wisconsin. (Washington, D. C.: U. S. Government Printing Office, 1963), p. 309.

26. "In May 1904 in Paris, five nations got together to found the F.I.F.A. (Federation Internationale de Football Association) .... Those five nations—France, Holland, Belgium, Switzerland, and Denmark ... have increased and multiplied." There were eighty-one countries controlled by F.I.F.A. in 1954. Batchelor, Dengil: Soccer—A History of Association Football. London, Batsford Ltd., 1954, p. 139. In 1963, there were "... 119 National Associations affiliated to it (F.I.F.A.) ...." Doggart, A. G.: (Chairman of the English Football Association), in Fiftieth Anniversary Golden Jubilee Journal. New York, 1963 U.S.S.F.A. Convention Committee, July, 1963. Hackensmith makes explicit reference to soccer on the five continents. Hackensmith, C. W.: History of Physical Education. New York, Harper and Row, 1966, pp. 59, 89, 159, 233, 235, 258, 266, 280, 292, 303, 368.

27. Personal interview with the committee of Club I, April 11, 1967.

28. Personal interview with the committee of Club J. April 20, 1967.

29. Gordon, Milton M.: Assimilation in American Life. New York, Oxford University Press, 1964, p. 81.

30. Ibid.

31. Ibid.

32. See Table 4.

33. Ibid.

further readings for part two

Section One: Sport Groups

Bird, A.M.: Team structure and success as related to cohesiveness and leadership. J. Soc. Psychol., *103*:217–223, 1977.

Bird, A.M., *et al.*: Convergent and incremental effects of cohesion on attributions for self and team. Sport Psychol. *2*:181–194, 3/1980.

Carron, A.V.: Social Psychology of Sport. Ithaca, N.Y., Mouvement Publications, 1980.

Chelladurai, P., and Carron, A.: Leadership. C.A.H.P.E.R. Monograph Series, Ottawa, C.A.H.P.E.R., 1978.

Cooper, R., and Payne, R.: Personality orientations and performance in soccer teams. J. Soc. Clin. Psychol., *11*:2–9, 1972.

Donnelly, P., Carron, A., and Chelladurai, P.: Group Cohesion in Sport. C.A.H.P.E.R. Monograph Series, Ottawa, C.A.H.P.E.R., 1978.

Emerson, R.M.: Mount Everest: A case study of communication feedback and sustained group goal striving. Sociometry, *29*:213–227, 1966.

Eitzen, D.S.: The effect of group structure on the success of athletic teams. Int. Rev. Sport Sociol., *8*:7–17, 1973.

Fiedler, F.E.: Assumed similarity measures as predictors of team effectiveness. J. Abnorm. Soc. Psychol., *49*:381–388, 1954.

Gill, D.: Cohesiveness and performance in sport groups. *In* Exercise and Sport Sciences Reviews. Edited by R. Hutton. Vol.

5. Santa Barbara, Cal., Journal Publishing Affiliates, 1977, pp. 131–155.

Hendry, L.B.: Human factors in sport systems: Suggested models for analyzing athlete-coach interactions. Hum. Factors, *16*:528–544, 1974.

Klein, M., and Christiansen, G.: Group composition, group structure and group effectiveness of basketball teams. *In* Sport, Culture and Society. Edited by J.W. Loy and G.S. Kenyon. 1st Edition. New York, Macmillan, 1969, pp. 397–408.

Landers, D., and Lüschen, G.: Team performance outcome and cohesiveness of competitive co-acting groups. Int. Rev. Sport Sociol., *9*:57–69, 1974.

Landers, D., Brawley, L., and Landers, D.: Group performance, interaction and leadership. *In* Handbook of Social Science of Sport. Edited by G. Lüschen and G. Sage. Champaign, Ill. Stipes, 1981, pp. 297–315.

Lenk, H.: The giving up of values in the case of top-class oarsmen under socio-dramatic simulated stress. Int. Rev. Sport Sociol., *3*:137–148, 1968.

Lenk, H.: Team Dynamics: Essays in the Sociology and Psychology of Sport Including Methodological and Epistemological Issues. Champaign, Ill., Stipes, 1977.

Loy, J.W.: Socio-psychological attributes associated with the early adoption of a sport innovation. J. Psychol., *70*:141–147, 1968.

Loy, J.W., Curtis, J., and Sage, J.: Relative Centrality of Playing Position and Leadership Recruitment in Team Sports. *In* Exercise and Sport Sciences Reviews. Vol. 6. Edited by R. Hutton. Philadelphia, The Franklin Institute Press, 1979, pp. 257–284.

Lüschen, G.: Small group research and the group in sport. *In* Aspects of Contemporary Sport Sociology. Edited by G.S. Kenyon. Chicago, The Athletic Institute, 1969, pp. 57–66.

McGrath, J.E.: The influence of positive interpersonal relations on adjustment and effectiveness in rifle teams. J. Abnorm. Soc. Psychol., 65:365–375, 1962.

Myers, A.: Team competition, success, and the adjustment of group members. J. Abnorm. Soc. Psychol., 65:325–332, 1962.

Nixon, H.L.: Cohesiveness and team success: A theoretical reformulation. Rev. Sport Leisure, 2:36–57, 1977.

Roberts, J.M., and Kundrat, D.F.: Variation in expressive balances and competence for sports car rally teams. Urban Life, 7:231–51, 276–80, 1978.

Roberts, J.M. and Chick, G.E.: Butler County eight ball: A behavioral space analysis. *In* Sports, Games and Play. Edited by J.H. Goldstein. Hillsdale, N.J., Lawrence Erlbaum Associates, 1979, pp. 65–99.

Roberts, J.M., and Nattrass, S.: Women and trapshooting: competence and expression in a game of physical skill with chance. *In* Play and Culture. Edited by H.B. Schwartzman. West Point, N.Y., Leisure Press, 1980, pp. 262–291.

Sage, G.H.: An assessment of personality profiles between and within intercollegiate athletes from eight different sports. Sportwissenschaft, 2:408–415, 1972.

Slepicka, P.: Interpersonal behavior and sports group effectiveness. Int. J. Sport Psychol. 6:14–27, 1975.

Tropp, K. and Landers, D.M.: Team interaction and the emergence of leadership and interpersonal attraction in field hockey. J. Sport Psychol. 1:228–240, 1979.

Widmeyer, W.N., and Martens, R.: When cohesiveness predicts performance outcome in sport. Res. Q. 49:372–388, 1978.

Widmeyer, W.N., Loy, J.W., Roberts, J.M.: The relative contributions of action styles and ability to the performance outcome of tennis teams. *In* Psychology of Motor Behavior and Sport—1979. Edited by G. Nadeau, W. Halliwell, K. Newell, and G. Roberts. Champaign, Ill., Human Kinetics, 1980, pp. 200–208.

Section Two: Sport Organizations

Ball, D. W.: Replacement processes in work organizations: Task evaluation and the case of professional football. Sociology of Work and Occupations, 1:197–217, 1974.

Chelladurai, P., and Carron, A.: A reanalysis of formal structure in sport. Can. J. of Appl. Sport Sci., 2:9–14, 1977.

Curtis, J., and Loy, J.W.: Positional segregation in professional baseball: Replications, trend data and critical observations. Int. Rev. Sport Sociol., 13:5–21, 1978.

Curtis, J., and Loy, J.W.: Race/ethnicity and relative centrality of playing positions in team sports. *In* Exercise and Sport Sciences Reviews. Edited by R.S. Hutton. Vol. 6. Philadelphia, The Franklin Institute Press, 1979.

Dunning, E., and Sheard, K.: The bifurcation of Rugby Union and Rugby League: A Case study of organizational conflict and change. Int. Rev. Sport Sociol., 11:31–72, 1976.

Eitzen, D.S., and Yetman, N.R.: Managerial change, longevity and organizational effectiveness. Administrative Sci. Q., 17:110–116, 1972.

Gamson, W.A., and Scotch, N.A.: Scapegoating in baseball. Am. J. Sociol., 70:69–72, 1964; with reply by Grusky, 72–73.

Gross, E.: Sport leagues: A model for a theory of organizational stratification. Int. Rev. Sport Sociol., 14:103–112, 1979.

Loy, J.W., and Sage, J.: Athletic personnel in the academic marketplace: A study of the interorganizational mobility patterns of college coaches. Sociol. Work Occup., 5:446–469, 1978.

Lüschen, G.: The Analysis of Sport Organizations. *In* Handbook of Social Science of Sport. Edited by G. Lüschen and G. Sage. Champaign, Ill., Stipes, 1981, pp. 316–329.

McPherson, B.D.: Involuntary turnover: A characteristic process of sport organizations. Int. Rev. Sport Sociol., 11:1–15, 1976.

McPherson, B.D.: Involuntary turnover and organization effectiveness in the National Hockey League. *In* Canadian Sport: Sociological Perspectives. Edited by R. Gruneau and J. Albinson. Don Mills, Ontario, Addison-Wesley, 1976, pp. 259–275.

McPherson, B.D.: Retirement from professional sport: The process and problems of occupational and psychological adjustment. Sociol. Symp., *30*:126–143, Spring, 1980.

Oglesby, C.: Social conflict theory and sport organizational systems. Quest, *22*:63–73, 1974.

Rosenberg, E.: Sports as work: Characteristics and career patterns. Sociol. Symp., *30*: 39–61, 1980.

Stern, R.N.: The development of an interorganizational control network: The case of inter-collegiate athletics. Administrative Sci. Q., *24*:242–266, June, 1979.

Stewart, D.W.: A preference mapping of organizational objectives of sports franchise executives. *Applied Psychol., 65*:610–615, 5/1980.

Theberge, N., and Loy, J.W.: Replacement processes in sport organizations: The case of professional baseball. Int. Rev. Sport Sociol., *11*:73–93, 1976.

Section Three: Sport Subcultures

Allison, M.T., and Lüschen, G.: A comparative analysis of Navajo Indian and Anglo basketball sport systems. Int. Rev. Sport Sociol., *14*:75–85, 3–4/1979.

Ball, D.W.: Failure in sport. Am. Sociol. Rev., *41*:726–739, 1976.

Birrell, S., and Turowetz, A.: Character work-up and display in collegiate gymnastics and professional wrestling. Urban Life, *8*:219–246, 1979.

Charnofsky, H.: The major league professional player: self-conception vs. the popular image. Int. Rev. Sport Sociol., *3*:39–56, 1968.

Csikszentmihalyi, M.: The Americanization of rock climbing. The University of Chicago Magazine, *61*:21–26, 1969.

Dunning, E., and Sheard, K.: Barbarians, Gentlemen and Players: A Sociological Study of the Development of Rugby Football. New York, New York University Press, 1979.

Faulkner, R.: Making violence by doing work: Selves, situations and the world of professional hockey. Sociol. Work Occup., *1*:288–312, 1974.

Fine, G., and Kleinman, S.: Rethinking sub-culture: An interactionist analysis. Am. J. Sociol., *85*:1–20, July, 1979.

Fine, G.: Small groups and culture creation: The idioculture of Little League Baseball Teams. Am. Sociol. Rev., *44*:733–745, October, 1979.

Hall, M.A.: Sport and physical activity in the lives of Canadian women. *In* Canadian Sport: Sociological Perspectives. Edited by R.S. Gruneau and J.G. Albinson. Don Mills, Ontario, Addison-Wesley, 1976, pp. 170–199.

Harris, D., and Eitzen, D.S.: The consequences of failure in sport. Urban Life, *7*: 177–188, July, 1978.

Ingham, A.: Occupational subcultures in the work world of sport. *In* Sport and Social Order. Edited by D.W. Ball and J.W. Loy. Reading, Mass., Addison-Wesley, 1975, pp. 337–389.

Iso-Ahola, S.: A Social Psychological Analysis of Little League Baseball. *In* Social Psychological Perspectives On Leisure and Recreation. Edited by S. Iso-Ahola. Springfield, Ill., Charles C. Thomas, 1980, pp. 171–218.

Lüschen, G.: Cheating in sport. *In* Social Problems in Athletics. Edited by D. Landers. Urbana, Ill., University of Illinois Press, 1976, pp. 67–77.

Pearson, K.: Surfing Subcultures of Australia and New Zealand. St. Lucia, Queensland, University of Queensland Press, 1979.

Phillips, J., and Schafer, W.: Sub-cultures in sport: A conceptual and methodological approach. *In* Sociology of Sport: Theoretical and Methodological Foundations. Edited by R. Albonico and K. Pfister-Bing Basel, Birkhauser Verlag, 1971.

Polsky, N.: The hustler. Social Problems, *12*: 3–15, 1964.

Smith, M.D.: Hockey violence: A test of the violent subculture hypothesis. Social Problems, *27*:235–247, 1979.

Stone, G.: Wrestling: The great American passion play. *In* Sport: Readings From a Sociological Perspective. Edited by E. Dunning. Toronto, University of Toronto Press, 1972, pp. 301–335.

Tejada-Flores, L.: Games Climbers Play. *In* The Games Climbers Play. Edited by K. Wilson. London, Piadem, 1978, pp. 19-27.

Taylor, I.: 'Football mad': A speculative

sociology of football hooliganism. *In* Sport: Readings From a Sociological Perspective. Edited by E. Dunning. Toronto, University of Toronto Press, 1972, pp. 353–377.

Theberge, N.: The system of rewards in women's professional golf. Int. Rev. Sport Sociol., *15*:27–41, 1980.

Thomson, R.: Subcultural Analysis In Sport. Can. J. Appl. Sport Sci., *2*:195–200, 1977.

Weinberg, S.K., and Arond, H.: The occupational culture of the boxer. Am. J. Sociol., *57*:460–469, 1962.

Whyte, W.F.: Street Corner Society: The Social Structure of an Italian Slum. Chicago, University of Chicago Press, 1955.

Williams, T.: A Goffmanian analysis of professional wrestling. Rev. Sport Leisure, *5*:35–48, 2/1980.

PART THREE

sport and macro-social systems

We turn now to social organization as it is found on a larger scale, the macro-social system level. The readings are grouped into four sections, with the first three addressed to social institutions (e.g., the family, the church, the school) or those social systems "organized around enduring patterns and practices developed about a set of values, norms, and sanctions."* In Sections One, Two, and Three, respectively, three main institutional spheres are considered: *socializing* institutions, *regulative* institutions, and *cultural* institutions. Section Four is concerned with a macro-level phenomenon characteristic of all social systems—*social stratification.*

Such organizations as the family, the school, and the community are dynamic social systems in that within them a number of social processes occur. *Section One: Sport and Socializing Institutions* includes two articles addressed to the process of socialization, i.e., the acquisition of various knowledges, skills, and dispositions enabling persons to participate in society, both collectively and individually. In the article by Loy and Ingham there is a description of the socialization process in general, followed by a review of how play, games, and sport serve as settings for the development of personality and the learning of various social roles; that is, the extent to which sport provides the means for achieving some generalized ends. However, one can also consider socialization *into* sport roles

*Loy, McPherson, and Kenyon, *Sport and Social Systems,* p. 35.

per se. Thus, the Kenyon and McPherson piece provides a conceptual framework and describes the results of its application to the learning of a variety of sport roles, from spectator to high performance athlete.

As increasing numbers are socialized into a wide array of sport roles, the magnitude of the sport order increases accordingly. Although it is debatable as to how well sport has retained its "playful" characteristics, its regulation and control has greatly increased and become highly formalized. Thus, *Section Two: Sport and Regulative Institutions,* provides a taste of the place of sport in society from the perspective of three kinds of regulative institutions: economic, legal, and political. As the reader will quickly discover, the three are often highly interrelated.

The magnitude of sport business, directly and indirectly, has become enormous. As with any enterprise of substantial proportions, sport, too, is governed by regulation, most of which is based on existing legislation. Thus, it was not surprising to find a number of scholars addressing themselves to the intertwining of law and economics such as in the landmark publication, *Government and the Sports Business* (Noll, 1974). Although any single chapter is too lengthy to reprint here, the interested reader should consult at least the introduction by the editor, in which he describes the distribution of economic resources in various professional sport contexts, and in doing so, illustrates the legal implications that arise.

In Section Two, two papers on economics and law in sport are reprinted; the first by Daymont (anti-trust laws and professional sport), the second by Koch and Leonard (the use of economic cartel theory and sociological social movement theory to explain the workings of the major intercollegiate sport organization in the United States—the NCAA). Although the number and depth of studies in these areas has increased in the past few years, more work is needed, particularly as we see an increase in both civil and criminal suits brought against both individuals (spectators, players, and team officials) and organizations (professional and amateur sport leagues and specific teams). Nevertheless, compared to ten years ago, some excellent material is available (see *Further Readings,* and in particular, Lowell, 1973). In fact, some of today's scholars are touching upon some very fundamental tenets of Western civilization, such as "freedom of opportunity" and "protection from the criminal acts of others."

Many persons, from citizen consumers to recent presidents of the International Olympic Committee, have lamented the linkage of sport and politics. Given the global proportions of sport today, however, students of sport should not be surprised at this development, both within sport itself and in the many wider political arenas. As usual, it is easier to condemn than to explain. Since our concern is with the latter, the remaining papers in Section Two deal with the sport-politics link. First, Kiviaho describes the close correspondence between political orientations and sport organizations within a single country—Finland. In a broader context, Grimes, Kelly, and Rubin report that, while demographic and economic factors are important, communist countries do perform better in Olympic competitions, although the relationship is by no means well understood.

In *Section Three: Sport and Cultural Institutions,* the reader is invited to become acquainted with the relationship between sport and certain elements of culture, from technology to politics. In the first contribution, Betts shows the historical linkage between sport and technology, citing a variety of examples from the latter half of the nineteenth century. In more comprehensive terms, Lüschen examines hypotheses explaining sport in terms of such cultural products as industrialization and technology; ideology (particularly "protestantism" and achievement values); and social differentiation. In addition, he analyzes both functional and dysfunctional attributes of sport, and concludes with an analysis of sport and the process of social change.

Although space is not sufficient to reprint studies based on an anthropological framework, the interested reader should consult such authors as Fox, Roberts, and Sutton-Smith. Fox describes the consequences when competitive baseball is introduced to the Pueblo Indians— a culture whose institutions stress harmony and cooperation. From another perspective, Roberts, Sutton-Smith and Kendon (1963) report how game differentiation paralleled differentiation in other cultural realms. Using comparative methods they showed that games of "strategy" are found in cultures revealing a strategic mode in their folk tales. Their "conflict enculturation" hypothesis should bring to mind the socialization processes as described in the readings of Section One. A number of other articles have been published by Sutton-Smith and Roberts, not all of which are listed under *Further Readings.*

Among the most persuasive elements of contemporary civilization are the mass media, although no extensive literature has accumulated on their relation to sport. In addition to Betts' historical material, we have included a recent article by Birrell and Loy, who draw heavily upon McLuhan's theory to account for the significance of the sport event once removed from its venue. With media technology widely disseminating news and live accounts of various high-risk or "vertigo" events, Donnelly, in the next paper, speculates upon the cultural factors that account for the increase in high-risk sports in recent years.

The proposition that man is inherently aggressive receives periodic reinforcement (for example, Ardrey's *Territorial Imperative,* and Lorenz's *On Aggression*). At the same time, the question of the role of sport in augmenting or discharging aggression is often raised, by layperson and scholar alike. The reader may wish to consult Sipes (1973), who, using two rival models of behavior in sport contexts, reported that aggression in humans is more likely to be a cultural product than one of man's inherent "drives."

Despite a range of concerns presented in this section, the reader should be aware that space restrictions prevent the inclusion of papers related to other aspects of cultural institutions, particularly those associated with the arts and religion. Again, the reader is advised to consult both *Further Readings* and *Sport and Social Systems*.

Probably the most common theme running through the literature of sociology in general, and sport sociology in particular, is *social inequality* or *social differentiation*. Since stratification within all societies has become highly institutionalized, it is fitting that Part Three close with *Section Four: Sport and Stratification Systems*. The first two papers focus upon the question of opportunity in higher education settings. Eggleston found that in England, students attending Oxford or Cambridge were at a disadvantage in achieving recognition through sport if they were graduates of tax-supported rather than independent secondary schools, both absolutely and in relation to their proportion among all students enrolled. Ten years later, Berryman and Loy replicated the study in the United States—an act too seldom seen in sport sociology, or sociology in general, for that matter—and obtained similar results after examining data based upon the secondary school background of Harvard and Yale athletes. The findings from such studies cast doubt upon the alleged democratization function of sport in higher education.

If certain inequalities persist *within* colleges and universities, what about the case for improving life chances after graduation as a consequence of sport achievement and success in college sport? Loy's study (1972) of UCLA athletes showed a "relatively high degree of social mobility," at least for those athletes with "blue collar" social origins. However, without a control group of nonathletes, it was difficult to assess the effects of sport involvement *per se*. In a paper not reproduced here, Dubois (1978) took this factor into account, and found that sport achievement in college does not account for high status attainment in terms of either occupational prestige or earnings, at least for a sample of California graduates. From another perspective, i.e., the significance of organizational prestige in facilitating career mobility, Loy and Sage obtained data from basketball and football coaches in American colleges and universities. They found a close parallel between organizational prestige and career contingency, similar to that of academic personnel. Finally, Gruneau, after noting the restricted contexts of much of the previous work on sport and social stratification, concentrates on accounting for the social structure of sport organizations in terms of broader societal characteristics. Using Canadian society as a framework he concludes that while the "organizational 'elite' in sport has become more complex, mobility into this elite has not increased appreciably."

In conclusion, the readings in *Part Three* should leave the reader better able to appreciate the reciprocal relationship between sport and society. That is, while sport may be considered a social institution in itself, at the same time it is intimately related to a wide variety of other social structures.

SECTION ONE
sport and socializing institutions

play, games, and sport in the psychosocial development of children and youth

JOHN W. LOY AND ALAN G. INGHAM

I. THE SOCIALIZATION PROCESS

Albeit brief, this first part of the chapter attempts to (a) define the term "socialization," (b) set forth the fundamental consequences of socialization, (c) outline the major modes and basic mechanisms of socialization, (d) describe the primary agencies of socialization, and (e) summarily characterize the socialization process.

A. SOCIALIZATION DEFINED

The concept of socialization is manifestly broad and complex and thus not readily definable. As Clausen (1968) has written:

> Socialization may be viewed from the perspective of the individual or from that of a collectivity (be it the larger society or a constituent group having a distinct subculture). Further, individual development may be viewed generically within a given society or it may be viewed in terms of the experiences and influences that lead to significant differences among persons (both social types and unique personalities).

Human beings learn to be social beings. It appears that little of the social behavior of the human being can be traced to genetic or hereditary sources. Nurture outweighs nature in its

Reprinted from Physical Activity—Human Growth and Development. Edited by G. Lawrence Rarick. New York, Academic Press, 1973. Copyright, 1973, by Academic Press, New York, New York 10003.

contribution to social development. The individual has to learn to participate effectively in social groups. Thus, Elkin (1960) defined socialization "... as the process by which someone learns the ways of a given society or social group so that he can function within it." According to Becker (1962) socialization is an interactional process because the human being is self-reflexive and symbolizes and must not only learn to place himself in a social group but must also learn the social definitions of behavior which enable him to confront a multitude of individuals without creating anxiety by an inappropriate presentation of self.

In short, then, socialization is a process that involves interaction and learning. On the one hand, it centers attention on the adaptation of individuals to their social situations; on the other hand, it centers attention on how individuals develop social identities as a result of their participation in various social situations. Taking these several themes into account, *socialization* may be defined for present purposes as an interactional process whereby a person acquires a social identity, learns appropriate role behavior, and in general conforms to expectations held by members of the social systems to which he belongs or aspires to belong.

The human being affiliates and reaffiliates with social groups throughout life. "Life (may) be viewed as continuous socialization, a series of careers, in which old identities are sacrificed as new identities are appropriated, in which old relations are left behind as new relations are 'joined'" (Stone, 1962). Each reaffiliation requires a redefinition of the situation. However, one should not assume that affiliation with one group necessarily denies affiliation with another. Each individual occupies many places or positions in many groups. This matrix of statuses with their contingent roles demands that the individual be capable of transforming his identities. In any given day the typical individual experiences many transformations; he may change from boss to employee, from father to son, from salesman to customer, etc. In sum, socialization is a process of preparing the social actor to perform appropriately in all of his social settings.

B. CONSEQUENCES OF SOCIALIZATION

Caplow (1964) stated . . . "In every situation in which a member or an aspirant is to be transformed into a successful incumbent, there are at least four requirements that must be met. The candidate must acquire: (a) a new self-image, (b) new involvements, (c) new values, and (d) new accomplishments." These requirements outlined by Caplow may be viewed as the major consequences of socialization.

1. A New Self-Image

"Identities are socially bestowed. They must also be socially sustained, and fairly steadily so" (Berger, 1963). As the individual takes a position (status) in a group, he learns to define himself in response to the expectations which the group has of a person occupying that status. That is, the person attempts to introject a group-defined identity into his own identity. The more congruent the projected self is with the group-defined self, the more social sustenance (reinforcement) one expects. Once having established one's claim to an identity, one works to preserve it, and if possible to enhance it. Therefore, it is suggested that the more established the claim to an identity becomes through adequate performance, the more an individual can feel secure in assuming that identity.

2. New Involvements

When an individual joins a new group he encounters new people. He finds that he must modify his performance, as a social actor, to the interests of the new audience which in all cases demands that the individual be that which he portrays (Berger, 1963; Goffman, 1959). That is,

his new affiliates demand sincerity in the acting out of a social role. "When an actor takes on an established social role, usually he finds that a particular front has already been established for it" (Goffman, 1959). The performance required of a role in a group has probably been group-defined before an individual joins the group. Not only has the role been group-defined but in a task-oriented group, such as a football team, the reciprocal behaviors of other roles have probably also been defined. Socialization may be considered successful when a candidate for the role has learned to present an identity and fulfill the behavioral obligations to the satisfaction of the group. To borrow a concept from Hollander (1958), the individual attempts to secure, by conformity to group expectations, a good credit rating. Thus credit ". . . represents an accumulation of positively-disposed impressions residing in the perceptions of relevant-others. . ." In the initial phases of membership in a new group, the individual seeks to establish an identity through conduct which is acceptable to his new affiliates. New involvements are anxiety producing until the social actor has sufficient credits for his performance to be taken for granted.

3. New Values

Through accepting and internalizing the communicated values and norms of the group which is acting as a reference, the social actor is able to ". . . visualize his proposed line of action from this generalized standpoint, anticipate the reactions of others, inhibit undesirable impulses, and thus guide his conduct" (Shibutani, 1961).

Socializing a neophyte into a group involves the lengthy process of imbuing the neophyte with the necessary ideology to enable him to justify to nongroup members what is done by the group. Thus, the professionally oriented physical education student is indoctrinated through such courses as "Principles of Physical Education" which supposedly prepare him to cognitively handle those outsiders who question his existence. This sharing of a perspective with a reference group is, in Mead's (1964) terms, taking the attitudes of "generalized others."

4. New Accomplishments

Berger (1963) suggested that ". . . identity comes with conduct and conduct occurs in response to a specific social situation." When we assume a status (position) it is often necessary to work at occupying that status. When we assume a status within a group we not only work to maintain our own identity but also to preserve the performance of the whole group. As Goffman (1959) suggested: "... it would seem that while a team-performance is in progress, any member of the team has the power to give the show away or to disrupt it by inappropriate conduct." In some cases this simply means an observance of professional etiquette, in others, it requires that a whole series of complex skills must be learned to maintain the group performance at an adequate level.

C. MECHANISMS OF SOCIALIZATION

Every neophyte in any given social system is exposed to one or more principal modes of socialization. These fundamental means of socialization include training, schooling, apprenticeship, mortification, trial-and-error, assimilation, and anticipatory socialization (Caplow, 1964). Common to each of these major modes of socialization are patterned forms of social learning, control, and influence.

New members of a group are asked to learn the prevalent definitions or meanings upon which the social reality of the organization is based. The new members learn to act out the identities which are designated to them. They learn the roles that are contingent with the assumption of such identities. And, in general, they learn the culture of their new social system. However, socialization is not merely a learning process. "The individual not only learns objectivated meanings but identifies with them and is shaped by them. He draws them into himself and makes them his meanings" (Berger, 1969). In sum, all modes of socialization imply attitudinal and behavioral changes resulting from certain basic mechanisms of social influence.

Processes of social influence have long been of central concern for behavioral scientists, and many theories and models have been set forth explaining the nature of social influence. One such theory is that proposed by Kelman (1961).

Kelman's theory suggests the circumstances under which attitude change will or will not occur and identifies the conditions leading to either temporary or permanent attitude change. Kelman distinguished three primary processes of social influence which he called (1) compliance, (2) identification, and (3) internalization.

1. Compliance

"Compliance can be said to occur when an individual accepts influence from another person or from a group because he hopes to achieve a favorable reaction..." (Kelman, 1961). That is to say, a person learns the appropriate responses to situations as defined by others in order to obtain reinforcement or avoid punishment. Initially, "the child's dependency and needs for affection established during early infancy provide a positive basis for maternal authority and for the child's compliance with it" (Deutsch and Krauss, 1965). The individual responds to influence from his significant others and eventually learns that groups also have authority over him and can reward or punish him similarly. Compliant behavior leads to reinforcement (the presentation of a reward or the removal of noxious stimuli). Noncompliant behavior leads to punishment. This orientation to the study of learning has been labeled "operant conditioning." "In operant conditioning we 'strengthen' an operant in the sense of making a response more probable or, in actual fact, more frequent" (Skinner, 1968). A response must be emitted before it can be reinforced. How this response is elicited is not clear. One possible method is direct tuition, as tuition engenders the intentional guidance of behavior and the manipulation of reinforcement (Secord and Backman, 1964). However, direct tuition presupposes that an individual knows the contingencies between the behavior and the cue-producing word or symbol (Miller and Dollard, 1941).

Compliant behavior is largely a function of the patterns of reward presented to an individual. By patterns we refer to the schedules of reinforcement. Under laboratory conditions, reward schedules can be manipulated. Some schedules (e.g., continuous) facilitate the rapid acquisition of responses. Other schedules (e.g., intermittent) while not resulting in such rapid acquisition render the response, once acquired, more resistant to extinction (Bandura and Walters, 1963).

Intermittent reinforcement can be presented in a variety of ways. One main mode of experimental reinforcement is a "fixed-ratio schedule" where only every other, or every nth response of the subject is reinforced. Another main mode of experimental reinforcement is a "fixed-interval schedule" where selected time intervals intervene between presentations of rewards. Bandura and Walters (1963) observed that:

> Examples of fixed-ratio schedules of reinforcement in everyday life, particularly in child-training procedures, are difficult to find. On the other hand, in most modern social systems the socializing agents, who are dispensers of reinforcers, have to organize their lives on the basis of the time schedules of others. Consequently, in most families some responses of the children are reinforced on a relatively unchanging fixed-interval schedule. Feeding, the availability of the father or school-age siblings for social interaction, and, in general, events associated with household and family routines may serve as reinforcers, positive or negative, that are dispensed at relatively fixed intervals.

In terms of compliant behavior it must be recognized that an individual may upon occasion learn that when one particular preferred response is reinforced, other responses contiguous in time and space may also be simultaneously reinforced. Effective social learning thus requires sharp discrimination and adequate generalization of learned patterns of responses. Generalization enhances the efficiency of the socialization process in that social situations which are defined similarly can be handled using the same set of responses. However, an individual sometimes learns responses other than those intended by his tutor. This may be the result of overgeneralizing or generalizing on the basis of cues not relevant to the situation in which he is placed. Fine discrimination among stimuli must often be exercised in the selection of a response which is appropriate to the situation as it is socially defined. For example, a young child must learn that physical aggression is particularly appropriate in some situations but most inappropriate in other social settings.

2. Identification

"Identification can be said to occur when an individual adopts behavior derived from another person or group because this behavior is associated with a satisfying self-defining relationship to this person or group" (Kelman, 1961). Identification is one explanation of imitative behavior. An individual attempts to establish himself in an identity by imitating persons who already possess that identity. Secord and Backman (1964) presented seven principles which account for the choice of a model. Suffice it here to merely generalize these seven principles into reinforcement terminology. Models are chosen for imitation mainly because they have coercive power (i.e., they can reward or punish) or because they are capable of obtaining rewards or approval which the individual also desires but does not have access to (the identifier is vicariously reinforced).

Two other theoretical orientations which have utilized the mechanism of identification are "role theory" and "reference group" theory.

A. ROLE THEORY. Role theory conceives of society as a stage and views the individual as a social actor. Accordingly, the task of socialization is to insure adequacy of performance from each and every actor. From this dramaturgical perspective role theory considers the ways in which an individual presents himself and his performance to others. In short, it is concerned with the management of impressions and the sustaining of identities (Goffman, 1959).

The individual learns to share definitions of the situations in which he places himself. Through interaction he attempts to perfect his performance in the identities he assumes. "The term role is usually applied to situations in which the prescriptions for interaction (i.e., the script for the performance) are culturally defined..." (Deutsch and Krauss, 1965). "A role, then, may be defined as a typified response to a typified expectation" (Berger, 1963). Conventional ethics demand that the prescribed role and the subjective role be in symmetry. That is, the individual should render a sincere playing of the role.

As a child we imitate our significant others (those with whom we identify) who aid us in self definition. In taking the role of others the child begins to develop a self-system, that is, he begins to view himself as a social object. Through imitative interaction and performance he learns the prescribed behavior for the statuses he occupies and he realizes that the prescribed behavior patterns are bolstered by social norms. He learns that only a range of behavior is acceptable to his significant and generalized others.

B. REFERENCE GROUP THEORY. The major problem for reference group theory is centered on the process whereby "... a person orients himself to groups and to other individuals and uses them as significant frames of reference for his own behavior, attitudes or feelings" (Deutsch and Krauss, 1965). Merton (1963) distinguished several types of reference groups. One of his major distinctions was between positive and negative reference groups. The former's standards are valued and adopted. The latter's standards are rejected. "Reference-group theory indicates that social affiliation or disaffiliation normally carries with it specific cognitive commitments" (Berger, 1963).

In brief, the degree of influence a reference group exerts in the formation of attitudes among its members is dependent on the degree to which any individual member identifies with the group. It should be recognized that by means of "anticipatory socialization" nonmembership groups may also serve as important reference groups and thus substantially influence attitude development.

For example, the son of an unskilled worker who aspires to middle-class status will tend to accept middle-class values and attitudes. His middle-class outlook will embrace such diverse objects as sexual practices and political issues. Upwardly mobile, he will reject the values and attitudes of his lower-class family (Krech *et al*, 1962).

As can be surmised from the preceding discussion, the effect of groups on social learning and attitude development is often indirect and typically complex.

3. Internalization

Internalization can be described as the appropriation of social reality and its transformation "... from structures of the objective world into structures of the subjective consciousness" (Berger, 1969). That is, society has outposts stationed in our heads (this metaphor is attributed to Kempton, 1970) which enable us to regulate our own behavior. Obviously, the external society reified in our own consciousness is rarely in a state of symmetry. Individuals modify collective definitions in the light of their idiosyncratic definitions of social reality. However, the more successful the socialization process is, the more symmetrical they become (Berger, 1969). The internalization of social norms and values enables us to confront our actions and reflectively appraise them. This appraisal may result in feel-

ings of guilt (self-punishment) or esteem (self-reinforcement). Although many theories share the concept of internalization, we would like to focus very briefly on the psychoanalytic orientation.

Although biologistic and behavioristically interpretable, Freudian theory attempts to reinstate the organism as an intervening entity between the stimulus and the response. In fact, Freud attempts to move from stimulus-response reaction to ego-controlled reaction (Becker, 1962). The ego operates on a reality principle, it either represses or defers gratification of id impulses. By reality we refer to the social world. The ego tempers the demands of the id in terms of social reality. Both the ego and superego are generated by interaction. The superego *is* the introjected cultural value system. Introjection refers to the internalization of standards. Hence, through the introjection of cultural values and norms, the individual anticipates the reactions of others to his behavior and appraises his own behavior in the light of these introjections. Psychoanalytic theory entertains the possibility of an internal dialectic between the individual's impulses and society reified in consciousness. It might be assumed that Freud's concern with this internal dialectic is manifested in his discussions of cathexis and anticathexis, defense mechanisms (e.g., repression and fixation), and the origins of neurotic and moral anxiety.

D. AGENCIES OF SOCIALIZATION

At the moment of birth a child obtains membership in a number of social systems, including his family, community, and society. These social systems and all others in which he may acquire membership at a later date constitute agencies of socialization. Initially, of course, socialization is limited to the micro-social system of the family, composed of parents, siblings, and perhaps immediate relatives. Members of the family constitute the first "significant others" for the child and initially define the world for him. As the child's social circle gradually extends he comes under the influence of other social systems which come to constitute his "generalized others" (Mead, 1964). Although any given individual is influenced by a multitude of social systems during the course of his life cycle, the principal agents of socialization for children and youth are held to be the family, the peer group, the school, and the community.

1. The Family

In industrial nations the family's all-encompassing role as a socializing agent has been diminished. Other societal agencies have taken over many of its functions. However, the family still retains its importance in primary socialization in that the parents (significant others) provide the child with his first exposure to rules and role behaviors. Initially, the child is totally dependent upon the family and is subordinated by it (Parsons and Bales, 1955). In these initial stages of life (the oral stage—Freud), a child is dependent upon its mother for the relief of oral stress. Food and suckling reduce this drive and they become associated with love and approval which are generalized reinforcers. Parental authority is based upon this dependency relationship (Hall, 1954). The child complies in order to gain approval and to avoid punishment (Miller and Dollard, 1941). As the symbolizing capacity of the child increases, shaping of behavior through the reinforcement of approximate imitations (Skinner, 1968) is supplemented by direct tuition. The child can be taught values and sentiments. The family can now interpret the wider community to the child and transmit "... segments of the wider culture to the child, the particular segments being dependent upon (the family's) social positions in the community" (Elkin, 1960).

2. The Peer Group

The importance of the peer group as an agent of socialization in present-day society is increasing. During the latency period (Freud), the child extends his social circle beyond that of the family. The generations gradually move apart so that the peer group replaces the parents as a source of information on contemporary know-how (Broom and Selznick, 1963). In what Riesman called "the other-directed society" the peer group becomes a measure of all things (Riesman et al., 1953). The child channels his competitive drives into a constant searching for peer group approval.

Socialization in the peer group is not formalized. Membership consists of knowing the norms and values of the in-crowd and being able to perform adequately in those tasks or performances which involve the group. Peer groups are egalitarian in that there is no formal authority structure (Broom and Selznick, 1963; Chinoy,

1963). However, it is the task of the older members of the group to socialize the neophytes. The neophyte identifies with the group values in order to gain approval and maintain his relationship with the group. Because an individual chooses his affiliates in an act of self-definition, it is likely that a certain uniformity among group members prevails (Berger, 1963; Jones and Gerard, 1967). Uniformity and cohesiveness are maintained not only by sanctioning deviates but also by group idiosyncrasies such as "slanguage," dress codes, and the group's vantage points in the universe of social relationships.

3. The School

The industrialization of societies has necessitated the development of a formal (organized) system of education (Toby, 1964; Worsley et al., 1970). Historically traced, the family structure has slowly evolved from an extended system to a nuclear system and increasing geographic mobility has loosened kinship ties. As a consequence of these developments, the formal education of maturing individuals is a deliberate attempt to provide the knowledge and skills required by the technical and social roles of complex modern society (Worsley et al., 1970). The child spends most of each day within the confines of the school. The school "... is the theater in which much of the drama of the child's life is played" (Jersild, 1968). In dealing with the adult significant others (teachers) who stand in loco parentis, the child is provided with one more setting in which he must accommodate himself to adult authority. These adults have the same mechanisms of socialization available to them as have the child's parents. They can reward or punish. They provide models for imitation and suggest values for the child to internalize (Elkin, 1960). The teacher has available the generalized reinforcers of approval and praise or the formalized rewards of grades and trophies. Besides accommodating himself to adult authority, the child has to assimilate the experience presented to him in the school. Jersild (1968) suggested that "the learner perceives, interprets, accepts, resists, or rejects what he meets at school in the light of the social system he has within him." This statement recognizes the possibility of a potential conflict between the home and the school or the peer group and the school. What self-system does the child bring with him to school and will the social origins from which this self has emanated conflict with the middle-class orientations of the teachers within the school? Will the activities valued by the peer group coincide with the valued activities of the school (Coleman, 1961)?

4. The Community

Generally, the word "community" has been used as an ideal-typical concept which orientates us to a social setting usually defined by territorial boundaries, a specific subculture, a degree of autonomy, and a fairly homogeneous populace (Frankenberg, 1957; Minar and Greer, 1969; Sanders, 1958; Young and Willmott, 1967).

The child because he is placed in a community "... forms an appreciation of the manner in which various categories of people are evaluated and incorporates customary patterns into his way of approaching the world" (Shibutani, 1961). The child responds to both the recurrences in social behavior (customs) and to the value orientations which define the meaning of life. He responds to the institutions of community life which have been "established by some common will" (MacIver, 1917). Socialization attempts to fit man to his community. In essence, the socially produced personality is asked to endure the society and continually sacrifice some personal wishes to preserve it. The child is asked to believe the subcultural ideologies of his community as disbelief destroys the perceived unanimity upon which the community publicly operates.

E. SOCIALIZATION AND SOCIETY

In the preceding sections, the modes, mechanisms, and agencies of socialization have been presented, albeit in a somewhat mechanistic fashion. These sections have only alluded to the societal purpose of socialization. In the final part of Section I some reasons why the socialization process is necessary for society are presented.

Society is the most encompassing, comprehensive, and consequential group to which an individual belongs. All other groups may be viewed as integrated subsystems of society. Thus, the purpose of socialization can be defined in general terms as the process by which an individual "... learns the ways of a given society so that he can function within it" (Elkin, 1960). In order for socialization to occur, society must be conceived of as a reality, an object in itself (Durkheim, 1950). Reified in this way it can

proceed to exert influence over the individual. However, the "... individual is not molded as a passive inert thing. Rather he is formed in the course of a protracted conversation in which he is a participant. That is, the social world is not passively absorbed by the individual, but actively appropriated by him" (Berger, 1969). The socialization process conceived of in this way stresses the ongoing dialectic which exists between man and his society. Socialization is one side of this dialectic where the social reality attempts to impose itself on the individual so that he conforms to, and believes in, the behavioral dictates necessary to ensure stability in the society. Stability refers to a minimum consensus of beliefs in the "goodness" of the social reality, as it is presently constructed, so that it can be perpetuated. Hence, if socialization were successful in all cases, symmetry (Berger, 1969) would exist between the values of society and the values of the individual and social stability would be ensured. If socialization were successful and an introjected society were all that there was to the self "... the account of the relationship between man and society would be an extreme and one-sided one, leaving no room for creativity and reconstructive activity; the self would merely reflect the social structure, but would be nothing beyond that reflection" (Morris—introduction to Mead, 1970). In the mechanistic presentation which preceded, we ignored this essential criticism which makes the plea for a dialectical conception of socialization. Out of a need for brevity and convenience, rather than our background assumptions concerning the nature of man and society, the discussion was confined to a one-sided approach in that a picture was presented whereby man needs only to be capable of learning and internalizing to fit into a socially ordered reality.

Socialization is obviously not as successful as society might wish it to be. Social change does occur. Creativity is evident. To speak of a dialectic is to admit to a process whereby the individual not only learns established meanings but also contributes to those meanings. Although a minimum of symmetry seems to exist (that is, there is sufficiency of social order), complete symmetry is probably not humanly possible. This is to admit that the individual is capable of redefining situations using rules as guides but not mandates. It suggests, as was alluded to in the discussion of Freud, that a second dialectic can occur within the individual's own consciousness. Hence, confrontation can occur between the internalized social system and the self-system.

In the discussion of modes, mechanisms, and agencies, both levels of the dialectic were somewhat ignored. Such an approach rightfully should have led to criticisms that the discussion suffered from an oversocialized conception of man (Wrong, 1961). The discussion of agencies and mechanisms implied that human conduct is totally shaped by common norms or institutionalized patterns of interaction (Wrong, 1961). For instance, under Section I, C, 1, "Compliance," the basic tenets of operant conditioning ignore man's ability to interpret and define the situations in which he places himself. Rather the discussion concentrates with ratlike experimental simplicity on shaping the cognitions of man through reinforcement and punishment. Also, internalization should not be merely viewed as habit formation (Wrong, 1961). If internalization were merely habit formation, then it would deny the dialectic between the self-system and social system which occurs in consciousness.

The discussion which now follows is essentially aimed at indicating the role of play, games, and sports in the socialization process. It is assumed that the agencies of socialization see ludic activities as a means of portraying the value system of society to a child so that through participation he can learn it. (The phrase "ludic activities" is used throughout this chapter to represent all activities generally described as play, games, or sports). It is also necessary to make the assumption that games provide definitions of meaningful interaction which, if participation is encouraged in them, have some transformable values to other situations defined as meaningful to society.

II. PLAY, GAMES, AND SPORT IN SOCIALIZATION

As previously defined, "socialization is an interactional process whereby a person acquires a social identity, learns appropriate role behavior, and in general conforms to expectations held by members of the social systems to which he belongs or aspires to belong." Thus, every social system can be conceived of as an agent of social-ization modifying individuals' behavior through various processes of social influence.

The purpose of this part of the chapter is to show, suggest, and speculate as to how play, games, and sport serve the socialization process within selected micro- and macro-social systems. Specifically, Section II,A focuses on the role of play during early childhood socialization in the family. Section II,B examines the importance of games within peer groups for preadolescent development and analyzes the function of sport for adolescent development in school settings. Section II,C centers attention on the complex nature of the socialization process and illustrates its complexity by describing the dialectic between individuals and society in terms of game involvement. Finally, Section II,D deals with the utility of simulated agonistic activities in meeting explicit socialization objectives of particular physical education programs. (The phrase "agonistic activities" is used in this chapter to denote those ludic activities which are essentially competitive in nature, e.g., games and sports).

A. THE FAMILY

The first social system and thus the initial agent of socialization to which the newborn infant is exposed is that of the family. It is in the context of the family that an individual's fundamental concept of self is largely molded. In this section an attempt is made to show what function play fulfills in this particular process of socialization.

1. Development of Self

Mead (1934), in his eminent work titled *Mind, Self, and Society*, described in detail how an individual obtains a full development of self. In his theoretical treatment of the genesis of self he discussed two general sets of background factors and two general stages in the full development of self. The first set of background factors concerns the conversation of gestures between animals, and the acquisition of language and consequent communication among humans. The second set of background factors "is represented in the activities of play and the game." Mead (1934) depicted the two general stages of the development of self as follows:

At the first of these stages, the individual's self is constituted simply by an organization of the particular attitudes of other individuals toward himself and toward one another in the specific social acts in which he participates with them. But at the second stage in the full development of the individual's self, that self is constituted not only by an organization of these particular attitudes, but also by an organization of the social attitudes of the generalized other or the social group as a whole to which he belongs.

Play primarily relates to the first stage of development and games to the second stage of development in the genesis of self—conceptualized by Mead. In play, the child takes on and acts out roles which exist in his immediate, but larger, social world. By acting out such roles he organizes particular attitudes about them. Moreover, the child in the course of role playing becomes cognitively capable of "standing outside himself" and formulating a reflected view of himself as a social object separate from but related to others. In contrast, a child in a game situation must be prepared to take on the role of every player in the game. He must sense what all other players are going to do in order to make his own particular plays. Mead (1934) summarily stated that "The game is then an illustration of the situation out of which an organized personality arises. Insofar as the child does take the attitude of the other and allows that attitude of the other to determine the thing that he is going to do with reference to a common end, he is becoming an organic member of society."

2. Stages of Early Childhood Play

The influential role of play with respect to personality development in particular and the socialization process in general can first be seen in infancy, and its effects are well illustrated throughout early childhood. Erikson (1963) recognized three stages of infantile play which he labeled "autocosmic play," "microcosmic play," and "macrocosmic play." During the period of autocosmic play the child centers attention on his own body and play "... consists at first in the exploration by repetition of sensual perceptions, of kinesthetic sensations, of vocalizations, etc." Play in the microsphere is confined to "the small world of manageable toys." "Finally, at nursery school age playfulness reaches into the macrosphere, the world shared with others."

3. Autocosmic Play

Several recent studies by Call (1964, 1965, 1968, 1970; Call and Marschak, 1966; Work and Call, 1965) show the importance of autocosmic play in early ego development. Call (1968) observed that "The capacity for social play in infancy is developed only in the presence of a reciprocating party ... impressions (ideas and feelings) about the self are influenced from the beginning by the mother's contribution to play in infancy and the capacity to play is crucially dependent on being played with." He further noted that "In the infant's play there is obvious utilization of congenital ego equipment. There is a testing of this equipment, there is the exploration of environmental responses, a survey of environmental responses, and under special conditions a selection of certain reciprocal experiences which become institutionalized as a game."

An example of a type of play experience which is an early precursor to full game behavior is the playful interaction within the dyadic social system of mother and child in feeding situations. For instance: "Near the end of the feeding the mother often tests his hunger by withdrawing the nipple to see if he will go after it again. Or the infant may let go and turn away from the nipple then grab it again and suck or chew lightly without getting milk" (Call, 1970). Similar kinds of play experiences include various forms of lap and finger play in infancy (Call, 1968). These types of play experiences provide the foundation for the construction and conduct of relatively complex games between the child and either parent and or sibling within the wider social system of the whole family. In turn, such games assist the child in his struggle for self-identity and aid him in his resolution of inner conflicts arising from basic anxieties. The traditional game of "peek-a-boo," for example, "... gives the infant practice at separating himself from someone else, then experiencing delightful reunion" (Call, 1970). The game of peek-a-boo can be considered a way for the infant to master anxiety when the mother is absent, i.e., mastery of object loss (Call and Marschak, 1966). The major social function of low order games in the sphere of autocosmic play is perhaps revealed in Erikson's theory (1963) that "... child's play is the infantile form of the human ability to deal with experience by creating model situations to master reality by experiment and planning.''

4. Microcosmic Play

Social scientists have virtually ignored the microsphere of play and its realm of dolls and toys. This state of affairs is both surprising and dismaying in view of the socially significant nature of microcosmic play. The underlying social import of play in the microsphere is clearly pointed out in Ball's (1967) pronouncement that:

Almost from the moment of birth and for many years thereafter, children are in frequent and intense contact with toys in great variety, of diverse type, complexity, and composition. These toys are, from a very early age, an important part of the child's experientially perceived reality, operating in several related ways over and above their more manifest recreational purpose. For example, they function as socializing mechanisms, as educational devices, and as scaled down versions of the realities of the larger adult-dominated social world.

Ball further suggested that toys serve the socialization process in two major ways. First, toys function as role rehearsal vehicles for the practice of role-associated activities. Second, toys act as role models by representing diverse social categories. This second function is exemplified in the following quotation from Sessoms (1969):

The small girl playing with her doll, acting as the mother of Raggedy Ann, provides a case in point. Her caring for the doll may be viewed as preparation for the traditional role of mother-homemaker. She performs the tasks as she has observed her mother perform them. The values and concepts of motherhood are being internalized through the play process just as the boy participating in baseball is learning to conform to the rules of the group and assumes the role assigned to him by that body.

In addition to providing a means of role rehearsal and the learning of important cognitive styles of behavior, toys ''. . . also serve at the same time as surrogates for human companionship, as important targets for affective expression'' (Ball, 1967). Herein one calls immediately to mind the ''security blanket'' sported by Linus in *Peanuts*, the popular cartoon series drawn by Charles M. Schulz. Notwithstanding this humorous exam-

ple, one should not lightly dismiss the importance of early affective attachments to playthings. For as Call (1970) showed in his citation of a psychiatric case study:

Infantile attachments can remain strong and influential even into adult life. A 40-year-old woman talked in analysis about her ''wag-a-dollie,'' a little cloth doll she associated with her father. While she was 21 and away at college, her mother burned wag-a-dollie. When she learned of this she became confused and depressed, even dropped out of college for awhile. She tried a series of substitute transitional objects, and even called her doctor ''Doll'' for a time. It was possible for her, by tracing the origins of wag-a-dollie, to recapture the feelings of her earliest attachment to her father, which helped her to understand the nature of the difficulties she had been having both in her marriage and in the raising of her children.

In sum, the microsphere of play provides a vast universe of symbolic discourse which serves the socialization process in many diverse ways both manifest and latent, conscious and subconscious, temporarily and permanently.

5. Macrocosmic Play

When a child reaches the state of macrocosmic play he enters into a play world shared by others and becomes involved in a world characterized by social drama. As Stone (1965) pointed out, drama is ''. . . basic in the child's development of a conception of self as an object related to, yet different from, other objects. Drama is a vehicle for the development of identity.'' Stone (1962, 1965) suggested that there are two basic modes of socialization associated with drama which he termed ''anticipatory socialization'' and ''fantastic socialization.'' In the first case, the child plays roles that he will likely perform in later life; for example, the child may play at being father, salesman, customer, etc. In the second case, the child plays roles which he is highly unlikely to perform in later life; for example, a child may pretend to be a king, a cowboy, or a space cadet. Although anticipatory drama appears to hold greater import for later life experiences, fantastic drama is not without functional importance since it ''. . . often serves to maintain and keep viable the past of society—its myths, legends, villains and heroes" (Stone, 1965).

A third form of early childhood play associated with drama is what Stone (1965) referred to as "childish tests of poise." Stone observed that:

> It is not enough only to establish an identity for one's self it must be established for others at the same time. Identities are *announced* by those who appropriate them and *placed* by others. Identities must always be validated in this manner to have reality in social interaction.

It is suggested that childhood play related to tests of poise affords a suitable medium whereby a child may learn in a rudimentary manner the arts and techniques of "impression management" so crucial to role performance in adult careers. Goffman (1959), in his major work *The Presentation of Self in Everyday Life*, discussed in depth the arts of impression management. His dramaturgical perspective posits that each individual in the social intercourse of everyday life presents himself and his performances to others and attempts to influence the impressions others form of him by employing various techniques which help sustain his performance in a manner not unlike the actor's portrayal of a particular character before an audience. Goffman discussed the arts of impression management in terms of personal performances, team performances, and regions of behavior. He used the term "performance" to refer to all the activity of an individual which occurs during a period marked by his continuous presence before a particular set of observers and which has some influence on the observers. The two major elements of a "performance" are what Goffman referred to as "the setting" and the "personal front." The setting consists of the physical environment in which the performance takes place and includes any expressive equipment required for the performance. Personal front may include such things as "insignia of office or rank; clothing; sex, age, and racial characteristics; size and looks; posture; speech patterns; facial expressions; bodily gestures; and the like." Goffman dichotomized the stimuli which make up the personal front into "appearance" and "manner." Manner refers "to those stimuli which function at the time to warn us of the interaction role the performer will expect to play in the oncoming

situation." Appearance refers to "those stimuli which function at the time to tell us of the performer's social statuses."

The relationships between appearance, play, and self have been treated at length by Stone (1965). He showed how "child's play demands costume and body control, and is facilitated by props and equipment (toys) appropriate to the drama." Stone (1962) especially emphasized the importance of clothes in the meaning of appearance. He spoke of "investure" during the pre-play period, "dressing out" in the play period, and "dressing in" as related to the game stage of early socialization. An example of investure is a mother dressing her son in blue clothes and her daughter in pink in order to denote masculinity and femininity, respectively. Dressing out involves "costume" and is associated with acting out a social role in another's clothing (e.g., playing housewife in one of mother's old dresses or shoes). Dressing in requires a uniform and is related to a "real" identity (e.g., a boy wearing a Little League baseball uniform).

By way of summary, it may suffice to state that macrocosmic play serves the socialization process by the fact that "much of the drama of childhood replicates the interaction of the larger society in which it occurs" (Stone, 1965).

B. THE PEER GROUP AND THE SCHOOL

Following early childhood socialization experiences within the family, the peer group and the school are the next significant social systems to impinge upon the child. Although these two social structures are analytically distinguishable, they are often, if not usually, empirically intertwined in American society. Therefore, these two agencies of socialization are treated together in this section.

1. Types of Peer Groups

The earliest and most informal peer grouping to emerge is the *play group*. Children become involved in such groups as early as the third or fourth year of life and continue to interact in play groups during the early school years. Two chief characteristics distinguish play groups from other kinds of peer groupings: First, "The choice of playmates is relatively restricted, in kind and number"; second, the play group is the child's "*first* introduction to a group which assesses him as a child from a child's point of view, and teaches him the rules of behavior from the same point of view'' (Bossard and Boll, 1966).

Later age peer groups which the child usually enters between the ages of 8 and 12 are more formalized than play groups. They have a more complex social structure, a greater degree of permanency, and more rigid requirements for membership. According to Bossard and Boll (1966) there are two major types of later age peer groups, the *clique* and the *gang*. ''A clique may be defined as a small, intimate social participation group consisting of persons of the same social status and in agreement concerning the exclusion of others from the group.'' A gang is a more formal group than a clique, less exclusive, more permanent in nature, and usually has an identifying subculture marked by nicknames, symbols, slogans, passwords, particular dress styles, etc.

While several kinds of peer groups can be differentiated for special purposes of analysis, all forms of peer groups share three characteristics in common (Havighurst and Neugarten, 1957). First, unlike the adult world where a child occupies a subordinate status position, in his peer world he holds an equal status with others. Second, the interpersonal relationships among peers in any given group tend to have a transitory quality. While peer relationships and friendships are often intense in nature, they are also often of short duration. This is especially true in childhood and preadolescence. Third, the influence of the peer group increases as children grow older.

The peer group as a socializing agent fulfills many functions. But perhaps the three primary socializing functions performed by the peer group are teaching the culture, teaching new social roles, and teaching social mobility (Havighurst and Neugarten, 1957).

2. Teaching the Culture

While each particular peer group has its own special subculture, every peer group nevertheless tends to reflect in important ways the culture of the society at large. Perhaps the most critical cultural content imparted by the peer group are codes of moral conduct. ''A child learns through his peers the prevailing standards of adult morality—fair play, cooperation, honesty, responsibility—that, while they may at first be child-like versions, become adult-like with increasing age'' (Havighurst and Neugarten, 1957).

Undoubtedly, the most famous description of the role of play in the moral development of the child is contained in Piaget's (1965) classic work, *The Moral Judgment of the Child*. In the first part of his book, Piaget described how children gradually develop a mature understanding of the rules of a game. His account is based upon a series of observational studies of children engaged in the game of marbles which Piaget characterized as a microcosmic moral system.

Piaget focused his attention on two particular phenomena associated with game rules: first, the *practice* of rules; second the *consciousness* of rules. With respect to the practice of rules, Piaget (1965) distinguished three kinds of behavioral patterns which appear in successive stages; namely, motor behavior, egocentric behavior, and cooperative behavior. Corresponding to these three types of behavior are, according to Piaget, three kinds of rules. ''There is the *motor rule*, due to preverbal motor intelligence and relatively independent of any social contact; the *coercive rule* due to unilateral respect; and the *rational rule* due to mutual respect.'' As succinctly summarized by Berlyne (1969): ''Competitive games thus exemplify for Piaget the advance from a view of morality characterized by 'heteronomy' and 'moral realism,' based on one-sided respect for persons in authority and belief in immutable moral laws comparable to the laws of nature, toward a mature 'autonomous' moral sense, rooted in mutual respect among equals, and capacity for cooperation.''

Although recent research reveals that moral judgments made by children do not always conform to Piaget's analysis (Berkowitz, 1964; Hoffman, 1970: Kohlberg, 1963b), his investigations nevertheless offer significant insights into the role of games for ''internalization'' of moral values. Moreover, recent empirical findings strongly support the important implication of Piaget's work that play patterns and attitudes can be used as indices of socialization (Herron and Sutton-Smith, 1971; Seagoe, 1969; Webb, 1969).

An excellent empirical illustration of play as an index of socialization as well as an example of how cultural content is transmitted through play is Webb's (1969) study of the professionalization of attitudes toward play among adolescents. Webb observed that ''The transition from 'child's play' to games, and then to sport, involves increasing complexity and rationalization of the activities and increasing professionalization of attitudes." By professionalization Webb meant "... the substitution of 'skill' for 'fairness' as the paramount factor in play activity, and the increasing importance of victory."

The findings of Webb's investigation are based on questionnaire responses from random samples of students enrolled in the public and parochial schools of Battle Creek, Michigan in 1967, stratified by grades (three, six, eight, ten, and twelve). At each grade level he asked students to rank in order of importance what they thought was personally most important in playing a game: to play it as well as you can, to beat your opponent, or to play the game fairly. Results of his study show the diminishing importance of the fairness factor and the increasing importance of the "success" factor (i.e., beat one's opponent) as age increases.

Webb (1969) drew a number of interesting parallels between the business and economic institutions of Western society, emphasizing the work-oriented values of equity, skill, and success, and the world of sport, emphasizing the play-oriented values of fairness, skill, and victory. He suggested that sport is a reflection of society in that "... it provides in fact in one institution what is essentially ideology in another." In conclusion, Webb (1969) commented:

> Clearly, if nothing else, this investigation demonstrates that participation in the play world is substantially influential in producing that final result, the urban-industrial man. Although it is true that play attitudes, as demonstrated, are extensively influenced by other factors, it is the final isomorphism of the play arena to the economic structure, and the fact of participation in it, at a time when participation in other areas is virtually nonexistent, that makes that participation the significant factor it now appears to be. Thus to continue the sophomoric and even moronic insistence on play's contribution to the development of such "sweetheart" characteristics as steadfastness, honor, generosity, courage, tolerance, and the rest of the Horatio Alger contingent, is to ignore its structural and value similarities to the economic structure dominating our institutional network, and the substantial contribution that participation in the play arena thus makes to committed and effective participation in that wider system.

In summary, the work of Piaget and Webb indicates how play, games, and sport in peer group and school settings "fit the child to his society" through relatively indirect and nonobtrusive means of socialization.

3. Teaching New Social Roles

Associated with the transmission of the general culture by the peer group is the teaching of new social roles. The context of the peer group provides opportunities for youth to occupy a variety of statuses and social positions and offers a suitable situation for children to try out various behavioral styles. Since sports and games are an almost universal feature of peer groups, it can be assumed that they play an important part in the teaching of new social roles. That such is the case is shown by Helanko (1958, 1963, 1969) in his several studies of the developmental pattern of sports participation among Scandinavian children.

Helanko spoke of the "expansion of socialization" and described how children first learn to interact in pairs, then in larger primary groups, followed by small secondary collectivities, and finally by still larger social systems. He showed how children via sport involvement at different age levels are exposed to new social norms and roles as a result of interacting with peers in progressively more complex social systems.

In his examination of the interrelationships between the peer groups, sport, and socialization, Helanko described the socialization process in terms of three stages which he refers to as the pre-gang period, the gang period, and the post-gang period. These stages of socialization are outlined in Table 1 and contrasted with Piaget's stages of moral development. Sports participation within the gang serves two basic functions according to Helanko. First, sport involvement serves as a source of pleasure. Second, sports participation acts as a means of status definition. As Helanko (1963) observed: "Sports and the gang together constitute the social milieu in which, for the first time in his life, the boy is called upon to create a social position for himself among his equals."

Helanko and other investigators who have attempted to analyze the relations between sport and socialization in the peer group usually have not been very specific about what particular kinds of social roles are learned in the course of play with peers. It is evident, however, that one

TABLE 1
Stages of Socialization*

Ages (years)	Stages in learning how to play marbles, according to Piaget		Stages in the process of socialization among boys, according to Helanko
	Practice of rules	Consciousness of rules	
1			
	Stage I	Stage I	Yard-aggregation-stage
2	Motor behavior of	No comprehension	Egocentricity
	an individualistic	or rules	Primitive pairs appear
3	nature		No actual groups are formed
			No sports
4			
	Stage II		
5	Egocentricity		
		Stage II	Play-gang stage
6		Rules are regarded	Primitive groups are formed
		as "sacred" and	Weak solidarity
7		absolute	Primitive sports
8			
	Stage III		First period of gang age
9	Cooperation		Solid groups
			Strong in-group feeling
10			Centripetal interaction
			Clubs are formed within the
11			gang
			Sports (ballgames) appear
12	Stage IV	Stage III	Second period of gang age
	Codification of rules	Rules are regarded	At the outset of this period
13		as relative	solid groups still appear
14			At the termination of this
			stage interaction becomes
15	Termination of in-		centrifugal
	terest in marbles		Gangs and gang clubs begin
16			to dissolve
			Interest in sports continues
17			but becomes more indi-
			vidualistic
18			The gang age terminates
			Individuals who have left
			their gangs form pairs
			which aggregate

* Adapted from Helanko (1963).

of the most significant social roles largely learned in the peer group is an individual's sex role. Although gender is socially assumed at birth, and while sex role learning is an important part of the familial socialization process, peer groups extend and elaborate earlier sex role acquisition in profound ways. As expressed by Havighurst and Neugarten (1957): "... the peer group is a powerful agency in molding the behavior of males and females in accordance with current American versions of manhood and womanhood." But, as Tryon (1944) took care to point out in her discussion of adolescent peer culture: "It is a long, complex, and often confusing learning-task to achieve manhood or womanhood in our society with the skills and behaviors, the attitudes and values appropriate to the role which a given individual must take. For the most part boys and girls work at these tasks in a stumbling, groping fashion, blindly reaching for the next step without much or any adult assistance."

Tryon's comments concerning the difficulty which adolescents experience in achieving an adequate concept of masculinity or femininity while made in 1944 nevertheless seem particularly relevant today as the mass media's exclamatory treatment of such topics as "unisex," "women's liberation," and the "gay liberation front" has brought once again the whole matter of sexual identity to the fore. Winick (1968), for example, treated at length the process of desexualization in American life in his recent book titled *The New People.* He suggested that current modifications of sex roles may be "intimately related to our society's ability to survive." Winick further forecasted that "Archeologists of the future may regard a radical dislocation of sexual identity as the single most important event of our time."

Regretfully, "sex-role behavior is one of the least explored areas of personality formation and development" (Brown, 1956). Thus, while it is commonly assumed that boys and girls learn appropriate sex role behavior as a by-product of playing games in their peer groups (Brown, 1958; Gump and Sutton-Smith, 1955; Rosenberg and Sutton-Smith, 1960; Rosenberg and Sutton-Smith, 1964), relatively few empirical efforts have been made to determine the degree of learning and even fewer investigations have been made to determine the specific means whereby such learning takes place. Therefore, in view of the present state of research regarding sex-role socialization, one can at best only examine revealed sex differences in play activities and speculatively infer what socialization processes are associated with them.

One of the more extensive examinations of sex differences in play choices is Sutton-Smith's and Rosenberg's work (1961) titled "Sixty Years of Historical Change in the Game Preferences of American Children." Their investigation is based on the comparative analysis of similar studies of game preferences of children conducted in 1896, 1898, 1921, and 1959. One of the most marked findings of their investigation is the fact that the game preferences of girls have become increasingly like those of boys since the turn of the century. They noted that this finding was not unexpected "in light of the well known changes in woman's role in American culture during this period of time." They were surprised, however, to find that "boy's play roles have become increasingly circumscribed" and that girls currently engage in a wider variety of play activities than boys. They stated that "there is little doubt that boys have been steadily lowering their preference for games that have had anything to do with girl's play"; but they noted that this finding may be interpreted in various ways. On the one hand, "it contributes to clear-cut role definition of appropriate boys' behavior and perhaps facilitates the development of those boys who have particular skills required by the games that are in demand. On the other hand, it must as surely penalize those many other boys who find that there is a discrepancy between their own abilities and those required in the play roles of their own age sex category." In short, the findings of Sutton-Smith and Rosenberg implicitly support the results of other studies (Cratty, 1967) which indicate that there is less social stigma attached to the display of masculine behavior by girls than to the show of feminine behavior by boys.

Several social observers have commented on the fact that many boys have difficulty in achieving appropriate sex-role identification since they often lack exposure to male role models (Parsons, 1942, 1947). And a number of articles and books both popular and scholarly have expressed concern about the perceived decline of masculinity in American society (Winick, 1968). An extended treatment of these issues is given by Sexton (1969) in a book titled *The Feminized Male,* and subtitled *Classrooms, White Collars and the Decline of Manliness.*

Sexton (1969) persuasively argued that our school systems are effectively emasculating adolescent males. She pointed out that 68% of the teachers in our public schools are women and contends that women teachers set the standards for adult behavior, favoring those who most conform to their own behavior norms. She further observed that:

The feminized school simply bores many boys; but it pulls some in one of two opposite directions. If the boy absorbs school values, he may become feminized himself. If he resists, he is pushed toward school failure and rebellion. Increasingly, boys are drawn to female norms.

Sexton presented a good deal of empirical evidence to buttress her case. Primary data in her investigation consist of school records and interview and questionnaire responses of 1000 ninth grade boys and girls in a community which she refers to as Urbantown. Secondary data in her study consist of records of academic achievement and deviant behavior for all of Urbantown's 12,000 students. In addition, her data for ninth grade boys in Urbantown are compared with data from a national survey of ninth graders. Sexton focused her basic analyses on achievement and masculinity. High achievers were operationally defined as students with all A's on their report cards, middle achievers were those with mostly B's and C's, while low achievers were those with mostly D's and F's. Masculinity was assessed by means of Gough's masculinity scale from the California Personality Inventory.

Comparing her measures of masculinity and academic achievement, Sexton (1969) found that (1) "The less masculine boys had better marks in most school subjects"; (2) "Only in physical education and science did boys with middle masculinity scores tend to get the best marks"; and, (3) "the most masculine boys usually received their worst grades in English."

Having determined a relationship between masculinity and academic achievement, Sexton (1969) attempted to assess the relationship of sports to scholastic success and masculinity. In general she found that:

> In all sports except tennis, bowling, and volleyball (a popular sport with girls), the interest of the most masculine boys exceeds that of the least masculine boys. The pattern of interest tends to follow that of high- and low-achieving boys. The interests of low achievers are most like those of the highly masculine, and most unlike the interests of girls.

In particular, Sexton discovered that high achievers prefer sports stressing individual performance and involving minimal aggression and body contact, whereas low achievers prefer team sports of a physically demanding nature. Exceptions to the latter finding are the individu-

alistic sports of boxing and pool which Sexton found to be very popular among low-achieving, masculine boys and disliked by high-achieving, less masculine boys. Finally, with respect to sport involvement Sexton reported that:

> Low achievers were more likely to say they had been on a school athletic team, and that they regarded it as important to be among the first in sports (52 percent of low and 43 percent of high achievers felt it was *very important* to be first in sports). Highly significant differences were found in the time boys spend playing sports. Low achievers spend far more time on sports, both on weekend and weekdays (50 percent of low, 38 percent of middle, and 15 percent of high achievers spend *three hours or more* each weekday on sports). Girls spend very little time on sports. About one in three said she never or rarely played sports on weekdays, and about half spend less than a half-hour. In their aloofness from sports and their general use of leisure, high-achieving boys are more like girls than like other boys.

Sexton went on to outline the pros and cons of the place of sports in the schools. She forcefully concluded that "If sports are replaced by greater stress on the sedentary and passive academic work, the masculine quality of our males, already weakened, may collapse. Other masculine activities may be found, but they may not be able to carry such a heavy load."

4. Teaching Social Mobility

Related to the teaching of new social roles is the teaching of social mobility by the peer group. As Havighurst and Neugarten (1957) have suggested: "A lower-class boy or girl who, through an organized youth group or through the school, becomes friendly with middle-class boys and girls learns from them new ways of behaving. He may be encouraged to acquire the values and goals of his new friends, and this may eventuate in his moving up from the social position of his family." The importance of teaching social mobility is underscored by the fact that in our high schools "27 percent of boys who are in the *highest ability quartile* but the *lowest socioeconomic quartile* never go to college"; and, "in the *top ability half,* 82 percent of the poorest boys and 20 percent of the richest" do not go on to any kind of higher education (Sexton, 1969).

Few efforts have been made to determine the degree to which lower-class students informally interact with middle-class students in school and peer group settings, and even fewer investigations have been conducted to determine the social consequences of such interaction. On the basis of research to date one is led to conclude that boys and girls of diverse social strata interact to a very limited degree in our senior high schools. For example, Hollingshead (1949) in his study of *Elmtown's Youth* examined the clique relations of adolescent boys and girls enrolled in Elmtown High School. He stratified the students according to the socioeconomic background of their families into five prestige classes. Hollingshead reported that:

Analysis of the 1,258 clique ties when the factor of school status is ignored reveals that approximately 3 out of 5 are between boys or girls of the same prestige class, 2 out of 5 are between adolescents who belong to adjacent classes, and 1 out of 25 involves persons who belong to classes twice removed from one another.

Findings such as those of Hollingshead implicitly indicate that interscholastic sports may play a role in teaching social mobility since one might expect greater interaction to occur between lower-class and middle-class students in sport situations than in other types of peer settings in the school community. Data in support of this assumption are presented in a study by Schafer and Armer (1968) wherein they analyzed a number of relationships between athletic participation and academic achievement. Their study is based upon data obtained from the school records of 585 boys in two Midwestern high schools. They classified 164 (28%) of the boys in the sample as athletes, and they matched each athlete with a nonathlete in terms of intelligence test scores, occupational status of fathers, type of high school curriculum, and grade point averages (G.P.A.s) for the final semester of junior high school. Schafer and Armer (1968) found that:

More than half of the athletes in each category exceed their matches, and the average G.P.A.s of athletes is always higher than that of their matched nonathletes. Moreover, on father's occupation and curriculum, the gap is greater between athletes and their matches in the *lower* categories than in the higher. For example, greater percentages of blue-collar athletes than white-collar athletes exceed their matches in G.P.A.s (63.0 percent versus 53.7 percent). An even greater spread separates non-college-preparatory athletes from college-preparatory athletes (69.0 percent versus 53.7 percent). In short, the boys who would usually have the most trouble in school are precisely the ones who seem to benefit most from taking part in sports.

It is, of course, a yet-unanswered question as to why sports participation apparently has its greatest positive effect on the academic performance of blue-collar athletes. Schafer and Armer stated that "A plausible interpretation of this finding is that, compared to nonathletes with the same characteristics, blue-collar and non-college-bound athletes are more likely to associate and identify with white-collar and college-bound members of the school's leading crowd."

Another type of educational achievement examined by Schafer and Armer is graduation from high school. Their findings indicate that participation in interscholastic sports has a "holding influence" on students. They report that "whereas 9.2 percent of the matched nonathletes dropped out of school before graduating, less than one-fourth as many (2.0%) of the athletes failed to finish." Since social mobility is in part a function of high school graduation, it can be assumed that sport serves this process to some degree.

Although there are not as yet any systematic studies of the effects of athletic participation and upward mobility, several recent investigations report interesting results regarding the relationships between sports participation, educational expectations, and educational achievement (Bend, 1968; Rehberg and Schafer, 1968; Rehberg *et al.* 1970; Snyder, 1969; Spreitzer and Pugh, 1971). For example, Rehberg and Schafer discovered a positive correlation between athletic participation and educational expectations in their analysis of data obtained from 785 senior males in six urban Pennsylvania high schools in the spring of 1965. Moreover, they found that the relationship was strongest toward a college education. For instance, while only 36% of working class nonathletes stated that they expected to complete at least 4 years of college, 55% of the working class athletes reported that they planned to finish at least 4 years of college.

Longitudinal analyses of the relationship between perceived educational expectations and actual educational achievement (Bend, 1968; Snyder, 1969) imply that there may be long-term positive effects accruing from interscholastic athletic participation. Snyder made a 5-year follow-up study of the 1962 high school graduating class of the only high school in a Midwestern community of 38,000. Results of his study show that high school social participation (including sports participation) is positively correlated with both high school and post-high school educational achievement. In addition, findings of his investigation reveal a positive association between high school social participation and occupational status 5 years after graduation.

Snyder's findings at the local level are supported by the results reported by Bend (1968) at the national level. On the basis of data drawn from the Project Talent data bank, Bend made an extensive examination of the social correlates and possible consequences of interscholastic athletic involvement. The sample for his study consisted of approximately 14,000 senior males who completed questionnaires for Project Talent in 1960 and who returned follow-up questionnaires mailed to them in 1965. For purposes of analysis Bend designated four types of athletic groups, ranging from nonathletes to superior athletes. A superior athlete was defined as a student who was a member of more than four teams and who received more than two athletic awards during his high school years. In addition, each subject was classified into high or low endowment categories on the basis of a nine-item socioeconomic environment index. Among low-endowed subjects Bend found that superior athletes in comparison with nonathletes held greater educational, financial, and occupational expectations in 1960 and had achieved greater educational and occupational status by 1965. As an example, although only 6.2% of the nonathletes in the low endowment category attended college as full time degree students, 17% of the superior athletes in the lower socioeconomic group attended college as full time students.

As a final illustration of the longitudinal analysis of the relationship between athletic participation and academic variables related to upward mobility, reference is made to the work of Rehberg et al. (1970). Their investigation is based on data collected from a sample of 1170 high school males surveyed during both their freshman and sophomore years in seven public and parochial, urban, and suburban schools in southern New York.

In comparisons with non-athletes, the varsity and junior varsity participants were found: (1) to have higher educational aspirations and expectations, both as freshmen and as sophomores, (2) to be more likely to increase their educational goals from two years of college or less to four years of college or more during the one-year interim, (3) to spend as much time on homework, (4) to value academic competence, (5) to receive more advice from teachers and guidance counselors to enroll in a four-year college, and (6) to be as conforming to the official normative structure of the school.

Rehberg and associates stated in conclusion:

... our data do indicate a difference between athletes and non-athletes with respect to scholastic pursuits and the difference more often than not is a positive one favoring those who participate in interscholastic sports. Furthermore, our data lend themselves to the interpretation that at least a portion of this difference is a function of certain achievement-relevant socialization experiences encountered by the athlete but not by the non-athlete. It is toward the identification and measurement of these socialization experiences and their separation from associated selection variables that further research should be dedicated.

C. SOCIALIZATION AND SOCIETY

By centering our attention on only the family, peer group, and school we have no doubt inadvertently given the reader a rather simplistic overview of the socialization process since there are a number of other socializing agencies in society which impinge in important ways upon the family, peer group, and school. Within a given community, for example, there are such additional agencies as ethnic groups, neighborhoods, religious associations, social classes, and various forms of the mass media. The complexity of the socialization process is further compounded at the societal level by significant cross-cultural differences. Regretfully, space limitations preclude a detailed discussion of the relationships between agonistic activities and socialization processes associated with subcultural variations at the community level and cross-cultural variations at the societal level of analysis. Thus, it may suffice to present in conclusion a speculative summary of the dialectic between individuals and society in terms of game involvement.

The fundamental problem of social order is the Hobbesian puzzle of how every individual can intensely pursue his own self-interests without society having an internal war of all against all. Games of children and youth well illustrate the Hobbesian puzzle and afford many key insights into the nature of social order in society. "In particular, they demonstrate the process by which institutions with their elements of cooperation and morality and their concepts of right and justice can emerge from the actions of an originally unorganized aggregation of individuals each selfishly seeking to maximize his own personal satisfactions" (Lenski, 1966).

On the one hand, by providing a source of personal pleasure, games serve to express the needs of the people who choose to play them. On the other hand, games serve as models of cultural activities. Games are an important subset of a larger class of expressive models, including art, dance, drama, folktales, and music.

> They provide a way of teaching people in a society (particularly the young) some ways of getting important things done; they also provide a kind of therapy, in that individuals who are in conflict about getting their actual cultural work done can live for a time in an easier fantasy world of expressive models and evade the world of those things which are modelled until their feeling of conflict passes (Lambert and Lambert, 1964).

The findings of the several studies conducted by Roberts and Sutton-Smith (1959, 1962, 1966) offer a number of indications as to how games model the maintenance problems of societies, provide significant socialization situations, and act as a means of assuaging intrapersonal conflicts. In an early investigation, Roberts *et al.* (1959) established a threefold classification of games based on the major modes of game outcome. Their triparite game typology consists of (1) games of physical skill, (2) games of strategy, and (3) games of chance. Having established these basic game categories, Roberts *et al.* then determined the distribution of game types in 50 tribal societies and made an exploratory examination of the relations between the predominant game form of given societies and certain cultural characteristics. They discovered that (1) games of strategy are related to cultural complexity as assessed by degree of political integration and social stratification, (2) games of chance are associated with religious beliefs and matters of the supernatural, while (3) games of physical skill may be related to environmental conditions.

In a second study, Roberts and Sutton-Smith (1962) extended the previous cross-cultural analysis into the area of childhood socialization. Specifically, they studied the relationships between game types and child-training variables at two levels of generality. First, at the intercultural level, the investigators examined data from the Cross-Cultural Survey Files and Human Relations Area Files at Yale University for 56 tribal societies. Second, at the intracultural level, the investigators compared the game preference of 1900 elementary school boys and girls in 12 Midwestern communities. Analysis of the cross-cultural data showed that games of strategy are related to obedience training, games of chance are related to responsibility training, and games of physical skill are related to achievement training. Subsystem validation of these cross-cultural findings with data obtained from Midwestern children confirmed the researchers predictions that (1) girls with their higher training in obedience should show a greater preference for games of strategy than boys, (2) girls with their higher training in responsibility should show a greater preference for games of chance than boys, and (3) boys with their higher training in achievement should show a greater preference for games of physical skill than girls. Roberts and Sutton-Smith (1962) interpreted these findings in terms of a *conflict-enculturation model* which implies:

> (1) that there is an over-all process of cultural patterning whereby society induces conflict in children through its child-training processes; (2) that society seeks through appropriate arrays and varieties of ludic models to provide an assuagement of these conflicts by an adequate representation of their emotional and cognitive polarities in ludic structure; and (3) that through these models society tries to provide a form of buffered learning through which

the child can make enculturative step-by-step progress toward adult behavior.

The causal assumptions of Roberts and Sutton-Smith's conflict-enculturation model are schematically outlined in Fig. 1. Roberts and Sutton-Smith noted that the assumptions and hypotheses underlying their model have not as yet been fully validated. However, they observed that their model does provide an explicit theoretical foundation for future research. And in a third study with American adults they replicated their research as outlined with children (Sutton-Smith *et al.*, 1963). On the basis of a comparative analysis of three state and national survey polls made in 1940 and 1948, they reported that (1) games of strategy are preferred by higher status groups as compared with lower status groups, and by females as compared with males; (2) games of chance are associated with lower status rather than high status categories, and with women in contrast to men; and, (3) games of physical skill are preeminent among upper as compared with lower status groups, and are held in greater preference by men than women (Sutton-Smith *et al.*, 1963).

Finally, in yet a fourth study, Roberts and Sutton-Smith (1966) examined the cross-cultural correlates of games of chance with particular reference to their conflict-enculturation model. They presented and discussed a wide variety of findings, but stated by way of conclusion that:

It is our provisional formulation, then, that games of chance are linked with antecedent conflict, powerlessness in the presence of uncertainty, the possibility of both favorable and unfavorable outcomes within the area of uncertainty, and certain compatible projective beliefs, particularly in the area of religion. The motivations produced in this situation are assuaged by play with uncertainty models, and the resulting learning may give individuals and groups strength to endure bad times in the hope of brighter futures.

In sum, Roberts and Sutton-Smith's conflict-enculturation model of game involvement affords many exciting insights into the relationships between dominant game categories in a culture or subculture and selected socialization practices. The model as well provides a theoretical integration of diverse findings from several studies and gives explicit leads and directions for future research.

However, notwithstanding the several studies made by Roberts and Sutton-Smith, no definitive experiments have been conducted to date to test critically the hypotheses underlying the conflict-enculturation model. Perhaps the least investigated aspect of the Roberts and Sutton-Smith model is the notion that individuals, who are unable to resolve strong psychological conflicts through buffered learning in the normal course of game involvement, become addicted to certain games and thus remain obsessively involved in game play. Although research is limited, some empirical support can be found for Roberts and Sutton-Smith's assumptions regarding game addiction. For example, "... preliminary work points up the probability that college students who are addicted to such games of strategy as poker, even to the point of playing the game as

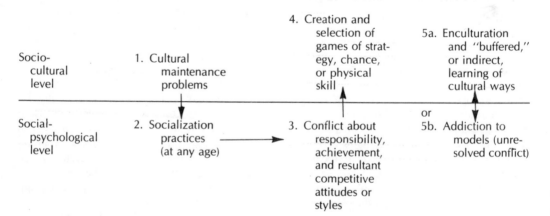

FIG. 1 CONFLICT-ENCULTURATION MODEL. REPRINTED FROM LAMBERT AND LAMBERT (1964).

much as 40 hours a week, are laboring under a particularly strong set of conflicts about their positions in the social system" (Lambert and Lambert, 1964). More in the realm of sport is Nicholi's (1970) work on the "motorcycle syndrome" which well illustrates the relationships between inner psychological conflicts and involvement in a motor sport. On the basis of in-depth psychiatric study of accident-prone student motorcyclists, Nicholi outlined the essential characteristics of a motorcycle syndrome as follows:

1. Unusual preoccupation with the motorcycle.
2. A history of accident-proneness extending to early childhood.
3. Persistent fear of bodily injury.
4. A distant, conflict-ridden relationship with the father and a strong identification with the mother.
5. Extreme passivity and inability to compete.
6. A defective self-image.
7. Poor impulse control.
8. Fear of and counterphobic involvement with aggressive girls.
9. Impotence and intense homosexual concerns.

Nicholi described how the motorcycle functions as a powerful emotional prosthesis and illustrated his description with the following colorful report of a patient:

You sit as tightly on it as you can ... and all of a sudden it responds to you. It's a throaty, gutsy kind of sound. To go from 30 to 70 miles per hour sends a quiver through you ... most people treat a motorcycle as an animal ... they're almost human you know ... it's a thrill, a joyous thing, like suddenly being free ... the noise is all you hear ... there is a strength and power in it. It's masculine and makes me feel strong. I approach a girl on a cycle and I feel confident. Things open up and I am much more at ease.

In summarizing his analysis of the motorcycle syndrome Nicholi stated that:

Suffering a serious ego defect that stems from a distant and difficult father-son relationship and results in a tenuous masculine identification, these patients experience the motorcycle as an integral part of their body image. The vehicle serves to confirm and delineate a shadowy inner definition of masculinity and to reinforce a fragile ego. Used adaptively to provide a sense of pleasure, virility, power, and freedom, the machine's primary use is defensive: The patient substitutes a sense of "getting somewhere" for substantive effort.

Thus, the results reported by Nicholi reveal how persons may become addicted to "expressive models," and his findings indicate how involvement with such models be they games or sporting machines may provide a kind of therapy. Moreover, Nicholi's examination of student motorcyclists graphically portrays the dialectic between the individual's search for self-identity and society's needs and pressures for adequate achievement and masculine performance on the part of its male members.

D. GAMES IN PHYSICAL EDUCATION

Numerous examples have been given throughout the chapter showing how games afford a significant social context for the "indirect" and "buffered" learning of important cultural content and positively sanctioned patterns of social behavior. The playing of games is, of course, an ancient and widespread form of learning and socialization. Yet it is only recently that games have received serious study with regard to their scientific and instrumental value. The recent attention given to games is, however, rather phenomenal. Presently, a number of academic disciplines offer courses on "game theory," and so-called serious games are being developed and utilized in several areas of education, industry, and the military. Thus we have educational games, management games, and war games which simulate important "real-life" activities within their respective institutional sectors (Abt, 1970; Avedon and Sutton-Smith, 1971; Boocock and Schild, 1968; D. L. Miller, 1970; Robinson, 1966; *Simulation and Games*, 1970–1971).

In view of the heightened interest in games by diverse scholars, it is a pathetic paradox that those professionals who traditionally have been most involved with games appear to have the least understanding of their nature and social import. Physical educators have professed for over a century that play, games, and sport provide a unique and particularly appropriate medium for meeting the main objectives espoused by our educational institutions. Similarly, they have made strong claims concerning the importance of participation in selected gross motor activities for the emotional, intellectual, physical, and social development of children and youth. Physical educators, however, have made few attempts to ascertain the nature of games, and they have done very little to confirm their assumption that participation in certain physical activities either directly or indirectly enhances learning in general or socialization in particular. Moreover, physical educators have virtually ignored the implications of the educational usage of games in other academic areas, business, government, and the military.

It seems apparent that physical educators have taken hold of selected recreative games for ostensibly educational purposes and have naively taken for granted that students somehow achieve a substantial degree of personal growth as a result of undergoing significant learning and socialization experiences assumed to be inherently associated with their participation in such games. It is suggested that if physical educators seriously wish to pursue educational objectives (especially those related to social development) through physical activity, then they must attempt to operationalize their particular educational aims and explicitly design, develop, and conduct innovative games and sports which are likely to aid the student in attaining these specific goals.

Needless to say, the design, development, and conduct of special games and sports related to particular educational objectives are a major undertaking since they require an understanding of both the structure of games and the nature of the socialization process. More specifically, the physical educator must be cognizant of (1) the intrinsic virtues of games as teaching devices, (2) the developmental syntax of games, (3) the primary stages of moral development, and (4) the basic mechanisms of social influence. By way of concluding this epilogue, the nature of these four factors is briefly described.

1. Characteristics of Academic Games

In commenting on the substantive consequences of the research on which his book *The Adolescent Society* is based, Coleman (1967a) wrote the following:

> ... perhaps the major problem that must be faced in socialization of neophytes into re-

sponsible members of the system is how and when to give over autonomy and responsibility to the neophyte. It is this problem, I propose, that is the most difficult one educational institutions of industrial societies have to solve today.

This has led in a direction in which I would never have anticipated going: toward experimentation in schools. The research in which I am presently engaged involves the construction of social and economic games to be used in schools. For a variety of reasons, games appear to me to be extremely interesting socializing devices: the reward structure they furnish, the self-governing system they establish, the autonomy they provide without dire consequences, the lack of necessity for outside judges.

In a later article titled "Learning through Games," Coleman (1967b) extended and elaborated upon this list of intrinsic virtues of games. His work and that of others suggest that games make good teaching devices because they possess the following characteristics.

a. Active Learning. Unlike most classroom situations wherein the student is largely a passive participant, games involve nearly total involvement on the part of students. As Coleman (1967b) has stated the case: "(an) important asset of simulation games is that they constitute an approach to learning that starts from fundamentally different premises than does the usual approach to learning in schools. The first premise is that persons do not learn by being taught; they learn by experiencing the consequences of their actions."

b. Rewards. In game situations a student receives immediate reinforcement from his peers for performance of successful acts. Moreover, the reward structure of games focuses on group achievement as well as individual achievement. Thus, unlike many classroom situations wherein the success of one student implies the failure of another, in game situations individual success often results in team success.

c. Attention and Motivation. It is often difficult in a classroom to motivate students and to hold their attention for relatively long spans of time. Games, however, seem to have an intrinsic attention-focusing quality. "The depth of involvement in a game, whether it is basketball, *Life Career,* or bridge, is often so great that the players are totally absorbed in this artificial world" (Coleman, 1967b). This intensive involvement is no doubt a function of immediate pleasure and perceived utility in gaining future pleasure.

d. Teacher's Role. Classrooms tend to be teacher-dominated. During the course of games "the teacher's role reverts to a more natural one of helper and coach." Thus, games are uniquely student-oriented.

e. Discipline. Closely associated with the factor of teacher's role is the matter of discipline. In game situations the teacher's role of judge and jury is greatly diminished. Furthermore, one seldom encounters discipline problems as peer sanctions are so strong. Young players do not permit game disruptions by spoilsports and can usually effectively cope with cheaters.

f. Self-Instruction and Testing. It is often difficult to adopt classroom materials to the ability levels of all students in a given course. Games may be developed at almost any level of complexity, and they more readily allow both high and low achievers to participate in the same social context. Games encompass a wide range of skills, and their rules and structure can be easily modified. In short, "... possibilities for creativity are opened up that the classroom situation often inhibits" (Coleman, 1967b).

g. Modeling. Because children have a certain familiarity with games in general, because games typically entail no life or death consequences, and because games present a unique time perspective in terms of such variables as frequency, duration, and intensity, games are consequently a highly suitable medium for conveying abstract ideas and concepts. "When a game situation simulates aspects of a student's present or future life, the student begins to see how his future depends very directly upon present actions, and thus gives meaning to these actions," (Coleman, 1967b).

h. Self-Development. Games require communication and role playing abilities; they stress rational decision-making and the understanding of cause-and-effect relationships; and they reward impulse control and self-restraint; consequently, games provide a medium for self-development. As Coleman (1967b) has written:

A special value of academic simulation games appears to be the capacity to develop in the player a sense that he can effect his own future. A massive study conducted by the U.S. Office of Education shows that one attribute strongly related to performance on standard achievement tests is a child's belief that his future depends on his own efforts rather than on a capricious environment. Many disadvantaged pupils appear to lack this belief.

In summary, it is clearly evident that the special pedagogical properties of simulated games make them useful devices for learning and socialization. Although simulated games are admittedly not an educational panacea, they nevertheless appear to be particularly suited for teaching the various contemporary categories of disadvantaged youth. Most surprisingly, few, if any, efforts have been made to determine the relative merits of educational games involving large amounts of physical activity with educational games involving only a minimal degree of gross motor activity. Moreover, few physical educators have used learning games as opposed to recreative games in their adaptive and special physical education programs. The work of Cratty (Cratty and Martin, 1970; Cratty, 1971) is an important exception to the preceding statement. His work well illustrates the nature and use of "active learning games" by physical educators to enhance the academic abilities of children handicapped by various learning disorders.

2. The Structure of Games

The discussion of the preceding section implies that an analysis of simulated games may give important insights into the nature of games and sport in general. In this section the other side of the case is taken up. Specifically, it is suggested that an analysis of general games and sport should be a prerequisite for the design and development of particular learning games. In addition, it is argued that if better inferences are to be made regarding the socializing functions of games and sport then greater knowledge is required concerning the basic structural dimensions of agonistic activities at different age levels.

While several attempts have been made to outline the general structure of sports and games (Avedon and Sutton-Smith, 1971; Loy and Kenyon, 1969), it is difficult to discover developmental accounts of the structural dimensions of games. One of the few behavioral scientists to have studied play, games, and sport from both a developmental and a structural perspective is Brian Sutton-Smith (Herron and Sutton-Smith, 1971).

An illustration of Sutton-Smith's developmental approach to play, games, and sport is given in a recent paper presented at the *Second World Symposium on the History of Sport and Physical Education* (Sutton-Smith, 1971). In this paper he examined the developmental sequence of "approach-and-avoidance" games played by children between the ages of 5 and 12. He discussed "the particular spatial and temporal relationships in games at different age levels, the approach and avoidant actions that are special to particular categories of games, and the relationships between the players as actors and counteractors." Sutton-Smith's analysis is schematically outlined in Table 2. With respect to the material given in the table, Sutton-Smith stated the following:

What is occurring across these four levels is a testing of powers first against "magical" IT figures, and finally against other players of relatively the same skill. The actions in this sequence are those of chasing, escaping, capturing and rescuing with the final game of prisoner's base containing both sets of elements. There is a new form of spatial and temporal arrangement at each level. We know that these arrangements of space and time correspond to

parallel forms of cognitive organization in children of these age levels. But we may assume that when presented in these exciting forms, the spatial and temporal qualities take on a vividness which they may not have when presented more impersonally.

Professor Sutton-Smith observed that "similar levels can be illustrated for other types of games"; and he noted that "When game progress is viewed in this developmental fashion it is difficult to resist the view that important qualitative properties in the understanding of social relations, social actions, space and time are being learned by the children that proceed through the series."

3. Stages of Moral Development and Processes of Social Influence

Since physical educators have been particularly concerned with the "character development" aspects of games and sports, it is both surprising and dismaying that they have not given greater attention to recent research in the behavioral and social sciences regarding moral development. It seems sensible to assume that unless physical education teachers acquire an adequate knowledge of the developmental nature of moral behavior, they will have difficulty in either assuring or assessing the moral values and conduct associated with the play and games

TABLE 2
Developmental Sequence of Approach–Avoidance Games*

Level	Sample game	Actors	Act	Space	Time
I 5–6 years	(a) Hide-and-seek (b) Tag	Central person of high power	Hide-and-seek Escape and chase	Hideways	Episodic
II 7–8 years	Release	Central person of lower power	Capture and rescue	Hideways and prisoner's base	Cumulative
III 9–10 years	Red rover	Powers change between central and others	Capture	Two home bases	Climax
IV 11–12 years	Prisoner's base	Diffuse teams	Capture-rescue Chase-escape	Home and Prisoner's bases	Team-cumulative

* Adapted from Sutton-Smith (1971).

of children and youth. In addition to a knowledge of the levels of moral development, physical educators must attain an understanding of the processes of social influence underlying the stages of moral behavior.

Kohlberg (1963a,b, 1964, 1966, 1968) has perhaps made the most extensive contemporary analysis of moral development. On the basis of an examination of Piaget's work and as a result of data collected in several longitudinal and cross-cultural studies, Kohlberg has established a highly comprehensive outline of the evolution of moral behavior. He distinguished three levels of development, divided into six stages as follows (Kohlberg, 1968; Maccoby, 1968):

A. Pre-conventional Level
1. Punishment and obedience orientation (obey rules to avoid punishment)
2. Naive instrumental hedonism orientation (conform to obtain rewards, have favors returned)
B. Conventional Level
3. Good-boy, good-girl orientation (conform to obtain approval from others)
4. Authority orientation (conform to avoid censure by legitimate authority and the resulting guilt)
C. Post-conventional Level
5. Social contract orientation (conform to maintain the respect of the impartial spectator judging in terms of community welfare)
6. Individual conscience orientation (conform to avoid self-condemnation)

Maccoby suggested that Kohlberg's three levels represent different degrees of internalization of moral values, and her treatment of his typology reveals what appears to be a close correspondence between Kohlberg's three levels of moral development and Kelman's description of three primary processes of social influence. For example, Maccoby stated that at the preconventional level, "standards of judgment are external to the child, and the motivation for conforming to the standards is also external in the sense that the child is governed by external rewards and punishments" (1968). Kelman (1961), in a parallel manner, stated that in the case of *compliance* an individual is "... interested in attaining certain specific rewards or in avoiding certain specific punishments that the influencing agent controls." At the conventional level the individual accepts the rules and norms from identified-with authority figures (Maccoby, 1968). Similarly, "*identification* can be said to occur when an individual adopts behavior derived from another person or a group because this behavior is associated with a satisfying self-defining relationship to this person or group" (Kelman, 1961). Finally, at the postconventional level, "the standards as well as the motive to conform have become inner; they are felt as emanating from the self, and no longer depend upon the support of external authority" (Maccoby, 1968). And as Kelman (1961) concluded: "Finally, *internalization* can be said to occur when an individual accepts influence because the induced behavior is congruent with his value system."

Regretfully, studies have not been conducted to date which attempt to relate Kohlberg's typology of moral development and Kelman's typology of processes of social influence to attitudinal and behavioral changes correlated with play and games. Their conceptual frameworks though provide the needed theoretical foundations for conducting critical experiments to test the claims made by professional physical educators regarding the importance of sport involvement for the social development of youth. Does moral conduct in sport situations, for example, represent compliance, identification, or internalization? Does athletic participation further or retard mature moral development?

Although the functional effects of play, games, and sport upon the socialization process have been stressed throughout the chapter, it must be recognized that involvement in agonistic activities may also have dysfunctional consequences for socialization. Richardson (1962), for example, reported rather disheartening results in his study of ethical conduct in sport situations. He ascertained the beliefs of 233 senior male physical education majors in 15 institutions regarding sportsmanship in sport situations by means of Haskins and Hartman's Action-Choice Tests for Competitive Sport Situations. Richardson found that (1) "non-letter winners indicated a higher degree of sportsmanship than did letter winners," (2) "those students receiving no athletic grants scored much higher than respondents receiving athletic grants," and (3) "football players ranked below all other sports in test scores."

Richardson's results and recent autobiographical accounts of "dropouts" from professional sports (Meggysey, 1970; Sauer and Scott, 1971) indicate that the ethical nature of the competitive world of sport is one of conventional morality. That is to say, socialization into or via sport may be largely a matter of compliance and identification rather than internalization. For instance, Sauer (Sauer and Scott, 1971), the recent outstanding wide receiver for the New York Jets, in speaking about his retirement from professional football, stated:

I think that ... most anybody who plays football on the college and professional levels is doing something he's done ever since he was preadolescent ... Given all the rewards that an athlete can get, it's alluring to a kid to want to be a good athlete. It's a means of identity, and as long as you stay in organized athletics, your identity is based on something you wanted to be back when you were a very young person ... The bad thing about football is that it keeps you in an adolescent stage, and you are kept there by the same people who are telling you that it is teaching you to be a self-disciplined, mature and responsible person. But if you were self-disciplined and responsible, they wouldn't have to treat you like a child.

In conclusion, socialization via play, games, and sport is a complex process having both manifest and latent functions, and involving functional and dysfunctional, intended and unintended consequences. Since research on the topic is limited, one must regard with caution many present empirical findings and most tentative theoretical interpretations of these findings.

REFERENCES

Abt, C.C.: Serious Games. New York, Viking Press, 1970.

Avedon, E.M., and Sutton-Smith, B., eds.: The Study of Games. New York, Wiley, 1971.

Ball, D.W.: Sociol. Quart., 8:447–458, 1967.

Bandura, A., and Walters, R.H.: Social Learning and Personality Development. New York, Holt, 1963.

Becker, E.: Amer. J. Sociol., 67:494–501, 1962.

Bend, E.: The Impact of Athletic Participation on Academic and Career Aspiration and Achievement. National Football Foundation, New Brunswick, New Jersey, 1968.

Berger, P.L.: Invitation to Sociology: A Humanistic Perspective. New York, Doubleday (Anchor Edition), 1963.

Berger, P.L.: The Sacred Canopy: Elements of a Sociological Theory of Religion. New York, Doubleday (Anchor Edition), 1969.

Berkowitz, L.: The Development of Motives and Values in the Child. New York, Basic Books, 1964.

Berlyne, D.E.: In The Handbook of Social Psychology. Edited by G. Lindzey and E. Aronson. 2nd ed., Vol. 3, Chapter 27, pp. 795–852. Reading, Massachusetts, Addison-Wesley, 1969.

Boocock, S. and Schild, E.O., eds.: Simulation Games in Learning. Beverly Hills, California, Sage, 1968.

Bossard, J.H.S., and Boll, E.S.: The Sociology of Child Development. 4th ed. New York, Harper, 1966.

Broom, L. and Selznick, P.: Sociology. 3rd ed. New York, Harper, 1963.

Brown, D.G.: Psychol. Monogr, 70(14):1–19 (Whole No. 421), 1956.

Brown, D.G.: Psychol. Bull., 55:232–242, 1958.

Call, J.D.: Int. J. Psycho-Anal., 45:286–294, 1964.

Call, J.D.: Sobrefiro Cuaderno Psicoanal., 1:237–256, 1968.

Call, J.D.: Int. J. Psycho-Anal., 49:375–378, 1968.

Call, J.D.: Psychol. Today, 3(8):34–37 and 54, 1970.

Call, J.D., and Marschak, M.: J. Amer. Acad. Child Psychiat., 5(2):193–210, 1966.

Caplow, T.: Principles of Organization. New York, Harcourt, 1964.

Chinoy, E.: Society. 4th ed. New York, Random House, 1963.

Clausen, J.A.: In Socialization and Society. Edited by J.A. Clausen. Chapter 1, pp. 1–17. Boston, Little, Brown, 1968.

Coleman, J.S.: The Adolescent Society. Glencoe, Ill. Free Press, 1961.

Coleman, J.S.: In Sociologists at Work. Edited by P.E. Hammond. Chapter 8, pp. 213–243. New York, Doubleday, 1967a.

Coleman, J.S.: NEA J. (January), 69–70, 1967b.

Cratty, B.J.: Social Dimensions of Physical Activity. Englewood Cliffs, N. J., Prentice-Hall, 1967.

Cratty, B.J.: Active Learning. Englewood Cliffs, N. J., Prentice-Hall, 1971.

Cratty, B.J., and Sister Martin, M.M.: The Effects of a Program of Learning Games upon selected Academic Abilities in Children with Learning Difficulties. [Evaluation of a Program Grant awarded by the U.S. Office of Education, (0–0142710) (032).], 1970.

Deutsch, M. and Krauss, R.M.: Theories in Social Psychology. New York, Basic Books, 1965.

Durkheim, E.: The Rules of Sociological Method. New York, Free Press, 1950.

Elkin, F.: The Child and Society. New York, Random House, 1960.

Erikson, E.H.: Childhood and Society. 2nd rev. ed. New York, Norton, 1963.

Frankenberg, R.: Village on the Border. London, Cohen & West, 1957.

Goffman, E.: The Presentation of Self in Everyday Life. New York, Doubleday, 1959.

Gump, P.V., and Sutton-Smith, B.: Group, 17:3–8, 1955.

Hall, C.S.: A Primer of Freudian Psychology. New York, New American Library, Inc., (Mentor Edition), 1954.

Havighurst, R.J., and Neugarten, B.L.: Society and Education. Boston, Allyn & Bacon, 1957.

Helanko, R.: Theoretical Aspects of Play and Socialization. Turan Yliopiston Kustantama, Turku, Finland, 1958.

Helanko, R.: *In* Personality and Social Systems. Edited by N. J. Smelser and W.T. Smelser. pp. 238–247. New York, Wiley, 1963. [article reprinted from Acta Sociol. 2:229–240 (1957)].

Helanko, R.: Int. Rev. Sport Sociol., 4:177–187, 1969.

Herron, R.E., and Sutton-Smith, B., eds.: Child's Play. New York, Wiley, 1971.

Hoffman, M.L.: *In* Carmichael's Manual of Child Psychology. Edited by P.H. Mussen. 3rd ed., Vol. 2, Chapter 23, pp. 261–359. New York, Wiley, 1970.

Hollander, E.P.: Psychol. Rev., 65:117–127, 1958.

Hollingshead, A.B.: Elmtown's Youth. New York, Wiley, 1949.

Jersild, A.T.: In Search of Self. 6th ed. New York, Teachers' College Press, Columbia University, 1968.

Jones, E.E., and Gerard, H.B.: Foundations of Social Psychology. New York, Wiley, 1967.

Kelman, H.C.: Pub. Opinion Q. 25:57–78, 1961.

Kempton, S.: *In* Sociology 101 Study Guide. Edited by P. Barber and T.O. Wilkinson. pp. 39–52. Amherst, Mass., Univ. of Massachusetts, 1970.

Kohlberg, L.: Vita Humana, 6:11–33, 1963a.

Kohlberg, L.: *In* Child Psychology—62nd Yearbook of the National Society for Education. Edited by H.W. Stevenson. Chapter 7, pp. 277–332. Chicago, Illinois, Univ. of Chicago Press, 1963b.

Kohlberg, L.: *In* Review of Child Development Research. Edited by M.L. Hoffman. Vol. 1, pp. 383–431. New York, Russell Sage Foundation, 1964.

Kohlberg. L.: Sch. Rev., 74:1–30, 1966.

Kohlberg, L.: Psychol. Today, 2:(4)25–30, 1968.

Krech, D., Crutchfield, R.S., and Ballachey, E.L.: Individual in Society. New York, McGraw-Hill, 1962.

Lambert, W.W., and Lambert, W.E.: Social Psychology. Prentice-Hall, Englewood Cliffs, New Jersey, 1964.

Lenski, G.: Power and Privilege. New York, McGraw-Hill, 1966.

Loy, J.W., and Kenyon, G.S., eds. Sport, Culture and Society. New York, Macmillan, 1969.

Maccoby, E.E.: *In* Socialization and Society. Edited by J.A. Clausen. Chapter 6, pp. 227–269. Boston, Little, Brown, 1968.

MacIver, R.M.: Community: A Sociological Study. New York, Macmillan, 1917.

Mead, G.H.: Mind, Self and Society. Edited by C.W. Morris. Chicago, Ill., Univ. of Chicago Press, 1934.

Mead, G.H.: George Herbert Mead on Social Psychology. Edited by A. Strauss. Univ. of Chicago Press, Chicago, (Phoenix Edition), 1964.

Mead, G.H.: Mind, Self and Society. Edited by C.W. Morris. 7th ed. Chicago, Univ. of Chicago Press, 1970.

Meggysey, Dave: Out of Their League. Berkeley, Ramparts Press, 1970.

Merton, R.K.: Social Theory and Social Structure, 8th ed. Glencoe, Ill., Free Press, 1963.

Miller, D.L.: Gods and Games—Toward a Theology of Play. New York, World Publ., 1970.

Miller, N.E., and Dollard, J.: Social Learning and Imitation. Yale Univ. Press, New Haven, 1941.

Minar, D.W., and Greer, S.: The Concept of Community. Chicago, Aldine, 1969.

Nicholi, A.M., II.: Am. J. Psychiat., 126:1588–1595, 1970.

Parsons, T.: Am. Sociol. Rev., 7:604–616, 1942.

Parsons, T.: Psychiatry, 10:167–181, 1947.

Parsons, T., and Bales, R.F.: Family, Socialization, and Interaction Process. Glencoe, Illinois, Free Press, 1955.

Piaget, J.: The Moral Judgment of the Child (transl. by M. Gabain). New York, Free Press, 1965.

Rehberg, R.A., and Schafer, W.E.: Amer. J. Sociol., 73:732–740, 1968.

Rehberg, R.A., Charner, I., and Harris, J.: Unpublished paper, Dept. Sociol., SUNY at Binghamton, New York, 1970.

Richardson, D.E.: Proc. Nat. Col. Phys. Educ. Assoc. Men, 1962, 66:98–104, 1962.

Riesman, D., Denny, R., and Glazer, N.: The Lonely Crowd. New York, Doubleday, (Abridged Anchor Edition), 1953.

Roberts, J.M., and Sutton-Smith, B.: Ethnology, 1:166–185, 1962.

Roberts, J.M., and Sutton-Smith, B.: Behav. Sci. Notes, 3:131–144, 1966.

Roberts, J.M., Arth, M.J., and Bush, R.R.: Amer. Anthropol., 61:597–605, 1959.

Robinson, J.A.: *In* The New Media and Education. Edited by P.H. Rossi and B.J. Biddle. Chapter 3, pp. 93–135. Doubleday, New York, 1966.

Rosenberg, B.G., and Sutton-Smith, B.: J. Genet. Psychol., 96:165–170, 1960.

Rosenberg, B.G., and Sutton-Smith, B.: J. Genet. Psychol., 104:259–264, 1964.

Sanders, I.T.: The Community: An Introduction to a Social System. New York, Ronald Press, 1958.

Sauer, G., and Scott, J.: Interview by Jack Scott with George Sauer on the Reasons for Sauer's Retirement from Professional Football while at the Height of his Career. Printed by Dept. of Physical Education, California State College at Haywood, 1971.

Schafer, W.E., and Armer, J.M.: Trans-Action, 6:21–26 and 61–62, 1968.

Seagoe, May V.: Proc. 77th Annu. Conv. Amer. Psychol. Assoc., Vol. 4, Part 2, pp. 683–684, 1969.

Secord, P.F., and Backman, C.W.: Social Psychology. New York, McGraw-Hill, 1964.

Sessoms, H.D.: *In* Recreation—Issues and Perspectives. Edited by H. Brantley and H.D. Sessoms. pp. 58–68. Wing Publ., Columbia, South Carolina, 1969.

Sexton, P.C.: The Feminized Male. New York, Vintage Books, 1969.

Sexton, P.C.: Psychol. Today, 3:(8)23–29 and 66–67, 1970.

Shibutani, T.: Society and Personality. Prentice-Hall, Englewood Cliffs, New Jersey, 1961.

Simulation and Games: A Quarterly International Journal of Theory, Design, and Research, Beverly Hills, Cal., Sage, 1970–1971.

Skinner, B.F.: Science and Human Behavior, 6th ed. New York, Free Press, 1968.

Snyder, E.E.: Sociol. Educ., 42:261–270, 1969.

Spreitzer, E.A., and Pugh, M.D.: Pap., Ohio Valley Sociol. Soc., 33rd Annu. Meet., 1971.

Stone, G.P.: *In* Human Behavior and Social Processes. Edited by A.M. Rose. Chapter 5, pp. 86–118. Boston, Houghton Mifflin, 1962.

Stone, G.P.: Quest, 4:23–31, 1950.

Sutton-Smith, B.: Pap., 2nd World Symp. Hist. Sport Phys. Educ., Banff, Alberta, Canada, 1971.

Sutton-Smith, B. and Gump, P.V.: Recreation, 45:172–174, 1955.

Sutton-Smith, B., Roberts, J.M., and Kozelka, R.M.: J. Soc. Psychol., 60:15–30, 1963.

Sutton-Smith, B., and Rosenberg, B.G.: J. Am. Folklore, 74:17–46, 1961.

Toby, J.: Contemporary Society. New York, Wiley, 1964.

Tryon, C.M.: *In* The 43rd Yearbook of the National Society for the Study of Education. Edited by N.B. Henry. Part 1, Chapter 12, pp. 217–239. Chicago, Univ. of Chicago Press, 1944.

Webb, H.: *In* Aspects of Contemporary Sport Sociology. Edited by G.S. Kenyon. Chapter 8, pp. 161–187. Chicago, Athletic Institute, 1969.

Winick, C.: The New People. Pegasus, New York, 1968.

Work, H.H., and Call, J.D.: A Guide to Preventive Child Psychiatry: The Art of Parenthood. New York, McGraw-Hill, 1965.

Worsley, P., Fitzhenry, R., Mitchell, J.C., Morgan, D.H.J., Pons, V., Roberts, B., Sharrock, W.W., and Robbin, W.: Introducing Sociology. Middlesex, England, Penguin Books, 1970.

Wrong, D.H.: Am. Sociol. Rev., 26:183–193, 1961.

Young, M. and Willmott, P.: Family and Kinship in East London, 5th ed. Middlesex, England, Penguin Books, 1967.

becoming involved in physical activity and sport: A process of socialization

GERALD S. KENYON AND BARRY D. MCPHERSON

For well over 50 years, psychologists, anthropologists, and sociologists have been addressing themselves to the social process whereby persons learn to become participants in their society—the process of *socialization*. Most of their efforts have focused upon the socialization of the child, and as a result the consequences of the process which have interested many investigators have been relatively broad behavioral dispositions. Recently, however, there has been a trend toward the study of socialization as it occurs not only during childhood but also throughout the life cycle. Moreover, attention is being directed to more limited aspects of the phenomenon such as occupational socialization and political socialization; consequently, researchers are able to concentrate upon a narrower set of behaviors and dispositions, i.e., those associated with more definitive social roles. Not only have these newer approaches made research on socialization more manageable, but also they have facilitated a more efficacious study of the consequences of socialization.

This chapter is an attempt to build further upon the study of socialization in a focused sense—in this case, *socialization into roles associated with institutionalized physical activity or sport*. Our approach will, in many respects, present the other side of the coin. While Loy and Ingham elsewhere in this volume have dealt primarily with socialization via play, games, and sport, most of our efforts will center upon socialization into sport. Section I consists of an attempt to provide a conceptual frame of reference, that is, our view of what it is to be socialized into sport involvement. Section II describes some findings related to the socialization process drawing upon data acquired from a variety of sport role players. Section III concludes the chapter with a brief consideration of future research needs by presenting a set of propositions based upon one approach to modeling the socialization process.

I. SPORT SOCIALIZATION: A CONCEPTUAL FRAME OF REFERENCE

Given, then, our concern for socialization into rather than via sport, the scope of our topic becomes more manageable. However, considerable diversity remains. Although the learning of sport roles is likely to occur in about the same way as the learning of nonsport roles, the complexity of the process in sport contexts is often greater since sport is engaged in throughout the life cycle, and in a wide variety of interrelated forms.[1] Such complexity becomes obvious when the various dimensions of the sport socialization process are enumerated:

1. Socialization of the elite performer
2. Socialization of the sub-elite performer
3. Socialization of the sport consumer
4. Socialization of the sport producer
5. Socialization of the sport leader

Reprinted from Physical Activity—Human Growth and Development. Edited by G. Lawrence Rarick, New York, Academic Press, 1973, pp. 304–333. Copyright 1973 by Academic Press, New York, New York, 10003.

6. Sport resocialization
    Sport to sport (i.e., from one sport to
      another)
    Sport to nonsport (i.e., the withdrawal
      from sport to learn nonsport roles)
    Role to role, within sport (i.e., changing
      roles within a given sport)
7. Sport socialization and social change
8. Socialization via sport

A. EXPLAINING THE SOCIALIZATION PROCESS: A SOCIAL ROLE–SOCIAL SYSTEM APPROACH

A summary of the several approaches to socialization has been presented by Loy and Ingham (See preceding article). For us, however, we note that among the several theoretical orientations used to study the process including psychoanalysis, psychoanalytically oriented social anthropology, the normative-maturational approach, the developmental-cognitive approach, the genetic and constitutional approach, and the various learning theory approaches, the latter, and particularly the social learning orientations, have become the most popular and most productive in both theory and empirical findings (Bandura and Walters, 1963; Brim and Wheeler, 1966; Clausen, 1968). Thus, given the nature of sport, and given that the major characteristics associated with sport roles are probably acquired after early childhood, a social learning approach, utilizing both psychological and sociological variables, would seem to be most fruitful for the study of sport socialization. However, there are variations within this approach. For example, sport role learning can be studied using as a frame of reference the three main elements of the socialization process (see Fig. 1), namely, *significant others,*[2] (socializing agents) who exert influence within social situations (socializing agencies) upon role learners (actors or role aspirants) who are characterized by a wide variety of relevant personal attributes. Some findings using this model are presented in Section II. There is an inherent weakness in such a general approach however, namely, the difficulty of specifying a manageable number of variables from a great many plausible ones, that is, the "specification problem" (Heise, 1969).

A more definitive rationale than the foregoing for the selection of variables is the "social role–social system" approach (Sewell, 1963). Role learning is accounted for by exposure of the role aspirant, who is already characterized by a set of physical and psychological traits, to a variety of stimuli and reinforcements provided by significant others, who act within one or more norm-encumbered social systems. Thus, a careful analysis is needed of the nature of both social roles and social systems. The social role, and more particularly its characteristics, which becomes the dependent variable in any explanatory system, is treated first.

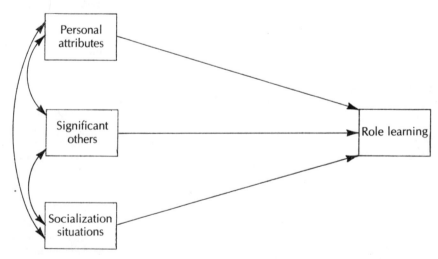

FIG. 1.　THE THREE ELEMENTS OF THE SOCIALIZATION PROCESS.

1. Sport Roles:
The Dependent Variable Problem

When it comes to specifying the consequences of sport socialization, after only a little reflection one quickly realizes that potentially there are many. Even though the discussion herein is restricted to socialization into sport involvement, and thus eschews considering socialization via sport (whereby the enactment of sport roles become independent variables for such dependent variables as social integration, community identification, social mobility, and social control), the complexity of the dependent variable remains great. To cope with this problem we have found the dramaturgical approach of "role theory" to be helpful.

As one becomes involved in sport he can be characterized as playing one of several roles. A sport role, like any role, implies that the role incumbent possesses knowledges, skills, and dispositions characterizing the role in question. Obviously, a clear definition of these dimensions is required for each sport role. More difficult, however, is the identification and classification of the many sport roles. While some role players actually participate in the contest (primary involvement), others "consume" sport (secondary involvement) either directly (as spectators) or indirectly (as consumers of the mass media). Still others produce sport through the enactment of leadership, organizational, and entrepreneurial roles (A general classification of sport roles is given in Fig. 2.). Moreover, sports themselves differ greatly in kind (e.g., exercise-oriented activity, gamelike activity, expressive activity), social environment [from involvement in the presence of many others to involvement in the absence of all others; or involvement oriented to varying combinations of reference groups such as Kemper's (1968) "normative," "role model," and "audience" groups], and complexity (from unstructured to highly structured).

Clearly, each sport role is conceptually complex. Nevertheless, to be able to specify the characteristics of a particular role is an essential prerequisite to the study of the learning of that role and thus deserves far greater attention than heretofore received.

2. Social Systems and Socialization:
The General Case

Having paid some attention to the role aspects of the social role–social system approach, we turn now to a brief consideration of how certain institutions or social systems such as the family, the school, the church, and the peer group might contribute to role learning. With respect to such systems then, it is argued that given the nature, complexity, and pervasiveness of sport roles, each relevant social system should be treated separately as a potential role learning situation. This takes advantage of considerable knowledge already available concerning the structure and function of institutionalized social systems. Moreover, such a procedure recognizes that factors accounting for socialization are likely to be

Mode	Primary	Secondary				
		Consumer		Producer		
		Direct	Indirect	Leader	Arbitrator	Entrepreneur
Role — Contestant	Contestant	Spectator	Viewer	Instructor	Member of —Sports governing body	Manufacturer
Athlete	Athlete		Listener	Coach	—Rules committee	Promoter
			Reader	Manager	Referee	Wholesaler
Player	Player			Team Leader	Umpire Scorekeeper Other officials	Retailer

FIG. 2. SOME SOCIAL ROLES ASSOCIATED WITH PRIMARY AND SECONDARY MODES OF SPORT INVOLVEMENT.

more salient within, rather than between, systems (Sewell *et al.,* 1969).

If the social system is made central in characterizing the socialization process, it is suggested that a general model of this process can be constructed consisting of a simple causal chain. Thus, in the proposed model: Given a degree of role aptitude (cognitive and motoric) the role aspirant is variously influenced within each of the social situations in which he inevitably finds himself, with the net effect being the acquisition of a propensity for learning the role in question. Furthermore, this motivates him to rehearse the role, which in turn leads to the learning of the role. In propositional form:

1. The greater the role aptitude, the greater the system-induced propensity for role learning.
2. The greater the system-induced propensity for role learning, the greater the role rehearsal, and vice versa.
3. The greater the propensity for role learning, the greater the role learning, i.e., degree of socialization.

These propositions are illustrated in Fig. 3. Central to the second stage of this model, obviously, are the socializing processes or mechanisms which occur within each relevant system. These are given more attention below. However useful the system context may be, it is recognized that ultimately it may be possible to strip away the institutional barriers and utilize only those few variables that reflect the sum total of influence within a system. For example, the Blau and Duncan (1967) model of the occupational attainment process relies on only two status variables (father's education and occupational attainment) and two behavioral variables (individual's education level and prestige of first job).

Sewell *et al.* (1969, 1970), in explaining occupational attainment, have shown that it is possible, and indeed useful, to characterize significant others' influence as a single variable. At the moment, then, it is suggested that the best strategy for identifying the influential variables is through a careful analysis of each relevant social system as illustrated in Fig. 4. Although one might desire parsimony, the selection of a small number of variables is premature with respect to sport socialization since too little is known at this time.

Given the present state of knowledge, then, it would seem that the best research strategy would be somewhat akin to McPhee's "modular" concept of model building (1963), and in particular, Blalock's "block-recursive system" (1969).

3. Relevant Factors in Relevant Social Systems

The general model proposed above would likely account for socialization into most social roles and not just those associated with sport. What is needed, then, is a careful consideration of the sport-relevant factors in those social systems likely to be important in inducing a propensity for sport involvement.[3] An alternative would be to begin with a highly theoretical analysis of the nature of social systems (e.g., Parsons, 1961) and try to show how sport may be functional or dysfunctional for a particular system and the consequent implications for the socialization process.[4] However, insofar as our objective is not to explain the nature of social systems per se, but rather to account for the processes precipitating sport socialization, it is suggested that only those factors likely to be useful in explaining the socialization process be considered. Therefore, it is proposed that the following elements, drawn largely from Smelser (1962), serve as a frame of reference when considering system-level factors:

Values
Norms
Sanctions
Situational facilities

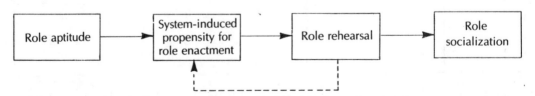

FIG. 3.   POSTULATED SOCIAL ROLE-SOCIAL SYSTEM MODEL OF SOCIALIZATION PROCESS.

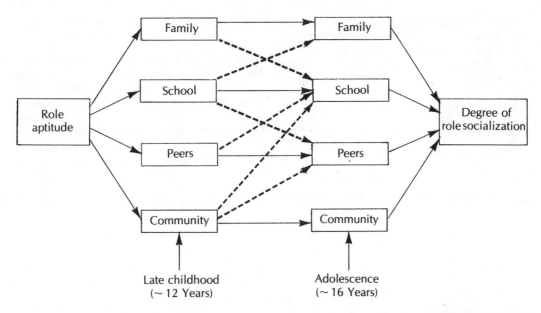

FIG. 4.   POSTULATED SOCIAL ROLE–SOCIAL SYSTEM TWO-STAGE BLOCK-RECURSIVE MODEL FOR SPORT SOCIALIZATION.

Thus, for a given social system, both in general and with regard to sport, the social learning that occurs, whether in the form of imitation, identification, or various forms of reinforcement (Bandura and Walters, 1963), would be governed by each of the foregoing elements, separately and in combination.

4. Explaining Sport Socialization at the System Level

If explanation is taken as theory and if theory is considered as a set of logically interrelated propositions (Zetterberg, 1966), then explanation of socialization should be in propositional form. By way of illustrating this point, a small number of propositions will be presented that reflect sport socialization as a consequence of a social role–social system approach. In each case the dependent variable (intervening variable in the larger system) will be propensity for sport involvement.

First, consider the family as an institutionalized social system. Although Reiss (1966) suggested that the transmission of behavioral patterns through the family may not be as great as in other institutions, in sport socialization it appears that the family is of some importance (Kenyon, 1970b) and therefore should not be ex-

cluded from the general model. For example, in the context of values as a social system element, achievement is often associated with both family socialization and sport role enactment. Thus, an analysis of achievement training may lead to a better understanding of the family's contribution to sport socialization, particularly for those sport roles where achievement and role enactment are closely related. Considering only a few variables (Rehberg *et al.*, 1970; Rosen, 1956; Turner, 1970; Zigler and Child, 1969), we might have, in propositional form, something as follows:

1. The greater the independence training, the greater the achievement motivation.[5]
2. The more democratic the parents, the greater the achievement motivation.
3. The greater the father's entrepreneurial role behavior associated with his occupational status, the higher the son's achievement motivation.
4. The greater the achievement motivation, the greater the propensity for sport involvement.
5. Therefore, the greater the independence training, the more democratic the parents, and the greater the father's entrepreneurial behavior, the greater the propensity for sport involvement.

Again, using an element common to all social systems, namely, situational facilities, but again within the context of the family, the following propositions are a few of the several that might help to explain sport socialization (Spady, 1970):

1. The higher the family socioeconomic status, the greater the social participation.
2. The higher the family socioeconomic status, the greater the propensity for involvement.
3. Therefore, the greater the social participation, the greater the propensity for sport involvement.

Still in the context of situational facilities, but more particularly with regard to role models (Brim, 1958; Stone, 1969), we have:

1. Sport involvement reflects masculinity (at least in North America).
2. Siblings frequently serve as powerful role models.
3. Children take on the personality traits of siblings of the opposite sex.
4. Therefore, as the number of male siblings increases, and the number of female siblings decreases, the propensity for sport involvement increases.

Shifting to the elements, norms and sanctions, the following propositions are presented, again in the context of the family (Campbell, 1969; McCandless, 1969), and again with achievement motivation considered a factor:

1. The less autocratic, the less authoritarian (particularly the father) and the more permissive the parents, the greater the likelihood of their being used as role models.
2. The greater the warmth and nurture provided by the parents, the greater the likelihood of their being used as role models.
3. The less autocratic, the less authoritarian, the more permissive, and the greater the warmth and nurture provided by the parents, the greater the offspring's need to achieve.
4. The greater the need to achieve, the greater the propensity for sport involvement.
5. Thus, given the capability of modeling sport roles, as parents become less autocratic and authoritarian, and more permis-

sive, nurturant, and warm, the propensity for sport involvement increases.

Although the foregoing propositions do not exhaust the factors accounting for family-induced propensity for sport involvement, they do suggest that it is possible to consider sport socialization at the social system level. Moreover, from the point of manageability, they also illustrate the desirability of a social system approach.

Other institutionalized social systems could be analyzed in a similar way, including those reflecting various educational, political, economic, military, and religious institutions. Moreover, if the adolescent peer group is taken as a social system, drawing upon the work of Helanko (1957), Homans (1950), and Spady (1970) it might be possible to partially account for peer influence with the following propositions:

1. The greater the aggregation, the greater the interaction.
2. The greater the interaction, the greater the mutual liking.
3. The greater the mutual liking, the more effective the peer influence (sport provides the means for achieving peer group goals—e.g., "status definition"—Helanko, 1957).
4. The greater the involvement in youth aggregates (groups and clubs), the greater the propensity for sport involvement.

When the contribution to sport socialization by each of several institutions is more completely analyzed, it is likely that some propositions would be system-specific while others would emerge as applicable in all systems. For example, from existing knowledge (LeVine, 1969; Webb, 1969) the following propositions, although somewhat general, would likely apply to all or most social systems having any bearing on sport socialization:

1. The greater the similarity between the values associated with sport and those associated with the institution, the greater the system-induced propensity for sport involvement.
2. The more deliberate the socialization effort, the greater the effect.
3. The more the role learner is aware of the socialization process, the greater the socialization.

4. The greater the number of positive sanctions (and the earlier they are applied) and the fewer the negative sanctions, the greater the system-induced propensity for sport involvement.

5a. The greater the situational facilities (number and kind), the greater the chances for success.

5b. The earlier success is experienced, the greater the propensity for sport involvement.

5c. As the degree of success increases, propensity for sport involvement increases.

5. National Differences in the Socialization Process

In assuming a social role–social system orientation to socialization, it is obvious that national differences exist in the nature of both sport roles (kind, milieu, and complexity) and relevant social system elements (values, norms, sanctions, and situational facilities). Consequently, cross-national research would provide a medium for testing the generality of any model of the sport role learning process. By way of example, consider the following propositions:

1. The earlier the success, the greater the propensity for sport involvement.
2. The more diverse the opportunity structure, the greater the chance of early success.
3. The more diverse the opportunity structure, the greater the propensity for sport involvement.

With wide between-nation differences in opportunity structure and public policy (e.g., achievement-oriented vs. participation-oriented, or, as in Moore and Anderson's terms (1969), "performance" societies vs. "learning" societies) it can be expected that national variations will exist. Again, however, the significance of these for explaining sport socialization can only be ascertained through careful cross-national investigations.

B. SUMMARY

In view of the nature of sport and those involved in it, it has been suggested that a social learning approach would be the most efficacious paradigm in the study of sport socialization. Upon acknowledging the complexity of the process, it was argued that a social role–social

system model would be best suited to studying the nature of sport role learning. On the assumption that socialization is situation-dependent, and by analyzing each institutionalized social system separately, the process becomes more manageable. Moreover, advantage can be taken of the considerable knowledge already available related to the structure and function of specific systems.

Thus, it is suggested that the degree to which actors are socialized into sport roles is dependent upon the propensity for sport involvement which has been generated by each system. In operational terms, specific system-related propositions need to be deduced relating relevant factors to system-specific propensities. The dependent variable—degree of socialization into a sport role—also requires careful delineation before data can be collected. As will be seen in the next section, the degree to which the foregoing conceptual considerations have been translated into empirical findings is small at this time.

II. SPORT SOCIALIZATION: SOME FINDINGS

Until recently, few sociologists of sport have concentrated their research efforts on problems associated specifically with socialization into sport roles. Some of the findings of studies that have been undertaken however are reported here, using a classification of roles approximating that given in Fig. 2. Thus, results are presented under the headings *Socialization into Roles Associated with Primary Involvement* (Section II, A), and *Socialization into Roles Associated with Secondary Involvement* (Section II, B).

At this point in time (1971), a small number of sport roles have been studied from a socialization perspective. Unfortunately, the empirical work to date has not mirrored the theoretical efforts presented in Section I (i.e., the social role–social system model). Therefore, the findings are discussed in the context of the "elements of socialization" model (personal attributes, significant others, and socialization situations).

A. SOCIALIZATION INTO ROLES ASSOCIATED WITH PRIMARY INVOLVEMENT

Researchers studying the socialization process as it is applied to primary involvement, for the most part have been interested in the "elite" performer. Although the term "elite" has many connotations, athletes who have reached a level of competition at or near a national standard are arbitrarily labeled elite performers. Data from two (but not entirely mutually exclusive) populations are discussed: first, Olympic aspirants and, second, college athletes. The section on primary involvement is concluded with a brief review of other studies.

1. Olympic Aspirants

In a project coordinated at the University of Wisconsin (Kenyon, 1968), data were acquired from two sets of Olympic aspirants: track and field athletes and gymnasts.[6]

In the first study 113 athletes, who were competing for a position on the 1968 United States Olympic Track and Field Team, completed a questionnaire designed to gather data concerning the influence of personal attributes, significant others, and the social situation on the learning of a sport role. The sample consisted of 96 white and 17 black athletes. Although only 30% of these were eventually chosen for the national team, performances were remarkably homogeneous.

For most, involvement in sport per se began early in life with 96% indicating that they participated in football, basketball, or baseball in elementary school. This early general involvement in a number of sports, plus the fact that over 65% were "winners" the first time they competed in a sport event, suggests that a high level of sport aptitude was present at an early age. However, ability does not totally account for their involvement and later success in the role of track and field athlete. For example, 50% of the subjects did not participate or compete in track and field as such until after they entered high school. Therefore, the learning of the role must have been situationally influenced by significant others who taught and reinforced the specific role behaviors within specific social settings. For example, over 75% of the respondents indicated that their interest in the activity was first aroused at school by either watching others compete, talking to a peer or teacher about the activity, or receiving instruction in a physical education class. In addition, they reported that they attended a school where 88% of the students and 83% of the teachers valued track and field and considered it to be an important extracurricular activity for students. Similar findings were reported for the years they attended college.[7] Thus, a social situation which values a pattern of behavior, and provides opportunities for the learning of the behavior, determines which roles will be learned.

The influence of significant others in generating an interest in a sport role appears to be not only important but also sport specific (Table 1). For example, when asked who was most responsible for arousing an interest in track and field, 30% indicated their peers, 25% indicated their teachers or coaches, and 21% felt that members of the family were responsible. However, when asked a similar question concerning interest in the traditional team sports of baseball, basketball, and football the results were: peers, 44%; family, 33%; and teachers or coaches, 16%. Whereas peers are important contributors to arousing interest in most sports, teachers and coaches appear to be more influential than peers in stimulating an interest in track and field. In contrast, the family is more influential than school faculty in generating interest in the traditional spectator sports.

In addition to generating interest in a role, significant others also reinforce the enactment of the role and thereby facilitate the learning of appropriate role behaviors. Figure 5 indicates the percentage of significant others who offered positive sanctions for competing in track and

TABLE 1
Relative Contribution of Classes of Significant Others in Generating an Interest in Sport Among Elite Athletes

| Significant other | % Responsible for first interest in | |
	Track and field	Traditional Spectator sports
Peer group	30	44
Teachers or coaches	25	16
Family	21	33

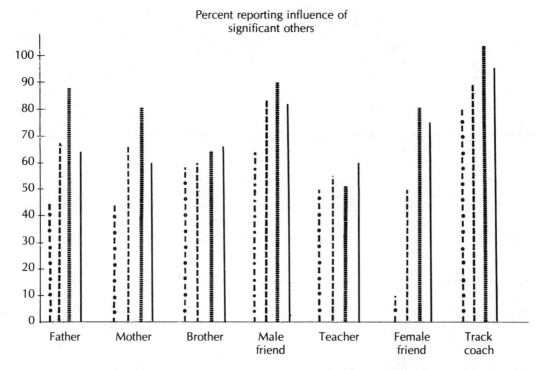

FIG. 5.   RELATIVE PROPORTION OF SIGNIFICANT OTHERS PROVIDING POSITIVE SANCTIONS AT FOUR STAGES OF THE LIFE CYCLE [Olympic track and field aspirants ($n = 113$)]. (———) on the job, (ıııııııı) during college, (- - -) during high school, and (— • —) before high school.

field at each of the four stages in the athlete's competitive career. It should be noted that male peers and track coaches were the most influential at all four stages. It is also interesting to note that while the athlete is in school or college, the number of significant others who offer encouragement increases in a linear fashion. This appears to coincide with the increasing amount of success experienced by the athletes; however, a cause–effect relationship is not implied, nor can it be substantiated with the present data. This latter finding does suggest, however, that the influence of significant others may be differential in a temporal sense, that is, it may increase or decrease over time.

In addition to significant others, reinforcement for continued involvement, and therefore further learning, is derived from other sources. For example, publicity from the mass media and personal satisfaction derived from successful competition (i.e., winning or improving personal times or distances) were found to be important factors in maintaining an interest in track and field throughout the athlete's competitive career.

In general, then, it would appear that the elite track and field athlete receives encouragement and reinforcement from many sources, several of which act simultaneously.

The results presented to date have been based upon the data of black and white athletes combined. However, it has been suggested that minority group members may be differentially socialized into sport roles (McPherson, 1971). Thus, when the data from black and white athletes were separated, differences in the socialization process appeared. Considering the social situation first, and recognizing the limitations of extrapolations based on a minimal sample of 17 subjects, it was found that compared to white athletes, black athletes were members of larger families (4.5 children compared to 2.4 for white families), were from a lower socioeconomic background, and were raised in large urban centers to a greater extent (56% vs. 29%). Moreover, they became involved in track at an earlier age, developed their first interest in the sport in the neighborhood and home, rather than in the school as the white athletes did, and perceived track to be more highly valued by students at school and by members of the community.

An examination of the influence of significant others suggests that the black athletes (a) *before high school* received more encouragement and reinforcement from the family than from others, received more positive sanctions from the mother than the father, and considered their peers to be more influential than a teacher or coach; while (b) *in high school* they received the most reinforcement from track coaches, peers, and their mother, were discouraged (negative sanction) from competing by "girl friends" whereas the white athletes reported that their girl friends were for the most part indifferent, and considered the opportunity to earn a college scholarship, the admiration of male peers (status), and publicity for success as positive reinforcement essential to maintaining their interest in track; and while (c) *in college* they received the greatest amount of reinforcement from peers, track coaches, and the father. This late appearance of the father as a source of reinforcement suggests that perhaps the fathers' desire is to identify with a success model. Thus, it appears that different role models serve as significant others for blacks, that the role models differ at each stage of the athlete's career, and that economic rewards related to track (scholarships) are more important to the black athlete.

Finally, when comparing the differences in the personal attributes of the two groups, it was noted that the black athletes were more successful in making a team on their first attempt; experienced success (won a race or event) at an earlier age, especially in the track events; appeared willing to sacrifice more in the realm of cultural pursuits and part-time jobs in order to compete in sports (were more successful in making the Olympic team); had less need for social support; were less religious; and had similar levels of aspiration as to their anticipated future socioeconomic level.

In view of the foregoing, and within the limitations of the data, it appears that there is at least minimal support for the hypothesis that the process accounting for sport socialization may differ from one subgroup to another.

In a second study (Roethlisberger, 1970) of United States Olympic Team aspirants, all the "all-around" gymnasts (competitors in six events), who had scored 104.00 points or more in

National meets in 1968, completed a questionnaire similar to that used in the track and field study. Of the 16 aspirants, 8 were eventually selected for the Olympic team. The data were treated for both the combined group ($n = 16$) and the two separate groups, classified according to whether or not they were chosen for the Olympic team. Similar to the track and field study, a "nonsystem" model (see Fig. 1) was employed, which considered personal attributes, socializing situations, and significant others.

It was found that with respect to their personal attributes, taken collectively, gymnasts apparently were skillful in a number of sports, having participated in several individual sports before they specialized in gymnastics. In terms of social values, they were not disposed toward social activism such as boycotting or demonstrating at the Olympic games; they had high educational and occupational aspirations; they were not highly committed to religion; and they considered themselves moderate to liberal in terms of their value orientations. A comparison of the chosen and unchosen gymnasts on such personal values revealed that the chosen somewhat more vigorously defended the civil rights of minorities, adhered less to conventional religious thought and attended religious services less often.

An analysis of the early socialization setting indicated that compared with other institutions, the educational system was primarily responsible for socializing an individual into the elite gymnast role; that the elite gymnasts were raised in an upper-middle or upper-class environment; that unlike the track athletes the mass media was of little importance in reinforcing the respondent's interest in gymnastics; that they learned the role in an environment that did not consider gymnastics to be important; and that initial primary involvement usually occurred between the sixth and tenth grade. A comparison of the chosen versus the unchosen indicated that the former were both interested in, and competed in, gymnastics at an earlier age. Those who were selected for the national team came from smaller families and had more older male siblings and fewer female siblings than those who were not selected.

Finally, an analysis of the role of significant others suggested that fathers and coaches were the most influential significant others, followed in order of importance by peers and brothers.

Mothers, sisters, and other relatives were not particularly influential. At all stages of the gymnast's competitive career, success was perceived to be the most important factor in maintaining interest in the sport. A comparison of the chosen and unchosen indicated that the fathers and older brothers were even more important as significant others for the chosen gymnasts.

In comparing the data from Olympic aspirants in two sports, it would appear that the school is the most important socializing milieu and the peer group and coaches the most influential significant others.

2. College Athletes

In view of the fact that most Olympic aspirants in the United States are college students or college graduates, it is likely that the overall socialization experiences of elite college athletes and Olympic aspirants are similar in many respects. However, as suggested above, sport differences can be expected. Therefore, the results of two studies which investigated socialization into elite college athlete roles are noted here.

A study of Canadian college ice hockey ($n = 52$) and tennis players ($n = 19$) focused upon the psychosocial factors accounting for college athletes becoming involved in sport (McPherson, 1968). A number of similarities and differences were discovered in the socialization experiences of the two groups. For example, it was found that 96% of the respondents were interested in sport by the age of 10, and that 63% were involved as consumers prior to their participation in sport. Again, this suggests that socialization into sport roles begins early in life. However, specialization in one sport may not occur until later. Whereas hockey players competed on organized teams before 9 years of age, competition in tennis was not attempted until a mean age of 12.7 years. Similar to the Olympic aspirants there was a trend toward specialization in one or two sports as they progressed through high school, with competition at college being restricted to the one sport.

In terms of the social situation, and in particular, class background and residence location, the tennis players were raised in a middle or upper-middle social class milieu and all lived in urban or suburban areas. The hockey players came from a middle-class or lower-middle-class milieu, with 30% having attended a rural or small community school.

The influence of significant others tended to follow a similar pattern for both groups, with the single exception being that mothers were more influential for tennis players than for hockey players. It was noted that interest in sport was initially aroused within the family and mainly by the father. However, during the high school years familial influence decreased and any interest in a new activity was aroused mainly by peers, coaches, and physical education teachers. Again, there appears to be a temporal factor whereby influence is differential over time. In addition, it appears that the initial stimulus to become interested in sport is received from involved peers and more so from a home environment which considers sport to be an important facet of life.[8] Among the Canadian athletes, peers were second in importance during the elementary and high school days but became less important at the university. Similarly, teachers and coaches were important significant others early in life and then declined in importance. A final significant other was the professional athlete—almost all respondents reported that they had an "idol." In view of the sample being Canadian, it is not surprising that most of the idols listed by both hockey and tennis players were outstanding professional hockey players. However, as the tennis respondents reached college age, a highly ranked tennis player tended to replace the hockey idol. It was interesting to note that for hockey there was a positive relationship, which increased with age, between the position played by the idol and that played by the respondent.

In a related study (Kenyon and Grogg, 1969) in the United States, 87 athletes in eight sports at the University of Wisconsin were interviewed to determine the factors influencing their socialization into the role of elite college athlete.[9] Since many of the results are similar to that of the study previously reported, only unique differences will be presented here. The social situation in which interest in a specific sport is first generated varies by sport. For example, interest in baseball was initiated about equally in the home and the school; for fencing and crew, almost entirely in the school; for football, in the home and neighborhood; for hockey, in the home and neighborhood; for swimming, in the home and club or recreational agency; for tennis, in the school and club or recreational agency; and, for track, in the home and school.

Sport and Macro-Social Systems

TABLE 2
Place of Residence during High School as a Function of Sport (in Percent of Subjects)

Sport	Large city	Suburb of large city	Middle-sized city or small town	Open country (not a farm)	Farm	n
Baseball	25.0	33.3	33.3	0.0	8.3	12
Crew	7.7	23.1	53.8	7.7	7.7	13
Fencing	37.5	25.0	12.5	12.5	12.5	8
Football	40.0	0.0	30.0	10.0	20.0	10
Hockey	36.4	0.0	63.6	0.0	0.0	11
Swimming	30.8	46.2	23.1	0.0	0.0	13
Tennis	22.2	66.7	11.1	0.0	0.0	9
Track	18.2	9.1	54.5	9.1	9.1	11
$\bar{X}$	26.4	25.3	36.8	4.6	6.8	87

Similarly, the means by which the respondents first became interested varied somewhat by sport. For example, baseball, football, hockey, and tennis players, together with swimmers and track and field athletes, reported that actual participation was the most important influencing factor in developing a serious commitment to their sport. For fencers and participants in crew, their initial interest was stimulated by personal conversation with those already committed to the sport in question. Exposure to television, reading, or attending contests as a spectator did not contribute significantly to arousing interest in competing. Interestingly, a number of athletes attributed their initial interest not to any of the foregoing factors but rather to a perceived self-motivation. Finally, the data suggest "opportunity set" differences. For example, the athlete's place of residence during high school varied among sports (Table 2). For instance, none of the hockey players, swimmers, or tennis players lived in the open country or on a farm, indicating, as one might expect, that certain facilities and a motivational climate generally necessary for learning and perfecting a specific sport role are not readily available in rural areas.

With regard to encouragement provided by significant others, Table 3 shows the relative influence of several socializing agents and also suggests that the total amount of encouragement increases over time. However, as shown in Table 4, the amount of reinforcement received

TABLE 3
Mean Rating of Socializing Agents on Encouragement to Participate before High School, during High School, and during College (Scale Values 1–5)

Socializing agents	Before High school		High school		College	
	n	$\bar{X}$	n	$\bar{X}$	n	$\bar{X}$
Father	57	4.05	69	4.26	85	4.24
Mother	57	3.96	70	4.07	87	4.14
Brother	49	3.92	63	4.06	76	4.10
Sister	44	3.39	55	3.53	68	3.74
Other relative	46	3.59	58	3.91	72	3.90
Male friend	57	4.28	70	4.38	87	4.20
Female friend	50	3.32	69	3.77	84	3.88
Classroom teacher	55	3.40	69	3.75	71	3.41
School coach	49	4.08	69	4.65	85	4.60
School counselor	39	3.28	64	3.59	60	3.33
Nonschool personnel	40	4.05	47	4.15	51	3.84
Other	26	3.81	32	4.00	44	3.86

TABLE 4

Mean Rating of Socializing Agents on Encouragement to Participate before High School as a Function of Sport (Scale Values 1–5)

Socializing agents	Baseball		Football		Hockey		Swimming		Tennis		Track	
	n	$\bar{X}$	n	$\bar{X}$	n	$\bar{X}$	n	$\bar{X}$	n	$\bar{X}$	n	$\bar{X}$
Father	12	4.08	9	3.33	11	4.36	12	4.42	5	4.20	8	3.75
Mother	12	4.17	9	3.11	11	3.91	12	4.42	5	4.00	8	4.00
Brother	12	3.92	6	4.00	9	4.22	9	4.00	5	3.80	8	3.50
Sister	8	3.38	9	3.44	7	3.43	9	3.56	4	3.00	7	3.28
Other relative	10	3.80	9	3.78	7	3.57	8	3.12	4	3.50	8	3.62
Male friend	12	4.25	9	4.44	11	4.55	12	4.17	5	3.60	8	4.38
Female friend	10	3.20	7	3.57	9	3.44	12	3.17	4	3.00	8	3.50
Classroom teacher	11	3.73	9	3.56	11	3.45	12	3.00	4	3.00	8	3.50
School coach	8	4.62	8	4.12	8	3.75	12	3.50	5	3.60	8	5.00
School counselor	8	3.50	4	3.50	8	3.38	9	3.00	3	3.00	7	3.28
Nonschool personnel	9	4.33	4	3.00	11	4.64	7	4.14	3	4.00	6	3.17
Other	6	4.00	4	3.50	5	4.00	6	4.33	1	3.00	4	3.00

by significant others during the critical pre-high school period varies by sport. Taken collectively, these data reveal that college athletes seem to receive encouragement from many agents and that it would be unusual to find socialization occurring when only a single agent functions.

3. Other Studies

In a study of the culture of young ice hockey players (Vaz, 1970), it was found that certain criteria were essential for initiation into the role of professional hockey player. For example, Vaz reported that aggressive fighting behavior is normative institutionalized conduct and as such is an integral facet in socializing future professional hockey players. Because this behavior is institutionalized, it becomes an integral facet of the role obligation of young hockey players and is learned by subsequent novices via formal and informal socialization.

In a study concerned with female college athletes, Malumphy (1970) reported that family influence is a major factor in college women competing in sport. She noted that the typical female athlete has family approval for her participation and competition and is encouraged by at least 50% of her significant others.

Finally, in a recent consideration of socialization into primary involvement (Kenyon, 1970b),[10] the path analysis technique[11] was utilized to attempt to explain the factors precipitating primary sport involvement (Fig. 6). According to this system, and for data of these kinds, a sizable portion of the variance was accounted for. Upon examination of the path coefficients, it appears that in order of importance the most influential factors were encouragement from nonschool personnel (e.g., neighbors and relatives outside the nuclear family) to participate in sport (.361), encouragement from school personnel (i.e., teachers, coaches) to participate in sport (.217), primary sport aptitude (.200), the type or size of the community (.198), and the sex (i.e., male) of the subject (.182). Thus, if an individual is a male, has a high level of sport aptitude, lives in a large city or town which has adequate facilities and instructors (i.e., a good opportunity set), and receives encouragement from significant others within and outside the school, the likelihood of his being socialized into a primary sport role is increased considerably.

In summary, it appears that college athletes and Olympic aspirants become interested and involved in sport by age 8 or 9; that they participate, usually with a great deal of success, in a number of sports before they begin to specialize in one sport; that they receive positive sanctions to become involved and to compete from a number of significant others, of which the family, peer group, and coaches appear to be the most influential; and, that although the general

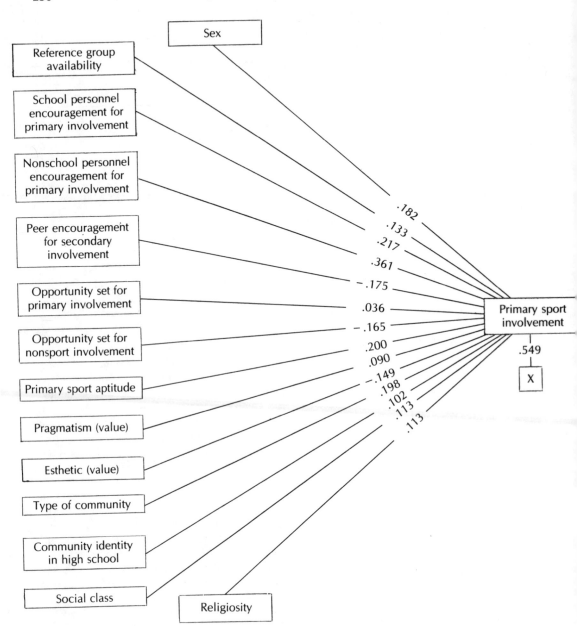

FIG. 6.   FACTORS INFLUENCING PRIMARY SPORT INVOLVEMENT.

socialization process has a number of common elements, noticeable between-sport, between-level, and between-life cycle stages occur.

B. SOCIALIZATION INTO ROLES ASSOCIATED WITH SECONDARY INVOLVEMENT

In addition to the study of primary involvement roles, a number of studies have been ad-dressed to the problem of socialization into secondary sport roles. These are described here in terms of consumer roles and leader roles.

1. Socialization of the Sport Consumer

Recent attempts to understand the sport socialization process have been concerned with the role of sport consumer, that is, the viewer, listener, reader, or discussant. Since these studies have attempted to be somewhat more theoretical than some earlier attempts to describe socialization into primary roles, they have lent themselves to the use of path models and path analysis. For example, in a study designed to explain the degree of present enactment of two consumer sport roles, data were collected from 177 college juniors and seniors (Kenyon, 1970a). The observations for 13 variables were placed into the path model shown in Fig. 7, which represents the factors accounting for consumption of major league baseball, and into the model depicted in Fig. 8, which represents the factors influencing the consumption of the Mexico Olympic Games. The causal functioning of each variable is represented in the multistage (high school and college), multivariate (13 variables) models. Upon an analysis of the path coefficients and the residuals it is apparent that much of the variation in each system remains unexplained. Nevertheless, Fig. 7 suggests that the most influential factors, in order of importance, leading to baseball consumption are sport aptitude (.186), general sport interest in high school (.303), involvement by the same sex peers in sport consumption (.143), and secondary involvement in baseball during high school (.290). Similarly, Fig. 8 indicates that the most important factors accounting for the consumption of the Mexico Olympic Games include involvement in the Tokyo Olympics (.720) and familiarity with athletes who participated in the Tokyo Olympic Games (.144).

It would appear that in comparing the baseball with the Olympic data, some differences emerge. For example, general sport interest in high school appears to contribute to secondary involvement in baseball in college but not to one's later interest in the Olympic games. In short, the factors which generate interest in one form of sport may not be the same factors which generate interest in other forms. Thus, as in primary sport role socialization, it may be necessary to account for considerable sport differences. Moreover, enactment of secondary sport roles as a young adult may not be very heavily dependent upon enactment as an adolescent. As shown in Fig. 7, to be interested in baseball during high school is only weakly related to interest in college.

In a secondary analysis of some factors hypothesized to be important in the sport socialization of male adolescents in Canada, the United States, and England, Kelly (1970) found that frequency of attendance at sport events was directly related to family size and indirectly related to age. For winter sports only, attendance at sporting events was positively related to social class background in Canada and the United States but negatively related in England.

In a study conducted at the University of Wisconsin in 1970 (Kenyon, 1970b), 96 college sophomores and juniors were interviewed to determine the factors accounting for socialization into the role of sport consumer. Although considerable unexplained variance remained, it was found that the major factor accounting for the learning of the role was primary sport involvement (Fig. 9); that is, the more they enacted primary sport roles, the greater their interest in other facets of sport, and, therefore, the greater their consumption of sport.

In a study of the sport consumer, Toyama (1971) investigated the influence of the mass media on the learning of sport language—specifically, football terminology. She found that 65% of her sample spent more than 3 hours per week consuming televised sport, and, of these, 36% spent 5 hours or more. It was not surprising then to find that 65% of the sample reported that they learned football terms by watching television. Another 16% learned the terms while actually playing the game. Thus, it appears that the mass media, especially television, is an important agent in cognitive sport socialization.

2. Socialization of the Sport Leader

Although many leadership roles can be found in a sport system, few of these have been the subject of empirical inquiry. Two exceptions, however, are the studies by Bratton (1970) and Pooley (1971).

Bratton (1970) investigated the demographic characteristics of executive members of two amateur sport associations. Although this study was limited to a descriptive analysis, it does suggest how and when one becomes a sport executive. Again, it should be noted that there are sport differences. For example, volleyball executives were 10 years younger than the swimming executives (29.5 vs 40.6 years), with the majority still active as players. It was also observed that fewer than 10% had occupations that fell below 65 (range 34–96) on the NORC occupational status scale, that Catholics were underrepresented, and that people of British origin held a larger proportion of the positions. Thus, it

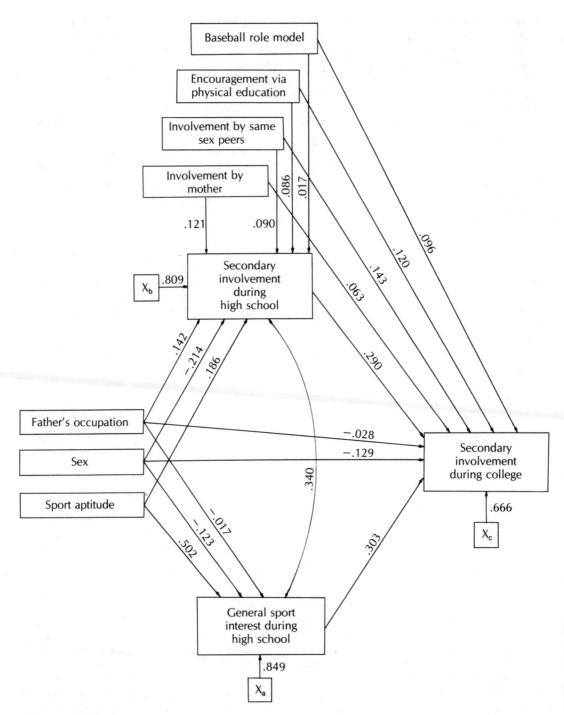

FIG. 7. TEST OF CAUSAL MODEL ACCOUNTING FOR SOCIALIZATION INTO SECONDARY INVOLVEMENT IN SAN FRANCISCO BAY AREA MAJOR LEAGUE BASEBALL.

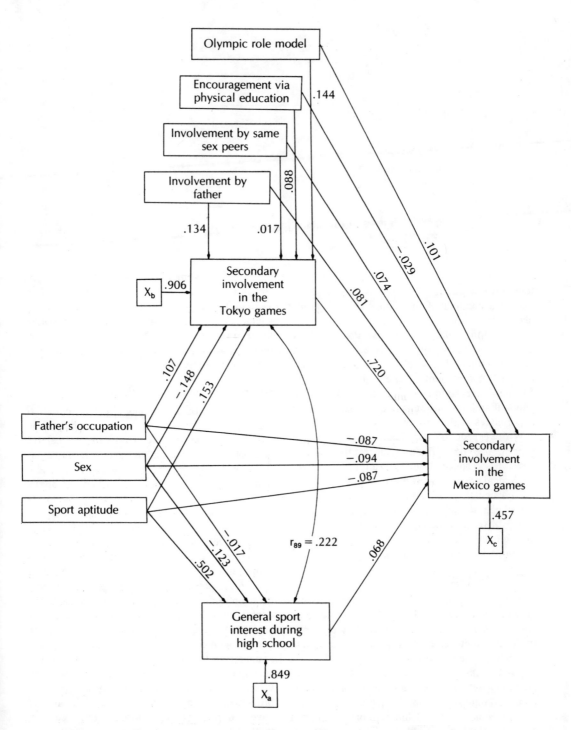

FIG. 8. TEST OF CAUSAL MODEL ACCOUNTING FOR SOCIALIZATION INTO SECONDARY INVOLVEMENT IN MEXICO OLYMPIC GAMES.

233

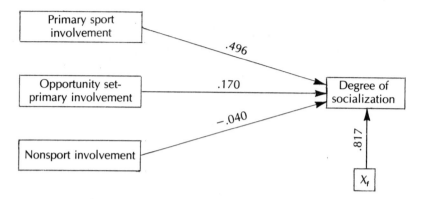

FIG. 9.   FACTORS ACCOUNTING FOR SOCIALIZATION INTO THE ROLE
OF SPORT CONSUMER.

appears that to become an executive for an amateur sport association it is almost essential that one be a member of the higher socioeconomic class.

In a more detailed analysis, Pooley (1971) investigated the sociopsychological elements involved in the professional socialization of physical education students in the United States and England. He found a number of significant national and sex differences in the socialization experiences of the role recruits.

With respect to sport leader socialization in general, the Pooley findings suggest that the process differs cross-nationally as a function of psychological and sociocultural factors operating in the particular social situation, while Bratton's work suggests that the possession of social characteristics and the occupancy of certain roles are prerequisites for gaining access to executive positions in the sport system.

C. SUMMARY

Although the study of sport socialization has only just begun, the findings to date already suggest a number of generalizations. For example, the elite athlete emerges from an environment which was highly supportive; that is, he was exposed from an early age to an abundant opportunity set (middle-class values and ample facilities, equipment, and leadership) and much encouragement, reward, and reinforcement from a variety of meaningful others. The consumer of sport is likely to be or have been active as a contestant, but his consumption is dependent upon the social situation in which he finds himself. The sport leader, in addition to considerable

primary involvement, tends to have emerged from a background laden with middle-class values. There are important differences in the socialization process for all forms of involvement. For example, the process varies somewhat from sport to sport and also differs for each stage in the life cycle.

III. A BASIS FOR FUTURE RESEARCH

Since most of the studies cited in Section II were not based upon a social role–social system approach, it has not been possible to test the general model presented in Section I. However, by considering the evidence already reported, and through a degree of conceptual extrapolation, we provide below a combination summary of present knowledge and a partial list of hypotheses requiring further empirical testing, using our general model (Figs. 3 and 4) as a frame of reference. In each case, it will be assumed that some minimal degree of motoric and cognitive aptitude is present; that is, the greater the motoric aptitude (sport aptitude), the greater the degree of primary role socialization, and the greater the cognitive aptitude (e.g., ability to comprehend and retain rules, strategy, statistics, and names), the greater the degree of primary or secondary role socialization. The major intervening variable in the model is "system-induced propensity for sport involvement." Thus, we have grouped the propositions around each of the four social systems: the family, the school, the peer group, and the community. Primary and secondary involvement socialization are treated separately. In each case only a few of the many possible propositions are given.

PROPOSITIONS RELATED TO SOCIALIZATION INTO A PRIMARY SPORT ROLE

A. *Family-Induced Factors*

1. The greater the parental primary involvement in sport, the greater the degree of sport role socialization among offspring.
2. The higher sport is placed in the parental value hierarchy, the greater the degree of sport role socialization among offspring.
3. The earlier the involvement in sport, the greater the family support, and thus the greater the level of attainment.
4. The higher the ordinal position, the greater the degree of sport role socialization.
5. The higher the social class background, the more favorable the sport socialization situation, and thus the greater the degree of socialization.

B. *School-Induced Factors*

1. The higher sport is placed in the school's hierarchy of values, the greater the degree of sport role socialization.
2. The less sport that is presented in the mass media, the greater the socializing function of teachers and coaches.
3. The greater the frequency of positive sanctions received from school personnel for participation in school sport, the greater the propensity for sport involvement.
4. The greater the success of school athletic teams, the greater the propensity for sport involvement.

C. *Peer-Induced Factors*

1. The greater the peer involvement in sport, the greater the propensity for sport involvement.
2. The greater the positive sanctions from peers, the greater the propensity for sport involvement.
3. The greater the amount of sport-oriented face-to-face interaction with peers, the greater the propensity for sport involvement.
4. The higher sport is placed in the peer group's hierarchy of values, the greater the degree of sport role socialization.

D. *Community-Induced Factors*

1. The greater the role player's success, the greater the reinforcement from significant others.
2. The greater the role player's publicity, the greater the propensity for sport involvement.
3. The more urban the place of residence, the greater the degree of sport role socialization.
4. The greater the opportunity for direct and indirect consumption of sport, the greater the propensity for sport involvement.
5. The larger the community, the greater the propensity for sport involvement.

PROPOSITIONS RELATED TO SOCIALIZATION INTO A SECONDARY SPORT ROLE

A. *Family-Induced Factors*

1. The greater the parental identification with individuals or groups in the sport system, the greater the novice's degree of consumer role socialization.
2. The greater the size of the family, the greater the degree of consumer role socialization.
3. The higher the social class, the greater the degree of consumer role socialization.
4. The greater the number of sport-consuming significant others in the nuclear family, the greater the degree of consumer role socialization.
5. The greater the amount of direct and indirect consumption of sport by significant others in the nuclear family, the greater the degree of consumer role socialization.
6. The greater the number of males in the nuclear family, the greater the degree of consumer role socialization.

B. *School-Induced Factors*

1. Among their hierarchy of values, the higher sport is ranked by the school's instructional and administrative personnel, the greater the degree of consumer role socialization.
2. The greater the number of interscholastic sport teams, the greater the degree of consumer role socialization.
3. The greater the success of interscholastic

sport teams, the greater the degree of consumer role socialization.

4. The greater the consumption of interscholastic sport by school personnel, the greater the degree of consumer role socialization.

C. *Peer-Induced Factors*

1. The greater the peer consumption of sport, the greater the degree of consumer role socialization.

2. The greater the peer propensity for sport involvement (e.g., a loyalty for, or an identity with, an entity or group in the sport system), the greater the degree of consumer role socialization.

3. Among their hierarchy of values, the higher sport is ranked by members of the peer group, the greater the degree of consumer role socialization.

D. *Community-Induced Factors*

1. The greater the primary involvement in sport, the greater the degree of consumer role socialization.

2. The greater the access to the mass media, especially television, the greater the degree of cognitive sport socialization.

3. The greater the identification with one sport team, the greater the degree of consumer role socialization.

IV. IN CONCLUSION

The reader will have concluded by now that the "state of the art" explaining socialization into the many roles associated with sport involvement is not well advanced. Indeed, in 10 years' time, much of that which has been reported in this article will seem elementary, at best. The success of future efforts, however, will depend upon a judicious combination of the best theoretical and empirical methods, the willingness to make many observations over time, the concentration upon smaller more manageable social systems (but always within the context of a larger model),[12] and an abiding pursuit of parsimony (such as Heise's "theory trimming" approach, 1969). Finally, in view of the evidence suggesting sport and national differences, much comparative work will be needed to test the generality of explanatory models.[13]

REFERENCES

Bandura, A.: *In* Handbook of Socialization Theory and Research. Edited by D.A. Goslin. pp. 213–262. Chicago, Rand McNally, 1969.

Bandura, A., and Walters, R.H.: Social Learning and Personality Development. New York, Holt, 1963.

Blalock, H.M., Jr.,: Theory Construction: From Verbal to Mathematical Formulations. Englewood Cliffs, N.J., Prentice-Hall, 1969.

Blau, P.M., and Duncan, O.D.: The American Occupational Structure. New York, Wiley, 1967.

Bratton, R.: Can. Ass. Health, Phys. Educ., Recreation, *37*:26–28, 1970.

Brim, O.G.: Sociometry, *21*:343–364, 1958.

Brim, O.G., and Wheeler, S.: Socialization After Childhood: Two Essays. New York, Wiley, 1966.

Campbell, E.O.: *In* Handbook of Socialization Theory and Research. Edited by D.A. Goslin. pp. 821–859. Chicago, Rand McNally, 1969.

Clausen, J.A., ed.: Socialization and Society. Little, Brown, Boston, 1968.

Duncan, O.D.: Amer. J. Sociol., *72*:1–16, 1966.

Heise, D.R.: *In* Sociological Methodology. Edited by E.F. Borgatta. pp. 38–73. Jossey-Bass, San Francisco, 1969.

Helanko, R.: Acta Sociol., *2*:229–240, 1957.

Homans, G.C.: The Human Group. New York, Harcourt, 1950.

Kelly, C.: Unpublished M. Sc. Thesis, University of Wisconsin, Madison, 1970.

Kemper, T.D.: Am. Sociol. Rev., *33*:31–45, 1968.

Kenyon, G.S.: Unpublished study, University of Wisconsin, Madison, 1968.

Kenyon, G.S.: *In* Aspects of Contemporary Sport Sociology. Edited by G.S. Kenyon. pp. 77–100. Chicago, Athletic Institute, 1969.

Kenyon, G.S., and Grogg, T.: Unpublished study, University of Wisconsin, Madison, 1969.

Kenyon, G.S.: Int. Rev. Sport Sociol., *5*:191–203, 1970a.

Kenyon, G.S.: Unpublished study, University of Wisconsin, Madison, 1970b.

LeVine, R.A.: *In* Handbook of Socialization Theory and Research. Edited by D.A. Goslin. pp. 503–542. Chicago, Rand McNally, 1969.

Lüschen, G.: *In* Aspects of Contemporary Sport Sociology. Edited by G.S. Kenyon. pp. 57–76. Athletic Institute, Chicago, 1969.

McCandless, B.R.: *In* Handbook of Socialization Theory and Research. Edited by D.A. Goslin. pp. 791–819. Chicago, Rand McNally, 1969.

McPhee, W.N.: Formal Theories of Mass Behavior. New York, Free Press, 1963.

McPherson, B.D.: Unpublished study, University of Wisconsin, Madison, 1968.

McPherson, B.D.: Pap., Int. Symp. Sociol. Sport, 3rd, 1971.

Malumphy, T.M.: Quest, *14*:18–27, 1970.

Moore, O.K., and Anderson, A.R.: *In* Handbook of Socialization Theory and Research. Edited by D.A. Goslin. pp. 571–614. Chicago, Rand McNally, 1969.

Parsons, T.: *In* Theories of Society. Edited by T. Parsons et al. pp. 30–79, New York, Free Press, 1961.

Pooley, J.C.: Unpublished Ph.D. Dissertation. Madison, University of Wisconsin, 1971.

Pudelkiewicz, E.: Int. Rev. Sport Sociol., 5:73–103, 1970.

Rehberg, R.A., Sinclair, J., and Schafer, W.E.: Am. J. Sociol., 75:1012–1034, 1970.

Reiss, A.J., Jr.: Unpublished manuscript, University of Michigan, Ann Arbor (cited by Bandura, 1969), 1966.

Roethlisberger, F.A.: Unpublished M.Sc. Thesis, University of Wisconsin, Madison, 1970.

Rosen, B.C.: Am. Sociol. Rev., 21:203–211, 1956.

Sewell, W.H.: Ann. Am. Acad. Political Soc. Sci., 394:163–181, 1963.

Sewell, W.H., Haller, A.O., and Portes, A.: Am. Sociol. Rev., 34:82–92, 1969.

Sewell, W.H., Haller, A.O., and Ohlendorf, G.: Am. Sociol. Rev., 35:1014–1027, 1970.

Smelser, N.J.: Theory of Collective Behavior. New York, Free Press, 1962.

Spady, W.G.: Amer. J. Sociol., 75:680–702, 1970.

Stone, G.P.: In Aspects of Contemporary Sport Sociology. Edited by G.S. Kenyon. pp. 5–16. Chicago, Athletic Institute, 1969.

Toyama, J.S.: Unpublished M.Sc. Thesis, University of Wisconsin, Madison, 1971.

Turner, J.H.: Sociometry, 33:147–165, 1970.

Vaz, E.: Pap. World Congr. Int. Sociol. Ass., 7th, 1970.

Webb, H.: In Aspects of Contemporary Sport Sociology. Edited by G.S. Kenyon. pp. 161–187. Chicago, Athletic Institute, 1969.

Woelfel, J., and Haller, A.O.: Am. Sociol. Rev., 36: 74–87, 1971.

Zetterberg, H.L.: On Theory and Verification in Sociology. Totowa, N.J., Bedminister Press, 1966.

Zigler, E., and Child, I.L.: In The Handbook of Social Psychology. Edited by G. Lindzey and E. Aronson. 2nd ed., Vol. 3, pp. 450–589. Reading, Mass., Addison-Wesley, 1969.

NOTES

1. The reader will note the frequent allusion to role theory in this section. We attempt to justify this in Section I,A,1.

2. Those persons who exercise major influence over the attitudes and behavior of individuals (after Woelfel and Haller, 1971).

3. It is proposed that the construct "propensity for sport involvement" (PSI) be considered as an intervening variable in the basic model. Each institutionalized social system considered would be assumed to contribute to, or detract from, the development of PSI.

4. For an example of this approach and a discussion of its strengths and weaknesses see Lüschen (1969).

5. This proposition should not be taken as axiomatic in view of the recent work of Rehberg et al. (1970).

6. The data were collected at the South Lake Tahoe, California altitude training camp through the cooperation of Dr. Jack Daniels who served as research physiologist for the United States Olympic Committee. (See F. A. Roethlisberger, "Socialization of the Elite Gymnast," unpublished Master of Science thesis, University of Wisconsin, 1970.)

7. Data were obtained on another situational variable, namely, birth order. Fifty percent of the respondents reported that they were first born.

8. This finding was also suggested by Pudelkiewicz (1970) who noted that a positive evaluation of sport by Polish parents gives rise to sport interests among their children.

9. These data were collected in 1969 by members of a graduate class in the sociology of sport at the University of Wisconsin and analyzed by Mr. Tom Grogg. Their assistance is gratefully acknowledged.

10. These data were collected in 1970 by members of a graduate class in the sociology of sport at the University of Wisconsin and analyzed by Mr. Tom Grogg. Their assistance is gratefully acknowledged.

11. The basic purpose of path analysis is to estimate ". . . the paths which may account for a set of observed correlations on the assumption of a particular formal or causal ordering of the variables involved" (Duncan, 1966). In developing such a system the researcher is greatly aided by the construction of a path diagram which represents graphically the causal theory underlying the system. In the diagram causal relations are represented by unidirectional arrows, while noncausal relations, i.e., correlational, are represented by two-headed curvilinear arrows. Residual variables, also depicted by unidirectional arrows, represent the unmeasured variation in the system which may consist of unknown variables, error, or both. Given the path model, it is possible to set up a system of regression equations which in turn supply standardized regression coefficients (betas) which are taken as the path coefficients. Thus, the path coefficient is the proportion of the standard deviation in the dependent variable for which the antecedent variable is directly responsible, with all other variables, including residuals, held constant.

12. See B. D. McPherson, "Socialization into the Role of Sport Consumer: A Theory and Causal Model." Unpublished Ph.D. Dissertation, University of Wisconsin, 1972.

13. A cross-national study on leisure role socialization was initiated by the International Committee for Sociology of Sport in 1972.

SECTION TWO

sport and regulative institutions

the effects of monopsonistic procedures on equality of competition in professional sport leagues

THOMAS N. DAYMONT

INTRODUCTION

There has been increasing interest by the public and government concerning the organization and operating procedures of the professional team sport business. This is especially true for those procedures which give the team owners monopsony power in the labor market, i.e. create conditions whereby the employee (player) can negotiate with only one employer (team owner). The interest is a consequence of such factors as the uniqueness of some of these procedures, the degree to which the business has grown financially, and the enormous public interest in its product, i.e. professional sport games. This paper examines three unique operating procedures: specifically, the effects of the free agent draft, the reserve system, and the player draft on equality of competition.

OVERVIEW

The relationship between the monopsonizing procedures and equality of competition is part of a broader debate concerning whether these operating procedures should be permitted. Proponents contend that these procedures are necessary for the viability of professional team sports, while critics assert that they violate federal antitrust laws. With respect to the use of these procedures by business organizations, the United

States Congress has noted that such procedures exist in no other business and can only be justified by exceptional circumstances. Team owners and league officials have maintained that professional sports *are exceptional* and that these procedures are necessary for the survival of professional sports. One of their primary contentions is that these procedures are essential in order to balance competition among teams. On the other hand, players dispute their necessity, and assert that they constitute a conspiracy among employers (i.e. team owners) which infringes on the freedom of players and violates antitrust laws. Thus far, the arguments of the owners have been efficacious. Both Congress and the Judiciary have allowed the practices to continue, thereby implying their agreement with the owner's contention that these procedures are essential for balanced competition.

Table 1 summarizes the league-years during which each of the restrictive procedures existed in the four major sports of baseball, basketball, football, and hockey. In general, these procedures were designed to alter the contractual arrangements between team owners and players from those occurring in a competitive market.

Specifically, the reserve system is a procedure whereby only one team owner negotiates for the future services of a player already under contract.[1] The owner also has the option of selling, trading, or transferring these rights to another team. Thus, under an effective reserve system a player has only two options: (1) continue to play for the team which owns his contract; or (2) not play for any team in the league. In short, the

Reprinted from International Review of Sport Sociology, *10*(2):83–99, 1975. Copyright 1975 by International Review of Sport Sociology, Warsaw, Poland.

241

TABLE 1
Years in which the Reserve System, Free Agent Draft, and Player Draft Were Effective in the Major Sports

Sport	Procedures[a]	1951	1954	1957	1960	1963	1966	1969	1972
Baseball	RES								
	FAD								
	PLD								
Basketball	RES								
	FAD								
	PLD								
Football	RES								
	FAD								
	PLD								
Hockey	RES								
	FAD								
	PLD								

[a] RES = Reserve System; FAD = Free Agent Draft; PLD = Player Draft.
Note: The vertical lines denote the beginning and end of the sample for the sport.

team owners have the power to unilaterally determine for which team a player will perform.

The reserve system is incorporated into the league by the inclusion of either a "reserve clause" or "option clause." Both clauses provide that a team owner may unilaterally renew the contracts of his players. The difference between the two is that whereas the former stipulates that the renewed contract also contain a reserve clause, the latter provides for no further options on the part of the owner. Because of this difference, it is sometimes claimed that the option clause is less restrictive than the reserve clause, but this has not proved to be the case. For instance, the option clause in the NFL provides that if a player and owner cannot come to terms, the player can choose to play for a year under the renewed contract and become a free agent. (Such a player is said to be "playing out his option"; actually he is playing out the owner's option). However, such a free agent does not have as advantageous a bargaining position as it initially appears. He could sign a standard contract with any club with which he could come to terms, but the team with which he signed would be required to compensate his former team with players and/or future draft choices. If the two teams could not agree on appropriate compensation, the Commissioner of Football would arbitrate, and in his sole discretion, decide upon the players and/or draft

choices to be awarded to the former club by the team which signed the so-called free agent.[2] In cases which have been decided by the Commissioner, the player compensation has been quite substantial. As a result teams have been extremely reluctant to sign free agents. Consequently, the procedures of the NFL, i.e., the option clause and enforced compensation for free agents, constitute an effective reserve system within the league.

The critical consideration with regard to the effectiveness of a reserve system is the degree to which the team owners in a sport refrain from bidding for the services of players on other teams. This becomes apparent when one compares the effectiveness of the reserve systems of baseball and basketball in the early 1970's. Despite the fact that the wording of the two is almost identical, baseball's reserve system has been effective, while that of basketball has not.[3] This is because all baseball team owners refuse to negotiate with players on other teams, but due to the war between the National Basketball Association (NBA) and the American Basketball Association (ABA), basketball owners do recruit players from teams in other leagues.[4] Prior to 1967 the NBA was the only basketball league, and teams did not compete with each other for players already in the league. However, in 1967, the ABA began to challenge the NBA as a major league. In an effort to reach parity with the established league, the new league "raided" the roster of the older league attempting to lure quality players to "jump" to the new league. Thus, Wilt Chamberlain was not restricted to bargain with only one team as in the past—he could negotiate with at least one team in each league. Two developments testify to the ensuing ineffectiveness of the reserve system. First, and most significant, was the relatively large number of players who have switched teams and leagues without the consent of their owners. A list of these players includes such names as Rick Barry, Zelmo Beatty, John Brisker, Joe Caldwell, Billy Cunningham, Connie Hawkins, Spencer Haywood, Jim McDaniels, and Charlie Scott. Second, the average salary for NBA players has risen from about $25,000 in 1968 to about $90,000 in 1973.

The free agent draft is a procedure whereby only one team within a league negotiates for the services of individual prospective professional players. The football and basketball drafts of college players are examples of the free agent draft. Each player is picked by one team and he must either sign with that team or not play within the league. For example, in 1969 the Buffalo Bills picked O. J. Simpson in the college draft even though he desired to play for a west coast team. However, when the Bills refused to trade the rights to him, Simpson had to either play for Buffalo or not play in the NFL.

The National Hockey League (NHL) introduced its free agent draft, called the "amateur draft" in 1962. Rewritten in 1966, the draft has been effective in permitting prospective professionals to negotiate with only one team. Players in leagues of the Canadian Amateur Hockey Association who have reached their 21st birthday are eligible for the draft. The free agent draft in baseball, instituted in 1964, controls the recruitment of players who have finished high school and of college players who have completed their first two years. [5] The baseball free agent draft is different from those in the other sports in that it is the only one in which draft rights are not perpetual. In each of the other sports the team retains the rights to a player until they either trade or sell those rights to another team. However, in baseball three separate drafts occur each year with each team selecting players not yet under contract to other teams. A team then has the exclusive right to negotiate with a particular player; however, if the team fails to sign him prior to the next it loses all rights to the player, who then can be drafted by a second club. This second club would then have exclusive rights to the player until the next draft. Hence, a player has some freedom, i.e. he can wait a few months until the next draft and negotiate with another team. Nevertheless, this procedure has been effective in limiting the ability of free agents to negotiate with more than one team at one point in time. This efficacy is supported by the fact that free agents received smaller payments after the draft was introduced.

In the past two decades, there were two periods in which a free agent draft existed according to the league rules but was ineffective. In both cases it was a result of competition for free agents by teams from opposing major leagues. One occurrence was in basketball from 1968 to the present. This was the same period that the reserve system was ineffective and it was because of the same reason—the struggle between the ABA and the NBA. With the emergence of this conflict, both leagues conducted a draft, choosing essentially the same players. Consequently, a prospective player could bargain with two teams instead of one, thereby nullifying the effectiveness of the free agent draft as well as the reserve system. A similar situation existed in football from 1960 to 1966 when the American Football League (AFL) was attempting to attain equality with the National Football League (NFL). Each league had a free agent draft and one team from each league bid for the top graduating college players. In 1967 both leagues initiated a common draft and once again free agents could negotiate with only one team. The ineffectiveness of the free agent draft in basketball and football during these periods of conflict was evidenced by the dramatic rise in payments made to free agents at these times. Top football prospects such as Joe Namath and Donny Anderson received bonuses in the neighborhood of $500,000 and several basketball stars have commanded over a million dollars for their talents. For the most part, the AFL limited its competition with the NFL to graduating college players and did not vie for players already on NFL teams; therefore, the reserve systems in football remained effective. Although the ABA and the AFL were not the only leagues other than the established major leagues in the sports of baseball, basketball, football, and hockey, they were the only challengers which caused the reserve system and/or free agent draft to become ineffective. The majority of the other leagues operating during the last two decades were clearly minor leagues. Even such a quality league as the Canadian Football League did not often vie with the major leagues for the best players.

The above discussion illustrates that the reserve system and the free agent draft function in essentially the same manner, the only difference being to which players each is applicable. The free agent draft binds free agents who are not yet part of the league to one team, while the reserve system binds players already in the league to one team.

The player draft is a procedure whereby teams are required to sell certain players to other teams at a constant price per contract. A team can name a certain number of players who cannot be selected by other teams, but any other players under contract can be chosen by other teams. Chosen players must be sold to the selecting team at a specified constant price which is designed to be, and usually is, below the market value of most players. This procedure was instituted by those sports with extensive minor league systems, i.e. hockey and baseball, to restrain the wealthy teams from hoarding large numbers of quality players in efficient farm systems. The player draft in the National Hockey League (NHL) provided that each team could protect 20 players, but other players could be drafted by other teams. The drafting order for all unprotected players was in the reverse order of the teams in the league standings (Jones, 1969. As of 1967, the drafting price was $30,000). The major leagues of baseball have had a player draft since 1921, and although this draft has been amended many times and is fairly complex, it is similar to the draft in hockey. As of 1970, baseball clubs were allowed to protect their entire 40 man roster plus some minor league players (Canes, 1970).

REVIEW OF LITERATURE

Because government policy has been based, at least partially, on the argument that the monopsonizing procedures promote balanced competition, it is desirous that this contention be supported by facts and evidence; however, supporting evidence is meager. Most of the research has been done by economists who have used microeconomic theory to analyze the consequences of these procedures. The approach has been to assume that team success would vary according to the distribution of player talent; i.e. the teams with the best players would win the most games. They then analyzed the effects which these procedures might have on the distribution of player talent; the majority being of the opinion that there would be a negligible effect.

With respect to the reserve system, Rottenberg (1956) provides a representative analysis by which possible effects of this procedure take place:

> Players under contract to make a team may be used by that team itself, or they may be sold to another team. Each team determines whether to use a player's services itself or to sell him, according to the relative returns on him in the two uses. If the return will be higher from sale, he will be sold, and vice versa. Now, if he can be sold to another team for a price higher than his worth to his present team, it is because he is worth more to the team that buys him than to the team that sells him. It follows that players will be distributed among teams so that they are put to their most "productive" use; each will play for the team that is able to get the highest return from his services. But this is exactly the result which would be yielded by a free market. The difference is only that in a market subject to the reserve rule part of the price for the player's services is paid to the team that sells his contract; in the free market the player gets his full value.

It was asserted that players will end up on the team for which they have the highest value by means of two fairly common practices: (1) the sale of players for cash; and (2) the trading of players of unequal ability. (El Hodiri and Quirk, 1971 and Noll and Okner, 1971). In contrast to these theorists, Topkis (1967) contended that in the absence of restraints such as the reserve system, wealthiest teams would buy the best players, thereby dominating the league and eventually driving the poorer teams out of existence.

Because the free agent draft is based on the same principle as the reserve system, several of the theorists asserted that it too would have no effect on equality of competition (e.g. Noll and Okner, 1971). El Hodiri and Quirk (1971) claimed that the poorer clubs would act as a "conveyor belt", obtaining new talent at low prices and selling or trading these players to those willing to pay higher prices. Canes (1971) presented a similar argument, but added that the selection of draft choices according to the reverse order of position in the league standing may produce a small equalizing effect. However, Topkis (1967) and Jones (1969) contended that the free agent draft would promote more balanced competition by allowing the poorer teams a better opportunity of obtaining quality players.

Jones (1969) maintained that the player draft would enhance balanced competition among teams because it would prohibit rich teams from stocking their top farm teams with players who were talented enough to play for other teams. Canes (1971) stated that because the player draft enables weaker teams to buy players at a price below that in a competitive market, their potential financial position is enhanced relative to that of stronger teams. However, he continued that because of the difficulty in determining player talent and the ability of teams to avoid the provisions of the draft, it may be ineffective in equalizing competititon.

In the only empirical investigation, Canes (1970) compared sport situations with the procedures, with sport situations without them, and concluded that equality of competition is independent of each of the restrictive procedures. Although some of his comparisons were made between various time periods within the same professional league, for the most part, Canes compared competitiveness in different professional leagues, and between professional and college leagues. Also, he used some data prior to 1900. The relevance of these latter comparisons to modern professional leagues seems somewhat limited. The present investigation is significant in that it restricted comparisons to major professional leagues and used data from the most recent league-years.

PROCEDURES

The sample for the study consisted of the league-years (a league-year is a single playing season of a particular league, e.g. the 1972 season of the NHL) in the major professional sports of baseball, basketball, football and hockey from 1951 to 1972.

The independent variables, the reserve system, the free agent draft, and the player draft were conceptualized as dichotomies; they either were present in the league rules *and* effective or they were absent *or* ineffective (Table 1).

The dependent variable, equality of competition, was the degree to which teams of a league were equal in their success in organized competition, i.e. their ability to win games in league play. Equality of competition can vary within as well as between league-years; hence, equality of competition was analyzed from two perspectives.

Static equality of competition was the degree to which teams of a league were equal in their success at winning games during a season. The degree to which teams in a single league were equal at one point in time was reflected in the distribution of winning percentages of the teams for that year. In a league with balanced competition, each team will win approximately the same number of games as it loses. The winning percentages of each team will be near .500, and the standard deviation of such a distribution of winning percentages will be relatively small. The more unequal the success of teams, the greater the likelihood that the winning percentages of some teams will approach the extremes, either .000 or 1.000. The standard deviation of such a distribution will be relatively large. Hence, static equality of competition was measured by the standard deviation of the distribution of winning percentages of teams for a league-year.

Dynamic equality of competition was the degree to which teams of a league were equal in their success over time, i.e. their relative success at winning games from one season to another. Changes in the success of teams over time are reflected by the year-to-year variability in the final team standings. In a league in which the relative success of teams remains fairly constant, final team rankings in the league show few changes from one year to another, and the correlation between the final rankings of teams in different years will approach unity. In a league in which the relative success of teams changes frequently, team rankings will often change, and the correlation between final team rankings in different years will be lower, approaching zero or a negative value. Therefore, one-year lagged correlations between the final team rankings in the league from one year to the next were used to measure dynamic equality of competition. However, possible changes in competitiveness due to these procedures may take a longer period than one year to become apparent. To detect these long-range changes in equality of competition, three-year lagged correlations were also used.

To ascertain the main and interaction effects of the restrictive procedures, additive and subclass regression equations based on the general linear model were computed. Since each of the independent variables were dichotomies, the basic model was a $2 \times 2 \times 2$; however, only 5 of the 8 possible combinations of effective procedures existed in the sample. This model gave rise to binary coded dummy variables which were included in the regression equations. To control for differences between sports which might confound the results in the analysis of data across all leagues, the data from each league were also analyzed individually.

RESULTS AND DISCUSSION

There was a significant positive relationship between the player draft and static equality of competition when analyzed across all sports. However, the relationship in the NHL, the only league in which the effects of the player draft could be tested, was negligible (Table 2). This discrepancy can possibly be reconciled by noting the league-years in which the player draft was present. Although present in each year in baseball and most of the years in hockey, the player draft was not present in basketball and football for any year. The results of the overall sample show that the standard deviation of the distribution of winning percentages was substantially higher in basketball and football than in baseball and hockey. However, this may be a result of differences between sports other than the presence of the player draft such as the number of games played in a season and the manner in which teams divide their revenue. Because these factors did not vary within a single league, the results of the NHL were a more valid indicator of the relationship than the results across all sports. In contrast to static equality of competition, there was a significant negative relationship between the player draft and dynamic equality of competition in the overall sample. Again, however, the lack of a relationship in the NHL suggests that this relationship was spurious. Since it was only possible to test the player draft in one league, the finding of a negligible relationship must be considered tentative.

The regression coefficients assessing the rela-

TABLE 2
The Relationship Between the Player Draft and Equality of Competition

League	Indicator[a]	Mean Score of Indicator of Equality of Competition		Regression Coefficient (b)[b] (Standard error of b)	Partial Coefficient of Determination (r^2)
		Player Draft Present	Player Draft Absent		
A. Static Equality of Competition					
NHL	SDWP	.108	.125	.013 (±.014)	.037
All	SDWP	.088	.173	.090 (±.007)[c]	.648
B. Dynamic Equality of Competition					
NHL	Cor-1	.595	.730	.045 (±.154)	.003
	Cor-3	.398	.703	.368 (±.266)	.077
All	Cor-1	.606	.504	−.090 (±.056)	.030
	Cor-3	.446	.252	−.178 (±.073)[c]	.064

[a] Cor-1 and Cor-3 are the one- and three-year lagged correlations between final standings, respectively.

[b] The sign of b was reversed in order that a positive (negative) relationship between the player draft and equality of competition would be indicated by a positive (negative) b. This was necessary because a lower score on each of the indicators of equality of competition represented more equal competition.

[c] Significant at .05 level of probability.

tionship between the free agent draft and equality of competition varied in sign, and the proportion of explained variation (r^2) was very low in most leagues (Table 3). Only in the American League (AL) of baseball was there a significant relationship. The absence of a relationship in the other five leagues suggests that the relationship in the AL was not due to a systematic effect of the free agent draft. Overall, the results indicate that equality of competition was independent of the free agent draft.

The effects of the reserve system could be tested in one league, the NBA. However, a complicating factor was that the free agent draft was ineffective during the same period as the reserve system; thus, the test was really of the combined effects of the reserve system and free agent draft. The results fail to indicate a relationship between these procedures and competitiveness (Table 4). Given that the free agent draft did not affect equality of competition, the combination of the free agent draft and the reserve system did not affect equality of competition, and that the two procedures are similar in their function, it is probable that the reserve system did not affect equality of competition.

TABLE 3

The Relationship Between the Free Agent Draft and Equality of Competition

| League | Indicator[a] | Mean Score of Indicator of Equality of Competition | | Regression Coefficient (b)[b] (Standard error of b) | Partial Coefficient of Determination (r^2) |
		Player Draft Present	Player Draft Absent		
		A. Static Equality of Competition			
AL	SDWP	.072	.092	.020[c] (±.008)	.227
NL	SDWP	.069	.078	.009 (±.008)	.055
NFL East	SDWP	.191	.202	.011 (±.017)	.030
NFL West	SDWP	.197	.201	.004 (±.020)	.003
NHL	SDWP	.104	.116	.008 (±.012)	.020
NBA	SDWP	.132	.142	.010 (±.019)	.016
All	SDWP	.132	.124	−.010 (±.007)	.018
		B. Dynamic Equality of Competition			
AL	Cor-1	.516	.773	.257[c] (±.086)	.309
	Cor-3	.285	.674	.389[c] (±.096)	.450
NL	Cor-1	.517	.559	.042 (±.118)	.006
	Cor-3	.360	.424	.064 (±.154)	.008
NFL East	Cor-1	.497	.381	−.116 (±.157)	.035
	Cor-3	.301	.143	.158 (±.198)	.041
NFL West	Cor-1	.334	.534	.200 (±.185)	.072
	Cor-3	.154	.100	−.054 (±.165)	.007
NHL	Cor-1	.523	.700	.162 (±.154)	.062
	Cor-3	.447	.458	.112 (±.206)	.015
NBA	Cor-1	.588	.608	.020 (±.104)	.002
	Cor-3	.294	.258	−.036 (±.230)	.002
All	Cor-1	.497	.618	.102 (±.056)	.028
	Cor-3	.305	.404	.073 (±.073)	.009

[a] Cor-1 and Cor-3 are the one- and three-year lagged correlations between final standings, respectively.

[b] The sign of b was reversed in order that a positive (negative) relationship between the player draft and equality of competition would be indicated by a positive (negative) b. This was necessary because a lower score on each of the indicators of equality of competition represented more equal competition.

[c] Significant at .05 level of probability.

TABLE 4

The Relationship Between the Reserve System and Equality of Competition

League	Indicator[a]	Mean Score of Indicator of Equality of Competition		Regression Coefficient (b)[b] (Standard error of b)	Partial Coefficient of Determination (r^2)
		Player Draft Present	Player Draft Absent		
A. Static Equality of Competition					
NBA	SDWP	.132	.142	.010 (±.019)	.016
All	SDWP	.127	.142	.040[c] (±.018)	.046
B. Dynamic Equality of Competition					
NBA	Cor-1	.588	.608	.020 (±.104)	.002
	Cor-3	.294	.258	−.036 (±.230)	.002
All	Cor-1	.556	.608	.049 (±.140)	.001
	Cor-3	.294	.258	−.041 (±.183)	.001

[a] Cor-1 and Cor-3 are the one- and three-year lagged correlations between final standings, respectively.

[b] The sign was reversed in order that a positive (negative) relationship between the player draft and equality of competition would be indicated by a positive (negative) b. This was necessary because a lower score on each of the indicators of equality of competition represented more equal competition.

[c] Significant at .05 level of probability.

This study supports the arguments of Rottenberg (1956), El Hodiri and Quirk (1971), and Noll and Okner (1971) that the restrictive procedures alter the initial allocation of rights to players from what they would be in a free market, but these procedures do not alter the final distribution of player talent enough to affect the ability of teams. With or without these procedures a player will tend to play for the team for which he has the highest value. Two practices facilitate the redistribution of talent when the free agent draft and the reserve system are in effect: the selling of players for cash and the trading of players of unequal ability. For example, team A may have a player who, for any number of reasons, is of more value to team B. Team A may sell the player to team B for cash or team A may trade the player to team B for a player who is of lesser value but also has a lower salary. This redistribution may occur when a financially weak team trades a star player, especially one in the twilight of his career, with a very high salary for a journeyman player with a smaller salary. Examples of such transactions abound in pro sports. The San Francisco Giants recently sold stars Sam McDowell and Juan Marichal for cash and traded Willie Mays to the New York Mets for another player and cash. This was done to bolster the Giants' financial position which had been weakened by low attendance. In basketball the financially troubled Virginia Squires sold Julius Erving to the New York Mets, a team better able to pay his high salary. It is interesting to note that clubs often trade players before they even have them; that is, they trade draft choices. By doing so, the distribution of player talent can be altered substantially. This was made evident when the Miami Dolphins, the previous Super Bowl winner, was tied for the most picks (22) in the 1974 college draft, and the worst team, the Houston Oilers, had the fewest choices (11). It is doubtful that such a distribution of selections will equalize talent.

In summary, the most plausible explanation for the findings of this study is that when owners have monopsony power, the distribution of player talent and consequently, the relative ability of teams, will be determined by the same forces as in a competitive market, namely the relative values of players to team owners.

THE FUTURE

Within the past few years there were significant changes in the free agent drafts and the reserve systems of the various sport leagues. These alterations are even more dramatic because these procedures had previously remained stable for so long. The following developments have occurred in the early 1970's.

1. Baseball's reserve system has been modified in two ways. As of 1974, baseball teams can no longer unilaterally determine the salary of players. Under the new rules if there is a disagreement concerning salary between the team and the player, the latter may demand that the dispute be brought before an arbitrator. The arbitrator is not to consider the financial positions of the two parties, only the player's physical, mental, and leadership abilities, his public appeal, and the length and consistency of his performance as a player. An interesting feature of this rule is that instead of reaching a compromise figure, the arbitrator must choose either the last offer by the club or the last demand by the player.

   Under the second modification, a player who has spent ten years in the major leagues can nullify a trade if he does not wish to play for a particular team. An example of this recently occurred when Ron Santo of the Chicago Cubs refused to be traded to the California Angels because he preferred to remain in Chicago. Subsequently, he agreed to be traded to the Chicago White Sox.

2. Hockey preceded baseball by four years in providing for arbitration in salary disputes between team owners and players. The arbitrator in this instance is an independent agent jointly agreed upon by the owners and the NHL's player association.

3. In 1973 a new hockey league, the World Hockey Association (WHA), was formed and began to compete with the NHL for players and spectators. The situation parallels that of the ABA-NBA struggle in basketball. The existence of two leagues provides a player with the opportunity of bargaining with more than one team for a higher salary. Consequently, the reserve systems and free agent drafts of the league have become ineffective. As in basketball, player salaries have soared so that they more accurately reflect the value of players to their team owners. The results of this study suggest that these events will not cause less equal competition among teams in the NHL.

4. The World Football League (WFL) was founded in 1974 and its founders, encouraged by the success of other challengers to establish leagues, have declared their intentions to compete with the NFL as a major league. If the WFL is successful, the reserve system and free agent draft in the NFL will probably be weakened as was the case in basketball and hockey.

Considering these changes and considering the changing views toward these monopsonistic procedures by the players, the Congress, the courts, and the fans, it is a distinct possibility that effective reserve systems may become a thing of the past. The improvement in the bargaining position of the player resulting from these changes may affect other aspects of these sports such as player salaries and ticket prices. The findings of this study suggest that equality of competition among teams will *not* be an aspect of sport which is affected.

REFERENCES

1. Canes M. E.: The Economics of Professional Sports. Unpublished Doctor's dissertation, University of California, 1970.
2. Canes, M. E.: Public Policy Toward Professional Team Sport. Paper presented at Conference on Government and Sports, the Brookings Institution, Washington, D.C., December 1971.
3. Coase R. H.: The problem of social cost. J. Law Econ., *3*:1–44, 1960.
4. Davis L.: The Ostriches: A Study in Cartel Leadership, Strategy, and Tactics. Paper presented at Conference on Government and Sports, the Brookings Institution, Washington, D.C., December 1971.
5. Durso J.: The All-American Dollar: The Big Business of Sport. Boston, Houghton Mifflin, 1971.
6. El Hodiri M., and Quirk J.: On the Economic Theory of a Professional Sports League. Paper presented at Conference on Government and Sports, the Brookings Institution, Washington, D.C., December 1971.
7. *Flood v. Kuhn et al.*, Supreme Court of the United States, Office of the Clerk, slip opinion, June 19, 1972, cetiorari to the United States Court of Appeals for the Second Circuit.
8. Jones J. C. H.: The economics of the National Hockey League. Canadian Journal of Economics, *2*:1–20 1969.
9. Koppett L.: In pay, N.B.A. is biggest league. The New York Times, March 11, 1973.
10. Noll R., and Okner B. A.: Statement before U.S. Senate Hearings, Professional Basketball, September 1971.
11. Rottenberg S.: The Baseball players' labor market. J. Polit. Econ., *64*:242–258, 1956.

12. Topkis J. H.: Monopoly in professional sports. The Yale Law Journal, *58*:692–712, 1949.
13. Topkis J. H.: The Superbowl and the Sherman Act: Professional Team Sports and the Antitrust Laws. Harvard Law Review, *81*:418–433, 1967.
14. U.S. Congress. Senate. Committee on the Judiciary, Subcommittee on Antitrust and Monopoly. Professional Basketball, Hearings, 92nd Cong., 2nd Sess., September 1971 to May 1972. Washington: Government Printing Office, 1972.
15. U.S. Congress. Senate. Committee on Commerce. *Federal Sports Act of 1972.* Hearings, 92nd Cong., 2nd Sess., June 1972. Washington: Government Printing Office, 1973.
16. Voight D. C.: American Baseball. Norman, Oklahoma, University of Oklahoma Press, 1966.

NOTES

1. E.g. The reserve system of baseball is contained in the "reserve clause" (paragraph 10/a/ of the Uniform Players' Contract). It stipulates that if a player and club cannot agree on the terms of a new contract for the next year then . . . the Club shall have the right by written notice to the player . . . to renew this contract for a period of one year for the same terms, except that the amount payable to the Player shall be such as the Club shall fix in said notice; provided, however, that said amount, if fixed by a Major League Club, shall be an amount payable at a rate not less than 80% of the rate stipulated for the preceding year.

2. For example, in 1968 Dave Parks played out his owner's option with the San Francisco 49ers and signed with the New Orleans Saints, and the two teams could not agree upon compensation. Commissioner Pete Rozelle prescribed that New Orleans give San Francisco their first round draft choice for the next two years. Most knowledgeable observers believe this decision was designed to discourage teams from signing players who had played out their option with other teams. Regardless of the intent, this was the effect, for players have since been unsuccessful in signing with other clubs after they have played out the options of their owners.

3. Compare the reserve clause of the National Basketball Association (NBA)—paragraph 22 of the Uniform Player Contract—with that of baseball (presented in footnote 1). The reserve clause in the NBA provides that if a player and club cannot agree on the terms of a new contract for the next year then ". . . this contract shall be deemed renewed and extended for one year, upon the same terms and conditions in all respects as provided herein, except that the compensation payable to the Player shall be the sum provided in the contract tendered to the Player pursuant to the provisions hereof, which compensation shall in no event be less than 75% of the compensation payable to the Player for the last playing season covered by this contract. . ."

4. Another factor which might be considered as a partial explanation of the difference in their effectiveness is the Supreme Court's anomalous exemption of baseball from antitrust laws and its concomitant sanctioning of baseball's reserve system. The applicability of antitrust laws to baseball was first considered by the Supreme Court in 1922 *(Federal Baseball Club of Baltimore. Inc. v. National League of Professional Baseball Clubs, et al.).* In what has been described as not one of Oliver Wendell Holmes' finest decisions, the Court found that the business of baseball was a purely state affair, not interstate commerce, and therefore immune from antitrust laws. This ruling has been upheld in subsequent cases, including Curt Flood's challenge of baseball's reserve clause *(Curtis C. Flood v. Bowie K. Kuhn, et al.,* 1972). In a 4–3 decision, the Supreme Court decided that, even though baseball ". . . is a business and it is engaged in interstate commerce," its immunity from antitrust should not be terminated by the Court. This action was taken despite the fact that in none of the cases involving other sports (football, boxing, basketball, hockey, and golf) was such an exemption permitted. Thus baseball's reserve system was sustained, thereby according team owners perpetual options on the service of players under contract. In contrast, it has been ruled the NBA's reserve system can only restrict players of teams for one additional year, making it, in effect, an option clause (e.g. *Lemat Corporation v. Richard F. Barry,* Illinois, 1969). However, this time restriction would not necessarily weaken the reserve system of NBA if the team owners in basketball refrained from bidding for the service of players who had become free agents. As described above, the National Football League is an example of a league in which an option clause has constituted an effective reserve system; this effectiveness is a result of the reluctance of team owners to negotiate with free agents. Thus, the different treatment of the reserve systems of baseball and basketball by the judiciary does not explain the difference in their effectiveness.

5. Davis, Lance: The Ostriches: A Study in Cartel Leadership, Strategy, and Tactics (preliminary paper prepared for the Conference on Government and Sports, The Brookings Institution, December 1971, Washington, D.C., p. 13). The major leagues of baseball have experimented with many procedures for the most economical method of recruitment of new players. They were quite successful as indicated by the ability of minor league teams to extract payments from the major leagues for players and the high payments made to some "bonus babies" between World War II and the reinstitution of an effective free agent draft in 1964.

the ncaa: a socio-economic analysis: the development of the college sports cartel from social movement to formal organization

JAMES V. KOCH and WILBERT M. LEONARD, 2D

"... the NCAA is a body primarily designed to protect and defend its member institutions from the professional sports world and to make sure that collegiate sports get its share of the sports business pie."

—Senator Marlow Cook of Kentucky (1973)

The National Collegiate Athletic Association (NCAA) is the dominant organizational force in intercollegiate athletics today. Over 840 colleges and universities maintain some type of membership in the NCAA. All universities which operate "big-time" intercollegiate athletic programs are members of this voluntary association.

The financial status of the NCAA is hardly threatened. The ABC television network paid the NCAA 36 million dollars in 1975 and 1976 for the privilege of televising collegiate football games. [1] This payment rises to 118 million dollars in the years 1978 through 1981. [2] Hence, there is ample reason to examine the NCAA as a socio-economic phenomenon.

In the following pages we examine the evolution of the NCAA from a social movement to a formal organization which today is a centerpiece of the sports establishment. Pervasive tensions that afflict the NCAA are examined in light of the theory of social movements and economic cartel theory. The following specific issues are ad-

Reprinted from the American Journal of Economics and Sociology, *37*:225–239, 1978. Copyright 1978 by the American Journal of Economics and Sociology, Inc., 50 East 69th Street, New York, New York 10021.

dressed: 1) the heterogeneity of the NCAA's membership; 2) financial aid to athletes and the matter of "need"; 3) the NCAA versus other sports cartels; 4) the financial problems which strain the NCAA; 5) the tendency of the NCAA's membership to pursue legal action to accomplish ends that the NCAA frustrates; and 6) present and anticipated future adjustments undertaken by the NCAA to shore up its hesitant existence as a formal organization and economic cartel.

We argue that it is necessary to weld together both the sociological and the economic perspectives in order to understand the development of the NCAA. Two often noted features of modern collegiate sports—commercialization and bureaucratization—serve as the focus of this multidisciplinary approach. It is interesting to note that both sociological and economic models suggest similar explanations for the evolution of the NCAA. This is encouraging in an age where the methods and logics of an increasingly large number of academic disciplines are often held to be incommensurate. Understanding of the unity of science is not yet at hand; however, this should not discourage us from attempts to probe and identify whatever interfaces may exist between and among academic disciplines.

I. THE NCAA AS A SOCIAL MOVEMENT

Social movements—collectivities acting with some continuity to promote or resist change in society—come in a myriad of different sizes and forms. Among the most common types are migratory, expressive, utopian, reform, revolutionary, and resistance movements.[3] The NCAA, originating as a reformist movement, has matured to the point where either the outright death of the NCAA, or its substantial restructuring, can now be expected.

The reform genre of social movements is characterized by an attempt to modify some component of society without radically transforming the entire social order. That part of society that the NCAA originally attempted to remedy was the unfashionable violence and other abuses that were occurring in intercollegiate athletics, football in particular, during the late 19th and early 20th centuries. It is not unreasonable to suggest, particularly in view of the supporting data presented below, that the mayhem associated with intercollegiate football's "flying wedge" was primarily responsible for the formation of the NCAA in 1905.

Social movements have a life cycle. It is seldom that two social movements have the same life history; however, there are sufficient common denominators among social movements to enable us to advance a typical life cycle hypothesis for a social movement. Most "mature" social movements transverse through four stages: 1) unrest; 2) excitement; 3) formalization; and 4) institutionalization. Movements, such as the NCAA, which pass through these formal stages become the formal organizations which comprise the institutional fabric of society.

UNREST. The catalyst to all social movements is the perception that something is wrong and must be rectified. Social unrest is often in the vanguard as a precipitating factor. In the early years of the 20th century, intercollegiate athletics were disreputable and struggling. The rugged, violent nature of intercollegiate football, typified by mass formations and gang tackling, and desperately inadequate equipment, led to many injuries and deaths. In the 1905 season, 18 football players were killed on the intercollegiate gridiron. Unfortunately, colleges and universities were not organized in such a way that they could constructively change football's rules and regulations; therefore, many academic institutions reacted by eliminating football as a sponsored intercollegiate sport. It is accurate to state that the public at large was somewhat revolted at the violence which permeated intercollegiate football.

Midway through the 1905 football season, President Theodore Roosevelt became the cata-

lyst for important changes in intercollegiate football. It is reported that after "T.R." viewed a picture of a badly mauled football player, he threatened to abolish the game if remedial steps were not taken to modify its most objectionable aspects.

EXCITEMENT. The transition from the unrest to the excitement stage is characterized by a clear identification of the problem needing attention. Whereas during the stage of unrest conditions are vague and ill-defined, during the stage of excitement conditions are sufficiently identified that specific action can be taken. To convert the unrest into action, a skillful and persuasive leader is needed—a Teddy Roosevelt. Roosevelt's threat to discontinue intercollegiate football was taken seriously. As a result, an initial meeting of Ivy League schools to consider a course of action blossomed into a larger meeting attended by representatives of 62 colleges and universities.

FORMALIZATION. On December 28, 1905, a committee of the 62 schools was appointed to seek merger with an already existing Football Rules Committee which had no real connection to academia. This resulted in the formation of the Intercollegiate Athletic Association, the forerunner of the NCAA. The formalization stage of the life cycle of a social movement is characterized by delegation and clarification of authority over business matters and rules, and a general statement of the organization's ideology. This is almost precisely what occurred during the formative years of the NCAA. One important product of this process was the approval of a dramatic innovation, the forward pass. Sanctioning of the forward pass clarified an otherwise murky situation in terms of football rules. More important, it opened up the game of intercollegiate football, and ultimately rendered obsolete the mass physical mayhem which had characterized the flying wedge. Finally, it also tremendously increased spectator interest in intercollegiate football and thereby hastened the development of big-time, commercialized intercollegiate football as we know it today.

INSTITUTIONALIZATION. When a social movement such as the NCAA becomes a part of the established social order, it ceases to be a social movement in the traditional sense. Instead, it becomes a formal organization with characteristic bureaucratic structures, specific goals, highly specialized division of labor, a complex set of formal and informal rules and regulations, hierarchical authority, frequent impersonality, and visible concern for the perpetuation of its own existence. In the case of the NCAA, a thick book of regulations prescribe a multitude of activities that never entered the minds of most athletes and coaches.

DISSOLUTION. Some social movements never reach this stage; there is some evidence that the NCAA as we know it may be developing intolerable internal fissures and stresses which will result in its dissolution as an organization. It is not outlandish to suggest that the NCAA may permute itself into a large number of sect-like bands, each doggedly pursuing parochial goals that have been found to be unrealistic for the entire NCAA community.

II. THE NCAA AS A CARTEL

In its social intercourse the NCAA attempts to maintain the fiction that it is the stronghold of amateur athletics and collegiate physical fitness. In fact, the NCAA is a ". . . business-like cartel composed of university-firms which have varying desires to restrict competition and maximize profits in the area of intercollegiate athletics". [4]

A cartel has been defined as ". . . a group of independent firms attempting, via collusive agreement, to behave as a collective monopoly". [5] The NCAA qualifies as a business cartel because it (1) sets input prices that can be paid for student-athletes; (2) regulates the usage of those student-athletes in terms of duration and intensity; (3) regulates output in terms of the number and length of athletic contests; (4) occasionally pools and distributes the profits of the cartel earned from activities such as the television football package; (5) disseminates information concerning transactions, market conditions, and business accounting techniques; and (6) polices the behavior of cartel members and levies penalties for infractions. [6]

The NCAA has been noticeably less successful as a cartel than other well-known cartels such as the Organization of Petroleum Exporters (OPEC). The major causes of this are the organizational structure and diverse membership of the NCAA. The NCAA has so many members with such diverse interests that the membership can seldom unite in common interest upon any subject of financial or competitive substance. The large number of universities involved, and the numerous means by which the universities can

undertake clandestine actions (for example, via faithful alumni) make enforcement of the cartel's rules not only selective, but also substantially ineffective.

The NCAA is a relatively ineffective cartel primarily because of the market structure in which it operates. The most destructive feature of this market structure, from the NCAA's standpoint, is the heterogeneity of member interests. What pleases Ohio State University does not necessarily please Valdosta State College, much less Shimer College. When the verbiage of amateurism and physical fitness is stripped away, the votes of individual universities and the actions of the NCAA seem nearly always to be indicative of financial self-interest. That is the core of the NCAA's problems.

What an economist refers to as a cartel is typically labeled a bureaucratic, large-scale social organization by a sociologist. The organizational structure of the NCAA cartel evinces three important ingredients of any social structure, namely, specialization, centralization, and formalization. The specialization of the NCAA can readily be seen in the growth of its professional personnel. The NCAA's "enforcement team"—those individuals whose jobs are devoted to uncovering violations of cartel rules—now numbers eleven and includes five lawyers and a former agent of the Federal Bureau of Investigation. [7]

The centralization of the NCAA is physically represented by the NCAA headquarters building in Mission, Kansas. Structurally, the 18-member NCAA Council directs the Association between its annual January meetings, and an Executive Committee of 10 members transacts daily business. The formal authority of the 800-plus members of the NCAA is therefore highly centralized where day-by-day operations are concerned.

The formalization of the NCAA's roles and authority is best symbolized by the thickness of the annual *NCAA Manual*, [8] which laboriously details how many paid visits a high school basketball player may make to a college campus, under what circumstances a school may pay for flying lessons if an athlete is enrolled in an aviation course, and so forth. At first glance it appears that the NCAA has a rule for every situation that could conceivably occur. The richness of human behavior, however, quickly disposes of that notion.

III. DIVISIONS IN THE NCAA: HOW MANY?

The NCAA has maintained three legislative divisions since 1973. Division I (University Division) membership numbers almost 140. Division I schools operate big-time football and/or basketball programs. The NCAA defeated a proposal at its January, 1977, meetings which would have further subdivided the organization into four separate legislative branches. A similar proposal, this one endorsed by the NCAA Council, was considered at the January, 1978, meetings. This latter proposal allows the super football powers considerable latitude in molding their own rules and financial requirements. One requirement for membership in this division would be that the university's football team must have averaged at least 17,000 attendance at its home football games over the previous four years. This requirement would reduce the membership of the top division to approximately 65 members.

The NCAA would not be so responsive to the demands of a small minority of its membership for a new division were it not for the threat of the football super powers withdrawing from the NCAA and later negotiating their own television contract. This possibility has been bandied about and openly threatened recently because of a revenue-sharing proposal submitted by Stephen Horn, President of California State University at Long Beach.[9] President Horn has asked the NCAA to divide the lucrative football contract television revenues among the entire NCAA membership. Each Division I school would have received 49,000 dollars in 1976 under President Horn's proposal.[10]

The revenue sharing proposal of President Horn has been labeled a "Robin Hood" proposal and was soundly defeated at the January, 1976, NCAA meetings. Had it passed, it is likely that the most important football schools which have already banded together under the guise of the "College Football Association," would have initiated withdrawal from the NCAA and later have negotiated their own television package. That television package would probably be worth more than the $18 million paid to the NCAA by the ABC television network in 1976 because the super football powers would guarantee that only the best teams and the most interesting games would be televised each week. The current NCAA television package limits the appearances of individual teams and guarantees that television appearances will be spread among conferences and geographic areas.

It is clear that the Robin Hood revenue-sharing proposal would be detrimental to the financial interests of the big-time football powers. The University of Notre Dame, for example, has appeared as part of the NCAA's regular season television package ten times in the past five years. Those appearances have earned the University of Notre Dame well over a million dollars.[11]

The creation of a "Super" Division of the NCAA is an open attempt to allow the big-time athletic powers to go their own way within the confines of the NCAA. It is not clear, however, that even the Super Division's membership is sufficiently homogeneous to achieve stability. Balkanization of the NCAA into numerous divisions cannot be accomplished without costs. The gap between the Super Division members and the remaining 750-plus members will only be accentuated. This possibility is already apparent in NCAA convention voting patterns where strong and almost irreconcilable differences have resulted in hot disputes. The proliferation of divisions may only accentuate the instability of the NCAA rather than reducing it.

IV. THE "NEED" ISSUE

A recurring proposal confronting the NCAA suggests that the NCAA eliminate "full-ride" athletic scholarships which universities are currently allowed to give to promising student-athletes without reference to the financial need of the student-athlete. The "need" system would tailor the size of the scholarship given the student-athlete to the ability to pay and income of the student-athlete's family.

A need-based financial aid system for Division I schools was narrowly defeated at the January, 1976, NCAA meetings. Need-based scholarships drew strong support from private schools and those schools in the lower competitive rungs of Division I. University of the Pacific President Stanley McCaffrey pointed out that ". . . need doesn't discriminate and it's fair in its provisions. The thing which students and faculties criticize most is making athletes special".[12]

The primary attraction of need-based scholarships, however, is the money that they would save athletic departments. Stanford University, it is estimated, would save 150,000 dollars annually if need-based scholarships were implemented. [13] The most fervent opponents of need-based scholarships were typically large state universities. Need-based scholarships would save them relatively less money. An unstated rationale for opposition to need-based scholarships probably also included the implicit threat that "need" contains for the current competitive balance. Need-based scholarships would help some schools, particularly private schools, far more than others. In the last analysis, a shift in competitive balance is ultimately reflected in gate revenues and similar financial variables.

The cleavages between the super and not-so-super powers regarding need-based scholarships bring to mind the "iron law" of oligarchy of Robert Michaels, the German sociologist. Michaels observed that "Who says organization says oligarchy". [14] Oligarchy, the power or rule of the few, is clearly extant in the domination of the NCAA by a minority of its membership (the big-time football powers) and the refusal of these members of the NCAA to agree to need-based scholarships.

V. THE NCAA VERSUS OTHER ATHLETIC CARTELS

The NCAA has engaged in continuous battle with other athletic cartels. At the collegiate level, the NCAA clearly dominates the field of men's intercollegiate athletics. Its only serious rival, the National Association of Intercollegiate Athletics (NAIA), claims as members only those schools operating small-time programs. The NAIA has no television contract.

In the area of women's intercollegiate athletics, however, the NCAA has repeatedly stubbed its toes in its drive for dominance. The predominant organization in women's intercollegiate athletics is the Association of Intercollegiate Athletics for Women (AIAW). The AIAW has resisted the NCAA's attempts to apply the entire body of men's regulations to female athletics. The NCAA purports to desire to do so because of the legal pressures of Title IX of the Civil Rights Act of 1972, as amended. The NCAA argues that it would be illegal to treat male intercollegiate athletes different than their female counterparts.

The AIAW's rules governing women's intercollegiate athletics are already quite different from those applied to male athletics. The AIAW

perceives, probably correctly, that the primary issue at stake is control of a burgeoning area of interest rather than Title IX requirements. The haste of the NCAA in this direction has been increased by the announcement that the AIAW will soon sign its own television contract involving as many as 16 sports. [15]

The NCAA had previously rejected a bid by the AIAW for a merger of equals. The key to that AIAW proposal was a provision that each institutional member of the merged organization have two votes—one for men's athletics and one for women's athletics. Such a power distribution is hardly what the NCAA has in mind when it talks of merger. As a result, a comprehensive intercollegiate athletic organization for both men and women is not in sight. It is possible that the intransigence of the NCAA will delay this possibility for such a length of time that the AIAW will no longer be interested in the merger. Such a paradigm is consistent with organization theory dealing with bureaucracies.

The NCAA has also conducted long-standing battles with the Amateur Athletic Union (AAU) and the United States Olympic Committee (USOC). These battles have stimulated action at the level of the United States Congress. Each of these organizations exhibits its share of petulance and parochiality in its relationships with the others. The NCAA, for example, routinely punishes athletes who participate in AAU-sanctioned meets which do not also have NCAA approval precisely because they are AAU-sanctioned. Patriotism is no barrier to such behavior. Visiting athletic teams from countries such as the Soviet Union have on several occasions played less than representative American teams because one or more of the above organizations refuses to sanction the competition. Individual athletes are caught in between.

The NCAA has been relatively more successful in its relations with the professional sports leagues. While the NCAA has not yet found the will and/or the way to force professional sports leagues to help finance the intercollegiate sports which act as development leagues for the professional leagues, the NCAA has been notably successful in maintaining its dominance over intercollegiate athletics.

The judicial battles involving the NCAA are evidence in favor of the sociological theory of structural functionalism. In this view, sport is viewed as an institution which maintains values, a network of social positions, roles, and norms. This institution is intimately related to, and affected by other institutions in society, for example, the family, the educational establishment, the courts, and so forth. What takes place in one institutional sphere, for example, intercollegiate athletics, will have reverberations on other institutions. The intercollegiate sports world cannot be viewed in isolation from the society in which it operates.

VI. FINANCIAL STRAINS

Like any cartel whose members have dissimilar revenues and costs, the NCAA finds it difficult to legislate a set of rules which are judged to be fair by its entire constituency. Nonetheless, in a time when there is mounting financial pressure being exerted upon all segments of higher education, there has been a strong incentive for the NCAA to introduce cost-cutting measures.

The need for cost-cutting measures has been exacerbated by the rising demand of women's intercollegiate athletics for increasing funding, if not outright equality in funding. At the University of Texas, the budget for women's intercollegiate athletics rose from $27,000 to $128,000 in three years. [16] The coverage of Title IX explicitly includes women's intercollegiate athletics. Directors of Men's Intercollegiate Athletics at "big-time" universities shudder to think that gate revenues from men's football will pay for the operation and travel of the women's field hockey team. John A. Fuzak, of Michigan State University, has labeled financial equality for men and women in intercollegiate athletics as "economic insanity". [17]

The impact of Title IX on both men's and women's intercollegiate athletics is typified by the situation at the University of Illinois. Eighty-two percent of the total budget for men's intercollegiate athletics of all types there is derived from gate revenues in men's football and men's basketball. [18] Cecil Coleman, the university's director of men's intercollegiate athletics, argues that such revenues belong to men's intercollegiate athletics and therefore cannot justifiably be disbursed to support women's intercollegiate athletics under the guise of equal treatment. In response to this type of problem, Senator John Tower of Texas has proposed amendments to Title IX regulations which would allow individual revenue-generating sports to retain all or most of the revenues directly attributable to those sports. The future of these amendments is in doubt at this juncture although the NCAA has made impassioned pleas in their support.

The financial strains of the NCAA are but one aspect of the precarious equilibrium which exists between the NCAA and broader society. Racism, sexism, and elitism also are causes of tension in the NCAA. However, these matters seem inevitably to take a back seat to financial issues when the NCAA seriously debates structural changes.

VII. EVOLUTION AND ADJUSTMENT BY THE NCAA

The NCAA has not passively accepted the financial difficulties which afflict most of its membership. Proposals for a Super Division and the need-based scholarships are examples of attempts to reduce the financial pressures felt by individual members. A record 225 amendments to existing regulations were submitted to the NCAA membership at the January, 1976, convention. [19] The great majority of the suggested changes dealt with cost reduction, but were not approved. The explanation for this seems to be that many of the changes would also have upset the perceived competitive balance in the NCAA in addition to possibly saving the entire membership money. The need-based scholarship proposal is one such example of this "prisoner's dilemma" type of situation.

The major cost-reducing rules adopted by the NCAA related to limiting the number of full-ride scholarships that can be legally granted by a particular university. In football, for example, the number of full-ride scholarships that a Division I team can offer is limited to 30 new scholarships per year, and a total of 95 scholarships overall. Such a rule may at first seem to injure schools with big-time programs by not allowing them to make as many scholarship offers as they would prefer. The key, however, is the 95 overall limitation on scholarships. Most schools have indicated satisfaction with this rule because it gives them the legal and moral sanction of the NCAA when they cancel the scholarship grants of those athletes who do not become stars. Such scholarship terminations have caused severe public relations problems in the past. Now, they are "required" for large numbers of student-athletes.

The NCAA has also adopted scholarship limitations for other sports. A maximum of 80 scholarships may be granted in all sports other than football and basketball by one university in one year. This is particularly important to universities which have felt that they have confronted the "prisoner's dilemma" in minor sports competition. This regulation, which is supplemented by limitations in each individual sport, enables each university to scale down its financial commitment to the non-revenue producing sports without suffering competitive humiliation.

In other cost-cutting moves, the NCAA has also placed new and stricter limits on the number of coaches that schools may employ, the number of times that coaches may visit a prospective student-athlete, and the number of visits that a prospective student-athlete may make to a particular campus at the expense of that particular institution. Coaches operating big-time athletic programs believe limits on visitations will favor them at the expense of less publicized opponents.

VIII. LEGAL CHALLENGES

The NCAA is a voluntary association, a formally organized social unit made up of members who belong by choice. It is important to be cognizant of this when analyzing the numerous legal suits involving the NCAA and student-athletes. Several judicial bodies have held that it is not appropriate for the courts to force the NCAA to alter its rules or actions if NCAA membership is voluntary and no apparent civil right has been violated.

An example in point is the recent dispute involving traveling squad limitations placed upon visiting teams by the NCAA convention in 1975. The number of athletes who might travel to an away game and dress for the game was limited to 48 in football and 10 in basketball. The University of Alabama in particular objected to the 48 player squad limit. It obtained a temporary injunction against the enforcement of this rule in a Tuscaloosa, Alabama, District Court.[20] This injunction was vacated shortly thereafter by the Fifth United States Court of Appeals in New Orleans.[21] The appellate court reasoned that the NCAA was a voluntary association with which the court should not interfere.

The empirical truth of the matter concerning legal suits against the NCAA is that the NCAA nearly always wins when the case is heard at the Federal District Court level or above. The strategy of the universities and individuals who sue the NCAA seems to be to find some state court which will issue a restraining order or injunction against the enforcement of some NCAA rule or dictum. Ideally, this forestalling of NCAA action should last sufficiently long that the student-athlete involved can finish the sports season.

The NCAA sometimes has unexpected problems even when it emerges victorious from a court test. In 1973, the NCAA declared ineligible Robert Parish, the superb basketball center at Centenary College. Centenary College was placed upon long-term probation for granting Parish a full-ride scholarship when according to the rules then in force (which were changed a week afterward) Parish was not eligible for one. Hence, the college was put on probation and Parish was held ineligible. Nonetheless, the college continued to play Parish for four seasons. The NCAA reacted by refusing to include any performances of Parish or Centenary College in its official statistical summaries. This has inspired the comment that both Parish and Centenary College really do not exist.[22] They do, however, and the college has played a full schedule of NCAA members each season. Parish was among the first collegiate basketball players drafted by the professional basketball teams in 1976.[23]

The NCAA leadership has proposed that member universities be required to pay all the NCAA's legal expenses if the member university ultimately lost its suit *and* the member university had not first exhausted internal NCAA appeals procedures. This amendment was defeated at the January, 1976, NCAA meetings, primarily, it seems, because some universities thought that they would have to pay for legal expenses regardless of the outcome of the suit. That was not the intent.

IX. SUMMARY AND EVALUATION

An athletic organization which attempted to write common rules for, and include under one roof, the Cincinnati Redlegs baseball team, and the Little League baseball teams of Cincinnati, Ohio, would doubtless have problems. This, however, is the type of circumstance in which the NCAA finds itself. Its membership contains universities which operate athletic programs which are professional in everything except name; the membership also includes colleges which field club teams composed of amateurs in the traditional sense.

It is not clear that the NCAA can, despite its amoeba-like tendency to create new divisions, survive the tremendous heterogeneity of its membership. Very few cartels have ever succeeded in similar situations. Further, certain of the members of the NCAA are sufficiently well-heeled financially that they are able to delay and frustrate the NCAA with innumerable Lilliputian legal suits. The NCAA typically wins such legal battles in the end, but only after the subject of controversy has often become moot.

As early as 1910, the NCAA adopted the following formal objective: ". . . the regulation and supervision of college athletics throughout the United States in order that the athletic activities of the colleges and universities of the United States may be maintained on an ethical plane in keeping with the dignity and high purpose of education." While it is tempting to argue that goal displacement has taken place, a more realistic scrutiny of the chronology of the NCAA must question whether this objective was ever realized at any time in any form.

The NCAA has evolved over time from a small, lower pressure organization composed of members with similar interests. Such was the case prior to 1947. Today the NCAA is a large, unwieldy organization which seldom achieves consensus on any topic of substance. The "Golden Years" of the life cycle of the NCAA have probably passed. The future is likely to bring with it the demise of the NCAA as we now know it. In its place is likely to arise either a series of separate organizations with more homogeneous memberships, or an NCAA which has decentralized nearly all important powers to its constituent divisions. The key to this development will be, as in the past, the financial character of modern day big-time intercollegiate athletics. The irony is that the very forces responsible for the growth of the NCAA—the commercialization, bureaucratization, and professionalization of collegiate sports—may be responsible for its demise.

REFERENCES

1. Van Dyne, Larry: ABC will pay 118 million to televise college football. The Chronicle of Higher Education, June 27:6, 1977.
2. Ibid.
3. The definition and views of social movements which are developed here are consistent with the classic statements on social movements of Blumer. See Blumer, Herbert: Collective behavior. *In* New Outline of the Principles of Sociology. 2nd Edition. Edited by A. E. Lee. New York, Barnes and Noble, 1951.
4. Koch, James V.: A troubled cartel: The NCAA. Law and Contemporary Problems, *38*:135–150, 1973.
5. Hirshleifer, Jack: Price Theory and Applications. Englewood Cliffs, New Jersey, Prentice-Hall, Inc., 1976, p. 296.
6. The character of the NCAA as a cartel and its production function are discussed in greater detail in Koch, James V.: The economics of "big-time intercollegiate athletics. Soc. Sci. Q., *52*:248–260, 1971.
7. Van Dyne, Larry: College sports' enforcement squad. Chron. Higher Educ., *14*:1, 1977.
8. For example, the NCAA Manual, 1977-1978. Kansas City, Missouri, National Collegiate Athletic Association, 1977.
9. Van Dyne, Larry: Behind those Saturday football telecasts. The Chronicle of Higher Education, October 20:3, 1975.
10. Ibid., p. 6.
11. Ibid.
12. Keith, Larry: A narrow defeat for need. Sports Illustrated, *44*:52–53, 1976.
13. Ibid., p. 52.
14. Michaels, Robert: Policat Parties: A Sociological Study of the Oligarchical Tendencies of Modern Democracy. Glencoe, Ill., The Free Press, 1949.
15. Watkins, Beverly T.: Pact offered for televising women's sports. Chron. Higher Educ., January 26:8, 1976.
16. Scorecard. Sports Illustrated, *43*:18, 1975.
17. Fuzak, John A.: NCAA News, *12*:17, 1975.
18. NCAA News, *12*:6, 1975.
19. NCAA News, *13*:1, 1976.
20. The original injunction was handed down on September 8, 1975, in the District Court of Tuscaloosa, Alabama.
21. University of Alabama v. National Collegiate Athletic Association, Fifth United States Court of Appeals, Louisiana, September 17, 1975.
22. Moses, Sam: Invisible in the Post. Sports Illustrated, *43*:67–68, 1975.
23. The Parish incident is a good example of the sociological distinction between manifest and latent functions. Manifest functions are those that are acknowledged, foreseen, and generally agreed upon. Latent functions are unanticipated and unforeseen. The Parish case vividly illustrates the latent consequences of an action.

the regional distribution of sport organizations as a function of political cleavages

PEKKA KIVIAHO

Regional variation is observed in the distribution of social activity which is manifested not only as quantitative accumulation but also as qualitative differences. In modern sport the quantitative regional variation in industrialized societies is connected with the regional variation particularly with the degrees of industrialization (Euler 1953, 175–180). This means for instance in Finland the quantitative relative accumulation of all kinds of sport activities in the cities and urban areas of the industrial southern Finland (Kiviaho 1970b, 1971). Besides quantitative accumulation, sport has undergone qualitative regional differentiation. In a study dealing with the relative support of national central sport federations, the Finnish Central Sports Federation (SVUL), the Workers' Sport Federation (TUL), the Central League of Workers' Sport Clubs (TUK), the Central Federation of Swedish Sports Organizations in Finland (CIF), and the Finnish Football Association (SPL), within economic areas (Kiviaho 1970b, 25) it was found that the support varies fairly much between the different economic areas.

A detailed examination of the various central organizations' support areas which has been done at the level of communes, indicates that the relative support of the different central organizations is almost entirely independent of the distribution of the membership density [1] of all organizations and can be explained by a different kind of approach.

A more detailed examination revealed another fact, which has a relevant bearing on the present study, namely that the municipalities in which the different organizations are strongly or weakly supported are regionally grouped into separate areas, and each is a stronghold of some of the organizations. SVUL is most strongly supported in southern, western and southwestern Finland, TUL in the urban areas of southern and central Finland and in the rural communes of eastern and northern Finland, TUK in the urban areas of southern and southwestern Finland, CIF in the Swedish-speaking coastal areas, and SPL in the towns and urban areas of southern and central Finland and the adjoining municipalities (Kiviaho 1971).

The present study is based on the notion that the changes of social structure and the features of social structure are related to the spreading and organizing of the sport movement. The study will concentrate on those factors that cause regional differences in the support of different central organizations. The purpose is to create a descriptive model in which certain features of social structure and behaviour can be related to features which describe the support of central sport organizations.

FACTORS AFFECTING THE CHOICE OF SPORT ORGANIZATION

The birth of separate sport organizations is also in Finland linked with the differences between linguistic and social groups due to social circumstances. At the end of the last century sport spread first among the middle and upper social classes through their own associations, youth and pupil organizations. The labour sport movement also became part of the political labour movement towards the end of the 19th century through clubs which were established by workers' associations and trade unions (Halila 1959, 73–87).

The organizational division of the Finnish sport movement into the Workers' Sport Federation (TUL) and the Finnish Gymnastic and Sports League (SVUL, from 1961 called the Finnish Central Sport Federation) dates back to the civil war of 1918. SVUL was officially established in 1906, and TUL in 1919 through the initiative of 56 clubs expelled from SVUL, because they took an active part in the civil war on the red side. In addition to these two central organizations Finland has a separate Swedish organization the Central Federation of Swedish Sports Organizations in Finland (CIF) formed in 1912, a central organization for soccer and bandy called the Finnish Football Association (SPL) set up in 1907, and the central League of Workers' Sports Clubs (TUK) which was formed in 1959 by the clubs that were expelled or withdrew from TUL.

Historically the organizational division of the Finnish sport movement into several central sport federations is thus connected with linguistic and social group differences caused by social circumstances, which differences still appear to affect the regional support of central sport federations. The support of sport organizations appears to have a close connection with the support of political ideologies and with the regional differences between the two linguistic groups, as is shown by cartograms which illustrate the distribution of political support and the location of the different organizations' support and core areas (Rantala 1971) and by preliminary analyses and by interview questionnaire results (Kiviaho 1970a, 138–143, 1971, 1972). Historically it is evident that the birth and stabilization of the Finnish political system and the birth and stabilization of sport organizations are related events both in terms of time and substance. The social set-up as it was shaped at the beginning of the century, i.e. the differences between linguistic and social groups, is reflected in and affects both present political life and the organizational activities of sport (see e.g. Lipset and Rokkan 1967, 50). In fact, it has been found in many connections also in Finland that political tradition is one of the most central factors that determine and account for political behaviour (Allardt and Pesonen 1967; Sänkiaho 1968, 112–173) together with certain structural variables (Allardt 1963; Sänkiaho 1958, 173). Therefore, it appears natural to assume that political tradition has a great effect also on the present support of sport organizations. It is equally obvious that neither political nor organizational tradition nor political and organizational support can survive in a situation in which the structural preconditions, i.e. the social basis of support, are totally lacking (Allardt and Pesonen 1967). The political cleavages of a given period measured, for instance, by means of the support of the left and the right are the result of different kinds of structural and traditional factors, as is the distribution of organizational support. Thus politial tradition and social structure influence organizational distribution both directly and through political cleavages. In Figure 1 these connections are indicated by dotted lines. One may, however, alternatively assume that while a suitable political cleavage has been necessary at the initial stage of different organizations, it still ultimately determines organizational distribution and precedes it. These relationships have been indicated by unbroken lines.

If the assumptions incorporated in the model are valid, the correlation between political cleavages and organizational distribution should be higher than the correlations of political tradition and social structure with organizational distribution, in other words $r_{34} > r_{14}$ or r_{24}.

Similarly, the control of political cleavages should account for the correlations between organizational distribution and political tradition or social structure i.e. $r_{14.3} = 0$. and $r_{24.3} = 0$. Further, the political cleavages should account for a larger proportion of the variance of organizational distribution than political tradition and social structure combined and approximately as much as all the factors together, i.e. $R^2_{4(3)} > R^2_{4(21)}$ and $R^2_{4(3)} \approx R^2_{4(321)}$.

The purpose of the study is, therefore, to examine to what extent political cleavages can be regarded as the mechanism through which the effects of political tradition and social structure on organizational distribution are reflected, and what are the direct and indirect relations between these factors and organizational distribution.

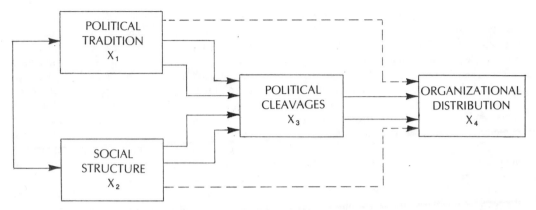

FIG. 1. The effects of political tradition, social structure and political cleavages on organizational distribution

RESEARCH MATERIAL AND VARIABLES

The research material covers all Finnish communes with the exception of the communes of the island of Ahvenanmaa and four minor municipalities according to the commune division of 1960. The material consists of 73 towns, 455 rural communes, or the total of 528 communes. The data concerning the support of sport organizations have been obtained from the club-wise information collected and filed by central sport federations and their district organizations. The variables that describe the number of organization members by commune are mainly from 1965, but in some cases the data had to be complemented with the corresponding data of 1964 or 1966. A more detailed description of data collection and its reliability has been presented elsewhere (Kiviaho 1970b, 2–5).

The study is limited to organized sport activities of central sport federations and their members, and only the Finnish Central Sports Federation (SVUL) and the Workers' Sport Federation (TUL). The other smaller central organizations have been omitted from the analysis: The Central League of Workers' Sport Clubs (TUK), the Finnish Football Association (SPL) whose member clubs represent all central organizations, and the Central Federation of Swedish Sports Organizations in Finland (CIF) which is the sport organization of the Swedish-speaking population only. The omission of these central organizations naturally makes it more difficult to obtain a general idea of the role of political factors in the organizational life of sport. The deci-

sion can, however, be motivated by the simplification of the methods of analysis and by the fact that the combined membership of SVUL and TUL covers about 85% of sport organization membership and their district organizations cover roughly the whole country. There were a total of 344 communes or 67% of all communes, in which only SVUL and/or TUL were represented. Since the analysis contains only such communes in which only SVUL and/or TUL are represented, the dependent variable—organizational distribution—has been measured with the proportion of TUL supporters from the total number of sport club members in a commune.

Voting behaviour has been chosen instead of party membership to describe political tradition and cleavages, because participation in party activities varies in different social classes. Thus, for instance, the supporters of the leftist parties have generally been found to be more active in party affairs than the supporters of the rightwing parties who in turn are more active in voluntary organizations (Blom 1971).

Political cleavages have been measured with the proportion of the votes for the leftist parties, the Social Democratic Party (SDP), the Social Democratic League (TPSL), the Finnish People's Democratic League (SKDL), from the total amount of votes in the national election of 1966 (SVT XXIX A:29) or a year later than the data of organizational distribution. Political tradition has been measured with the proportion of the votes for the leftwing parties from the total amount of votes in the national election of 1929 (SVT XXIX A:14). The election of 1929 has been chosen as the indicator of political tradition mainly because a second leftist party (the present SKDL) in addition to the Social Democratic Party took part in the national election.

The selection of the factors of social structure is difficult because it has been found in several studies that the social background of organizational and party support is heterogeneous and complex (Allardt and Pesonen 1967; Kiviaho 1970a, 140; Sänkiaho 1968, 173). Earlier it has been found, however, that the support of SVUL is connected with agricultural predominance and the support of TUL with industrialization, and the correlations between the variables of organization support and structural factors indicated that other structural variables have clearly lower correlations with organizational support (Kiviaho 1970a, 138–143). Similarly, social class has been found to be significant in the selection of sport organization, SVUL being mainly the organization of farmers and middle or upper classes and TUL almost exclusively the organization of industrial workers and the lower class (Kiviaho 1972). On the basis of these studies social structure has been measured here with a variable which shows the proportion of the population employed in industry (SVT VI, C: 103, IV).

METHODS OF ANALYSIS

At an earlier stage of the present study (Kiviaho 1970b, 1971) the cartogram technique has been mainly used to describe regional differences, since compared with statistical methods it has been found to simplify and illustrate better the observed phenomena. In this part, however, the relations between groups of variables are analyzed by statistical methods. The purpose of the study is to account for the regional differences in the support of central sport organizations by analyzing how organizational distribution is related to political factors. The relations of organizational distribution to polit-

ical cleavages, political tradition and social structure are first examined on the basis of correlation coefficients. In further analyses, however, the statistical methods must be such that they make it possible (1) in the analysis of the relationship between organizational distribution and political cleavages to control or partition off other factors which affect organizational distribution, in this case political tradition and social structure and (2) to examine the mediating role of political cleavages in the relations of political tradition and social structure to organizational distribution. The former problem is examined with the partial correlation method by controlling the effects of political tradition and social structure and the latter problem—the causal relations between variables—using the same technique by controlling political cleavages (see e.g. Blalock 1962; 1964, 61–94). In addition, the proportion from the total variance accounted for by the variables is analyzed by means of multiple correlation coefficients, and the variables' relative direct and indirect effects on organizational distribution by means of path analysis (see e.g. Duncan 1966). [2]

RESULTS

The intercorrelations of the variables are presented in Table 1. They indicate that all correlations are positive and rather high. It appears that organizational distribution is more closely connected with political cleavages than with political tradition or social structure. Besides, political cleavages account for one third of the variance of organizational distribution. On the other hand, the result indicates that the variables are not only related with organizational distribution but also interrelated. On account of this, the connection between political cleavages and organizational distribution must be examined in a situation in which political tradition and social structure are controlled separately and at the same time. The results are presented in Table 2.

TABLE 1

Intercorrelations of the variable (N = 344)

		1.	2.	3.
1. Political tradition	(left)			
2. Social structure	(industr.)	.31		
3. Political cleavages	(left)	.76	.64	
4. Organizational distribution	(TUL)	.40	.33	.53

TABLE 2

The correlations and partial correlations of political cleavages with organizational distribution when political tradition and social structure are controlled separately and simultaneously (N = 344)

Independent variable	Dependent variable	Controlled variable	Partial correlation	Explained variance (%)
Political cleavages	Organizational distribution	—	.53	28
Political cleavages	Organizational distribution	Political tradition	.38	14
Political cleavages	Organizational distribution	Social structure	.44	19
Political cleavages	Organizational distribution	Political tradition and social structure	.31	10

The control of political tradition and social structure weakens the connection between political cleavages and social structure, the proportion of explained variance dropping from 28 per cent to 14 per cent when tradition is controlled, to 19 per cent when structure is controlled and to 10 per cent when both factors are controlled. However, the partial correlation and the amount of explained variance remain fairly high and indicate that political cleavages have a significant direct effect on organizational distribution.

The correlation .08 and .12 are significant at the 5% and 1% level of confidence, respectively, with a sample of 344 (one tail test).

So far the analysis has not clarified the position of political cleavages in the explanation of organizational distribution in relation to political tradition and social structure, which is the second purpose of the study. On the basis of the arguments presented above it was assumed that the causal relation between the variables is such that tradition and social structure affect organizational distribution directly and/or through political cleavages.

In the latter case it was assumed that $r_{14.3} = 0$ and $r_{24.3} = 0$. The computed value of the first equation is .00, and that of the second equation—.02. Therefore, at least in the present material the effect of political tradition and social structure on organizational distribution seems to be channeled entirely through political cleavages. In addition to testing the validity of the model, it is worthwhile to examine the relative strengths of the various variables' direct and in-

direct connections with organizational distribution by means of path coefficients (which in this case are partial regression coefficients) (Figure 2).

The model makes no assumption about the relation between political tradition and social structure, although political tradition might well be assumed to influence the social structure of the commune e.g. through the encouragement of industrialization which is typical of the political left.

The result supports the above correlational analysis and indicates that the effects of political tradition and social structure on organizational distribution are mediated entirely through political cleavages. The same result is oatined in the multiple correlation analysis, because as assumed political cleavages alone account for the same amount (28%) of the variance of organizational distribution as together with political tradition and social structure (28%). The latter, in turn, account for less (20%) of the variance of organizational distribution than political cleavages alone, but as much as 76 per cent of the variance of political cleavages. In addition to the fact that path analysis confirms the presented causal interpretation and shows the various distribution, the size of the last-mentioned residual path coefficient as well as the smallness of the explained variance of the multiple correlation show that the employed variables can account for only part of the variance of the dependent variable. This may be due to several factors. First, it is possible that the reliability of the

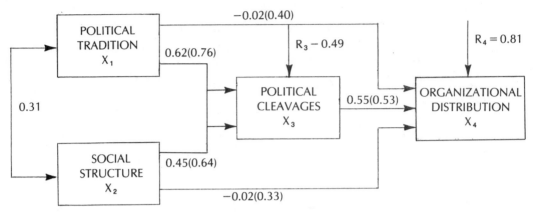

FIG.2. Path analysis concerning the effects of political tradition, social structure and political cleavages on organizational distribution (correlation coefficients within brackets and path coefficients without brackets)

variable measuring organizational distribution is not very good, which, however, is difficult to check, because it represents the data obtained from the central sport federations' files collected by local sport clubs. The data may contain both erroneous and incomplete observations. Second, the model may lack some factor or factors which have significant effects on organizational distribution, which have not come up in previous analyses containing several explanatory variables (Kiviaho 1970a). Such a factor might be, for instance, the fact that in some commune or area there may be active club officials whose influence may be so great that it partly cancels the effects of political-ideological and structural factors.

SUMMARY AND DISCUSSION

The initial stage of industrialization in Finland, which dates back to the middle of the 19th century, created the material conditions necessary for the organization and spreading of the international sport movement in Finland. Also the differentiation of sport organizations based on the then prevailing political-ideological circumstances is linked with the same social situation, though at a later stage. The clash of interests between the working class and the burgeois led to a situation in which the working class and the middle class became self-sufficient in sport as well as in many other fields of social life. The effect of social situation on the birth of sport organizations and the effect of political situation on their differentiation has been essential. The

purpose of this study was to examine to what extent sport organizations at the moment reflect social and political reality and to what extent they represent "the past in the present," i.e. are out of touch with the present situation (Kekkonen 1971).

The starting point of the present study has been the assumption that political factors are essential in sport organization policy. The material was gathered from all Finnish communes (both urban and rural) with the exception of the communes of Ahvenanmaa island and four small rural communes, but final analysis contains only those communes in which only SVUL and/or TUL were represented. Although the purpose was to make causal inferences about the effects of political factors on organizational support, the dependent variable does not represent a longitudinal variable but a cross section variable of one period, because longitudinal material concerning sport organization activities is not easy to collect due to the lack or inadequacies of local data and to the differences in the data of different central sport federations, and the difficulties in tracking down missing data over a longer period of time.

The results indicate that the political cleavages of a region have an essential role in accounting for the distribution of the region's sport organizations support. Political cleavages have, in the first place, a rather great main effect on organizational support, but at the same time they seem to mediate practically all the influence of political tradition and social structure. However, it is to be noted that these variables account for approximately only one third of the total variance of organizational distribution, which means that some factor or factors have been omitted which are central factors in explaining organizational support. However, the main purpose of the present study was to examine specifically the position and effects of political factors rather than to give a thorough account of all factors involved in organizational alignment.

REFERENCES

1. Allardt, E.: Traditional and emerging radicalism. Publication No. 21 of the Institute of Sociology, University of Helsinki, 1963.
2. Allardt, E. and Pesonen, P.: Cleavages in Finnish politics. *In* Party systems and Voter Alignments. Edited by M. Lipset and S. Rokkan. New York, 1967, pp. 325–366.
3. Blalock, H. M.: Four-variable causal models and partial correlations. Am. J. Sociol. *68*(2):182–194, 1962.
4. Blalock, H. M.: Causal inferences in non-experimental research. Chapel Hill, 1964.
5. Blom, R.: Järjestökiinnitymisen luokkaluontei-suus, Sosiologia, *8*(5):247–261, 1971.
6. Duncan, O. D.: Path analyses: sociological examples. Am. J. Sociol. *72*(1):1–16, 1966.
7. Euler, R. von: Idrottsrörelsen i dag, *In* Svensk Idrott 1903–1953, Edited by S. Svensson. Malmö, 1953, pp .149–278.
8. Halila, S.: Suomen miesvoimistelu- ja urheiluseu-rat vuoteen 1915 (The early history of Finnish gymnastics and athletics for men, English summary), Helsinki, 1959.
9. Kekkonen, U.: Urheilun tilan tarkastelua, The speech of the president at the inauguration of the Faculty of Physical and Health Education in the University of Jyväskylä 30.10.1971, Mimeograph.
10. Kiviaho, P.: Urheilu ja yhteiskunta: Tutkimus urheiluliikkeen alueellisista ominaisuuksista ja niihin vaikuttavista tekijöistä Suomessa, Unpublished licentiate thesis, University of Jyväskylä, 1970a.
11. Kiviaho, P.: Urheilujärjestöjen kannatuksen alueelinen levinneisyys Suomessa vuonna 1965 (Regional distribution of sport association membership in Finland in 1965, English summary), Report No. 74, Institute for Educational Research, University of Jyväskylä, 1970b.
12. Kiviaho, P.: Urheilupoliittinen aluejako Suomessa (Sports politics territorial division in Finland, English summary), Stadion, *8*(3) pp. 90–118. 1971.
13. Kiviaho, P., Urheilujärjestöt ja politiikka Suomessa (Sport association and politics in Finland, English summary). Politiikka, *14*(3):172–190, 1972.
14. Lipset, M. and Rokkan, S., Cleavage structures, party systems, and voter alignments: An introduction. *In* Party Systems and Voter Alignments. Edited by M. Lipset and S. Rokkan. New York, 1967, pp. 1–64.
15. Rantala, O.: Suomen poliittiset alueet I, Turku, 1971.
16. Sänkiaho, R., Puolueiden alueellinen kannatus Uudenmaan läänissä, Helsinki, 1968.
17. SVT, Suomen Virallinen Tilasto XXIX A:14, Vaalitilasto, Eduskuntavaalit v. 1929, Helsinki, 1930.
18. SVT, Suomen Virallinen Tilasto VI C:103, IV, Yleinen väestönlaskenta 1960, Väestön elinkeino ja ammattiasema, Helsinki, 1963.
19. SVT, Suomen Virallinen Tilasto XXIX A:29, Kansanedustajain vaalit v. 1966, Helsinki, 1966.

NOTES

1. In the whole country the membership density correlated with SVUL—.15, with TUL .17, with TUK .14, with SPL .16 and with CIF—.05.
2. Path analysis is a method which enables the testing of causal relations between variables. It makes it possible to estimate the direct and indirect effects of the independent variable on the dependent variable by means of path coefficients. Where the correlation coefficient expresses how much of the relationship between variables has been explained, the path analysis expresses the nature of the relationship.

a socioeconomic model of national olympic performance [1]

A. RAY GRIMES, JR., WILLIAM J. KELLY and PAUL H. RUBIN

The Olympic games have been extolled by some as personal contests in which individuals compete against other individuals, but others view them as political contests in which the honor of one nation is pitted against that of another. [2] While this nationalistic competition has been decried as a recent development, [3] it seems to be an old phenomenon: Mandell, for example, argues that this attitude was prevalent in the ancient Olympics. [4] Baron Pierre de Coubertin, the father of the modern Olympic Games, viewed the games as a means of reinvigorating the youth of France. [5] The 1936 Olympics in Berlin were seen by Hitler as a test of the powers of German youth and Nazism. [6] Since World War II the United States and the Soviet Union have viewed the games as tests of their respective political systems [7] while developing countries have sought nationalistic benefits from the Olympics. [8]

It has frequently been asserted that communist nations make efforts which go far beyond those of most noncommunist nations. Johnson, for example, reports that the Russians spent millions to prepare for the 1952 Helsinki games while East Germany had created a "Brave New World breeding factory" environment in which athletes were trained like "thoroughbred horses or racing dogs." [9]

The primary purposes of this paper are to construct a socioeconomic model of national Olym-

pic performance and to determine whether communist countries have performed better than noncommunist countries after allowance is made for key demographic and economic factors. Subsidiary purposes are to suggest an approach for investigating the impact of political systems on the sports and other spheres of activity, to present evidence on "n-achievement," and to suggest new avenues of research.

FORMULATION OF THE MODEL

Assuming that national performance in the Olympics is a function not only of political ideology, but also of other variables, political ideology should manifest itself as a *systematic deviation* from the national performance one would expect on the basis of nonpolitical variables such as demographic and economic characteristics. To test for this we formulated a regression model containing one demographic, one economic, and one ideological variable based on the following reasoning:

To become a world class athlete, an individual must have the genetic potential for this level of performance and must receive adequate nutrition to develop this potential. He must be willing and able to spend time training. Complementary inputs—coaches and equipment—must be available. Once one has developed the ability to be a competitor, state subsidization of costs of participation would be significant. Finally, the individual must be willing to remain an amateur.

Assuming that the necessary genetic potential is randomly distributed throughout the world's population, we would expect the number of

Reprinted from Social Science Quarterly, 55(3):777–783, 1974. Copyright 1974 by the University of Texas Press, P.O. Box 7819, Austin, Texas 78712.

medals won to be directly related to an individual country's total population. [10] We therefore selected national population size as our first variable.

The second variable chosen—per capita GNP—was expected to be significant for several reasons. First, it should be a good proxy for nutrition. [11] Second, increased discretionary income would enable a person to spend time outside of the labor force (perhaps in college) in training for athletics. Also, one would expect complementary inputs to be normal goods and thus related directly to income. The effect of income on amateur status is less clear. Higher income might be correlated with higher salaries for professional athletes, and thus reduce the incentive to remain an amateur. But the possibility of earning such higher incomes might induce one to spend the time training for Olympic performance; many athletes seem to participate in one Olympiad and then become professional. On balance, we believe there should be a positive relationship between per capita GNP and number of medals won by a country.

The third variable, which was designed to detect systematic deviations due to political ideology, was a dummy variable which took on the value 1 for a communist country and 0 otherwise. It was felt that this variable would capture several effects. Communist countries make special efforts to systematically recruit, train, and subsidize athletes. Also, there are no professional athletes in communist countries; therefore, Olympic athletes do not have the alternative of becoming professional, and hence would remain eligible for longer periods of time. [12] We expect these factors to operate by heightening the influence of our population and income variables. From a demographic viewpoint we expect communist countries to make a greater effort to cull their populations for quality athletes and to encourage such athletes to compete. From an economic viewpoint, we expect them to devote more resources to training Olympic athletes than would the average noncommunist country with the same level of per capita income. We therefore expect that the effects of population and per capita income will be stronger for communist countries and that, as a result, they will win more medals than would a comparable noncommunist country.

The measure of national performance chosen was the sum of gold, silver, and bronze medals won by each country. Since all weighting schemes are arbitrary, the three types of medals were assigned equal weights.

THE DATA

This model was used to explain the results of the 1972 Olympic Games. Medal totals were computed from a newspaper tabulation. [13] The totals for the 48 countries which won at least one medal are shown in column (C) of Table 1. Complete data on total population and per capita GNP were found for all 48 medal winning countries and for 47 of the other participants. [14]

STATISTICAL PROCEDURES

Because many countries won no medals, a regression fit to the number of medals won would violate the assumption of normality of errors. We therefore used Tobin's hybrid of regression and probit analysis. [15] The "Tobit" method, unlike probit analysis, does not waste information about the dependent variable, and, unlike regression analysis, does not yield predicted values which fall below the lower limit of the dependent variable (zero in this case). This technique is an iterative procedure for getting maximum likelihood estimates for a non-limited dependent variable. The resulting estimates are used together with the probabilities of limit and non-limit values of the dependent variable to compute the expected value of the limited dependent variable.

Our hypothesized model may be stated as:

(1) $M = L$ $(W - \epsilon < L)$,
       $M = W - \epsilon$ $(W - \epsilon \geq L)$,

where M is the number of medals won by a country, L is the lower limit of M (here $L = 0$), W is a non-limited dependent variable which is a combination of the independent variables to which M is by hypothesis related, and ϵ is independently and normally distributed with mean zero and variance σ^2.

In this problem W is hypothesized to be of the form

(2) $W = B_0 + B_1 P + B_2 Y + K(B_3 Y + B_4 P)$

where P is population in millions, Y is per capita GNP in hundreds of dollars, and K is the communist dummy variable. The multiplicative role of K allows the communist dummy to modify the effects of P and Y, as we hypothesize it should. [16]

The probability density function is

(3) $f(\times | W, L) = \frac{1}{\sigma} Z\{(W - \times)/\sigma\}$

and the expected value of M for given values of W and L is given here by

$$(4) \quad E(M|W,L) = LQ\{(W - L)/\sigma\} + Wp\{W - L)/\sigma\} + \sigma Z\{(W - L)/\sigma\},$$

where $p(\times)$ represents the value of the cumulative unit-normal distribution function at $\times$, $Q(\times) = 1 - p(\times)$, and $Z(\times)$ is the value of the unit-normal probability density function at $\times$.

RESULTS

The iterative solution for the maximum likelihood estimates yielded the following equation:

$$(5) \quad W = - 15.51825 + .08454P + .01357Y +$$
$$\qquad (3.55) \qquad (6.07)$$
$$\qquad .03261(KY) + .21543(KP).$$
$$\qquad (4.52) \qquad (3.01)$$

The t-values are shown in parentheses. All coefficients are significant at the .01 level. [17] The expected values of M were computed from equations (4) and (5) and are listed in column (B) of Table 1. [18] A regression of the actual number of medals won on the number expected to be won yielded an R^2 of .70 indicating that our model fits the data well.

With reference to the second major objective of this paper, there is good evidence that communist countries *did* perform better in the 1972 Olympics than comparable noncommunist countries. The communist dummy variable was significant when entered in a multiplicative fashion, supporting our hypothesis that much of the success of communist countries is due to a better use of their available population and a stronger effect of income. The success of this multiplicative form of the communist dummy variable may be judged by the model's prediction of total communist winnings of 289 medals—a deviation of only one percent from the actual figure of 286 medals.

TABLE 1

(A) Country [a]	(B) EM	(C) AM	(A) Country	(B) EM	(C) AM
U.S.S.R.	98	99	Denmark	10	1
U.S.A.	49	94	Switzerland	16	3
East Germany	46	66	Canada	17	5
Japan	5	29	Iran	0	3
West Germany	12	40	Belgium	7	2
Australia	10	17	Greece	0	2
Poland	28	20	Austria	5	3
Hungary	25	35	Colombia	0	3
Bulgaria	16	21	Mexico	0	1
Italy	3	18	Pakistan	0	1
Sweden	16	16	Tunisia	0	1
Great Britain	11	18	Argentina	0	1
Romania	20	16	South Korea	0	1
Finland	7	8	Lebanon	0	1
Cuba	3	8	Turkey	0	1
Netherlands	5	5	Mongolia	3	1
France	12	13	Brazil	0	2
Czechoslovakia	35	8	Ethiopia	0	2
Kenya	0	9	Spain	0	2
Yugoslavia	14	7	Jamaica	0	1
Norway	8	4	India	31	1
North Korea	1	5	Niger Republic	0	1
New Zealand	11	3	Ghana	0	1
Uganda	0	2	Nigeria	0	1

[a] The countries are listed in order of winnings of gold medals, then silver, and finally bronze. EM = expected medals; AM = actual medals.

SUGGESTIONS FOR FURTHER RESEARCH

The subsidiary purposes of this paper may best be considered under this heading. We feel that our model is a successful representation of the effects of selected variables on Olympic performance. But we are able to explain only 70 percent of the variance in the actual medal series. Among the noncommunist countries our model has substantially underpredicted the winnings of some countries and overpredicted the winnings of others. There are similar, though less severe, discrepancies for communist countries. Some of the discrepancies must be due to unquantifiable variables. However, the underprediction of winnings by countries noted for their emphasis on personal accomplishments —the United States, the two Germanies, and Japan—suggests that there are important characteristics of societies which have been omitted. We therefore constructed a two-by-two contingency table to investigate the correlation between our unexplained residuals and McClelland's estimates of national "n-achievement" levels. We were able to obtain n-achievement information for 33 of the 95 countries in our sample. [19] These 33 countries were distributed in the contingency table shown as Table 2 on the basis of (1) their classification by McClelland as having either high or low n-achievement levels and (2) the signs of their residuals in our statistical tests—i.e. whether our model (a) underpredicted their Olympic performance (residuals with minus signs) or (b) either overpredicted (plus signs) or exactly predicted (no sign) their performances. [20]

Table 2 suggests that there is a correlation between the signs of our residuals and national n-achievement levels and that our model underpredicts the performances of countries with high n-achievement scores. A chi-square test of the table confirmed this, yielding a value of 5.08 which is significant at the .05 level. [21]

We have not incorporated these results into our model because n-achievement scores were available for only one-third of our sample countries. Also, the possibilities of success in this area seem great enough that the topic should be tackled by social scientists who are more experienced with this method. In view of the success of our multiplicative dummy variable we suggest specifically that future researchers investigate the possibility that n-achievement enters models in a multiplicative fashion, heightening the influence of more basic variables. We suspect that the multiplicative form may prove useful in a variety of socioeconomic models which call for measures of social or political philosophy or ideology.

Finally we suggest an investigation of the correlation between success in the Olympics and success in national power conflicts such as war. In the course of our research we have been struck by several things. First, there is the assertion by Edwards that "Sports and war are born from man's same needs." [22] Second, the three variables which we have used to explain success in the Olympics are almost identical to the factors which Organski argues are the key determinants of national power. [23] As a simple test of the correlation between success in the Olympics and success in war we have computed the medal winnings in the 1936 Olympics for the Allied and Axis powers. The Axis powers won a total of 165 medals while the Allies (excluding the Soviet Union which did not participate) won only 133 medals. [24] However, if Italy and Romania are shifted to the Allies' side (as happened in 1943 and 1944, respectively) the medal balance shifts in favor of the Allies: 156 versus 142. This exam-

TABLE 2

Olympic Performance [a]

	Overpredicted or Exactly predicted	Underpredicted
High n-achievement	4 (7.2)	13 (9.8)
Low achievement	10 (6.8)	6 (9.2)

[a] Actual frequencies are shown without parentheses; expected frequencies with parentheses.

ple proves nothing but suggests that it might be interesting to see whether similar results are obtained for other wars.

NOTES

1. The authors wish to thank Thomas Lindley for providing the computer program used in this paper, to thank H. Gregg Lewis, Joseph Ableman, and Edward Meeker for helpful comments, and to absolve them from responsibility for any remaining deficiencies.

2. Johnson, William O. Jr.: All that Glitters Is Not Gold: The Olympic Game. New York, G. P. Putnam's Sons, 1972, pp. 33–39; Mandell, Richard D.: The Nazi Olympics. New York, Macmillan, 1971; Edwards, Harry: Sociology of Sport. Homewood, Ill., Dorsey Press, 1973, pp. 51, 264–265; and McClelland, David C.: The Achieving Society. New York, Free Press, 1961, pp. 322–324.

3. See the remarks of Henry Wittenberg in Johnson, p. 30.

4. Mandell, p. 4.

5. Ibid., p. xii.

6. See: Mandell, pp. ix–xvi and Johnson, pp. 172–207.

7. Edwards, p. 51 and Johnson, pp. 34–35.

8. Johnson, Harry G.: A theoretical model of economic nationalism in new and developing states. Political Science Quarterly, 80:169–185, 1965.

9. Johnson, pp. 37–38.

10. We are assuming that international migration and mixing of the world's populations have proceeded to such an extent that forces (e.g. mutation pressure, selection pressure, selective migration, etc.) which might create qualitative differences between national gene pools and hence national athletic potential have been counterbalanced. For a theoretical discussion see: Rasmuson, Marianne: Genetics on the Population Level. Stockholm, Svenska Bokförlaget, 1961, particularly Chaps. 3 and 4.

11. On the correlation between nutrition and Olympic performance, see: Paparescos, N.: Environmental Factors Affecting the Athletic Activity and Career. In Report of the Twelfth Session of the International Olympic Academy at Olympia, Athens, Hellenic Olympic Committee, 1973, pp. 226–233. On the relationship between nutrition and per capita income, see: Kindleberger, Charles P.: Economic Development. New York, McGraw-Hill, 1958, p. 211.

12. This variable might work either way: since athletes in communist countries cannot ultimately become professionals, they might have less incentive to train

for world class competition. However, relative income of athletes in communist countries (including status and prestige) may be high enough to compensate for this. If so, the main difference between communist and noncommunist athletes may be that the latter have the option of making electric shaver commercials and thus losing their eligibility for future Olympic participation.

13. The Atlanta Constitution (September 12, 1972), p. 4-D.

14. Population Reference Bureau, 1969 World Population Data Sheet. Washington, Population Reference Bureau, 1969.

15. Tobin, James: Estimation of relationships for limited dependent variables. Econometrica, 26:24–36, 1958.

16. A form of W in which K played only a simple additive role was estimated and rejected because of the objectionable effect of K in that form. In the additive form the fact that a country was communist implied that W would be 31 medals higher whatever the population or per capita GNP of the country.

17. Early analysis was also carried out using Y^2 instead of Y to ascertain whether athletic performance acted as a superior good. That model yielded similar t-scores but a slightly lower coefficient of determination.

18. The actual and expected number of medals are not listed for the 47 countries which won no medals. In all but two of these countries the expected number of medals was also zero.

19. McClelland, p. 100.

20. The "overpredicted" and "exactly predicted" categories had to be combined in order to raise all expected cell frequencies to the minimum level of five which is recommended for chi-square analysis of contingency tables. See Freund, John E.: Modern Elementary Statistics. 2nd ed., Englewood Cliffs, N.J., Prentice-Hall, 1960, p. 281.

21. McClelland found a positive but insignificant correlation between unofficial team scores per capita and national n-achievement scores. The difference between his and our results is probably due to our improved correction for the influence of other variables. See: McClelland, pp. 322–323.

22. Johnson, p. 31.

23. Organski, A. F. K.: World Politics 2nd ed. New York, Alfred A. Knopf, 1968, p. 208.

24. The medal computations were made from Mandell, Nazi Olympics, p. 207; the list of participants in World War II is taken from Singer, J David, and Small, Melvin: The Wages of War, 1816–1965: A Statistical Handbook. New York, John Wiley 1972, pp. 67–68.

SECTION THREE
sport and cultural institutions

the technological revolution and the rise of sport, 1850–1900

JOHN RICKARDS BETTS

The roots of our sporting heritage lie in the horse racing and fox hunting of the colonial era, but the main features of modern sport appeared only in the middle years of the nineteenth century.[1] Organization, journalistic exploitation, commercialization, intercommunity competition, and sundry other developments increased rapidly after 1850 as the agrarian nature of sport gave way gradually to the influences of urbanization and industrialization. Just as the Industrial Revolution was to alter the interests, habits, and pursuits of all classes of society, it was to leave a distinct impression on the development of sport.

Many other factors were responsible for the directions taken by sport in the half century from 1850 to 1900. Continuing rural influences, the decline of Puritan orthodoxy, the English athletic movement, the immigrant, frontier traditions of manliness and strength, and the contributions of energetic sportsmen were to have a significant effect on the sporting scene. Industrialization and urbanization, however, were more fundamentally responsible for the changes and developments in sport during the next generation than any other cause. Manufacturers, seeking cheap labor, encouraged immigration; factories were most efficiently run in larger towns and cities; urban masses, missing the rustic pleasures of hunting and fishing, were won to the support of commercialized entertainment

and spectator sports; the emergence of a commercial aristocracy and a laboring class resulted in distinctions every bit as strong in sport as in other social matters; and the urgency of physical exercise as life became more sedentary was readily recognized.

The revolution in manufacturing methods, which had such profound social consequences for the American way of life, derived from a powerful inventive spirit which flourished throughout the nineteenth century. From England and western Europe we borrowed many mechanical innovations and most of our scientific theory, but Americans demonstrated a native ability soon recognized everywhere as "Yankee ingenuity." These inventions were to revolutionize transportation, communication, manufacturing, finance, and all the many facets of economic life. Although the tendency in narrating the history of sport has been to emphasize the role of individuals, the changing social scene was of equal importance in directing sport into the channels it eventually took in modern society. The impact of invention had a decisive influence on the rise of sport in the latter half of the century. By 1900 sport had attained an unprecedented prominence in the daily lives of millions of Americans, and this remarkable development had been achieved in great part through the steamboat, the railroad, the telegraph, the penny press, the electric light, the streetcar, the camera, the bicycle, the automobile, and the mass production of sporting goods.

The transformation of the United States from a rural-agrarian to an urban-industrial society, of

Reprinted from Mississippi Valley Historical Review, *40*:231–256, 1953. Copyright 1953 by The Journal of American History, Indiana University, Bloomington, Indiana 47405.

course, affected the development of sport in other ways. Urbanization brought forth the need for commercialized spectator sports, while industrialization gradually provided the standard of living and leisure time so vital to the support of all forms of recreation. But it is the relationship of invention to sport, and that alone, which constitutes the theme of this study.

Early American interest in outdoor exercise was largely confined to hunting, fishing, horse racing, field sports, and the informal games of the local schoolyard. As the nation became more commercially minded in the decades after the War of 1812, many of those who lived in rapidly growing cities became concerned over the sedentary habits of clerks, office workers, and businessmen. In the years before 1850 there emerged a limited interest in rowing, running, prize fighting, cricket, fencing, and similar activities, but the only organized sport which excited the minds of most Americans was the turf. A more general interest in horse racing appeared in the 1820's and 1830's, and many jockey clubs held meetings attended by throngs of spectators in their carriages and barouches.[2]

From the early years of the century steamboat captains engaged in racing on the Hudson, Ohio, Mississippi, and other rivers, and the steamboat served as a common carrier of sports crowds. By the 1850's it became an indispensable means of transport to the races along the eastern seaboard and in the Mississippi Valley. As one of the first products of the age of steam it played a significant role in the rise of the turf and outdoor games.[3]

In the years preceding the Civil War the turf was also encouraged by the development of a railroad network. As early as 1838 Wade Hampton was transporting race horses to Charleston by rail;[4] in 1839 the Nashville Railroad was carrying New Orleans crowds to the Metairie Course;[5] in 1842 the Long Island Railroad was already suffering the abuse of irate passengers swarming to the races; and three years later it carried some 30,000 passengers to the Fashion-Peytona race at more than fifty cents each.[6] Kentucky became the leading breeding center for thoroughbreds and Louisville could announce in 1851: "Lexington, Georgetown, Frankfort, Paris and other towns in this State, are now but a short ride from our city by railroad conveyance. Horses can come from Lexington here in five hours."[7] The famous trotter Flora

Temple began barn-storming tours; racing and trotting benefited from the cooperation of railroad lines; and "speed trials" at agricultural fairs during the 1850's were attended by excursionists.[8] Other outdoor sports also profited from the interest shown by certain lines. When excitement over rowing began to catch on in the late 1830's the first boat shipped west of the Appalachians went by the way of the Erie Canal.[9] It was a railroad, however, which encouraged the holding of the first intercollegiate rowing race between Harvard and Yale in 1852.[10] Baseball clubs were organized throughout the East and Midwest during the decade and the National Association of Base Ball Players was formed in 1857, soon after both sections had been connected by rail. Chicago had its first baseball team in 1856, two years after it was linked by rail to Baltimore, Maryland, and Portland, Maine. In 1860 the Excelsior Club of Brooklyn made a tour of upper New York state. Most of the early prize fights were held along the rivers served by steamboats; the Harlem Railroad carried fight crowds in the early 1850's to the Awful Gardiner-William Hastings (*alias* Dublin Tricks) match sixty miles north of New York City and to a highly publicized championship fight at Boston Four Corners, New York;[11] and the John Morrissey-John Heanan match on the Canadian shore near Niagara Falls in 1858 was advertised by the Erie Railroad.[12]

The Civil War failed to halt turf meetings and outdoor recreation in the North. It was, however, only with the return of peace that the nation felt a new sporting impulse and began to give enthusiastic support to the turf, the diamond, the ring, and other outdoor activities. The game of baseball, spreading from cities to towns and villages, became a national fad, and matches were scheduled with distant communities. A tournament at Rockford, Illinois, in 1866 was attended by teams from Detroit, Milwaukee, Dubuque, and Chicago.[13] In 1869 Harry Wright's Cincinnati Red Stockings were able to make a memorable transcontinental tour from Maine to California; a New Orleans club visited Memphis, St. Louis, and Cincinnati; and eastern teams condescended to travel as far west as the Queen City. The Erie line offered to convey a New Orleans club, then visiting Cincinnati, to New York and return at half-fare rates. When the Cincinnati Red Stockings made their tour by boat, local lines, and the Union Pacific in 1869 it was reported: "The boys have received every attention from the officers of the different roads. . . . At all the stations groups stare us almost out of countenance, having heard of the successful exploits of the Club through telegrams of the Western Associated Press." [14]

Baseball clubs made use of the rapidly expanding network of the 1870's, and the organization of the National League in 1876 was only possible with the continued development of connecting lines. In the 1886 edition of *Spalding's Official Base Ball Guide* the Michigan Central advertised: "The cities that have representative clubs contesting for the championship pennant this year are—Chicago, Boston, New York, Washington, Kansas City, Detroit, St. Louis and Philadelphia. All of these cities are joined together by the MICHIGAN CENTRAL Railroad. This road has enjoyed almost a monopoly of Base Ball travel in former years." Throughout the 1870's and 1880's the expanding railroad network played an indispensable role in the popularization of the "national game." [15]

A widespread interest in thoroughbred and trotting races also was in great part sustained by railroad expansion. In 1866 the Harlem, Rensselaer and Saratoga Railroad Company, realizing the advantage of encouraging the racing public, arranged to convey race horses at cost by express train from New York to Saratoga. *Turf, Field and Farm* pointed to the need for better transportation arrangements and predicted, "The completion of the Pacific Railroad will not be without effect upon the blood stock interests of the great West." [16] Jerome Park, Long Branch, and Gravesend catered to New York crowds, Baltimore attracted huge throngs of sportsmen, and in California racing was encouraged by the building of lines into the interior of the state. In the 1870's western turfmen began sending their horses by rail to eastern tracks, the Grand Circuit linked Hartford, Springfield, Poughkeepsie, and Utica with Rochester, Buffalo, and Cleveland, and racing associations formed in virtually every section. When Mollie McCarthy and Ten Broeck raced at Louisville in 1877, "Masses of strangers arrived by train, extra trains and steamboats." People from "all over the land" attended the Kentucky Derby in 1885, the City Council declared a holiday, and sixteen carloads of horses were sent from Nashville to Louisville. [17] Agricultural fairs, with the cooperation of numerous companies, drew thousands to their fairground tracks, and the railroads encouraged intersectional meetings by introducing special horse cars in the middle eighties. [18]

In the decades after the Civil War an apologetic but curious public acquired a "deplorable" interest in prize fighting, and railroad officials were not slow to capitalize on the crowd appeal of pugilism despite its illegality. When Mike McCoole met Aaron Jones in 1867 at Busenbark Station, Ohio, "Tickets were openly sold for excursion trains to the bout" and sporting men from the East were in attendance, while another McCoole fight in 1869 encouraged the lines to run specials from Cincinnati and other nearby cities. [19] After 1881 John L. Sullivan, the notorious "Boston Strong Boy," went on grand tours of the athletic clubs, opera houses, and theaters of the country, his fights in the New Orleans area with Paddy Ryan, Jake Kilrain, and James J. Corbett luring fans who jammed the passenger coaches. When the Great John L. met Kilrain near Richburg, Mississippi, in 1889, the Northeastern Railroad carried a tumultuous crowd from New Orleans to the site, even though Governor Robert Lowry of Mississippi issued a proclamation against the affair and called out armed guards to prevent any invasion of the state. After the brawl the Governor requested the attorney general "to begin proceedings to forfeit the charter of the Northeastern railroad." [20] Railroad companies expressed only a minor concern for such sporadic events, it is true, but the prize ring was greatly aided by their cooperation. [21]

Poor connections, uncomfortable cars, and the absence of lines in rural sections remained a problem for some years. [22] Many of the difficulties and inconveniences of travel remained throughout these expansive years of railroading, but all sports were encouraged by the improved transportation of the post-bellum era. Immediately after the war a New York crew visited Pittsburgh to participate in a regatta held on the Monongahela River. [23] The first intercollegiate football game between Rutgers and Princeton was attended by a group of students riding the train pulled by "the jerky little engine that steamed out of Princeton on that memorable morning of November 6, 1869." [24] Intercollegiate athletics depended on railroad service for carrying teams and supporters to football, baseball, and rowing, as well as track and field contests.

Harvard's crack baseball team made the first

grand tour in 1870, "the most brilliant in the history of college baseball," according to Henry Chadwick almost two decades later. Playing both amateur and professional clubs, Harvard won a majority of the games played in New Haven, Troy, Utica, Syracuse, Oswego (Canada), Buffalo, Cleveland, Cincinnati, Louisville, Chicago, Milwaukee, Indianapolis, Washington, Baltimore, Philadelphia, New York, and Brooklyn.[25] Amateur and professional cycling races were held throughout the country,[26] while rod and gun enthusiasts relied on branch lines into rural preserves.[27] By the closing years of the century virtually every realm of sport had shared in the powerful impact of the railroad on American life.

Almost contemporaneous with the development of a continental railroad system came the diffusion of telegraph lines throughout the nation. From its invention in 1844 the electric telegraph rapidly assumed a significant role in the dissemination of news.[28] When the Magnetic Telegraph Company's line reached New York, James Gordon Bennett's *Herald* and Horace Greeley's *Tribune* installed apparatus in 1846. Direct contact was made between the East and New Orleans two years later, largely to meet the urgent demand for quicker news from the Mexican War front. By 1861 San Francisco was connected by wire with the Atlantic coast, and throughout the war years use of the telegraph was extended in military operations.

During the pioneer years telegraphic messages were both costly and brief, and sports events were reported on a limited scale. One of the first reports by wire was that of the Tom Hyer-Yankee Sullivan brawl at Rock Point, Maryland, in 1849. A New York dispatch read, "We hope never to have to record a similar case of brutality in this country," and even Greeley, an inveterate foe of the prize ring, permitted the printing of dispatches of this brutal encounter. Interest was not confined to Baltimore, Philadelphia, and New York, for some newspapers in the West noticed it. In the next decade several fights were widely reported by telegraph. When Morrissey and Heanan fought for the American championship in Canada in 1858, anxious crowds waited at Western Union offices for the news; when Heanan met Tom Sayers in England two years later the news was spread by wire after it was brought to America by the *Vanderbilt*.[29] Horse racing and yachting news was less novel and less sensational, but Lady Suffolk's appearance on the course at the Rochester, New York, fair in 1851, the victory of Commodore John Cox Stevens' yacht *America* at Cowes in the same year, and the exciting trotting races of the decade were given extensive wire coverage.[30] When Lexington met Lecomte at New Orleans in 1855, however, there seems to have been little reporting of the race in the North. Newspapers of that section were primarily concerned in that year with the trouble in Kansas, the rise of the Republican party, the heat of the abolitionist crusade, and the public furor over the murder of pugilist William Poole.

The expansion of sporting news in ensuing years was directly related to the more general usage of telegraphy, which made possible instantaneous reporting of ball games, horse races, prize fights, yachting regattas, and other events. Box scores, betting odds, and all kinds of messages were relayed from one city to another, and by 1870 daily reports were published in many metropolitan papers. In that year the steamboat race of the *Natchez* and the *Robert E. Lee* was reported throughout the country in one of the most extensive telegraphic accounts of any nonpolitical event prior to that time.[31] Not only did the newspapers make a practice of publishing daily messages from all corners of the sporting world, but crowds formed around Western Union offices during any important contest.[32] When the Associated Press sent its representatives in 1889 to the Sullivan-Kilrain fight in New Orleans, reporters appeared from "every prominent journal in the Union," and Western Union was said to have employed 50 operators to handle 208,000 words of specials following the fight. Poolrooms and saloons were often equipped with receiving sets to keep customers and bettors posted on baseball scores and track results, while newspapers set up bulletin boards for the crowds to linger around.[33] And the business transactions of sporting clubs and associations were often carried on by wire.

Sport had emerged into such a popular topic of conversation that newspapers rapidly expanded their coverage in the 1880's and 1890's, relying in great part on messages sent over the lines from distant points. Among the leaders in this field during these formative years of "yellow journalism" were such New York papers as Bennett's *Herald*, Charles Dana's *Sun*, and Joseph Pulitzer's *World*. The sports page was not solely the result of improvements in telegraphy, however, for popular interest had encouraged the employment of specialists who were extremely quick, as were the publishers, to capitalize on the news value of sporting events. Chicago produced the pioneers in baseball writing in such masters of breezy slang and grotesque humor as Leonard Washburne, Charles Seymour, and Finley Peter Dunne. Cincinnati newspapers, staffed by experts like Harry Weldon, O.P. Caylor, and Byron (Ban) Johnson, were among the most authoritative journals in the diamond world. In 1895, when William Randolph Hearst invaded the New York field and bought the *Journal*, he immediately brought in western writers and, within a few years, developed the first sports section.[34] The telegraph retained its functional importance in recording daily box scores and racing statistics, but it was no longer the one indispensable factor it had been in earlier decades.

The Atlantic cable, successfully laid in 1866 by Cyrus Field, had overcome the mid-century handicap of reporting two- or three-weeks-old English sporting news. At the end of that year James Gordon Bennett, Jr., with the aid of the Associated Press, featured cable dispatches of the great ocean race. When the Harvard crew rowed against Oxford in a highly publicized race in 1869, "the result was flashed through the Atlantic cable as to reach New York about a quarter past one, while the news reached the Pacific Coast about nine o'clock, enabling many of the San Franciscans to discuss the subject at their breakfast-tables, and swallow the defeat with their coffee!"[35] The combination of cable and telegraph aroused a deeper interest in international sport. Nor must we ignore that forerunner of the modern radio, the wireless which was demonstrated publicly in America for the first time in the yacht races of 1899. From Samuel F.B. Morse to Guglielmo Marconi the revolution in communication had encouraged the rise of sport.

Public interest in sport was also aroused by the enlarged format and greater circulation achieved by numerous inventions which revolutionized the printing process. By 1830 the Napier double-cylinder press was imported from England and developed by R. Hoe and Company, printing those cheap and sensational papers which were the first to feature horse races, prize fights, and foot races—the New York *Sun*, the New York

Transcript, and the Philadelphia *Public Ledger*.[36] James Gordon Bennett, Sr., recognized the value of catering to the whims of the masses and occasionally featured turf reporting in the *Herald* of the 1840's.[37] In 1846 the Hoe type-revolving cylinder press was introduced by the *Public Ledger*, enabling newspaper publishers, after improvements were made in the machine, to print 20,000 sheets an hour.[38] Other inventions facilitated the mass publication of the daily paper, making possible the sensationalized editions of Bennett, Pulitzer, and Hearst.[39] With the arrival of the new journalism of the 1880's, sporting news rapidly became a featured part of the metropolitan press.[40]

Publishers also aided in the popularization of outdoor sport throughout this whole era. From the 1830's onward sporting books appeared, the most famous of prewar authors being Henry William Herbert, whose illustrious pseudonym was Frank Forester. After the Civil War cheap methods of publication gave a great stimulus to the dime novel and the athletic almanac. While the vast majority of the thrillers and shockers concerned the Wild West or city crime, athletic stories and manuals were put out by Beadle & Adams, the leading publisher of the paper-backed dime novel.[41] After the establishment of A. G. Spalding & Brothers the *Spalding Guide* developed into the leading authority on rules of play, and all sorts of handbooks were included in the *Spalding Library of Athletic Sports*. The *New York Clipper* began publishing a theatrical and sporting *Clipper Almanac* in the 1870's, while newspapers like the New York *World*, the New York *Tribune*, the Chicago *Daily News*, the Washington *Post*, and the Brooklyn *Daily Eagle* issued almanacs listing athletic and racing records and sporting news. Richard Kyle Fox of the *National Police Gazette* published *Fox's Athletic Library* and sporting annuals. By the end of the century book publication had grown to astronomic proportions when compared to the Civil War era, and the Outing Publishing Company issued more than a hundred titles on angling, canoeing, yachting, mountain climbing, hunting, shooting, trapping, camping, cycling, and athletics.

A few dime novels had taken up the athletic theme in the 1870's, but more mature stories like Mark Sibley Severance's *Hammersmith: His Harvard Days* (1878), Noah Brooks's *Our Baseball Club* (1884), and, of course, Thomas

Hughes's English classics, *Tom Brown at Rugby* and *Tom Brown at Oxford*, were responsible for the rising desire for sports fiction. By the 1890's a demand for boys' athletic stories was met in the voluminous outpouring of the heroic sporting achievements of Gilbert Patten's "Frank Merriwell." [42] Along with the newspaper and the sporting journal the field of publishing, with its improved techniques and expanded output, did much to attract attention to athletics at the turn of the century.

Much of the angling and hunting equipment and horseman's supplies came from England in the colonial era, but in the years before and after the American Revolution several dealers in sporting wares appeared in Philadelphia, New York, and Boston. From the early years of the nineteenth century merchants and gunsmiths in Kentucky supplied the settlers west of the Appalachian range. [43] Field sports were still enjoyed mainly by schoolboys and sportsmen with their simple rods in the 1840's and 1850's, but from the 1830's onward fishing and hunting purely for recreation developed into a sporting fad, the end of which is not in sight. Charles Hallock, noted sportsman, conservationist, and journalist of the post-Civil War era recalled how the rural folk of Hampshire County, Massachusetts, responded to a visiting sportsman of the 1840's who brought with him a set of highly finished rods, reels, and fly-fishing equipment.

> Ah! those were halcyon days. No railroads disturbed the quiet seclusion of that mountain nook.... Twice a week an oldfashioned coach dragged heavily up the hill into the hamlet and halted in front of the house which was at once post-office, tavern, and miscellaneous store. ... One day it brought a passenger.... He carried a leather hand-bag and a handful of rods in a case. The village *quidnuncs* said he was a surveyor. He allowed he was from Troy and had "come to go a-fishing." From that stranger I took my first lesson in fly-fishing. [44]

By the 1850's the manufacture of cricket bats and stumps, billiard tables, archery equipment, guns, fishing tackle, and other sporting accessories was carried on by a host of individual craftsmen and by such concerns as J. W. Brunswick & Brothers of Cincinnati, Bassler of Boston, Conroy's of New York, and John Krider's "Sportsmen's Depot" in Philadelphia.

Mass-production methods of manufacture were still in their infancy in post-Civil War dec-

ades, but the factory system became ever more deeply entrenched. While the sporting goods business never attained any great economic importance in the nineteenth century, [45] much of the popularity for athletic games and outdoor recreation was due to standardized manufacturing of baseball equipment, bicycles, billiard tables, sporting rifles, fishing rods, and various other items. [46] Although most American youths played with restitched balls and a minimum of paraphernalia, college athletes, cycling enthusiasts, and professional ballplayers popularized the products of George B. Ellard of Cincinnati, Peck & Snyder of New York, and other concerns. [47]

By the end of the century A. G. Spalding & Brothers was the nationally recognized leader in this field. As a renowned pitcher for the Boston and Chicago clubs and then as the promoter of the latter, Albert Spalding had turned to the merchandizing of athletic goods in 1876. [48] One of the most avid sponsors of the national game, he branched out into varied sports in the 1880's, and acquired a virtual monopoly over athletic goods by absorbing A. J. Reach Company in 1885, Wright & Ditson in 1892, as well as Peck & Snyder and other firms. By 1887 the Spalding "Official League" baseball had been adopted by the National League, the Western League, the New England League, the International League, and various college conferences, and balls were offered to the public ranging in price from 5 cents to $1.50. To gain an even greater ascendancy over his rivals A. G. Spalding published a wide range of guides in *Spalding's Library of Athletic Sports*, in which his wares were not only advertised but those of rivals were derided as inferior.

The sewing machine was one of many inventions which made possible the more uniform equipment of the last decades of the century when local leagues and national associations took shape throughout the United States. Canoeing and camping were other diversions which gave rise to the manufacture of sporting goods on an ever larger scale. In the latter years of the century the mail-order house and the department store began to feature sporting goods. Macy's of New York began with ice skates, velocipedes, bathing suits, and beach equipment in 1872, although all sporting goods were sold by the toy department. By 1902, with the addition of numerous other items, a separate department was established. Sears, Roebuck and Company, meanwhile, devoted more than eighty pages of its 1895 catalogue to weapons and fishing equipment, and within a decade not only hunting and fishing equipment but also bicycles, boxing gloves, baseball paraphernalia, and sleds were featured.[49]

When Thomas A. Edison developed the incandescent bulb in 1879 he inaugurated a new era in the social life of our cities. Although the first dynamo was built within two years, gas lighting did not give way immediately, and the crowds which jammed the old Madison Square Garden in New York in 1883 to see John L. Sullivan fight Herbert Slade still had to cope not only with the smoke-filled air but also with the blue gas fumes. The Garden had already installed some electric lights, however. At a six-day professional walking match in 1882 the cloud of tobacco smoke was so thick that "even the electric lights" had "a hard struggle to assert their superior brilliancy" over the gas jets. Even "the noisy yell of programme, candy, fruit and peanut venders who filled the air with the vilest discord" failed to discourage the crowd, according to a philosophically minded reporter who wondered what Herbert Spencer would think of "the peculiar phase of idiocy in the American character" which drew thousands of men and women to midnight pedestrian contests.[50]

Within a few years electric lighting and more comfortable accommodations helped lure players and spectators alike to Y.M.C.A.s, athletic clubs, regimental armories, school and college gymnasiums, as well as sports arenas. In 1885, at the third annual Horse Show in Madison Square Garden, handsomely dressed sportswomen reveled in the arena, "gaudy with festoons of racing flags and brilliant streamers, lighted at night by hundreds of electric lights," while visitors to the brilliantly lighted New York Athletic Club agreed that "fine surroundings will not do an athlete any harm."[51] The indoor prize fight, walking contest, wrestling match, and horse show were a far cry from the crude atmosphere of early indoor sport. In 1890 carnivals were held at the Massachusetts Mechanics' Association by the Boston Athletic Association and at the new Madison Square Garden in New York by the Staten Island Athletic Club; the horse show attracted fashionable New Yorkers to the Garden; and indoor baseball, already popular in Chicago, was taken up in New York's regimental armories.[52] A decade of electrification, paralleling improvements in transportation and commu-

nication, had elevated and purified the atmosphere of sport. The saloon brawls of pugilists in the 1850's and 1860's were gradually abandoned for the organized matches of the 1880's and 1890's. At the time of the Sullivan-Corbett fight in the New Orleans Olympic Club in 1892, an observer wrote in the Chicago *Daily Tribune,* September 8, 1892: "Now men travel to great boxing contests in vestibule limited trains; they sleep at the best hotels . . . and when the time for the contest arrives they find themselves in a grand, brilliantly lighted arena."

Basketball and volleyball, originating in the Y.M.C.A. in 1892 and 1895, were both developed to meet the need for indoor sport on winter evenings. The rapid construction of college gymnasiums and the building of more luxurious clubhouses after the middle eighties stemmed in great part from the superior appointments and more brilliant lighting available for athletic games, and much of the urban appeal of indoor sport was directly attributable to the revolution which electric lighting made in the night life of the metropolis.

Electrification, which transformed everything from home gadgets and domestic lighting to power machinery and launches, exerted an influence on the course of sport through the development of rapid transit systems in cities from coast to coast. Horse-drawn cars had carried the burden of traffic since the 1850's, but the electric street-car assumed an entirely new role in opening up suburban areas and the countryside to the pent-up city populace. Soon after the Richmond, Virginia, experiment of 1888, the streetcar began to acquaint large numbers of city dwellers with the race track and the ball diamond.[53] Experimental lines had been laid even earlier in the decade, and Chicago crowds going to the races at Washington Park in 1887 were jammed on "the grip," one reporter noting the "perpetual stream of track slang," the prodding and pushing, and the annoying delay when it was announced that "the cable has busted."[54] Trolley parks, many of which included baseball diamonds, were promoted by the transit companies; ball teams were encouraged by these same concerns through gifts of land or grandstands; and the crowds flocked to week-end games on the cars.[55] At the turn of the century the popular interest in athletic games in thousands of towns and cities was stimulated to a high degree by the extension of rapid transit systems, a development which may possibly have been as significant in the growth of local sport as the automobile was to be in the development of intercommunity rivalries.

Numerous inventions and improvements applied to sport were of varying importance: the stop watch, the percussion cap, the streamlined sulky, barbed wire, the safety cycle, ball bearings, and artificial ice for skating rinks, among others. Improved implements often popularized and revolutionized the style of a sport, as in the invention of the sliding seat of the rowing shell, the introduction of the rubber-wound gutta-percha ball which necessitated the lengthening of golf courses, and the universal acceptance of the catcher's mask.

Vulcanization of rubber by Charles Goodyear in the 1830's led to the development of elastic and resilient rubber balls in the following decade, and eventually influenced the development of golf and tennis balls as well as other sporting apparel and equipment. The pneumatic tire, developed by Dr. John Boyd Dunlop of Belfast, Ireland, in 1888, revolutionized cycling and harness racing in the next decade. Equipped with pneumatic tires, the sulky abandoned its old highwheeler style, and the trotter and pacer found it made for smoother movement on the track. Sulky drivers reduced the mile record of 2:08¾ by Maud S. with an old highwheeler to 1:58½ by Lou Dillon in 1903 with a "bicycle sulky." According to W. H. Gocher, a racing authority, the innovation of pneumatic tires and the streamlining of the sulky cut five to seven seconds from former records, which was "more than the breeding had done in a dozen years." [56] The pneumatic tire, introduced by racing cyclists and sulky drivers, went on to play a much more vital role in the rise of the automobile industry and the spectacular appeal of auto racing.

The camera also came to the aid of sport in the decades following the Civil War. Professional photography had developed rapidly in the middle period of the century, but nature lovers became devotees of the camera only when its bulkiness and weight were eliminated in the closing years of the century. Development of the Eastman Kodak after 1888 found a mass market as thousands of Americans put it to personal and commercial use. Pictorial and sporting magazines which had been printing woodcuts since the prewar era began to introduce many pictures taken from photographs, and in the late 1880's and early 1890's actual photographic prints of ath-

letes and outdoor sportsmen came into common usage. *Harper's Weekly, Leslie's Illustrated Weekly, Illustrated American*, and the *National Police Gazette* featured photography, and by the end of the century the vast majority of their pictures were camera studies.[57] Newspapers recognized the circulation value of half-tone prints, but because of paper and technical problems they were used sparsely until the New York *Times* published an illustrated Sunday supplement in 1896, soon to be imitated by the New York *Tribune* and the Chicago *Tribune*. The year 1897 saw the half-tone illustration become a regular feature of metropolitan newspapers, rapidly eliminating the age-old reliance on woodcuts. At the turn of the century sport was available in visual form to millions who heretofore had little knowledge of athletics and outdoor games.[58]

It was in 1872 that Eadweard Muybridge made the first successful attempt "to secure an illusion of motion by photography." With the help of Leland Stanford, already a noted turfman, he set out to prove whether "a trotting horse at one point in its gait left the ground entirely."[59] By establishing a battery of cameras the movements of the horse were successively photographed, and Muybridge later turned his technique to "the gallop of dogs, the flight of birds, and the performances of athletes." In his monumental study entitled *Animal Locomotion* (1887) he included thousands of pictures of horses, athletes, and other living subjects, demonstrating "the work and play of men, women and children of all ages; how pitchers throw the baseball, how batters hit it, and how athletes move their bodies in record-breaking contests."[60] Muybridge is considered only one among a number of the pioneers of the motion picture, but his pictures had presented possibly the best illusion of motion prior to the development of flexible celluloid film. A host of experimenters gradually evolved principles and techniques in the late 1880's which gave birth to the true motion picture. Woodville Latham and his two sons made a four-minute film of the prize fight between Young Griffo and Battling Barnett in 1895, showing it on a large screen for an audience, an event which has been called "the first flickering, commercial motion picture."[61] When Bob Fitzsimmons won the heavyweight championship from James J. Corbett at Carson City Nevada, in 1897, the fight was photographed for public distribution. With the increasing popularity in succeeding years of the newsreel, the short subject, and an occasional feature film, the motion picture came to rival the photograph in spreading the gospel of sport.[62]

When sport began to mature into a business of some importance and thousands of organizations throughout the country joined leagues, associations, racing circuits, and national administrative bodies, it became necessary to utilize on a large scale the telephone, the typewriter, and all the other instruments so vital to the commercial world. Even the phonograph, at first considered a business device but soon devoted to popular music, came to have an indirect influence, recording for public entertainment such songs as "Daisy Bell," "Casey at the Bat," "Slide, Kelly, Slide," and, early in the present century, the theme song of the national pastime, "Take Me Out to the Ball Game." All of these instruments created a great revolution in communication, and they contributed significantly to the expansion of sport on a national scale.

The bicycle, still an important means of transport in Europe but something of a casualty of the machine age in the United States, also had an important role. After its demonstration at the Philadelphia Centennial, an interest was ignited which grew rapidly in the 1880's and flamed into an obsession in the 1890's.[63] Clubs, cycling associations, and racing meets were sponsored everywhere in these years, and the League of American Wheelmen served as a spearhead for many of the reforms in fashions, good roads, and outdoor exercise. Albert H. Pope was merely the foremost among many manufacturers of the "velocipede" which became so popular among women's clubs, temperance groups, professional men, and, at the turn of the century, in the business world and among the trades. Contemporary observers speculated on the social benefits to be derived from the cycle, especially in enticing women to the pleasures of outdoor exercise. Bicycling was discussed by ministers and physicians, it was considered as a weapon in future wars, police squads in some cities were mounted on wheels, mail carriers utilized it, and many thought it would revolutionize society.[64]

As a branch of American industry the bicycle was reputed to have developed into a $100,000,000 business in the 1890's. Mass-production techniques were introduced, Iver Johnson's Arms and Cycle Works advertising "Every part interchangeable and exact." The Indiana Bicycle Company, home of the Waverley cycle, maintained a huge factory in Indianapolis and claimed to be the most perfect and complete plant in the world: "We employ the highest mechanical skill and the best labor-saving machinery that ample capital can provide. Our methods of construction are along the latest and most approved lines of mechanical work."[65]

Much of the publicity given to competing manufacturers centered around the mechanical improvements and the speed records of their products. Between 1878 and 1896 the mile record was lowered from 3:57 to 1:55$^1/_5$. While recognizing the effect of better riding styles, methodical training, improved tracks, and the art of pacemaking, one critic contended, "The prime factor ... is the improvement in the vehicle itself. The racing machine of 1878 was a heavy, crude, cumbersome affair, while the modern bicycle, less than one-sixth its weight, equipped with scientifically calculated gearing, pneumatic tires, and friction annihilators, represents much of the difference."[66] Roger Burlingame has pointed out the impact of the bicycle on the health, recreation, business, and the social life of the American people and on the manufacture of the cycle he claimed that "it introduced certain technical principles which were carried on into the motor car, notably ball bearings, hub-breaking and the tangential spoke."[67] Little did cycling enthusiasts realize that in these same years a much more revolutionary vehicle, destined to transform our way of life, was about to make its dramatic appearance on the national scene.

One of the last inventions which the nineteenth century brought forth for the conquest of time and distance was the automobile. During the 1890's the Haynes, Duryea, Ford, Stanley Steamer, Packard, and Locomobile came out in quick succession, and the Pierce Arrow, Cadillac, and Buick were to follow in the next several years.[68] Manufacturers of bicycles had already turned to the construction of the motor car in a number of instances. As early as 1895 Herman H. Kohlsaat, publisher of the Chicago *Times-Herald*, sponsored the first automobile race on American soil. One of the features of this contest, run through a snowstorm and won by Charles Duryea, was the enhanced reputation achieved for the gasoline motor, which had not yet been recognized as the proper source of motor power. A number of European races inspired American drivers to take to the racecourse, and the experimental value of endurance or speed contests was immediately recognized by pioneer manufacturers. Nor were they slow to see the publicity value of races featured by the newspapers.[69]

Henry Ford "was bewitched by Duryea's feat," and he "devoured reports on the subject which appeared in the newspapers and magazines of the day." When other leading carbuilders sought financial backing for their racers, Ford determined to win supremacy on the track. After defeating Alexander Winton in a race at Detroit in 1902, "Ford's prowess as a 'speed demon' began to appear in the columns of the widely circulated trade journal *Horseless Age*."[70] In later years he was to contend, "I never thought anything of racing, but the public refused to consider the automobile in any light other than as a fast toy. Therefore later we had to race. The industry was held back by this initial racing slant, for the attention of the makers was diverted to making fast rather than good cars." The victory over Winton was his first race, "and it brought advertising of the only kind that people cared to read." Bowing to public opinion, he was determined "to make an automobile that would be known wherever speed was known," and he set to work installing four cylinders in his famous "999." Developing 80 horse power, this machine was so frightening, even to its builders, that the fearless Barney Oldfield was hired for the race. Oldfield had only a tiller with which to drive, since there were no steering wheels, but this professional cyclist who had never driven a car established a new record and helped put Ford back on his feet. The financial support of Alex Y. Malcomson, an admirer of "999," gave him a new start: "A week after the race I formed the Ford Motor Company."[71]

The next few years witnessed the establishment of Automobile Club of America races, sport clubs in the American Automobile Association, the Vanderbilt Cup, and the Glidden Tour. Reporting on the third annual Glidden Tour in 1906, *Scientific American* defended American cars, heretofore considered inferior to European models: "Above all else, the tour has demonstrated that American machines will stand fast driving on rough forest roads without serious damage to the cars or their mechanism. Engine and gear troubles have practically disappeared, and the only things that are to be feared are the breakage of springs and axles and the giving out of tires. Numerous shock-absorbers were tried out and found wanting in this test; and were it not for the pneumatic tires, which have been greatly improved during the past two years, such a tour would be impossible of accomplishment."[72]

The Newport social season featured racing, Daytona Beach soon became a center for speed trials, and tracks were built in various parts of the nation, the first of which may have been at Narragansett Park in 1896.[73] Not until the years just prior to World War I did auto racing attain a truly national popularity with the establishment of the Indianapolis Speedway, but the emphasis on speed and endurance in these early years spurred manufacturers to build ever faster models and advertisers to feature the record performances of each car. Henry Ford had long since lost interest, while the Buick racing team was discontinued in 1915. By then mass production had turned the emphasis toward design, comfort, and economy. Racing was not abandoned and manufacturers still featured endurance tests in later years, but the heated rivalry between pioneer builders had become a thing of the past.[74]

Technological developments in the latter half of the nineteenth century transformed the social habits of the Western World, and sport was but one of many institutions which felt their full impact. Fashions, foods, journalism, home appliances, commercialized entertainment, architecture, and city planning were only a few of the facets of life which underwent rapid change as transportation and communication were revolutionized and as new materials were made available. There are those who stress the thesis that sport is a direct reaction against the mechanization, the division of labor, and the standardization of life in a machine civilization,[75] and this may in part be true, but sport in nineteenth-century America was as much a product of industrialization as it was an antidote to it. While athletics and outdoor recreation were sought as a release from the confinements of city life, industrialization and the urban movement were the basic causes for the rise of organized sport. And the urban movement was, of course, greatly enhanced by the revolutionary transformation in communication, transportation, agriculture, and industrialization.[76]

The first symptoms of the impact of invention on nineteenth-century sports are to be found in the steamboat of the ante-bellum era. An intensification of interest in horse racing during the 1820's and 1830's was only a prelude to the sporting excitement over yachting, prize fighting, rowing, running, cricket, and baseball of the 1840's and 1850's. By this time the railroad was opening up new opportunities for hunters, anglers, and athletic teams, and it was the railroad, of all the inventions of the century, which gave the greatest impetus to the intercommunity rivalries in sport. The telegraph and the penny press opened the gates to a rising tide of sporting journalism; the sewing machine and the factory system revolutionized the manufacturing of sporting goods; the electric light and rapid transit further demonstrated the impact of electrification; inventions like the Kodak camera, the motion picture, and the pneumatic tire stimulated various fields of sport; and the bicycle and automobile gave additional evidence to the effect of the transportation revolution on the sporting impulse of the latter half of the century. Toward the end of the century the rapidity with which one invention followed another demonstrated the increasingly close relationship of technology and social change. No one can deny the significance of sportsmen, athletes, journalists, and pioneers in many organizations, and no one can disregard the multiple forces transforming the social scene. The technological revolution is not the sole determining factor in the rise of sport, but to ignore its influence would result only in a more or less superficial understanding of the history of one of the prominent social institutions of modern America.

NOTES

1. Among the most useful works to be consulted on early American sport are Krout, John A.: Annals of American Sport. New Haven, 1929; Holliman, Jennie: American Sports, 1785–1835. Durham, 1931; Dulles, Foster R.: America Learns To Play: A History of Popular Recreation, 1607–1940. New York, 1940; Weaver, Robert B.: Amusements and Sports in American Life. Chicago, 1939; and Manchester, Herbert: Four Centuries of Sport in America, 1490–1890. New York, 1931. For certain aspects of ante-bellum sport, see Schlesinger, Arthur M., and Fox, Dixon R.: (eds.), A History of American Life, 13 vols. New York, 1927–1948.

2. See the New York American, May 27, 1823; New Orleans Daily Picayune, March 27, 1839; New York Weekly Herald, May 17, 1845, July 11, 1849; and accounts of many races in the Spirit of the Times (New York) for prewar years. In an era when bridges were more the exception than the rule the ferry was an indispensable means of transportation. See, for example, Roberts, Kenneth, and Roberts, Anna M.: (eds.), Moreau de St. Mery's American Journey, 1793–1798. Garden City, 1947, 173; New York American, May 27, 1823.

3. For examples of the steamboat in early sport, see the New York Herald, June 17, 1849; Wilkes' Spirit of the Times (New York), XII (August 5, 1865), 380; New Orleans Daily Picayune, December 1, 1855, December 10, 1859; Spirit of the Times, XX (June 19, 1869), 276; New York World, June 19, 1869. When the passenger lines began converting to steam in the Civil War era, the development of international sport was facilitated to a considerable degree. In the latter decades of the century the steam yacht became the vogue among American millionaires.

4. Hervey, John: Racing in America, 1665–1865, 2 vols. New York, 1944, II, 101.

5. New Orleans Daily Picayune, March 27, 1839.

6. American Turf Register and Sporting Magazine (Baltimore), XIII (July, 1843), 367; New York Daily Tribune, May 14, 1845.

7. Spirit of the Times, XXI (July 12, 1851), 246.

8. Demaree, Albert L.: The American Agricultural Press, 1819–1860 (New York, 1941), 203–204. Specific instances of such aid can be found in the Cultivator (Albany), IX (March, 1842), 50; American Agriculturist (New York), II (October 16, 1843), 258; New York Daily Tribune, September 18, 1851; Transactions of the Illinois State Agricultural Society (Springfield), I, 1853–54 (1855), 6; II, 1856–57 (1857), 24–32; Report and Proceedings of the Iowa State Agricultural Society ... October, 1855 (Fairfield, 1856), 24; Fifth Report of the Indiana State Board of Agriculture ... For the Year 1856 (Indianapolis, 1858), 34, 482–83; Kentucky Farmer (Frankfort), I (July, 1858), 12; Wisconsin Farmer and North-Western Cultivator (Madison), IX (October, 1857), 873; XI (October, 1859), 386–87; Springfield Weekly Illinois State Journal, September 5, 19, 1860. The "ploughing matches" of the ante-bellum era attracted large crowds seeking both entertainment and the latest improvements in agricultural implements.

9. Crowther, Samuel, and Ruhl, Arthur: Rowing and Track Athletics. New York, 1905, 11.

10. James N. Elkins, superintendent of the Boston, Concord and Montreal Railroad, agreed to pay all transportation costs for the crews and their equipment to the New Hampshire lake where the race was to be held. Kelley, Robert F.: American Rowing: Its Background and Traditions. New York, 1932, 100–101.

11. New York Daily Times, October 13, 1853; Boston Advertiser, October 14, 1853.

12. New York Herald, October 23, 1858.

13. Wilkes' Spirit of the Times, XIV (July 7, 1866), 294. More rural areas felt the impact somewhat later, Warrenton, Mississippi, holding a tourney in 1885 to which special trains were sent. New Orleans Daily Picayune, July 19, 1885.

14. New York World, August 21, 1869; Cincinnati Commercial, September 22, 1869; San Francisco Evening Bulletin, October 5, 1869. Their use of Pullman cars set a precedent in sports circles. Advertising by local lines for an approaching game appeared in the Cincinnati Commercial, August 24, 1869.

15. See Spalding's Official Base Ball Guide (New York, 1886), appendix. The Memphis Reds Base Ball Association sent a printed circular to Harry Wright of the Boston team in 1877 in which it stressed the reduced rates to any club visiting St. Louis or Louisville. Harry Wright Correspondence, 7 vols., I (1865–1877), 40, Spalding Baseball Collection (New York Public Library). In the 1880's enthusiastic crowds turned out to the railroad station to welcome home the victorious nines. Frank Leslie's Boys' and Girls' Weekly (New York), XXXV (October 6, 1883), 174; New York Sun, September 7, 1886.

16. Turf, Field and Farm (New York), I (September 2, 1865), 69; VIII (May 28, 1869), 344.

17. Wilkes' Spirit of the Times, XIV (May 19, 1866), 185; San Francisco Evening Bulletin, October 15, 1869; Baltimore American and Commercial Advertiser, October 25, 1877; New Orleans Daily Picayune, April 20, 1884, May 9, 15, 1885; Charles E. Trevathan, The American Thoroughbred (New York, 1905), 371.

18. New York World, April 29, 1884.

19. Johnston, Alexander: Ten—And Out! The Complete Story of the Prize Ring in America. New York, 1947, 42–43.

20. Rowland, Dunbar: (ed.), Encyclopedia of Mississippi History, 2 vols. Madison 1907, II, 142; St. Paul and Minneapolis Pioneer Press, February 8, 1882; New Orleans Daily Picayune, August 6, 1885; New York Sun, May 12, 1886.

21. Railroad interest in sport was illustrated by the New York Railroad Gazette: "Horse-racing tracks of the violest [sic] character are encouraged (indirectly, it may be) in more than one case by railroads normally law-abiding. Sunday excursions patronized chiefly by roughs who conduct baseball games of a character condemned by all decent people are morally the same as prize fights in kind though not in degree." Quoted in the New Orleans Daily Picayune, August 6, 1885.

22. For illustrations of the difficulties of railroad travel, see Walter Camp Correspondence, Box 64 (Yale University, Library, New Haven).

23. Wilkes' Spirit of the Times, XIII (October 14, 1865), 102.

24. Davis, Parke H.: Football, The American Intercollegiate Game. New York, 1911, 45.

25. Outing (New York), XII (August, 1888), 407–408.

26. By the 1890's many railroads carried bicycles as free freight and professional cyclists could tour their National Circuit in luxury cars. New York Journal, September 18, 1897.

27. Scores of railroads in every section of the country served those seeking to hunt or fish in the rustic countryside. See, particularly, Hallock, Charles: (ed.), The Sportsman's Gazetteer and General Guide. New York, 1877, Pt. II, 1–182. See also the Chicago and Northwestern Railway advertisement in the Spirit of the Times, XCII (August 19, 1876), 53.

28. For the early development of the telegraph, see Reid, James D.: The Telegraph in America and Morse Memorial. New York, 1887; Kaempffert, Waldemar: (ed.), A Popular History of American Invention, 2 vols. New York, 1924; and Thompson, Robert L.: Wiring a Continent: The History of the Telegraph Industry in the United States, 1832–1866. Princeton, 1947.

29. Boston Daily Journal, February 7, 8, 9, 1849; New York Daily Tribune, February 8, 9, 1849; Milwaukee Sentinel and Gazette, February 10, 1849; Boston Daily Courier, October 21, 1858; New York Times, October 21, 1858; New Orleans Daily Picayune, May 6, 7, June 29, 1860; Nashville Daily News, April 29, 1860.

30. New York Daily Tribune, September 19, 1851; Natchez Courier, September 19, 1851.

31. New Orleans Daily Picayune, July 6, 1870.

32. Ibid. See also New York Times, October 21, 1858; Harper's Weekly (New York), XXVII (October 13, 1883), 654.

33. Gramling, Oliver: AP; The Story of News. New York, 1940, 232; New Orleans Daily Picayune, July 10, 1889. For poolrooms, saloons, and bulletin boards, see the New York Sun, October 6, 1878; New York Herald, February 7, 1882; New Orleans Daily Picayune, May 17, 1884, July 6, 1885; New York World, September 8, 1892. Also see Harper's Weekly, XXVII (October 13, 1883), 654; XXXVI (April 2, December 17, 1892), 319, 324, 1210. Henry L. Mencken, in Happy Days, 1880–1892 (New York, 1940), 225, nostalgically recalled how, since there were few sporting "extras" in Baltimore in the 1880's, "the high-toned saloons of the town catered to the [baseball] fans by putting in telegraph operators who wrote the scores on blackboards."

34. The New York Transcript and the Sun sensationalized the news as early as the 1830's and began reporting prize fights. James Gordon Bennett's Herald exploited sporting interest in pre-Civil War years and his son continued to do so in the period following the war. Magazines which capitalized on sport included the American Turf Register and Sporting Magazine, the Spirit of the Times, the New York Clipper, and the National Police Gazette (New York), as well as a host of fishing and hunting journals. Through the 1880's and 1890's the New York Sun and the World competed for the sporting public, only to be outdone by the Journal at the end of the century. Among the prominent writers of the era were Henry Chadwick, Timothy Murnane, Harry Weldon, Harry C. Palmer, Al Spink, Sam Crane, Walter Camp, Caspar Whitney, and Charles Dryden. See Nugent, William H.: The sports section. American Mercury XVI (February, 1929), 329–38; and Fullerton, Hugh: The fellows who made the game. Saturday Evening Post, CC (April 21, 1928), 18 ff.

35. New York Herald, December 30, 31, 1866; Cincinnati Commercial, August 24, 28, 1869; Frank Leslie's Illustrated Newspaper (New York), XXIX (September 28, 1869), 2.

36. The origins of the penny press are ably discussed in Bleyer, Willard G.: Main Currents in the History of American Journalism. Boston, 1927, 154–84; and in Mott, Frank L.: American Journalism, A History (New York, 1941), 228–52.

37. Bleyer, History of American Journalism, 197, 209; Lee, Alfred M.: The Daily Newspaper in America. New York, 1937, 611; New York Weekly Herald, May 15, 17, 1845, and Herald files for the 1840's.

38. Bleyer, History of American Journalism, 394.

39. Ibid., 394–98.

40. Joseph Pulitzer's New York World began an intensive exploitation of sport as a front-page attraction almost immediately after its purchase in 1883, and by

the following year first-page accounts of pedestrian matches, dog shows, and similar topics became regular features.

41. Johannsen, Albert: The House of Beadle and Adams and its Dime and Nickel Novel: The Story of a Vanished Literature, 2 vols. Norman, 1950, I, 260, 377–79.

42. Cutler, John L.: Gilbert Patten and His Frank Merriwell Saga, University of Maine Studies (Orono), Ser. II, No. 31 (1934).

43. Goodspeed, Charles E.: Angling in America: Its Early History and Literature. Boston, 1939, 285 ff.

44. Hallock, Charles: The Fishing Tourist: Angler's Guide and Reference Book. New York, 1873, 18.

45. In 1900 the value of sporting goods manufactured was only $3,628,496. United States Bureau of the Census, Statistical Abstract of the United States (Washington, 1909), 188.

46. See the Spirit of the Times, XX (May 4, 1850), 130; Natchez Courier, November 26, 1850; Madison Daily State Journal, March 26, 1855; New Orleans Daily Picayune, April 4, 1856. As midwestern merchants began to purchase large stocks from the East, John Krider advertised widely. Madison Daily State Journal, April 13, 1855. Michael Phelan, who in 1854 developed an indiarubber cushion permitting sharp edges on billiard tables, joined with Hugh W. Collender in forming Phelan and Collender, the leading billiards manufacturer until the organization of the Brunswick-Balke-Collender Company in 1884. Gymnastic apparatus, created by Dudley A. Sargent and other physical educators, was featured by many dealers, while the readers of American Angler (New York), Forest and Stream (New York), and other sporting journals were kept informed of the latest models of rifles, shotguns, and fishing rods and reels.

47. George B. Ellard, who sponsored the Red Stockings, advertised his store as "Base Ball Headquarters" and "Base Ball Depot," with the "Best Stock in the West." Cincinnati Commercial, August 24, 1869. Other merchandisers included Horsman's Base Ball and Croquet Emporium in New York and John H. Mann of the same city. Peck & Snyder began dealing in baseball equipment in 1865 and by the 1880's claimed to be the largest seller of sporting goods.

48. King, Moses: (ed.), King's Handbook of the United States. Buffalo, 1891, 232; Bartlett, Arthur: Baseball and Mr. Spalding: The History and Romance of Baseball. New York, 1951 passim: Fortune (New York), II (August, 1930), 62 ff.; Bartlett, Arthur, They're just wild about sports. Saturday Evening Post, CCXXII (December 24, 1949), 31 ff.; Spalding's Official Base Ball Guide for 1887 (New York and Chicago, 1887), passim.

49. It was on mass manufacture of baseballs and uniforms that Spalding gained such a leading position in the sporting goods field. Since the business was restricted in these early years certain difficulties had to be overcome. To make the most out of manufacturing bats Spalding bought his own lumber mill in Michigan, while Albert Pope received little sympathy from the rolling mills in his first years of manufacturing bicycles. Wheelman (Boston), I (October, 1882), 71. For department and mailorder stores, see Ralph M. Hower, History of Macy's of New York, 1858–1919 (Cambridge, 1946), 103, 162, 234–35, 239; Emmet,

Boris, and Jeuck, John C.; Catalogues and Counters: A History of Sears, Roebuck and Company. Chicago, 1950, 38; Cohn, David L.: The Good Old Days. New York, 1940, 443–60.

50. New York Herald, October 23, 1882; New York Sun, August 7, 1883. The introduction of electric lighting in theaters was discussed, while the opposition of gas companies was recognized. Scientific American, Supplement (New York), XVI (November 10, 1883), 6535–36.

51. Harper's Weekly. XXIX (February 14, November 14, 1885), 109, 743.

52. See Ibid., XXXIV (March 1, 8, 1890), 169, 171, 179. A new Madison Square Garden with the most modern facilities was built in the years 1887–1890; the California Athletic Club in San Francisco featured a "powerful electric arc light" over its ring; and electric lights in the Manhattan Athletic Club's new gymnasium in 1890 "shed a dazzling whiteness." Ibid., XXXIV (April 5, 1890), 263–64; New York Daily Tribune, November 2, 30, 1890.

53. After the completion of the Richmond line rapid transit spread throughout the country. Although in 1890 there were only 144 electric railways in a national total of 789 street lines, by 1899 there were 50,600 electric cars in operation as contrasted to only 1,500 horse cars. Willets, Gilson: et al., Workers of the Nation, 2 vols. New York, 1903, I, 498. For the suburban influence, see the Street Railway Journal (New York), XVIII (November 23, 1901, 760–61).

54. Chicago Tribune, July 5, 1887.

55. Street Railway Journal, XI (April, 1895), 232; XII (May, November, 1896), 317, 319, 708; Cosmopolitan (New York), XXXIII (July, 1902), 266; Collier's (New York), CXXV (May, 1950), 85; Oscar Handlin, This Was America (Cambridge, 1949); 374; New Orleans Daily Picayune, February 27, 1899.

56. Gocher, W. H.: Trotalong. Hartford, 1928, 190.

57. Taft, Robert: Photography and the American Scene: A Social History, 1839–1889. New York, 1938, 441.

58. Photography developed throughout the nineteenth century as an adjunct of the science of chemistry. Chemical and mechanical innovations were also responsible for the improvements of prints and all kinds of reproductions. Woodcuts were featured in the press, engravings were sold widely, and lithographs were found in the most rural home. Nathaniel Currier (later Currier & Ives) published hunting, fishing, pugilistic, baseball, rowing, yachting, sleighing, skating, trotting, and racing scenes for more than half a century. Cheap prints, calendars, and varied reproductions of sporting scenes did much to popularize the famous turf champions and sporting heroes of the era. See Peters, Harry T.: Currier & Ives: Printmakers to the American People. Garden City, 1942.

59. Dyer, Frank L., and Martin, Thomas C.: Edison: His Life and Inventions, 2 vols. New York, 1910, II, 534–35.

60. Kaempffert, Popular History of American Inventions, I, 425.

61. Morris, Lloyd: Not So Long Ago. New York, 1949, 24.

62. The pioneer years of the motion picture industry are described by numerous other works, among them Taylor, Deems: A Pictorial History of the Movies.

New York, 1943, 1–6; Wood, Leslie: The Miracle of the Movies. London, 1947, 66 ff.; Bryan, George S.: Edison: The Man and His Work. Garden City, 1926, 184–94; Eder, Josef M.: History of Photography, trans. by Edward Epstean. New York, 1945, 495 ff.; Taft, Photography and the American Scene, 405–12; Morris, Not So Long Ago, 1–35.

63. There was a brief craze in 1869, during which year, according to Albert H. Pope, "more than a thousand inventions were patented for the perfection and improvement of the velocipede." Wheelman, I (October, 1882), 70. Interest declined, however, until the Philadelphia celebration of 1876. Although race meetings and cycling clubs were widely reported in the 1880's, there were only 83 repair establishments in 1890 and the value of products in bicycle and tricycle repairs was only about $300,000. By 1900 there were 6,378 repair shops and the value in repairs exceeded $13,000,000. United States Bureau of the Census, Statistical Abstract of the United States (Washington, 1904), 516.

64. For summaries of the impact of the bicycle, see Andrews, E. Benjamin: History of the Last Quarter-Century in the United States, 1870–1895, 2 vols. New York, 1896, II, 289–90; Schlesinger, Arthur M.: The Rise of the City, 1878–1898. New York, 1933, 312–14; Burlingame, Roger: Engines of Democracy: Inventions and Society in Mature America. New York, 1940, 369–74.

65. Harper's Weekly, XL (April 11, 1896), 365. It is interesting that the "father of scientific management," Frederick W. Taylor, a tennis champion and golf devotee, was said to have learned through sport "the value of the minute analysis of motions, the importance of methodical selection and training, the worth of time study and of standards based on rigorously exact observation." De Fréminville, Charles: How Taylor introduced the scientific method into management of the shop. Critical Essays on Scientific Management, Taylor Society Bulletin (New York), X (February, 1925), Pt. II, 32. Mass-production techniques, however, were only partially responsible for the outpouring of athletic goods which began to win wider markets at the turn of the century. The manufacture of baseball bats remained a highly specialized trade, while Scotch artisans who came to the United States maintained the personalized nature of their craft as makers of golf clubs. Despite the great improvements in gun manufacture, Elisha J. Lewis asserted in 1871 that there were thousands of miserable guns on the market: "The reason of this is that our mechanics have so many tastes and fancies to please, owing principally to the ignorance of those who order fowling-pieces, that they have adopted no generally-acknowledged standard of style to guide them in the getting up of guns suitable for certain kinds of sport." Lewis, Elisha J.: The American Sportsman. Philadelphia, 1871, 435. Although numerous industries had taken up the principle of interchangeable parts, mass-production techniques were to come to the fore only with the assembly lines of Henry Ford and the automobile industry in the years before World War I.

66. Harper's Weekly, XL (April 11, 1896), 366.

67. Burlingame, Engines of Democracy: Inventions and Society in Mature America, 3.

68. Duncan, Herbert O.: World on Wheels, 2 vols. Paris, 1927, II, 919 ff.

69. Seltzer, Lawrence H.: A Financial History of the American Automobile Industry. Boston, 1928, 91; Sauvestre, Pierre: Histoire de l'Automobile (Paris, 1907), passim; Epstein, Ralph C.: The Automobile Industry, Its Economic and Commercial Development. Chicago, 1928, 154; Cleveland, Reginald M. and Williamson, S. T.: The Road Is Yours. New York, 1951, 175–76, 194–97.

70. Sward, Keith: The Legend of Henry Ford. New York, 1948, 14.

71. Ford, Henry, and Crowther, Samuel: My Life and Work. Garden City, 1927. 36–37, 50–51.

72. Scientific American, XCV (August 11, 1906), 95.

73. Baright, G. F.: Automobiles and automobile races at Newport. Independent, (New York), LIV (June 5, 1902), 1368.

74. In these years the motorcycle and the motorboat also created interest, Sir Alfred Harmsworth (later Lord Northcliffe) establishing the Harmsworth Trophy for international competition in 1903. Air races also won widespread publicity in the press from 1910 onward. Glenn H. Curtiss achieved an enviable reputation as an aviator, newspapers sponsored air meets, and considerable attention was given to the "new sport of the air." Ibid., LXIX (November 3, 1910), 999.

75. Mumford, Lewis: Technics and Civilization. New York, 1934, 303–305; Toynbee, Arnold J.: A Study of History, 6 vols. London, 1934–1939, IV, 242–43.

76. Technological developments throughout the business world transformed the pattern of city life. The electric elevator and improvements in the manufacture of steel made possible the skyscrapers of Chicago and New York in the late 1880's. Concentration of the business community in the central part of the city was increased also by the telephone switchboard and other instruments of communication. Less and less open land remained for the youth living in the heart of the metropolis, and it was to meet this challenge that the Y.M.C.A., the settlement house, the institutional church, the boys' club, and other agencies expanded their athletic facilities. The playground movement and the public park grew out of the necessity for recreational areas for city dwellers, and public authorities early in the twentieth century began to rope off streets for children at play. The subway, the streetcar, and the automobile made possible the accelerated trend toward suburban development, where the open lot or planned play area offered better opportunities to participate in sport. The more general implications of the impact of the technological revolution on society, already considered by several outstanding scholars, are not discussed here, the principal aim of this study being to describe the interrelationship of sport and invention in the latter half of the nineteenth century. Although the account of the auto slightly transgressed the limits of this study, it was felt necessary to give it an abbreviated treatment. The twentieth century, and the role of improved sporting equipment, racing and training devices, the radio, television, improved highways, and bus and air transport, would require an equally extensive study.

the interdependence of sport and culture *

GÜNTHER LÜSCHEN

I INTRODUCTION

Sport is a rational, playful activity in interaction, which is extrinsically rewarded. The more it is rewarded, the more it tends to be work; the less, the more it tends to be play.[1] If we describe it in an action system frame of reference, this activity depends on the organic, personality, social, and cultural systems. By tradition, physical education has tried to explain this action system largely on the grounds of the organic system, and sometimes making reference to the personality system. Only on rare occasions has it been approached systematically from the social and cultural systems as well. Yet it seems obvious that any action going on in this system ought to be explained with reference to all of the subsystems of the action system.

Even such a simple motor activity as walking is more than a matter of organic processes initiated by the personality system. It is determined by the social and cultural systems as well, as is most evident in the way the Israelis from the Yemen walk. Since in their former society in the Yemen, the Jews were the outcasts, and every Yemenite could feel free to hit a Jew (whenever he could get hold of one), the Yemenite Jew would always run in order to escape this oppression. This way of walking finally became an in-

Reprinted from International Review of Sport Sociology, 2:127–139, 1967. Copyright 1967 by International Review of Sport Sociology, Warsaw, Poland.

* A paper presented to the National Meeting of the American Association of Health, Physical Education and Recreation in Las Vegas, 1967.

tegrated pattern of his culture. And though the environment in Israel no longer is hostile to him, the Yemenite Israeli still carries this pattern with him as part of his culture and walks in a shy and hasty way. This example shows in addition that the different subsystems of action are not independent from one another; they are structurally related. Thus, in dealing with the cultural system of sport and its interdependence with general culture, we will not always be able to explain the culture of sport and that of its environment in terms of the cultural system, and therefore should refer as well to the social and personality system to describe and explain what we call culture. It was Radcliffe-Brown who stressed the point that culture should be explained through its social structure. Furthermore, one should discuss the function of a unit within general culture, as well as cultural process and change.[2]

II. CONCEPTS OF CULTURE AND REVIEW OF RESULTS

Culture as a concept does not refer to behavior itself. It deals with those patterns and abstractions that underlie behavior or are the result of it. Thus culture consists of cognitive elements which grow out of everyday or scientific experience. It consists of beliefs, values, norms, and of signs that include symbols of verbal as well as non-verbal communication.[3]

Anthropologists have sometimes held a broader view of culture and given more attention to the material results of human behavior. Leslie White in a critique of the above-stated concept of culture has called for more attention to "acts, thoughts and things dependent upon symboling." These would include not only the study of the above-mentioned elements, but also those of art, tools, machines, fetishes, etc.[4] As attractive as White's critique may be, especially for cultural anthropology as an independent science, this approach as related to the cultural study of sport has led more to mere curiosity about things than to theoretical insights. This methodological approach has also dealt more with the cultural diffusion of sport and games than with the social structure of which they are a part. For decades we have learned about all types of games in all types of societies (especially primitive ones), which may well lead to the conclusion that we know more about the games and sports displayed by some Polynesian tribe than those of our own children and ancestors. For an understanding of sport it is less important to find the same games in different cultures as Tylor did.[5] It is more important to analyze, for example, the different meaning of baseball in the United States and Lybia, which in the one culture has at least latent ritualistic functions, while it has also economic functions in the other.[6]

Another concept of culture, mainly held in Central Europe, has almost led to the same results for sport. In this concept "higher" culture was separated from civilization and expressed itself significantly in the arts and sciences. On the basis of values attributed to sport *a priori*, it was related either to "Zivilisation" or to Kultur.[7] Physical educationalists through Huizinga's theory on the origin of culture in play saw in the latter approach their main support.[8] Thus defining sport as a special form of play, physical educationalists felt safe in their implicit attempt to justify sport for educational purposes. Yet Huizinga's theory has not only been criticized on the basis of ethnological findings,[9] but he himself was very critical about the play element in sport.[10] Those that believed in the role of sport within higher culture were hardly able to prove their hypothesis. So, as recently as Rene Maheu,[11] they often expressed their hope that sport in the future would contribute to "Kultur."

One can hardly deny that sport has indeed some impact on "higher" culture, as may be shown by symbolic elements from sport to be found in script and language. In an analysis of the cultural meaning of the ballgame of the Aztecs and Maya, Krickeberg found that in their script there were elements related to this game. The symbol for movement, for example, was identical with the I-shape of the ball court.[12] "To get (take) a rain check" refers to baseball, but has now become in American English symbolic for any situation where you get another chance. "That's not cricket" refers to a dishonest procedure in everyday life. And though German is not as idiomatic as English, it contains elements which originated in sport and games as well. "Katzbalgerei," and the phrase "sich gegenseitig die Bälle zuspielen," refer to a game which today is still known in the Netherlands as "Kaatsen" and perhaps appears in the New York children's game of one-o-cat. As did football in Shakespeare's "King Lear," so appeared this game and its terminology in the 16th century poetry of J.G. Fischart.[13]

How weak these relationships of sport indeed are to "higher" culture may be shown by the relatively unsuccessful attempts to establish, through special contests in modern Olympics, a relationship between sport and the arts. Sport only rarely expresses itself in the material aspects of culture. It is what I would like to call a momentary activity. Just from a certain level on, an event may have its appearance on such a short range cultural element as the sports page of the next day's newspaper.[14] This appearance of sport in the media of mass communication, in language, poetry, and the arts is significant for the overall meaning of sport within society, but these manifestations tell us little about sport itself and its interdependence with general culture as we define it.

It may also be interesting to discuss cognitive elements such as scientific insight coming out of sport. Also religious beliefs and ritual found in sport would be an interesting point of analysis. Yet after showing how sport is indeed bound to society and structured by general culture, we will mainly discuss our problem on the level of cultural values and their related social structure.

III. SPORT AS PART OF CULTURE AND SOCIETY

That sport is structurally related to culture and society has sometimes been questioned. Yet it is quite easy to show how strong this relationship is. Sport is indeed an expression of that sociocultural system in which it occurs. David Riesman and Reuel Denney describe how American football was changed through the American culture from rugby to a completely different game. It is now well integrated and quite obviously shows in its vigor, hard contact and a greater centrality on the individual, the basic traits of the culture of American society.[15]

On the level of the so-called primitive societies we see the same dependence of sport and games on culture and its underlying social structure. The Hopi Indians had 16 different terms for foot races which nearly all referred to one aspect of the social organization of that tribe.[16] A recent socio-historical study on three Illinois subcultures finds the same close relationship between socio-cultural system and sport.[17] And Käte Hye-Kerkdal outlines the tight structural relation between the log-races of the tribe of the Timbira in Brazil and their socio-cultural system. This ritualistic competition between two teams has symbolic meaning for nearly every aspect of the dual-organization of this tribe. It refers to all kinds of religious and social polarities and is so strongly imbedded in this religious-dominated system that winning or losing does not have any effect on the status of the team or individual, nor are there any other extrinsic rewards. Yet these races are performed vigorously and with effort.[18]

Now that we have proven that there is a structural relationship between sport and culture, the first question is that of sport's dependency on culture. What factors make for the appearance of sport? Or more specifically, what are the underlying cultural values?

IV CULTURAL VALUES AND SPORT

By values we mean those general orientations in a socio-cultural system that are not always obvious to its members, but are implicit in actual behavior. On the level of the personality system they are expressed partly in attitudes. Values should be separated from norms which are derived from values and are actual rules for behavior. For instance, health is a high value in the American culture, as it seems to be in all young cultures, while death is higher in the hierarchy of values in old cultures like India.[19] On this continuum we may explain why sport as an expression of the evaluation of health is more important in American than in Indian society. The whole emphasis on physical fitness in the United States may well be explained by this

background, and the norm "run for your life" is directly related to it.

1. SPORT, INDUSTRIALIZATION AND TECHNOLOGY

In comparing the uneven distribution and performance level of sport all over the world, one widely accepted hypothesis is that sport is an offspring of technology and industrialization. The strong emphasis on sport in industrialized societies seems to show that industrialization and technology are indeed a basis for sport. This would be a late confirmation of Ogburn's theory of social change, as well as of Marxian theory that society and its structure depend on its economic basis. However, there are quite a number of inconsistencies. Not all sport-oriented societies or societal subsystems show a relation to technology and industrialization, and historically games and sport have been shown to have existence prior to industrialization. Yet it can hardly be denied that certain conditions in the later process of industrialization have promoted sport, and technology has at least its parallels in modern sport. The above-stated hypothesis may, despite its obvious limitations, lead us to the independent variables.

2. SPORT, A PROTESTANT SUBCULTURE?

In an investigation that because of its methodological procedure turned out to be a profound critique of Marxian materialism, Max Weber studied the interrelationship of what he called "The Protestant Ethic and the Spirit of Capitalism."[20] This investigation about the underlying values of capitalism in Western societies quoted data on the overrepresentation of Protestants in institutions of higher learning, their preference for industrial and commercial occupations and professions, and the stronger trend towards capitalism in Protestant-dominated countries (most obvious in the United States). Weber found not the material basis but Protestant culture, with achievement of worldly success and asceticism held as the basic values, caused industrialization and capitalism. In accordance with the Calvinistic belief in predestination, the Protestant felt that he was blessed by God once he had achieved success. Thus, need for achievement became an integrated part of his personality and a basic value in Protestantism.

Together with the value of asceticism this led to the accumulation of wealth and to Western capitalism. If we turn to sport, we find the same values of achievement and asceticism. Even the Puritans, generally opposed to a leisurely life, could therefore justify sport as physical activity that contributed to health.[21] Today we find significance for this relationship in the YMCA, in a group like the American Fellowship of Christian Athletes, and also in the Protestant minister who in Helsinki became an Olympic medal winner in the pole vault. He showed the consistency between Protestantism and sport in his prayer right after his Olympic winning vault. Max Weber's findings about the relationship between the Protestant ethic and the spirit of capitalism may thus well be extended to the "spirit" of sport. Not only Weber was aware of this relationship, but also Thorstein Veblen who described the parallels in religious and sport ritual.[22]

The relationship between sport and Protestantism is not only to be observed in the emphasis on sport in the Scandinavian and other Protestant countries. A rough compilation of the probable religious preference of Olympic medal winners on the basis of the percentage of different religious groups in their countries also shows the dominance of Protestantism up to 1960. Protestantism accounted for more than 50 per cent of the medal winners, while its ratio among the world population is less than 8 per cent.[23] Furthermore, in 1958 a survey of young athletes in West Germany revealed a distribution according to religious preference as shown in Table 1:[24]

among those that have achieved a higher level of performance. Thus it may be concluded that there is a correlation between Protestantism and sport and the culture of both. This was obvious for individual sports, but less for team sports where in the German sample Catholics appeared quite often. Since in Catholicism collectivity is highly regarded, this inconsistency is to be explained by the value of collectivity in team sports. It is consistent with this hypothesis that Catholic Notre Dame University has been one of the innovators of football in America. At present, it is a leading institution in this discipline. And internationally Catholic-dominated South America is overall rather poor in individual sports, but outstanding in team sports like soccer and basketball.

This result on the overall, strong relationship between sport and Protestantism is, despite support by data, theoretically insufficient. As was the case with sport in its relationship to industrialization, there are many exceptions. The high achievement in sport of the Russians, the Poles, the Japanese, the Mandan Indians, the Sikhs in India, or the Watusi in Africa can not be related to Protestantism, though in Japanese Zen-Buddhism there are parallels.

3. THE CENTRALITY OF THE ACHIEVEMENT-VALUE

Since again Protestantism can not be specifically identified as being the independent variable, we may hypothesize that there is a more general system of values as the basis for Protestantism, capitalism and sport. In his critique of

TABLE 1

	Whole Population West Germany	Sport Club Members 15–25	Track; Swimming	High Achievers Track/Swimming
Protestants	52%	60%	67%	73%
Catholics	44%	37%	31%	26%
Others	4%	3%	2%	1%
n =	universe	1,880	366	111

These figures indicate the overrepresentation of Protestants in German sport. Moreover, they indicate a higher percentage in individual sports, and an even higher percentage of Protestants

Max Weber, McClelland has considered the ethic of Protestantism as a special case of the general achievement orientation of a system, this being the independent variable. Achievement orientation (or, as he puts it on the personality-system-level, need achievement) precedes all periods of high cultural achievement in ancient Greece, in the Protestant Reformation, in modern industrialism[25] and, as we may conclude, in modern sport. He referred in his analysis also to the related social structure of the achievement value (such as family organization), which should also be studied in relationship to sport.

If we turn again to the cross-cultural comparison of those systems that participate and perform strongly in sport, we find that in all of these societies achievement-orientation is basic. In Russia this value is expressed in the norm that social status should depend only on achievement. The Sikhs and the Watusi are both minority groups in their environment. In order to keep their position, they have to achieve more than the other members of the societies they live in. The Japanese[26] and the Mandan Indians[27] also place a heavy emphasis on achievement.

Similar results appear in cross-cultural investigations of different types of games as related to basic orientations in the process of socialization. Roberts and Sutton-Smith find in a secondary analysis of the Human Relation Area Files of G.P. Murdock that games of chance are related to societies that emphasize routine responsibility in the socialization process. Games of strategy are found in societies where obedience [is stressed], games of physical skill in those where achievement is stressed.[28] Individual sports would mainly qualify as games of physical skill and again show achievement as their basic cultural value. Team sports as well are games of strategy. Their relation to training of obedience would support exactly what we called earlier the value of collectivity.

It remains an open question, for further research into the value structure of sport, as to which other values are related to this system. It is to be expected that the structure of values will be more complex than it appears on the basis of our limited insight now. Roberts and Sutton-Smith briefly remark that games of physical skill are related to occupational groups that exert power over others.[29] Thus, power orientation may be another value supporting sport. This would cross-culturally be consistent with power-oriented political systems that strongly emphasize sport. Here we could refer to countries like Russia or the United States, as well as to a tribe like the Mandan Indians.

4. THE CULTURE OF SOCIETAL SUBSYSTEMS AND ITS RELATION TO SPORT

Within a society we find subsystems that have their own subculture, which will be another influence on (condition for) sport. The female role in modern societies still depends on a culture that stresses obedience as the main value-orientation, while the male culture is strongly oriented towards achievement. Thus we find a disproportionately high participation of men in sport which in most of the disciplines is a male culture. One of the most male-oriented sports, however, is pool, a game supported mainly by the subculture of the bachelor. This has, with the general change in the number of people marrying, lost its main supporting culture.[30]

Another subsystem which in its culture shows a strong relationship to sport is that of the adolescent age group.[31] Sport is dependent more on the culture of the adolescent than on that of any other age group. Helanko raises the point, referring to his studies of boys' gangs in Turku, that sport has its origin in the gang-age and in boys' gangs. The fact that there are no rules for early sports to be found is seen as one of the supporting factors.[32] Generally speaking, achievement is again more central as a value in adolescence and early adulthood than later, where the main response to sport goes not so much towards achievement but towards values of health and fitness.

The different social classes have a culture of their own. The greatest emphasis on achievement, and thus the highest sport participation, is to be found in the upper-middle class. It is considerably less important in the lower class where routine responsibility is valued. The notion that there is no way to gain higher status accounts for the high regard for games of chance or those sports where one may just have a lucky punch, as in boxing.[33] Loy has related the different types of games and the passive and active participation in sport to different modes of adaptation and to the members of social classes.[34] His theoretical analysis as to "innovation" found in the lower class, ritualism in the lower-middle class and conformity in the upper-middle class is supported by data[35] that show the same ways of adaptation in sport. However, in responding to the social class system and its culture as related to sport one should have in mind that class determined behavior may not follow the traditional class lines in sport. Sport may indeed show or promote new orientations in the class system.[36]

Finally, sport is organized within, or relates to different institutions whose cultures sometimes have a profound influence on sport itself. This is especially true for physical education in schools where, with the same skills and rules, we may find a completely different culture as compared to sport in the military establishment. And while intercollegiate and interscholastic athletics are overall a surprisingly well integrated subculture within American schools and universities, the different values held by an educational (the school or university) and a solely success-oriented unit (the team) may well lead to strong value conflicts. This could result in a complete separation of school and athletics.[37]

V. FUNCTIONS AND DYSFUNCTIONS

After we have found achievement, asceticism in individual sports, obedience (collectively) in team sports, and exertion of power, the basic value orientations that give structure to this activity, we may then proceed to the second question: How does sport influence the socio-cultural system at large? Though we have little evidence through research, we may on the basis of structural-functional methodology be able to outline the basic functions of sport for pattern maintenance, integration, adaptation and goal attainment.

1. THE FUNCTIONS OF SPORT WITHIN CULTURE AND SOCIETY

As in the case of the Timbira, Hye-Kerkdal states that the basic values of that culture were learned through the log-race. Furthermore, the participants were functionally integrated into the social system.[38] Thus, we may hypothesize that the main functions of sport are pattern mainte-nance and integration.

Since sport implies (as we saw) basic cultural values, it has the potential to pass these values on to its participants. We know from studies of the process of socialization that the exposure of children to competitive sport will cause these children to become achievement-motivated; the earlier this exposure occurs, the more achieve-ment-motivated they become.[39] And the child's moral judgment may, for instance, be influenced through games such as marbles. Again, accord-ing to Piaget, the child not only becomes social-ized to the rules but at a later age he also gets an insight into the underlying structure and function of the rules of a game, and thus into the structure and function of social norms and values as such.[40] Overall, from the level of primitive socie-ties to modern societies, sport not only social-izes to the system of values and norms but in primitive societies it socializes towards adult and warfare skills as well.

Since we mentioned that sport is also struc-tured along such societal subsystems as different classes, males, urban areas, schools and com-munities, we should say it functions for integra-tion as well. This is obvious in spectator sports where the whole country or community identi-fies with its representatives in a contest. Thus, sport functions as a means of integration, not only for the actual participants, but also for the represented members of such a system.

Sport in modern societies may function for goal-attainment on the national polity level. In primitive societies, sport functions for adapta-tion as well as goal-attainment since the sport skills of swimming, hunting, and fishing are used to supply food and mere survival.

2. POSSIBLE DYSFUNCTIONS OF SPORT AND SOCIAL CONTROL

A question should be raised at this point ask-ing whether sport is dysfunctional for culture and society as well. Th. W. Adorno called sport an area of unfreedom ("ein Bereich der Unfrei-heit"),[42] in which he obviously referred to the differentiated code of rules which earlier led Huizinga to his statement that excluded sport from play.[43] Both seem to overlook what Piaget called the reciprocity and mutual agreement on which such rules rest.[44] And they may also be considered as an expression of a highly struc-tured system.

Another dysfunctional element for culture and for the sport system itself could be the centrality of achievement. It has such a high rank in the hierarchy of values of sport that, by definition, the actual objective performance of a member of this system will decide the status he gets. In the core of sport, in the contest on the sports field, there only is status achieved. It seems that there is no other system or any societal subsystem, with the exception of combat, where achieve-ment ranks that high. It may create conflict once this value-orientation is imposed on the whole culture, and it may create conflict within the system of sport itself since its members bring other values into this system as well. M. Mead in an investigation of competition and cooperation (the first concept of which is related to achievement) of primitive peoples, however, finds that there seems to be no society where one of these principles existed alone.[45] And on the microsociological level, small groups seem to control this value by discriminating against those that deviate from the group norm of a fair performance.[46] Thus, one would notice some kind of a mechanism built into a social system that keeps it in a state of balance. Exactly this seems to happen within sport where the sporting groups themselves and their differentiated organizational and institutional environment exert social control on those participants achieving beyond a certain level.

In a survey of sport club members in Germany it was found that the norms expressed for an athlete's behavior referred surprisingly less to the achievement value but more often to a value of affiliation, which is to be defined as a positive orientation towards other group members or opponents. Fair play was the one mentioned most frequently. The value of affiliation expressed by the respondents was found more in normative statements the higher their level of performance. On the basis of the hypothesized mechanism of social control, they are under stronger pressure to affiliate with others.[47] Similar results were found in a field experiment with two school classes.[48] This may explain (on the basis of this structural relationship) why in the culture of sport we find not only the value of achievement but also that of fair play and other affiliative orientations.

However, achievement and affiliation may not necessarily be related. It depends on the amount of social control imposed on sport from the internal as well as external system, whether this relationship will be strong or weak. In professional boxing these controls are very weak; while in golf, with the handicap rule, they seem to be comparatively strong.

How much this pattern would influence the culture as such is an open question. Yet it seems not so mis-oriented as Litt and Weniger thought when Oetinger stated that sport would provide a good model for political partnership.[49] We may on the basis of our findings hypothesize that also on the political level the amount of social control will decide whether two or more systems will coexist or not.

VI CHANGE AND EVOLUTION

1. SPORT AND SOCIO-CULTURAL CHANGE

After we have discussed the culture and underlying social structure of sport and its function, we are left with Radcliff-Brown's third programmatic point—that of social and cultural change. We know little about the role of sport in socio-cultural change, though we hypothesized earlier that it may have a function of innovation, or at least structural relationship to changes in the system of social classes. Sport has also functioned as an initiator for the diffusion of technical inventions, such as the bicycle or the automobile.[50] The same holds true to a degree for conduct in regard to fashion and a healthy life. Typically, this question of change has been highly neglected so far.

2. SPORT AND CULTURAL EVOLUTION

If we finally try to explain the different cross-cultural appearance of sport on the basis of an evolutionary theory, it is hard to justify on the basis of our present knowledge about the appearance of sport that there are such things as primitive and developed cultures of sport. The Mandan Indians had a highly developed sport culture, the Australian aboriginals, as perhaps the most primitive people known to us today, knew quite a variety of recreational activities and physical skills, and the variety of competitive games in Europe and America in the past was probably richer than today.

An evolution can only be seen on a vertical level which on the one hand shows in a state of mechanic solidarity rather simple rules in sport and games, while in a state of organic solidarity, as in modern industrialized societies, the code of rules and the structure of games get more differentiated.

What we may furthermore state is that, on the level of primitive cultures, sport's function is universal, often religious, collectively oriented, and in the training of skills, representative and related to adult and warfare skills; while modern sport's function may be called specific for pattern maintenance and integration, is individual oriented and nonrepresentative in the training of skills. The rewards are more intrinsic in primitive cultures, while they are more extrinsic in the sport of modern cultures. Thus, referring to our definition at the beginning, one may well differentiate between physical and recreational activities of primitive cultures and sport in modern cultures.[51]

VII SUMMARY AND CONCLUSION

The interdependence of sport and culture, up to now mainly outlined on the basis of sport's contribution to higher culture (Kultur), was discussed on sport's relation to culture with the emphasis on values, sport's function for the socio-cultural system and its relation to change and evolution.

The system of sport, an integrated part of the socio-cultural system, seems to depend on the industrialized, technological or Protestant religious system. Yet cross-culturally it appears that these systems as intermediate variables are just special cases of a more general system. This is determined for sport by the achievement-value, a value of collectivity and supposedly power orientation. On the basis of these cultural value orientations one may explain the uneven distribution of sport as such, and of team sports versus individual sports in certain socio-cultural systems.

Sport's function for a socio-cultural system can mainly be seen for pattern maintenance and integration, in modern polity dominated societies [also] for goal attainment. In primitive cultures it is universal and thus functions for adaptation as well.

Though a relation of sport to social change is obvious (sport fulfills a certain role for innovation), this neglected question of social change needs more careful investigation. Evolutionary theories applied to sport need more study as well; this might contribute to evolutionary theories as such. It appears that physical activity on the level of "primitive" cultures should be kept apart from sport in modern cultures since meaning and manifest functions are as universal on the one level as they are specific and segmentary on the other.

REFERENCES

1. I owe much of this definition to a discussion with my colleague, G.P. Stone, University of Minnesota.

2. Radcliffe-Brown, A.R.: Structure and Function in Primitive Society. Glencoe, Ill., The Free Press, 1952.

3. This refers to a concept held by Kluckhohn/Kroeber and Talcott Parsons. For a general reference as to culture and the action frame of reference within structural functionalism see Johnson, Harry M.: Sociology: A Systematic Introduction. New York, Harcourt, Brace and World, 1960.

4. White, Leslie.: The concept of culture. Am. Anthropol., 61:227–251, 1959.

5. Cf. Tylor, F.B.: On American lot-games. Internationales Archiv für Ethnographie, Suppl. 9. Leiden, 55–67, 1896.

6. Gini, C.: Rural ritual games in Lybia. Rural Sociol., 4:283–299, 1939.

7. Most significantly to be found in an unpublished lecture of Diem, C.: Sport und Kultur, 1942 at the University of Halle.

8. Huizinga, J.: Homo Ludens. Boston, The Beacon Press, 1955.

9. Cf. Jensen, A.F.: Spiel und Ergriffenheit. Paideuma, 3:124–139. 1942.

10. Huizinga, p. 196.

11. Maheu, R.: Sport and culture. Int. J. Adult Youth Educ., 14(4):169–178, 1962.

12. Krickeberg, W.: Das mittelamerikanische Ballspiel und seine religiöse Symbolik. Paideuma, 1944, 3.

13. Cf. articles Katzball and Katzenspiel. Grimm, J. and Grimm, W.: Deutsches Wörterbuch. Leipzig: Hirtz, 5:279 and 302, 1873.

14. For one of the few content analyses of the special jargon of sport language see Tannenbaum, P.H. and Noah, J.E.: Sportugese: A study of sports page communication. Journalism Q., 36(2):163–170, 1959.

15. Riesman, D. and Denney, R.: Football in America. In Individualism Reconsidered. Edited by D. Riesman. Glencoe, Ill., The Free Press, 1954, pp 242–251.

16. Culin, S.: Games of the North American Indians. 24th Annual Report. Bureau of American Ethnology. Washington, D.C. 1907, p. 801.

17. Hill, Ph. J.: A Cultural History of Frontier Sport in Illinois 1673–1820. Unpl. Ph.D. Thesis. Urbana, University of Illinois, 1966.

18. Hye-Kerkdal, K.: Wettkampfspiel und Dualorganisation bei den Timbira Brasiliens. In Die Wiener Schule der Völkerkunde. Edited by J. Haekel Wien, 1956, 504–533.

19. Cf. Parsons, T.: Toward a healthy maturity. J. Health Hum. Behav., 1(3):163–173, 1960.

20. Weber, M.: Die protestantische Ethik und der Geist des Kapitalismus. Gesammelte Aufsätze zur Religionssoziologie, Tübingen, Bd. 1, 1920.

21. Cf. McIntosh, P.C.: Sport and Society. London, Watts, 1963, 35–45.

22. Veblen, Th.: The Theory of the Leisure Class. Chicago, University of Chicago Press, 1899.

23. Lüschen, G.: Der Leistungssport in seiner Abhängigkeit vom sozio-kulturellen System. Zentralblatt für Arbeitswissenschaft, 16(12):186–190, 1962.

24. Unpublished investigation of German Sport's Youth by Lüschen, 1958. Data obtained by random sample of sportsclub members 15–25 in West Germany and West Berlin.

25. McClelland, D.C.: The Achieving Society. New York, Van Nostrand, 1961.

26. Bellah, R.N.: Tokugawa Religion: The Values of Pre-Industrial Japan. Glencoe, Ill., The Free Press, 1957, p. 57.

27. McClelland, p. 491.

28. Roberts, J.M. and Sutton-Smith, B.: Child training and game involvement. Ethnology. 1(2):166–185, 1962.

29. Sutton-Smith, B., Roberts, J.M., and Kozelka, R.M.: Game involvement in adults. J. Soc. Psychol., 60(1):15–30, 1963.

30. Polsky, N.: Poolrooms and poolplayers. Transaction, 4(4):32–40, 1967.

31. Coleman, J.S.: The Adolescent Society. Glencoe, Ill., The Free Press, 1961.

32. Helanko, R.: Sports and socialisation. Acta Sociol., 2(4):229–240, 1957.

33. Weinberg, S.K. and Arond, R.: The occupational culture of the boxer. Am. J. Sociol., 57(5):460–463, 1952.

34. Loy, J.W. Sport and Social Structure. Paper at the AAHPER Convention, Chicago, 1966.

35. Lüschen, G. Soziale Schichtung und soziale Mobilität. Kölner Zeitschrift für Soziologie und Sozialpsychologie. 15(1):74–93, 1963.

36. Kunz, G. and Lüschen, G.: Liesure and Social Stratification. Paper at Int. Cong. Sociol., Evian/France, 1966.

37. This institutional influence is so strong that it may well be advisable to treat informal (recreational), formal (organized for sport purpose only) and institutional sport (physical education and athletics in school) separately.

38. Hye-Kerkdal.

39. Winterbottem, M.R.: The Relation of Childhood Training in Independence to Achievement Motivation. Unpl. Ph.D. Thesis. University of Michigan, 1953.

40. Piaget, J.: The Moral Judgment of the Child. New York, Free Press, 1965.

41. Stumpf, F., Cozens, F.W.: Some aspects of the role of games, sports and recreational activities in the culture of primitive peoples. Res. Q., 18(3):198–218, 1947; and 20(1):2–30, 1949.

42. Adorno, Th. W.: Prismen. Frankfurt, Suhrkamp, 1957.

43. Huizinga.

44. Piaget.

45. Mead, M.: Competition and Cooperation Among Primitive Peoples. Berkeley, University of California Press, 1946.

46. Roethlisberger, F.J., Dickson, W.J.: Management and the Worker. Cambridge, Mass., Harvard University Press, 1939.

47. Lüschen, G. Soziale Schichtung.

48. Lüschen, G. Leistungsorientierung und ihr Finfluss auf das soziale und personale System. In Kleingruppenforschung und Gruppe im Sport. Edited by G. Lüschen. Köln und Opladen, Westdeutscher Verlag, 1966, 209–223.

49. Oetinger, F.: Partnerschaft. Stuttgart, 1954. Litt and Weniger in Die Sammlung, Göttingen 1952 attacked the concept of partnership as a mode of political conduct which would not provide a way of socialization towards political power.

50. Kroeber, A.L.: Anthropology. New York, Harcourt, Brace and World, 1963, 163–165.

51. Cf. Damm, H.: Vom Wesen sogenannter Leibesübungen bei Naturvölkern. Studium Generale, 13(1):3–10, 1960.

media sport: hot and cool *

SUSAN BIRRELL and
JOHN W. LOY, JR.

As long as organized sport has existed, it has provided popular subject matter for the media, and each new medium has been accepted enthusiastically by both the producers and consumers of the sporting world. The media, likewise, has understood the attractiveness of sport as content matter. Within five years of its invention in 1844, the telegraph was spreading results of horse and yachting races and boxing bouts.[1:152] Sport fans clustered eagerly around Western Union offices where sport results were posted as quickly as they became available. Twenty years later, the Atlantic Cable joined the sporting worlds of two continents, carrying results of international yachting and rowing contests from Europe.[1:153] The newspapers, bolstered by telegraphed stories, were quick to serve the growing interest of the sport fan, and by the turn of the twentieth century, the sport page and the sport section had risen to prominence. Radio was not slow to follow the pattern and was broadcasting local baseball and football games in the early 1920's. By 1926, "NBC started the first regular network with twenty-four stations. Its first coast-to-coast hookup, in 1927, broadcast a football game."[14:244]

In 1939, televised sport made its debut when NBC sent sportcaster Bill Stern and a one-

camera crew to cover the battle between Columbia and Princeton for fourth place in the Ivy League baseball standings. The action proved too much for one clumsy camera to handle:

> Its field of vision was like peering down a small drain pipe that was mounted on a swivel. It could not take in both the pitcher and the batter for the same shot. On every pitch, it was swinging constantly back and forth, describing dizzy, blurry arcs across the screen as it hurried to follow the path of the ball to the plate.[19:36]

Less than a month later, NBC broadcast the first boxing match, an unimpressive bout between Max Baer and Lou Nova. Boxing fared far better than baseball had at the hands of the Iconoscope camera:

> Where it had been painfully awkward and nearly blind when it tried to cover the huge acreage of a baseball diamond, the camera easily focused on the tiny lighted patch of a boxing ring. It beamed out steady, sharp pictures and an easily comprehended version of the fight.[19:42]

If the first baseball telecast had not been an overwhelming success, at least its failure was witnessed in only moderate proportions—there were only 400 working television sets in the United States at the time.[19:37]

Today, about 70 million households own at least one television set. And networks no longer send only one camera to cover an event. Football games are covered by five or six cameras,[36:3]

Reprinted with adaptations from International Review of Sport Sociology, *14*(1):5–18, 1979. Copyright 1979 by International Review of Sport Sociology, Warsaw, Poland.

* A portion of this paper is reworked from a paper presented at the Popular Culture Association Meetings in 1974.

and ABC used fourteen cameras to cover the downhill ski events in the 1976 Winter Olympics.[29:48]

The boom in media sport, particularly the prominence of sport on television, has effects on the media, the fan, and the entire world of sport. The media has become such an integral part of the sport experience of the nation that the fortunes of one closely affect the fortunes of the other. The networks pay a big price for the privilege of bringing sport to the fan. Network sport budgets totalled $260 million in 1973,[47:4] and figures for 1976 would probably dwarf that: rights to the Summer Olympics alone cost ABC $25 million in 1976.[28:47] These costs are passed along to advertisers, who will pay up to $250,000 per minute for a spot on the 1977 Super Bowl.[11:10]

The TV sport fan—"super spectator" as *Sports Illustrated* writer William Johnson has labelled him—is offered more and more sport every year, and he consumes more and more. Over 73 million people watched the Super Bowl in 1976;[10:84] almost 76 million saw the last game of the 1976 World Series;[10:84] and 45 million saw the "Battle of the Sexes" tennis match between Billie Jean King and Bobby Riggs.[42:21]

But the world of sport itself has undergone perhaps the greatest transformation. Not only are sport events rescheduled for the benefit of the television audience,[6:13] and rule changes adopted to provide a more exciting game for this crowd,[13] but the very existence of a sport or league may depend on its exposure or overexposure by television. Many believe that minor league baseball and boxing were all but destroyed by indiscriminate broadcasting of bigger events.[8] And while the old American Football League owed its success to its television backers,[19] the World Football League suffered the opposite fate when no major television network would broadcast its games.

For better or for worse, the marriage of television and sport is here to stay, and no one can deny that television's treatment of sport has had tremendous and probably irrevocable impact on the sport experience of the nation. The purpose of this paper is to explore the media, and television in particular, as a major factor in the changing nature of the sporting experience of the fan. First, a model of possible functions of media sport is proposed. Next, some theories of Marshall McLuhan are invoked as a foundation for understanding the appeal of certain television

sports. Finally, some speculation about the future of media sport is offered.

THE FUNCTIONS OF MEDIA SPORT

Probably the most ambitious attempt to classify individual needs and assess the relative contribution of the different forms of media in gratifying each group of needs is the recent study by Katz, Gurevitch and Haas.[23] At the outset of their investigation they reviewed the social and psychological functions of the media reported in the literature and compiled a list of thirty-five needs which they classified as follows:

1. Needs related to strengthening information, knowledge, and understanding—these can be called cognitive needs;
2. Needs related to strengthening aesthetic, pleasurable and emotional experience—or affective needs;
3. Needs related to strengthening credibility, confidence, stability, and status—these combine both cognitive and affective elements and can be labelled integrative needs;
4. Needs related to strengthening contact with family, friends, and the world. These can also be seen as performing an integrative function;
5. Needs related to escape or tension-release which we define in terms of the weakening of contact with self and one's social roles.[23:166-7]

A factor analysis based upon Israeli data confirmed this *a priori* model.

Another recent factor analysis[15] of media use by British school children revealed six clear factors related to television viewing: (1) to learn, (2) as a habit, (3) for arousal, (4) for companionship, (5) to relax, and (6) to forget. As can be seen by these two exemplary studies, a variety of uses and gratifications are discussed in media literature. In order to get a perspective on the functions of sport via the media, a consensus model might be used to summarize these media theories. Four uses or functions are discussed in the literature:

1. information—surveillance of the environment [17,22,26,35,37,51]
2. integration—correlation of the individual with the environment [16,17,22,26,27,35,51]
3. escape—entertainment [21,22,17,25,27,35,45,51]

4. pattern maintenance—transmission of cultural patterns.[3,16,17,26,27,51]

Of similar scope in sport research is a factor analysis of attitudes held toward physical activity of which Kenyon found six distinct dimensions of individual involvement in physical activity:[24] (1) for health and fitness, (2) as an ascetic experience, (3) as the pursuit of vertigo, (4) as catharsis, (5) as a social experience, and (6) as an aesthetic experience. Although the first two dimensions clearly pertain only to overt behavioral involvement in sport, the last four fit well within a model based upon the consensus model, the Katz research, and the Greenberg research. Table 1 shows the areas of congruence of these four models and four proposed uses that media sport might serve for the individual.

The following four functions of media sport are proposed:

1. *information functions*—increasing knowledge of the game itself, the outcome of particular games, or statistical breakdowns of games, teams, or players
2. *integration functions*—providing an affiliative or other social experience between the spectator and other spectators
3. *arousal functions*—providing pleasurable, aesthetic, or arousing experiences—an affective function
4. *escape functions*—allowing a release from pent up emotions or from personal problems—an affective function

The research of Katz and his colleagues indicated a media specialization effect with some

TABLE 1
Review of Functions and Uses of the Media and Proposed Media Sport Functions

Proposed Media Sport Functions	Consensus Model[a]	Katz, Gurevitch and Haas[23]	Greenberg[15]	Kenyon[24]
Information	surveillance of the environment	providing information, knowledge or understanding of society, self or others— cognitive needs	learning	
Integrative	correlation of the individual with the environment	creating credibility, confidence or status— integrative needs strengthening contact with world, friends, family—integrative needs	companionship	sport as a social experience
Arousal	entertainment	providing aesthetic, pleasurable and emotional experiences— affective needs	arousal	sport as an aesthetic experience sport as vertigo
Escape		weakening contact with world, self, others	relaxation to forget habit	sport as catharsis

[a] Based on models of Breed,[3] Hartley and Hartley,[16] Head,[17] Katz, Blumler and Gurevitch,[22] Katz and Foulkes,[21] Klapper,[25] Lasswell,[26] Lazersfeld and Merton,[27] McQuail,[35] Mendelsohn,[37] Stephenson,[45] and Wright.[51]

media fulfilling certain functions better than others. For example, "Books cultivate the inner self; films and television give pleasure; and newspapers, more than any other medium, give self-confidence and stability."[23:169] Perhaps by his choice of a specific media form for secondary sport consumption, the fan acknowledges such a specialization among sport media. Considering the four event-oriented media experiences—live attendance at a game, watching on television, listening to the radio, and reading the sport page—a definite relationship can be discerned. The four media can be located along a time dimension. Attending a sport event is an *immediate* sport experience; television and radio are *simultaneous*; and newspapers offer a *delayed* review of the event.

When this time factor is considered along with media sport uses proposed above, some interesting relationships are evident (see Figure 1). While escape needs are served equally well by all four modes, an inverse relationship exists between integrative and arousal modes on the one hand and information modes on the other.

Figure 1 suggests that needs related to information, knowledge and other cognitive concerns are best met through delayed kinds of media. Information content tends to increase as the modes of media become further removed in space and time from the sport event itself. Support for this supposition is given by the proportion of statistical data conveyed through the different forms of media. Except for limited facts provided by the game program, scoreboard results, or the perfunctory remarks of an announcer, little information is offered the fan at the sport event itself. On the other hand, while newspapers occasionally present interesting feature stories, they typically are the medium sought by the most statistically oriented sport consumer.

In contrast to informational content, integra-tion experiences tend to decrease across the time dimension. This relationship is perhaps best explained in terms of the degree of sociability associated with each medium of communication. Newspaper reading is a solitary experience, while a sporting event, even when attended alone, reflects an affiliative experience.

Arousal or aesthetic needs related to sport situations are assumed to be primarily a visual matter in combination with auditory stimuli, and thus are likely to be better met by means of live attendance or television viewing, rather than by listening to radio broadcasts or reading sport accounts in the daily newspaper.

What particular media best provide for escapist needs is a moot matter as a case can be made that every form of medium can serve to gratify such needs. Interestingly, Katz et al. state that "... consistency in mass media use is not evident in 'escapist' items," and add that "the dimensions of the concept of 'escape' obviously require further clarification."[23:169]

Further elucidation of these relationships might be gained from an examination of the theories of Marshall McLuhan.[34]

SPORT: HOT AND COOL

McLuhan's celebrated statement, "the medium is the message," represents the essence of his thinking. McLuhan's basic thesis is that the real message of any medium is not the content, but what the form of the medium itself reveals about the society. McLuhan discerns fundamental relationships between historical development and media forms, and he divides human history into three eras, *pre-literate*, *literate*, and *post-literate*, each of which is typified by the media found within it. Pre-literate society is primarily an oral tradition society. The invention of the printing press ushered in the literate era, and in recent years the invention of television, com-

Needs \ Media	Immediate Event	Simultaneous Television Radio	Delayed Newspapers
Information	LOW——————————————————————————►HIGH		
Integration	HIGH◄—————————————————————————LOW.		
Arousal	HIGH◄—————————————————————————LOW		
Escape	◄————————STABLE THROUGHOUT————————►		

FIG. 1   TIME DIMENSIONS AND FUNCTIONS OF MEDIA SPORT

puters, and other electronic devices marked the beginning of the post-literate period. Pre- and post-literate societies, however, have much in common, particularly the sensory experience associated with their respective media. Both feature a diffused pattern of sensory stimulation, while the print-oriented experience of the literate phase of society features a linear, step-by-step progression,

McLuhan's term for media suited for literate society is "hot" media, while post-literate media are classified as "cool." The basic criterion for McLuhan is the sensory participation demanded from the audience. Hot media, such as books, newspapers, and films, are media of high definition, requiring low participation from the audience. The low definition of cool media such as television, theatre, and cartoons calls for a higher sensory participation.

The time dimension discussed above parallels McLuhan's hot and cool classification (see Figure 2). Attendance at an event is the coolest medium, demanding the most sensory participation from the spectator. Television is less cool, radio hotter, and the newspaper the hottest medium included.

In adapting a McLuhan-type dichotomy as a classification system for media sport, the essential concept is degree of diffusion. Media sport experience then can be seen as relatively more diffuse or more focused—*diffusion* being defined as a function of the demands put on the secondary participant in terms of sensory acuteness and sensory involvement. Thus diffusion can be understood as a sensory variety show: the spectator is bombarded by many aspects which demand his attention, but he must limit himself to only one. The more diffuse the choices, the more demanding the involvement experience for the spectator is.

The basic concept can be further clarified along two dimensions: locational diffusion and action diffusion. *Locational diffusion* is simply the amount of space required by the sport. Diving and boxing are low on this dimension, golf and football are high. *Action diffusion* is inverse-

ly related to the degree of linear progression of the game. Sports in which the ball moves freely between two teams, as in soccer and hockey, are the best examples of high action diffusion. Baseball, on the other hand, features a distinctly linear type action sequence. As McLuhan observed, "baseball is a game of one-thing-at-a-time." [34:211]

To a degree, action diffusion is a function of the pace of the game action and the proportion of unexpected or unpredictable action. Races in general are linear by nature and thus low in action diffusion. But auto racing is an exception because of the potential for action and accidents to occur anywhere on the track. For the fan intent on experiencing the sport event most fully, highly diffused action demands a great deal of attention and acuteness. A football fan, for instance, is called on to make some important decisions at each play in order to enjoy the game experience to its fullest.

Table 2 presents ratings of some sports. Those high in diffusion across both dimensions, like hockey and soccer, are most diffuse overall, while sports such as wrestling, diving and bowling are the most focused or linear.

The diffusion rating of a sport may help to explain why some are better spectator sports than others. Based on McLuhan's thesis, one would expect diffuse sports to translate best to cool media such as television. Figures from television audience data collected by the A.C. Nielsen Company offer some support for this hypothesis (see Table 3).

The average per cent of the television audience captured by sports of Class I (most diffuse) is higher than the average for Classes II and III. The hybrid category is second overall. These trends are constant for the three years sampled. Further elucidation of this idea might be obtained by comparing gate attendance figures and radio audience figures for sport broadcasts.

An analysis of the relationship between sport and the media raises an interesting problem: what is the effect of translating the live sport event, a very cool medium, into another, hotter

Time Dimension	Immediate	Simultaneous		Delayed
Sport Occurrence	Event	TV	Radio	Newspaper
Degree of Coolness	Cool —————————————————————————————►Hot			

FIG. 2   RELATIVE "COOLNESS" OF SPORT MEDIA

TABLE 2
Diffusion Ratings of Most Major Sports

Sports	Diffusion Dimensions	
	Locational diffusion	Action diffusion
Class I		
soccer, basketball, lacrosse, rugby, hockey, football, roller derby, auto racing	high	high
Class II		
baseball, golf, tennis, most races	high	low
Class III		
boxing, wrestling, pool, bowling, fencing, diving, gymnastics, field events	low	low

medium? Specifically, what changes in the sport experience arise when the spectator follows sport through television rather than live attendance? In short, what does television do to the sport experience of the fan in terms of McLuhan's theory?

The coolness or diffusion of television as a medium, relative to the medium of the event itself, must therefore, be examined. The model in Figure 2 suggests that movement from the event as a medium to television as a medium should change the nature of the sport experience somewhat, through a focusing of diffuse action, unavoidable due to limitations of broadcasting translation.

In the earlier days of television, effectiveness of sport coverage with only one camera varied from sport to sport. The singular focus was disastrous for sports such as baseball but had an almost negligible effect on a relatively more focused event such as boxing. Increasing the number of cameras used to cover an event might appear to foster greater diffusion. But the action is still previewed by the producer who selects exactly which part of the total picture will be broadcast.

Other complex advances in technology have continued to limit the diffusion effect of television. Instant replay, isolated camera, stop action, slow motion, wide-angle lens and split screen have all transformed the sport spectacle, disrupting the natural rhythm of the game and synthesizing the action through highlighting to enhance the excitement value.

In general, television produces the following effects which are unavailable to the live event audience:

1. changing the size of the image and permitting a greater range of vision (wide-angle lens, split screen)
2. concentrating time-diffuse events into a more manageable time span (highlights)
3. manipulating time to dramatize action (instant replay, slow motion, stop action, highlights)
4. focusing on one isolated action (isolated camera, instant replay)
5. providing more statistical information.

What television can *not* do is allow the spectator the freedom to choose the segment of action he wishes to follow. In addition, television does not provide the fan with the high degree of social integration with other fans and, more important, integration with the nature of the game experience itself. As Orrin E. Dunlop, Jr., a writer for

TABLE 3

Average U.S. Audience Per Cent by Sport Type for Three Years[a]

Year Diffusion Ratings	1970		1973		1975	
	%	N	%	N	%	N
CLASS I						
football[b]	13.9	101	15.2	110	15.5	116
basketball[b]	8.0	47	7.4	72	8.0	71
auto racing	4.7	2	11.1	3	10.0	6
ice hockey	4.2	16	5.0	24	3.9	21
soccer					4.6	2
class average	11.2	166	11.3	209	11.7	216
CLASS II						
horse racing	13.7	3	9.3	9	10.8	6
baseball	11.4	36	13.4	53	12.0	52
golf	5.6	69	5.5	81	6.8	58
tennis	4.2	5	5.1	32[a]	4.1	64
skiing	5.8	16	5.2	1		
class average	7.4	129	8.0	176	7.5	180
CLASS III						
bowling	7.2	13	8.9	14	8.6	18
boxing			5.2	6	5.3	8[a]
fishing	8.1	1				
class average	7.3	14	7.8	20	7.6	26
HYBRID TELECASTS						
multi sport	9.2	54	8.9	84	9.2	113
track and field	5.6	15			6.0	1
Pan Am Games					5.8	1
World Games			5.4	8		
class average	8.4	69	8.6	92	9.1	115

Figures compiled from A.C. Nielsen Company data[31, 32, 33]
[a] These figures include both regular season games and special events such as the Super Bowl, the World Series, the Stanley Cup. The Riggs-King tennis match is included in the 1974 figures and the Ali-Lyle heavyweight boxing championship is included in 1975.
[b] These figures include both professional and college games.

the *New York Times*, lamented in the early days of televised sport:

(The fan) does not see the half of what is going on to make baseball the pleasure it has become in 100 years. The televiewer lacks freedom; seeing baseball by television is too confining, for the novelty would not hold up for more than an hour, if it were not for the commentator ... What would ... old-timers think of such a turn of affairs—baseball from a sofa!

Television is too safe. There is no ducking the foul ball.[19:39]

A more recent interpretation continues in the same vein:

The networks with their zeppelins and zoom lenses, their dreamlike instant replays of color and violence have changed football watching from a remote college pastime to something very much like voyeurism ... No matter how fine his TV reception, no beer and armchair quarterback can hope to see the true game. For all the paraphernalia, the tube rarely shows an overview; pass patterns and geometric variations are lost in a kaleidoscope of close-ups and crunches.[20:54]

Live sport spectation is a diffuse experience; media sport are focused events. How the spectator has resisted or adjusted to such shifts serves as a basis for speculation as to the future of media, sport, and the sport experience of the fan.

THE FUTURE OF MEDIA SPORT

With McLuhan as prophet, one might assume that the new electronic age with its diffuse and demanding nature drives us further and further from a linear interpretation of the world. Surely, the wave of the future must carry on its crest increasingly diffuse media experiences, even for the media sport consumer. But will super spectator ever abandon his television set? Will the media sport experience of the future be hot or cool? Speculative models for both positions exist; surprisingly, some are beginning to creep into reality as well.

Through its technological breakthroughs, television is bringing a higher and higher degree of focus to a diffused sport world. In effect, television is providing the fan with a greater amount of information, both visually and through statistical recitations, and depriving him of the integrative aspects of the sport experience. Thus, the close link with the game in its natural spectatorial form is broken in order to provide a higher informational picture of the game. Taken to an extreme, this will eventually lead to a homogenization effect on the media.

But contrary to McLuhan's theory, the new techniques of sport broadcasting seem to enhance the sport experience for the fan rather than diminish it. Although it removes him from the true context of the sport situation, the American spectator seems more than happy to accept the television sport experience.

If McLuhan's literate/post-literate society theory is correct, this first generation of television children to come of age—those in their early thirties, the first wave of the post-literates—should be expected to shun a hotter media experience for a cooler one. This does not seem to be the case. Instead, it is more likely the case that the first television generation has been weaned

on the television sport experience, and that this has fostered a linear orientation to sport. Television has trained America to focus on particular bits of action and ignore, or perhaps never come into meaningful contact with, a live event experience. Perhaps this explains why many disgruntled fans leave a live game complaining that they could have seen it better on television.

Techniques such as isolated camera, instant replay, stop action, and split screen are designed to provide the spectator with knowledge, not an integrative sensory experience. Perhaps the American fan with his increasing mania for statistical information is being fed the diet of data he requests. Other revolutionary techniques or practices may go even further to satisfy him.

One innovation which has yet to make its actual debut is a method of telecasting sport events called "retarded live action television."[40:43] According to the news report of the invention, "At regular intervals, a frame of perhaps one second duration is discarded, and the blank space is filled by stretching out the others. The action can be slowed by 15 or 20 per cent without the viewer being conscious of any delay."[40:43]

Another potential change in sport due to television lies in the area of officiating. It has become obvious to the fan as well as the coaches that instant replay can not only recapture isolated action but rule violations as well. A replay can either confirm or contradict the judgment of the referee, and nowadays a referee is often more relentlessly monitored than the players. The camera can be used not only to confirm a rules decision but to make one. During the 1974 NFL play-offs, the most memorable and spectacular play was the controversial last minute catch of a deflected pass by Pittsburgh Steeler Franco Harris. To be legal, the ball had to touch an opposing player between the initial contact with the intended Steeler receiver and Harris. The referee was not quite sure; he ran to the sidelines to confer with relay men in contact with the television production box. For the first time in media sport history, instant replay and slow motion techniques were used to confirm the officials' decision.

Despite agitation from many coaches, including Woody Hayes, to make regular use of instant replays for officiating purposes,[4:26] the issue has not yet been seriously discussed. In fact, arenas such as Capital Center in the Washington, D.C. area which are equipped with Telescreens for instant replay purposes generally refrain from replaying controversial calls by the referees.[4: 16]

On the other hand, in 1973 the American Horse Show Association introduced an experimental system for judging dressage championships. The system involves the video-taping of events at locations around the country and submitting them for review to a panel of judges. The measure is intended to allow riders to compete without the inconvenience and expense of transporting horses across country.[48: 7]

Weibe[50] has attributed America's appetite for the media to the difficulty individuals find in trying to divest themselves of their fundamental ego-centrism and acquire the concept of the "other." Their reluctance to deal with others is manifested in their susceptibility to the media. The media provides the illusion of interaction while actually removing the other and replacing it with "printed symbols or sounds or images, but never persons."[50: 210] Perhaps this theory is personified by super spectator.

Followed to an extreme, this high information/low interaction–low arousal orientation results in studio sport. Studio sport or scripted sport would eliminate all chance elements and all integrative aspects of sport contests. All that would remain would be the distillation of the contest, the result and the data. Sport, like the entertainment product it is, would become an athletic "Playhouse 90," with the Super Bowl featured as "Masterpiece Theatre." Plays would be repeated until the perfect take had been satisfactorily accomplished. Several examples can be cited which indicate that this orientation to sport is not as unrealistic as one might suppose.

To some extent, television already controls important game elements such as time outs. One special individual is designated to walk along the sidelines and signal the referee when the station needs time for a commercial.[30: 73] Often these arbitrary interruptions can work to the detriment of the game. When Bill Russell was player-coach of the Celtics, he was once fined $50 for refusing to call time out for the broadcasters because his team was enjoying the momentum of a catch-up victory and he realized that an interruption at that point could cost him the game.[46] The extreme of this sort of manipulation occurred during the Super Bowl when the half time kick and return were replayed because the audience had been detained by a commercial message. Who knows how the live audience dealt with their bewilderment at the repetition.

Evidence to support a trend toward "process theatre" is exemplified in the coverage of the USC-UCLA football game in 1974. During one running play, one instant replay camera followed USC back Anthony Davis to the line where the second smoothly picked up the coverage. The resulting spliced tape was highly effective and similar to techniques presently being used by sport movie producers.

But the most undeniable and overwhelming piece of evidence supporting a belief in the continuing and increasing focus of media sport is the effect that lifting of the black-out in home-team areas when an NFL game is sold-out has had: the no-show phenomenon. For the early part of the 1973 season, the no-show rate was about ten per cent,[39: 58] a figure which represents a considerable financial loss to owners in terms of auxiliary profits such as concessions, parking and programs. For whatever reasons, the no-show fan preferred to remain at home and consume his sport experience through the medium of television rather than to experience it live. An afternoon of television football is apparently more attractive an alternative than the long drive to the stadium, the unsure weather conditions, the jostling of the crowds. The reaction of the fans to the lifting of the blackout clearly shows that "given a choice, onlookers now prefer a two-dimensional view of the game."[20: 54]

On the other hand, perhaps Americans are still captivated by sport on television only because a cooler medium has not yet presented itself. Future developments in television or in other media used to cover sport events might provide a more diffuse and demanding experience for the spectator.

Forty years ago, essayist E.B. White speculated about the sport experience of the future. His concept of sport in the future was a totally diffuse one. "Not only did sport proliferate but the demands it made on the spectator became greater. Nobody was content to take in one event at a time, and thanks to the magic of radio and television nobody had to."[49: 41] White illustrates the development of media sport through a super spectator who sits in the stands viewing the Yale-Cornell football game while simultaneously listening to the radio broadcast of the World Series from New York, monitoring the horse race presented on video sets located at either goal line, and glancing occasionally at the scores of other major or minor sporting contests being constantly revised by skywriters. "The effect of this vast cyclorama of sport was to divide the spectator's attention, over-subtilize his appreciation, and deaden his passion."[49:42]

Aldous Huxley's conception of the "feelies," his medium of the future, is in many ways similar. Apparently no senses are left unstimulated by the future total-experience medium. Society has progressed through an oral and a visual stage. Soon taste, feel, and smell will also be incorporated, or as Huxley advertises: "Three Weeks in a Helicopter, An All-Super Singing, Synthetic-Talking, Coloured, Stereoscopic Feely. With Synchronized Scent-Organ Accompaniment."[18:113]

Amusing as their ideas must have seemed years ago, White and Huxley have proved to be accurate prophets. "Sensurround," the cinema technique used to enhance the viewer's experience of *Earthquake* and *Midway*, is the first step in the direction of Huxley's "feelies," and many practices and innovations can be cited as evidence of White's perceptiveness: the fan who buys two televisions so he can watch two sport programs at once, the armchair fanatic who watches the video on television but takes the audio from the radio coverage because it gives him an added dimension. Charles Sopkin[43] experienced the ultimate in this regard. He closeted himself in a room with seven televisions, each tuned to a different network, and monitored all for "seven glorious days, seven fun-filled nights."

Wherever possible, the media keeps pace with these demands. The sport fan can now buy a device which will tape a television show so that he can enjoy it at his leisure: the sport fan doesn't have to miss a thing. Telescreen, the huge replay screen in the Capital Center, makes it possible to fulfill White's predictions, for it is not limited to replaying action occurring on the floor below but might be used to broadcast another game altogether.

The skyboxes in the Astrodome in Houston may well be on the forefront of a diffusion trend. Partly because the ridiculous distance from the live action all but prohibits the box owner from viewing the sporting event, partly because Astrodome entrepreneur Hofheinz considers the sport event only a minor aspect of a total entertainment experience, box owners are virtually forced to watch the closed circuit broadcast of the live event in order to follow the game. The Astrodome was designed "not so much as a sport stadium as a consumer's complete pleasure palace with the athletic events proceeding on the field below but one of the diversions."[12]

Similarly, because of a contract conflict during the 1973 season, CBS found itself in the unwitting position of presenting to its viewers their most diffuse sport experience to date. The lifting of the blackout required CBS to broadcast into the Oakland area both the Detroit-San Francisco and the Giants-Raiders games in the same time slot.

The network does not plan to let momentum govern its coverage staying with long drives and periodic swingbacks. Instead it plans constant changing to show as much action as possible just as dial switchers of the past did before affluence led to two television set families and the piggyback concept.[5:88]

The best model of the super spectator of the future is the sport show producer. Anyone who has seen *Two Minute Warning* would have to be impressed by the cacophony and confusion of the sport producer's world. Seated in a control booth, he continually monitors the image from each camera being used while receiving a constant relay of information through an earphone. His function is to predigest sport for the viewer. He determines when to insert instant replay and which camera's image gives the most effective picture. It is he who sees the diffusion and makes the focus decision. He is perhaps the only person for whom the media sport experience matches the live event in terms of diffusion. Roone Arledge is the archetype of the media man of the future.

SUMMARY

Why the individual feels less removed from the sport event beamed into his living room than the experiences of being physically present at the event is a function of the way in which he defines the sport experience. Several possible factors such as information, integration, arousal, and escape have been considered above. A model based on McLuhan's theory of media has been presented suggesting that an informational predisposition fosters an affinity toward linearity, focus and hot media sport experiences, whereas integrative and arousal predispositions incline the individual toward a more diffuse or cool experience. With that dichotomy in mind, speculation about the media sport experience of the future was presented. If this is truly a post-literate society, with all that implies in terms of focus and diffusion, innovations aimed at an increasingly diffuse media experience will appear and take their place in the consciousness of the sports fan. Some such innovations have already made their entry. In general, however, American sport fans are fed a greater and greater diet of predigested, focused sport events. And so far, none of the post-literates is complaining.

BIBLIOGRAPHY

1. Betts, John R.: The technological revolution and the rise of sport, 1850–1900. *In* Sport, Culture and Society. Edited by John W. Loy, Jr., and Gerald S. Kenyon. New York, Macmillan, 1969, 145–165.
2. Birrell, Susan and John W. Loy, Jr.: Sport Consumption Via the Mass Media: Patterns, Perspectives and Paradigms. Paper presented at the Fourth National Meeting of the Popular Culture Association, Milwaukee, May 1974.
3. Breed, Warren: Mass communication and sociocultural integration. Social Forces, 37:109–116, 1958.
4. Carry, Peter: New big E for a big new eye. Sports Illustrated, March 11, 1974, pp. 16–17.
5. Craig, Jack: CBS juggling act: 2 games in 1 slot. Boston Sunday Globe, November 4, 1973, p. 88.
6. Creamer, Robert W., ed.: Scorecard: Selling yourself. Sports Illustrated, October 27, 1975, p. 13.
7. Defleur, Melvin L.: Theories of Mass Communication, 2nd edition. New York, David McKay Company, 1970.
8. Einstein, Charles.: TV slugs the boxers. Harpers Magazine, August 1956, pp. 65–68.
9. Eye in the storm. Sports Illustrated, November 18, 1974, p. 26.
10. Forkan, James P.: Nets, sponsors ready to 'play ball.' Advertising Age, March 15, 1976, p. 84.
11. Forkan, James P.: Networks put up sold-out sign for most football. Advertising Age, August 23, 1976, p. 10.
12. Frady, Marshall: Hofheinz and the Astrodome. Holiday, 45:42–45ff. 1969.
13. Furst, Terry: Mass media and the transformation of spectator team sports. Canadian Journal of History of Sport and Physical Education, 3:27–41, 1972.
14. Gillingham, George O.: The ABC's of radio and TV. *In* Mass Media and Communication. Edited by Charles S. Steinberg. New York, Hastings House, 1966, pp. 243–256.
15. Greenberg, Bradley S.: Gratifications of television viewing and their correlates for British children. *In* The Uses of Mass Communications. Edited by Jay G. Blumler and Elihu Katz. Beverly Hills, Calif., Sage, 1974, pp. 71–92.
16. Hartley, Eugene L. and Hartley, Ruth E.: The importance and nature of communication. *In* Mass Media and Communication. Edited by Charles S. Steinberg. New York, Hastings House, 1966, pp. 8–27.
17. Head, Sydney W.: Broadcasting in America: A Survey of Television and Radio. Boston, Houghton Mifflin Company, 1972.
18. Huxley, Aldous: Brave New World. New York, Bantam Books, 1932.
19. Johnson, William O. Jr.: Super Spectator and the Electric Lilliputians. Boston, Little, Brown and Company, 1971.
20. Kanfer, Stephen: Football: Show business with a kick. *Time*, October 8, 1973, pp. 54, 56.
21. Katz, Elihu and Foulkes, D.: On the use of the mass media as "escape:" Clarification of a concept. Pub. Opinion Q., 26:377–388, 1962.
22. Katz, Elihu, Blumler, Jay C., and Gurevitch, Michael: Utilization of mass communication by the individual. *In* The Uses of Mass Communications. Edited by Jay C. Blumler and Elihu Katz. Beverly Hills, Calif., Sage, 1974, pp. 19–32.
23. Katz, Elihu, Gurevitch, Michael, and Haas, Hadassah: On the use of the mass media for important things. Am. Sociol. Rev., 38:164–181, 1973.
24. Kenyon, Gerald S.: A Conceptual model for characterizing physical activity. *In* Sport, Culture and Society. Edited by John W. Loy, Jr. and Gerald S. Kenyon. New York, MacMillan, 1969, pp. 71–81.
25. Klapper, Joseph T.: The Effects of Mass Communication. New York, Free Press, 1965, pp. 166–205.
26. Lasswell, Harold D.: The Structure and Function of Communication in Society. *In* The Communication of Ideas. Edited by Lyman Bryson. New York, Cooper Square Publishing, 1964, pp. 37–51.
27. Lazersfeld, Paul F. and Merton, Robert K.: Mass communication, popular taste and organized social action. *In* Mass Culture: The Popular Arts in America. Edited by Bernard Rosenberg and David Manning White. New York, Free Press, 1957, pp. 457–473.
28. Leggett, William: Commercializing the games. Sports Illustrated, August 9, 1976, p. 47.
29. Leggett, William: He was right on the button. Sports Illustrated, February 23, 1976, p. 48.
30. Leggett, William: Stop the game, I want to go on. Sports Illustrated, October 21, 1974, p. 73.
31. Let's Look at Sports 1975. Nielsen Television Index Special Release. Media Research Division, A.C. Nielsen Company, 1976.
32. Let's Look at Sports: The 1973 Season. Nielsen Television Index. Media Research Division, A.C. Nielsen Company, 1974.
33. A Look at Sports: 1969–1970 Season. Nielsen Television Index, Media Research Division, A.C. Nielsen Company, 1970.
34. McLuhan, Marshall: Understanding Media. New York, New American Library, 1964.
35. McQuail, Denis: Towards a Sociology of Mass Communications. London, Collier-Macmillan, 1969.
36. Menaker, Daniel: How TV tackles football. New York Times, November 25, 1973, Section 2, pp. 1, 3.
37. Mendelsohn, Harold: Socio-psychological perspectives on the mass media and public anxiety. Journalism Q., 40:511–516, 1963.
38. Miller, Jonathan: Marshall McLuhan. New York, Viking, 1971.

39. NFL no shows. Boston Globe. October 3, 1973, p. 58.
40. Retarded live television. New York Times. April 14, 1973, p. 43.
41. Rosenthal, Raymond: McLuhan: Pro and Con. New York, Funk and Wagnalls, 1968.
42. Shain, Percy and Craig, Jack: Sexes match had TV sets humming. Boston Globe, September 22, 1973, p. 21.
43. Sopkin, Charles: Seven Glorious Days, Seven Fun-Filled Nights. New York, Ace Publishing, 1968.
44. Stearn, Gerald Emanuel: McLuhan: Hot and Cool. New York, Dial, 1967.
45. Stephenson, William: The Play Theory of Mass Communications. Chicago, Univ. of Chicago Press, 1967.

46. TV influences sports. Newsweek. June 5, 1967, p. 66.
47. TV pays price to show sports. New York Times. May 19, 1974, p. 4.
48. Video-tape helps judges pick dressage champion. New York Times. December 16, 1974, p. 73.
49. White, E.B.: The decline of sport. In Second Tree from the Corner. New York, Harper and Row, 1954, pp. 41–45.
50. Weibe, Gerhart D.: Two psychological factors in media audience behavior. In Mass Media and Society. Edited by Alan Wells. Palo Alto, Calif., National Press Book, 1972, pp. 208–217.
51. Wright, Charles: Functional analysis and mass communication. Pub. Opinion Q., 24:605–620, 1960.

vertigo in america: a social comment

PETER DONNELLY

Participation in high-risk sports which are characterized by the pursuit of vertigo appears to have increased markedly in the United States during the 1970's. Colleges and universities have begun to offer courses in rock climbing, scuba diving, sport parachuting, hang gliding and white water kayaking, and stores and private schools offering equipment and instruction for these sports have proliferated. Additional evidence for the increased participation in hazardous sports may be found in various aspects of the communications media. In recent years there have been a large number of articles, films, television programs and mass-market and trade paperback books which have taken high-risk sports as their subject.[1] In the light of recent discussions by sport sociologists regarding the two-way interaction between sport and society, each being a reflection of the other, the increasing interest in the vertigo sports may be an important phenomenon of interest to both sport sociologists and students of American society.

Roger Caillois (1961) has emphasized the relationship between sport and society and the belief that sport may be employed as a "culture club." Caillois' inferences about culture are based on his typology of games which is in turn purported to represent the psychological attitudes underlying play. Play and games are classified into four categories; agon (competition), alea (chance), mimicry (simulation) and ilinx (vertigo), and two combinations of these categories are considered

to be of particular interest for the study of society. Caillois hypothesized that games of simulation and vertigo are associated with primitive societies and that games of competition and chance are associated with more advanced societies:

> In the first type there are simulation and vertigo or pantomime and ecstasy which assure the intensity and, as a consequence, the cohesion of social life. In the second type, the social nexus consists of compromise, of an implied reckoning between heredity, which is a kind of chance, and capacity, which presupposes evaluation and competition. (Caillois, 1961, 87)

The emergence of an advanced culture is believed to be associated with the repression of simulation and vertigo and the ascendance of competition and chance. Belief in a stable and orderly universe is the basis of the emergence of an advanced society and leads to the condemnation of simulation and vertigo and their displacement to the periphery of society. The Puritan suppression of witchcraft (which contains major elements of simulation and vertigo), mime and ritual dances, and many forms of play and games may be seen as an example of this process in action. Loy (1969) has noted that, in present day society, simulation and vertigo are associated with the "pseudo-rebellion" of youth but not specifically with any other social group. "Without resorting to G. S. Hall's recapitulation theory, it is conjectured that the social reality of youth is greatly characterized by simulation and

Reprinted from Quest, 27:106–113, 1977. Copyright 1977 by Human Kinetics Publishers, Champaign, Illinois 61820.

vertigo, but the reality of the adult world has place for only competition and chance" (Loy, 1969, 193).

However, the occurrence of simulation and vertigo appears to have become far more widespread in the United States in the few years since Loy's paper was written. Whether this is a result of the spread of the youth culture to other age groups or evidence of some more basic change in society (e.g. a reversion to a more primitive form of society) is not readily apparent. Examples of the re-emergence and spread of simulation (s) and vertigo (v) are plentiful. One might note the widespread use of drugs to alter perception (v), the colorful styles of dress for both sexes (s), and the interest in the occult, Eastern mysticism and altered states of consciousness (s and v). Further examples include the identification with sports and popular music stars (s) which is often associated, at athletic events and concerts, with the abandonment of individual perception for a form of group perception or consciousness (v), and finally the rapidly growing interest and participation in high-risk vertigo sports noted previously.

If one accepts both Caillois' assertion that games and other forms of simulation and vertigo are associated with more primitive types of society and the examples presented here of a recent increase in manifestations of simulation and vertigo, then additional evidence should be available to support the contention that we are witnessing a reversion to a simpler or more primitive type of society. Several examples are available which lend suppport to this view. The lawlessness in major cities is generally acknowledged ("the streets are a jungle") suggesting that urban society at least is becoming more primitive. The movement against "big government" is gaining support and appears to indicate a harking back to simpler and more conservative times. There is a growing consciousness of the disadvantages of advanced technology which has led to the environmental and conservationist movements, health foods, an interest in plants and vegetable gardening, a trend towards handcrafted rather than mass-produced consumer goods where possible and a search for the simpler life-style of farm or commune.

On the other hand Caillois has hypothesized that, with the development of an advanced society, simulation and vertigo would be suppressed or shifted to the fringes of society. American society today is the archetype of an advanced society and competition and chance predominate. Thus one may postulate that the recent increase in manifestations of simulation and vertigo would lead to a certain amount of conflict within American society, and consequently, the suppression of simulation and vertigo may be quite evident.

Public reaction to high-risk sports provides an ideal example of the conflict between the suppression and admiration of vertigo in present day American society. The death or near death of individuals involved in voluntary or unnecessary pursuits may serve some function in society. Haskell has noted that "in each of us there is something base—the need, for example, to see someone else's death to certify our own aliveness" (Haskell, 1976, 60). But in most circumstances it is not an approved function and may be considered to be the result of a deviant act.

There appears to be a balance between admiration and criticism when individuals risk their life for some approved or officially sanctioned purpose. The pursuit of fame and wealth has strong elements of competition and chance which may outweigh the fact that a high-risk vertigo activity is being employed as the vehicle to those ends. A great deal of admiration may be attached to this form of "rugged individualism" in American society where fame and wealth are admirable goals with little concern for the means. Risking one's life for the entertainment of others may be associated with the pursuit of fame and wealth but whether an individual is admired or criticized may depend on the nationality of the observer. British visitors to Spain have been known to cheer for the bull at bullfights.

Risk may be officially sanctioned if it brings national prestige. Ascents of the world's highest mountains, circumnavigations of the world by lone yachtsmen, or voyages into space or to the moon may all bring prestige to a nation, but the acts may also be criticized as being foolhardy or wasteful. Criticism may be most pronounced when individuals risk their lives solely for their own entertainment.

Public and official reactions to some recent highly publicized manifestations of risk and vertigo were mixed. Evel Knievel's attempt to jump the Snake River Canyon in 1975 met with reactions ranging from admiration to indifference, from morbid curiosity to harsh criticism.[2] Phillipe Petit's tightrope walk between the towers of the World Trade Center (also in 1975) led to his prosecution by the New York City police and therefore to a criminal record. However, his sentence was to perform his act in Central Park for the people of New York without financial remuneration. It should be noted that both Knievel and Petit had a great deal to gain by their acts, Knievel financially and Petit in terms of publicity. But both had a great deal to lose. Their pursuit of wealth and fame exemplified the admirable qualities of competition and chance in American society. Their manner of pursuing fame and wealth—risking their lives in the pursuit of vertigo—may be less admirable and consequently led to the mixed public and official responses.

The increasingly popular high-risk vertigo sports such as mountain climbing, sky diving, hang gliding and scuba diving are among those activities in which individuals participate largely for their own pleasure. Unlike the more commercial high-risk vertigo activities (e.g. auto and motor cycle racing, high diving or circus stunts) they are rarely performed for the entertainment of non-participants and they seldom lead to fame or large financial rewards. It is these attributes which may lead to such activities being perceived somewhat differently or more negatively than the more commercial high-risk vertigo activities and these activities may not be entirely sanctioned by society.

The non-commercial vertigo sports appear to have a negative public image because of a number of highly publicized accidents. Because they are not spectator sports the public rarely hears about them unless there is an accident thereby giving the impression that the participants are somehow suicidal. The relationship between the pursuit of vertigo for personal pleasure and the apparently suicidal deaths that occur becomes established in the public's mind and lends reinforcement for the suppression of vertigo in this advanced society. The problem is magnified because a large proportion of the population has little understanding of the sports in question. A great many people believe that rock climbers climb up the rope. The question most often asked of mountaineers and rock climbers is "why do you climb?" and as Lester has noted, "the question is not too often asked seriously; it is more often asked as a way of asserting something; namely, that mountain climbing is foolish, or perhaps mad" (Lester, 1964, 394).

Such feelings are probably associated with the suicide taboo in Western society. Life was sanctified by Christianity because of the blatant disregard for life encountered in ancient Rome. Suicides were not allowed to be buried in sanctified ground. Legislation against suicide, and imprisonment for attempted suicide, is attributable to economic causes. To take one's life was to deprive the King (in England) of one's body and ability as a soldier, and of one's taxes. Twentieth century enlightenment in either repealing the suicide laws or not enforcing them has done little to lift the stigma associated with suicide and this stigma may be attached to participants in the non-commercial vertigo sports. Those who do get killed may be perceived as rather exotic suicides, while those who survive do so because of good luck rather than good judgement. Some Freudian psychologists have even intimated that the survivors may be frustrated suicides.

However, when the facts regarding fatal accidents in sports are examined one finds that there are fewer deaths among participants in the non-commercial vertigo sports than the publicity might suggest. The fatality figures for mountain climbers, hang glider pilots and sky divers are fairly similar in the United States—approximately 20–25 a year in each sport. In scuba diving there are approximately 120 fatalities each year but this figure should be compared with the large number of participants—some 250,000 in southern California alone. No accurate figures have been discovered for the various white water sports (canoeing, kayaking and rafting) but one report indicates that, in the three years following the release of "Deliverance" (the film version), there were 19 deaths on the Chattooga River.

When compared with the fatality rates in other sports these figures do not appear to be excessive. Michener has noted that "swimming, with enormous participation, accounts for about 600 (deaths each year), but this figure includes accidents to people who were not intentionally in the water" (Michener, 1976, 86). Football accounts for some 28 deaths each year but is perhaps more remarkable for its injury rate. A recent television documentary reported that 86% of high school football players could expect at least one injury. Perhaps the most remarkable fatality rate of all is found in motor racing, and particularly in that best attended of all American sporting events, the Indianapolis 500. Verigan reports that:

> Over the years, 23% of the men who drove in the 500 have been killed in racing. There may be even more deaths, because many of these drivers are still active. Only 48 men have won the 500, and 14 of them died in race cars, a depressing 29%. (Verigan, 1976, 17).

Referring to Grand Prix racing one racing driver, John Morton, was overheard to say that "if you took all the Grand Prix drivers and gave them eternal youth so they could race for a hundred years, they would all kill themselves" (Wilkinson, 1973, p. 55).

Risk of injury is generally perceived to be a part of many sports and it is a risk which is accepted. Even in the nineteenth century the English poet, Adam Lindsay Gordon, was able to quip that:

> No game was ever worth a rap
> For a rational man to play,
> Into which no accident, no mishap
> Could possibly find its way.

There are normally ongoing attempts to modify rules and equipment in sport in order to decrease the risk of injury but in some cases (e.g. football) equipment modifications which were originally intended to reduce the risk of injury have not worked. Pads and helmets which were designed to reduce injuries have come to be used as offensive weapons, thereby increasing injuries. In other cases (e.g. ice hockey) there has been a reluctance to modify the rules in order to make the sport less dangerous. Risk of death is somewhat of an anathema to the very concept of sport since sport is generally considered to be an aspect of the non-serious side of life. Consequently, the vertigo sports which involve a risk of death are intriguing, particularly since modifications in equipment which are designed to increase safety in the sports do not lead to fewer accidents but to increased performance.

In the United States the injuries and deaths associated with football are lamented but lead to little in the way of efforts to eradicate them and no attempts whatsoever to suppress the sport. Football exemplifies competition and chance and the technological society within which it exists. It is seen to provide the opportunity for upward mobility and possibly wealth and fame. Swimming is the premier recreational activity in the United States. It is an activity in which many people have both the ability and the opportunity to participate. The ownership of a private pool is a status symbol. In all aspects except diving the sport is not characterized by vertigo and even diving is not considered to be a high-risk sport. Major efforts are made to promote water safety but the inevitable crop of drownings each year are considered to be unfortunate accidents. Again there is no thought of suppressing the activity. Neither football nor swimming are perplexing to non-participants who believe they can readily discern the motives for participation.

Motor racing is more perplexing because of its characteristic vertigo and high-risk, but it also exemplifies competition and chance, it is glamorous and may lead to wealth and fame, and it is close to the experience of most spectators who have driven automobiles. None of the justifications outlined above can be made for the non-commercial high-risk vertigo sports and, as Tiger has noted:

> Amateur sport behavior is genuinely extraordinary. Persons who could otherwise enjoy comfort and leisure willingly engage in violent exertions which may involve considerable danger. This willingness to experience danger is a perplexingly unrational manifestation (Tiger, 1970, 154).

Attempts to explain such behavior have occupied social scientists for a number of years and they have met with remarkably little success.

Elias and Dunning (1970) have given a very general explanation by suggesting that the 'tension' associated with all mimetic leisure activities represents "the quest for excitement in unexciting societies." Klein (1975) and Martin and Berry (1975) offer similar hypotheses with regard to such sports as motocross racing, snowmobiling and sport parachuting. They suggest that risky and rugged sports attract low-status participants who are compensating for the tedium experienced in their work. This hypothesis lacks support when one considers the number of scientists, lawyers and members of the medical profession who participate in high-risk sports. Donnelly (1976) has proposed that individuals who participate in high-risk sports are characterized by a high need for stimulation, but notes that there are other ways of expressing a high need for stimulation. Similarly, Ogilvie (1973) believes that participants in high-risk sports are characterized by stimulus addiction. Finally, Csikszentmihalyi (1975) has suggested that rock climbers are motivated to experience a state which he has termed "flow" but shows that flow may be experienced in a variety of activities including those not involving risk.

We are left with a pattern of behavior that is difficult to justify or understand even by the participants who only know that they enjoy their particular activity. In return for their enjoyment the participants may have families who worry about them, friends and acquaintances who think they are crazy, and state and local government officials who wish to control or restrict their activity. For the most part the participants in the non-commercial vertigo sports are not irresponsible. Safety procedures are well thought out and occupy much of the time during the training of novices, and the governing bodies of each of the sports attempt to practice a certain amount of self-regulation of the activities.

However, elected representatives of the people who have recently been involved in seat-belt and air-bag legislation for automobiles and crash-helmet legislation for motor cyclists are beginning to turn to the vertigo sports because of the increasing numbers of participants. The Federal Aviation Administration is taking responsibility for sky diving and hang gliding; the Los Angeles County board of supervisors has recently passed strict controls for the sport of scuba diving; and the National Park Service of the Department of the Interior has attempted to control rock climbing and mountaineering. There are now quotas for the number of people who are allowed to climb Mount Rainier, and the new Master Plan for the Yosemite National Park, one of the most famous rock climbing areas in the country, does not even make provision for rock climbers.

How does one account for these apparent attempts to suppress the pursuit of vertigo and at the same time account for the increasing number of participants in vertigo sports? Perhaps a characteristic of the advanced societies described by Caillois is their desire to control all of the activities of their citizens. Individuals who are manifesting the various aspects of competition and chance are under control because they are reflecting the values of an advanced society. When

a few individuals opt for simulation and vertigo they pose no threat to the society and may easily be accommodated at the fringes of society. When the number increases to the point where they are beginning to attract attention as they have in recent years they begin to pose a threat to society because they are manifesting values which are not sponsored by that society. Controls are justified in terms of protecting the citizen from himself.

During the 1960's American society began to lose control of its younger citizens. The counterculture or youth movement was much more than the "pseudo-rebellion" of youth and it had a major impact on society. It is possible that governmental control had gone too far and some individuals became aware of the nearness of 1984. When the Vietnam War finally ceased to be an issue energies were turned to the various manifestations of simulation and vertigo described previously. What began as elements of the youth movement, and what can now be seen as clearly countercultural because of its involvement with simulation and vertigo in a culture which values competition and chance, has since been accepted by a much broader segment of the population. Whether this is simply a spreading of the youth movement to other parts of society which values youth highly, or whether the overzealousness of governmental control has led to a reaction which is causing some more fundamental change in society remains to be seen.

NOTES

1. Few actual figures are available which demonstrate the increased participation in vertigo sports in recent years and the increase must be deduced from a number of secondary sources. The writer has contacted long-time participants in each of the sports cited and all have commented on the remarkable increase in numbers in their particular sport since approximately 1970. Some of the long-time participants, as instructors or equipment dealers, have actively worked to promote their sport. Another source of data is the number of magazines which have appeared catering to participants in each of the sports. Although some have folded or merged and others only appear in a mimeographed form, many are expensive and glossy productions with growing circulations. The advertisements in these magazines provide another source of data. In 1972, Mountain (a mountaineering magazine with a wide circulation in English-speaking countries) listed 12 stores in the United States which supply mountaineering equipment; in 1976 they list 58 stores.

Various aspects of the communications media have reflected the growing interest in vertigo sports. Recent feature films have had plots based around mountain climbing, canoeing, scuba diving, hang gliding and sky diving. Articles on the sports have appeared in various sources, from Harper's and New York Magazine to the New York Post and the weekly news magazines. An article in Newsweek (July 12, 1976) provided some evidence for the increase in scuba diving. They report that there are about 1,000,000 scuba divers in the United States and that this figure is now increasing with about 200,000 new divers each year. The Professional Association of Diving Instructors had 500 members in 1966 and has 7,000 members today. Newsweek also provides figures for the growth in hang gliding which only became a sport in 1971 in California. On September 17, 1973 they reported that the Southern California Hang Gliding Association had 3,000 members; two years later (August 18, 1975) they estimated that there were 25,000 hang gliding enthusiasts throughout the United States. The other vertigo sports have probably experienced a similar increase and an accurate survey of the number of participants in each of the sports would be invaluable.

2. It is interesting to note that the event was accompanied by a demonstration against the repression of the pursuit of vertigo. Motor cyclists protesting against the compulsory helmet wearing laws used the occasion to blatantly ride around the area without wearing helmets.

REFERENCES

Caillois, Roger: Man, Play, and Games. (Trans. by Meyer Barash) New York, Free Press, 1961.

Csikszentmihalyi, Mihaly: Beyond Boredom and Anxiety: The Experience of Play in Work and Games. San Francisco, Jossey-Bass, 1975.

Donnelly, Peter: A study of need for stimulation and its relationship to sport involvement and childhood environment variables. (Unpublished Master's thesis, University of Massachusetts, 1976.)

Elias, Norbert and Dunning, Eric: The quest for excitement in unexciting societies. In The Cross-Cultural Analysis of Sport and Games. Edited by Günther Lüschen. Champaign, Ill., Stipes Publishing Company, 1970, pp. 31–51.

Haskell, Molly: The night porno films turned me off. New York Magazine (March 29, 1976) 55–60.

Klein, David: The relationship of risk-taking to recreational injury. Paper presented at the Conference on the Mental Health Aspects of Sports, Exercise and Recreation, American Medical Association, Atlantic City, N.J., June 14, 1975.

Lester, James L.: Psychology. In James R. Ullman, Americans on Everest. Philadelphia, Lippincott, 1964, pp. 390–395.

Loy, John W.: Game forms, social structure, and anomie. In New Perspectives of Man in Action. Edited by R.C. Brown and B.J. Cratty. Englewood Cliffs, N.J., Prentice-Hall, 1969, pp. 181–199.

Martin, Thomas W. and Berry, Kenneth J.: Competitive sport in post-industrial society: the case of the motocross racer. J. Popular Culture. VIII:107–120, 1974.

Michener, James A.: Sports in America. New York, Random House, 1976.

Ogilvie, Bruce C.: The stimulus addicts. The Physician and Sports Medicine, November: 61–65, 1973.

Tiger, Lionel: Men in Groups. New York, Vintage Books, 1970.

Verigan, Bill: Viewpoint: an auto racing writer is haunted by ghosts of those who died at Indy. Sports Illustrated May 10:17, 1976.

Wilkinson, Sylvia: The Stainless Steel Carrot: An Auto Racing Odyssey. Boston, Houghton Mifflin, 1973.

SECTION FOUR
sport and stratification systems

secondary schools and oxbridge blues

JOHN EGGLESTON[1]

A number of studies have been undertaken to examine the relationship between pre-university schooling and achievement at the university.[2] Almost without exception, however, these studies have been concerned with academic achievement in the undergraduate or post-graduate course and, especially, achievement in final first degree examinations. This is curious in view of the widely held beliefs in the social and other non-academic advantages to be gained from university life. Indeed concentration on a narrow range of largely examination-based criteria of achievement is something of an ideational and methodological problem in the sociology of education. There are some obvious reasons for this, notably the problems and hazards of measurement of achievement in student societies, extra-curricular activities and the other intangibles of student life.[3]

An area where such problems may be overcome is that of athletic performance, where identifiable and measurable marks of achievement exist. Notable amongst these are the "colours" which are awarded in most universities by the student body, for membership of a representative team or club. Of particular interest in Britain are the colours of Oxford and Cambridge, known as "Blues." They are of interest not only for their indication of student achievement but also for their elitist associations within the university and their repute as counters in the

subsequent occupational and social status of their holders. University lore is rich in tales which equate the value of an Oxbridge blue with that of a "First" and the reputed composition of the upper echelons of some occupational groups, notably the Church of England ministry, suggests that this may not be entirely without foundation.[4] Certainly the situation is of considerable interest as a model of non-expanding status availability in conditions of expanding demand which has many parallels in education.

Several studies exist which list the scores of blues obtained by ex-pupils of the various schools in the major university sports.[5] Such studies, though indicating a lengthening of the list of schools from which blues emerge, none the less reveal the persistence of a striking concentration of blue awards to the ex-pupils of some of the major public schools. Blues from ex-pupils of the local education authority schools, though increasing in number are rarely concentrated in a small range of schools, rather they tend to be widely spread and non-recurring.

This study involves examination of the evidence in a different way, to discover if the well-established differential in chance of admission to Oxbridge between the public school and local education authority grammar school population[6] is matched by similar differences in chance of award of a blue.

Investigation of schools of origin of blues presents no major research problem, membership of university teams on qualifying for the award of blues is recorded, with the names of the members' school in parenthesis, in the national

Reprinted from The British Journal of Sociology, 16(3):232–242, 1965. Copyright 1965 by Routledge & Kegan Paul Ltd., London, England.

press and the appropriate sporting almanacs.[7] Using these sources an investigation of the schools of origin of Oxford and Cambridge blues over a ten-year period—1953/4 to 1962/3—was undertaken. To facilitate subsequent comparison the schools of origin were classified in the manner used by Kelsall in the study of admissions to universities in 1955.[8] This classification contained four categories of home schools:

1. Independent schools in membership of the Headmasters' Conference. Schools in membership of the Conference but which were aided by direct grant from the Ministry of Education or fully maintained by Local Education Authorities were not included in this category. Schools in this category are predominantly public schools and will be described by this name (PUBLIC).

2. Direct grant schools. As all direct grant schools featured in the ten-year survey were, interestingly, in membership of the H.M.C. these schools will be referred to as H.M.C. DIRECT GRANT.

3. Secondary grammar schools maintained by local education authorities. Schools described as 'transitionally assisted', 'voluntarily controlled' and 'voluntarily aided' were included in this category (MAINTAINED GRAMMAR SCHOOLS).

4. Other schools. Most of the schools included in this category are the independent schools not in membership of the H.M.C. (PRIVATE).

So that the larger variables in sporting tradition and facilities between the different categories of schools could be minimized the survey was confined to three major sports: association football, rugby football, and cricket, the most generally available sports in home schools providing full-time education for boys prior to university entrance. Cricket is common to all but a tiny handful of such schools and rugby became increasingly so as many maintained grammar schools adopted this code during the survey period. Association football is the least general of the three; it is played by only 13 of the 80 independent boarding schools in Category 1 and by decreasing numbers of Category 3 schools. It is included because of its complementary relationship to rugby football. No school plays neither code and it is possible for rugby schools to produce soccer blues (there is no record of the converse). The inclusion of association football also offered an opportunity to ascertain if categories of schools under-represented in rugby

blues had compensating over-representation in association blues.

This selection of sports has involved the elimination of a number of notable university sports, including rowing, where there is still widely differing opportunity for participation between different categories of schools and where "blue opportunity" is still strikingly concentrated on the ex-pupils of a small group of public schools.[9] Athletics was also eliminated as the wide range of track and field events involves a wide range of facilities making useful comparison of the kind envisaged difficult.

The results of the survey are set in Table 1 and summarized in Table 2. The numbers are numbers of blues not numbers of individuals as it is possible for one individual to be capped for two, three, or even four years in succession, competing anew each year. Award of blues in more than one sport is possible. A notable case in recent years is that of an ex-pupil of Tadcaster Grammar School, M. Ralph, who won six blues—three for association football, three for athletics.

The tables indicate interesting variations in the membership of the teams in each sport and between the universities. In both universities for all the survey years public schools predominate in cricket and rugby, in both sports the representation of the maintained grammar schools is small, 20·4 per cent and 17·3 per cent respectively in rugby and only 0·93 per cent and 8·4 per cent respectively in cricket. The small showing of the maintained grammar school in cricket is particularly notable in view of the widespread availability of this sport in the schools. Their score during the survey period amounted to nine Cambridge cricket blues and only one Oxford blue, in neither university had there ever been more than one ex-maintained grammar school boy in any team. Only in association football does the maintained grammar school pupil appear in large numbers. In almost all the teams in this sport he has comprised the largest group, often holding an absolute majority of places over players from all other types of school.

It is noticeable that only in rugby has Oxford offered a greater number of blues to the maintained grammar school pupils than has Cambridge. In association football Cambridge has offered slightly more, in cricket nine times as many. At both universities the H.M.C. direct grant schools are well represented, notably in cricket, where despite a substantially smaller

TABLE 1

(a) Schools of Origin of Oxford and Cambridge Blues in Association Football, 1953/4–1962/3 Seasons

| | Oxford | | | | | | Cambridge | | | | | |
Year	1	2	3	4	Over-seas	All	1	2	3	4	Over-seas	All
53/4	3	—	8	—	—	11	3	1	6	1	—	11
54/5	3	—	8	—	—	11	4	2	5	—	—	11
55/6	3	—	8	—	—	11	4	3	5	—	—	12
56/7	3	1	7	—	—	11	3	2	6	—	—	11
57/8	5	1	5	—	—	11	—	2	9	—	—	11
58/9	5	2	4	—	—	11	—	4	7	—	—	11
59/60	3	2	6	—	—	11	1	4	6	—	—	11
60/1	5	1	5	—	—	11	2	3	6	—	—	11
61/2	7	—	4	—	—	11	2	1	7	1	—	11
62/3	2	1	8	—	—	11	2	—	8	1	—	11
Totals	39	8	63	—	—	110	21	22	65	3	—	111
%	35·5	7·3	57·2	—	—	100	18·9	19·8	58·6	2·7	—	100

(b) Schools of Origin of Oxford and Cambridge Blues in Rugby Football, 1953/4–1962/3 Seasons

| | Oxford | | | | | | Cambridge | | | | | |
Year	1	2	3	4	Over-seas	All	1	2	3	4	Over-seas	All
53/4	4	—	1	1	9	15	13	1	—	1	—	15
54/5	5	2	1	1	6	15	10	1	—	2	2	15
55/6	6	1	2	5	3	17	8	—	2	5	—	15
56/7	7	3	2	—	3	15	9	1	1	3	1	15
57/8	6	3	5	—	1	15	9	—	2	3	1	15
58/9	3	3	6	—	3	15	9	—	3	3	—	15
59/60	6	1	7	—	1	15	8	2	2	3	—	15
60/1	8	—	5	—	2	15	4	2	6	3	—	15
61/2	11	—	1	2	1	15	8	—	6	1	—	15
62/3	9	—	1	2	3	15	10	1	4	—	—	15
Totals	65	13	31	11	32	152	88	8	26	24	4	150
%	42·7	8·6	20·4	7·2	21·1	100	58·7	5·3	17·3	16·0	2·7	100

(continued on p. 320)

TABLE 1 (continued)

(c) Schools of Origin of Oxford and Cambridge Blues in Cricket, 1953/4–1962/3 Seasons

	Oxford						Cambridge					
Year	1	2	3	4	Over-seas	All	1	2	3	4	Over-seas	All
53/4	6	1	—	—	4	11	7	—	—	—	4	11
54/5	7	—	—	—	3	10	6	2	—	—	3	11
55/6	8	1	—	—	2	11	6	2	—	—	3	11
56/7	7	2	—	—	1	10	4	2	—	1	2	9
57/8	7	3	—	—	1	11	3	2	1	1	4	11
58/9	3	5	1	—	2	11	6	1	1	—	2	10
59/60	3	5	—	—	3	11	7	1	1	1	1	11
60/1	5	3	—	—	3	11	6	—	2	1	2	11
61/2	7	1	—	—	3	11	5	2	2	1	1	11
62/3	8	—	—	—	3	11	7	1	2	—	1	11
Totals	61	21	1	—	25	108	57	13	9	5	23	107
%	56·5	19·4	0·9	—	23·2	100	53·3	12·1	8·4	4·7	21·5	100

TABLE 2

Summary of Schools of Origin of Oxford and Cambridge Blues in Association Football, Rugby Football and Cricket, 1953/4–1962/3 Seasons

Oxford

School of origin	1		2		3		4		Overseas		Survey nos. (=100%)
	n	%	n	%	n	%	n	%	n	%	
Assn. Football	39	35·4	8	7·3	63	57·2	—	—	—	—	110
Rugby Football	65	42·7	13	8·6	31	20·4	11	7·2	32	21·1	152
All Football	104	39·7	21	8·0	94	35·9	11	4·2	32	12·2	262
Cricket	61	56·5	21	19·4	1	0·9	—	—	25	23·2	108
All blues in these sports	165	44·6	42	11·4	95	25·7	11	2·9	57	15·4	370

Cambridge

School of origin	1		2		3		4		Overseas		Survey nos. (=100%)
	n	%	n	%	n	%	n	%	n	%	
Assn. Football	21	18·9	22	19·8	65	58·6	3	2·7	—	—	111
Rugby Football	88	58·7	8	5·3	26	17·3	24	16·0	4	2·7	150
All Football	109	41·2	30	11·5	91	34·9	27	10·3	4	1·5	261
Cricket	57	53·3	13	12·1	9	8·4	5	4·7	23	21·5	107
All blues in these sports	166	45·1	43	11·7	100	27·2	32	8·7	27	7·3	368

number of undergraduates their score of blues exceeds that of the maintained grammar schools, strikingly so at Oxford. Table 1 indicated however that the strength of the H.M.C. direct grant schools may be declining; this is discussed later. The private schools play little part as a source of blues with the exception of the rugby XVs at Cambridge—an exception largely accounted for by the notable ex-pupils of Marling school.

It is possible to compare the survey figures with the contribution of the various categories of schools to the total male undergraduate population of Oxford and Cambridge on two occasions during the period under consideration and calculate the relative chances of achieving a blue for students from different schools of origin. The first of these is in the mid-50's. For the year 1955–6 Kelsall provides a breakdown of the total first-year undergraduate population by schools of origin. To achieve a basis of calculation it has been assumed that these figures are representative of the total undergraduate population of the year following 1956–7, that is of the total entry for the years 1954, 1955, and 1956. Recent evidence [10] of the slow change of the relative distribution of the schools of origin of Oxford and Cambridge undergraduates suggests that the error involved in this assumption is likely to be more an absolute one than a relative one. Accordingly the numbers of 1955–6 first-year students have been increased threefold to form a basis for calculating the rates shown in Table 3(a). (This is still not an entirely adequate base as the period eligibility for a blue can extend to a fourth undergraduate or post-graduate year. It has proved impossible to achieve any adequate basis for calculating this small additional population and it has therefore been ignored. There is some suggestion, however, that it offers a relatively greater 'blue advantage' to the fee-paying student—most generally of independent or overseas school origin.)

For the year 1961–2 details of the schools of origin of the total undergraduate population are available from the Robbins Report. [11] The figures quoted in the Report are based on a sampling fraction of 1 in 22 and to provide a basis of calculation the figures are therefore multiplied by 22. The assumption this time may be justified by the very close reported correspondence of the achieved sample to the sample population envisaged. [12] The rates thereby calculated are shown in Table 3(b). The qualification concerning fourth-year eligibility applied to Table 3(a) also applies here.

Table 3(a) and (b) indicates interesting variations in the chance of achieving a blue for boys

TABLE 3

Oxford and Cambridge Blues per 1,000 Undergraduate Population Originating from the Home School Categories

(a)

School of origin	Number of men per 1,000 * in each school category achieving Blues in				
	Soccer	Rugby	All Football	Cricket	All 3 sports
1	1·1	3·0	4·1	2·1	6·2
2	2·5	3·3	5·8	3·3	9·1
3	3·9	0·9	4·8	0·0	4·8
4	0·0	4·7	4·7	1·5	6·3
All	2·1	2·5	4·6	1·5	6·1

(b)

School of origin	Number of men per 1,000 * in each school category achieving Blues in				
	Soccer	Rugby	All Football	Cricket	All 3 sports
1 and 4	1·5	3·4	4·9	2·0	6·9
2	0·5	0·0	0·5	1·7	2·2
3	3·2	2·0	5·2	0·6	5·8
All	1·9	2·4	4·3	1·5	5·9

*See comment on basis of calculation in text.

from different categories of school. Perhaps the most striking result, however, is the decline in the chances of the H.M.C. direct grant pupils—from a dominance in all sports in 1956-7 to an inferior chance in football to all other schools and a much reduced chance in cricket in 1962-3. Though the small numbers of pupils from these schools accentuate the apparent significance of small fluctuations, inspection of Table 1 suggests that these are not a-typical years and that the position of these schools had declined since the late 1950's.

Major interest centres on the relative chances of the public and the maintained grammar school boy. In both years the public school boys in close association with the small number of private school boys had a greater chance of winning a blue once at Oxbridge. If his considerably greater chance of entry to Oxbridge is taken into account along with this, his far greater opportunity of winning a blue, with its short term and long term rewards, becomes clearly evident. Within the university the absolute chance of the independent school pupil is greater in 1961-2 than in 1956-7. His relative chance compared with the maintained grammar school boy is however slightly diminished; indeed the chance of the maintained grammar school boys shows a modest absolute and relative improvement, both categories benefiting from the decline of the H.M.C. direct grant schools performance. But the maintained grammar school boys' main source of blue opportunity is concentrated in both years in the lower-status sport of association football. This has indeed compensated for their lower chance in rugby and has given them a higher overall chance of football blues than the independent schools. As the maintained grammar schools adopt rugby there is some evidence of improvement in the chance of their pupils in this sport. It is in cricket, the sport common to all the schools, that the disadvantage of the maintained grammar school boy is most marked. Indeed the chance of a cricket blue can hardly be said to exist for the maintained grammar school boy—inspection of Table 1 indicates that the situation in the years under discussion is representative of the total survey period. This inferior chance of a blue in cricket seems the major factor in the overall inferior chance of boys from the maintained grammar schools within the universities.[13]

The study indicates that type of school attended is identified as being associated with differential chances of blues and that these chances are further differentiated as between different sports of different status. The full extent of these differences is, of course, only incompletely brought out in this study because of the incomplete range of sports considered, and particularly by the elimination of rowing where the chance of achieving a blue is still strikingly associated with having been a pupil at one of a limited number of public schools.

It must be emphasized that there is no evidence of any kind of overt bias in the selection procedures of any university teams. (This might be tested by examining the number of blues achieving "caps.") Indeed the selection procedure is usually carried out in a highly public manner in the various trial games and seems to embody a genuine attempt to ensure objective assessment of the candidates' prowess.

It is suggested that the disadvantages of the maintained grammar school pupil in rugby and cricket springs from differences in social experience rather than sporting ability. The nuances of team play at university, communication between players, rhythm and pattern of play may be familiar to the boy from the independent school but subtly different from those to which the boy from the maintained grammar school is accustomed. These differences may be reinforced by the coaching techniques and even the coaching language employed. There is also the problem of 'outside' feeling by the grammar school boy in a group largely comprised of and often led by boys from a different educational and social background, backgrounds which are often shared in view of the tight concentration of 'blue producing' schools in Category 1 in each sport—often with interlocking and exclusive fixture lists. This is in marked contrast with the diffusion of maintained grammar schools producing blues, where a potential blue may have never encountered a blue, and may never consider the possibility of aspiring to be one or even to go to Oxbridge.[14] Even in association football where the maintained grammar school boys predominate the largest single group of old blues and aspirant blues may well be the ex-pupils of one of the public schools which specialize in this sport.

There are also differences in the sporting opportunities of boys from the different educational backgrounds, even though cricket and one of the football codes are common to all. The boy from the public school is far more likely to have been under the influence of a former blue as a consequence of the staffing policy of these schools which leads to the appointment of old blues and international players as games specialists. The maintained grammar school however tends to favour the college-trained physical education teacher and may even regard some old blues as unqualified teachers. Furthermore the boy from the independent school is likely to have spent considerably more time on sport—if only because he is more likely to have been a boarder with consequent advantages in experience and physique. Moreover he is also likely to have attended a boys' preparatory school giving a degree of attention to games—and especially cricket—which is seldom matched in the state system. Conversely the maintained grammar school boy destined for Oxbridge is even less likely to spend a considerable time on sport than his own peers in view of his commitment to the time-consuming competition for Oxbridge places. Certainly, he is unlikely to be a boy for whom sporting achievement is of equal importance to academic achievement or who sees sporting opportunity as a main attraction of university life. Indeed, in many maintained grammar schools, an academically able boy whose life is focused on sporting achievement is far more likely to be deflected to a college for teachers of physical education than receive encouragement to apply for a university place, particularly if, as is probable, he heeds the advice of his physical education trained games master. Expenditure on games also distinguishes the schools, notably in cricket where the condition of 'the square' in most public and preparatory schools is incomparably better than the average state school. At university the ex-maintained grammar school boy, more frequently depending for his continued financial support on satisfactory reports on his academic performance, tends to be less willing to renounce maximum academic achievement in order to devote substantial time to sport, and this constitutes a particular barrier in cricket where major participation is called for in examination terms. The immediate economic obligations of university team membership, both in actual expenses and forfeited vacation work earnings, also tend to constitute a greater problem to the pupil from the maintained grammar school.

It is finally suggested that in the present intensified competition for Oxbridge places, the conditions of academic competition for pupils of the direct grant schools are becoming similar to those of the maintained schools, involving a diminution of the chances of entry for the outstanding sportsman whose prowess in sport is not matched by academic excellence.

CONCLUSION

The study of the awards of Oxford and Cambridge University blues in three major sports indicates that the ex-pupils of the maintained grammar schools are at a disadvantage to ex-pupils from the public schools in cricket and rugby, both absolutely and relative to their total representation in the university population.

It has been suggested that causal factors include covert disadvantages in selection situations, differentials in sporting opportunity at school and differentials in the evaluation of sport made by the pupils and by the school—differentials probably reinforced by economic differences.

Type of school attended thus becomes associated with differences in a further area of performance at university—an area which seems to be of considerable importance in view of its likely association with social opportunities in university life and social and occupational prospects in later life.

NOTES

1. The writer wishes to acknowledge his gratitude to Mr. Paul Gaskin, physical education master at Great Barr Comprehensive School, Birmingham, for collecting much of the data used in the survey, also to the following persons for their helpful criticism and advice: Miss F. Conway, Dept. of Economics, University of Leicester; E. Dunning, Dept. of Sociology, University of Leicester; J. S. Hardie, Principal, Loughborough Training College; G. Murray, Marlborough College; C. S. Sayer, Head of Physical Education Dept., Loughborough Training College; R. Wight, School of Education, University of Leicester.

2. For example Furneaux, W. D.: The Chosen Few, 1961; Newfield, J. G. H.: The academic performance of British university students. *In* Sociological Studies in British University Education, Sociological Review Monograph No. 7, University of Keele, 1964; Worswick, G. D. N.: Anatomy of Oxbridge. Times Educ. Suppl., 3.5.57, pp. 596–7.

3. Such problems have of course been overcome by some workers in this field, for example Coleman, J.: The Adolescent Society, 1961.

4. It is hoped to undertake subsequent work in this field.

5. For example: Schools behind the boat race, Times Educ. Suppl., 27.3.64, p. 798, and McKelvie, R.: Blues and the schools. The Field, 2.4.64, pp. 625–6. The article lists the top ten 'blues producing' schools in five sports for the years 1946–63 as follows:

Cricket: Dulwich 18; Charterhouse 15; Winchester 15; Repton 12; Eton 9; Radley 8; Rugby 8; Harrow 7; Manchester G. S. 7; Sherborne 7.

Athletics: Eton 17; Manchester G. S. 16; Epsom 13; Oundle 13; Kingswood 12; Marlborough 12; Wellington 12; Sherborne 11; Malvern 10; Dulwich 10.

Rowing: Eton 51; Shrewsbury 35; Radley 23; Winchester 17; Oundle 14; Bedford 13; St. Paul's 13; St. Edward's 11; Bryanston 9; Monkton Coombe 9.

Association Football: Repton 21; Shrewsbury 15; Manchester G. S. 14; Malvern 13; Royal Liberty, Romford 13; Barnsley G. S. 12; Brentwood 11; Charterhouse 9; Winchester 8; Alleyn's 8; Forest 8; St. Clement Danes 8.

Rugby: Oundle 28; Fettes 15; Sedborgh 14; Marling 13; Clifton 10; Rugby 9; Bristol G.S. 8; Blundell's 8; Tonbridge 7; Stonyhurst 7; Birkenhead 7.

6. Kelsall, R. K.: Report on an enquiry into applications for admission to Universities, Association of Universities of the British Commonwealth, 1957; Robbins Report. Higher Education, Appendix 2B, 'Students and their education,' H.M.S.O., 1964.

7. For this study the sources used were the annual issues of Wisden *Cricketers' Almanack* and Playfair *Rugby Annual* and the issues of *The Times* appearing on days following the annual University Association Football match.

8. Kelsall, R. H., op. cit., pp. 7–8.

9. The concentration of schools producing rowing blues is discussed in "Schools Behind the Boat Race." It is reported that of the 180 rowing blues awarded between 1955 and 1964, 120 went to ex-pupils of 10 public schools.

10. Robbins Report, Higher Education, Appendix 2B, 'Students and their education', H.M.S.O., 1964, p. 12.

11. Ibid., p. 9.

12. Ibid., p. 553.

13. Further analysis, suggested during the survey, indicates:

(*a*) In rugby, position of play may possibly be related to school of origin, forwards coming mainly from the public schools.

(*b*) Some Oxbridge colleges may offer the grammar school boy a more favourable chance of a blue—notably St. Edmund's Hall.

14. An interesting parallel with the conditions of student entry to Oxbridge is described in a recent article by Michael Brook:

"Suppose two boys of comparable ability, both fit to be commoners at Oxford, one at a famous public school, the other at a two-stream maintained school. The first headmaster has candidates for Oxford every year and is known in several colleges. He is an expert on which college to approach and on how to play his cards. Spurred on by parents who will consider no university except Oxford or Cambridge he makes persistent efforts to place his boy, and at last finds a college to take him.

"The second headmaster has not had a candidate for several years and has no Oxford contacts. He puts the boy in for Oxford once, and when this fails settles for a modern university. Indeed, to say that the "selection" system favours the first headmaster is to put the case too narrowly. The second one may not give the system a chance: he may never enter his boy at all. He has no difficulty in spotting a potential Oxford scholar among his pupils; but he may have a good deal in spotting the potential commoner, and the boy's parents are unlikely to demand a shot at Oxford." Brook, M.: Are Oxbridge selections biased? The Guardian, 2.6.62.

secondary schools and Ivy League letters: a comparative replication of Eggleston's "Oxbridge Blues" [1]

JACK W. BERRYMAN and JOHN W. LOY

Numerous studies within the sociology of education have examined the relationship between secondary school background and academic achievement at the college or university level. But markedly few sociological investigations have studied the relationship between pre-university schooling and achievement in several important non-academic sectors of higher education, as for example, student government and undergraduate societies. As Eggleston [2] cogently observes: "This is curious in view of the widely held beliefs in the social and other non-academic advantages to be gained from university life. Indeed concentration on a narrow range of largely examination-based criteria of achievement is something of an ideational and methodological problem in the sociology of education." [3]

Eggleston further observes that one obvious reason for the research hiatus in educational sociology with respect to the analysis of achievement in non-academic areas of university life is the hazards and problems associated with the measurement of non-academic forms of achievement. He notes, however, that measurement problems may be overcome in at least one non-academic area, namely athletic performance. Support for this latter observation is provided by his own investigation of the secondary school origins of Cambridge and Oxford university students between 1953/4 and 1962/3 who were awarded blues for their athletic achievement in

association football, cricket and rugby football. Results of his socio-historical survey clearly show that different educational backgrounds afford differential chances of earning blues and "these chances are further differentiated as between different sports of different status." [4]

The purpose of this study was to replicate, in so far as possible in an American setting, Eggleston's study of "Secondary Schools and Oxbridge Blues." Specifically, an effort was made to discover whether the secondary school origins of students earning varsity letters [5] at Harvard and Yale are matched by the well-established differential admissions of students in general from the private and public school [6] populations of the United States to these élite universities.

While the main objective of this study was to provide a comparative replication, a secondary goal of some importance was to make an exploratory examination of the premise that intercollegiate athletics promote democratization. Although Eggleston's findings run somewhat counter to the argument, several social observers of the American sporting scene have placed special emphasis on the role of sport in educational settings as a means of sustaining the creed of egalitarianism, as an avenue of social mobility, and as an agent of democratization. Havighurst and Neugarten assert in their sociology of education text that "athletic prowess combined with education often provides a very good base for mobility in a lower class boy." [7] More explicitly, Hodges in his text on social stratification footnotes that "college football has functioned as a highly effective status elevator

Reprinted from The British Journal of Sociology, 27(1):61–77, 1976. Copyright 1976 by Routledge & Kegan Paul Ltd., London, England.

for thousands of boys from blue-collar ethnic backgrounds."[8] In a similar manner, Earnest in his informal history of the American college writes that football

> ... broke the pattern of snobbishness based on race, religion, and wealth. Students and alumni alike recruited team candidates from all ranks and races ... and because of the prestige of football heroes, such men tended to become big men in college. Perhaps football's greatest achievement is its contribution to social democracy in the colleges.[9]

And more generally speaking, Baltzell contends that: "changing sporting mores, and changing social origins of the sportsmen, are often sensitive seismographs of social upheaval."[10] Thus in addition to its comparative nature, the underlying significance of the present study is the examination of the widely held assumption that involvement in sport advances democratization.

PROCEDURE

SAMPLES

INSTITUTIONS. It is generally acknowledged that the most élite cluster of institutions of higher education in the United States is the constituent colleges of the so-called "Ivy League." These institutions include Brown, Columbia, Cornell, Dartmouth, Harvard, Princeton, Pennsylvania, and Yale universities. For purposes of this study, data collection was confined to Harvard and Yale in view of (1) their special eminence within the Ivy League, (2) their traditional athletic rivalry, (3) their extensive archives, and (4) their comparable stature with Cambridge and Oxford. Like Oxford and Cambridge, Harvard (1638) and Yale (1701) are the two oldest universities in their country, retain very selective admission standards and are internationally renowned centres of learning. Moreover, it is relevant to note that intercollegiate athletic competition between English and American universities has been largely confined to matches between Cambridge, Oxford, Harvard, and Yale.[11]

SPORTS. Data concerning the secondary school background and athletic achievements of students at Harvard and Yale were largely limited to athletes participating in baseball, basketball, crew, and football. These sports were selected because of (1) their wide popularity, (2) their relatively large number of participants, and

(3) the ready availability of accurate records of athletic achievements. Unfortunately, in terms of their basic game structure, these selected sports are not directly comparable to those sampled by Eggleston. However, they do represent a range of sports of different status with respect to sporting traditions and athletic facilities found among private and public secondary schools.[12]

YEARS. For the selected colleges and sports, data were gathered for the seventy-year period 1901–72 in order to assess certain parameters of social change. Special emphasis is placed on the period 1951–70 as these two decades encompass the time period covered in Eggleston's study and afford the most complete and comparable records of secondary school background and athletic achievement.

MEASURES

SECONDARY SCHOOL ORIGINS. For purposes of most comparisons, lettermen were classified according to secondary school background as follows:

1. *Private Schooling*: graduation from a secondary school supported by private funds and endowments. Private secondary schools are usually designated by the phrase "preparatory schools."[13]

2. *Public Schooling*: graduation from a secondary school supported by public funds such as federal, state, and municipal monies. Public secondary schools are usually identified by the words "high schools."[14]

3. *Mixed Schooling*: secondary education acquired at both public and private institutions.[15]

4. *Unclassified*: the secondary school background for several subjects could not be determined for various reasons. For example, during the period of World War II, many students did not graduate with their college 'class' and thus their student biographies (including secondary school background) were not reported in the yearbook for their senior class.

ATHLETIC ACHIEVEMENT. Athletic achievement was assessed by ascertaining whether a student had earned a *letter award* as a result of his successful participation in a particular sport. Harvard and Yale annually award an "H" or "Y," respectively, to students excelling in various intercollegiate sports. The requirements for earning a letter are relatively standard among institutions of a given athletic conference, but vary from sport to sport. Thus to earn a letter for crew an athlete must participate in a certain number of races; in baseball an athlete must play a selected number of innings during the course of a season; and, similarly in basketball and football an athlete must play so many minutes during a season. As an additional measure of athletic achievement, *team captaincy* was recorded for selected sports for each year considered in the study.

OVERALL ADMISSION RATES. Figures regarding the percentage of private and public secondary school students annually admitted to Harvard and Yale were obtained for each year from 1911 to 1970.

SOURCES OF DATA

HARVARD. The primary sources used to obtain names of lettermen were *The H Book of Harvard Athletics 1852–1922* and *The Second H Book of Harvard Athletics 1923–1963*. Names of Harvard athletes from 1964–72 were obtained from annual sport brochures prepared by the Department of Athletics. The name of each athlete was located in the Class Album of his graduating class. On the basis of biographical data reported for each student in the class albums it was possible to determine the secondary school background of most lettermen. The overall percentage of private and public school students annually admitted to Harvard was ascertained from "The Report of the Committee of Admissions" located in the *Official Register of Harvard University—Issue Containing the Report of the President of Harvard College and Reports of Departments*.

YALE. The names of football lettermen from 1901–60 were obtained from the *Football Y-Men (Men of Yale Series)* edited by Albert Crawford. This excellent three-volume series encompassing the years 1872–1960 gives biographic data for every football letterman, including the secondary school attended by each player. The names of football lettermen from 1961–70 and the names of lettermen in baseball, basketball and crew were obtained from the files of the Department of Athletics at Yale University. The secondary school origin of "Y" winners was determined from data contained in the *Class Books* for a given athlete's graduating class. The percentage of private and public school students annually admitted to Yale from 1911 to 1952 was obtained from George Pierson's two volumes:

Yale College: An Educational History 1871–1921 and *Yale: The University College 1921–1937* (with appendices for 1938–52). Admission information for the years 1953–70 was acquired from the Office of Undergraduate Admissions at Yale University.

FINDINGS

The major findings of the study are summarized in Tables 1 through 5. With the exception of Tables 3 and 5, the figures within the tables represent the number of letters granted and not the number of individuals awarded letters. A given athlete may have earned as many as three letters in a single sport, and may, of course, have lettered in more than one sport. Findings are briefly reported in terms of past, present and comparative perspectives.

PAST PERSPECTIVE

Results regarding the secondary school background of Harvard and Yale lettermen in baseball, basketball, crew and football from 1901 to 1970 are summarized in Tables 1A to 1D. These tables reveal three major findings. First, the majority of letter winners at Harvard and Yale acquired their secondary education at private schools. Second, there was no marked change in the secondary school origins of lettermen in any given sport until after World War II. Third, although most athletes were drawn from preparatory schools throughout the seven decades studied, the ratio of private to public school lettermen consistently varied from sport to sport. Specifically, since the beginning of the century, crew noticeably has had the highest percentage of private school lettermen, followed by football, baseball and basketball.

As might be expected, the patterns of secondary school origin of lettermen from 1901–70 are reflected in a parallel manner for team captains (see Table 4). In short, with the notable exception of basketball, the majority of letter winners and team captains at Harvard and Yale since the turn of the century have been recruited from private schools.

PRESENT PERSPECTIVE

Data presented in Table 2 permit an analysis of the schools of origin of Harvard and Yale lettermen for the last two decades (i.e., 1951/2 to 1970/1). On the one hand, the table shows that in

TABLE 1A
Schools of Origin of Harvard and Yale Baseball Lettermen (1901/2–1970/1 Seasons)

School[a]	HARVARD									YALE								
	1		2		3		4			1		2		3		4		
Decade	n	%	n	%	n	%	n	%	N	n	%	n	%	n	%	n	%	N
1901–10	84	62·7	39	29·1	2	1·5	9	6·7	134	Data not available								
1911–20	90	68·2	32	24·2	4	3·0	6[b]	4·5	132	54	47·0	11	9·6	24	20·9	26	22·6	115
1921–30	126	76·4	29	17·6	4	2·4	6	3·6	165	56	36·6	13	8·5	40	26·1	44	28·8	153
1931–40	129	80·6	22	13·8	4	2·5	5	3·1	160	62	49·6	22	17·6	22	17·6	19	15·2	125
1941–50	77	60·2	32	25·0	0	·0	19	14·8	128	46	41·8	27	24·5	17	15·4	20	18·2	110
1951–60	61	38·9	93	59·2	1	·6	2	1·3	157	75	44·4	70	41·4	15	8·9	9	5·3	169
1961–70	53	40·2	79	59·8	0	·0	0	·0	132	50	33·8	80	54·1	12	8·1	6	4·1	148
Totals[c]	536	61·3	287	32·8	13	1·5	38	4·3	874	343	41·8	223	27·2	130	15·9	124	15·1	820

a 1 = private; 2 = public; 3 = mixed; 4 = unclassified   b Including three foreign students   c For 1911/12–1970/1 seasons only

TABLE 1B
Schools of Origin of Harvard and Yale Basketball Lettermen (1937/8–1970/1 Seasons)

School[a]	HARVARD									YALE								
	1		2		3		4			1		2		3		4		
Decade	n	%	n	%	n	%	n	%	N	n	%	n	%	n	%	n	%	N
1937–40[b]	16	43·2	20	54·1	0	·0	1	2·7	37	13	26·0	13	26·0	22	44·0	2	4·0	50
1941–50	32	33·0	53	54·6	0	·0	12	12·4	97	20	18·3	33	30·3	19	17·4	37	33·9	109
1951–60	15	15·6	79	82·3	0	·0	2	2·1	96	18	17·5	65	63·1	20	19·4	0	·0	103
1961–70	18	17·6	84	82·4	0	·0	0	·0	102	12	13·3	66	73·3	9	10·0	3	3·3	90
Totals	81	24·4	236	71·1	0	·0	15	4·5	332	63	17·9	177	50·3	70	19·9	42	11·9	352

a 1 = private; 2 = public; 3 = mixed; 4 = unclassified   b Letters were periodically awarded in basketball by Harvard 1933–7 and by Yale 1932–7

TABLE 1C

Schools of Origin of Harvard and Yale Crew Lettermen (1901/2–1970/1 Seasons)

School[a]	HARVARD									YALE								
	1		2		3		4			1		2		3		4		
Decade	n	%	n	%	n	%	n	%	N	n	%	n	%	n	%	n	%	N
1901–10	104	70·3	22	14·9	3	2·0	19[b]	12·8	148	Data not available								
1911–20	100	84·0	7	5·9	5	4·2	7[c]	5·9	119	51	56·7	7	7·8	7	7·8	25	27·8	90
1921–30	125	91·9	4	2·9	5	3·7	2	1·5	136	75	56·8	2	1·5	14	10·6	41	31·1	132
1931–40	126	94·0	5	3·7	0	·0	3	2·2	134	88	70·4	6	4·8	11	8·8	20	16·0	125
1941–50	93	78·2	17	14·3	0	·0	9	7·6	119	42	55·3	9	11·8	6	7·9	19	25·0	76
1951–60	134	85·9	20	12·8	0	·0	2	1·3	156	96	76·8	19	15·2	9	7·2	1	·8	125
1961–70	76	69·7	32	29·4	0	·0	1	·9	109	78	62·9	39	31·5	4	3·2	3	2·4	124
Totals[d]	654	84·6	85	11·0	10	1·3	24	3·1	773	430	64·0	82	12·2	51	7·6	109	16·2	672

a 1 = private; 2 = public; 3 = mixed; 4 = unclassified b Including six foreign students c Including five foreign students d For 1911/12–1970/1 seasons only

TABLE 1D

Schools of Origin of Harvard and Yale Football Lettermen (1901/2–1970/1 Seasons)

School[a]	HARVARD									YALE								
	1		2		3		4			1		2		3		4		
Decade	n	%	n	%	n	%	n	%	N	n	%	n	%	n	%	n	%	N
1901–10	143	74·5	12	6·3	3	1·6	34[b]	17·7	192	182	85·0	22	10·3	3	1·4	7	3·3	214
1911–20	143	82·7	16	9·2	6	3·5	8[c]	4·6	173	192	91·9	15	7·2	2	1·0	0	·0	209
1921–30	173	71·8	42	17·4	8	3·3	18	7·5	241	237	84·3	36	12·8	7	2·5	1	·4	281
1931–40	179	70·5	63	24·8	4	1·6	8	3·2	254	233	83·5	45	16·1	1	·4	0	·0	279
1941–50	122	43·6	102	36·4	0	·0	56	20·0	280	208	56·7	147	40·1	12	3·3	0	·0	367
1951–60	107	34·0	208	66·0	0	·0	0	·0	315	107	33·6	194	61·0	15	4·7	2[d]	·6	318
1961–70	124	36·8	205	60·8	0	·0	8	2·4	337	91	36·5	158	63·4	0	·0	0	·0	249
Totals	991	55·3	648	36·2	21	1·2	132	7·4	1792	1250	65·2	617	32·2	40	2·1	10	·5	1917

a 1 = private; 2 = public; 3 = mixed; 4 = unclassified b Including four foreign students c Including three foreign students d Two foreign students

TABLE 2
Summary of Schools of Origin of Ivy League Lettermen in Baseball, Basketball, Crew, and Football 1951/2–1970/1

Harvard

| School[a] | 1 | | 2 | | 3 | | 4 | | Total no. |
Sport	n	%	n	%	n	%	n	%	(=100%)
Baseball	114	39·4	172	59·5	1	·4	2	·7	289
Basketball	33	16·7	163	82·3	0	·0	2	1·0	198
Crew	210	79·2	52	19·6	0	·0	3	1·1	265
Football	231	35·4	413	63·3	0	·0	8	1·2	652
Total number of letters for all sports	588	41·9	800	57·0	1	0·1	15	1·1	1404

Yale

| School[a] | 1 | | 2 | | 3 | | 4 | | Total no. |
Sport	n	%	n	%	n	%	n	%	(=100%)
Baseball	125	39·4	150	47·3	27	8·5	15	4·7	317
Basketball	30	15·5	131	67·9	29	15·0	3	1·6	193
Crew	174	69·9	58	23·3	13	5·2	4	1·6	249
Football	198	34·9	352	62·1	15	2·6	2[b]	0·4	567
Total number of letters for all sports	527	39·7	691	52·1	84	6·3	24	1·9	1326

[a] 1 = private; 2 = public; 3 = mixed; 4 = unclassified   [b] Two foreign students

TABLE 3
Summary of Schools of Origin of Harvard Athletes In All Varsity Sports 1971/2

| School | Preparatory | | Parochial | | Public | | Total no. |
Sport	n	%	n	%	n	%	(=100%)
1. Squash	13	100·0	0	0·0	0	0·0	13
2. Lacrosse	23	82·1	1	3·6	4	14·3	28
3. Hockey	16	76·2	1	4·8	4	19·0	21
4. Skiing	13	72·2	0	0·0	5	27·8	18
5. Golf	5	62·5	0	0·0	3	37·5	8
6. Crew (heavyweight)	12	57·1	0	0·0	9	42·9	21
7. Crew (lightweight)	11	47·8	0	0·0	12	52·2	23
8. Tennis	10	47·6	0	0·0	11	52·4	21
9. Football	28	40·6	6	8·7	35	50·7	69
10. Baseball	12	38·7	1	3·2	18	58·1	31
11. Basketball	5	38·5	3	23·1	5	38·5	13
12. Fencing	6	31·6	1	5·3	12	63·1	19
13. Swimming	7	29·2	0	0·0	17	70·8	24
14. Wrestling	6	28·6	0	0·0	15	71·4	21
15. Track	15	25·4	9	15·3	35	59·3	59
Totals	182	46·8	22	5·7	185	47·6	389

TABLE 4

A Comparison of the Differential Admission Rates and the Differential Athletic Achievements of Private and Public School Students at Harvard and Yale 1911–70[a]

Decade	General Student body		Baseball lettermen		Basketball lettermen		Crew lettermen		Football lettermen		Team captains[b]	
	Harvard	Yale	Harvard	Yale	Harvard	Yale	Harvard	Yale	Harvard	Yale	Harvard	Yale
	%	%	%	%	%	%	%	%	%	%	%	%
1911–20	55·2	75·1	68·2	47·0	No team		84·0	56·7	82·7	91·9	72·0	55·2
1921–30	53·7	74·8	76·4	36·6	No team	26.0	91·9	56·8	71·8	84·3	82·8	43·3
1931–40	55·7	76·0	80·6	49·6	43·2	18·3	70·4	70·4	70·5	83·5	80·0	52·5
1941–50	50·4	65·8	60·2	41·8	33·0	17·5	78·2	55·3	43·6	56·7	50·0	40·0
1951–60	47·1	42·8	38·9	44·4	15·6	13·3	85·9	76·8	34·0	33·6	40·0	27·5
1961–70	42·3	44·2[e]	40·2	33·8	17·6		69·7	62·9	36·8	36·5	37·5	37·5

[a] All %'s = percentage of students from preparatory school backgrounds   [b] For the sports of baseball, basketball, football and crew   [c] Excluding female students matriculating in 1970

331

TABLE 5
Summary of Schools of Origin of All Ivy League Football Players for the 1972 Season

University	Secondary School Preparatory n	%	Parochial n	%	Public n	%	Total no. (=100%)
1. Harvard	28	40·6	6	8·7	35	50·7	69
2. Yale	15	23·4	11	17·2	38	59·4	64
3. Brown	12	17·6	26	38·2	30	44·1	68
4. Princeton	10	17·2	8	13·8	40	69·0	58
5. Pennsylvania	10	16·4	10	16·4	41	67·2	61
6. Columbia	11	12·9	17	20·0	57	67·1	85
7. Cornell	6	9·4	16	25·0	42	65·6	64
8. Dartmouth	3	5·0	5	8·3	52	86·7	60
Totals and average (%)	95	18·0	99	18·7	335	63·3	529

comparison to previous decades there is a much greater percentage of athletes of public school origin participating in intercollegiate athletics at Harvard and Yale. On the other hand, the table shows that the percentages of public school lettermen is markedly differentiated according to type of sport. Thus while less than one-fifth of the basketball lettermen were drawn from private schools, over one-third of the football lettermen, nearly two-fifths of the baseball lettermen, and approximately three-fourths of the crew lettermen were selected from preparatory schools during the last twenty years.

The fact that athletic achievement at America's élite universities has been, and to a lesser degree still is, a function of secondary school background is most strikingly illustrated in Table 3. This table gives a summary of schools of origin of Harvard athletes in all varsity intercollegiate sports for the 1971/2 season. Thus while only twenty-five percent of the trackmen and less than one-third of the fencers, swimmers and wrestlers are from private schools, one-hundred percent of the squash players and over seventy-five percent of the hockey and lacrosse players were prepared at private schools.

COMPARATIVE PERSPECTIVE

In order to calculate the relative chances of earning a blue for students from different types of secondary schools, Eggleston compared his survey figures for sportsmen with the contribution of the various categories of schools to the total male undergraduate population of Oxford and Cambridge for two selected years.[16] A simi-

lar comparison was made for the seven decades considered in this study. Table 4 offers a comparison of the differential admission rates and the differential athletic achievements of private and public school students on selected sports at Harvard and Yale from 1911 to 1970.

Inspection of Table 4 indicates that, with the exception of basketball lettermen, students from preparatory schools were substantially overrepresented on athletic teams in comparison to the student body as a whole from 1911 to 1940; whereas in the last thirty years, with the exception of lettermen in crew, the percentage of private school students excelling in athletics is similar to or less than the percentage of private school students found in the general student bodies at Harvard and Yale.

A final observation is that among élite universities opportunities for sport success are differentially associated with secondary school background relative to the status of a given university within its particular organizational-set. Evidence supporting this observation is given in Table 5 which shows the schools of origin of all Ivy League football players for the 1972 season. Table 5 clearly reveals that the "élite of the élite" (i.e., Harvard and Yale) recruit more athletes from preparatory schools than Ivy League universities of slightly less stature.

In sum, this study in an American setting replicates Eggleston's investigation in an English setting and provides confirmation for his major conclusion that within élite universities, opportunities for athletic achievement are differentially associated with secondary school origins and further differentiated between different sports of different status.

DISCUSSION

Social observers have long recognized the class and ethnic overtones of Ivy League athletics. For example, the noted American artist George Biddle who attended Harvard at the turn of the century records in his biography:

At Harvard, then, the New England boarding-school boy went in for clubs—social success. If that were not one's line, one opted for major athletics—although even in the field of major athletics there were social overtones. Football and rowing were of course the *ne plus ultra*. About the baseball squad there was something a little—well you know. Very few Grotties went in for baseball at Harvard. The track team was quite all right and of course tennis, golf and soccer; but one hardly knew the fellows who played lacrosse or basketball; or for that matter the members of the Pierian Sodality; and never, never, never, the members of the wrestling or debating teams. They were probably Jews and one might as well go to Columbia University.[18]

In an often cited study titled "Football in America: a study in culture diffusion,"[19] Riesman and Denney examined the ethnic significance of intercollegiate football by documenting "the shift in the typical origins of player names on the All-American Football Teams since 1889." On the basis of their analysis they state that:

There is an element of class identification running through American Football since its earliest days, and the ethnic origins of players contain ample invitations to the making of theory about the class dimensions of football. Most observers would be inclined to agree that the arrival of names like Kelly and Kipke on the annual All-American list was taken by the Flanagans and the Webers as the achievement of a lower-class aspiration to be among the best at an upper-class sport.[20]

Similar statements might be made in the present study for the several sports examined in terms of the secondary school origins of players, granting, of course, that secondary school origin is an indirect index of social class in the same sense that ethnic origin is a secondary measure of social class. Unfortunately, the social class background of the athletic alumni of Harvard and Yale sampled in this study could not be ascertained.

While there is no doubt a moderate correlation between an individual's social class and secondary school matriculation, the fit is likely far from perfect for a number of reasons. First, preparatory schools have always recruited some working-class students and their base of recruitment has increasingly broadened over the decades. Thus many prep school athletes competing at Harvard and Yale may have come from underclass backgrounds. Second, many public school athletes in the Ivy League may have come from upper-class backgrounds, and attended public schools which possess the advantages of private schools. Riesman, for example, cites model public schools ". . . such as New Trier or Scarsdale, where a suburban community, prosperous and enlightened, chooses to run its own private school at its own public expense."[21] Third, there are many cases of athletes of mixed-schooling, i.e., those who shifted from public-to-private, or *vice-versa*, during the last year or two of secondary education. A possible bias in the data reported in this investigation is the fact that some mixed-school athletes may have only listed the preparatory school they attended and failed to note previous attendance at a public secondary school. Notwithstanding the stated limitations of examining the social class aspects of democratization, results of this study permit a more narrow analysis of democratization of sport with respect to the increased participation of public school students in intercollegiate athletics at Harvard and Yale over the years surveyed.

In general, results of this study discount the thesis that intercollegiate athletics act as active agents of democratization at élite universities, in that, the percentage of preparatory school students participating in athletics is typically greater than the percentage of private school students in the general student body populations at Harvard and Yale. However, the findings do show that a relatively high degree of democratization has taken place *within* sport teams. It is evident from Tables 1 and 2 that an increasing number of public school graduates have excelled in athletics at Harvard and Yale in recent decades. Perhaps the best example of democratization in sport is the changing secondary school background of football lettermen at Yale. As is shown in Table 1D, 88 per cent of Yale's football lettermen were of private school origin during the period 1901–20; 84 per cent from 1921–40; but only 46 per cent from 1941–60; and for the decade of 1961–70, the percentage of football lettermen of preparatory school origin dropped to an all-time low of 36·5 per cent. Another striking example of democratization in sport is the introduction of basketball as a varsity sport during the 1930s and the marked participation of public school athletes in the sport from its inception to the present.

CONCLUSION

Results of the present study reveal marked changes in the social origins of intercollegiate athletes in the Ivy League when pre-World War I and post-World War II comparisons are made of the secondary school background of lettermen. But, an overall analysis of the findings strongly suggests that the changing social origins of collegiate sportsmen provide merely a mirror of social change and not a prognosis of social upheaval within élite institutions of higher education.

Specifically, this study of athletic awards at Harvard and Yale since the turn of the century of four major sports indicates that graduates of public schools have been at a decided disadvantage to graduates of preparatory schools concerning opportunities to letter in baseball, crew and football, both absolutely and relative to their total representation in the university population.

To quote Eggleston's conclusion to his study which this study replicates: "Type of school attended thus becomes associated with differences in a further area of performance at university—an area which seems to be of considerable importance in view of its likely association with social opportunities in university life and social occupational prospects in later life." [22]

NOTES

1. This article is a greatly revised version of a paper presented at the 3rd International Symposium on the 'Sociology of Sport', Waterloo, Ontario, Canada, 22–8 August, 1971, entitled: 'Democratization of Intercollegiate Sports in the Ivy League: a study of secondary school background and athletic achievement at Harvard and Yale.' Thanks is given to the following personnel of Yale University: Miss Nancy Gunneson, Office of Undergraduate Admissions; Mr. James C. Holgate, Associate Director of Athletics; and Miss Judith A. Schiff, Research Librarian in Historical Manuscripts and Archives. Appreciation is also accorded to the staff of the Department of Athletics and the Archives of Widener Library of Harvard University: especially, Mr. Robert B. Watson, Director of Athletics; Mr. David Matthews, Sports Information Director; Mrs. Jean Maciver, Secretary for the Department of Athletics. Special thanks is extended to Professor David Riesman of Harvard University for an unsolicited and thoughtful critique of an earlier draft of this paper.

2. Eggleston, John: Secondary schools and Oxbridge blues. Brit. J. Sociol., *16:*232–42, 1965.

3. Ibid., p. 232.

4. Ibid., p. 239.

5. Varsity letters such as the "H's" and "Y's" awarded for athletic excellence at Harvard and Yale are equivalent to the 'blues' awarded for outstanding athletic performance at Oxford and Cambridge.

6. Somewhat ironically, the term 'public school' in British usage may be equated with the term 'preparatory school' or 'private boarding school' in American usage.

7. Havighurst, Robert J. and Neugarten, Bernice: Society and Education, Boston, Allyn and Bacon, 1957, p. 45.

8. Hodges, Harold M.: Social Stratification—Class in America. Cambridge, Mass., Schenkman Publishing Company, 1964, p. 167.

9. Earnest, Ernest: Academic Procession: An Informal History of the American College, 1936 to 1953. New York, Bobbs-Merrill Co., Inc., 1953, p. 229.

10. Baltzell, E. Digby: Philadelphia Gentlemen: The Making of a National Upper Class. New York, The Free Press, 1958, p. 360.

11. The first American-British intercollegiate sport competition was a rowing contest between Harvard and Oxford universities in 1869.

12. For example, private schools sponsor sports seldom sanctioned by public schools such as crew, fencing, hockey, lacrosse and squash.

13. No attempt was made to distinguish among the various gradations of private schools, nor was a distinction made between boarding and day students at private schools, and private parochial schools (e.g. St. John's) were not considered separately from other private boarding schools. The major private schools whose graduates have gone on to Harvard and Yale include: Groton School, Noble and Greenough School, Phillips-Andover Academy, Phillips-Exeter Academy, Milton Academy, Pomfret School, St. George's School, Cambridge Latin School, Roxbury Latin School, Browne and Nichols School, St. Mark's School, St. Paul's School, Deerfield Academy, Volkmann School, Boston Latin School, Middlesex School, Worcester Academy, Choate School, Hotchkiss School, and the Hackley School.

14. Urban nonboarding parochial schools (e.g., St. Xavier High School) were also classified as high schools.

15. With only a couple of exceptions, all cases of mixed-schooling consisted of prior attendance at a public school before matriculation at a private school.

16. Eggleston, op. cit., Table 3, p. 238.

17. Spatial limitations preclude speculation as to

why preparatory school graduates have been so predominate in Ivy League athletics since the turn of the century. Discussion is thus confined to the democratization of intercollegiate sports at Harvard and Yale.

18. Biddle, George: An American Artist's Story. Boston, Little, Brown, 1939, p. 82.

19. Riesman, David and Denney, Reuel: Football in America: A study in culture diffusion. Am. Qt., *3*:309–19, 1951.

20. Ibid., p. 310.

21. Riesman, David: Teachers amid changing expectations. Harvard Educ. Rev., *24*:106–17, 1954. Quote from p. 117.

22. Eggleston, op. cit., p. 241.

athletic personnel in the academic marketplace: a study of the interorganizational mobility patterns of college coaches*

JOHN W. LOY and GEORGE H. SAGE

INTRODUCTION

BACKGROUND

Higher education in the United States is comprised of several hundred colleges and universities. Taken together, these institutions of higher education constitute a giant organizational set, composed of numerous organizational sub-sets. According to Caplow (1964: 224): "What enables us to identify a set is the presence of a prestige order that is recognized by most participants, the interchangeability of *some* personnel, and the engagement of each organization in *some* important activities common to all members of the set." It is evident that colleges and universities do exchange some personnel and do share some significant activities. Moreover, the "... various colleges and universities commonly are ranked in a hierarchical fashion"; [and] "the basis of this ranking is usually ex-

pressed in terms of notions of institutional 'quality' or 'prestige'...." (Hargens 1969: 18). An illustration of such a prestige order within higher education is Caplow and McGee's (1958) colloquial ranking of colleges and universities according to whether they belong to the "major league," the "minor league," the "bush league," or "academic Siberia."

The sociological significance of organizational prestige and institutional affiliation is that: "Prestige differences between institutions have consequences for interorganizational relations, particularly the flow of personnel between organizations and the distribution of other resources among the institution, and for the careers of professionals employed in these organizations" (Gross 1971: 1–2). Sociologists have long recognized the interrelationship between institutional and individual prestige patterns. Over thirty years ago, Logan Wilson, in *The Academic Man* (1942: 171) observed that a

... professor's prestige is connected with his institutional affiliation, and a faculty member at one of the leading universities has some prestige attached to him regardless of his personal standing among the elite of his field. A fortunate institutional connection is a double asset to the teacher or research man: First, it gives prestige to him by signifying (if status is permanent) that he has already 'arrived'; and second, it places him in an advantageous position further to enhance his reputation.

In a similar vein, nearly twenty years ago, Cap-

Reprinted from Sociology of Work and Occupations, 5(4):446–469, 1978. Copyright 1978 by Sage Publications, Inc., Beverly Hills, California.

*This article is a greatly revised and corrected version of a paper presented at the 36th annual meeting of the Southern Sociological Society (cf., Loy and Sage, 1973). Appreciation is accorded Ira E. Robinson, George Gross, Richard Rehberg, and an anonymous reviewer for thoughtful criticisms of an earlier draft of this article. The first author is indebted to the University of Pittsburgh for an award of an Andrew Mellon Postdoctoral Fellowship in the Department of Anthropology (1876) which has provided the needed time and resources to prepare this article.

low and McGee in *The Academic Marketplace* (1958: 76) observed that: "The value of a position to its incumbent is determined not only by his status within the organization but by the prestige of the whole organization in its external environment."

The connection between organizational prestige and career contingencies suggested by the observations of Wilson, and Caplow and McGee, is well documented in relatively recent research regarding the academic stratification system in American higher education. For example, several studies have found significant relationships between organizational prestige (institutions and/or departments) and (1) the average salary of faculty members (Cartter 1966); (2) the number of formal honorary awards received by faculty members (Crane 1965; Cole and Cole 1967); (3) the scholarly productivity of faculty members (Berelson 1960; Cole and Cole 1967; Crane 1965; Hargens and Hagstrom 1967; Lazarsfeld and Thielens 1958); and, (4) the quality of research publications by faculty members (Cole and Cole 1967; Cole 1968; Shamblin 1970). Other studies have shown that unless an individual receives his doctorate from an elite institution he has little likelihood of obtaining a faculty position at a leading university (Crane 1970; Gross 1970, 1971; Hurlbert 1976; Shichor 1970).

PURPOSE

The purpose of this study was to determine whether the marked relationship between organizational prestige and career mobility of scholars also obtains in the case of another group of individuals in the academic community, namely, college coaches. Although there are at present over 20,000 men employed as intercollegiate coaches (Sage 1975: 395), and while coaches are probably the most highly visible and publicized members of institutions of higher education, little is known about their occupational mobility patterns.

This study presents an exploratory examination of the "directions" and "mechanisms" of interorganizational mobility patterns of college coaches. The investigation also serves to replicate in part past studies of faculty mobility, and provides an empirical illustration of the utility of the concept of organizational set for understanding the relationship between institutional affiliation and career patterns.

CONTEST VS. SPONSORED MOBILITY

Although the nature of the data collected permitted only an indirect comparison, particular emphasis was placed in this study on examining the relative influence of achieved and ascribed attributes on the upward career mobility of coaches. These two sets of factors were analyzed in terms of Turner's (1960) two "ideal" modes of social ascent labeled "contest mobility" and "sponsored mobility." As described by Turner (1960: 856):

Contest mobility is a system in which elite status is the prize in an open contest and is taken by the aspirants' own efforts.... Since the "prize" of successful upward mobility is not in the hands of an established elite to give out, the latter cannot determine who shall attain it and who shall not.

Whereas,

Under *sponsored* mobility elite recruits are chosen by the established elite or their agents, and elite status is *given* on the basis of some criterion of supposed merit and cannot be *taken* by any amount of effort or strategy. Upward mobility is like entry into a private club where each candidate must be "sponsored" by one or more of the members.

Turner's model has been employed in several studies of mobility in academic settings (see, e.g., Crane, 1969; Hargens and Hagstrom, 1967; Kinloch, 1969; and, Kinloch and Perrucci, 1969); but it has not been utilized in the study of intercollegiate athletics, where it would appear quite appropriate for analysis of career mobility.

On the one hand, the case can be made that the domain of intercollegiate athletics with its norms of personal achievement in competitive situations governed by fair play and sportsmanship is a suitable setting for "contest mobility." It would follow that the best means to a head coaching job at a major university is to earn a degree in physical education, produce championship teams at the interscholastic level, and move upward in the coaching ranks by obtaining in turn positions at the junior college, senior college, and university levels on the basis of winning records.

On the other hand, a strong case can be made that the greatest social ascent in collegiate coaching circles is acquired through "sponsored mobility." Some authorities in athletics have suggested that the coaching profession has the basic characteristics of a craft guild. Thus the individual who wishes to reach the top must participate as an athlete at a major university and receive the recommendation of his coach to understudy as an assistant coach with a well known head coach. Following a successful apprenticeship with a renowned coach, the individual asks for the sponsorship of his mentor in seeking his own head coaching position at a major university. This latter case implies that organizational prestige as well as individual status affects upward career mobility; therefore, attention was directed to the concept of "organizational-set" in the course of the investigation.

ORGANIZATIONAL SETS

"An organizational set consists of two or more organizations of the same type, each of which is continuously visible to every other" (Caplow, 1964:210). Moreover, "*all* organizational sets develop a prestige order by which the members of each organization and interested audiences outside the set can rank-order the member organizations of each set" (Gross, 1970: 25). The basic premises underlying the concept of organization set have been set forth by Gross (1970:26) as follows:

1. Nearly every organization belongs to a set of organizations which generates a prestige order that is recognized by participants and, usually, outsiders as well.
2. Organizations belong to a number of organizational sets. Some of these sets are more important than others, but in each set there is a prestige ordering.
3. Organizational sets can be more or less easily recognized as being composed of organizations that are visible to one another, share a common prestige order, engage in similar activities, and have personnel many of whom are functionally interchangeable.
4. Organizational prestige affects interorganizational relations in that the most prestigious organizations have some influence on the less prestigious organizations. They formulate the standards by which prestige is evaluated and they get the lion's share of resources from sources external to the set. They come out better in the process of recruiting and exchanging personnel because of their more favorable bargaining

position. And they can bargain for new personnel by offering more prestige in exchange for less money, security, or authority than their less prestigious counterparts.
5. How prestige is determined has a bearing on organizational goals. If an organization can appeal to a professional audience for resources, then its goals will be oriented toward meeting existing professional standards. However, if it is dependent upon favorable opinions by nonexpert groups for financial support, then it must bid for prestige by visible symbols of performance.

This study draws upon these notions of organization sets and tests a number of hypotheses related to the interchange of personnel among institutions within the realm of intercollegiate athletics.

HYPOTHESES

While intercollegiate athletics often appears to hold a tenuous position and to possess a marginal status in the academic community, the patterns of social differentiation among the academic and athletic domains of higher education have a number of similarities. For example, with respect to individual status, parallels can be drawn between the rank and authority of athletic directors and deans, the roles and responsibilities of head coaches and department heads, and the universalistic norms of achievement held for coaches and professors. Similarly, with respect to organizational prestige, there is the obvious parallel of being associated with a major or minor sport on the one hand, and a major or minor department on the other. More importantly, for purposes of this study, is the fact that various colleges and universities commonly are ranked in hierarchical fashion in terms of their athletic quality or prestige as well as in terms of their academic quality or prestige.

The concern for athletic prestige is reflected in the current controversy surrounding the proposal of the National Collegiate Athletic Association to create a new "super division" for a very select sample of big-time college football teams (Van Dyne 1976a, 1976b).[1] Other examples of preoccupation with athletic prestige are given in Crase's (1972) discussion of the inner circles of intercollegiate football in terms of (1) perennial powers, (2) near-perennial powers, (3) marginal powers, and (4) opportunists. In short, the connection between institutional and individual prestige found in various academic disciplines may well obtain in various intercollegiate sports.

In this study the investigators sought to determine the degree to which universities having high athletic prestige recruit their coaching staffs from other institutions possessing similar status. It was hypothesized that:

1. Coaches who participated as varsity athletes at high prestige institutions are more likely to have served as assistant coaches at high prestige institutions than coaches who participated as varsity athletes at low prestige institutions.
2. Coaches who served as assistant coaches at high prestige institutions are more likely to have obtained their first head coaching position at high prestige institutions than coaches who served as assistant coaches at low prestige institutions.
3. Coaches who held their first head job at high prestige institutions are more likely to presently hold head jobs at high prestige institutions than coaches whose first head jobs were at low prestige institutions.
4. The coaching career pattern implied by the assumptions underlying hypotheses 1–3 tends to be linear, additive, and unidirectional (i.e., the hypothesized career pattern constitutes a "weak" causal order).

In addition to the variables of individual status and institutional prestige associated with the preceding hypotheses, the variables of academic achievement, athletic achievement, and coaching success were also taken into account for purposes of exploratory analysis.

METHODOLOGY

POPULATIONS AND SAMPLES

Findings of the study are based on data obtained from questionnaires mailed in the Spring of 1971 to all head basketball coaches (n = 536) and football coaches (n = 416) employed by colleges and universities affiliated with the National Collegiate Athletic Association (NCAA). Questionnaires were returned by 348 basketball and 276 football coaches. Thus reported findings are based on data obtained from 65 percent of all NCAA head basketball coaches, and 66 percent of all NCAA head football coaches. However, due to missing and incomplete data, the specific number of cases considered varies from one analysis to another. A comparison of expected and obtained questionnaire returns by samples with respect to college and university categories is presented in Table 1.

VARIABLES AND MEASURES

Most of the variables treated were operationally measured in a straightforward manner and will be defined in context where appropriate. However, a brief description of the assessment of *athletic prestige* is in order as this variable is central to the study and was operationally measured somewhat differently for the two sports. First, institutions of higher education engaged in intercollegiate athletics under the auspices of the NCAA were classified as either university or college division institutions as defined by the NCAA. A given institution could be placed in one category for basketball and in another category for football. Second, the institutions placed in the university division were further grouped

TABLE 1
A Comparison of Populations and Samples of NCAA Coaches

Institution Level of Present Position	Head Basketball Coaches				Head Football Coaches			
	total NCAA institution population		returned questionnaires		total NCAA institution population		returned questionnaires	
	n	%	n	%	n	%	n	%
College Division	335	62.50	246	70.69	298	71.63	199	72.10
University Division	201	37.50	102	29.31	118	28.37	77	27.90
TOTALS	536		(348)		416		(276)	

according to their respective athletic conference. Third, athletic conferences for university division institutions were rank-ordered in terms of "athletic prestige."[2]

In *the case of basketball* an analysis was made of the Associated Press (AP) and United Press International (UPI) annual rankings of the top ten teams nationwide for the years 1950 to 1970. For any given year a specific conference was awarded two points for each of its constituent institutions which was ranked in the "top 5" and one point for each of its constituent institutions which was ranked in the "second five." The total summation of points from the two press polls for the two decades provided the basis for the rank-ordering of conferences in terms of athletic prestige as follows: (1) top 1–5 conferences, (2) top 6–10 conferences, (3) major independent institutions, (4) other universities not in the top 10 conferences, and, (5) college division institutions.[3]

In the *case of football* the athletic prestige of a given conference was ascertained from an analysis of conference ratings reported in the Harmon Football Forecast for the years 1963–1972. A conference's rating in Harmon's poll is based on the average athletic performance of its member institutions against all opposition throughout an entire season. Caliber of competition rather than won/lost records *per se* is the primary criterion for Harmon's ratings. Although a given conference was found to fluctuate in its annual rating over the ten-year period, such fluctuation only occurred with a given category in the following scale of athletic prestige: (1) top 1–5 conferences, (2) top 6–10 conferences, (3) major independent institutions, (4) top 11–20 conferences, (5) other university division institutions, and (6) college division institutions.

DATA TREATMENT

Descriptive statistics, cross-tabulations, correlations and regression analyses (including path analyses) were computed using various programs of the *Statistical Package for the Social Sciences* (Nie et al. 1975). In order to insure adequate frequencies per cell, most cross-tabulations and related measures of association were calculated on the basis of 2×2 contingency tables. In all analyses missing data were handled by means of listwise deletion.

Parametric statistical techniques were employed in regression analysis with the awareness

that certain assumptions such as the use of interval level measures were not fully met.[4] However, the robustness of the data was assessed by means of numerous comparisons of nonparametric measures of association and parametric measures of correlation using both "raw data" and "binary coded data." Several of these comparisons are shown below for the reader's personal analysis. Of the several measures obtained in these comparative statistical analyses only the most conservative were used for purposes of hypothesis testing. Moreover, regression and path analyses were viewed as exploratory and heuristic in the sense of examining trends and patterns rather than establishing population estimates and determining the precise degree of variance explained *per se*.

FINDINGS AND DISCUSSION

CONFIRMATION OF HYPOTHESES

Results of the primary phase of data analysis are summarized in Tables 2 and 3, and Figures 1 and 2, and are reported in terms of the hypotheses stated above.

1. *Hypotheses 1–3* were tested by means of nonparametric correlation analysis. Table 2 presents rank-order correlation matrixes for the four variables of athletic prestige related to the three hypotheses for the two samples of college coaches. It is evident from Table 2 that each hypothesis received empirical support as all correlations between the defined independent and dependent variables[5] are statistically significant beyond the .0001 level. More specifically, with respect to Hypothesis 1, the moderate tau of .40 for basketball coaches and the relatively high tau of .61 for football coaches indicates a fairly substantial relationship between the athletic prestige of a coach's undergraduate college and the athletic prestige of the employing institution where he served as an assistant coach on the college level. Secondly, as concerns Hypothesis 2, the relatively high tau of .59 for basketball coaches and the moderate tau of .47 for football coaches reveals a marked relationship between the athletic prestige of the institution where a coach served his apprenticeship and the athletic prestige of his initial employing institution as a head coach. Finally, as regards Hypothesis 3, the relatively high tau of .60 for basketball coaches and the high tau of .68 for football coaches suggests a strong relationship between

TABLE 2
Rank Order Correlations Between Athletic Prestige Measures for NCAA Coaches*

(a) Basketball Coaches

Variables	Correlation	Coefficients		(tau)
	1	2	3	4
1. Athletic Prestige of Undergraduate College	(348)	.40	.30	.18
2. Athletic Prestige of Coaching Apprenticeship	0.0000	(320)	.59	.47
3. Athletic Prestige of First Head Job	0.0000	0.0000	(325)	.60
4. Athletic Prestige of Present Head Job	0.0367	0.0000	0.0000	(97)

(b) Football Coaches

Variables	Correlation	Coefficients		(tau)
	1	2	3	4
1. Athletic Prestige of Undergraduate College	(276)	.61	.47	.36
2. Athletic Prestige of Coaching Apprenticeship	0.0000	(220)	.47	.42
3. Athletic Prestige of First Head Job	0.0000	0.0000	(222)	.68
4. Athletic Prestige of Present Head Job	0.0021	0.0010	0.0000	(64)

*Values along diagonal denote the number of cases from which data were obtained on each respective variable; values above diagonal are Kendall Tau$_b$ correlation coefficients; values below diagonal are levels of significance for respective correlations.

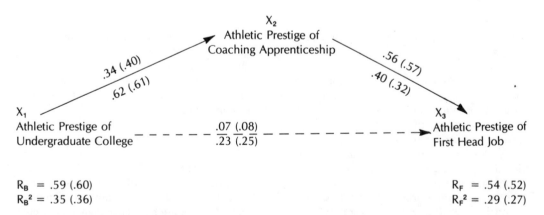

$R_B = .59 (.60)$ $R_F = .54 (.52)$
$R_B^2 = .35 (.36)$ $R_F^2 = .29 (.27)$

FIG. 1   PATH DIAGRAM FOR CAUSAL MODEL OF INTERORGANIZATIONAL MOBILITY. Path coefficients for basketball coaches are shown above the arrows and those for football coaches below the arrows. Path coefficients *not* in parentheses are based on "raw data" (i.e., standard scales), while those in parentheses are based on "binary coded data" (i.e., dummary variables). Multiple correlations and coefficients of determination are placed on the left for basketball coaches (R_B) and on the right for football coaches (R_F). The hyphenated lines and arrows denote indirect influences.

TABLE 3
Product-Moment Correlations Between Athletic Prestige Measures for NCAA Coaches*

(a) Basketball Coaches

Variables	Correlation		Coefficients	(r)
	1	2	3	4
1. Athletic Prestige of Undergraduate College	(348)	.34	.26	.22
2. Athletic Prestige of Coaching Apprenticeship	.40	(320)	.59	.43
3. Athletic Prestige of First Head Job	.30	.60	(325)	.60
4. Athletic Prestige of Present Head Job	.15	.47	.60	(97)

(b) Football Coaches

Variables	Correlation		Coefficients	(r)
	1	2	3	4
1. Athletic Prestige of Undergraduate College	(276)	.62	.47	.30
2. Athletic Prestige of Coaching Apprenticeship	.61	(220)	.54	.41
3. Athletic Prestige of First Head Job	.45	.48	(222)	.72
4. Athletic Prestige of Present Head Job	.36	.41	.70	(64)

*Values along diagonal denote the number of cases from whom data were obtained for each respective variable; values above diagonal are correlation coefficients based on "raw data" (i.e., five and sixfold category scales of athletic prestige for basketball and football coaches, respectively); values below diagonal correlation coefficients based on "binary coded data" (i.e., on a created set of dummy variables).

the athletic prestige of a coach's first head position and present head position at the college level.

2. *Hypothesis 4* was tested by the use of path models representing the several stages of an individual's coaching career in a temporal sequence. The utilization of path models required the treatment of ordinal variables as interval level measures. A comparison of the parametric correlation matrixes in Table 3 and the nonparametric correlation matrixes in Table 2 provides some justification for this procedure as the two sets of correlation coefficients are very similar in magnitude.[6]

Because the present head coaching position of a majority of coaches was discovered to be their first head coaching position, two sets of path models were calculated. The first set of path models (cf., Fig. 1) is based on data obtained from all subjects in each sample and analyzes the sequence of interorganizational mobility from undergraduate college (X_1), to "best" coaching apprenticeship (X_2), to first head coaching position (X_3). The second set of path models (cf., Fig. 2) is based on data obtained from selected subjects in both samples who have held more than one head coaching position at the college level.

The data schematically illustrated in Figures 1 and 2 offer a good deal of empirical support for Hypothesis 4 in that they show the significant direct effects of a temporal sequence of interorganizational mobility and account for 37 to 53 percent of the variance in the dependent variable of athletic prestige of present position (X_4) in terms of only three independent variables: athletic prestige of first head job (X_3), athletic prestige of "best" coaching apprenticeship (X_2), and

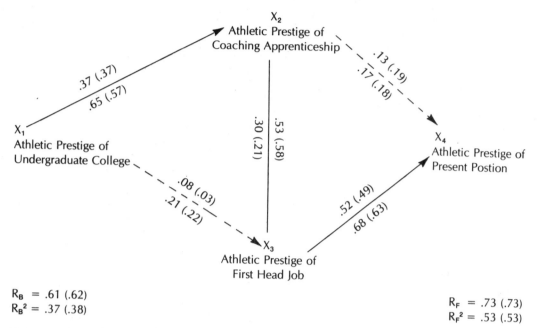

X_2
Athletic Prestige of
Coaching Apprenticeship

.37 (.37)
.65 (.57)

.13 (.19)
.17 (.18)

X_1
Athletic Prestige of
Undergraduate College

.30 (.21)   .53 (.58)

X_4
Athletic Prestige of
Present Postion

.08 (.03)
.21 (.22)

.52 (.49)
.68 (.63)

X_3
Athletic Prestige of
First Head Job

R_B = .61 (.62)
R_B^2 = .37 (.38)

R_F = .73 (.73)
R_F^2 = .53 (.53)

FIG. 2   PATH DIAGRAM FOR CAUSAL MODEL OF INTERORGANIZATIONAL MOBILITY. Path coefficients for basketball coaches are shown above the arrows and those for football coaches below the arrows. Path coefficients *not* in parentheses are based on "raw data" (i.e., standard scales), while those in parentheses are based on "binary coded data" (i.e., dummy variables). Multiple correlations and coefficients of determination are placed on the left for basketball coaches (R_B) and on the right for football coaches (R_F). The hyphenated lines and arrows denote indirect influences.

athletic prestige of undergraduate college (X_1). With the exception of the influence of the athletic prestige of undergraduate college on the athletic prestige of the first head job for football coaches, the indirect effects of the several variables of the path models are relatively insignificant. The major difference between the samples is that the athletic prestige of undergraduate college has more influence on the career mobility patterns of football coaches than basketball coaches; whereas the athletic prestige associated with coaching apprenticeship has greater influence on the career mobility patterns of basketball coaches than football coaches. These latter findings suggest that the community of football coaching has more caste characteristics, and the stamp of one's status is firmly established by the choice of an undergraduate college. Moreover, since there are some 22 percent more head basketball coaching positions, basketball coaches have a better opportunity to attract the attention of the high prestige colleges through their coaching achievements.

CONTEST VS. SPONSORED MOBILITY

The results reported above provide some indication that the greatest social ascent in collegiate coaching circles is acquired through sponsored rather than contest mobility. Further indirect evidence supporting the thesis of sponsored mobility is given by the regression analyses of selected achievement variables summarized in Tables 4 and 5. Data reported in these tables indicate that such seemingly relevant factors as educational status, athletic achievement, coaching experience, and even coaching success have little, if any, apparent effect on the athletic prestige of an individual's first or present job. The nine independent variables employed in the regression analyses account for only one to sixteen percent of the variance of the dependent variables of athletic prestige of coaching position, and thus imply that the variance might be better accounted for by ascribed rather than achieved attributes.

These regression analyses, however, must be

TABLE 4

Stepwise Multiple Regression Analysis of Selected Achievement Variables for NCAA Head Basketball Coaches

Independent Variables	R*	R²*	R**	R²**
1. Subject's Educational Status	0.06811	0.00464	0.06852	0.00469
2. Number of Varsity Sports Played	0.06811	0.00464	0.06852	0.00469
3. Number of Varsity Letters Earned	0.08000	0.00640	0.14969	0.02241
4. Athletic Achievement in Primary Sport	0.08752	0.00766	0.15062	0.02269
5. Professional Achievement in Primary Sport	0.08786	0.00772	0.22320	0.04982
6. Professional Achievement in Secondary Sport	0.08787	0.00772	0.23175	0.05371
7. Total Years of Coaching Experience	0.08804	0.00775	0.24282	0.05896
8. Years of Head Coaching Experience	0.13358	0.01784	0.24602	0.06052
9. Winning Percentage as Head Coach	0.13358	0.01784	0.24602	0.06052

*Dependent variable = Athletic Prestige of First Head Job (n = 348)
**Dependent variable = Athletic Prestige of Present Head Job (n = 97)

TABLE 5

Stepwise Multiple Regression Analysis of Selected Achievement Variables for NCAA Head Football Coaches

Independent Variables	R*	R²*	R**	R²**
1. Subject's Educational Status	0.01404	0.00020	0.24832	0.06166
2. Number of Varsity Sports Played	0.01404	0.00020	0.24832	0.06166
3. Number of Varsity Letters Earned	0.02565	0.00066	0.26376	0.06957
4. Athletic Achievement in Primary Sport	0.05542	0.00307	0.32761	0.10733
5. Professional Achievement in Primary Sport	0.07459	0.00556	0.32910	0.10831
6. Professional Achievement in Secondary Sport	0.07584	0.00575	0.34470	0.11882
7. Total Years of Coaching Experience	0.07660	0.00587	0.34892	0.12175
8. Years of Head Coaching Experience	0.08166	0.00667	0.36214	0.13115
9. Winning Percentage as Head Coach	0.08615	0.00742	0.39750	0.15800

*Dependent variable = Athletic Prestige of First Head Job (n = 276)
**Dependent variable = Athletic Prestige of Present Head Job (n = 65)

viewed with some caution as they are based on data which are descriptive and cross-sectional in nature, and thus preclude any direct inferences about the causes and consequences of the interorganizational mobility patterns discussed above. In short, the data permit no conclusions about patterns over time. For example, "winning percentage" may be critical at different stages of a coach's career but not of major importance in terms of his overall record. This is to say, a coach with a lifetime .500 won/lost record may remain employed at a major institution if he has very successful seasons periodically to establish "professional credit" on which he may draw during "lean years." This performance contingency of a coaching career has a similar parallel with the performance contingency of an academic career. Most college and university professors do not have substantial productivity records but an occasional article or a book now and again provides them with a degree of professional credit that they draw upon for some amount of time for purposes of promotion, tenure, and salary increases. Unlike professors, however, no matter how much professional credit a coach establishes at any given time he seldom receives tenure for his successful performance, only a renewed contract of varying duration.[7]

IMPLICATIONS

The high degree of association found between institutional prestige and coaching career patterns provides a strong but indirect indication that upward career mobility within intercollegiate coaching circles is largely a function of sponsored rather than contest mobility. However, the concept of institutional prestige and its correlation with coaching career patterns gives only limited insight into the direction and mechanisms of interorganizational mobility patterns of college coaches. Greater attention needs to be given to the precise forms of sponsorship involved. A number of factors are likely associated with the sponsored mobility of college coaches.[8]

First, there is the factor of friendship and the "old boy network." In recruiting new assistant coaches, head coaches tend to favor their former athletes who excelled under their leadership, and they tend to sponsor assistant coaches for jobs who have loyally served a long apprenticeship under their guidance.

Second, there is the related factor of athletic farm systems. A major consequence of organization sets ". . . is the phenomenon of 'feeder' subsets which link together with different types of organizational sets" Tausky (1970: 170) noted:

> For example, the very prestigious law firms draw primarily on the graduating students of prestigious law schools; prestigious private firms engaged in scientific research, recruit science graduates from eminent university departments of chemistry, physics, and so forth; and prep schools channel their graduates to private colleges which give them preference in admission.

There are indications that the phenomenon just illustrated is also characteristic of intercollegiate athletics as reflected, for instance, in the number of current college coaches who are alumni of the University of Oklahoma and Miami University of Ohio (Benagh 1976).

A third factor associated with sponsorship is the matter of publicity. A college or professional athlete who has received the favorable endorsement of the mass media provides immediate prestige to the institution that employs him on its coaching staff. Needless to say a talented athlete at a relatively unknown institution will not receive the press of an equally or even lesser talented athlete at a major university.[9]

Fourth, there is the factor of collegial *quid pro quo*. The credits and debits of social exchange in coaching circles often entail the hiring of personnel from an institution that formerly hired candidates sponsored by one's own institution.

A fifth factor is the "halo effect" associated with high prestige institutions. Given the choice of two candidates with approximately equal credentials, the candidate from the more prestigeful institution will likely get the job.

Finally, there is the factor of "inexplicit criteria." Because college athletes and assistant coaches have established no coaching "record" of their own, it is difficult to determine their potential as head coaches and thus institutional prestige becomes an important variable in recruitment procedures due to its assumed connection with the other factors outlined above.

SUMMARY

Findings of the study show a close connection between organizational prestige and career contingencies and suggest that the interorganizational mobility patterns of athletic personnel in institutions of higher education are similar to those of academic personnel in various disciplines such as anthropology (Hurlbert 1976), economics (Crane 1970), English (Crane 1970, Gross 1971), mathematics (Gross 1971), philosophy, physics and psychology (Crane 1970), and sociology (Gross 1970, 1971; Shichor 1970).[10] In general, it was found that the athletic prestige of undergraduate institutions is positively associated with the athletic prestige of the institutions in which coaches carry out their careers. In particular, it was discovered that: (1) alumni of more prestigeful undergraduate institutions are more likely to serve as assistant college coaches at high prestige institutions than are alumni of less prestigeful undergraduate institutions; (2) assistant coaches at more prestigeful institutions are more likely to obtain their initial head coaching jobs at high prestige institutions; and, (3) coaches who obtained their first head job at prestigeful institutions are more likely to be currently employed by high prestige institutions than are coaches who obtained their first head job at less prestigeful institutions.

In conclusion, we suggest that the further study of intercollegiate athletics would be a fruitful line of research for empirically assessing other implications of the concept of organizational set in addition to its import for the exchange of personnel.[11]

NOTES

1. Most recently it was announced that the NCAA abandoned its proposal for a football super-division as "plans would have moved 41 teams from top tier, leaving 97 super-powers; demoted institutions blocked the realignment, *fearing serious loss of prestige*" (Van Dyne 1976c: 3) (italics ours).

2. It is perhaps a moot matter as to whether the operational measures discussed below reflect "institutional quality" rather than "institutional prestige" per se. We prefer the concept of "athletic prestige" rather than what might be termed "athletic quality" because the "athletic quality" of an institution of higher education is, unlike its "academic quality," rather unstable in the short run. But notwithstanding a winning record one year and a losing record the next, the "athletic prestige" of an institution remains relatively stable across time. The stability of "athletic prestige" of a given institution derives in large measure from the prestige of the organizational-set (i.e., conference) of which it is a member.

3. Although the college division institutions are grouped into a seemingly homogeneous mass, there was very little choice, first because none of them has much athletic status, when compared to the major universities, and second, since there are several hundred of them, only a few of which compete against each other or against common opponents, there is no viable way to rank their athletic status. This holds for both basketball and football.

4. The reader interested in the rationales, techniques, and limitations of using ordinal variables as interval level measures in regression and multivariate analysis is referred to Allen (1976), Blalock (1964), Bohrnstedt and Carter (1971), Boyle (1970, 1971), Cohen (1968), Kim (1975), Labovitz (1967), Lyons (1971), Lyons and Carter (1971), and Werts and Linn (1971).

5. That is, variables contained in the stated hypotheses.

6. Computed phi-coefficients and Spearman rank-order correlation coefficients were virtually identical to the Pearson product-moment correlation coefficients reported in Table 3.

7. This observation, of course, does not apply to cohorts who hold faculty status in departments of physical education. Moreover, some head coaches at selected institutions hold professorships in escrow which they may claim upon the termination of their coaching careers.

8. The list of factors discussed is suggested by Gross (1971: 106–7).

9. This is well illustrated by the great publicity given Heisman award candidates who have been notable for their lack of success in professional football, and by the lack of publicity given talented black athletes at small southern colleges who have achieved notable success in professional basketball and football.

10. See Sturgis and Clements (1973) for a critique of the ranking systems employed in the rating of departments in the studies cited.

11. Other implications include "... (a) the transmission and refinement of the institutional model, (b) the allocation of scarce resources, (c) procedural experimentation, (d) comparative appraisal of achievement, (e) diffusion of inventions and discoveries..." (Caplow 1964: 203–4).

REFERENCES

Allen, Michael Patrick: Conventional and optimal interval scores for ordinal variables. Sociol. Methods Res., *4*(May): 475–94, 1976.

Benagh, Jim: Miami: Football's tight little gene pool. Signature, (October): 40–43, 1976.

Berelson, Bernard: Graduate Education in the United States. New York, McGraw-Hill, 1960.

Blalock, Hubert M.: Causal Inferences in Nonexperimental Research. Chapel Hill, N.C., University of North Carolina Press, 1964.

Bohrnstedt, George W., and Carter, T. Michael: Robustness in regression analysis. *In* Sociological Methodology. Edited by Herbert L. Costner. San Francisco, Jossey-Bass, 1971, pp. 118–146.

Boyle, Richard P.: Path analysis and ordinal data. Am. J. Sociol., *75*(January): 461–80, 1970.

Boyle, Richard P.: Rejoiner to Werts and Linn, Lyons and Carter. Am. J. Sociol., *76*(May): 1132–34, 1971.

Caplow, Theodore: Principles of Organization. New York, Harcourt, Brace & World, 1964.

Caplow, Theodore, and McGee, Reece J.: The Academic Marketplace. New York, Basic Books, 1958.

Cartter, Allan M.: An Assessment of Quality in Graduate Education. Washington, D.C., American Council on Education, 1966.

Cohen, Jacob: Multiple regression as a general data-analytic system. Psychol. Bull., 70(December): 426–43, 1968.

Cole, Jonathan R.: Patterns of intellectual influence in scientific research. Paper presented to the American Sociological Association. August, 1968.

Cole, Stephen, and Cole, Jonathan R.: Scientific output and recognition: A study in the operation of the reward system in science. Am. Sociol. Rev., 32(June): 377–90, 1967.

Crane, Diana: Scientists at major and minor Universities: A study of productivity and recognition. Am. Sociol. Rev., 30(October): 699–714, 1965.

Crane, Diana: Social class origin and academic success: The influence of two stratification systems on academic careers. Sociol. Educ., 42(Winter): 1–17, 1969.

Crane, Diana: The academic marketplace revisited: A study of faculty mobility using the Cartter ratings. Am. J. Sociol., 75(May): 953–64, 1970.

Crase, Darrell: The inner circles of intercollegiate football. Sport Sociol. Bull., 1(Fall): 3–7, 1972.

Evan, William M.: The organization-set: Toward a theory of interorganizational relations. In Approaches to Organizational Design. Edited by James D. Thompson. Pittsburgh, University of Pittsburgh Press, 1966, pp. 173–191.

Gross, George R.: The organization set: A study of sociology departments. Am. Sociol., 5(February): 25–29, 1970.

Gross, George R.: Organizational prestige and academic career patterns. Ph.D. Dissertation, Department of Sociology. University of Massachusetts, Amherst, Mass., 1971.

Hargens, Lowell L., and Hagstrom, Warren O.: Sponsored and contest mobility of American academic scientists. Sociol. Educ., 40(Winter): 24–38, 1967.

Herlbert, Beverley McCelligott: Status and exchange in the profession of anthropology. Am. Anthropol., 78(June): 272–284, 1976.

Kim, Jae-On: Multivariate analysis of ordinal variables. Am. J. Sociol., 81(September): 361–98, 1975.

Kinloch, Graham C.: Sponsored and contest mobility among college graduates: Measurement of the relative openness of a social structure. Sociol. Educ., 42(Fall): 350–67, 1969.

Kinloch, Graham C., and Perrucci, Robert: Social origins, academic achievement and mobility channels: Sponsored and contest mobility among college graduates. Soc. Forces, 48(September): 36–45, 1969.

Labovitz, S.: Some observations on measurement and statistics. Soc. Forces, 46(December): 151–69, 1967.

Lazerfeld, Paul F., and Thielens, W., Jr.: The Academic Mind. Glencoe, Ill., Free Press, 1958.

Loy, John W., and Sage, George H.: Organizational prestige and coaching career patterns. Paper presented at the 36th annual meeting of the Southern Sociological Society, Atlanta, 1973.

Lyons, Morgan: Techniques for using ordinal measures in regression and path analysis. In Sociological Methodology. Edited by Herbert L. Costner. San Francisco, Jossey-Bass, 1971.

Lyons, Morgan, and Carter, T. Michael: Further comments on Boyle's "Path Analysis of Ordinal Data." Am. J. Sociol., 76(May): 1112–32, 1971.

Nie, Norman H., et al.: Statistical Package for the Social Sciences. 2nd ed. New York, McGraw-Hill, 1975.

Sage, George H.: An occupation analysis of the college coach. In Sport and Social Order. Edited by Donald W. Ball and John W. Loy. Reading, Mass., Addison-Wesley, 1975, pp. 391–455.

Shamblin, Don H.: Prestige and the sociology establishment. Am. Sociol., 5(May): 154–156, 1970.

Shichor, David: Prestige of sociology departments and the placing of new Ph.D.'s. Am. Sociol., 5(May): 157–60, 1970.

Shichor, David: Prestige and regional mobility of new Ph.D.'s in sociology. Am. Sociol., 8(November): 180–86, 1973.

Sturgis, Richard B., and Clemente, Frank: The productivity of graduates of 50 sociology departments. Am. Sociol., 8(November): 169–80, 1973.

Tausky, Curt: Work Organizations. Itasca, Ill., F.E. Peacock, 1970.

Turner, Ralph H.: Sponsored and contest mobility in the school system. Am. Sociol. Rev., 25(December): 855–67, 1960.

Van Dyne, Larry: Lyman Hits NCAA on Super-Division Poll. Chron. Higher Educ., (May 3): 6, 1976a.

Van Dyne, Larry: Ranking the powers in college football. Chron. Higher Educ., (May 24): 6, 1976b.

Van Dyne, Larry: NCAA abruptly abandons football superdivision. Chron. Higher Educ., (July 26): 3, 1976c.

Werts, Charles E., and Linn, Robert L.: Comments on Boyle's 'Path Analysis and Ordinal Data.' Am. J. Sociol., 76(May): 1109–11, 1971.

Wilson, Logan: The Academic Man. New York, Oxford University Press, 1942.

elites, class and corporate power in canadian sport: some preliminary findings

RICHARD S. GRUNEAU

INTRODUCTION

Within the last three decades, sociologists have paid considerable attention to the changing social origins of sportsmen and the implications of these changes for broader themes and issues in the literature on inequality and stratification, but they have paid much less attention to the changing significance of sport at the highest levels of the class structure. Moreover, where sociologists have sought to explore the relationships between sport and the privileged, they have tended to emphasize the role of sports in the life styles and psychology of the upper classes [6, 82], or the nature of the values and recruitment patterns characterizing the executives of sports organizations [15, 38, 54], *without* linking such considerations to a critical analysis of the general framework of state and economy within which elite groups are recruited and structured. [a] In this working paper I attempt to respond to this deficiency, first, by outlining some of the theoretical and ideological biases which have limited the scope of research into the relationship between sport, class inequality and political order and, second, by suggesting some linkages between the recruitment of elite organizational figures in Canadian sport and changing patterns of class structuration and decomposition in Canadian society.

Reprinted from Sociology of Sport. Edited by F. Landry and W. Orban. Symposia Specialists, Inc., Miami, 1978, pp. 201–242. Copyright 1978 by Symposia Specialists, Inc., P.O. Box 610397, Miami, Florida 33161.

BACKGROUND PERSPECTIVES ON SPORT, CLASS AND POWER

A feature common to much of the writing on sports and social class is the failure of researchers to differentiate adequately between socioeconomic changes which have occurred at the level of *athletic participation* and those which have occurred at the level of *organizational leadership*. The effects of historical forces which appear to have figured significantly in the democratization of sports participation at the individual level are frequently echoed in the assertion that there have been parallel or compensatory changes at the "top" of the institutional hierarchies, even though evidence to support such trends is rarely presented. Nowhere is this tendency more pronounced than in the American literature on the relationship between sport and social class. Betts [11], for example, bases his claim that the relationship of American sport to capitalism has been "productive" and that its contribution to social democracy has been "significant" almost solely on the basis of evidence suggesting the massive expansion of athletic facilities and the democratization of individual sports participation. Given the consistency of findings which outline continuing class and status group differences in many forms of American sport [17, 53, 85], such a conclusion may overstate the scope of the democratization of individual sports participation in American society, but a far greater weakness in Betts' argument stems from the narrowness of his approach.

In the first place, it is rather misleading to make general inferences about the changing character of class arrangements in any society, based on a consideration of changes in athletic participation, without referring to changes in the control and administration of sport's organizational spheres as well. The dimensions of "social upheaval" which have ostensibly affected athletic participation are poor standards by which to gauge either the dissolution of class barriers at the highest levels of the institutional structure or the apparently democratic character of a particular nation-state.

Second, and possibly more important, such an approach characteristically ignores basic questions of power and changes in the role that sport has played in either consolidating or attenuating the hegemony of dominant groups. By limiting the analysis to benign questions of involvement rather than the themes of domination and subordination which have more traditionally stood at the core of class analysis and the study of the dynamics of capitalist society, Betts and others have been led too easily to the conclusion that sport reflects universal democratizing trends which testify to the "success" of capitalism as a form of political-economic organization.

In an ideological sense, the importance of this last point should be relatively clear. Both the *optimism* [b] of those who have seen sport as a dimension of the "classlessness" of capitalism and their *concentration on sport's leveling character,* not only typify the commonly accepted image of sport suggested in the literature on American society, but more generally mirror the concern of American intellectuals over the last half-century with middle class issues of status and status-striving rather than broad theories of class and society [13, 67]. Writing from a sociology of knowledge standpoint, Page [67] has argued that such emphases are compatible with long-standing themes in American culture: "an individualism that resists structural interpretations of social arrangements and processes, a voluntarism that rejects deterministic explanations of social action, a pragmatism that suspects abstract theories," all of which have crystalized into a focus on the "distributive" rather than the "relational" characteristics of inequality [c] and a concern for interpersonal ranking at the expense of an understanding of the structural arrangements which tend to guarantee continuity in the advantaged positions of specific groups. These themes, which are undoubtedly rooted to the historical development of both the American class structure and ideological system, have frequently intruded into and influenced the shape of sociology as a global scholarly enterprise. In the case of the sociological study of sport, the implied "theory" of the relationship between sport, class and capitalism contained in them seems to take as resolved some of the most significant questions which must be asked about the changing character of sport as an institution [d] in all of the capitalist societies and about its meaning for the issues surrounding the analysis of elites and power within them.

The most obvious response to the challenge posed by such unanswered questions can be found within Marxism, for Marx always recognized the necessity of understanding the effects of class relationships in their totality. In contrast to the "leveling" characteristics that liberal-democratic theorists have attributed to the growth of industrial capitalism, Orthodox and Neo-Marxists have emphasized the continuing relevance of class as an analytic category for the study of modern social relationships. From this perspective, it has been suggested [16, 51, 83] that there is a striking similarity between the internal logic of "institutionalized" sport and the logic of capitalist social organization itself. Since capitalism is depicted as an inherently class-based type of society, it is argued that sport must certainly be contoured by existing material relationships and is, therefore, clearly integrated into existing patterns of domination. Thus, Brohm [16] argues that the future of sports as an institutionalized component of life in the West must be seen as inextricably linked to the future of capitalism itself. [e]

However accurate such an interpretation may be, it must be emphasized that much of the Marxist literature, like liberal-democratic "theory," also has been subject to its own brand of ideological shortsightedness. By tending to define automatically the owners of the means of production as capable of extending their hegemony to all forms of social organization, Western Marxists have generally overlooked the in-depth empirical analysis of those who now control the sporting enterprise in the capitalist nations. When Western Marxists have examined sport, they have concentrated on how the dominant class translates its economic power into ideological hegemony, when they might better have questioned the extent to which a dominant class in the classical Marxist sense exists at all. The comparative neglect by Western Marxists of widespread changes in the reward structures of advanced capitalist societies seems, as Giddens [30] reminds us, like the posturing of "the blind man who insists he has not lost his sight even while blundering into the furniture and unable to make sense of his surroundings."

Yet, the real failure of much of the Marxist literature may lie in the degree to which its dogmatic rigidity has stimulated a rash of contemporary theories which suggest that industrial capitalism, with its inherent class divisions, has been virtually superseded by a newer form of "post-industrial" or "post-capitalist" order. Under conditions which Marxists have been unable to interpret adequately as identifiable features of "classical" capitalist social organization, many sociologists have all but rejected the use of class analysis as a viable approach to the comprehension of issues and problems of societal development.

At the general level, this most recent rejection of class theory tends to take on two different forms [30]. In one case, writers like Marcuse [58], Habermas [36] and Touraine [80] hold that the transformation of 19th-century capitalism into a "one dimensional" or "totalitarian" form of post-industrial society has not totally eliminated classes, but it has effectively undermined the broad contours of class relationships, reconstituting them in the form of technocratic forms of domination. In the second case, as typified in the works of Bell [8] and, to a large extent, Dahrendorf [25], class analysis no longer becomes relevant because of the increasing specialization and autonomy of individual institutional orders, thereby guaranteeing a diversification of the sources of economic and political power. At the same time, a graduated socioeconomic hierarchy where recruitment is based on technical expertise comes to supplant the existing pattern of property-based access to privilege. [f]

There is considerable debate, however, over both the degree to which such developments can be substantiated in all advanced capitalist societies and the extent to which they represent a significant evolution beyond capitalism rather than merely fluctuations and adaptations within its basic form and structure. Robert Heilbroner has emphasized the danger in assuming that

either objective changes in the life conditions of manual laborers, or meritocratic standards of recruitment into the burgeoning "technical" elites of modern life have eliminated the dramatis personae of the Marxian drama. [g] Indeed, he concludes that:

> the organizational character of industrial capitalism with its hierarchies, bureaucracies, and above all its trend toward concentration, seems likely to continue in the post-industrial society [37].

Unfortunately, one does not sense this degree of caution in the majority of the writings of contemporary "sport sociologists." Those few analyses of sport and social class which adventure beyond the traditional analytic legacies of liberal-democratic idealism or vulgar Marxism tend often to reveal a generally uncritical acceptance of basic post-industrial assumptions. An especially concise statement of the most basic of these assumptions is demonstrated in the following passage from Gregory Stone's influential essay:

> As our organization has shifted from a system of estates, through a system of production and classes, to an arrangement of consumption and masses, play and sport have always been affected by the cleavages and processes built into such patterns [76].

In true post-industrial fashion, Stone does not see the dissolution of class relationships in sporting activities as a *condition of capitalism* as Betts does; rather, he sees class decomposition as a *partial supercession* of the capitalist mode of production itself. As the "leisure and class" becomes the "leisure mass," one gains the distinct image of a social setting wherein any control the classes may have exerted in sport during the era of production must be reassessed in view of current patterns of mass consumption. Stone fails to relate these patterns to possible changes in the structure of elites and power in the new period of "consumption and masses," but such implications are easily derivable from more general post-industrial theories.

Let us consider an example of some of the effects of post-industrial conditions as they conceivably relate to the study of elites and power in the control and administration of sport. The first point has to do with the increasing influence of technical "elites" and changing patterns of administration. Just as Auf der Maur [5] has argued that the "feudal lords" of professional hockey were replaced by a group of bourgeois entrepreneurs with the further development and expansion of capitalism in post-war Canadian society, the logic of post-industrialism suggests that this class of entrepreneurs is being challenged (or increasingly controlled) by new forms of bureaucratic organization. These "new forms" ostensibly symbolize a democratization of sorts, in that they transcend the class interests of the previous period. Also implicit is the idea that with the expansion of service industries and an increased concern by the state for health, welfare and "cultural" activities, the state political apparatus will increasingly provide the thrust of this organization. The control and administration of sport then becomes more and more subjected to the principles of bureaucratic and technical organization both in the context of big business and big government, reflecting a shift from patrimonial to legalistic [h] forms of administration, an increase in the role of the technical "expert" and, therefore (in theory), increasingly meritocratic standards for entrance into a bureaucratic hierarchy which features a largely autonomous power structure. Most of these themes in some form or another have found general expression in recent assessments of the changing role of sport in industrial societies, and they are all compatible with broader post-industrial frameworks.

Now it is not my intention in this discussion to suggest that post-industrial theories are totally unacceptable, since it is readily apparent that they encapsulate some of the most striking organizational tendencies of sports and leisure activities in advanced capitalist societies. Rather, following the arguments of Giddens [30], Heilbroner [37] and others, it seems necessary only to point out how the reification of such theories has biased or skewed discussion. The case can be made that just as in those instances where writings have been influenced by a belief in the "success" of capitalism in achieving social democracy, or by the commitment to the developmental theory of Orthodox Marxism, the blanket-usage of the post-industrial thesis has, in its turn, become a substitute for the in-depth empirical analysis of changing class relationships in specific institutional settings.

What has this tendency meant for social scientific studies of sport? The answer to this question is given simply by the existence of a state of affairs where the fundamental and emergent characteristics of organizational development in sport are assumed to be *known* and where certain key issues and problems, particularly those pertaining to class and power, are either ignored or taken to be resolved. Yet, such a position must be rejected if our understanding of the meaning of sport for the dynamics of capitalist society is to be enhanced. To this end, it should be emphasized that writings based on the assumption that changes in the upper levels of sport's organizational spheres reflect trends of class decomposition variously labeled as either "democratic," "technocratic," or "post-industrial," take as given what should really be considered as *problematic* —the nature of objective changes in the basic organizing structures of sport in advanced capitalist societies; the social backgrounds of elite organizational figures in sport during specific periods in the history of these societies; and finally, the relationship between the sport of these periods and the values and life-styles of the dominant classes. When researchers have concentrated on these issues they have tended to re-affirm, rather than reject, the relevance of class analysis as a framework for understanding the historical development and the current structure of organizational leadership in the sport of individual societies.

An excellent example of this last point can be found in a recent longitudinal analysis of the recruitment of sports leaders in Finland conducted by Kiviaho and Simola [50]. [i] Kiviaho and Simola began their analysis by noting that the national organization of Finnish sport began as a reflection of upper and middle class interests in the late 19th century, but, by the end of World War I, parallel, national sports organizations for workers had developed in conjunction with the increasing "solidarism" [j] of the Finnish working class. As indicated in Table 1, the subsequent patterns of recruitment into the executive positions of these organizations do not seem to suggest any great swing to meritocratic recruiting principles, nor do the data suggest any significant effects of bureaucratically induced class decomposition. The Finnish commercial (notably finance capitalists, especially in fundraising "support" organizations) and professional bourgeoisie have not only *increased* rather than *decreased* their representation in the executive positions of the bourgeois sports organizations, but they also appear to have made

TABLE 1

Class Origins of Finnish Sports Leaders (%) *

	1900–1918		1919–1944		1945–1973	
	Bourgeois Organizations	Workers' Organizations	Bourgeois Organizations	Workers' Organizations	Bourgeois Organizations	Workers' Organizations
Upper class	59	—	78	13	88	30
Middle class	19	—	20	44	12	49
Agrarians	—	—	—	—	—	—
Working class	7	—	—	39	—	17
Not classified	15	—	2	5	—	4
Sample size (n)	(27)	—	(41)	(39)	(57)	(53)

*Adapted from Kiviaho and Simola [50].

inroads into the administrative spheres of the working class sports organizations as well. The extent to which this latter trend is the result of encroachment by the bourgeoisie related to the perceived necessity of having "professional" administrators in today's complex sports organizations, or alternatively represents an "embourgeoisement" [k] of the workers' organizations themselves is not immediately clear from Kiviaho and Simola's analysis. However, what is clear is that control over capital and high occupational pedigree remain unchallenged as the dominant characteristics of Finnish sports leaders.

Problems of interpretation in Kiviaho and Simola's fascinating study stem primarily from the fact that their research lacks a detailed historical-interpretive framework. While their study is useful in drawing attention to a possible crystallization rather than decomposition of class factors affecting the recruitment of Finnish sports leaders, it is not really an adequate class analysis. Still, to my knowledge, their research represents the only systematic attempt to combine an analysis of the changing social origins and business interlocks of sports' leaders with a discussion of the class structure and political economy of a given society. [1] Herein lies an additional problem, however, since it seems rather obvious that because of the unique manner in which the Finnish class structure has developed, there is considerable danger in attempting to make any generalized conclusions about increasing or decreasing class closure in the administrative hierarchies of sports organizations in other capitalist societies. Yet, in similar research on the changing character of organizational elites in Canadian sport, I have noticed occasional parallels between patterns of recruitment in Canadian society and those outlined by Kiviaho and Simola. For example, the strong role played by *financial* as opposed to *industrial* capital in contouring organizational development is a pattern common to both Canada and Finland which may differ from patterns of organizational development in Britain or the United States. In order to clarify this somewhat elliptical observation, it is necessary to turn now to a brief political-economic analysis of the organizational development of Canadian sport.

CLASSES, ELITES AND ORGANIZATIONAL DEVELOPMENT IN CANADIAN SPORT

As noted in the title of this paper, the discussion that follows should be considered as a "preliminary" analysis. Only a portion of my biographical and content data on organizational elites has been tabulated at this point and in many cases, it has been necessary to draw conclusions based on impressions generated during the collection of data which have yet to be "reduced" for tabular presentation. At the same time, in order to keep some limits on what already threatens to be an extended discussion, I have had to avoid the lengthy accounting of primary source data as "evidence" of certain relationships that are postulated. Yet, despite these limitations, I am confident that the analysis represents a thematically accurate, albeit simplified, portrayal of the development and changing character of the relationships between organizational tendencies and structures in Canadian sport and broader issues of class inequality in Canadian society.

For purposes of clarity, the analysis is organized into a condensed overview of several *overlapping* "periods" in the progressive "structuring" of sport. The word "overlapping" is used deliberately here, for I do not want to convey the impression that these periods can be completely "set off" from one another either as direct evolutionary derivatives or as radical antitheses. As Dunning [26] has correctly pointed out in his analysis of "stages" in the "incipient modernization" of football, even the most radical changes in social and economic organization do not create situations where a newer set of patterns merely replaces an older set of patterns, rather, the changes cause *structural elaborations* which lead to new forms and patterns which vie for dominance with existing ones. The danger of "ideal-typing" in the fashion chosen here lies in the relegation of nonemergent or hypothetically declining social conditions to a marginal status that may overlook their continuing importance (see my discussion in Gruneau [32]). On the other hand, the designation of key "periods" has not occurred in a completely random fashion. For each period, I have attempted to suggest how the development of new social and productive forces and relationships has demarcated a progressively dominant "form," or set of conflicting "forms," for sport's organizational character and relationship to the class structure. Since each "form" tends to establish a certain organizational legacy, I indicate how the conflict and accommodation occurring between them have led to an increasingly complex structure of organizational leadership—a structure whose complexity and apparent "pluralism" in the present day belies a continuing association with the dominant classes and status groups in Canadian society.

ASCRIPTIVE FOUNDATIONS (1760–1840)

The "making" of the Canadian class structure occurred in the context of a clash between French and British mercantile empires and the establishment of a set of institutional arrangements appropriate to Canada's colonial status. Dominant among these arrangements were the implementation of ascriptive colonial policies of land allocation and the institutionalization of a mercantile system, heavily funded by foreign portfolio investment and designed to extract staples from the Canadian hinterland in the service of European markets.[m] The significance of this pattern of social, economic and political organization for the early structure of class relationships in Canada can be primarily measured in three areas.

First, as Naylor [63, 64] has recently stressed, by gearing to the international movement of staples rather than the abetment of secondary processing in domestic markets, the growth of industry and manufacturing was retarded and financial institutions became "overdeveloped." Second, a conscious attempt to maintain traditional European patterns of "landed" power combined with the overdevelopment of financial institutions to allow for the entrenchment of a strong merchant class in the fledgling Canadian urban areas which aligned itself with the remains of the colonial ruling class of the Conquest era, the Church and the Empire Loyalist elite. Finally, the close connection under colonial rule between the merchant class and the state generally opposed in principle both the "laissez-faire" political-economic philosophy commonly associated with industrial capitalism and the rational utilitarian ethics which were later to become the cornerstone of liberal-democratic sentiment in industrial Britain.

It is against the background of such an environment that one must understand the social organization of sport in Canada at the turn of the 19th century. While it has been popular among Canadian "sport historians" to emphasize the close association between the patterns and ethos of sport and the supposedly democratic "frontier spirit" of the time [43, 74], it is even more important to understand that the influence of this "spirit" was mediated by the effects of a conservative political economy and a semifeudal class structure. Under these conditions, sporting pastimes represented more than just the idle play of the colonial squire or a periodic attempt by farmers and artisans to relieve the monotony of the almost constant work of frontier life. In their various "folk" and "elite" forms,[n] sporting activities were also symbolic statements of differential life chances and life styles and notable components in the existing patterns of domination.[o] For example, the upper class, many of whom viewed the aristocracy and gentry of late 18th century Britain as a reference group, stressed in play, anti-utilitarian attitudes toward consumption and toward life itself which reinforced the ascriptive character of the class structure through the conscious exclusion of all forms of utilitarian rationality. The values of manly character and conspicuous leisure which had characterized the traditional martial games and field sports of European life were, in part, imported and adapted to suit the colonial situation. In addition to being the mere "spontaneous enjoyment of life," such activities also functioned as a means of self-assertion and [as] weapons in the struggle for power.

However, by the 1820s conditions in Canadian society had altered considerably. The lack of an industrial base in the colony (the merchant and landed classes preferred to *trade* in staples rather than *produce* manufactured goods) combined with discriminating land practices and heavy immigration to create a growing class of propertyless laborers and "would-be" farmers [19, 64, 75, 77]. At the same time, the imperially oriented commercial policy of the dominant class, which prohibited the export of manufactured goods and the emigration of skilled artisans [64], increasingly antagonized growing petite bourgeois interests in the colony. These tensions were further aggravated by the frustrations of frontier farmers over high interest rates and the shortage of available land and, as well, by a growing religious pluralism which resulted in criticisms of the colonial linkage between church and state [61].

One of the important aspects of the first contact between the dominant colonial-mercantile class and ascendant and contending groups in Canadian society was a gradual shift in attitudes about the lower classes as a possible "problem" and threat to established traditions and privileges. In a vast and comparatively "empty" frontier, members of the dominant class in Canada saw their subordinates as "curious but harmless beings" [24] and sought to maintain a measure of traditional tory "disinterest" in their affairs. [p] But, the growing contact with the expanding and increasingly less docile "lower orders" led to an advocacy and acceptance of mechanisms for controlling the ostensibly "unruly" impulses of lower class groups. An apparent manifestation of these "impulses" was seen to lie in the steady growth of taverns in the colony and in the proliferation of gambling and other "idle" activities which might serve to encourage the "degeneration" of physical activity into "amusements" and "moral levity."

Several writers have commented on the movements for moral reform which swept through the colony during the 1830s [18], and it has been common to interpret such concerns as an indication of the growing significance of middle class Methodist religious sentiment as a social force. [q] Certainly there is an element of truth in this argument, but it is a mistake to interpret the erosion of tory disinterest and the elevation of Methodist moral concerns to the level of public policy as any indication of a decline in the strength of the conservative colonial-mercantile dominant class. Indeed, in a manner similar to earlier developments in England, the moral reform movements merely bonded middle class ascetic values onto the political fears of the dominant class. Commenting on the British situation, Thompson has argued that the composition of church and state to primarily underclass forms of recreation combined the "ethos of Methodism with the unction of the establishment." Moral control was not a clergical dictum that developed "sui generis"; rather, it can be seen as closely associated with class conflicts and a clearly articulated strategy of political domination. The "grand law of subordination" laid down by William Pitt's "moral lieutenant" Wilberforce was a response to the belief that "moral levity" among the underclasses (and the large gatherings often associated with popular amusements) led to political sedition. Accordingly, through law and theological edict, Wilberforce carried on an elaborate campaign of moral control against "sabbath-breakers" and idle "amusements" [79]. In late 18th century England, such policies can be interpreted as a specific response to the perceived threat of Jacobinism, but they contain as well a broader antidemocratic bias that continued to guarantee rather distinct class differences in the "rate" and "type" of participation in sporting activities and in the comparative meaning of these activities within the existing pattern of domination. That the legacy of this tradition should become at least partly transplanted into the moral ethos of Canada's dominant class is not entirely surprising given the growing class tensions in the colony and the perceived "threat" of the spread of American democratic values from the south.

Notably, the standard of tory disinterest continued to erode on all fronts during the 1830s. Much of this erosion was based on a fear of political movements like European Jacobinism; part of it no doubt occurred in response to utilitarian critiques of both the gentry and lower class styles of life; it was likely stimulated by the conflicts over mercantile economic policy; and it was certainly hastened by the entrance of the lower classes into recreational activities which had previously been the exclusive preserve of the upper class. Faced with a situation where traditional constraints and distinctions appeared to be breaking down, the upper class responded by introducing more formalized regulatory statutes which were designed to exorcise the "lower orders" from areas where they were not welcome. Guay [35], for example, has shown how the progressive "structuring" and regulation of horseracing in Lower Canada in the 1830s was essentially a response to the perceived threat posed by the swelling numbers of francophone workers at previously "elite" events.

Organization of a different sort was also occurring within the confines of other elite pastimes. The focus for this new emphasis on organization, and ultimately the focus of much of the upper class recreational activity in Canadian society, was the "private school" generally modeled after Britain's reformed public school system. [r] Recently, Dunning [26] has argued that the British public school reform movement represented an important break from traditional anti-utilitarian attitudes toward sporting pastimes. The emphasis on discipline, religion and "civilized" team sports that emerged as a part of Dr. Thomas Arnold's program of "muscular christianity" at Rugby School, ostensibly represented a "mid-Victorian compromise" and "mutual accommodation" between growing industrial bourgeois and declining aristocratic interests. Dunning notes how this process of "embourgeoisement" [s] led to the "incipient modernization" of team games (notably football) by stimulating the development of codified rules designed to civilize the game by "equalizing" the participants.

Dunning's reasoning is masterful on this issue, but his entire analysis overstates, I believe, the degree to which the reformed "public school" was a concession to middle class criticism of the aristocratic style of life. For example, Wilkinson [91] and Arnstein [4] have each pointed out that rather than becoming increasingly middle class, the reformed public schools merely captured middle class talent in the promotion of gentry class power. By indoctrinating the sons of the bourgeoisie as "gentlemen," the public schools really acted as a safety valve in the social system. They helped to avert class conflict, not by instilling the values of "self-help" and the entrepreneurial ethos into the sons of aristocrats but, rather, by educating the young bourgeoisie in a sense of gentlemanly propriety which would subvert their individualistic tendencies and integrate them into a broader more organic commitment to the collectivity. Arnstein concedes that the "reformed" public schools rejected undisciplined chivalric and aristocratic attitudes, but he argues that they continued to emphasize the non-utilitarian virtues of a classical education, the values of continuity and tradition more than those of utilitarian rationalism and the belief in hierarchy rather than social equality [4].

Arnstein's conclusions are especially applicable to an understanding of the Canadian scene in the early 1830s, where the private school was designed to solidify a Canadian ruling class which could model itself after the British gentry and nobility and thereby provide leadership and stability in the "new society." The comparatively "tory" approach to team games in the first Canadian private schools is suggested by the attention paid to cricket instead of football. Certainly, a type of football was played at the Canadian private schools, but its formal "organization," progression beyond oral tradition and subsequent codification of rules lagged well behind such developments in England until well into the latter part of the 19th century. The industrial bourgeois "push" that Dunning argues was so significant in the "incipient modernization" of football in England during the 1840s and 1850s was retarded by the hegemony of finance capital and lack of an industrial base in the colony. By contrast, the social organization and "common" rules of cricket had arisen "within" the development of the British aristocracy rather than out of the conflict between industrial bourgeois and aristocrat. Accordingly, the game became especially palatable to Canada's self-styled colonial aristocrats and "merchant princes" [92].

COMMERCIAL EXPANSION AND "NASCENT" INDUSTRIALISM (1840–1870)

The conscious attempt by colonial rulers to establish semi-aristocratic traditions and institutions only intensified the class tensions that had been building in the colony during the 1820s.

These class tensions erupted into open class conflict in the rebellions of 1837–1838, but the rebels were easily controlled. Nonetheless, while politically unsuccessful, the rebellions revealed growing liberal and reformist strength in the colony and the rise of the interests of laborers and independent commodity producers as a new social force [75]. Within the confines of the political superstructure imposed by the "victorious" colonial-mercantile ruling class, the reformers achieved a measure of organizational legitimacy and they would eventually form governments [64]. Moreover, repeal of the British Corn Laws in 1846 provided the material conditions necessary for the ascendancy of a "liberal-tory" component to the upper class by effectively ending the colonial-mercantile domination of the "first commercial empire of the St. Lawrence" [23].

To suggest, however, that the decline of the dominant colonial-mercantile class of the 1820s and 1830s generally ushered utilitarian ethics and liberal democratic political principles into the colony would be as misleading as to assume that the power of the large Canadian merchants was completely destroyed. While the "first" commercial empire of the St. Lawrence was crippled by the loss of imperial preference, a "second empire" soon emerged to replace it [19]. Conditions became more favorable for Canada's petite bourgeoisie to develop as an indigenous capitalist class, and "responsible government" free from *direct* British control was achieved, but the colony remained a conservative staple-producing economy where "elite" commercial interests, usually funded by British capital, maintained a firm hold on the state. [t]

The post-rebellion, but pre-confederation, era in Canada was a significant transitional period in the "structuring" and organizational development of sport. Most importantly, the regulative tendencies begun in earlier decades, rather than "easing" with the apparent infusion of middle class ethics into social and political life, continued to intensify. The rebellions themselves had reinforced the fear a of population with "time on its hands," and as the frontier began to "fill in" even more with massive immigration during the 1840s and 1850s, the view of the "lower orders" hardened accordingly [24]. Concerned over the possible spread of disease from an impoverished lower class and not quite so secure in their sociopolitical dominance, members of the new commercial-political ruling class sought to formally design programs which would maintain order, discipline and health among the working population.

One area where such programs were quickly established was in the tax-supported free school systems. Houston [42] has noted that in Ontario, Ryerson and his followers deeply feared the unfettered forces of urbanism and industrialization and saw the "spirit" of underclass "insubordination" abroad threatening the "honest independence of the working and labouring classes, particularly servants" [42]. Based on such attitudes and on a concern for the necessity for a "fit" population for military service, "recreational" activities in the schools emphasized discipline and regimentation through the teaching of military drill and gymnastic exercise [22, 29, 71]. By contrast, the private schools continued to emphasize the values of leadership, fair play and the disciplined but spontaneous enjoyment of games.

An even more significant dimension of sport's "transitional" development during the 1840s and 1850s was the growth of the urban sports club. Field sports flourish among a landed upper class, but they are less suited to the recreational aspirations of a bourgeois class which must locate close to where the "commercial action" is. In conjunction with "incipient industrialization" in Canada and the growth of new indigenous commercial (primarily banking and retailing) activities, the recreational sports club developed as a new organizational "form" for Canadian sporting activity. At first, as Metcalfe [59] has pointed out in his ground-breaking study of sport and social stratification in 19th century Montreal, the leadership of these clubs was limited to the professional, commercial and military elite in the community, and their focus was clearly social rather than competitive.

Table 2, which is reproduced from Metcalfe's study, outlines the occupations of executives and players from a sample of the major Montreal clubs in 1860. The strong role played by high ranking bourgeois interests in the community is clearly shown in the table. Commercial businessmen, professionals and store owners make up 85% of the sample. Metcalfe does not provide "class of origin" data for these individuals, but from Tulchinsky's [81] discussion of the Montreal business community we can infer, perhaps, that few of the club executives and players came from working class backgrounds. Tulchinsky ar-

TABLE 2

Occupations of a Sample of Club Executives and Players in 1860, Compared to the Montreal Labor Force of the Period *

Occupation	Club Executives and Players (N = 40) (%)	Montreal Labor Force (%)
Professional	20	4
Commercial		
(a) Businessmen, merchants and store owners	65 ⎱	22
(b) Bookkeepers, clerks, salesmen	8 ⎰	
Domestic	0	16
Industrial	0	41
Agriculture	0	1
Not classified	7	16

*Adapted from Metcalfe [59].

gues that most of the leaders of the Montreal business community were not men of modest beginnings; they frequently combined control over capital with solid family connections and a classical education. Accordingly, while clearly a bourgeois class, it seems likely that their approach to sport and recreation would be tempered by lingering tory biases—a belief in the spirit of fair play and the legacy of anti-utilitarian sentiments about the role of games in life.

Actual membership in the elite clubs of the 1840s and 1850s was clearly limited by ascriptive criteria [59], but a few of the clubs began to sponsor "open" competitions. Open competitions featured contact between social classes in athletic contests and demanded the formulation of universalistic rules that "equalized" all participants. However, even in such "open" competition, when lawyers often competed against Indians and working men, class distinctions were implicitly recognized by the provision of trophies for "gentlemen" and cash prizes for others [59]. Sport was expanding and beginning to commercialize, but only within the context of limits defined by the dominant class.

Yet, the democratizing force of incipient industrialization in Canada altered class relationships by the late 1860s to the extent that the entire organizational development of sport was affected. In a *material sense*, incipient industrialization allowed for a quantitative expansion of the middle class; it created the necessary conditions for the wider production of manufactured goods; it allowed for the all-important "rationali-

zation" of working time [79]; and it allowed for the technological developments in transportation and communications which were necessary for sport to grow beyond its localized character. In an *ideological sense*, industrial development stimulated the growth of more "pure" type of bourgeois values in the Canadian business community: rational utilitarian and, frequently, Darwinist values that were generally "unsullied" by the direct contact with ascriptive gentry class attitudes or the "gentlemanly" methods of professionals and administrators. These new values differed from the "liberal-toryism" that had evolved into the dominant ideology in Canada by the 1860s and they created the normative environment for the transformation of loosely organized social and recreational activities into more highly structured achievement-based competitive sports.

ORGANIZED COMMERCIAL SPORT AND AMATEURISM AS CLASS CLOSURE (1870–1910)

By the mid-1860s, the urban club movement had begun to democratize, not on the basis of the elimination of discriminatory patterns of membership selection and recruitment, but rather through the proliferation of the clubs themselves. Yet, the "democratization" of clubs through proliferation merely reinforced existing class distinctions and shaped them into new organizational forms. These forms served to reflect symbolically the hierarchical arrangements of social groups and the solidification of new forms of domination which were based on the equation of personal worth with position in the market-place. Consider along these lines the development of "amateurism" and "professionalism."

During the 1840s, as noted previously, elite sporting clubs occasionally sponsored "open" competitions where upper class individuals would compete against working men. Upper class "trend setters," as Dunning and Sheard [27]have called similar groups in England, were relatively secure in their positions and competed in sport for fun. Their identities and statuses were not at stake in a race or other athletic contest and there was little concern about losing to "inferiors." Losing was nonproblematic, since it did not affect the established order in any way. Moreover, professionalism was not seen as a problem since it was assumed that it would always be controlled [27]. Metcalfe [59] reminds us that such occasional cross-class athletic contact should not be interpreted as a "utopian" view of friendly competition; competitions were not that frequent and class distinctions were still evident. But the point is that "open" competitions sponsored by elite clubs did exist and facilitated contact between classes within the sporting world.

However, during the 1850s and 1860s there were fewer of these elite sponsored "open" competitions. As the Canadian class structure elaborated and as meritocratic liberal values began to develop widespread support, members of the dominant class apparently became unable to tolerate the possibility of defeat at the hands of groups which they defined as their social infe-riors. They also became progressively more alarmed at the prospect that commercialism in sport could very easily get out of hand and vulgarize the nobility of play. There were two possible responses to such developments: (a) withdraw completely from the world of competitive sports and establish social clubs which could be easily defended against the forces of democratization or (b) set up formal organizations designed to provide particularistic standards for insuring that the nobility of play would remain uncontaminated by the unfettered forces of crass commercialism or *unrestricted* meritocratic principle [32]. Members of different strata within the dominant class tended to pursue one or the other of these strategies: many of the traditional tory "establishment" withdrew to the socially oriented hunt and tandem clubs and vigorously

defended entry against "lower status" bourgeois accessibility (for example, entry by the indigenous industrial bourgeoisie). The other component of the upper class consolidated their "Victorian legacy" through the cult of the "amateur" [56]. Thus, as Dunning and Sheard [27] have pointed out in the case of English rugby football, the concept of amateurism seems to have evolved in a dialectical fashion as a conscious strategy of "social closure" in class formation.[u] In this form, it became a major policy feature of the early national[v] sports governing bodies which developed during the 1870s and 1880s.

By the mid-1880s, the key organizational structures in the sport world were dominated by amateur agencies. Central among these were the early national sporting associations alluded to above, the newly formed Amateur Athletic Union of Canada, and the powerful Montreal Amateur Athletic Association. The executives of these agencies, in conjunction with those of the provincial jockey clubs and racing associations (which remained bastions of ascriptive tradition), and select individuals from the private school, clubs and university sports environment, might be seen as defining an organizational "elite" for this period. The occupational backgrounds of these "elite" organizational figures are presented in Table 3. Individuals in high status bourgeois occupations dominated the elite, but the group as a whole seems somewhat more democratized than Metcalfe's 1860 sample of club executives in Montreal. In the 1885 elite sample there are fewer professionals and independent merchants and more people from lower ranking, bookkeeping, sales and clerical positions.

Beyond a straightforward occupational description, what else may be noted about the incumbents of elite organizational figures in the sport world in 1885? One thing that seems to be important is the comparatively *low level* of interlocking with other elites in Canadian society. For example, with only seven or eight exceptions (out of 71 cases), members of the 1885 organizational elite in sport did not appear to come from the highest stratum of the Canadian upper class. Among the sample in question here, I could only identify slightly over 15% of the sporting "elite" as people who have been designated in biographies and available newspaper accounts as members of the Canadian economic and political "establishment" of the pe-

TABLE 3

Sample of Executives of Major Sporting Clubs and Associations in 1885 *

Occupation	1885 Club and Association Executives (%) (N = 71)
Professional	11
Commercial	
(a) Businessmen, bankers, merchants, store owners	48
(b) Managers and company executives	15
(c) Bookkeepers, clerks, sales personnel	17
Military	7
Skilled labor	2

Data collected from Lovell's Montreal Directory (1885); Polk's Toronto Directory (1885); Wise and Fisher (1974); and Athletic Life (1896).

*Includes Executive of M.A.A.A. and affiliates; A.A.A. of C.; Ont. and Montreal Jockey; National Lacrosse Association; Canadian Wheelman's Association; Canadian Association of Amateur Oarsmen; Canadian Rugby Union; and select elite individuals from other clubs and associations identified by newspapers and periodicals.

riod.ʷ When the sample list was compared to Acheson's list [2] of the Canadian industrial "elite" of 1880–1885, there was no overlap whatsoever. Such patterns are important, for they appear to provide a measure of support for the argument that I have developed thus far. By 1885, the highest stratum of the Canadian upper class was not greatly involved in the "amateur" organizations. Rather, the major amateur organizations were the province of a loose coalition of younger and less "established" members of the upper and middle class commercial community [59].

Perhaps an even more important pattern is discovered when one focuses on those executive members engaged in commercial occupations and examines their occupational backgrounds. Given that the 1880s in Canada represented what

Acheson [2] has called the "halcyon" days of Canadian industrial development, one might hypothesize that many of the upper and middle class executives of the amateur sports organizations would come from the dynamic industrial sector of the Canadian business community. That this hypothesis is flawed is clearly revealed in Table 4. Only about 10% of the executive members of the amateur associations who worked in commercial occupations were involved in industry and manufacturing. By far, the major concentration among the sample lies in the areas of finance and retail trade.

The underrepresentation of the industrial sector of the economy in the occupations of sport's organizational elite in 1885 is easily explained within the framework of the history of Canadian political economy that I have outlined. Consider

TABLE 4

Classification by Economic Sector for Sports Executives in Commercial Occupations (1885)

Sector of Economy of Primary Occupations	1885 Executives in Commercial Occupations (%) (N = 54)
Financial	30
Retail and wholesale trade	15
Manufacturing and transport	11
Utilities	6
Media	6
Real estate	6
Unclassified	26

the following points. First, while the major amateur organizations did not generally recruit their leadership from the highest stratum of the Canadian upper class, they were nonetheless unabashedly Victorian in focus and organization and rooted to an ascriptive liberal-tory conception of play, social organization and hierarchy. The laissez-faire and rational utilitarian standards of industrial interests were not generally compatible with such traditions and views. Second, and because of the historical dominance of finance capital in Canada, the indigenous Canadian industrial bourgeoisie had never been in a position to develop as a full-fledged component of the Canadian upper class. Acheson [2] notes that while few of the 1885 industrial elite were men of humble origins, industrialists generally considered themselves as the "proletariat" of the Canadian business community. Moreover, despite the economic nationalism of the National Policy (1879) period, the domination of Canadian industrial production by Americans that had been stimulated by the Reciprocity Act of 1854 continued to act as a serious limiting factor to the development of *indigenous* and independent industrial power.

But, to note that the industrial development of Canada was retarded by the branch-plant character of production and that "progressive" industrial bourgeois interests were rarely reflected in the activities of the dominant class in Canada is not to argue that industrialization as a social force should be trivialized. Similarly, the fact that the small manufacturer or plant owner was not generally a part of the organizational "structuring" of amateur sport should not be taken as an indication that these individuals failed to play a role in the organizational development of sport. Certainly, some of the upwardly mobile industrialists became actively involved in amateur clubs across the country, but for the most part their contribution to sport's organizational development lay in the "commercial" sphere of sport rather than the "ascriptive" amateur sphere.

Dunning and Sheard [27] have noted how the presence of the ascendent industrial component of the bourgeoisie in England stimulated an "open," more meritocratic and commercial approach to sport. The small scale industrialists were often self-made men who kept in direct touch with the manufacturing process from a small office attached to the workshop. Close

contact with employees and a feeling of commonalty in production were conducive to a low degree of status-exclusiveness and class distance and hence formed the foundation for "open" Rugby clubs, often associated with the plant. Similar patterns in Canada are easily identified in some of the sports clubs of the 1870s and 1880s, and it is frequently within these clubs that the emphasis on skill and winning begins to rival the "amateur" ideal of fair play as a legitimate standard for participation.

However, this last point must be accompanied by a caveat. Much of the production in Canada was based on an impersonal type of industrial organization, and given the long hours and lingering policies against sabbath-breaking and amusements, there was little in the way of *organized sport* for the industrial laborer or worker in Canada's primary industries. Moreover, the prevailing standards for "amateur" and "gentlemanly" play were, if not always discriminating, at least beyond the means of time and money of the majority of the working population. [x] In fact, as I have tried to suggest, the increasingly discriminatory standards of "amateur" sport seemed to evolve in direct proportion to commercialism and the growth of "open" competitively oriented clubs.

The establishment of industrial middle class and working class clubs and the increase of distinctly commercial forms of sport after the 1850s represent the beginnings of a "nascent" parallel organizational structure in Canadian sport. The first "challenge" series and semi-structured "leagues" stimulated the "monetization" of games, and the progressively wide open and Horatio Alger-like dimensions of entrepreneurial activity in Canada reinforced the idea of the overriding importance of "success" in all walks of life, including the playing field. More importantly, the adulation and national pride associated with new "professional athletes" like Ned Hanlan [24] helped to integrate sport into the marketplace and partially legitimate it as an area of "open" competition and entrepreneurial activity. Yet, however such developments influenced spectatorship and offered limited careers in organized sport to individuals with exceptional abilities, the 19th century did not, in any organizational sense, represent the triumph of rational meritocratic values in the sport world. Commercial sport was generally chaotic and in constant conflict with "amateurism," and as late as the turn of the century the Victorian legacy of the "gentleman-amateur" continued to dominate as the axis around which organization in the sport world revolved.

THE GROWTH OF THE CORPORATE ETHOS (1910–1960)

The conflict between amateur and commercial sport at the turn of the 20th century raises some interesting questions about the relationships of ideology to changing conditions of social organization. Amateur and commercial sport shared certain structural similarities but differed markedly in ideology. For example, members of the major amateur agencies objected to commercial sport primarily on the basis of four principles: (a) commercial sport was seen to debase play by allowing the representative character of play to take precedence over the act of playing itself; (b) commercial sport was seen to emphasize "ends" more than traditional "means"; (c) commercial sport was viewed as involving passion rather than restraint; and finally (d) commercial sport was seen to be closely associated with gambling, drinking and frivolity—all of which offended middle class Protestant sentiment.

Yet, given the contingencies of industrial development and democratization, many of the clubs, teams and individual competitors who were associated with the major "amateur" organizations had a good deal of trouble "living up" to the ideals that amateurism defined. As clubs proliferated and as many of them became increasingly involved in intense local rivalries, challenge series and more formalized leagues, they often became transformed from "exclusive" to "open" and finally to "gate-taking" organizations in a manner similar to the British rugby clubs studied by Dunning and Sheard [27]. At the same time, while it was still in no way ideologically legitimate for a gentleman to want to win above all else, "scientific play" was beginning to replace "fair play" as an accepted standard for judging the sporting experience [89]. The move from an emphasis on "fairness" to an emphasis on "technique" *within* amateurism itself seemed to make some of the distinctions between amateur sport and commercial sporting activities less "real" and more arbitrary. The development of superior technique, whether pursued as an end in itself or as a means to an end, essentially has only one outcome—improved performance.

These transformations introduced a difficult and highly ambiguous situation within amateur sports, for they suggested on the one hand that sport was quintessentially a "democracy of ability" yet, on the other hand, was a *subordinate* area of life where the development of ability could only be pursued on a casual and part-time basis. In other words, the guardians of the amateur ethos embraced and assimilated some of the advancing sentiments of 19th century utilitarianism, but only within the limits imposed by a conservative view of social organization which stressed *moral* rather than *rational* utility (see my discussion in Gruneau [32]). The use-value of amateur sport lay in its contribution to personal growth and development whereas the use-value of professional sport came to be increasingly defined in economic terms. But, as Metcalfe [60] has correctly pointed out, over the last two decades of the 19th century there was increased bureaucratization in sport which facilitated differentiation between the executives in the major amateur sport organizations and the players themselves. Given this, it seems the case that the meritocratic side of the amateur equation was being overly credited at the level of actual play, thus introducing a situation where many clubs defined themselves nominally as "amateur," but began to coverge progressively with more commercialized forms of sporting activity. This consequence provided one of the major conditions that stimulated the development of a parallel organizational structure in commercial sport in Canada. Influenced by the success of commercial sport in both Canada and the United States and finding the "elite" in the major amateur sport organizations inaccessible and unresponsive, members of the "open" and "gate-taking" clubs created organizational alternatives to domination by middle and upper class business and professional men. The organizers of the first professional leagues in baseball, lacrosse and, later, hockey included promoters and fast-buck artists, local "athletic facility" owners, small manufacturers and local businessmen. In short, they were a far more broadly based group than the upwardly mobile businessmen and professionals who controlled the major amateur organizations. However, the leadership in commercial sport itself began to crystallize after the first decade of the 20th century as team owners and league organizers moved from an *entrepreneurial* to a *corporate* orientation.

The period of entrepreneurial development in sport paralleled an intense period of entrepreneurial activity in Canada generally. Despite the recessions of the latter third of the 19th century, the Canadian economy continued to expand and "opened up" avenues of mobility within the class structure. Bliss [12] argues, for example, that most of the great finance capitalists who dominated the Canadian upper class after the turn of the century had begun their careers as clerks and subcontractors a generation before. Bliss clearly overstates the degree of actual mobility into the Canadian upper class during this period [1] and his argument should not be taken to imply that great inequalities in condition had dissolved by the turn of the 20th century [20], but there can be no denying that substantial mobility did occur as Canada went through a phase of entrepreneurial capitalism. In the sport world, many of the upwardly mobile clerks and white collar workers who identified with the Victorian values of the middle class and saw in sport an agency which helped strengthen temperance and the business-related virtues of hard work and dedication moved into executive positions in the amateur sports organizations as they worked their way toward increased power and privilege. At the same time, as I have tried to indicate, commercial sport opened up as an area of business opportunity and mobility itself.

Yet, the period of intense and "open" entrepreneurial capitalism in Canada did not last much beyond World War I. The increased involvement of established financial capitalists in certain areas of the industrial sector (the area of the economy featuring the highest degree of mobility) and the accelerated rate of American direct investment in other areas of the industrial sector worked, in the shape of corporate concentration, to solidify a more stable and rigid class structure. Thus, Clement [19] argues:

> During one brief period the manufacturing sector was open and immigrants with skills and some capital were able to establish themselves as a new social force, but as the ruling class moved in and consolidated these emerging firms, avenues began to close, manufacturing became concentrated and opportunities were limited.

The period of "open" competitive capitalism which is so commonly depicted as occurring within the transformation from feudal or colonial systems to industrial capitalist systems was generally ended by the establishment of a highly structured bureaucratic approach to production, an accompanying emphasis on "specialization" within the division of labor and the overall shift to modern corporationism.

The effects of such developments in the world of commercial sport can be measured by two basic developments. First, as clubs and individuals entered into market relationships with one another in and through sport, it became a necessity to *formally* incorporate clubs and sport businesses. Thus, the number of federal charters on record issued to sports organizations of various types rose from one in the period between 1890 and 1910 to 30 in the period between 1911 and 1920.^{y} Second, there developed a growing recognition of the necessity of creating mechanisms which could regulate "economic competition" between teams and protect the developing labor and product markets in sport. In the early years of "structured" commercial sport (the period between 1870 and 1910) promoters and team owners usually acted in an *individualistic* entrepreneurial fashion and struggled for dominance in the labor and product markets surrounding early professional sport. Such struggles were ultimately counterproductive since they made it difficult to keep leagues together for any period of time. Arguments over gate receipts, stadium and rink sizes and franchise rights posed continuing threats to financial success in the sports business and, while professional sport in itself was popular, individual teams developed and faded with almost predictable regularity.

The first major shift from an entrepreneurial to a corporate orientation in the Canadian sport world occurred, I believe, with the formation of the National Hockey League. By the 1920s, hockey had replaced lacrosse as Canada's major "team" sport, and by 1930 the owners of N.H.L. franchises had learned (after years of bidding wars for players) that profit maximization could only be hampered by unrestricted individual "economic" competition. In other words, as Jones [47] indicates, the owners recognized that in order to maximize *individual profits* they had to maximize *joint profits*. The period following this realization has been characterized by concentration and growing league control over both the product and labor markets in hockey. At the same time, as the league solidified it consolidated massive capital gains based on the appreciation of franchise values and on windfall profits.[z] By contrast, Canadian professional football developed within the "ambiguity" of amateurism that I described earlier and was in constant contact with the upper and middle class university sport programs. Most of the "professionalizing" forces in football developed in the West, and the C.F.L. did not undergo a partial move to profit-maximizing corporationism until after 1950.[aa]

The success and stability of commercial team sports created a clearly defined organizational elite in the 20th century that paralleled the older (and rapidly changing) amateur structures. In the early stages of organizational development this elite represented a combination of promoters, small businessmen and wealthy entrepreneurs who had been convinced that they should financially support local teams. For the most part, these early organizers and owners of franchises were self-made men who lacked extensive business contacts, and they were frequently from modest family backgrounds. However, as commercial teams became more profitable and cartel structures were created, mobility into the upper echelons of the organizational structures of commercial sport became limited to those having access to capital.

A somewhat similar crystallization was occurring within the organizational structure of amateur sport. The growth of the Olympic movement in Canada after 1920 and the accompanying prestige associated with international sport attached a rejuvenated form of "status-exclusiveness" to executive positions in selected amateur organizations, particularly the national amateur athletic union and, later, the Canadian Olympic Association. By contrast, as the number of single-sport national associations grew to accommodate the popularity of new sports in Canada, the organizational significance of the national associations was lessened, as was the power of the urban sports clubs like the M.A.A.A. Paralleling these developments in organized amateur sport, the depression and two world wars had reaffirmed the deep concern on the part of Canada's dominant class about the necessity for a physically "fit" and "industrious" population. As I have argued throughout this paper, these concerns have their roots deep in the 19th century, and in our modern era they have combined with the notion of "participation" as a "right" of citizenship to stimulate a more formal connection between public policy in sport and recreation and the state political structure.[bb]

CORPORATE INTERLOCKING AND THE STATE STRUCTURE (1960–PRESENT)

Since the late 1950s the organizational structure of Canadian sport has elaborated to include three basic forms: (a) amateur organizational agencies including national associations and international amateur sports governing bodies; (b) commercial organizations, including the Canadian Football League, National and World Hockey Leagues and American professional baseball; and (c) a state bureaucratic structure where government agencies at both the provincial and federal levels play a mediating role between the public and private spheres of sport and where they design recreational and competitive programs in conjunction with voluntary associations whose interests lie in the sport area.

It is not possible in the analysis at hand to discuss in detail the characteristics of the current organizational "elite" in each of these three areas or to outline how and why formal government agencies like *Sport Canada* developed over the last decade. What is necessary to emphasize, however, is simply that we are dealing now with an organizational elite in sport that is far more complex than in earlier periods of Canadian history. At the same time, given my comments at the outset of this paper, it is also necessary to ask whether recruitment into the elite positions of this complex structure represents any real democratization from patterns of recruitment in the past. To do this correctly would require "social origin" data on organizational elites at several points in Canadian history. Since I have only a smattering of social origin data available at this point, I shall merely try to summarize the trends and shifts in patterns that have occurred. These trends and patterns are outlined at the end of this paper in Table 7.

Taking the corporate sphere first, developments since 1960 seem to have emphasized the increased "interlocking" of professional team sports with larger corporations. This pattern has been stimulated, as Okner [66] notes, by the tax advantages a professional franchise can offer a large corporation, but in Canada the pattern seems even more closely related to the desire of businessmen to support popular, highly visible and market-related activities from within a parent corporation. There are obvious advantages for a brewery to own a baseball team or a broadcasting company to own a football or hockey team. But even within some of the old "family" owned teams, interlocking has become an enduring feature of modern corporate life. To cite but one example, the Bronfmans transformed the old Canada Arena Company which owned the "Canadiens" into Carena-Bancorp, a holding company which has controlling interests in a variety of companies including Trizec Corporation, one of the largest development companies in the country.

In Table 5, I have attempted to outline some of the interlocks for the C.F.L. and N.H.L. (Canadian franchises) by economic sector. It can be seen from the table that the executives and directors of these teams interlock heavily with corporations in the financial, trade, transportation and communication sectors of the economy—areas where Canadian capital has been strongest. These patterns do not indicate in themselves any relationship between sport and what Clement [19] identifies as "dominant corporations" in Canada, but with few exceptions most of the sports corporations had individuals on their boards who interlocked with dominant corporations and who could be classified as members of Canada's corporate elite.[cc]

The issues of interlocking and the diversification of corporate interests raise further questions

about the changing character of organizational leadership in commercial sport. In an era when effective control over a corporation can be maintained through as low as 5% to 10% of preferred shares, economists have argued that power in the modern corporation has been passed on to management through the diffusion of stock ownership. Thus, a dimension of the diversification of corporate interests through interlocking is seen to be the separation of ownership from control and an increased dependence on the technical expert [8]. Yet, regardless of what one thinks about this argument in its broadest sense, it does not seem that such developments have occurred in commercial sport in Canada. Except for the "community teams" that I mentioned above, the role of the manager and "expert" has not appeared to supersede the power of ownership.

At this stage I have conducted ten of 20 planned in-depth interviews with "elite" organizational figures in commercial sport and all of the respondents have indicated support for the idea that the effective "power" of management and experts may have actually declined rather than increased with modern developments. The professional hockey leagues in particular prefer "full-time owners" rather than absentee shareholders, and the lower-level management does not participate in major decisions at the *league level*. Indeed, it seems obvious that the manner

TABLE 5

Interlocking Directorships by Economic Sector for C.F.L. and N.H.L. (Canadian Franchises)

Economic Sector	C.F.L. * (%) (N = 73)		N.H.L. * (%) (N = 18)	
	N	%	N	%
Financial	105	(34)	45	(37)
Trade (retail and wholesale)	12	(4)	4	(3)
Utilities, transport and communication ·	47	(15)	17	(14)
Resources	33	(11)	7	(6)
Food and beverage indus.	13	(4)	—	
Manufacturing and const.	47	(15)	12	(10)
Services	12	(4)	18	(15)
Printing and publishing	4	(1)	3	(2)
Unclassified	35	(11)	15	(12)
Total directorships	308		121	

*In the C.F.L. there are a total of 210 Board positions (excluding General Managers). These are held by 194 individuals, 73 of whom I have thus far been able to gather data on. The three N.H.L. Canadian franchises have a total of 28 positions held by 22 people. Data are presented for 18.

in which owners approach the goals of an organizational structure devoted to the maximization of joint profits is qualitatively different from the goals of team management. The general manager of a hockey club, for example, is concerned with organizational efficiency and administration—particularly in the case of contracts and player performance; but the major shareholders must be concerned with the broad contours of profit-maximization and league success itself. Similarly, for all the "influence" general managers may wield, it is unlikely that they possess effective power. Moreover, since management and ownership have become increasingly separate in recent years, mobility into the elite through prior involvement at the managerial level seems to have narrowed rather than opened up.

The recent trends in the organizational development of the state bureaucratic sphere of sport also raises significant questions about the forces of democratization in modern life and changing patterns of elite recruitment. The growth of an ostensibly rational bureaucratic structure where recruitment is based on "credentials" appears on the surface to open up new avenues of mobility into positions of influence within the sport world. Yet as Parkin [69] argues in his discussion of strategies of "social closure" in class formation, "credentialism" itself is only as democratized as the educational system which guarantees it.[dd] I do not have a complete set of quantitative data on Canada's new sport's

bureaucrats, but preliminary interviews suggest that they are essentially middle class people with "professional" training. Since data exist that outline the overwhelmingly upper and middle class backgrounds of students in professional programs in Canadian universities [57, 70, 72], it seems reasonable to infer that this pattern is maintained among "professionals" in the civil service.

In fact, it seems to be the case that individuals in professional occupations have made inroads into all levels of sport's organizational structure. In Table 6, for instance, socioeconomic data from a recent unpublished study of the executive members of 26 of Canada's national sporting associations reveal that in 1975 nearly 70% of all executives were involved in professional occupations and that the majority came from solid middle class family backgrounds [7]. Given the high turnovers in these voluntary positions, one would be hard pressed to call this group of executives an "elite" in amateur sport; but this group certainly provides a "pool" of administrative talent for the recruitment of executives of the national sports federation and international amateur associations. Earlier in this paper, I included the executives of the first "national" sports governing bodies in my 1885 organizational "elite" sample and it was noted how upper and middle class businessmen rather than "professionals" dominated. By contrast, the commercial sector of the labor force has been replaced in the present national associations by the

TABLE 6

Present Occupations and Fathers' Occupations of the Executive Members of 26 National Sporting Associations (1975) * (1971 Canadian Labor Force % in brackets) †

Type of Occupation	Present Occupation of Executives (%) (N = 145)		Occupations of Executives' Fathers (%) (N = 141)
Professional	68	(15)	35
Managerial	14	(8)	17
Clerical	8	(20)	8
Service	3	(22)	14
Transport and communication	1	(4)	14
Crafts and production, skilled and unskilled labor	1	(25)	12
Other	5	(6)	—

*Source: Beamish [7].

†Census data (average of Male and Female Labor Force percentages) from Perspective Canada (1974).

teacher, lawyer, doctor and engineer. The implications of this transformation can be debated, but it does not suggest that executives of the amateur sports governing bodies are in any way representative of the population.

While the executives of the national associations are hardly a completely "democratized" group, the international amateur associations are even more exclusive. Indeed, it is in these associations that the "Victorian legacy" of liberal-toryism has managed to maintain itself the longest. Helmes [39] has noted from a comparative content analysis of sports publications that the rhetoric of the Canadian Olympic Association is far more "traditionally" liberal-tory in focus than that displayed in the publications of other amateur organizations. The Olympic focus especially has allowed for a close working relationship between the Olympic association and Canada's corporate elite—a relationship that is demonstrated by the comparative ease with which the C.O.A. Olympic "Trust" was established and grew to include some of the most powerful individuals in the Canadian business community. Operating as an "elite forum" [19], the Olympic Trust was able to make strong linkages to available capital in Canada. The "Trust" itself is an impressive assembly of members of Canada's dominant class and reveals a predictable association with established Canadian financial capital. Of the 43 members of the trust, 30 can be classed as members of Clement's "corporate elite." These 30 hold 85 "dominant" directorships in 113 dominant corporations in Canada including notable interlocks with commercial sport and with 23 major corporations who have more than one director on the Olympic Trust. Among the banks alone, the Canadian Imperial Bank of Commerce is represented by eight directorships, the Royal Bank by seven, the Bank of Nova Scotia with three, and the Toronto Dominion and Bank of Montreal with two each.

SUMMARY AND CONCLUSION

In summary, it must be emphasized that my conclusions on these and other issues can be regarded as somewhat speculative until I have completed the over-all data analysis. The patchwork of preliminary data that has been presented provides only some impressionistic guidelines for further study. However, until the data analysis is complete I suspect that the patterns displayed in Table 7 can be seen as a first step in defining sport's relationship to the general framework of state and economy within which elites in Canada are recruited. As noted in Table 7, the organizational "elite" in sport has elaborated and become more complex, but mobility into the elite does not appear to have been "opened up" to any great extent. In the commercial sphere of sport, control over capital seems to have increased rather than decreased its significance and in the amateur sphere ascriptive elitism has merely been replaced by "credentialism"—a credentialism that has been reinforced by the involvement of the state in organized sport and has yet to transcend the traditional categories of capitalism.

But are such patterns in the sport world really surprising? Indeed, they seem merely to be reflective of the colonial legacy and patterns of social closure that frame so much of the history of the Canadian class structure. The linkages between elite positions in voluntary associations, the structure of state power and the dominant class have always been intimate and, as Clement [19] has indicated, despite the measure of democratization which accompanied Canada's growth as a liberal democracy, access to the command posts of Canada's institutional elites has become even more limited since World War II. The Canadian "corporate elite," for example, is more exclusive in social origins, more upper class and more closely knit than it was when Porter [70] studied it first in the 1950s.

Questions as to why this restriction seems so graphic in Canada fall beyond the limits of what I have set out to do in this paper. It may be that, like many colonial societies, third world dependency models will be useful tools in helping to relate issues of class and political economy to problems of cultural development. In this, perhaps, there is a line of similarity between countries whose industrial bourgeoisie has been retarded by the dominance of foreign interests. Can we draw, for example, a similarity between the stunted "democratization" of organizational leadership in Canadian sport and the patterns Kiviaho and Simola [50] have noted in Finland, based on an historical understanding of each country's developments? Has the role of the state as a coordinating agency between varying subelites in sport differed appreciably in each society? [ee] These are important questions and I have sought to raise rather than to answer them.

TABLE 7

Preliminary Outline of the Changing Structure of the Organizational Elite in Canadian Sport

Time Frame	Elite	Administrative Stratum of Elite	Primary Recruitment Base of Elite
1850	Directors of major urban sports clubs and administrators of school programs	Same as elite	Members of other elites; military officers, upper class professionals and colonial administrators, merchants and gentry
1885	Executives and directors of major urban clubs and amateur governing bodies	Same as elite	Merchants, military officers, upper class professionals, upwardly mobile middle class individuals in commercial occupations
1915	(a) Amateur Sphere: Directors of amateur sport governing bodies and international amateur associations	(a) Same as elite	(a) Military officers, professional, commercial middle and upper classes
	(b) Commercial Sphere: Executives and directors of league franchises in major "professional" team sports (especially Canadian Rugby Union and N.H.L.), directors of organizations regulating other forms of commercial activity in sport (i.e., racing associations)	(b) Executives and senior management	(b) Urban middle classes, small businessmen, industrial entre-preneurs and promoters
1950	(a) Amateur Sphere: Executives of international sport associations (i.e., C.O.A. and executives of selected national associations)	(a) Same as elite	(a) Middle and upper class profes-sionals and businessmen
	(b) Commercial Sphere: Executives of C.R.U. & N.H.L. franchises, directors of jockey and racing associations	(b) Senior management	(b) Middle and upper class busi-nessmen, members of other elites (i.e., corporate elite)
1975	(a) Amateur Sphere: Executives of international amateur associations and sport federation	(a) Amateur associations and executive directors of national associations	(a) Upper and Middle class pro-fessionals, members of corporate elite
	(b) State Sphere: Bureaucrats, directors in federal and provincial government agencies dealing with sport	(b) Civil service	(b) Middle class university graduates
	(c) Commercial Sphere: Executives of franchise members of professional team sports, jockey and racing associations	(c) Senior management	(c) Members of corporate elite, other corporate executives, upper class lawyers and businessmen

But I will conclude by noting that such questions are empirical problems that cannot be solved by the uncritical acceptance of available theories of "postcapitalist" or "postindustrial" evolution. As I have suggested throughout my presenta-tion, these theories might very well be prema-turely and falsely disillusioned with the utility of class analysis as a viable approach to the study of sport, and the comprehension of general is-sues and problems of societal development.

ACKNOWLEDGMENTS

This paper is a trend report based on conclusions drawn during the first stages of data collection for my forthcoming doctoral thesis [34]. Several people have helped in the shaping of the analytic framework used in the paper, and some of the data cited have come out of the research efforts of students at Queen's University. I especially want to thank Charles Page, Rob Beamish, and Rick Helmes for their comments, and Jim Lidstone, Greg Vaz, Susan Stewart and Lee Wetheral for their help with historical research. Alan Metcalfe was kind enough to send me some of his historical data which helped shape my arguments about amateurism as "class closure." Finally, I want to thank all the people in the sport world who have granted me interviews, as well as Mr. Gord Walker of the Canadian Football League, Carol Randal and Ron Andrews of the National Hockey League.

REFERENCES

1. Acheson, T. W.: Changing social origins of the Canadian industrial elite, 1880–1910. *In* Enterprise and Moral Development. Edited by G. Porter and R. Cuff. Toronto, Hakkert, 1973.
2. Acheson, T. W.: The social origins of the Canadian industrial elite, 1880–1885. *In* Canadian Business History. Edited by D. S. Macmillan. Toronto: McClelland and Stewart, 1972.
3. Adams, G. M. (ed.): Prominent Men. Toronto, 1892.
4. Arnstein, W.: The survival of the Victorian aristocracy. *In* The Rich, the Well Born and the Powerful. Edited by F. C. Jaher. Urbana; University of Illinois Press, 1973, p. 236.
5. Auf der Maur, N.: The N.H.L. power play. *In* Corporate Canada. Edited by M. Starowicz and R. Murphy. Toronto: James Lewis and Samuel, 1972, p. 120.
6. Baltzell, E. D.: Philadelphia Gentlemen. New York, Free Press, 1958.
7. Beamish, R.: An Analysis of the Composition of the National Executives of Selected Amateur Sports: A Meadian Perspective. Unpublished B.A. thesis, Department of Sociology, Queen's University, 1976.
8. Bell, D.: The Coming of Post-Industrial Society. New York, Basic Books, 1973.
9. Bendix, R.: Max Weber: An Intellectual Portrait. New York, Doubleday, 1962.
10. Béteille, A.: Social Inequality. Baltimore, Penguin Books, 1969, p. 13.
11. Betts, J. P.: America's Sporting Heritage, 1850–1950. Reading, Addison-Wesley, 1974.
12. Bliss, M.: A Living Profit: Studies in the Social History of Canadian Business, 1883–1911. Toronto, McClelland and Stewart Ltd., 1974.
13. Bottomore, T. B.: Classes in Modern Society. New York, Vintage Books, 1966.
14. Brailsford, D.: Sport and Society: Elizabeth to Anne. Toronto, University of Toronto Press, 1969.
15. Bratton, R. D.: Consensus on the Relative Importance of Association Goals and Personal Motives Among Executive Members of Two Canadian Sports Associations. Unpublished Ph.D. dissertation, University of Illinois, 1970.
16. Brohm, J. M.: Sociologie politique du sport. *In* Sport, Culture et répression. Edited by G. Berthaud. Paris: petite maspero, 1972.
17. Burdge, R.: Levels of occupational prestige and leisure activity. *In* Sport and American Society. Edited by G. Sage. Reading, Addison-Wesley, 1974.
18. Burnet, J. R.: The urban community and changing moral standards. *In* Urbanism and the Changing Canadian Society. Edited by S. D. Clark. Toronto, University of Toronto Press, 1961.
19. Clement, W.: The Canadian Corporate Elite. Toronto, McClelland and Stewart, 1975, pp. 54, 73.
20. Copp, T.: The Anatomy of Poverty: The Condition of the Working Class in Montreal, 1897–1929. Toronto, McClelland and Stewart, 1974.
21. Cosentino, F.: Canadian Football: The Grey Cup Years. Toronto, Musson, 1969.
22. Cosentino, F. and Howell, M.: A History of Physical Education in Canada. Toronto, General Publishing, 1971.
23. Creighton, D.: The Empire of the St. Lawrence. Toronto, Macmillan, 1970.
24. Cross, M.: The Workingman in the Nineteenth Century. Toronto, Oxford University Press, 1974, p. 225.
25. Dahrendorf, R.: Class and Class Conflict in Industrial Society. Stanford, Stanford University Press, 1959.
26. Dunning, E.: Industrialization and the incipient modernization of football. Arena, *1*(1), 1976.
27. Dunning, E. and Sheard, K.: The bifurcation of rugby union and rugby league: a case study of organizational conflict and change. Int. Rev. Sport Sociol., *11*(2), 1976.
28. Easterbrook, W. T. and Watkins, M. H.: Approaches to Canadian Economic History. Toronto, McClelland and Stewart, 1967.
29. Gear, J.: Factors influencing the development of government sponsored physical fitness programmes in Canada from 1850–1972. Can. J. Hist. Sport Phys. Educ., *IV*(2), 1973.
30. Giddens, A.: The Class Structure of the Advanced Societies. London, Hutchinson Books, 1973, pp. 18, 269.
31. Goldthorpe, J. et al.: The Affluent Worker (3 Vols.). London, Cambridge Press, 1968.
32. Gruneau, R.: Sport, social differentiation and social inequality. *In* Sport and Social Order. Edited by D. Ball and J. W. Loy. Reading, Addison-Wesley, 1975, pp. 125–127, 129–132, 155–168.
33. Gruneau, R.: Sport as an area of sociological study. *In* Canadian Sport: Sociological Perspec-

tives. Edited by R. S. Gruneau and J. Albinson. Toronto, Addison-Wesley, 1976, pp. 20, 21.

34. Gruneau, R.: Elites, Class and Corporate Power in Canadian Sport. Unpublished doctoral dissertation, University of Massachusetts, 1981.

35. Guay, D.: Problèmes de l'intégration du sport dans la société Canadienne 1830–1865: Le cas des courses de chevaux. Can. J. Hist. Sport Phys. Educ., IV(2), 1973.

36. Habermas, J.: Toward a Rational Society. Boston, Beacon Press, 1970.

37. Heilbroner, R. L.: Economic problems of a 'postindustrial' society. Dissent, Spring 1973, p. 169.

38. Heinila, K.: Survey of the value orientations of Finnish sport leaders. Int. Rev. Sport Sociol., (7), 1972.

39. Helmes, R. C.: Canadian Sport as an Ideological Institution. Unpublished M.A. thesis, Queen's University, 1977.

40. Hoch, P.: Rip Off the Big Game. New York, Doubleday, 1972.

41. Hodges, H. M.: Social Stratification. Cambridge, Mass., Schenkman Publishing Co., 1964, p. 167.

42. Houston, S. E.: Politics, schools and social change in Upper Canada. Can. Hist. Rev, III(3)1972, p. 251.

43. Howell, N. and Howell, M.: Sports and Games in Canadian Life. Toronto, Macmillan, 1969, pp. 54–56.

44. Ingham, A. G.: Occupational subcultures in the work world of sport. In Sport and Social Order. Edited by D. Ball and J. W. Loy. Reading, Addison-Wesley, 1975.

45. Ingham, A. G. and Loy, J.: The social system of sport: A humanistic perspective. Quest, XIX Fall, 1973.

46. Innis, H.: The Fur Trade in Canada. Toronto, University of Toronto Press, 1956.

47. Jones, J. C. H.: The economics of the National Hockey League. In Canadian Sport: Sociological Perspectives. Edited by R. S. Gruneau and J. Albinson, Toronto, Addison-Wesley, 1976.

48. Kando, T.: Leisure and Popular Culture in Transition. St. Louis, C. V. Mosby, 1975.

49. Kaplan, M.: Leisure in America. New York, Wiley, 1960.

50. Kiviaho, P. and Simola, M.: Who leads sport in Finland? Eripainos Sosiologia, N:05–6/74.

51. Laguillaumie, P.: Pour une critique fondamentale du sport. In Sport, culture et répression. Edited by G. Berthaud et al. Paris: petite collection maspero, 1972.

52. Laxer, R.: Canada Ltd: The Political Economy of Dependency. Toronto, McClelland and Stewart, 1973.

53. Loy, J.: The study of sport and social mobility. In Aspects of Contemporary Sport Sociology. Edited by G. S. Kenyon. Chicago: The Athletic Institute, 1969.

54. Lüschen, G.: Policy-making in sport organizations and their executive personnel: a proposal for a cross-national project. In Current Research in Sociology. The Hauge, Mouton, 1974.

55. Mackintosh, W. A.: Economic factors in Canadian history. Can. Hist. Rev., IV:March, 1923.

56. Mallea, J.: The Victorian sporting legacy. McGill J. Educ., Vol. (2), 1975.

57. Marchak, P.: Ideological Perspectives on Canada. Toronto, McGraw-Hill Ryerson, 1975.

58. Marcuse, H.: One Dimensional Man. Boston, Beacon Press, 1964.

59. Metcalfe, A.: Organized sport and social stratification in Montreal: 1840–1901. In Canadian Sport: Sociological Perspectives. Edited by R. S. Gruneau and J. Albinson. Toronto: Addison-Wesley, 1976, pp. 80–84.

60. Metcalfe, A.: Working Class Organized Physical Recreation in Montreal, 1860–1895. Presented at the annual meetings of the North American Association for the Study of Sport History, 1976.

61. Moir, J. S.: Church and State in Canada 1627–1867. Toronto, McClelland and Stewart, 1967.

62. Myers, G.: A History of Canadian Wealth. Toronto, James Lewis and Samuel, 1972, p. 140.

63. Naylor, R. T.: A History of Canadian Business (2 Vols.). Toronto, James Lorimer, 1975.

64. Naylor, R. T.: The rise and fall of the third commercial empire of the St. Lawrence. In Capitalism and the National Question in Canada. Edited by G. Teeple. Toronto: University of Toronto Press, 1972, p. 9.

65. Neuberg, L. G.: A Critique of Post-Industrial Thought. Social Praxis, 3(1–2), 1975.

66. Okner, B.: Taxation and sports enterprises. In Government and the Sports Business. Edited by R. Noll. Washington, The Brookings Institution, 1974.

67. Page, C. H.: An introduction thirty years later. In Class and American Sociology. New York: Schocken Books, 1969, p. xvii.

68. Panitch, L.: The role and nature of the Canadian state. Presented at the Annual Meetings of the Canadian Political Science Association, Quebec City, June 1976.

69. Parkin, F.: Strategies of social closure in class formation. In The Social Analysis of Class Structure. Edited by F. Parkin. London: Tavistock, 1974, p. 5.

70. Porter, J.: The Vertical Mosaic. Toronto, University of Toronto Press, 1966.

71. Roberts, T.: The influence of the British upper class on the development of the values claim for sport in the public education system of Upper Canada. Can. J. Hist. Sport Phys. Educ., 4(1), 1973.

72. Rocher, G.: Formal education: The issue of opportunity. In Issues in Canadian Society. Edited by D. Forcese and S. Richer. Scarborough: Prentice-Hall of Canada, 1975.

73. Rose, G. M. (ed.): The Cyclopedia of Canadian Biography. Toronto, 1866.

74. Roxborough, H.: One Hundred—Not Out; The Story of Nineteenth Century Canadian Sport. Toronto, Ryerson Press, 1966.

75. Ryerson, S.: Unequal Union. Toronto, Progress Books, 1973, p. 133.

76. Stone, G.: American sport: Play and display. In

Sport and Society. Edited by J. Talamini and C. Page. Boston, Little Brown, 1973, p. 67.

77. Teeple, G.: Land labour and capital in pre-Confederation Canada. *In* Capitalism and the National Question in Canada. Edited by G. Teeple. Toronto: University of Toronto Press, 1972.

78. Thompson, E. P.: The Making of the English Working Class. Hammondsworth, Pelican Books, 1968.

79. Thompson, E. P.: Time, work-discipline and industrial capitalism. Past and Present, *38*, December 1967, p. 442.

80. Touraine, A.: La société post-industrielle. Paris, Ed. Denoël, 1969.

81. Tulchinsky, G.: The Montreal Business Community, 1837–1853. *In* Canadian Business History. Edited by D. S. Macmillan. Toronto: McClelland and Stewart, 1972.

82. Veblen, T.: The Theory of the Leisure Class. New York, Mentor Books, 1953.

83. Vinnai, G.: Football Mania. London, Ocean Books, 1973.

84. Watkins, G.: Professional Team Sports and Competition Policy: A Case Study of the Canadian Football League. Unpublished doctoral dissertation, University of Alberta, 1972.

85. Webb, H.: Reaction to Loy's Paper. *In* Aspects of Contemporary Sport Sociology. Edited by G. S. Kenyon. Chicago: The Athletic Institute, 1969.

86. Weber, E.: Gymnastics and sports in fin-de-siècle France: opium of the classes. Am. Hist. Rev., *76*(1), 1971.

87. Weber, M.: The Theory of Social and Economic Organization. New York, The Free Press, 1964.

88. Weber, M.: The Protestant Ethic and the Spirit of Capitalism. New York, Charles Scribner, 1958, pp. 167, 168.

89. Weiler, J.: The idea of sport in late Victorian Canada. Presented at The Canadian Historical Association Meetings, Kingston, June 1973.

90. West, T.: Physical fitness, sport and the Federal Government 1909 to 1959. Can. J. Hist. Sport Phys. Educ., *IV* (2) December, 1973.

91. Wilkinson, R.: Gentlemanly Power: British Leadership and Public School Tradition, New York, Oxford University Press, 1964.

92. Wise, S. F.: Sport and class values in nineteenth century Canada. *In* His Own Man: Essays in Honour of A. R. R. Lower. Edited by W. H. Heide and R. Grahm. Montreal, McGill-Queen's Press, 1974.

NOTES

a. Veblen [82], for example, does not *adequately* link status to power. See my discussion of Veblen [32].

b. Typical of this optimism is Kaplan's [49] comment that in "no area of American life more than its leisure activity is the outdated concept of class made apparent." Hodges [41] is more guarded when he suggests that class differences in sports and leisure are still often of "transcendent" consequence, but he concludes by suggesting that the barriers are "diminishing in importance as we become an ever more homogeneous people."

c. "Distributive" characteristics refer to the variety of underlying objective and symbolic factors that contribute to structured social ranking and inequality, that is, those factors such as income, wealth, occupation, skill, prestige or social esteem. "Relational" characteristics refer to the ways in which "individuals differentiated by these criteria are related to one another within a system of groups and categories" [10].

d. On the institutional character of sport, see my discussion [33] as well as Ingham and Loy [45] and Kando [48].

e. This is an especially problematic point, because it seems that the "logic" of rationalized sport is common to both capitalist and state-socialist societies.

f. Further developments accompanying the transition from industrial-capitalist to post-industrial and post-capitalist forms of organization that are common to both of the above cases, include a decline in the relevance of "industrialism" as the core of the capitalist order; the bloating of the "service" sector of the labor force; and the growing importance of communicative technology in attenuating the distinctions between individuals who are differentially ranked in the reward structure. However, the "meaning" of all of these conceptions tends to be differently interpreted by "liberal" and "radical" post-industrial thinkers.

g. See also Giddens [30] and Neuberg [65].

h. See Weber's discussion of patrimonial and legalistic forms of bureaucratic administration [87]. A brief discussion of the application of these concepts to the organizational development of sport can be found in Ingham [44].

i. The original article by Kiviaho and Simola is in Finnish. However, Kiviaho was kind enough to translate large parts of it into English for use in my research. It was a gesture of friendship and scholarly interest that I am happy to acknowledge.

j. Solidarism refers to the collective responses of excluded groups that are unable to maximize their own resources within a class structure by adopting practices of exclusion [69].

k. Stated most simply, the term "embourgeoisement" refers to the spread of bourgeois values, customs and goals within the working class.

l. There are, however, some popular journalistic efforts on this topic. Perhaps the best known is Hoch's provocative, but facile, Rip Off the Big Game [40].

m. The staples approach has dominated Canadian economic history. See Mackintosh [55]; Innis [46]; Easterbrook and Watkins [28] and Creighton [23] for an overview of the basic characteristics of "staples" theory. An attempt to transform some of the principles of the staples approach into radical political economy can be found in Laxer [52] and Naylor [63, 64].

n. Elite sports refer to such activities in history as manorial hunting, early tennis and organized equestrian events ("the hounds" or polo), (this list is hardly exhaustive). Folk sports refer to wrestling, some early forms of ball games, cock-fighting (and other "blood" sports) and foot-racing. A discussion of such activities in Elizabethan England can be found in Brailsford [14].

o. See the discussion of Weber's conception of "traditional domination" in Bendix [9].

p. It should be noted that the degree to which English Canada could be seen to represent a purely "tory" fragment of Britain is difficult to ascertain. English Canada was a commercial state by design and, as such, the aristocratic style of life continually came into conflict with the short-term goals of colonial extraction. But were these commercial goals overly reflective of anti-aristocratic bourgeois attitudes in the colony? I think not. As Marx has noted in his discussion of merchant's capital, the existence of a mercantile system does not necessarily symbolize progressive bourgeois interests; rather, merchant capitalists have tended to be "reactionary" aligning with traditional landed interests against the spread of liberal values (see Marx's discussions in Vol. III of Capital).

q. See Weber's discussion [88] on the conflicts between aristocrats and Protestants over sport. Methodists echoed reformist sentiments about moral virtue and, during the 1830s, they led a series of campaigns against moral "abuses."

r. University sports also developed at this time, but like the private school, their organization tended to reflect value premises surrounding the idea of the "amateur-gentleman."

s. Dunning [26] incorrectly uses the term "embourgeoisement" to refer to the penetration of middle class values into the aristocracy. He does recognize, however, that this definition runs contrary to established usage of the term as defined by Goldthorpe et al [31].

t. Capital-intensive expenditures in such areas as transportation (first canals and, later, railroads) could not be financed within the colony and brought the commercial capitalist and politician together in order to petition British financial houses which "demanded state guaranteed loans" [19]. The colonial connection was also maintained, as Myers [62] points out, by the continuing power of chartered mercantile companies like the Hudson's Bay Company.

u. Indeed, Dunning and Sheard [27] note that in this sense amateurism takes on what Durkheim would have regarded as a "collective representation."

v. Many of the first "national" associations were national in name only. They drew their executive primarily from the business community in Ontario and Quebec.

w. There is no single systematic study of the "establishment" of this period. This comment is based only on an informal list of key figures drawn from biographies, newspapers and sources like Myers [62]. I have primarily consulted G. M. Rose, (ed.), The Cyclopedia of Canadian Biography [73], the Encyclopedia of Canadian Biography (3 vols.) (1904) and G. M. Adams [3].

x. Weber [86] argues that since the economic slumps of the latter two decades of the 19th century meant higher relative incomes for the upper and middle classes in Europe, the "leisured young" could devote much of their time to sporting activity before joining the labor force. This argument is only partially applica-

ble to the Canadian scene, but there is no doubt that economic recessions helped to define the generally restricted upper and middle class character of amateur sport by limiting the "participation resources" of the working class.

y. Data from Canada Public Records, Division Holdings Inventory, The National Archives, Ottawa.

z. See Jones [47] for a discussion of this process in hockey. In addition, consider the following example: between 1966 and 1974, the Toronto Maple Leaf Hockey Club made $4,581,715 through expansion franchise fees and the selling of a farm club. This breaks down to an extra $572,714 per season in excess of normal operating profits.

aa. See Watkin's [84] analysis of the C.F.L. and competitive policy. A history of the C.F.L. is outlined in Cosentino [21].

bb. See Gear [29] and West [90]. The role of the state will be discussed further in Gruneau [34].

cc. Among major professional team franchises in hockey, football and baseball, only three teams failed to have at least one individual in senior management or on the board of directors who interlocked with a dominant corporation. Several teams had more than five interlocks among board members. Consider just one example: Jacques Courtois, who is President of the Montreal Canadiens Hockey Club, is also president and a director of Kukatush mining corporation, Carena-Bancorp, Canadian International Investment Trust Inc. and Elicon Development Company. In addition, he is chairman of the Board of Gaz du Quebec Inc., vice-chairman and a director of Eagle Star Insurance Co., vice-president and a director of the Bank of Nova Scotia and a director of Brinco Ltd., C.A.E. Industries, Canadian Life Assurance Co., Canadian Hydro-Carbons, Commonwealth International Corp., Commonwealth International Venture Fund, Eaton Commonwealth Fund, I.A.C. Ltd., McGraw-Hill Ryerson Ltd., Northern and Central Gas Corp., Quebec Iron and Titanium Corp., Trizec Corp. and the Rolland Paper Co. (the list is not exhaustive). Similar lists could be drawn up in many other cases. A complete listing and quantitative summary will be available in Gruneau [34].

dd. Following Parkin's [69] discussion, it seems likely that bureaucratization in the sport world parallels and reinforces class structuration rather than symbolizing any sort of class decomposition.

ee. A more important question might be asked about the relationship of the coordinating function of the state structure to changes in patterns of class domination in these societies. The growth of a "relatively autonomous" state structure in sport may do little more than serve to support existing patterns rather than undermine them. A good starting point for an analysis which would deal with this issue can be found in Panitch [68].

further readings for part three

Section One: Sport and Socializing Institutions

Bend, E. and Petrie, B.: Sport participation, scholastic success and social mobility. *In* Exercise and Sport Sciences Reviews. Edited by R. Hutton. Santa Barbara, California, Journal Publishing Affiliates, 1977, Vol. 5, pp 1–44.

Buhrmann, H.: Scholarship and athletics in junior high school. Int. Rev. Sport Sociol., 7:119, 1972.

Coakley, J.: Play, games and sport: developmental implications for young people. J. Sport Behavior, 3:99, 1980.

Feltz, D.: Athletics in the status system of female adolescents. Rev. Sport Leisure, 4:110, 1979.

Fine, G.A.: Preadolescent socialization through organized athletics: The construction of moral meanings in Little League Baseball. *In* The Dimensions of Sport Sociology. Edited by M. Krotee. West Point, New York, Leisure Press, 1979, pp 79–105.

Greendorfer, S.: Socialization into sport. *In* Woman and Sport: From Myth to Reality. Edited by C. Oglesby. Philadelphia, Lea & Febiger, 1977.

Greendorfer, S.: Differences in childhood socialization influences of women involved in sport and women not involved in sport. *In* The Dimensions of Sport Sociology. Edited by M. Krotee. West Point, New York, Leisure Press, 1979, pp 59–72.

Hall, M.A.: Sport and physical activity in the lives of Canadian women. *In* Canadian Sport: Sociological Perspectives. Edited by R. Gruneau and J. Albinson. Don Mills, Ontario, Addison-Wesley (Canada), 1976, pp 170–199.

Hanks, M.: Race, sexual status and athletic participation in the educational attainment process. Soc. Sci. Q. 60:482, 1979.

Hauser, W.J. and Lueptow, L.B.: Participation in athletics and academic achievement: A replication and extension. Sociol. Q., 19:304, 1978.

Helanko, R.: Sports and socialization. Acta Sociol., 2:229–240, 1957.

Ingham, A., Loy, J., and Berryman, J.: Socialization, dialectics and sport. *In* Women and Sport: A National Research Conference. Edited by D. Harris. University Park, Pennsylvania State University, 1972, pp 235–276.

Kenyon, G.S.: Sport and Career: Patterns of role progression. *In* Sport in the Modern World—Chances and Problems. Edited by O. Grupe et al. Berlin, Springer-Verlag, 1973, pp 359–364.

Kenyon, G.S., and McPherson, B.D.: The sport role socialization process in four industrialized countries. *In* Sociology of Sport. Edited by F. Landry and W. Orban. Miami, Symposium Specialists, 1978, pp. 5–34.

Landers, D.: Birth order in the family and sport participation. *In* The Dimensions of Sport Sociology. Edited by M. Krotee. West Point, N.Y., Leisure Press, 1979, pp 140–166.

Lee, B., and Zeiss, C.: Behavioral commitment to the role of sport consumer: an exploratory analysis. Sociology and Social Research, *64*:405, 1980.

Lever, J.: Sex differences in games children play. Soc. Prob., *23*:478, 1976.

Marmion, H.: (ed.), On collegiate athletics. Educ. Record, *60*:341, 1979.

McPherson, B.D.: The segregation by playing position hypothesis in sport: An alternative explanation. Soc. Sci. Q., *55*:960, 1975.

McPherson, B.D.: Socialization into the role of sport consumer: A theory and causal model. Can. Rev. Sociol. Anthropol., *13*:165, 1976.

McPherson, B.D.: The sport role socialization process for anglophone and francophone adults in Canada: Accounting for present patterns of involvement. *In* Sociology of Sport. Edited by F. Landry and W. Orban. Miami, Symposium Specialists, 1978, pp 41–52.

McPherson, B.D.: Socialization into and through sport. *In* Handbook of Social Science of Sport. Edited by G. Lüschen and G. Sage. Champaign, Ill., Stipes, 1981, pp 246–273.

Nixon, H.L., Maresca, P.J., and Silverman, M.A.: Sex differences in college students' acceptance of females in sport. Adolescence, *XIV*(56):755, 1979.

Orlick, T.D.: Sport participation—A process of shaping behavior. Hum. Factors, *16*:558, 1974.

Otto, L.B., and Alwin, D.: Athletics, aspirations and achievements. Sociol. Educ., *42*:102, 1977.

Picou, J.S.: Race, athletic achievement and educational aspiration. Sociol. Q., *19*:429, 1978.

Picou, J.S., and Curry, E.W.: Residence and the athletic participation—educational aspiration hypothesis. Soc. Sci. Q., *55*:768, 1974.

Rehberg, R.A., and Schafer, W.E.: Participation in interscholastic athletics and college expectations. Am. J. Sociol., *73*:732, 1968.

Rehberg, R.A.: Behavioral and attitudinal consequences of high school interscholastic sports: A speculative consideration. Adolescence, *4*:69, 1969.

Roberts, J.M., and Sutton-Smith, B.: Child training and game involvement. Ethnology, *2*:166, 1962.

Rosenberg, E.: Social disorganization aspects of professional sport careers. J. Sport Social Issues, *4*:14, 1980.

Sage, G.H.: Parental influence and socialization into sport for male and female intercollegiate athletes. J. Sport Social Issues, *4*:1, 1980.

Schafer, W.E., and Armer, J.M.: Athletes are not inferior students. Trans-action, November, 1968, p 21.

Schutz, R.: Academic achievement and involvement in hockey: A post-hoc longitudinal study. Canadian J. Appl. Sport Sci., *4*:71, 1979.

Snyder, E., and Spreitzer, E.A.: Participation in sport as related to educational expectations among high school girls. Sociol. Educ., *50*:47, 1977.

Snyder, E. and Spreitzer, E.A.: High school value climate as related to preferential treatment of athletes. Res. Q., *50*:460, 1979.

Snyder, E., and Spreitzer, E.A.: Sport, education and schools. *In* Handbook of Social Science of Sport. Edited by G. Lüschen and G. Sage. Champaign, Ill., Stipes, 1981, pp 119–146..

Spady, W.G.: Lament for the letterman: Effects of peer status and extracurricular activities on goals and achievement. Am. J. Sociol., *75*:5, 1970.

Spinrad, W.: Fandom and the functions of spectator sport. *In* Handbook of Social Science of Sport. Edited by G. Lüschen and G. Sage. Champaign, Ill., Stipes, 1981, pp 354–365.

Staniford, D.J.: Play and Physical Activity in Early Childhood Socialization. Ottawa, C.A.H.P.E.R., 1978.

Webb, H.: Professionalization of attitudes toward play among adolescents. *In* Aspects of Contemporary Sport Sociology. Edited by G.S. Kenyon. Chicago, The Athletic Institute, 1969, pp 161–178.

Wells, R., and Picou, J.S.: Interscholastic athletes and socialization for educational achievement. J. Sport Behavior, *3*:119, 1980.

Section Two: Sport and Regulative Institutions

Appenzeller, H.: Athletics and the Law. Charlottesville, Virginia, Michie, 1975.

Burr, K.J.: Player control mechanisms in professional team sports. Univ. Pittsburgh Law Rev. *34*:645, 1973.

Carr, G.A.: The involvement of politics in the sporting relationships of East and West Germany, 1945–1972. J. Sport History 7(1):40, 1980.

Cox, T.A.: Intercollegiate athletics and Title IX. George Washington Law Rev., 46:34, 1977.

Dauriac, C.: Social hierarchies regarding sport expenditures and practices. Int. Rev. Sport Sociol., 10:73, 1975.

Espy, R.: The Politics of the Olympic Games. Berkley, California, University of California Press, 1979.

Gillis, J.H.: Olympic success and national religious orientation Rev. Sport Leisure, 5:1, 1980.

Greendorfer, S.: Sport and the mass media. In Handbook of Social Science of Sport. Edited by G. Lüschen and G. Sage. Champaign, Ill., Stipes, 1981, pp 160–180.

Holahan, W.L.: The long-run effects of abolishing the baseball player reserve system. J. Legal Studies, 7(1):129, 1978.

Johnson, A.T.: Congress and professional sports: 1951–1978. Annals, 445:102, 1979.

Joyal-Poupart, R.: La Responsabilité civile en matière de sports au Québec et en France. Montreal, Presses de l'Université de Montreal, 1975.

Kiviaho, P. and Mekala, P.: Olympic success: A sum of non-material and material factors. Int. Rev. Sport Sociol., 13:5, 1978.

Lowell, C.H.: Collective bargaining and the professional team sport industry. Law and Contemp. Prob., 38:3, 1973.

Lowell, C.H.: Federal administrative intervention in amateur athletics. George Washington Law Rev. 43:729, 1975.

McPherson, B.D.: Sport consumption and the economics of consumerism. In Sport and Social Order: Contributions to the Sociology of Sport. Edited by D.W. Ball and J.W. Loy. Reading, Mass.: Addison-Wesley, 1975.

Meynaud, J.: Sport et Politique. Paris, Payot, 1966.

Morton, H.: Soviet Sport. New York, Cromwell-Collier, 1963.

Natan, A.: Sport and politics. In Sport, Culture and Society. 1st Edition. Edited by J.W. Loy and G.S. Kenyon. New York, Macmillan, 1969, pp 203–310.

Neale, W.C.: The peculiar economics of professional sports. Q. J. Econ. 76:1, 1964.

Niwa, T.: The function of sport in society today (with special reference to sport in Japanese business enterprise). Int. Rev. Sport Sociol., 8:53, 1973.

Noll, R.G., (ed.): Government and the Sports Business. Washington, D.C., The Brookings Institution, 1974.

Petrie, B.M.: Sport and politics. In Sport and Social Order: Contributions to the Sociology of Sport. Edited by D.W. Ball and J.W. Loy. Reading, Mass.: Addison-Wesley, 1975.

Quirk, J.: An economic analysis of team movements in professional sports. Law and Contemp. Prob., 38:42, 1973.

Riordan, J.: Soviet sport and soviet foreign policy. Soviet Studies, 26:322, 1974.

Riordan, J.: Sport Under Communism: A Comparative Study. Montreal, McGill-Queens University Press, 1978.

Rosentraub, M. and Nunn, S.: Suburban city investment in professional sports. Am. Behav. Sci., 21:393, 1978.

Scully, G.W.: Economic discrimination in professional sports. Law and Contemp. Prob., 38:67, 1973.

Seppanen, P.: Olympic success: A cross-national perspective. In Handbook of Social Science of Sport. Edited by G. Lüschen and G. Sage. Champaign, Ill., Stipes, 1981, pp 93–116.

Sigelman, L.: Win one for the giver: Alumni giving in big-time college sports. Soc. Sci. Q., 60:284, 1979.

Weistart, J.C., and Lowell, C.H.: The Law of Sports. Charlottesville, Va., Michie/Bobbs-Merrill Law Publishing, 1979.

Zollers, F.E.: From gridiron to courtroom to bargaining table: the new National Football League agreement. Am. Bus. Law J. (Summer 1979) 17(2):133, 1979.

Section Three: Sport and Cultural Institutions

Ardrey, R.: The Territorial Imperative; A Personal Inquiry Into The Animal Origins of Property and Nations. First Edition. New York, Atheneum, 1966.

Betts, J.R.: America's Sporting Heritage. 1850–1950. Reading, Mass., Addison-Wesley, 1974.

Fox, J.R.: Pueblo baseball: A new use for old witchcraft. J. Am. Folklore, *74*:9, 1961.

Greendorfer, S.: Sport and the mass media. *In* Handbook of Social Science of Sport. Edited by G. Lüschen and G. Sage. Champaign, Ill., Stipes, 1981, pp 160–180.

Guttman, A.: From Ritual to Record: The Nature of Modern Sports. New York, Columbia University Press, 1978.

Hamilton, L.C.: Modern American rock climbing—some aspects of social change. Pacific Sociol. Rev., *22*(3):285, 1979.

Hearle, R.: The athlete as single "moral" leader: Heroes, success themes and basic cultural values in selected baseball autobiographies, 1900–1970. J. Popular Culture, *8*:392, 1974.

Inglis, F.: The Name of the Game (Sport and Society). London, Heinemann, 1977.

Horowitz, I.: Sports telecasts: Rights and regulations. J. Communication, *27*:160, 1977.

Kiviaho, P.: Sport and intracultural social change: a longitudinal analysis. Acta Sociologica, *21*(1):3, 1978.

Lorenz, K.: On Aggression. New York, Harcourt, Brace, and World, 1966.

Lowe, B.: The Beauty of Sport: A Cross-Disciplinary Inquiry. Englewood Cliffs, N.J., Prentice-Hall, 1977.

McLuhan, M.: Understanding Media: The Extension of Man. New York, McGraw Hill, 1964.

Riesman, D., and Denney, R.: Football in America: A study in culture diffusion. Am. Q., *3*:309, 1951.

Roberts, J., Sutton-Smith, B. and Kendon, A.: Strategy in games and folk tales. J. Soc. Psychol., *61*:185, 1963.

Sage, G.: Sport and religion. *In* Handbook of Social Science of Sport. Edited by G. Lüschen and G. Sage. Champaign, Ill., Stipes, 1981, pp. 147–159.

Segrave, J., and Chu, D. (eds): Olympism. Champaign, Ill., Human kinetics, 1981.

Schloz, R., et al.; Sport and religions of the world. *In* Sport and the Modern World. Edited by O. Grupe et al. New York: Springer-Verlag, 1973.

Sipes, R.: War, sports and aggression: An empirical test of two rival theories. Am. Anthropol., *75*:64, 1973.

Smith, M.D.: Towards an explanation of hockey violence: A reference other approach. Can. J. Sociol., *4*:105, 1979.

Tannenbaum, P.H., and Noah, J.: Sportugese: A study of sports page communication. Journalism Q., *36*:163, 1959.

Theology. *In* Philosophy, Theology and History of Sport and Physical Activity. Edited by F. Landry and W. Orban. Miami; Symposium Specialists, 1978.

Weinberg, S.K., and Arond, H.: The occupational culture of the boxer. Am. J. Sociol., *57*:460, 1972.

Section Four: Sport and Stratification Systems

Abrahamson, M.: A functional theory of organizational stratification. Soc. Forces, *58*:128, 1979.

Allison, M.T.: On the ethnicity of ethnic minorities in sport. Quest, *31*:50, 1979.

Birrell, S.: An analysis of the inter-relationships among achievement motivation, athletic participation, academic achievement, and educational aspirations. Int. J. Sport Psychol., *8*:178, 1977.

Braddock, J.H.: Race, sports and social mobility: A critical review. Sociol. Symp., *39*:18, 1980.

Coleman, J.S.: The Adolescent Society. New York, The Free Press, 1961.

Curtis, J. and Loy, J.W.: Race/ethnicity and relative centrality of playing positions in team sports. *In* Exercise and Sport Sciences Review. Edited by R. Hutton. Philadelphia: The Franklin Press, 1979, Vol. 6, pp 285–313.

Dubois, P.E.: Participation in sports and occupational attainment: A comparative study. Res. Q., *49*:25, 1978.

Edwards, H.: Authority, power and intergroup stratification by race and sex in American sport and society. *In* Handbook of Social Science of Sport. Edited by G. Lüschen and G. Sage. Champaign, Ill., Stipes, 1981, pp 383–399.

Gruneau, R.S.: Sport, social differentiation and social inequality. *In* Sport and Social Order. Edited by D.W. Ball and J.W. Loy. Reading, Mass, Addison-Wesley, 1975.

Haerle, R.J.: Career patterns and career contingencies of professional baseball players: An occupational analysis. *In* Sport and Social Order. Edited by D.W. Ball and J.W.

Loy. Reading, Mass, Addison-Wesley, 1975, pp 457–519.

Hall, M. A.: Sport and Gender: A Feminist Perspective on the Sociology of Sport. Ottawa, C.A.H.P.E.R., 1978.

Kenyon, G.S.: The significance of physical activity as a function of age, sex, education and socio-economic status of northern United States adults. Int. Rev. Sport Sociol. *1*:41, 1966.

Lever, J.: Soccer: Opium of the Brazilian people. Trans-action, *7*:36, 1969.

Lever, J.: Sex differences in the complexity of children's play and games. Am. Sociol. Rev. *43*:471, 1978.

Loy, J.W.: Social origins and occupational mobility patterns of a selected sample of American athletes. Int. Rev. Sport Sociol., *7*:5, 1972.

Loy, J.W.: Implications of the Davis-Moore theory of social stratification for the study of social differentiation within sport. *In* The Dimensions of Sport Sociology. Edited by M. Krotee. West Point, New York, Leisure Press, 1979.

McPherson, B.D.: Minority group involvement in sport: The Black athlete. *In* Exercise and Sport Sciences Review. Edited by J. Wilmore. New York, Academic Press, 1977, Vol. 2, pp 71–101.

McPherson, B.D.: Aging and involvement in physical activity: A sociological perspective. *In* Physical Activity and Human Well-Being. Edited by F. Landry and W. Orban. Miami, Symposia Specialists, 1978, Vol. 1, pp 111–128.

McPherson, B.D. and Kozlik, C.A.: Canadian leisure patterns by age: Disengagement, continuity or ageism. *In* Aging In Canada: Social Perspectives. Edited by V. Marshall.

Toronto, Fitzhenry and Whiteside, 1979, pp 113–122.

Metcalfe, A.: Organized sport and social stratification in Montreal: 1840–1901. *In* Canadian Sport: Sociological Perspectives. Edited by R. Gruneau and J. Albinson. Don Mills, Ontario, Addison-Wesley (Canada), 1976, pp 77–101.

Oliver, M.L.: Race, class and the family's orientation to mobility through sport. Sociol. Symp., *39*:62, 1980.

Otto, L. B., and Alwin, D.: Athletics, aspirations, and attainments. Sociol. Educ., *42*:102, 1977.

Renson, R.: Social status symbolism of sport stratification. Hermes (Leuven), *10*:433, 1976.

Roberts, J. and Sutton-Smith, B.: Child training and game involvement. Ethnology, *1*:166, 1962.

Sack, A., and Thiel, R.: College football and social mobility: A case study of Notre Dame football players. Sociol. Educ., *52*:60–66, 1979.

Snyder, E., and Spreitzer, E.: Participation in sport as related to educational expectations among high school girls. Sociol. Educ., *50*:47, 1977.

Sutton-Smith, B., Roberts, J., and Kozelka, R.: Game involvement in adults. J. Soc. Psychol., *60*:15, 1963.

Tsai, Y.M. and Sigelman, H.: Stratification and mobility in big-time college football: A vacancy chain analysis. Sociological Methods and Research, *8*:487, 1980.

Yuchtman-Yaar, E. and Semyonov, M.: Ethnic inequality in Israeli schools and sports: An expectation-states approach. Am. J. Sociol., *85*:576, 1979.